Taxation

Finance Act 2012

Eighteenth edition

Alan Melville
FCA, BSc, Cert. Ed.

PEARSON

Harlow, England • London • New York • Boston • San Francisco • Toronto • Sydney • Auckland • Singapore • Hong Kong
Tokyo • Seoul • Taipei • New Delhi • Cape Town • São Paulo • Mexico City • Madrid • Amsterdam • Munich • Paris • Milan

Pearson Education Limited
Edinburgh Gate
Harlow
Essex CM20 2JE
England

and Associated Companies throughout the world

Visit us on the World Wide Web at:
www.pearson.com/uk

First published 1995
Eighteenth edition published 2013

ISBN: 978-0-273-77301-6

British Library Cataloguing-in-Publication Data
A catalogue record for this book is available from the British Library

Library of Congress Cataloging-in-Publication Data
A catalog record for this book is available from the Library of Congress

10 9 8 7 6 5 4 3 2 1
16 15 14 13 12

Printed and bound by Ashford Colour Press Ltd, Gosport

Website
A website to accompany the eighteenth edition of *Taxation* can be found at www.pearsoned.co.uk/melville

Contents

Preface

The main aim of this book is to describe the UK taxation system in sufficient depth and with sufficient clarity to meet the needs of those undertaking a first course of study in taxation. The book has not been written with any specific syllabus in mind but should be useful to anyone who is studying taxation as part of a university or college course in accounting, finance or business studies. The book should also be of value to students who are preparing for the taxation examinations of the professional accounting bodies. A list of relevant examinations is given on the back cover of the book.

Every effort has been made to explain the tax system as clearly as possible. There are numerous worked examples and each chapter (except Chapter 1) concludes with a set of exercises which thoroughly test the reader's grasp of the new topics introduced in that chapter. The book also contains four sets of review questions, drawn mainly from the past examination papers of the professional accounting bodies. The solutions to most of these exercises and questions are located at the back of the book but solutions to those exercises and questions marked with an asterisk (*) are provided in a separate Instructor's Manual.

This eighteenth edition incorporates the provisions of Finance Act 2012.

Alan Melville
June 2012

Acknowledgements

I would like to thank the following accounting bodies for granting me permission to use their past examination questions:

- Association of Chartered Certified Accountants (ACCA)
- Chartered Institute of Management Accountants (CIMA)
- Chartered Institute of Public Finance and Accountancy (CIPFA)
- Association of Accounting Technicians (AAT).

I must emphasise that the answers provided to these questions are entirely my own and are not the responsibility of the accounting body concerned. I should also point out that the questions which are printed in this textbook have been amended in some cases so as to reflect changes in taxation law which have occurred since those questions were originally published by the accounting body concerned.

I would also like to thank the Office for National Statistics for granting me permission to reproduce the table of Retail Price Indices given in Chapter 24.

Alan Melville
June 2012

Summary of Tax Data

Income Tax

	2012-13	2011-12
TAX RATES AND BANDS		
Basic rate	20%	20%
Higher rate	40%	40%
Additional rate	50%	50%
Basic rate limit	£34,370	£35,000
Higher rate limit	£150,000	£150,000
Starting rate for savings	10%	10%
Starting rate limit for savings	£2,710	£2,560

Note:
Rates of tax on dividends are 10%, 32.5% and 42.5%.

	2012-13	2011-12
ALLOWANCES	£	£
Personal allowance		
Age 0 to 64	8,105	7,475
Age 65 to 74	10,500	9,940
Age 75 or over	10,660	10,090
Blind person's allowance	2,100	1,980
Married couple's allowance†		
Born before 6 April 1935	7,705	7,295
Minimum amount	2,960	2,800
Income limit for basic personal allowance	100,000	100,000
Income limit for age-related allowances	25,400	24,000

†*This allowance is relieved at 10%.*

	2012-13	2011-12
PROPERTY INCOME		
Rent-a-room relief limit	£4,250	£4,250
CAR AND FUEL BENEFIT		
Upper limit for 5% charge	75g/km	75g/km
Upper limit for 10% charge	99g/km	120g/km
Upper limit for 15% charge	-	125g/km
Amount used in car fuel benefit calculation	£20,200	£18,800
PENSION SCHEMES	£	£
Annual allowance	50,000	50,000
Lifetime allowance	1,500,000	1,800,000

Capital Allowances

Writing Down Allowance (WDA):	
Main pool of plant and machinery†	18%
Special rate pool of plant and machinery†	8%
Annual Investment Allowance (AIA):	
AIA annual limit‡	£25,000
AIA rate	100%
First Year Allowance (FYA) on qualifying plant and machinery:	
Low emission cars (to 31 March 2015)	100%
Gas refuelling equipment (to 31 March 2015)	100%
Energy saving or water efficient technology	100%
Zero-emission goods vehicles (to 5 April 2015)	100%

† *WDA rates 20% and 10% before 6 April 2012 (1 April 2012 for companies)*
‡ *AIA limit £100,000 before 6 April 2012 (1 April 2012 for companies)*

National Insurance Contributions

	2012-13	*2011-12*
CLASS 1 (Not contracted out)		
Primary threshold (weekly)	£146	£139
Upper accruals point (weekly)	£770	£770
Upper earnings limit (weekly)	£817	£817
Employee contributions		
Rate on earnings between primary threshold and UEL	12%	12%
Rate on earnings beyond UEL	2%	2%
Employer contributions		
Secondary threshold (weekly)	£144	£136
Rate on earnings beyond secondary threshold	13.8%	13.8%
CLASS 1A		
Rate	13.8%	13.8%
CLASS 2		
Weekly contribution	£2.65	£2.50
Small earnings exception	£5,595	£5,315
CLASS 3		
Weekly contribution	£13.25	£12.60
CLASS 4		
Lower profits limit	£7,605	£7,225
Upper profits limit	£42,475	£42,475
Rate on profits between lower and upper limit	9%	9%
Rate on profits beyond upper limit	2%	2%

Capital Gains Tax

	2012-13	*2011-12*
Standard rate	18%	18%
Higher rate	28%	28%
Entrepreneurs' relief rate	10%	10%
Entrepreneurs' relief lifetime limit	£10,000,000	£10,000,000
Annual exempt amount	£10,600	£10,600

Corporation Tax

Financial Year	*FY2012*	*FY2011*	*FY2010*	*FY2009*
Main rate	24%	26%	28%	28%
Small profits rate	20%	20%	21%	21%
Lower limit	£300,000	£300,000	£300,000	£300,000
Upper limit	£1,500,000	£1,500,000	£1,500,000	£1,500,000
Marginal relief fraction	1/100	3/200	7/400	7/400

Note:
Main rate for FY2013 is 23%.

Inheritance Tax

Date of transfer	*0% Band*	*Rate on life-time transfers*	*Rate on death*	*Lower rate*
6 April 2005 to 5 April 2006	0 - £275,000	20%	40%	-
6 April 2006 to 5 April 2007	0 - £285,000	20%	40%	-
6 April 2007 to 5 April 2008	0 - £300,000	20%	40%	-
6 April 2008 to 5 April 2009	0 - £312,000	20%	40%	-
6 April 2009 to 5 April 2010	0 - £325,000	20%	40%	-
6 April 2010 to 5 April 2011	0 - £325,000	20%	40%	-
6 April 2011 to 5 April 2012	0 - £325,000	20%	40%	-
6 April 2012 to 5 April 2013	0 - £325,000	20%	40%	36%

Value Added Tax

Standard rate†	20%	(from 4 January 2011)
Reduced rate	5%	
Registration threshold	£77,000	(from 1 April 2012)
Deregistration threshold	£75,000	(from 1 April 2012)

†*Standard rate 17.5% prior to 4 January 2011*

Part 1

INCOME TAX AND NATIONAL INSURANCE

Chapter 1

Introduction to the UK tax system

Introduction

The purpose of this first chapter is to provide an overview of the UK tax system. The principal UK taxes are introduced and classified and the main sources of taxation law are explained. This chapter also deals with:

(a) the structure and the functions of Her Majesty's Revenue and Customs, which is the organisation responsible for the administration of the UK tax system

(b) the annual procedure which is used to determine the tax liability of an individual.

The chapter concludes by distinguishing between tax avoidance and tax evasion.

UK taxes

The UK taxation system is composed of a number of different taxes, some of which are *direct* taxes and some of which are *indirect* taxes:

(a) Direct taxes are charged on income, profits or other gains and are either deducted at source or paid directly to the tax authorities. The main direct taxes which are payable by individuals are income tax, capital gains tax and inheritance tax. The main direct tax payable by companies is corporation tax. All of these taxes are administered by HM Revenue and Customs (HMRC), which was formed in April 2005 when the Inland Revenue and HM Customs and Excise were merged. National Insurance contributions, which can also be looked upon as a form of direct taxation, are administered by the National Insurance Contributions Office (NICO) of HMRC.

(b) Indirect taxes are taxes on spending. They are charged when a taxpayer buys an item and are paid to the vendor as part of the purchase price of the item. It is then the vendor's duty to pass the tax on to the tax authorities. Indirect taxes include value added tax (VAT), stamp duty, customs duties and the excise duties levied on alcohol, tobacco and petrol. The only indirect tax considered in this book is VAT, which is also administered by HM Revenue and Customs.

Sources of tax law

There is no single source of UK tax law. The basic rules are laid down in Acts of Parliament but it is left to the courts to interpret these Acts and to provide much of the detail of the tax system. In addition, HMRC issues a variety of statements, notices and leaflets which explain how the law is implemented in practice. These statements have no legal backing but they explain the tax authorities' interpretation of the law and will be adhered to unless successfully challenged in the courts.

Statute law

The basic rules of the UK tax system are embodied in a number of tax *statutes* or Acts of Parliament. The main statutes currently in force for each tax are as follows:

Tax	*Statute*	*Abbreviation*
Income tax	Capital Allowances Act 2001	CAA 2001
	Income Tax (Earnings and Pensions) Act 2003	ITEPA 2003
	Income Tax (Trading and Other Income) Act 2005	ITTOIA 2005
	Income Tax Act 2007	ITA 2007
National Insurance	Social Security Contributions and Benefits Act 1992	SSCBA 1992
Capital gains tax	Taxation of Chargeable Gains Act 1992	TCGA 1992
Inheritance tax	Inheritance Tax Act 1984	IHTA 1984
Corporation tax	Taxation of Chargeable Gains Act 1992	TCGA 1992
	Capital Allowances Act 2001	CAA 2001
	Corporation Tax Act 2009	CTA 2009
	Corporation Tax Act 2010	CTA 2010
Overseas aspects of tax	Taxation (International and Other Provisions) Act 2010	TIOPA 2010
Value added tax	Value Added Tax Act 1994	VATA 1994
Administration of }	Taxes Management Act 1970	TMA 1970
the tax system }	Customs and Excise Management Act 1979	CEMA 1979

These statutes are amended each year by the annual Finance Act, which is based upon the Budget proposals put forward by the Chancellor of the Exchequer. Some of the tax statutes provide for the making of detailed regulations by *statutory instrument*. A statutory instrument (SI) is a document which is laid before Parliament and then automatically becomes law within a stated period unless any objections are raised to it.

European Union law

Membership of the European Union (EU) involves adherence to EU law. This applies as much to taxation as to any other category of law and the EU's influence on UK tax law may increase over time. At present, the main impact is on VAT, where the prevailing legislation takes the form of EU Directives. These Directives are binding on the UK and dictate the results which the internal legislation of the UK must bring about.

Case law

Over the years, taxpayers and the tax authorities have frequently disagreed over the interpretation of the tax Acts. As a result, many thousands of tax cases have been brought before the courts. The decisions made by judges in these cases form an important part of the tax law of the UK and some of the more significant cases are referred to in this book.

Statements made by the tax authorities

The main statements and other documents produced by HM Revenue and Customs as a guide to the law on taxation are as follows:

(a) **Statements of Practice**. A Statement of Practice (SP) sets out the HMRC interpretation of tax legislation and clarifies the way in which the law will be applied in practice. For example, SP 2/02 (the second SP issued in 2002) deals with the taxation treatment of exchange rate fluctuations.

(b) **Extra-Statutory Concessions**. An Extra-Statutory Concession (ESC) consists of a relaxation which gives taxpayers a reduction in liability to which they are not entitled under the strict letter of the law. In general, concessions are made so as to resolve anomalies or relieve hardship. For example, ESC C4 deals with the taxation treatment of charitable fund-raising events.

    A process of giving statutory effect to certain ESCs is currently underway. This is generally being done by means of statutory instruments.

(c) **Press releases**. These are issued throughout the year on a variety of tax-related subjects. Of especial interest are the press releases and notes which are issued on Budget day and which provide a detailed explanation of the Budget proposals.

(d) **Internal Guidance Manuals**. HMRC produces a comprehensive set of internal tax manuals for the guidance of its own staff. These manuals may be inspected at HMRC Enquiry Centres or accessed via the Internet.

(e) **Leaflets**. These are aimed at the general public and explain the tax system in non-technical language. For example, HMRC leaflet IR121 is a guide to tax and national insurance contributions for those approaching retirement.

Most of the information produced by the tax authorities is now available on the HMRC website, the address of which is www.hmrc.gov.uk.

The tax year

The changes to the tax system that are proposed in the annual Budget speech are usually intended to take effect as from the start of the next *tax year*. Tax years for individuals and for companies are identified as follows:

(a) For individuals, a tax year runs from 6 April to the following 5 April. For instance, tax year 2011-12 began on 6 April 2011 and ended on 5 April 2012. Tax years are also referred to as *fiscal years* or *years of assessment*.

(b) For companies, a corporation tax *financial year* runs from 1 April to the following 31 March and is identified by the year in which it begins. For instance, the financial year referred to as FY2011 began on 1 April 2011 and ended on 31 March 2012.

This book takes into account the provisions of Finance Act 2012 (which is based on the March 2012 Budget) and describes the UK taxation system for fiscal year 2012-13 and corporation tax financial year FY2012.

Structure of HM Revenue and Customs

Her Majesty's Revenue and Customs (HMRC) consists of a large body of civil servants headed by the *Commissioners for Revenue and Customs*. The Commissioners are appointed by Her Majesty The Queen in accordance with recommendations made by the *Treasury*. This Government department has overall responsibility for the public finances of the UK and is managed by the *Chancellor of the Exchequer*. The main duties of the Commissioners for Revenue and Customs are as follows:

(a) to implement the law relating to direct and indirect taxation

(b) to provide advice to the Chancellor of the Exchequer on taxation matters

(c) to administer the many divisions and offices into which HMRC is organised.

The routine work of HMRC is carried out by officials known as *Officers of Revenue and Customs*. With regard to direct taxation, the main function of these officials is to calculate or "assess" a taxpayer's tax liability and then to ensure that the correct amount of tax is paid. Under the Self Assessment system (see later in this chapter) a taxpayer may calculate his or her own tax liability, in which case HMRC officials will check that the taxpayer's self-assessment is correct. The functions of HMRC with regard to indirect taxation (and VAT in particular) are explained later in this book (see Chapter 30).

HMRC has specialist offices which deal with such matters as pension schemes, charities, trusts and so forth but most of the day-to-day work relating to direct taxation takes place in local area offices. These local offices are responsible for routine assessment and collection and for ensuring that taxpayers comply with tax regulations. There is also a network of HMRC Enquiry Centres. These provide a first point of contact for taxpayers with general queries and carry stocks of tax forms and leaflets.

Administration of the tax system

The remainder of this chapter describes the administration system which is used to assess an individual's liability to income tax and capital gains tax in each tax year. This system is known as "Self Assessment". Under this system, the taxpayer (*not* HMRC) is primarily responsible for ensuring that:

(a) the tax liability for each tax year is properly assessed, and

(b) the correct amount of tax is paid on the due date or dates.

Later chapters of this book explain the administration systems which are used for the purposes of corporation tax, inheritance tax and VAT.

Self Assessment

If an individual's tax liability for a tax year cannot be collected entirely by deduction at source (see Chapter 2) or via the PAYE system (see Chapter 7), then the liability must be formally assessed. The starting point in the assessment process is the completion of a *self assessment tax return*. The annual procedure is as follows:

(a) Tax returns are normally issued in April each year to those taxpayers who are likely to need them. Each tax return includes a formal notice requiring a return to be made and delivered to HMRC. Paper tax returns are not sent to taxpayers who submitted the previous year's return electronically (see below) but such taxpayers are still sent a notice requiring a return to be made and can request a paper tax return if they so wish. Returns can also be downloaded and printed from the HMRC website.

(b) The main tax return consists of a basic six-page form together with a four-page "additional information" form which covers some of the less common types of income and tax reliefs. The additional information form need not be filed if none of these types of income or tax reliefs apply to the taxpayer concerned.

There are also several sets of supplementary pages, each dealing with a different type of income or gains (e.g. income from self-employment). Taxpayers are sent only those supplementary pages which are thought to be relevant to their circumstances but can request further supplementary pages if necessary.

(c) A short tax return (STR) is available for taxpayers with simpler tax affairs.

(d) Rather than completing a paper tax return, taxpayers and their agents can file tax returns electronically by means of the Internet and are encouraged to do so. In fact, 7.65 million returns were filed electronically for tax year 2010-11. This represents more than 80% of all returns submitted.

(e) The information requested in a tax return relates to the tax year just ended. For example, the tax returns issued in April 2012 required taxpayers to declare their income and gains for tax year 2011-12.

(f) A tax return must be completed in full. It is not permissible to omit figures or to make entries such as "see accounts" or "as submitted by employer". Unless asked to submit accounts or other supporting documentation with the return, a taxpayer is under no obligation to do so. However, it is necessary to retain all supporting documentation in case HMRC enquires into the accuracy of a return.

(g) If a main tax return is submitted on paper, the taxpayer has the option of calculating his or her own tax liability (using "tax calculation summary" pages) and submitting this calculation to HMRC as part of the return. HMRC will calculate the tax liability for taxpayers who do not take up this option or for those who submit the short tax return (which does not include a self-calculation facility). However, if a paper return is submitted late (see below), HMRC does not guarantee to advise the taxpayer of the liability in time for the correct amount of tax to be paid on the correct date.

If a tax return is filed electronically, the tax liability is calculated by computer software. In all cases, the resulting assessment is referred to as a "self-assessment".

(h) Self assessment tax returns must normally be filed (i.e. submitted to HMRC) on or before the following dates:

- for paper returns, 31 October following the end of the tax year
- for returns filed electronically, 31 January following the end of the tax year.

However, if the return notice is issued after 31 July following the end of the tax year (but not after 31 October) the taxpayer has three months from the date of the notice to submit a paper return. The deadline for electronic filing in such a case remains at 31 January. If the notice is issued after 31 October, the taxpayer has three months from the date of the notice to submit the return either on paper or electronically.

(i) Penalties are imposed if a return is filed late. Furthermore, the submission of a late return may mean that the tax liability for the year is not determined until after the due date of payment (see below). A taxpayer who pays tax late will incur interest and may also incur a late-payment penalty (see Chapter 15).

(j) The 31 January which follows the end of a tax year is known as the "filing date" for that year. For example, the filing date for tax year 2012-13 is normally 31 January 2014. However, if a return notice is issued after 31 October, the filing date becomes the date which falls three months after the issue date of the notice.

(k) HMRC is empowered to correct a tax return (so as to rectify obvious errors or omissions or anything else that is believed to be incorrect) within nine months of the date on which the return is filed. Similarly, the taxpayer has the right to amend his or her tax return within 12 months of the filing date for that return.

(l) A taxpayer who has paid an amount of tax but now believes that this tax should not have been paid (a situation that could be caused by an error in a tax return) may make a claim for recovery of the overpaid tax. Such a claim must be made within four years of the end of the tax year to which it relates. Depending upon the circumstances of the case, HMRC may or may not accept the claim.

(m) The tax due in relation to a self-assessment is normally payable as follows:
   (i) A first payment on account (POA) is due on 31 January in the tax year to which the self-assessment relates.
   (ii) A second POA is due on the following 31 July.
   (iii) A final balancing payment is due on the following 31 January.

   For example, the tax due in relation to a 2012-13 self-assessment would normally be payable on 31 January 2013 (first POA), 31 July 2013 (second POA) and 31 January 2014 (balancing payment). Further information regarding the payment of tax is given in Chapter 15 of this book.

(n) An employed taxpayer who has an outstanding tax liability of less than £3,000 may request that this liability should be collected via the PAYE system (see Chapter 7). In these circumstances, taxpayers who file their returns electronically are advised to do so by 30 December (rather than 31 January) so as to give HMRC sufficient time to make the necessary arrangements.

Determinations

If an individual fails to submit a tax return by the required filing date for that return, an Officer of Revenue and Customs may make a determination of the tax due, calculated according to "the best of his information and belief". There is no right of appeal against a determination and the tax due cannot be postponed. A determination can be displaced only if the individual files the required return.

Notification of chargeability to tax

An individual who has not received a notice to submit a tax return, but has taxable income (or gains) of which HMRC is not aware, must notify HMRC of his or her chargeability to tax within six months of the end of the tax year in which the income arises. However, notification of chargeability is *not* required if *all* of the following conditions are satisfied:

(a) the individual has no capital gains

(b) the individual is not a higher-rate taxpayer (see Chapter 2)

(c) all of the individual's income has been subject to deduction of income tax at source (see Chapter 2) or has been dealt with via the PAYE system (see Chapter 7)

(d) the individual is not liable to a high income child benefit charge (see Chapter 7).

An individual who fails to notify chargeability within the permitted six-month period will incur a penalty (see Chapter 15).

Enquiries

HMRC is empowered to "enquire" into any tax return. The usual reason for opening an enquiry is that HMRC suspects that something is wrong with the information provided in the return. However, some enquiry cases are selected entirely at random and HMRC is under no obligation to justify the opening of an enquiry or to state whether or not the case has been chosen randomly. Note that:

(a) If a tax return is filed by the due date, an enquiry cannot usually begin more than 12 months after the date on which the return is filed. This means that the "enquiry window" for a return which is filed early closes correspondingly early.

(b) If a return is filed late or is amended after the date on which the return was due to be filed, the enquiry window is extended until the quarter day which follows the first anniversary of the date on which the return or amendment was filed. For this purpose, the quarter days are 31 January, 30 April, 31 July and 31 October.

EXAMPLE

In April 2012, HMRC issues a notice requiring an individual to submit a tax return for the year 2011-12. The return is submitted electronically to HMRC on 8 December 2012.

(a) State the date by which any enquiry into the above return must begin.
(b) How would the situation differ if a paper return was submitted on 8 December 2012?
(c) How would the situation differ if an electronic return was submitted on 1 March 2013?

Solution

(a) The return is filed before the due date (31 January 2013). Any enquiry must begin within 12 months of the date that the return is filed (i.e. by 8 December 2013).
(b) The return is filed after the due date (31 October 2012). Any enquiry must begin by the quarter day which follows the first anniversary of the date that the return is filed (i.e. by 31 January 2014).
(c) The return is filed after the due date (31 January 2013). Any enquiry must begin by the quarter day which follows the first anniversary of the date that the return is filed (i.e. by 30 April 2014).

Discovery assessments

HMRC may raise a "discovery assessment" if it is discovered that full disclosure has not been made in a tax return and that tax has been lost as a result.

The time limit for making a discovery assessment is normally four years after the end of the tax year concerned. This increases to six years if the taxpayer has been negligent and 20 years if the taxpayer has been dishonest.

Record keeping

Taxpayers are required to keep proper records so that they can make a correct tax return and (if necessary) substantiate the figures entered on the return. A taxpayer who is in business or who lets property must normally preserve these records for five years after the 31 January which follows the end of the tax year concerned. Otherwise, records must be preserved for 12 months after the 31 January which follows the end of the tax year. For example, records for tax year 2012-13 must normally be retained until 31 January 2019 by a taxpayer who is in business or who lets property and until 31 January 2015 otherwise.

Appeals

Under the Self Assessment system, taxpayers have the right of appeal in relation to a number of HMRC decisions. For example, a taxpayer may appeal against a discovery assessment or against an HMRC amendment to a self-assessment.

An appeal may involve an internal review of the decision by an HMRC official and/or a hearing before a tribunal. The main features of the appeals system are as follows:

(a) An appeal must be sent to HMRC in writing within 30 days of the disputed decision.

(b) The taxpayer may also apply to postpone payment of all or part of any tax which is payable as a result of the decision, though interest will continue to accrue on the postponed amount until the appeal is settled. Any non-postponed tax is payable on the due date in the usual way. If the appeal is subsequently settled in the taxpayer's favour, any overpaid tax is refunded.

(c) On receiving an appeal, HMRC considers the taxpayer's reasons for disputing the decision and may discuss the matter with the taxpayer. Most appeals are settled by agreement at this stage.

(d) If the taxpayer and HMRC are unable to agree, the taxpayer will be offered an internal review of the decision. A taxpayer who wishes to accept this offer must normally do so within 30 days. An internal review is carried out by an HMRC officer who has not previously been involved with the disputed decision and is usually completed within 45 days. The review officer then writes to the taxpayer to inform him or her of the review's conclusions.

(e) A taxpayer who rejects the offer of an internal review may appeal to a tribunal within 30 days of the date of the offer letter. Otherwise, an appeal to a tribunal may be made within 30 days of the date of the review conclusion letter.

(f) Most appeals to a tribunal are dealt with by the Tax Chamber of the First-tier Tribunal. However, very complex appeals may be heard by the Finance and Tax Chamber of the Upper Tribunal. The Upper Tribunal also hears appeals against decisions made by the First-tier Tribunal.

(g) If either HMRC or the person concerned is dissatisfied with a decision made by the Upper Tribunal, a dispute on a point of law may be referred to the Court of Appeal.

(h) The costs of bringing an appeal before the First-tier Tribunal are usually fairly modest. Parties bear their own costs and a taxpayer who loses an appeal is not normally required to pay HMRC's costs (unless the taxpayer has acted wholly unreasonably). The costs of taking an appeal to higher authority can be very high and an unsuccessful taxpayer may be required to pay HMRC's costs in defending the appeal as well as his or her own costs.

The HMRC Charter

The HMRC Charter sets out the rights and obligations of taxpayers. The Charter explains what the taxpayer can expect from HMRC and what HMRC expects from the taxpayer. In summary, the taxpayer can expect:

- to be treated even-handedly and with respect
- to be treated as honest
- to receive help and support from HMRC
- to be tackled if he or she breaks or bends the rules of the tax system
- that HMRC will be professional and act with integrity
- that HMRC will protect taxpayer information and respect taxpayer privacy
- that the costs of dealing with HMRC will be kept as low as possible.

In return, HMRC expects taxpayers to be honest, to take care to get things right and to treat HMRC staff with respect.

The Adjudicator

An independent and impartial Adjudicator considers complaints made by taxpayers who are not satisfied with the quality of the service they have received from HMRC. The Adjudicator writes an annual report and makes recommendations for improvements to HMRC procedures and practices. The Adjudicator is not empowered to hear tax appeals.

Tax evasion

Taxpayers are required to provide information which is correct and complete. Dishonest behaviour (such as concealing a source of income) is known as *tax evasion* and is against the law. On summary conviction in a magistrate's court, offenders may be sentenced to up to six months in prison and may be fined up to £5,000. On indictment in a higher court, the penalties are increased to a maximum of seven years in prison and/or an unlimited fine.

Tax avoidance

Taxpayers are entitled to organise their financial affairs in such a way that their tax burden is minimised. This perfectly legal activity is known as *tax avoidance*. For example, a taxpayer might legally avoid income tax by moving funds from a bank account which pays taxable interest to an ISA which pays tax-free interest (see Chapter 6). Tax avoidance (which is legal) should be contrasted sharply with tax evasion (which is not).

Tax avoidance is acceptable within limits but, over the years, tax advisors have shown great ingenuity in devising very complex and highly artificial tax avoidance schemes to exploit "loopholes" in the tax system. These schemes often result in a significant loss of tax revenue until eventually blocked by specific anti-avoidance legislation. So as to limit the effectiveness of tax avoidance schemes, a disclosure regime has been introduced which requires certain disclosures by those who devise such schemes or use them. A summary of the requirements is as follows:

(a) Those who promote and market schemes which bear certain "hallmarks" of tax avoidance are required to provide HMRC with details of each scheme. Promoters must provide a description of the scheme, including details of its tax consequences and the statutory provisions on which it relies. The scheme is then registered by HMRC and is allocated a registration number.

(b) Taxpayers using such a scheme are required to quote the registration number of the scheme in their tax returns. Taxpayers who develop their own "in-house" tax avoidance schemes must provide details of each scheme directly to HMRC.

These rules are intended to provide HMRC with advance warning of tax avoidance schemes, so enabling swifter and more effective investigation and counteraction.

General anti-abuse rule (GAAR)

The Government has announced that a "general anti-abuse rule" (GAAR) will be introduced in the UK in 2013. The intention of such a rule is to counteract *any* tax avoidance arrangement which is deemed to be abusive and so reduce the need to devise specific anti-avoidance legislation to deal with each new tax avoidance scheme as it arises.

Summary

- Direct taxes are charged on income, profits and other gains. The main direct taxes are income tax, capital gains tax, inheritance tax and corporation tax. National Insurance contributions are also a form of direct taxation. Indirect taxes are taxes on spending and are paid as part of the price of a bought item. Indirect taxes include VAT, stamp duty, customs duties and excise duties.
- Taxation law is a combination of statute law and case law. Statements made by the tax authorities have no legal force but provide information on the authorities' interpretation of the law.
- The fiscal year runs from 6 April to the following 5 April. The corporation tax financial year runs from 1 April to the following 31 March.
- HM Revenue and Customs (HMRC) calculates a taxpayer's tax liability or checks the taxpayer's own calculation of the liability. The calculation is based upon the information provided in an annual tax return.
- Paper tax returns must normally be filed by 31 October following the end of the tax year to which they relate. Returns submitted electronically must be filed by the following 31 January.
- A taxpayer who has not received a tax return notice, but has taxable income or gains of which HMRC is not aware, must notify HMRC of his or her chargeability to tax within six months of the end of the tax year in which the income arises.
- If a tax return is submitted on or before the required filing date, HMRC cannot initiate an enquiry into the return more than 12 months after the date on which the return is submitted. Discovery assessments may be made after the enquiry window has closed if it is discovered that the taxpayer has not made full disclosure of all relevant facts.
- Taxpayers have the right of appeal against certain HMRC decisions. Appeals which cannot be settled by agreement between the taxpayer and HMRC are dealt with by a two-tier tribunals system.
- Tax evasion should be distinguished from tax avoidance. The former involves dishonest conduct by the taxpayer and is illegal. The latter involves the sensible arrangement of the taxpayer's affairs so as to minimise the liability to tax and is perfectly legal.

Chapter 2

Introduction to income tax

Introduction

Income tax assessments are computed for a tax year (or "year of assessment") and are based on the taxpayer's total income for the year from all sources, ignoring any income which is exempt from income tax. This chapter explains the main features of an income tax computation, in preparation for the much more detailed information which is provided in subsequent chapters.

Most of the primary legislation relating to income tax used to be located in the Income and Corporation Taxes Act 1988, but this legislation has been rewritten in recent years and moved to new statutes. Income tax legislation can now be found mainly in the Income Tax (Earnings and Pensions) Act 2003, the Income Tax (Trading and Other Income) Act 2005 and the Income Tax Act 2007, as amended by subsequent Finance Acts.

Taxable persons

Individuals who are resident in the UK for a tax year are generally charged to income tax on all of their income for that year, including both income arising in the UK and income arising overseas. However, there are two main exceptions to this general rule:

(a) Some forms of income are exempt from income tax altogether (see below).

(b) UK residents who are not UK-domiciled (i.e. whose permanent home is not the UK) may claim that their overseas income should be subject to UK income tax only to the extent that the income is remitted to the UK. However, this may lead to an additional tax charge of £30,000 or more in some cases (see Chapter 32).

Individuals who are not UK residents are liable to pay income tax on their UK income only (see Chapter 32). Income tax is payable by:

(a) adults, on their own income and on their share of the income of a partnership

(b) children, if they have sufficient income to pay tax (see below)

(c) trustees, on the income of a trust or settlement

(d) personal representatives, on income arising from the estate of a deceased person.

Child's income derived from parent

If an unmarried minor child receives investment income which is derived from a parent, this income is treated for tax purposes as the income of the parent, not the child, unless the amount involved does not exceed £100 (per parent per child) in the tax year. This prevents parents from transferring income-bearing assets to a child so as to take advantage of the child's personal allowance (see Chapter 3).

However, income which is derived from parental contributions to a Child Trust Fund account (see Chapter 6) does not count towards the £100 limit.

Exempt organisations and individuals

Most organisations are generally exempt from income tax, subject to various restrictions and exceptions. Certain individuals are also exempt. Exempt organisations and individuals include the following:

(a) companies, which are liable to corporation tax rather than income tax
(b) clubs and societies, which are also liable to corporation tax
(c) registered pension schemes
(d) registered charities (on income used for charitable purposes)
(e) representatives of foreign countries (e.g. ambassadors)
(f) visiting members of foreign armed forces (on their service pay and on income arising from a source outside the UK).

Classification of income

Income is classified for income tax purposes into a number of types or categories, each with its own set of rules for calculating the amount of income of that type arising in a tax year. These rules are located in the Income Tax (Earnings and Pensions) Act 2003 and in the Income Tax (Trading and Other Income) Act 2005. The main classes of income which are subject to income tax are as follows:

Statute	*Type of income*	*Chapter of this book*
ITEPA 2003	Employment income	Chapters 7-8
	Pensions	Chapter 7
	Social security income	Chapter 7
ITTOIA 2005	Trading income	Chapters 9-13
	Property income	Chapter 5
	Interest	Chapter 6
	Dividends	Chapter 6
	Miscellaneous income	Chapter 6

Each of these classes of income is considered in some detail in later chapters of this book.

Exempt income

Certain types of income are specifically exempt from income tax and should be completely ignored when preparing an income tax computation. Some of the more important sources of exempt income are as follows:

(a) Exempt savings and investment income (see Chapter 6):
- income from Individual Savings Accounts
- income from National Savings Certificates
- interest arising from a certified SAYE (Save As You Earn) arrangement
- income from investments held in a Child Trust Fund account
- dividends received on shares held in a Venture Capital Trust, so long as certain conditions are satisfied

(b) Exempt employment income (see Chapter 7):
- certain minor benefits provided by employers for their employees
- statutory redundancy pay and the first £30,000 of compensation received for loss of employment
- certain lump sums payable under registered pension schemes (e.g. a lump sum payable at the commencement of a pension)
- the operational allowance paid to UK armed forces serving in specified locations

(c) Exempt property income (see Chapter 5):
- income of up to £4,250 per annum received under the "rent-a-room" scheme

(d) Other exempt income:
- winnings from betting, competition prizes and premium bond prizes
- maintenance payments (see Chapter 4)
- income from scholarships
- wound and disability pensions
- certain social security benefits (e.g. child benefit† and housing benefit)
- most commissions, discounts and cashbacks received by ordinary retail customers when purchasing goods, investments or services
- damages or compensation received for personal or professional injury and compensation received for mis-sold personal pension schemes
- receipts (not exceeding specified limits) from foster care and other qualifying care
- certain payments made to individuals who adopt children or care for children placed with them under a special guardianship order or residence order
- income from the sale of electricity generated by home microgeneration systems.

† *Although child benefit is exempt from income tax, a taxpayer who receives child benefit and has an income exceeding £50,000 p.a. may be subject to an income tax charge known as the "high income child benefit charge" (see Chapter 7).*

Structure of an income tax computation

In order to calculate a taxpayer's income tax liability for a tax year it is necessary to bring together *all* of the taxpayer's income into a single income tax computation. The structure of this computation is specified in the Income Tax Act 2007. A typical computation for the year 2012-13 might appear as follows:

			£
Business profits			43,410
Income from property			8,479
Building society interest taxed at source (pre-tax equivalent)			700
Total income			52,589
Less: Tax reliefs			1,200
Net income			51,389
Less: Personal allowance			8,105
Taxable Income			43,284
Income tax			
	34,370	@ 20%	6,874.00
	8,914	@ 40%	3,565.60
	43,284		10,439.60
Less: Tax reductions			0.00
Tax borne			10,439.60
Add: Tax withheld on payments			240.00
Tax liability for the year			10,679.60
Less: Tax paid by deduction at source			140.00
Tax payable			10,539.60

All of the terms used in this computation are explained in great detail in this chapter and in later chapters. For the time being it is sufficient to understand the main features of the computation, which are as follows:

(a) The taxpayer's "total income" for the year is calculated by adding together income from all sources, including the pre-tax equivalent of any income from which tax has already been deducted at source. However, any income which is exempt from income tax is excluded.

(b) Relief for certain payments made by the taxpayer (see Chapter 4) together with certain loss reliefs (see Chapters 5 and 12) and relief for certain pension contributions (see Chapter 14) are deducted from total income, giving "net income".

(c) Any personal allowance available to the taxpayer (see Chapter 3) is deducted from net income to give "taxable income". The basic personal allowance available to most taxpayers for tax year 2012-13 is £8,105 and this acts as a tax threshold, ensuring that those on very low incomes do not have to pay income tax. However, the allowance is reduced (possibly to zero) for those on high incomes.

(d) Income tax is charged on the taxable income, using the rates of tax in force for the year. The amount of tax calculated in this way is then subject to a number of adjustments and the result is the tax payable to HM Revenue and Customs.

(e) The *tax borne* by the taxpayer is the amount of income tax suffered for the year. This may be different from the *tax liability*, which is the amount of tax which must be accounted for to HMRC and the *tax payable* which is the tax remaining to be paid after deducting any tax already paid for the year. These distinctions will become clearer in the course of the next two chapters.

A formal tax computation is not required for every taxpayer. For example, a computation is not usually required for an individual whose income is derived entirely from employment, since the correct amount of tax is normally deducted automatically by the PAYE system (see Chapter 7). However, the only way to calculate the income tax liability in more complex cases is to prepare a tax computation.

Married couples and civil partners

Married couples are taxed independently, which means that the husband's income and the wife's income are taxed completely separately. This is also the case for same-sex civil partners who have entered into a legally-recognised civil partnership.

If a married couple (or civil partners) receive joint income, such as interest on a joint bank account, the amount of that income will normally be divided between them equally for tax purposes. But if the source of income is genuinely held between them in some other proportion, the couple may make a declaration to that effect and the income will then be divided between them as appropriate.

Dividends from jointly owned shares in close companies (see Chapter 27) are always taxed according to the actual proportions of ownership of the shares, rather than automatically being divided equally between the couple concerned.

Rates of income tax for 2012-13

An individual's taxable income is taxed according to the rates of income tax in force for the year in question. For 2012-13, the main rates of income tax are as follows:

First £34,370 of taxable income	20% (the "basic rate")
Next £115,630 taxable income (up to £150,000)	40% (the "higher rate")
Remaining taxable income after the first £150,000	50% (the "additional rate")

Note that:

(a) The point at which basic rate tax gives way to higher rate tax is known as the "basic rate limit". For 2012-13, this is £34,370 and the first £34,370 of taxable income is referred to as the "basic rate band". Similarly, the figure of £150,000 is known as the "higher rate limit" and taxable income lying between £34,370 and £150,000 may be referred to as the "higher rate band".

(b) The additional rate will fall from 50% to 45% in tax year 2013-14.

(c) Savings income and dividend income are treated specially, as explained below.

(d) The Scottish Parliament has the power to increase or decrease (by up to 3%) the basic rate of income tax set by the UK Parliament. The resulting "Scottish variable rate" (SVR) applies to Scottish taxpayers only. *The examples and exercises in this book all assume that the taxpayers concerned are liable to tax at unvaried UK rates.*

    Note, however, that the SVR is to be abolished. As from April 2016, the rates of income tax applicable to Scottish taxpayers will be derived by subtracting 10% from the UK basic rate, higher rate and additional rate and then increasing each of these rates by a new "Scottish rate" to be set by the Scottish Parliament.

(e) Calculations are made to the nearest pound when calculating taxable income. The amount of tax due on that income is calculated to the nearest penny in this book but HMRC will generally accept calculations made to the nearest pound.

EXAMPLE 1

Calculate the 2012-13 income tax liability of a taxpayer with taxable income (i.e. income remaining after deducting any available personal allowance) of:

(a) £11,250 (b) £34,370 (c) £45,706 (d) £231,400

Assume that none of the income is derived from savings or dividends.

Solution

(a) £11,250 @ 20% = £2,250.00.

(b) £34,370 @ 20% = £6,874.00.

(c) £34,370 @ 20% + 11,336 @ 40% = £11,408.40.

(d) £34,370 @ 20% + £115,630 @ 40% + £81,400 @ 50% = £93,826.00.

Income taxed at source

Certain types of income are *taxed at source*, which means that income tax is deducted from the income before the taxpayer receives it. For instance, banks and building societies are obliged by law to deduct income tax from interest paid to savers. Similarly, employers deduct income tax from wages and salaries paid to employees (see Chapter 7). Income which has been taxed at source must still be included in the taxpayer's income tax computation, despite the fact that tax has already been paid. This may seem unnecessary but there are two good reasons for including the income in the tax computation:

(a) It is important to derive correct figures for the taxpayer's "total income" and "net income", as will become clearer in later chapters.

(b) The amount of income tax which has already been deducted might not be the correct amount. The only way to check this is to aggregate the income concerned with all of the taxpayer's other income in a single computation.

In a tax computation, all income must be shown "gross". In other words, the amount of income shown must be the amount of the income *before* any income tax was deducted at source. When the tax liability has been calculated, tax paid by deduction at source is subtracted and the taxpayer is then required to pay only the balance of the liability. A tax refund is given if tax deducted at source exceeds the tax liability for the year.

Income which is taxed at source is often referred to as "income received net" and the amount actually received by the taxpayer after tax has been deducted is then referred to as the "net" amount of the income. This usage of the term "net" is very common but it must be carefully distinguished from the entirely different usage of the same term in the Income Tax Act 2007. As indicated earlier in this chapter, ITA 2007 defines "net income" as being equal to a taxpayer's total income less tax reliefs.

Grossing up

If income is received net of basic rate (20%) income tax, the gross amount of that income can be ascertained by multiplying the net amount received by 100/80. This calculation is known as "grossing-up" and the 100/80 fraction may be referred to as the "grossing-up fraction". The amount of income tax deducted at source is equal to the net amount multiplied by 20/80 (or 20% of the gross income). The main types of income which are received by individuals net of basic rate tax are:

(a) most forms of bank and building society interest (apart from interest on a National Savings Bank (NSB) investment account, which is received gross)

(b) debenture and other loan interest paid by UK companies

(c) the income element of a purchased life annuity (i.e. an annuity for life provided by an insurance company in exchange for a lump sum payment)

(d) patent royalties.

Interest on most UK Government securities ("gilt-edged" securities or "gilts") used to be received net of 20% tax but anyone receiving such interest may now choose whether to receive the interest gross or net.

When wages and salaries are received net of income tax, the gross pay and the amount of tax deducted can be ascertained by examining the end-of-year certificate supplied by the taxpayer's employer (see Chapter 7).

EXAMPLE 2

In 2012-13, an individual receives net building society interest of £1,248. Compute the equivalent gross income and the amount of tax deducted at source.

Solution

The equivalent gross income is £1,248 x 100/80 = £1,560 and the tax deducted at source is £1,248 x 20/80 = £312 (or 20% of £1,560).

Savings income

The tax liability on a taxpayer's "savings income" is calculated differently from the tax liability on non-savings income. The main categories of savings income are:

(a) interest from banks and building societies

(b) interest from gilt-edged securities and corporate bonds (i.e. debentures)

(c) the income element of purchased life annuities

(d) certain foreign income (see Chapter 32).

The important difference between the taxation of savings income and the taxation of non-savings income is that savings income which falls into the first £2,710 (for 2012-13) of the basic rate band is taxed at the *starting rate for savings* of 10% rather than at the basic rate of 20%. Therefore, if a taxpayer has both savings income and non-savings income, it is necessary to split taxable income between these two categories before the tax liability can be calculated. Note that:

(a) Non-savings income is regarded as the bottom layer or "slice" of taxable income and savings income is regarded as a higher layer. This means that the basic rate band is made available to non-savings income in priority to savings income.

(b) Tax reliefs and the personal allowance are set against income in the order which will result in the lowest tax liability. The best approach in 2012-13 is to make these deductions from non-savings income in priority to savings income, since non-savings income cannot benefit from the starting rate.

(c) The figure of £2,710 (for 2012-13) is known as the *starting rate limit for savings*. If a taxpayer's taxable income includes non-savings income of at least this amount, then the 10% rate will not be available for savings income at all. Otherwise, some or all of the taxpayer's savings income (if any) will fall into the first £2,710 of the basic rate band and will be taxed at 10%.

(d) Dividends from UK companies used to be regarded as savings income but this is no longer the case. The special tax regime which applies to UK dividends is explained later in this chapter.

EXAMPLE 3

In 2012-13, Robert has business profits of £41,310 and net bank interest of £360. He claims the personal allowance of £8,105. Calculate the income tax payable for the year.

Solution

	Total	*Non-savings*	*Savings*
	£	£	£
Business profits	41,310	41,310	
Bank interest £360 x 100/80	450		450
Total income	41,760	41,310	450
Less: Personal allowance	8,105	8,105	
Taxable income	33,655	33,205	450

Income tax due				
Non-savings income	: Basic rate	33,205	@ 20%	6,641.00
Savings income	: Basic rate	450	@ 20%	90.00
		33,655		
Tax borne				6,731.00
Less: Tax deducted at source				90.00
Tax payable				6,641.00

Taxable income includes non-savings income of more than £2,710 and so the starting rate is not available for savings income, all of which is taxed at the basic rate.

EXAMPLE 4

In 2012-13, Roberta has rental income of £9,805, net building society interest of £4,000 and net bank interest of £6,080. She claims the personal allowance of £8,105. Calculate the income tax payable for the year.

Solution

	Total	*Non-savings*	*Savings*
	£	£	£
Income from property	9,805	9,805	
BSI £4,000 x 100/80	5,000		5,000
Bank interest £6,080 x 100/80	7,600		7,600
Total income	22,405	9,805	12,600
Less: Personal allowance	8,105	8,105	
Taxable income	14,300	1,700	12,600

Income tax due

Non-savings income	: Basic rate	1,700	@ 20%	340.00
Savings income	: Starting rate	1,010	@ 10%	101.00
	: Basic rate	11,590	@ 20%	2,318.00
		14,300		
Tax borne				2,759.00
Less: Tax deducted at source				2,520.00
Tax payable				239.00

Non-savings income occupies £1,700 of the basic rate band. This allows £1,010 (£2,710 – £1,700) of the savings income to be taxed at the starting rate. The remaining £11,590 of savings income is taxed at the basic rate.

EXAMPLE 5

In 2012-13, Philip has business profits of £240,235 and net bank interest of £44,000. His personal allowance for the year is zero. Calculate the income tax payable for the year.

Solution

	Total	*Non-savings*	*Savings*
	£	£	£
Business profits	240,235	240,235	
Bank interest £44,000 x 100/80	55,000		55,000
Total income	295,235	240,235	55,000
Less: Personal allowance	0	0	
Taxable income	295,235	240,235	55,000

Income tax due

Non-savings income	: Basic rate	34,370	@ 20%	6,874.00
	: Higher rate	115,630	@ 40%	46,252.00
	: Additional rate	90,235	@ 50%	45,117.50
Savings income	: Additional rate	55,000	@ 50%	27,500.00
		295,235		
Tax borne				125,743.50
Less: Tax deducted at source				11,000.00
Tax payable				114,743.50

Non-savings income occupies the whole of the basic and higher rate bands, so savings income (and the balance of non-savings income) is taxed at the additional rate.

EXAMPLE 6

In 2012-13, Philippa has business profits of £7,510, National Savings Bank investment account interest (received gross) of £380 and net debenture interest of £41,880. She claims the personal allowance of £8,105. Calculate the income tax payable for the year.

Solution

	Total	*Non-savings*	*Savings*
	£	£	£
Business profits	7,510	7,510	
NSB interest	380		380
Debenture interest £41,880 x 100/80	52,350		52,350
Total income	60,240	7,510	52,730
Less: Personal allowance	8,105	7,510	595
Taxable income	52,135	nil	52,135

Income tax due				
Savings income	: Starting rate	2,710	@ 10%	271.00
	: Basic rate	31,660	@ 20%	6,332.00
	: Higher rate	17,765	@ 40%	7,106.00
		52,135		
Tax borne				13,709.00
Less: Tax deducted at source				10,470.00
Tax payable				3,239.00

Taxable income includes no non-savings income, so the first £2,710 of savings income is taxed at the starting rate. The next £31,660 (£34,370 – £2,710) is taxed at the basic rate and the remaining £17,765 is taxed at the higher rate.

Note that NSB investment account interest is received gross (i.e. without deduction of tax at source) and therefore should not be grossed-up.

Dividends from UK companies

At one time, dividends received from UK companies were regarded as savings income and were treated in a similar way to income received net of tax. However, a special tax regime now applies to UK dividends. The main points of this regime are as follows:

(a) UK dividends have an attached "tax credit" which is equal to *one-ninth* of the amount of the dividend received. A taxpayer's dividend income for a tax year is equal to the amount of the UK dividends received in that year plus the attached tax credits. For example, a taxpayer who receives UK dividends of £720 has dividend income for tax purposes of £800 (£720 plus the tax credits of £80).

(b) UK dividends are not classed as savings income or non-savings income. Dividends constitute a third layer which is treated as the top slice of taxable income, ranking above both non-savings and savings income.

(c) For 2012-13, dividends which fall into the basic rate band are taxed at the "dividend ordinary rate" of 10% and dividends which fall into the higher rate band are taxed at the "dividend upper rate" of 32.5%. Any dividends which lie above the higher rate limit are taxed at the "dividend additional rate" of 42.5%.

(d) Tax reliefs and the personal allowance should be set against non-savings income in priority to savings income and against savings income in priority to dividends.

(e) Tax credits relating to dividends which are charged to tax (i.e. dividends which are part of taxable income) may be deducted from the taxpayer's income tax liability on those dividends. However, it is *not* possible to claim payment of any tax credits which exceed this liability. Nor is it possible to deduct tax credits from the income tax which is due on other forms of income. Tax credits that relate to dividends which are not charged to tax are lost.

Note that the tax regime described above also applies to dividends received from non-UK companies (subject to certain conditions). The tax treatment of dividends received from non-UK companies is explained in Chapter 32 of this book.

Dividends from UK-REITs

A UK company which is a property investment company may elect to become a UK Real Estate Investment Trust (UK-REIT). Dividends received from a UK-REIT, to the extent that they derive from the company's tax-exempt property income or gains, are subject to a different tax regime than the one which is described above. Such dividends are received net of basic rate (20%) income tax and are treated as property income (see Chapter 5).

The examples and exercises in this book all assume that any dividends received are received from companies other than UK-REITs. A fuller description of the tax regime which relates to UK-REITs is given in Chapter 23.

EXAMPLE 7

In 2012-13, Ewan has rental income of £27,950, net bank interest of £3,240 and UK dividends of £183,690. Calculate the income tax payable by Ewan for the year, assuming that his personal allowance for 2012-13 is zero.

Solution

	Total	*Non-savings*	*Savings*	*Dividends*
	£	£	£	£
Income from property	27,950	27,950		
Bank interest £3,240 x 100/80	4,050		4,050	
UK dividends £183,690 + £20,410	204,100			204,100
Total income	236,100	27,950	4,050	204,100
Less: Personal allowance	0	0		
Taxable income	236,100	27,950	4,050	204,100

Income tax due

Non-savings income	: Basic rate	27,950	@ 20%	5,590.00
Savings income	: Basic rate	4,050	@ 20%	810.00
Dividend income	: Ordinary rate	2,370	@ 10%	237.00
	: Upper rate	115,630	@ 32.5%	37,579.75
	: Additional rate	86,100	@ 42.5%	36,592.50
		236,100		
Tax borne				80,809.25
Less: Tax credits on dividends				20,410.00
Tax payable				60,399.25
Less: Tax deducted at source				810.00
Tax payable				59,589.25

The dividends are treated as the top slice of income and are taxed at 10% to the extent (£2,370) that they occupy the basic rate band. Then the next £115,630 is taxed at the dividend upper rate of 32.5% and the remaining £86,100 is taxed at the dividend additional rate of 42.5%. The total tax due on dividends is £74,409.25, so the tax credits of £20,410 (i.e. the tax credits relating to dividends which are charged to tax) may be deducted in full.

EXAMPLE 8

In 2012-13, Charlie's only income consists of net bank interest of £3,640 and UK dividends of £4,140. He claims the personal allowance of £8,105. Calculate the income tax payable by Charlie for the year.

Solution

	Total	*Non-savings*	*Savings*	*Dividends*
	£	£	£	£
Bank interest £3,640 x 100/80	4,550		4,550	
UK dividends £4,140 + £460	4,600			4,600
Total income	9,150		4,550	4,600
Less: Personal allowance	8,105		4,550	3,555
Taxable income	1,045		–	1,045

Income tax due		
Dividend income : Ordinary rate	1,045 @ 10%	104.50
Tax borne		104.50
Less: Tax credits on dividends		104.50
Tax payable		0.00
Less: Tax deducted at source		910.00
Tax repayable		(910.00)

The dividends all fall into the basic rate band and are taxed at the dividend ordinary rate of 10%. Tax credits relating to dividends which are charged to tax are £104.50. The tax due on these dividends is also £104.50, so these tax credits may be deducted. But Charlie cannot claim payment of the remaining £355.50 of tax credits which relate to the dividends covered by the personal allowance.

Summary

- In general, income tax is chargeable on all of the income of UK residents and on the UK income of non-residents.
- Income is classified into a number of categories, each of which has its own rules for determining the amount of assessable income in a tax year.
- Certain types of income are specifically exempt from income tax.
- To calculate a taxpayer's income tax liability it is necessary to bring together all of the taxpayer's income into a single computation. The gross equivalent of income received net of income tax must be included in the computation.
- Husbands, wives and civil partners are assessed to income tax independently.
- In 2012-13, the main rates of income tax are the basic rate of 20%, the higher rate of 40% and the additional rate of 50%. Savings income which occupies the first £2,710 of the basic rate band is taxed at the starting rate for savings of 10%.
- UK dividends are accompanied by tax credits which generally may be set against the tax liability on those dividends. In 2012-13, dividends which fall into the basic rate band are taxed at 10% and dividends which fall into the higher rate band are taxed at 32.5%. Dividends which lie above the higher rate limit are taxed at 42.5%.
- If the tax credit attached to a UK dividend exceeds the tax liability with regard to that dividend, the excess tax credit cannot be paid to the recipient under any circumstances.

Exercises

2.1 Calculate the income tax payable in 2012-13 on a taxable income (i.e. income remaining after deducting any available personal allowance) of:

(a) £1,830 (b) £32,300 (c) £68,703 (d) £320,000.

Assume in each case that none of the income is derived from savings or dividends.

2.2 Calculate the income tax payable in 2012-13 on the following incomes:

(a) Business profits of £23,710 and net bank interest of £720.

(b) Business profits of £30,840, net building society interest of £8,000 and net bank interest of £2,300.

(c) Net bank interest of £130,604.

Assume that a personal allowance of £8,105 is claimed in cases (a) and (b). Assume that the personal allowance in case (c) is zero.

2.3 Stephanie has the following income in 2012-13:

	£
Income from employment	28,755
Rents received	13,330
Bank interest (net)	144
NSB investment account interest, received gross	20
UK dividends	225

Compute the income tax payable by Stephanie for the year (before deducting any tax paid under the PAYE system) assuming that the rents received are not within the "rent-a-room" scheme and that Stephanie is entitled to the personal allowance of £8,105.

2.4 Ernest has a retirement pension in 2012-13 of £7,395. He also receives net bank interest of £416. Compute the income tax payable by Ernest for the year, assuming a personal allowance of £8,105.

What difference would it make if Ernest had received UK dividends of £468 instead of the bank interest?

***2.5** Ivan's income for the tax year 2012-13 is as follows:

	£
Part-time salary	9,590
Building society interest (net)	9,360
Premium bond prize	50
NSB investment account interest, received gross	60

Compute the income tax payable by Ivan for the year (before deducting any tax paid under the PAYE system) assuming a personal allowance of £8,105.

***2.6** Mary's income for the tax year 2012-13 is as follows:

	£
Business profits	29,280
Rents received	3,750
UK dividends	109,890

Compute the income tax payable by Mary for the year, assuming that the rents received are not within the "rent-a-room" scheme and that Mary's personal allowance for 2012-13 is zero.

Chapter 3

Personal allowances

Introduction

One of the factors which must be taken into account when preparing an income tax computation is the taxpayer's entitlement to *personal allowances*. Most taxpayers can claim only the basic personal allowance but there are higher allowances for older taxpayers and extra allowances for blind taxpayers and for older married couples. The purpose of this chapter is to describe the allowances available in tax year 2012-13 and to explain the way in which each allowance is dealt with in a tax computation.

It is important to appreciate that personal allowances are indeed "personal". If all or part of a personal allowance cannot be used by the person to whom it is available, then any unused part of the allowance is generally lost. Excess allowances cannot normally be transferred to anyone else and cannot be carried back to previous years or forward to future years. However, some limited provisions exist for transferring excess allowances between spouses or civil partners (see later in this chapter).

Personal allowances for 2012-13

Personal allowances may be claimed by UK residents and by certain non-residents. The main classes of non-resident who may claim personal allowances and set these allowances against their UK income are:

(a) nationals of the European Economic Area (EEA), which comprises all EU states plus Norway, Iceland and Liechtenstein

(b) residents in the Isle of Man or the Channel Islands

(c) persons who used to reside in the UK but now reside abroad for health reasons

(d) Crown servants, ex-Crown servants and their widows/widowers

(e) missionaries.

The personal allowances for 2012-13 are as follows:

	£
Allowances which are deducted from net income:	
Personal allowance:	
Basic (age 0-64)	8,105
Age 65-74	10,500
Age 75 and over	10,660
Blind person's allowance	2,100
Allowances which are "tax reducers":	
Married couple's allowance:	
Born before 6 April 1935	7,705
Minimum amount	2,960
Income limit for age-related allowances	25,400

The personal allowance (PA)

Anyone who is entitled to claim personal allowances may claim at least the basic personal allowance. This allowance is deducted from the taxpayer's net income (i.e. total income less tax reliefs) when computing his or her income tax liability. The full amount of the personal allowance for 2012-13 is £8,105 but this is reduced (possibly to zero) if the taxpayer has income exceeding £100,000 (see below). Note also that:

(a) The personal allowance is fully available in the tax year in which a taxpayer is born or dies, apart from being reduced as usual if income for that year exceeds £100,000.

(b) The personal allowance for 2013-14 will be £9,205, but the basic rate limit for that year will fall to £32,245. Taken together with planned changes to National Insurance thresholds, most higher rate taxpayers will receive only one-quarter of the benefit that basic rate taxpayers will receive from the increase in the personal allowance.

Reduction in the basic personal allowance

The amount of the basic personal allowance for a tax year is reduced if the taxpayer's "adjusted net income" for the year exceeds £100,000. Adjusted net income is defined as the taxpayer's net income less the grossed-up amount of any Gift Aid donations made during the year (see Chapter 4) and the gross amount of any pension contributions relieved at source during the year (see Chapter 14).

If adjusted net income exceeds £100,000, the basic personal allowance is reduced by one-half of the excess. Therefore the allowance is reduced to zero in 2012-13 if adjusted net income is £116,210 (£100,000 + (2 × £8,105)) or more.

It is worth noting that the gradual withdrawal of the personal allowance means that a taxpayer with income in the range £100,000 to £116,210 is subject to a marginal rate of income tax of 60%. This surprising result is illustrated in the following example.

EXAMPLE 1

A taxpayer's adjusted net income for 2012-13 is £108,400. None of this is derived from dividends. Calculate the amount of the personal allowance and show that a £2 increase in adjusted net income would result in an increase of £1.20 in the income tax liability.

Solution

The PA is £3,905 (£8,105 – 1/2 x £8,400). If the taxpayer's income increased by £2, the PA would reduce by a further £1, so that taxable income would increase by £3. Income tax on an extra £3 of taxable income would be £1.20 (£3 @ 40%). This represents an effective income tax rate of 60% on the £2 increase in income.

Older taxpayers

As can be seen from the list of allowances given earlier, the amount of the personal allowance depends upon the taxpayer's age:

(a) A taxpayer who is over 65 years old, or who reaches the age of 65 during the tax year, is entitled to an increased personal allowance (£10,500 in 2012-13), and

(b) the allowance is higher still (£10,660 in 2012-13) for taxpayers who are over 75 years old or who reach the age of 75 during the tax year.

These higher personal allowances are granted *instead* of the usual personal allowance, not in addition to it. A taxpayer who dies in the tax year in which he or she would have reached the age of 65 or 75 is granted the higher allowance for the year of death.

However, age-related personal allowances are reduced if the taxpayer's adjusted net income exceeds a specified limit (£25,400 in 2012-13). If adjusted net income exceeds this limit, the personal allowance is reduced by one-half of the excess. But the allowance is not reduced to less than the personal allowance for those aged 0-64.

Note that, *in tax year 2013-14*, the age-related personal allowances for those aged over 65 (or 75) will be frozen at their 2012-13 levels and will be available only to those taxpayers who reach the age of 65 (or 75) before 6 April 2013. These allowances will then be kept at their frozen level in future years and will be abolished completely when they no longer exceed the basic personal allowance. This change will have no effect on an individual's entitlement to the married couple's allowance (see below).

EXAMPLE 2

Calculate the personal allowance due in 2012-13 to each of the following taxpayers:

(a) Born 31 July 1947, income £15,700

(b) Born 31 July 1937, income £15,050

(c) Born 22 April 1944, income £26,000

(d) Born 2 May 1943, income £33,400

(e) Born 22 April 1934, income £25,600

(f) Born 2 May 1933, income £103,150.

In each case, the stated income figure is the taxpayer's adjusted net income for the year.

Solution

(a) This taxpayer reaches the age of 65 during 2012-13, so PA for the year is £10,500.

(b) This taxpayer reaches the age of 75 during 2012-13, so PA for the year is £10,660.

(c) This taxpayer is in the 65-74 age group and has an income which exceeds the limit by £600, giving a PA of £10,200 (£10,500 – 1/2 x £600).

(d) This taxpayer is 65-74 and has an income which exceeds the income limit by £8,000. This would give a PA of £6,500 (£10,500 – 1/2 x £8,000) but the allowance is not reduced to less than the PA for those aged 0-64 so the taxpayer will claim £8,105.

(e) This taxpayer is over 75 and has an income which exceeds the limit by £200, giving a PA of £10,560 (£10,660 – 1/2 x £200).

(f) This taxpayer is over 75 and has an income which exceeds the limit by £77,750. This gives a negative PA (£10,660 – 1/2 x £77,750) so the allowance would normally be £8,105. However, adjusted net income exceeds £100,000, so the PA is reduced to £6,530 (£8,105 – 1/2 x £3,150).

Blind person's allowance (BPA)

The blind person's allowance (£2,100 in 2012-13) may be claimed by registered blind persons. This allowance is deducted from net income and is given in full in the tax year in which the taxpayer is first registered as a blind person.

If a husband or wife (or civil partner) who is granted the blind person's allowance cannot make full use of it, the unused part can be transferred to the other spouse or partner, even if that spouse is not a registered blind person.

Tax reducers

The personal allowance and the blind person's allowance are both deducted from net income when calculating taxable income. By contrast, the married couple's allowance (the only other allowance which is available in 2012-13) is ignored until the amount of income tax due on the taxpayer's taxable income has been calculated. The MCA is then relieved by reducing this tax liability by *10% of the amount of the allowance*. For this reason, the MCA is sometimes referred to as a "tax reducer". Note that:

(a) Certain payments and some types of investments made by a taxpayer also act as tax reducers (see Chapters 4 and 6).

(b) The amount of tax borne can never be reduced to less than zero as a result of the tax reduction process. If available tax reductions exceed the tax due on taxable income, there is no repayment of the excess. Any unused part of a tax reduction is generally lost. However, the tax reduction relating to the MCA may be transferred between spouses or civil partners in certain cases (see below).

Married couple's allowance (MCA)

The married couple's allowance is available to a legally married couple who live together for at least part of the tax year, *so long as at least one of the spouses was born before 6 April 1935*. MCA is also available to civil partners, so long as at least one of the partners was born before 6 April 1935. Note the following points:

(a) The allowance is not available to a married couple (or civil partners) who are separated for the whole of the tax year. A couple are regarded as "separated" for tax purposes if they are legally separated or if they are separated in circumstances which make it likely that separation will be permanent.

(b) The amount of the MCA for 2012-13 is £7,705, giving a maximum tax reduction of £770.50 (£7,705 @ 10%).

(c) For couples who were married before 5 December 2005, MCA is generally claimed by the husband. However, the couple may elect that the MCA should instead be claimed by the spouse with the higher net income. Such an election must be made before the start of the first tax year in which it is to have effect and then applies to all subsequent tax years. The election is irrevocable.

(d) For couples who marry on or after 5 December 2005 (and for civil partners) the MCA is claimed by the spouse or partner with the higher net income.

(e) In the same way as the age-related personal allowance is reduced if a taxpayer's adjusted net income exceeds a specified limit, the MCA is reduced if the *claimant's* adjusted net income exceeds the same limit (£25,400 in 2012-13). However, the allowance is never reduced to less than a specified minimum amount (£2,960 in 2012-13). It is noteworthy that the other spouse's (or other partner's) income is not taken into account for this purpose, even if the MCA is being given because of that spouse's or partner's age rather than because of the claimant's age.

(f) The procedure which is adopted if a taxpayer's adjusted net income needs to be taken into account when computing both that taxpayer's own PA (because he or she is over 65) and the MCA (because of the above rules) is as follows:

    (i) The excess of the person's adjusted net income over the income limit is divided by two, giving the required reduction in allowances.

    (ii) The person's own PA is reduced first, but not to an amount which is less than the personal allowance for those aged 0-64.

    (iii) If the reduction made in the personal allowance has not fully achieved the required reduction in allowances, the MCA is reduced next, but never to less than the specified minimum amount.

EXAMPLE 3

Calculate the allowances available in 2012-13 to the following husbands and wives:

	Husband	*Wife*
(a)	Born 5 July 1939, income £19,100	Born 1 March 1935, income £12,450.
(b)	Born 12 April 1948, income £nil	Born 5 April 1935, income £32,200.
(c)	Born 3 May 1932, income £25,550	Born 7 September 1938, income £nil.
(d)	Born 4 June 1938, income £31,760	Born 8 October 1933, income £13,950.
(e)	Born 5 July 1948, income £35,200	Born 9 November 1934, income £nil.

In each case, the stated income figure is the adjusted net income. All of the couples were married before 5 December 2005 and none of them have elected that MCA should be claimed by the spouse with the higher net income.

Solution

(a) The husband is over 65 and is entitled to a PA of £10,500. His wife is over 75 and is entitled to a PA of £10,660. An MCA of £7,705 is available because the wife was born before 6 April 1935.

(b) The husband is under 65 and is therefore entitled to a PA of £8,105, all of which is unused. His wife is over 75 but her income exceeds the limit by £6,800. This would give her a PA of £7,260 (£10,660 – 1/2 x £6,800) but the allowance is not reduced to less than the PA for those aged 0-64 so she will claim a PA of £8,105.

An MCA of £7,705 is available since the wife was born before 6 April 1935. The MCA is not reduced at all since the husband's income does not exceed the income limit.

(c) The husband is over 75 but his income exceeds the limit by £150. This gives him a PA of £10,585 (£10,660 – 1/2 x £150). His wife is over 65 and she is entitled to a PA of £10,500, all of which is unused.

An MCA of £7,705 is available because the husband was born before 6 April 1935. This is not reduced at all since the reduction required because of the size of his income has already been made in full against his own PA.

(d) The husband is over 65 but his income exceeds the limit by £6,360. Therefore he must lose a total of £3,180 in allowances. His PA is first reduced from £10,500 to £8,105 (a reduction of £2,395). The remaining £785 is deducted from the MCA of £7,705 (available because of his wife's date of birth). So MCA is £6,920.

The wife is over 75 and she is entitled to a PA of £10,660.

(e) The husband is under 65 and is therefore entitled to a PA of £8,105. His wife is over 75 and so she is entitled to a PA of £10,660, all of which is unused.

The wife was born before 6 April 1935 so MCA is available. But this must be reduced because the husband's income exceeds the limit by £9,800. None of the reduction in allowances (£4,900) can be subtracted from his own PA as he is claiming only the basic £8,105. So the whole of the reduction must be set against the MCA. This would give an MCA of £2,805 (£7,705 – £4,900) but the allowance is never reduced to less than the minimum amount (£2,960) so an MCA of £2,960 is available.

Allocation of the MCA

The tax reduction relating to the MCA is normally set against the tax liability of the *claimant*, but note that:

(a) The couple may elect jointly that the tax reduction relating to the MCA minimum amount (£2,960 for 2012-13) should be set against the tax liability of the claimant's spouse or civil partner.

(b) The claimant's spouse or civil partner may elect unilaterally that the tax reduction relating to 50% of the MCA minimum amount (£1,480 for 2012-13) should be set against his or her tax liability.

(c) If either spouse or partner is unable to use their MCA-related tax reduction in full or in part, the unused part may be transferred to the other spouse or partner.

The elections described in (a) and (b) must normally be made before the start of the tax year to which they relate, but they can be made during the tax year if this is the year of marriage or the year in which a civil partnership is registered. If either of these elections is made, any remaining part of the MCA is dealt with in the claimant's tax computation.

The transfer described in (c) must be claimed within four years of the end of the tax year to which it relates.

Year of marriage and year of separation or death

In the tax year in which a marriage occurs or a civil partnership is registered, MCA is reduced by one-twelfth for each full tax month which elapses between the start of the year and the date of the marriage or registration. A tax month runs from the 6th of one month to the 5th of the next month. An election to transfer all or 50% of the MCA minimum amount to the claimant's spouse or partner in the year of marriage or registration applies to that amount reduced in the same proportion as the MCA itself.

MCA is available in full in the tax year in which a couple separate or in which one of them dies.

EXAMPLE 4

Calculate the MCA available in 2012-13 to a husband and wife (both born in September 1934) who each have an adjusted net income not exceeding £25,400 and who marry on:

(a) 5 April 2012 (b) 9 April 2012 (c) 23 June 2012 (d) 4 April 2013

Solution

(a) A couple who marry on 5 April 2012 are already married by the start of 2012-13, so the MCA of £7,705 is available in full.

(b) A couple who marry on 9 April 2012 are not married for the whole of 2012-13 but no full tax months have passed between the start of the tax year and the date of the marriage. Therefore the full MCA of £7,705 is available.

(c) If the marriage takes place on 23 June 2012, two full tax months have passed since the start of the tax year (6 April 2012 to 5 May 2012 and 6 May 2012 to 5 June 2012). The MCA is reduced by two-twelfths, giving an MCA of £7,705 x 10/12 = £6,421.

(d) If the marriage takes place on 4 April 2013, eleven full tax months have passed since the start of the tax year. Therefore the MCA is reduced by eleven-twelfths, giving an MCA of £7,705 x 1/12 = £642.

EXAMPLE 5

Calculate the tax borne in 2012-13 by a husband and wife (both born in March 1935) given the information shown below. In each case, an election has been made for 50% of the tax reduction relating to the MCA minimum amount to be set against the tax of the claimant's spouse. None of the income is derived from savings or dividends.

(a) Married July 1960; husband's income £26,880, wife's income £21,750.

(b) Married 1 October 2012; husband's income £19,785, wife's income £15,855.

(c) Married July 1960 but husband dies 12 October 2012; husband's income £12,245, wife's income £22,415. The couple have not elected that MCA should be claimed by the spouse with the higher net income.

In each case, the stated income figure is the taxpayer's net income (i.e. total income less tax reliefs) and adjusted net income is the same as net income.

Solution

	(a)	(b)	(c)
	£	£	£
HUSBAND			
Net income	26,880	19,785	12,245
Less: Personal allowance	9,920	10,660	10,660
Taxable income	16,960	9,125	1,585
Income tax			
£16,960 @ 20%	3,392.00		
£9,125 @ 20%		1,825.00	
£1,585 @ 20%			317.00
Less: MCA £6,225 @ 10%	622.50		
MCA £3,632 @ 10%		363.20	
MCA £6,225 @ 10% = £622.50			317.00
Tax borne	2,769.50	1,461.80	nil

WIFE			
Net income	21,750	15,855	22,415
Less: Personal allowance	10,660	10,660	10,660
Taxable income	11,090	5,195	11,755
Income tax			
£11,090 @ 20%	2,218.00		
£5,195 @ 20%		1,039.00	
£11,755 @ 20%			2,351.00
Less: MCA £1,480 @ 10%	148.00		
MCA £863 @ 10%		86.30	
MCA £1,480 @ 10% + £305.50			453.50
Tax borne	2,070.00	952.70	1,897.50

Notes:

(i) In case (a), the husband's income is £1,480 over the income limit, therefore his PA is reduced to £9,920 (£10,660 – 1/2 x £1,480). MCA is available in full. £1,480 (one-half of the minimum amount) is claimed by the wife, leaving £6,225 for the husband.

(ii) In case (b), the available MCA is 7/12 x £7,705 = £4,495. The wife claims 7/12 x £1,480 = £863, leaving £3,632 for the husband.

(iii) In case (c), the MCA is available in full in the year of the husband's death. £1,480 is claimed by the wife, leaving £6,225 for the husband. The tax reduction that he cannot use (£305.50) is transferred to his wife.

Summary

- All UK residents and some non-resident taxpayers are entitled to claim at least the basic personal allowance. But this allowance is reduced if the taxpayer's adjusted net income exceeds £100,000.
- Older taxpayers are entitled to a higher personal allowance but this is reduced if adjusted net income exceeds a specified limit. The reduction is generally equal to one-half of the amount by which this limit is exceeded, but the allowance is not reduced to less than the basic personal allowance.
- The blind person's allowance is granted to registered blind persons.
- The married couple's allowance is available to a legally married couple who live together for at least part of the tax year, so long as at least one of the spouses was born before 6 April 1935. MCA is also available to civil partners.
- MCA is reduced if the claimant's adjusted net income exceeds a specified limit.
- All or part of the MCA may be transferred to the claimant's spouse or partner if an appropriate election is made.

- The personal allowance and the blind person's allowance are deducted from the taxpayer's net income when computing taxable income. The MCA reduces tax borne by 10% of the amount of the allowance.
- Personal allowances which cannot be used in the tax year to which they relate are lost. There is no provision for carrying unused allowances backwards or forwards.

Exercises

3.1 Calculate the basic personal allowance available in 2012-13 to a taxpayer with adjusted net income of:

(a) £90,000
(b) £110,000
(c) £120,000.

3.2 Calculate the personal allowance due in 2012-13 to each of the following taxpayers:

(a) Born on 28 August 1945, adjusted net income £16,100
(b) Born on 25 May 1936, adjusted net income £26,400
(c) Born on 2 February 1948, adjusted net income £34,000.

3.3 Calculate the allowances available to a husband and wife in 2012-13 (assuming that they were married before 5 December 2005 and that they have not elected for MCA to be claimed by the spouse with the higher net income) given the following information:

(a) Husband born 1934, income £18,500; wife born 1939, income £25,700
(b) Husband born 1934, income £26,100; wife born 1934, income £10,070
(c) Husband born 1934, income £31,800; wife born 1939, income £20,000.

In each case, the stated income figure is the adjusted net income.

3.4 Calculate the tax borne in 2012-13 by a husband and wife (both born in 1933), given the information shown below. No elections have been made in relation to the married couple's allowance and none of the income is derived from savings or dividends.

(a) Married in 1956; husband's income £17,300, wife's income £18,600
(b) Married 17 August 2012; husband's income £9,500, wife's income £14,535
(c) Married in 1956 but husband dies on 16 September 2012; husband's income to date of death £10,995, wife's income for the year £18,465.

In each case, the stated income figure is the taxpayer's net income (i.e. total income less tax reliefs) and adjusted net income is the same as net income.

3.5 Calculate the married couple's allowance available in 2012-13 to a married couple who marry on each of the following dates:

(a) 4 May 2012 (both born 1990)

(b) 14 February 2013
(husband born 1937, income £15,300; wife born 1934, income £10,300)

(c) 25 December 2012
(husband born 1934, income £12,700; wife born 1949, income £27,000).

In each case, the stated income figure is the adjusted net income.

3.6 Toby is a widower. He was born in August 1937 and his income for 2012-13 is as follows:

	£
Retirement pension	9,640
Bank interest (net)	912

Calculate the amount of income tax repayable to Toby for 2012-13.

3.7 Richard was born on 5 April 1935. His wife, Patricia, was born on 5 October 1938. They were married in 1968. Their income for 2012-13 is as follows:

	£
Richard:	
Business profits	31,760
Patricia:	
UK dividends	3,600

Calculate their tax borne and tax payable in 2012-13.

***3.8** A married man (born 3 November 1934) died on 8 July 2012. He received a retirement pension of £11,890 between 6 April 2012 and the date of his death. His wife (born 12 August 1940) had no income whilst her husband was alive but received a pension of £17,685 between 8 July 2012 and 5 April 2013. They were married in 1970 and made no elections in relation to the married couple's allowance.

Calculate their tax borne in 2012-13.

***3.9** Bill was born in 1973. He is married to Hazel who was born in 1977. In 2012-13, Bill received business profits of £45,160 and UK dividends of £4,680. Hazel received a salary of £220,570 and net bank interest of £2,432.

Calculate their tax payable for the year (before deducting any tax paid under the PAYE system).

Chapter 4

Payments and gifts eligible for tax relief

Introduction

Certain payments and gifts made by a taxpayer are eligible for tax relief. Some of these are subtracted from the taxpayer's total income when computing his or her tax liability. Others act as tax reducers and are relieved by reducing the amount of tax payable on the taxpayer's taxable income. A special tax regime applies to charitable donations which fall within the "Gift Aid" scheme.

The purpose of this chapter is to identify the main types of payments and gifts which attract tax relief in these ways and to explain how relief is given for each. However, this chapter does *not* deal with:

(a) payments and gifts which are deductible when computing a taxpayer's income from either employment (see Chapter 7) or self-employment (see Chapter 9)

(b) pension contributions (see Chapter 14).

Payments and gifts deductible from total income

The following payments and gifts are deductible from a taxpayer's total income for the tax year in which the payment or gift is made:

(a) eligible interest payments

(b) certain "annual payments" and patent royalties

(c) gifts of listed shares or securities to a charity

(d) gifts of land or buildings to a charity.

Each of these is explained later in this chapter. As indicated in Chapter 2, the income which remains after these items (and certain other reliefs) have been subtracted from total income is referred to by Income Tax Act 2007 as the taxpayer's "net income".

Tax relief for these payments and gifts is given at "marginal rate" (i.e. at the highest rates of income tax to which the taxpayer is liable). Deducting them from total income will automatically give the right amount of relief, since the effect of the deduction is to reduce the amount of taxable income which falls into the upper tax bands.

Payments made gross or net

Most of the payments which are deductible from total income are made gross (without deduction of income tax). Others are required by law to be paid net, after deduction of income tax calculated at the basic rate.

Payments made gross are deducted from the taxpayer's total income when computing his or her income tax liability, but it is tempting to ignore any payments made net since the taxpayer has already taken tax relief at source. However, the tax deducted at source is always calculated at the basic rate (20% for 2012-13) and this will not give the right amount of relief to a taxpayer whose highest rate of tax is not the basic rate. The only way to be sure that the right amount of tax relief is given for a payment made net is to:

(a) calculate the gross amount of the payment (net payment × 100/80)

(b) subtract the gross figure from the taxpayer's total income, thus giving the correct amount of tax relief

(c) increase the taxpayer's income tax liability by the amount of basic rate tax which was deducted from the payment when it was made.

In effect, the person making the payment is regarded as having collected basic rate income tax from the recipient on behalf of HM Revenue and Customs and must therefore account to HMRC for this tax as part of his or her income tax liability. Note the following points:

(a) This treatment of payments made net of tax is entirely consistent with the treatment of income received net of tax (see Chapter 2). Income received net is shown gross in the taxpayer's income tax computation and the amount of tax deducted at source is subtracted when calculating tax payable. Similarly, payments made net are shown gross in the taxpayer's income tax computation and the amount of tax deducted at source is added when calculating tax payable.

(b) Basic rate tax must be deducted at source from certain payments which are allowable when computing a taxpayer's income from self-employment (see Chapter 9). In this case, to ensure that tax relief is not given twice, these payments are not also deducted from total income. However, the amount of tax deducted at source must still be accounted for to HMRC and this is achieved by adding this amount to the taxpayer's income tax liability for the year.

EXAMPLE 1

(a) Bob has total income of £18,050 in 2012-13. None of his income is derived from savings or dividends and he claims only the basic personal allowance. He makes a deductible payment of £200 during the year (paid gross).

(b) Cathy's circumstances are precisely the same as Bob's except that her deductible payment is made net of basic rate tax, so that she pays a net amount of £160.

Compute Bob and Cathy's income tax liabilities for 2012-13. Does it seem to make any difference whether a deductible payment is made gross or net?

Solution

	Bob	Cathy
	£	£
Total income	18,050	18,050
Less: Payment	200	
Payment £160 x 100/80		200
Net income	17,850	17,850
Less: Personal allowance	8,105	8,105
Taxable income	9,745	9,745
Income tax		
£9,745 @ 20%	1,949.00	
£9,745 @ 20%		1,949.00
Tax borne	1,949.00	1,949.00
Add: Tax deducted from payment	0.00	40.00
Tax liability	1,949.00	1,989.00

Note:

Bob has made a payment of £200 and has a tax liability of £1,949.00, a total of £2,149.00. Cathy has made a payment of £160 and has a tax liability of £1,989.00, again a total of £2,149.00. Apart from the timing of the cash flows involved, it makes no difference whether a deductible payment is made gross or net and this is evidenced by the fact that tax borne is the same for both taxpayers.

Higher rate and additional rate taxpayers

A payment or gift which is deductible from total income costs a higher rate or additional rate taxpayer less than a basic rate taxpayer, since relief is given at the highest rate of income tax to which the taxpayer is liable. However, there is no need to adjust the method of computation to deal specially with such taxpayers. The method described above will give the correct result for all taxpayers.

EXAMPLE 2

Derek's total income for 2012-13 is £62,920 (entirely non-savings income). He makes a gross deductible payment of £3,000 during the year and claims only the basic personal allowance. He makes no Gift Aid donations or pension contributions. Show his income tax computation:

(a) with the deductible payment (b) as it would have been without the payment.

How much has the payment effectively cost him? How much would it have cost him if his total income for the year had been £162,920? And in what ways would the situation have differed if his income for the year had been £112,920?

Solution

			Income £62,920		Income £162,920	
			(a)	(b)	(a)	(b)
			£	£	£	£
Total income			62,920	62,920	162,920	162,920
Less: Payment			3,000		3,000	
Net income			59,920	62,920	159,920	162,920
Less: Personal allowance			8,105	8,105	0	0
Taxable income			51,815	54,815	159,920	162,920
Income tax						
34,370	34,370	@ 20%	6,874.00	6,874.00		
17,445	20,445	@ 40%	6,978.00	8,178.00		
51,815	54,815					
34,370	34,370	@ 20%			6,874.00	6,874.00
115,630	115,630	@ 40%			46,252.00	46,252.00
9,920	12,920	@ 50%			4,960.00	6,460.00
159,920	162,920					
Tax liability			13,852.00	15,052.00	58,086.00	59,586.00

Notes:

(i) With total income of £62,920, Derek's income tax liability is reduced by £1,200 if he makes the £3,000 payment, so in fact it costs him only £1,800. In effect, tax relief has been given at 40%, which is Derek's highest rate of tax.

(ii) With total income of £162,920, Derek's income tax liability is reduced by £1,500 if he makes the £3,000 payment, so it now costs him only £1,500. Tax relief has been given at 50%, which is Derek's highest rate of tax. The personal allowance is zero in this case because adjusted net income greatly exceeds £100,000 (see Chapter 3).

(iii) With total income of £112,920, the £3,000 payment reduces Derek's net income to £109,920 and his personal allowance is £3,145 (£8,105 – 1/2 x £9,920). Without the payment, the personal allowance is only £1,645 (£8,105 – 1/2 x £12,920). Therefore the combination of the £3,000 payment and the extra personal allowance of £1,500 reduces taxable income by £4,500.

Since Derek's highest rate of tax in this case is 40%, he saves tax of £1,800 (40% of £4,500). A tax saving of £1,800 on a payment of £3,000 amounts to an effective rate of tax relief of 60%. This exceptionally high rate of tax relief will always occur if a taxpayer has adjusted net income (for 2012-13) which lies between £100,000 and £116,210 (see Chapter 3).

Starting rate and dividend ordinary rate taxpayers and non-taxpayers

A taxpayer whose highest rate of income tax is the starting rate for savings (10%) or the dividend ordinary rate (10%) is entitled to tax relief on deductible payments and gifts at only 10%. Similarly, a non-taxpayer (with a total income which is covered by the personal allowance) is not entitled to any tax relief at all. But there is no need to adjust the method of computation to deal specially with such taxpayers. Once again, the method described above will automatically ensure that tax relief (if any) is given at the correct rate.

EXAMPLE 3

Esmé has total income of £8,660 in 2012-13 (all savings income) and she makes a gross deductible payment of £160 during the year. She claims only the basic personal allowance. Show her income tax computation:

(a) with the deductible payment

(b) as it would have been without the payment.

How much has the payment effectively cost her?

Solution

	(a)	(b)
	£	£
Total income	8,660	8,660
Less: Payment	160	
Net income	8,500	8,660
Less: Personal allowance	8,105	8,105
Taxable income	395	555
Income tax		
Tax liability @ 10%	39.50	55.50

Note:

Esmé's highest rate of income tax is the starting rate for savings and her tax liability is reduced by £16 if she makes the payment. This is logical since she is entitled to relief at 10% (10% of £160 = £16). The payment has cost her £144 (£160 – £16).

EXAMPLE 4

Glenda has total income of £7,980 in 2012-13. She makes a gross deductible payment of £50 during the year and claims only the basic personal allowance. Show her income tax computation:

(a) with the deductible payment

(b) as it would have been without the payment.

How much has the payment effectively cost her?

Gift Aid

The Gift Aid scheme provides a tax incentive for individuals and companies to make charitable donations. The way in which the scheme applies to individuals is explained here. The way in which the scheme applies to companies is explained in Chapter 23.

This scheme applies to any charitable donation (including donations made to community amateur sports clubs) so long as:

(a) the donor is either UK resident or is a Crown servant working overseas or a non-resident with income or gains charged to UK tax

(b) the donation takes the form of a gift of money and this gift is not repayable to the donor, is not covered by the payroll giving scheme (see Chapter 7) and is not deductible when computing the donor's income from any source

(c) the donor receives no benefit at all from making the gift, or receives a benefit which does not exceed the following limits:

   (i) 25% of the amount of the gift, if the gift does not exceed £100
   (ii) £25, if the gift exceeds £100 but does not exceed £1,000
   (iii) 5% of the amount of the gift, if the gift exceeds £1,000

   subject to a limit of £2,500 on the value of the benefits which the donor may receive in any one tax year as a consequence of donations to any one charity

(d) the donor makes a Gift Aid declaration with regard to the donation.

If these conditions are satisfied, the gift is treated as if made net of basic rate tax and the charity can recover the tax deemed to have been deducted at source. For instance, a £20 gift would be treated as a gross gift of £25 (£20 × 100/80) less tax deducted of £5. In this case, the charity would receive £20 from the donor and a further £5 from HMRC.

Gift Aid relief for donors

Gift aid donations are *not* shown in the donor's tax computation, but the following provisions apply:

(a) The donor must pay income tax and capital gains tax equal to at least the amount of tax deemed to have been deducted from the gift. If this is not the case, then the donor's entitlement to personal allowances is restricted to ensure that this amount of tax is in fact paid. If the restriction of personal allowances does not give the required result, the donor is charged to income tax at the basic rate on as much of the gift as is necessary to ensure that the required amount of tax is paid.

(b) The donor's basic rate limit and higher rate limit are both increased by the gross amount of the gift, so ensuring that relief at the higher rate or additional rate is automatically given to higher rate and additional rate taxpayers.

(c) The donor may elect that a qualifying Gift Aid donation should be treated for tax purposes as if paid in the previous tax year. Such an election must be made on or before the date that the tax return for the previous tax year is submitted and no later than the 31 January which follows the end of that year.

EXAMPLE 6

In 2012-13, Owen makes qualifying Gift Aid donations totalling £360. He claims only the basic personal allowance and he has no capital gains tax liability for the year. Show his income tax computation if his only income for the year consists of business profits of:

(a) £24,430 (b) £8,220 (c) £246,090.

Solution

					(a)	(b)	(c)
					£	£	£
Business profits					24,430	8,220	246,090
Less: Personal allowance					8,105	7,770	0
Taxable income					16,325	450	246,090
Income tax							
	(a)	(b)	(c)				
	16,325	450	34,820	@ 20%	3,265.00	90.00	6,964.00
			115,630	@ 40%			46,252.00
			95,640	@ 50%			47,820.00
	16,325	450	246,090				
Tax borne					3,265.00	90.00	101,036.00

Notes:

(i) The donations of £360 are grossed-up to £450 (£360 x 100/80) and are treated as if paid net of 20% tax. Deemed tax deducted is £90.

(ii) In case (a), Owen's income tax liability exceeds £90 so there is no more to be done.

(iii) In case (b), Owen's income tax liability will be only £23 if the full personal allowance is given i.e. (£8,220 – £8,105) = £115 x 20% = £23. This falls short of the required £90 by £67. Therefore he must pay a further £67 of income tax. This is achieved by reducing his personal allowance by £335 to £7,770.

(iv) In case (c), Owen's basic rate limit is increased by £450 to £34,820 and his higher rate limit is increased by £450 to £150,450. This moves £450 of taxable income from the additional rate to the basic rate and saves tax of £135 (£450 x 30%). Together with the £90 deemed to have been deducted at source, total tax relief is now £225 (i.e. £450 x 50%).

Summary

- Certain payments and gifts made by a taxpayer are either deducted from total income or act as tax reducers.
- Payments which are deducted from total income must always be shown gross in the tax computation. Any tax deducted when the payment was made is added to the tax liability of the payer.
- If a payment which ranks as a tax reducer is made gross, the appropriate tax reduction is given in the payer's income tax computation. But payments made net should be omitted from the computation entirely.
- The main deductible payments are eligible interest payments and certain annual payments and patent royalties. A charitable gift consisting of listed shares or securities (or land and buildings) may also be deducted from total income.
- Qualifying maintenance payments of up to the amount of the minimum married couple's allowance are relieved at 10%. This relief is available only if either the payer or the recipient was born before 6 April 1935.
- Interest paid on a home loan taken out before 9 March 1999 and used to buy a life annuity is relieved at 23%.
- The Gift Aid scheme covers charitable donations which satisfy certain conditions. Qualifying donations are deemed to have been made net of basic rate tax.
- A taxpayer making a Gift Aid donation must pay income tax and capital gains tax equal to at least the amount of tax deemed to have been deducted from the donation. Higher rate and additional rate taxpayers obtain higher rate and additional rate relief on such donations.

Exercises

4.1 Mabel has total income of £22,810 in 2012-13, none of which is derived from savings or dividends. During the year she makes a net deductible payment of £200. Show her income tax computation for the year.

4.2 Paul has total income of £46,580 in 2012-13, none of which is derived from savings or dividends. During the year he pays gross eligible interest of £1,600. Show his income tax computation:

(a) with the interest payment (b) as it would be without the interest payment.

How much has the interest effectively cost him?

4.3 Rose has total income of £8,095 in 2012-13. She makes a gross deductible payment of £25 during the year. Show her income tax computation for the year and determine the amount of tax relief given in relation to the payment.

4.4 At what rate of income tax is each of the following types of payment relieved in tax year 2012-13?

(a) interest on a qualifying home loan used to buy an annuity

(b) interest on a loan used to buy an interest in a partnership

(c) qualifying maintenance payments

(d) a gift of pre-eminent property to the nation.

4.5 A taxpayer with no capital gains tax liability makes a qualifying Gift Aid donation of £960 in tax year 2012-13. Explain:

(a) why this donation is worth more than £960 to the charity which receives it

(b) why this donation might cost the taxpayer more than £960

(c) why this donation might cost the taxpayer less than £960.

4.6 Raj was born in 1945 and is single. In 2012-13, he has business profits of £26,400 and no other income. He makes a qualifying Gift Aid donation of £280 during the year. Show his 2012-13 income tax computation.

4.7 Matthew dies on 23 December 2012, leaving a widow aged 63. He was born on 1 March 1935. His only income in 2012-13 is a retirement pension of £26,510. His wife has income from property of £17,900 and no other income. During the year, she gives shares to charity with a market value of £500 and she also makes a Gift Aid donation of £100.

They were married for many years and made no elections with regard to the married couple's allowance. Calculate their tax liabilities for 2012-13.

***4.8** Pauline (born March 1935) marries Adrian (born May 1939) on 17 October 2012. Their income for 2012-13 is as follows:

	£
Pauline:	
Retirement pension	11,950
Net building society interest	2,420
Adrian:	
Business profits	34,630
UK dividends	1,575

During 2012-13, Adrian pays maintenance of £3,000 to his former wife, as required by a court order. She was born in February 1935 and has not remarried.

Show Pauline and Adrian's income tax computations for 2012-13.

***4.9** Geoffrey's income for 2012-13 consists of a salary of £114,600 and UK dividends of £3,780. He makes qualifying Gift Aid donations of £7,200 during the year. Show Geoffrey's 2012-13 income tax computation.

Chapter 5

Income from property

Introduction

An individual's income from property is charged to income tax in accordance with the rules of the Income Tax (Trading and Other Income) Act 2005. The main purpose of this chapter is to explain those rules and to show how a taxpayer's UK property income is calculated. Income from overseas property is considered separately in Chapter 32.

Definition of property income

ITTOIA 2005 states that income tax is charged on the profits of a property business. This statute also states that a UK property business consists of a business which is carried on for generating income from land which is situated in the UK and that "generating income from land" means "*exploiting an estate, interest or right in or over land as a source of rents or other receipts*". This is a broad definition but, in practice, the main classes of property income are:

(a) rents

(b) lease premiums (if the length of the lease does not exceed 50 years)

(c) amounts receivable in respect of rights of way, sporting rights etc.

(d) income from the letting of fixed caravans or permanently moored houseboats.

Dividends received from a UK Real Estate Investment Trust (UK-REIT) are also treated as property income to the extent that they are derived from the company's tax-exempt property income or gains (see Chapter 23). Such dividends are received net of basic rate income tax and do not carry an attached tax credit (see Chapter 2).

Despite the use of the word "business" above, income from property is almost always treated as *unearned* income. The only occasion on which property income is treated as earned income is when the income derives from the commercial letting of furnished holiday accommodation (see later in this chapter). The distinction between earned and unearned income may be especially important if the taxpayer is hoping to obtain tax relief on pension contributions (see Chapter 14).

Basis of assessment and allowable expenditure

A taxpayer's property income for a tax year is normally calculated on the accruals basis, in accordance with generally accepted accounting principles. However, short lease premiums are subject to a special tax regime (see below) and dividends received from UK-REITs are taxed on the receipts basis.

Expenditure which is incurred wholly and exclusively for the purposes of a property business is deducted when computing property income. This "wholly and exclusively" rule is copied directly from the rules relating to trading income and is considered more fully in Chapter 9 of this book, but the types of expenditure which are likely to be deductible when computing property income include the following:

(a) repairs and maintenance to the property (excluding improvements)

(b) insurance of the property and/or its contents

(c) the cost of providing services to tenants

(d) administrative and management costs, including bad debts incurred

(e) rent paid to a superior landlord (if the property is sub-let)

(f) business rates, water rates or council tax (which are the legal responsibility of the occupier of premises, not the owner, but may be paid by a landlord on behalf of a tenant and then recouped via an increased rent)

(g) interest paid on a loan to buy or improve the property concerned.

If a property is partly let and partly owner-occupied, it is necessary to apportion the expenditure accordingly.

When a taxpayer derives income from two or more properties it is *not* necessary to calculate the amount of profit (or loss) arising on each property individually. In each tax year, total property expenditure is deducted from total property income, giving a single profit (or loss) figure for the year. However, dividends received from UK-REITs are *not* aggregated with other property income but are treated instead as income arising from a separate property business.

EXAMPLE 1

Ryan owns a house which he lets to a tenant. Rent is payable monthly in advance on the 6th day of each month. For some years the rent has been fixed at £7,200 per annum but this was increased to £7,800 per annum with effect from 6 December 2012. The rent due on 6 March 2013 was not paid until 7 April 2013. Compute Ryan's property income for 2012-13, given that his allowable expenditure for the year is £2,350.

Solution

The rent for 2012-13 is £7,400 ((£7,200 x 8/12) + (£7,800 x 4/12)). So property income for the year is £5,050 (£7,400 – £2,350). The fact that some of the rent was not received until early in the following year is irrelevant, since rents are assessed on the accruals basis.

Capital expenditure

Capital expenditure is normally not deductible when computing property income but tax relief may be obtained on certain types of capital expenditure as follows:

(a) Allowances for depreciation known as "capital allowances" are available in relation to capital expenditure on:

(i) plant and machinery which is used in the repair, maintenance or management of let property

(ii) the renovation/conversion of vacant or underused space above shops and other commercial premises to provide flats for rent (but these capital allowances are not available in relation to expenditure incurred after 5 April 2013)

(iii) the renovation of business premises in disadvantaged areas.

Capital allowances are considered in Chapter 11 of this book.

(b) A "wear and tear allowance" may be available in relation to expenditure on furniture and other equipment let to a tenant. The wear and tear allowance is commonly calculated as 10% of the rent for the year, net of any council tax or rates borne by the landlord on behalf of the tenant.

(c) An alternative to the wear and tear allowance is the "renewals basis". If this basis applies, no tax relief is available for the initial cost of providing furniture or equipment, but subsequent expenditure on replacements (not improvements) is allowed as a deduction when computing property income for the year in which the expenditure is incurred.

Capital expenditure on the acquisition and installation of certain energy-saving items in let residential property (e.g. loft insulation) may be deducted when calculating the landlord's income from property. This deduction is known as the "landlords energy saving allowance" (LESA) and cannot exceed £1,500 per dwelling per tax year. No deduction may be claimed for expenditure incurred after 5 April 2015.

EXAMPLE 2

Ursula owns a flat which she lets furnished. In 2012-13 the flat was let for 46 weeks at £200 per week. For the remaining 6 weeks of the year, Ursula occupied the flat herself. Her expenditure during the year was as follows:

	£		£
Council tax and water rates	2,480	Cleaning (whilst property let)	1,184
Minor repairs	540	Painting and decorating	1,000
Advertising for tenants	152	Insurance	480

Compute Ursula's property income for 2012-13, assuming that she claims the wear and tear allowance.

Solution

		£	£	£
Rents for the year £200 x 46				9,200
Less: Expenses allowed in full:				
Advertising for tenants			152	
Cleaning			1,184	
Apportioned expenses:				
Council tax and water rates		2,480		
Minor repairs		540		
Painting and decorating		1,000		
Insurance		480		
	46/52	x 4,500	3,981	
Wear and tear allowance (see note)			701	6,018
Property income				3,182

Note:

The wear and tear allowance is calculated at 10% of the rents, less any part of those rents which are deemed to reimburse Ursula for expenses incurred by her which are legally the tenants' responsibility (i.e. council tax and water rates). The tenants were in occupation for 46 weeks, so 46/52ths of the council tax and water rates were their responsibility. The wear and tear allowance is therefore 10% of (£9,200 – 46/52 x £2,480) = £701.

Losses

If a taxpayer's gross property income for a tax year is exceeded by the allowable expenditure, then the taxpayer has incurred a loss and taxable property income for the year is £nil. The loss is carried forward and relieved against the first available property income arising in subsequent tax years. Strictly speaking, relief is given by deduction from the taxpayer's total income (see Chapter 2), but the amount of relief given in any tax year cannot exceed the property income for that year.

Any loss incurred on an individual property in a tax year will automatically be set against profits arising on other properties in the same year, since property income and expenditure is generally pooled to give an overall profit or loss for the year. However (as explained earlier) dividends from UK-REITs are *not* pooled with other property income but are treated instead as income arising from a separate property business. Losses arising from a general property business cannot be set against such dividends.

EXAMPLE 3

Sandra's entire income is derived from the letting of property. She has the following income and expenditure in tax years 2010-11 through to 2012-13:

	2010-11	*2011-12*	*2012-13*
	£	£	£
Total rental income	49,320	51,400	76,100
Total allowable expenditure	78,510	25,430	17,540

Compute her net income for each year.

Solution

	2010-11	*2011-12*	*2012-13*
	£	£	£
Total rental income	49,320	51,400	76,100
Total allowable expenditure	78,510	25,430	17,540
Property income/(loss)	(29,190)	25,970	58,560
Total income	0	25,970	58,560
Less: Losses b/f	-	(25,970)	(3,220)
Net income	0	0	55,340

Note:

The 2010-11 loss must be set against the first available property income in subsequent years. This means that Sandra's net income for 2011-12 is reduced to £nil and that her personal allowance for that year is wasted. It would have been better if more of the loss could have been carried forward to 2012-13, so as to avoid wasting the 2011-12 personal allowance and to reduce the amount of higher-rate tax payable in 2012-13. However, it is not possible to restrict the amount of loss relief given in 2011-12.

Lease premiums

A premium is a lump sum paid by a tenant to a landlord on the grant of a lease. The income tax treatment of lease premiums is as follows:

(a) Premiums arising on the grant of a "long lease" (a lease of more than 50 years) are not charged to income tax at all.

(b) Premiums arising on the grant of a "short lease" (a lease of 50 years or less) are charged to income tax in the tax year in which the lease is granted. However, the amount of the premium is reduced for this purpose by 2% for each year of the lease except for the first year.

Note that these provisions apply only to the *grant* of a new lease, not to the *assignment* of an existing lease. Note also that lease premiums arising on the grant of a lease may give rise to a capital gains tax liability (see Chapter 19).

EXAMPLE 4

In tax year 2012-13, a landlord receives a premium of £36,000 when granting a 25-year lease to a tenant. How much of this premium is assessable to income tax?

Solution

For income tax purposes, the lease premium is reduced by 2% for each year of the lease except for the first year. Therefore 48% (24 x 2%) of the premium is not charged to income tax. The remaining 52% is taxable, so the assessable amount of the premium is £18,720 (52% of £36,000).

Relief for premiums paid

A tenant who pays a premium on being granted a short lease may obtain tax relief on the premium paid in one of two ways:

(a) If the tenant uses the property for business purposes then, throughout the duration of the lease, the tenant may claim an annual deduction from his or her trading profits which are charged to income tax (see Chapter 9). This annual deduction is equal to the amount of the premium on which the landlord is assessable to income tax, divided by the number of years of the lease.

(b) If the tenant sub-lets the property to someone else and receives a premium from the sub-lessee, then the assessable amount of the premium received is reduced by virtue of the premium paid. The reduction is equal to:

$$\text{Landlord's income tax assessment on premium paid} \times \frac{\text{Duration of sub-lease}}{\text{Duration of head-lease}}$$

If this reduction cannot be made in full (either because the premium received is too small or because no premium was received at all) the excess is spread evenly over the period of the sub-lease and set against the rents due from the sub-lessee.

EXAMPLE 5

Susan is granted a 20-year lease on a property, paying a premium of £76,000. Explain how tax relief will be given in relation to this premium if:

(a) she uses the property for trading purposes, or

(b) she grants a sub-lease to Timothy for five years, receiving a premium of:

   (i) £25,000

   (ii) £10,000.

Solution

(a) The amount assessable to income tax on Susan's landlord is £47,120 (£76,000 less 38% of £76,000). If Susan uses the premises for trading purposes she will be able to claim an annual deduction of £2,356 from her trading profits for each of the next 20 years (£47,120 divided by 20 = £2,356).

(b)

	(i)	(ii)
	£	£
Premium received	25,000	10,000
Less: 2% x 4 x £25,000	2,000	
2% x 4 x £10,000		800
	23,000	9,200
Less: Premium paid £47,120 x $\frac{5}{20}$	11,780	11,780
Assessable premium	11,220	nil

In case (ii), the reduction available in relation to the premium paid cannot be made in full. The amount unrelieved is £2,580 (£11,780 – £9,200). There will be no income tax assessment on the premium received in this case and a deduction of £516 will be made from Susan's property income for each of the five years of the sub-lease (£2,580 divided by 5 = £516).

Reverse premiums

It is not uncommon for a landlord to pay a so-called "reverse premium" to a potential tenant so as to induce that tenant to take out a lease. This arises most frequently when commercial premises are let to business tenants. The amount of any reverse premium paid by a landlord will usually be treated as enhancement expenditure for capital gains tax purposes when the landlord disposes of the property (see Chapter 18). But if the landlord is a property developer or dealer, the premium may be an allowable expense when computing the landlord's trading income (see Chapter 9).

From the point of view of a tenant who receives a reverse premium, this premium is chargeable to income tax (or to corporation tax for a corporate tenant). If the rented premises are used for business purposes, the amount received is treated as trading income (see Chapter 9). Otherwise the amount received is assessable as property income. In both cases, the timing of the tax charge will usually follow accepted accountancy practice, so that the tax liability arising on the receipt of a reverse premium will probably be spread over the period of the lease.

"Rent-a-room" relief

If a taxpayer lets furnished accommodation which forms part of his or her main residence, gross annual rents not exceeding a specified limit (£4,250 for 2012-13) are exempt from income tax. However, the taxpayer may elect to ignore this exemption and to apply the usual property income rules instead. This might be beneficial if the rents were exceeded by expenses, so that a loss could be claimed.

If gross rents for a tax year exceed the limit, rents less expenses are assessed to income tax in the normal way. However, the taxpayer may elect to be assessed instead on the excess of gross rents over the limit, without deducting expenses of any kind.

Both of the elections referred to above must be made by 31 January in the second tax year following the tax year to which the election relates. The first election applies only to the year for which it is made. The second election applies to all subsequent tax years until a year arises in which gross rents do not exceed the limit (or the election is withdrawn).

EXAMPLE 6

In 2012-13, Victor rents out a room in his house and receives rents of £4,900. He incurs allowable expenses of £820. No "rent-a-room" elections are currently in force. What elections (if any) should he make?

Solution

The rent-a-room exemption does not apply since gross rents exceed £4,250. If Victor does nothing, he will be charged to income tax on property income of £4,080 (£4,900 – £820).

If he elects to be assessed on the excess of gross rents over the rent-a-room relief limit, his property income for tax purposes will be only £650 (£4,900 – £4,250). He should make this election and he has until 31 January 2015 to do so.

Furnished holiday lettings

Subject to certain conditions, income derived from the "commercial letting of furnished holiday accommodation" is treated for most tax purposes as if it were trading income. The main beneficial effects of this treatment are as follows:

(a) The income is regarded as earned income when determining the extent to which tax relief is available in relation to pension contributions (see Chapter 14).

(b) Capital allowances may be claimed in respect of the furniture (see Chapter 11).

(c) Business-related capital gains tax reliefs may be available (see Chapter 22).

Until 6 April 2011, losses incurred in relation to furnished holiday lettings (FHL) were relieved as if they were trading losses (see Chapter 12). However, this treatment of FHL losses is not available in tax year 2011-12 or in subsequent tax years.

FHL conditions

Letting qualifies as the commercial letting of furnished holiday accommodation if *all* of the following conditions are satisfied:

(a) The property concerned is situated in the UK or elsewhere in the European Economic Area (see Chapter 3) and is let furnished with a view to profit.

(b) The property is available for letting to the general public as holiday accommodation for at least 210 days in the tax year and is actually let for at least 105 days, ignoring any periods of "longer-term occupation" (i.e. periods of more than 31 consecutive days during which the accommodation is in the same occupation).

(c) The property is not in longer-term occupation for more than 155 days in the tax year.

A taxpayer with furnished holiday lettings both in the UK and elsewhere in the EEA is treated as having two separate FHL businesses. All qualifying property in the UK forms one FHL business. All qualifying property elsewhere in the EEA forms a separate FHL business. A loss incurred in either of these FHL businesses may be set only against income arising from the same FHL business.

If a property qualifies as furnished holiday accommodation in one tax year, the taxpayer who owns the property may elect to treat the property as continuing to qualify for up to two further tax years (the "period of grace") even though it does not satisfy the 105-day condition in those years. Such an election may not be made for a tax year if an averaging election is made in respect of the same year for the property concerned (see below).

Averaging

If a taxpayer owns two or more properties, each of which qualifies for FHL purposes except that at least one property does not satisfy the "actually let" condition, all of these properties will qualify as furnished holiday accommodation if their average number of days let is such that (on average) they all satisfy that condition.

EXAMPLE 7

Yvonne owns four cottages, all let furnished with a view to profit. None of the cottages is ever let to the same tenant for more than 31 consecutive days. In 2012-13 the number of days each cottage was available for letting and the number of days actually let were:

	Days available	*Days actually let*
Cottage A	220	115
Cottage B	240	85
Cottage C	190	148
Cottage D	250	103

Show Yvonne's potential averaging claims.

Solution

Cottage C cannot be regarded as furnished holiday accommodation since it does not pass the 210-day test. Cottages A, B and D all pass this test but only Cottage A also passes the 105-day test. Without any averaging claims, therefore, only Cottage A will be regarded as furnished holiday accommodation. Possible averaging claims are:

(a) Average Cottage A with Cottage B. This is no use since the average number of days let is only 100.

(b) Average Cottage A with Cottage D. This would be beneficial since the average number of days let is 109.

(c) Average Cottage A with Cottage B and Cottage D. This is no use since the average number of days let is only 101.

Therefore, Yvonne should claim that Cottage A should be averaged with Cottage D, in which case both cottages would qualify as furnished holiday accommodation.

Summary

- Income tax is charged on the profits of a business which is carried on for the purpose of generating income from land situated in the UK.
- Property income is usually treated as unearned income unless it arises from the commercial letting of furnished holiday accommodation.
- A taxpayer's property income for a tax year is generally calculated on the accruals basis. Expenditure incurred wholly and exclusively for the purposes of a property business is deducted when computing property income.
- Capital allowances are available in relation to certain types of capital expenditure incurred in relation to a property business.
- Losses incurred by a property business are carried forward and set against the first available property income arising in subsequent years.
- A premium received on the grant of a lease is charged to income tax if the lease does not exceed 50 years. The assessable amount is the amount of the premium less 2% for each year of the lease except the first.
- A tenant paying a lease premium will receive tax relief on the premium if the property is sub-let or is used for the purposes of a trade.
- Rent-a-room relief is available if a taxpayer receives rents of up to £4,250 p.a. from the letting of furnished rooms in his or her main residence.
- Under certain conditions, the letting of furnished property qualifies as the commercial letting of furnished holiday accommodation and income from the property is treated as trading income. This offers a number of benefits to the taxpayer.

Exercises

5.1 Andrew owns a house which he lets to tenants. Rent is payable quarterly in advance on 1 January, 1 April, 1 July and 1 October. The rent was £8,000 per annum until it was increased to £8,800 per annum with effect from 1 January 2013. Rent received by Andrew during 2012-13 was as follows:

	£
2 July 2012	2,000
30 September 2012	2,000
3 January 2013	2,200
	6,200

Andrew did not receive the payment due on 1 April 2013 until 7 April 2013. Compute his property income for 2012-13, assuming that he incurred no allowable expenditure during the year.

5.2 Simon owns a country cottage which he uses as a holiday home for 4 weeks per year and lets furnished at £220 per week for the remaining 48 weeks of the year. Simon's expenses in relation to the cottage in 2012-13 were as follows:

	£
Council tax	1,400
Advertising	35
Repairs to furniture (damaged by tenant)	50
Gardener's wages (£20 per week)	1,040
Insurance	230

Compute Simon's property income for 2012-13.

5.3 In 2012-13, a landlord receives a premium of £12,000 when granting a lease to a tenant. Compute the amount of this premium which is chargeable to income tax if the length of the lease is:

(a) 60 years

(b) 50 years

(c) 20 years

5.4 In 2012-13, Jasper is granted a 10-year lease on a property, paying a premium of £15,000. He uses the property for trading purposes. Compute the tax relief which he will be allowed in respect of the lease premium.

5.5 Georgina owns three holiday flats, all of which she lets furnished with a view to profit. None of the flats is ever let to the same tenant for more than 31 consecutive days. In 2012-13 the number of days for which each flat was available for letting, and the number of days actually let, were:

	Days available	*Days actually let*
Flat 1	210	99
Flat 2	220	107
Flat 3	252	109

Show Georgina's potential averaging claims.

***5.6** In 2012-13, Peter is granted a 12-year lease on a property, paying a premium of £40,000 to his landlord. He immediately grants a 4-year sub-lease to Paula, receiving a premium of £14,000. Calculate the income tax assessment on the premium received by Peter.

***5.7** Melissa is single and was born in 1943. She owns a house which she lets unfurnished at a rent of £200 per week. Her allowable expenditure in 2012-13 was £4,100 and she had property losses brought forward from 2011-12 of £6,550. Her other income in 2012-13 was as follows:

	£
Retirement pension	12,784
Net building society interest	10,480

Compute the income tax payable by Melissa for the year.

Chapter 6

Income from savings and investments

Introduction

The main purpose of this chapter is to explain the tax treatment of income arising from savings and investments. The main options available to a taxpayer who wishes to save or invest are to deposit money in bank and building society accounts or to invest in shares and securities. Each of these courses of action has its taxation implications and this chapter explains those implications.

This chapter also briefly considers the taxation of income from trusts and settlements and the tax treatment of certain miscellaneous sources of income.

Interest received

Interest received by a taxpayer is charged to income tax by the Income Tax (Trading and Other Income) Act 2005. This Act states that tax is charged on the full amount of interest arising in the tax year and that interest "arises" when it is paid to the taxpayer or when it is credited to the taxpayer's account. Therefore, any interest which has accrued at the end of a tax year but has not yet been paid or credited to the taxpayer is ignored when computing the income for that year.

Interest ranks as savings income (see Chapter 2) and so any interest falling into the first £2,710 (for 2012-13) of the basic rate band is taxed at the starting rate for savings of 10%. No expenses are allowed against this form of income.

Interest received net

Interest is generally received net of 20% income tax. Some investments do pay gross interest but these are comparatively few (see later in this chapter).

The gross equivalent of any interest received net by a taxpayer during a tax year is included in the taxpayer's total income. The tax suffered by deduction at source is then subtracted when calculating tax payable.

Self-certification

Individuals resident in the UK who are unlikely to be liable to income tax for a given tax year may supply a certificate to this effect to their bank or building society. Interest is then paid to such individuals without deduction of tax at source, so avoiding the need for repayment claims at the end of the year. As might be expected, there are penalties for supplying such certificates fraudulently or negligently.

EXAMPLE 1

Alfred is single and 66 years old. He receives the following income in 2012-13:

	£
Retirement pension	9,560
Building society interest (net)	408

Calculate the amount of income tax reclaimed by Alfred at the end of 2012-13. Could the need to make a repayment claim have been avoided?

Solution

Alfred's total income for 2012-13 is £10,070 (£9,560 + (£408 x 100/80)). This is less than his over-65 personal allowance of £10,500, resulting in a zero income tax liability for the year. He may reclaim the £102 tax deducted at source from the interest.

Since it was probably evident at the beginning of the year that Alfred was going to be a non-taxpayer in 2012-13, he could have supplied his building society with a certificate to that effect. He would then have received his interest without deduction of tax.

Interest received gross

Certain types of interest are received gross (without deduction of tax at source). The amount of any such interest received by a taxpayer during a tax year is included in the taxpayer's total income. The main types of interest received gross are:

(a) National Savings Bank† (NSB) investment account interest

(b) National Savings Bank† (NSB) direct saver account interest

(c) interest on gilt-edged securities unless the recipient has opted for net interest.

†*NSB is operated by National Savings and Investments (NS&I).*

Accrued income scheme

The accrued income scheme exists in order to prevent a form of tax avoidance known as "bondwashing". Bondwashing involves selling securities "cum interest" (so that the buyer of the securities will receive the next interest payment) just before an interest payment is due. The price paid by the buyer reflects the fact that the sale is cum interest and so the seller of the securities is not disadvantaged. However, the effect of the transaction from the tax point of view is that the seller has converted what would have been income into a capital gain. Since capital gains arising on the disposal of certain securities are exempt from capital gains tax (see Chapter 20) the seller appears to have avoided tax.

The accrued income scheme overcomes this potential loss of tax by charging the seller income tax on the interest which has accrued up to the date of the sale. The buyer of the securities is entitled to tax relief on the same amount and this is given by deduction from the next interest payment the buyer receives. Similar arrangements apply if securities are transferred "ex interest" (so that the seller will receive the next interest payment). In this case, the buyer is taxed on the interest accruing from the date of the sale to the date of the next interest payment and the seller is entitled to tax relief on the same amount.

The accrued income scheme applies to securities such as gilts, local authority bonds and company debentures. It does not apply to ordinary or preference shares. Transfers made by individuals who have not held securities with a total nominal value exceeding £5,000 in the current tax year or in the preceding tax year are excluded from the scheme.

Dividends received

Dividends received by an individual from a UK resident company are charged to income tax by the Income Tax (Trading and Other Income) Act 2005. This Act states that tax is charged on the amount of dividends actually received in the tax year, with no adjustment for any accrued dividends. UK dividends have an attached tax credit which is equal to one-ninth of the amount of the dividend received (see Chapter 2) and an individual's dividend income for a tax year is equal to the UK dividends received in that year plus the attached tax credits. No expenses are allowed against dividend income.

For 2012-13, dividends which fall into the basic rate band are taxed at the dividend ordinary rate of 10% and dividends which fall into the higher rate band are taxed at the dividend upper rate of 32.5%. Any dividends which lie above the higher rate limit are taxed at the dividend additional rate of 42.5%. Tax credits relating to dividends which are charged to tax are set against the income tax liability on those dividends. Tax credits exceeding this liability cannot be paid to the taxpayer or set against the tax liability on any other income. Note also that:

(a) Subject to certain conditions, this tax regime also applies to dividends received from overseas companies (see Chapter 32).

(b) Any capital gain which arises on a disposal of shares is generally subject to capital gains tax (see Chapter 20).

Tax-efficient investments

A taxpayer who is seeking a tax-efficient means of investing in an interest-bearing account or in shares and securities may invest in any of the following:

(a) an Individual Savings Account (ISA)

(b) the Enterprise Investment Scheme (EIS)

(c) a Venture Capital Trust (VCT)

(d) a Child Trust Fund (CTF).

Each of these forms of investment is considered below. A further tax-efficient investment opportunity is offered by the Community Investment Tax Credits (CITC) scheme and the main features of this scheme are explained on the website which accompanies this book. The website address is www.pearsoned.co.uk/melville.

Individual Savings Accounts

Tax-free Individual Savings Accounts (ISAs) were introduced on 6 April 1999. The main features of these accounts are currently as follows:

(a) Individuals who are resident and ordinarily resident in the UK (see Chapter 32) and at least 16 years old may hold an ISA. The residence requirement is waived in the case of Crown servants serving overseas and their spouses (or civil partners).

(b) ISAs are of two types. These are "cash ISAs" and "stocks and shares ISAs". Money invested in a cash ISA is deposited with a bank or building society and is held in a savings account. Money invested in a stocks and shares ISA is used by the ISA provider to acquire stocks and shares on the saver's behalf. These stocks and shares may be listed on a stock exchange anywhere in the world. Savers under the age of 18 may invest in a cash ISA only.

(c) Each tax year, a saver may invest in a single cash ISA and/or a single stocks and shares ISA. Savers may start fresh ISAs each year or may continue to invest in ISAs started in previous years.

(d) The maximum amount which a saver may invest in ISAs during tax year 2012-13 is £11,280. No more than £5,640 of this may be saved in a cash ISA. The remainder of the £11,280 may be invested in a stocks and shares ISA, which could be managed by the same provider as the cash ISA or by a different provider.

(e) There is no cumulative limit on the total amount which an individual can save in ISAs during his or her lifetime. Nor is there a specified minimum level of saving.

(f) Interest and dividends arising from ISAs are exempt from income tax. Capital gains (and losses) arising from ISAs are exempt from capital gains tax.

(g) Withdrawals may be made from an ISA without loss of tax relief. But once the maximum amount has been subscribed to an ISA for a tax year, no further subscriptions will be allowed in that year, regardless of how much is withdrawn.

(h) Some or all of the money saved in cash ISAs in previous tax years may be transferred to stocks and shares ISAs without affecting the current year's ISA investment limit. Savers may also transfer money saved in a cash ISA in the current tax year to a stocks and shares ISA. Such a transfer must be for the whole amount saved in the cash ISA during the current year up to the date of the transfer. If money saved in the current year is transferred in this way, it is treated as if it had been invested directly in a stocks and shares ISA in the current year.

Junior ISAs

Junior ISAs (JISAs) were introduced on 1 November 2011. JISAs are available to children under 18 who are UK resident and do not have a Child Trust Fund account (see below). JISAs have many features in common with adult ISAs. They are tax-free and investments of up to £3,600 per annum may be made in cash or in stocks and shares. Funds invested in JISAs are owned by the child but are locked in until the child reaches the age of 18.

The fact that a child has a JISA does not prevent that child from also having an adult ISA as from the age of 16, in which case the existence of the JISA has no impact upon the adult ISA subscription limits.

EXAMPLE 2

Assume that all of the individuals referred to in this example are over 18 years old.

(a) An individual saves £500 in a cash ISA on 6 April 2012. What further investments in ISAs may this individual make during 2012-13?

(b) An individual saves £6,000 in a stocks and shares ISA on 21 May 2012. What further investments in ISAs may this individual make during 2012-13?

(c) An individual saves £1,000 in a cash ISA on 30 June 2012. A further £800 is saved in the cash ISA on 31 July 2012. On 31 December 2012, the individual decides to make a transfer from the cash ISA to a stocks and shares ISA. Is there any restriction on this transfer? How will the transfer affect further ISA investments during 2012-13?

Solution

(a) A further £10,780 may be saved during the year. Up to £5,140 of this may be saved in the same cash ISA and the remainder may be saved in a stocks and shares ISA.

(b) A further £5,280 may be saved during the year. This could all be saved in the same stocks and shares ISA or in a cash ISA or in a combination of both.

(c) The entire £1,800 must be transferred. A further £9,480 may then be saved in ISAs during the year. Up to £5,640 of this may be saved in a cash ISA and the remainder may be saved in the stocks and shares ISA to which the £1,800 was transferred.

Enterprise Investment Scheme

The Enterprise Investment Scheme (EIS) was established in 1994 to provide a means of encouraging investment in industry. The main features of the EIS are as follows:

(a) Income tax relief is available to taxpayers who subscribe for newly-issued ordinary shares in "qualifying companies". Essentially, these are unlisted companies (with less than 250 employees) which have a permanent establishment in the UK and which have gross assets not exceeding £15 million immediately before the share issue and not exceeding £16 million immediately after it. The company must have raised no more than £5 million under the EIS and other venture capital schemes in the previous 12 months.

(b) Relief takes the form of a reduction in the amount of tax due on the taxpayer's taxable income, equal to 30% of the amount invested in qualifying companies during the tax year. This reduction takes priority over the tax reductions relating to certain payments (see Chapter 4) and the MCA (see Chapter 3).

(c) A taxpayer's EIS investments of up to £1 million in each tax year are eligible for tax relief. Any of the EIS investments made in a tax year may be carried back and treated as if made in the previous year, but the total EIS investment that can attract income tax relief in any one tax year is subject to the £1 million limit.

(d) The taxpayer must not be connected with the company at any time during the two years prior to the date of the investment and the three years following that date. Broadly speaking, an individual is connected with a company for this purpose if he or she is an employee of the company or, together with associates, owns more than 30% of the company's ordinary shares.

(e) Dividends received on the shares are subject to income tax in the usual way.

(f) Any capital gain arising on the eventual disposal of the shares is exempt from CGT but any loss arising on the disposal is eligible for relief. A loss may be relieved:

    (i) as a capital loss, in the usual way (see Chapter 17), or

    (ii) against the taxpayer's total income of the year in which the loss is incurred or the previous year (see Chapter 12).

    When calculating the allowable loss, the shares are deemed to have been acquired for their issue price, less the tax reduction obtained when the shares were purchased.

The taxpayer must retain the shares for a minimum holding period of at least three years or both the income tax and capital gains tax reliefs are lost.

Seed Enterprise Investment Scheme

The Seed Enterprise Investment Scheme (SEIS) was launched in April 2012 as a means of encouraging investment in start-up companies. The main features of the scheme are:

(a) Subject to certain conditions, tax relief is available to investors who subscribe for ordinary shares in a company which is carrying on a new business. A new business is one which started no more than 2 years before the share issue. The share issue must take place on or after 6 April 2012.

(b) The company concerned must be an unlisted trading company with a permanent establishment in the UK. The company must have fewer than 25 employees and its total assets must be less than £200,000 before the SEIS investment is made. Also, the amount of all SEIS investment received by the company in the three years to the date of the latest investment must not exceed £150,000.

(c) During the period from the company's incorporation until the third anniversary of the share issue, the investor must not own 30% or more of the company's share capital. Also, the investor cannot be an employee of the company (other than a director).

(d) Tax relief takes the form of an income tax reduction equal to 50% of the amount invested up to a limit of £100,000 per annum. Relief is withdrawn if the shares are disposed of within 3 years. As with the main EIS, any SEIS investments made during a tax year may be carried back and treated as if made in the previous year.

(e) Furthermore, the capital gain arising on the disposal of any asset in tax year 2012-13 is exempt from capital gains tax if the amount of the gain is then invested through the SEIS during 2012-13 (see Chapter 22).

The scheme is scheduled to end on 5 April 2017 but may be extended to a later date.

Venture Capital Trusts

A Venture Capital Trust (VCT) is a company which is approved as such by HM Revenue and Customs. The main conditions which must be satisfied before HMRC approval can be obtained are as follows:

(a) The company's ordinary shares must be listed on an EU stock exchange.

(b) Its income must be derived wholly or mainly from shares or securities and no more than 15% of this income may be retained by the company.

(c) At least 70% of its total investments must consist of "qualifying holdings" and at least 70% of these holdings must consist of "eligible" shares. Broadly, shares or securities owned by a VCT rank as qualifying holdings if they were newly issued to the VCT and are shares or securities of a company which would be a qualifying company for the purposes of the EIS (see above). Eligible shares exclude redeemable shares.

(d) No holding in any one company (other than in another VCT) can represent more than 15% of a VCT's investments. At least 10% of a VCT's investment in a company must be held in the form of eligible shares.

Income tax relief is available to taxpayers who subscribe for newly-issued shares of a VCT. This takes the form of a tax reduction equal to 30% of the amount invested, subject to an investment limit of £200,000 per tax year. This reduction takes priority over the tax reductions relating to certain payments made by the taxpayer (see Chapter 4) and the tax reduction relating to the MCA (see Chapter 3). To qualify for income tax relief, the tax-payer must hold the shares for a minimum holding period of at least five years.

Dividends on the first £200,000 of VCT shares acquired in each tax year are exempt from income tax and any capital gain or loss arising on the disposal of these shares is exempt from capital gains tax, regardless of whether or not the shares have been held for the minimum holding period.

Child Trust Funds

Child Trust Fund accounts were introduced in 2005 as a tax-efficient means of building up a fund of assets for a young person to use (or re-invest) at the age of 18. The scheme involved the establishment of a CTF account for each child born on or after 1 September 2002. The Government would contribute funds into each CTF account and additional contributions could be made by the child and by his/her family and friends.

However, the Child Trust Funds scheme has now been wound down. Children born in 2011 or later do not qualify for CTF accounts and all Government contributions to existing accounts have ceased. But existing CTF accounts remain open and these accounts continue to offer the following tax advantages:

(a) Additional contributions of up to a total of £1,200 per annum may still be made into a CTF account. These contributions do not attract tax relief in themselves. But income and gains arising from CTF investments are tax-free and no tax liability arises when a CTF account reaches maturity on the child's 18th birthday.

(b) Any income derived from parental contributions to a CTF account does not count towards the £100 limit relating to income derived from a parent (see Chapter 2).

Note, however, that no funds may be withdrawn from a CTF account until maturity.

Income from trusts and settlements

A trust or settlement is an arrangement whereby property is held by persons known as *trustees*, for the benefit of other persons known as *beneficiaries*. Trusts fall into two main categories, as follows:

(a) If one or more persons are entitled to receive all of the income which is generated by the trust property, then those persons are "life tenants" and the trust is a "trust with an interest in possession".

(b) If there is no life tenant and the trustees have the discretion to distribute as much or as little of the trust income to the beneficiaries as they see fit, the trust is referred to as a "discretionary trust".

Trust taxation is a very complex matter and a full study of the subject is beyond the scope of this book. However, an introduction to trust taxation is given below.

Trusts with an interest in possession

For tax year 2012-13, the trustees of a trust with an interest in possession are liable to income tax at the dividend ordinary rate (10%) on the trust's dividend income and at the basic rate (20%) on all of its other income. Note that:

(a) The tax liability of the trustees is never calculated at the starting rate for savings, the higher rate, the additional rate or the dividend upper and additional rates.

(b) The general expenses of administering the trust are *not* allowed when computing the income tax liability of the trustees. However, expenses which relate to specific items of trust income (e.g. expenses normally deductible from property income) are set against that income.

(c) The trustees' tax liability is calculated without deduction of personal allowances.

(d) Relief is given for income tax deducted at source and tax credits on dividends.

The income which remains after tax and all expenses have been deducted (including general administration expenses) is paid to the life tenants and is dealt with in their personal tax computations. In those computations:

(a) trust non-savings income is treated as income received net of basic rate tax

(b) trust savings income is also treated as income received net of basic rate tax

(c) trust dividend income is treated as dividend income with an attached tax credit.

The general administration expenses of the trust are deemed to have been paid first out of dividend income, then out of savings income and then out of non-savings income.

EXAMPLE 3

An interest in possession trust with one life tenant has the following income in 2012-13:

	£
Rents receivable	30,200
Bank interest (net)	7,200
UK dividends	1,350

Expenses were incurred in the year as follows:

	£
Property expenses	6,900
Administration expenses	1,990

(a) Compute the trustees' income tax liability for 2012-13.

(b) How much income does the life tenant receive from the trust in 2012-13 and how will this be treated in his or her personal tax computation?

Solution

	Total £	*Non-Savings* £	*Savings* £	*Dividends* £
Property income £30,200 – £6,900	23,300	23,300		
Bank interest £7,200 x 100/80	9,000		9,000	
UK dividends £1,350 + tax credit £150	1,500			1,500
	33,800	23,300	9,000	1,500
Income tax @ 20%	(4,660)	(4,660)		
Income tax @ 20%	(1,800)		(1,800)	
Income tax @ 10%	(150)			(150)
Income after tax	27,190	18,640	7,200	1,350
Administration expenses	(1,990)		(640)	(1,350)
Income after tax and expenses	25,200	18,640	6,560	0

(a) The trustees' tax liability for the year is £6,610 (£4,660 + £1,800 + £150). The £1,800 of tax deducted at source and the £150 of tax credits are deducted, leaving tax payable by the trustees of £4,660.

(b) The income of the life tenant is:

	Gross £	*Tax deducted* £
Non-savings £18,640 x 100/80	23,300	4,660
Savings £6,560 x 100/80	8,200	1,640
Total	31,500	6,300

This income will be included in the life tenant's tax computation for 2012-13 and the tax deducted at source of £6,300 will be subtracted when computing tax payable for the year.

Discretionary trusts

In general, the income tax liability of the trustees of a discretionary trust is calculated at the "dividend trust rate" on dividend income and at the "trust rate" on all other income. For tax year 2012-13, these rates are 42.5% and 50% respectively. However, these rates do not apply to income which has been used to fund the expenses of administering the trust. Such income is taxed at the dividend ordinary rate (10%) or the basic rate (20%), depending upon the type of income involved.

Also, the first £1,000 of the income of a discretionary trust is not taxed at the special trust rates but is instead charged to tax at the income tax rate which generally applies to the class of income concerned (i.e. the dividend ordinary rate or the basic rate). When identifying the first £1,000 of a trust's income, non-savings income is considered first, then savings income, then dividends.

Any payments which are made to beneficiaries are deemed to have been made net of tax at the trust rate of 50% and must therefore be grossed-up at 100/50 in their personal income tax computations. The tax which is deemed to have been deducted from such payments is assessable on the trustees, but only to the extent (if any) that the amount of this tax exceeds the trustees' tax liability on the trust income. For this purpose, the tax liability of the trustees is deemed to exclude any tax which is satisfied by deduction of tax credits on dividends.

Trusts with vulnerable beneficiary

A special tax regime applies to trusts with a vulnerable beneficiary. This tax regime ensures that the tax liability of this type of trust is reduced to the amount of tax that would have been payable if the trust income and gains had accrued directly to the beneficiary concerned.

A "vulnerable beneficiary" may be either a disabled person or (in certain instances) a minor. Trustees who wish to claim the special tax treatment available under this regime must make an appropriate election to HM Revenue and Customs. Once made, such an election is irrevocable.

EXAMPLE 4

Assume that a discretionary trust has the same income and expenses in 2012-13 as the trust described in the above example. Assume also that a payment of £4,500 was made to a beneficiary during the year.

(a) Compute the trustees' income tax liability for 2012-13.

(b) Show how the £4,500 received by the beneficiary will be treated in his or her personal tax computation.

Solution

	Total	Non-Savings	Savings	Dividends
	£	£	£	£
Property income £30,200 – £6,900	23,300	23,300		
Bank interest £7,200 x 100/80	9,000		9,000	
UK dividends £1,350 + tax credit £150	1,500			1,500
	33,800	23,300	9,000	1,500
First £1,000 of trust income:				
Income tax at 20% on £1,000	(200)	(200)		
Remainder of trust income:				
Income tax @ 10% on £1,500	(150)			(150)
Income tax @ 20% on £800	(160)		(160)	
Income tax @ 50% on £8,200	(4,100)		(4,100)	
Income tax @ 50% on £22,300	(11,150)	(11,150)		
Income after tax	18,040	11,950	4,740	1,350
Administration expenses	(1,990)		(640)	(1,350)
Income after tax and expenses	16,050	11,950	4,100	0

Note:

The administration expenses of £1,990 are deemed to have been paid out of the trust's after-tax income, first out of dividends (£1,350) and then out of savings income (£640). As £640 of net savings income has been used for this purpose, gross savings income of £800 is taxed at only 20% and not at the special rate of 50%.

(a) The trustees' tax liability is £15,760 (£200 + £150 + £160 + £4,100 + £11,150). The tax deducted at source of £1,800 and tax credits of £150 are subtracted, leaving tax payable by the trustees of £13,810. This consists of £11,350 payable on the non-savings income and an extra 30% (50% – 20%) on the £8,200 of savings income which is taxed at the trust rate.

(b) The payment of £4,500 is grossed-up at 100/50, giving gross income of £9,000. This income is included in the beneficiary's tax computation for 2012-13 and the £4,500 of tax deducted at source is subtracted when computing tax payable for the year. The trustees' tax liability on the trust income (excluding the £150 which is satisfied by tax credits on dividends) is £15,610. This exceeds £4,500 so there is no further assessment on the trustees in relation to this payment.

Miscellaneous income

ITTOIA 2005 charges income tax on certain items of miscellaneous income to the extent that these items are not already taxed under another heading. The Act also provides rules for computing the amount of such income arising in the tax year.

Examples of miscellaneous income include certain royalties, receipts from the sale of patent rights and income from any source which is not otherwise charged to tax.

Summary

- Income tax is payable on the amount of interest received by a taxpayer during the tax year. Most interest is received net of tax but non-taxpayers may receive their interest gross if they certify themselves as non-taxpayers. The main source of gross interest is the National Savings Bank.
- Income tax is payable on UK dividends received. Such dividends have an attached tax credit. Tax credits relating to dividends which are charged to income tax are set against the tax liability on those dividends.
- Individual Savings Accounts (ISAs) provide a tax-free means of either saving cash or investing in stocks and shares. Junior ISAs were introduced in November 2011.
- The Enterprise Investment Scheme provides tax incentives for those who subscribe for the newly-issued shares of unlisted trading companies which have a permanent establishment in the UK.
- The Seed Enterprise Investment Scheme (SEIS) was launched in April 2012 as a means of encouraging investment in start-up companies.
- Subject to certain conditions, tax relief is available in relation to an investment in a Venture Capital Trust.
- Child Trust Fund (CTF) accounts provide a tax-free means of building up a fund of assets for a young person born between 1 September 2002 and 31 December 2010. But Government payments into CTF accounts have now ceased.
- Trustees must account for income tax on the income of a trust. The administration expenses of the trust are not allowed when computing the trustees' income tax liability. Special rates of tax apply to the income of a discretionary trust.
- Certain forms of miscellaneous income are charged to income tax.

Exercises

6.1 Edward has the following income in 2012-13:

	£
Building society interest (net)	15,772
UK dividends	36,468

Compute the income tax payable by Edward for the year, assuming that he claims only the basic personal allowance.

6.2 Anne is single and aged 76. She has the following income in 2012-13:

	£
Bank interest:	
Interest on deposit account (net)	384
Interest credited to cash ISA	83
UK dividends	585
Retirement pension	10,046

Compute the income tax payable by (or repayable to) Anne for the year.

6.3 Outline the income tax advantages of investing in:

(a) the Enterprise Investment Scheme

(b) the Seed Enterprise Investment Scheme

(c) a Venture Capital Trust.

6.4 Outline the main features of Individual Savings Accounts.

6.5 Bernice was born on 31 March 1948 and is unmarried. Her income for 2012-13 is as follows:

	£
Retirement pension	20,970
NSB investment account interest	60
Building society interest (net)	3,784

Compute the income tax payable by Bernice for 2012-13.

***6.6** An interest in possession trust with two life tenants has the following income in tax year 2012-13:

	£
Rents received	12,620
Bank deposit interest (net)	992
Gilt interest received gross	1,800
UK dividends	12,600

Property expenses incurred in the year were £2,220 and general administration expenses amounted to £2,700.

(a) Compute the trustees' income tax liability for 2012-13.

(b) Assuming that the trust income is divided equally between the two life tenants, calculate each life tenant's income from the trust in 2012-13.

Chapter 7

Income from employment (1)

Introduction

Income from employment is charged to tax in accordance with the rules of the Income Tax (Earnings and Pensions) Act 2003. The main purpose of the next two chapters of this book is to introduce these rules and to explain how an individual's income from employment is calculated for tax purposes.

This chapter begins by distinguishing between employment and self-employment and then deals with various aspects of the taxation of employment income, including the basis of assessment, non-taxable employment income and deductible expenses. There is also a brief description of the Pay As You Earn (PAYE) system which is used to collect both income tax and National Insurance contributions from employees. The chapter concludes by outlining the features of a number of tax-efficient employee incentive schemes. The tax treatment of benefits in kind is explained in the next chapter.

These two chapters are concerned with employees whose duties are performed wholly within the UK. The taxation of overseas earnings is considered in Chapter 32.

Employment and self-employment

As will become clear in subsequent chapters, self-employed people enjoy considerable tax advantages when compared with employees. Two of the main advantages of being self-employed are:

(a) A much wider range of expenses is allowed against the income of self-employed people than against the income of employees (see Chapter 9).

(b) Self-employed people pay their income tax by instalments (see Chapter 15) and effectively pay their tax much later than employees, who normally pay income tax under the Pay As You Earn system.

It is usually quite obvious whether someone is employed or self-employed but sometimes there are borderline cases. For example, it may be extremely difficult to distinguish between an employee with a number of part-time jobs and a self-employed person with a number of clients. In such cases, the taxpayer will usually wish to claim self-employed status, whilst HM Revenue and Customs will often insist that the taxpayer should be treated as an employee.

The key test to be applied when trying to establish a taxpayer's status in cases like these is concerned with the nature of the contract between the taxpayer and the person who is paying for the work done by that taxpayer. There are two possibilities:

(a) If it can be shown that a *contract of service* exists, then the taxpayer is regarded as an employee who is in service to an employer.

(b) If it can be shown that a *contract for services* exists, then the taxpayer is regarded as a self-employed person who is rendering services to a client.

A great deal of case law has accumulated on this subject over the years and several criteria have been established which may be used to distinguish between the two types of contract. The main criteria are as follows:

(a) **Control**. The more control that the person who is paying for the work has over the person who is doing the work, the more likely it is that a contract of service exists. Employees are usually unable to choose whether or not to do certain work, how to do the work, when to do the work or where to do the work. Self-employed people are usually able to decide these matters for themselves.

(b) **Remuneration and financial risk**. Employees usually receive a regular wage or salary; they are paid whether or not their employer is making a profit and do not risk their own capital in the business. Self-employed people are normally paid a separate fee for each job they do; they may make losses as well as profits and may lose their capital if their business fails.

(c) **Equipment**. In general, employees do not provide their own equipment but self-employed people do.

(d) **Work performance and correction**. Employees are usually expected to do their work themselves. If they make mistakes they will correct the work during working hours and get paid for both the original work and the corrections. Self-employed people often delegate their work to staff or subcontractors. If the work done is unsatisfactory, the client will not expect to pay for it to be corrected.

(e) **Holidays and sickness**. Employees are likely to receive holiday pay and sick pay from their employers. Self-employed people are paid by their clients only for the work that they do and do not get paid when on holiday or when ill.

(f) **Exclusivity**. In general, an employee is employed by just one employer and is an integral part of that employer's business. Self-employed people normally have a number of clients and are not integral to any of their clients' businesses.

There are exceptions to all of the general statements given above and therefore these criteria should be applied with caution. It is vitally important to consider the facts of each case as a whole and not to rely upon just one criterion when trying to decide whether a taxpayer should be regarded as employed or self-employed.

Personal service companies

One way in which an individual might seek to avoid being classed as an employee is to form a limited company (a "personal service company") and then to hire out his or her services in the name of that company. This would enable the individual to exploit the tax and National Insurance advantages offered by corporate status. However, anti-avoidance legislation (the "IR35" legislation) exists to thwart this kind of disguised employment. The main features of this legislation are as follows:

(a) The legislation applies to "relevant engagements" where a worker provides services to a client through an intermediary (usually a company) in circumstances such that the income arising from the engagement would have been treated as income from employment if it had not been for the presence of the intermediary.

(b) The legislation does *not* apply if the worker receives income from the intermediary only in a form which is taxable as employment income and has no other rights to income or capital from the intermediary.

(c) If an intermediary receives income from relevant engagements during a tax year and this income (less allowable expenses) is greater than the worker's employment income from the intermediary in that year, then the excess is treated as a deemed salary payment made on the last day of the year. This deemed payment is subject to both income tax and National Insurance contributions, collected via PAYE.

(d) The allowable expenses referred to above include all expenses generally allowable against employment income, plus any employer's pension and National Insurance contributions made by the intermediary, plus a further flat-rate 5% of the income arising from relevant engagements (to cover running costs of the intermediary).

(e) To the extent that the deemed salary is paid out to the worker as a dividend, the intermediary may claim that the dividend should not be liable to tax.

Managed service companies

Managed service companies (MSCs) are similar to personal service companies (see above) in that they act as intermediaries through which the services of workers are provided to end clients. However, whilst a personal service company is usually controlled by the individual who formed it, an MSC is a mass-marketed service company set up and controlled by an MSC provider. A number of workers (typically ten to twenty) may become shareholders in an MSC, which then offers their services to clients. The HMRC view of such schemes is that MSCs are "almost invariably disguising employment".

Since it was proving difficult to enforce the usual intermediaries legislation in the case of managed service companies, fresh legislation was introduced that was aimed directly at MSCs. The effect of this legislation is that income received by individuals who provide their services through MSCs is treated as employment income for tax purposes. MSCs are required to operate the PAYE system (see below) to collect income tax and National Insurance contributions in relation to such income.

Basis of assessment

An individual's employment income for a tax year is the income actually received in that tax year (the "receipts basis"). This is not necessarily the same as the income *earned* during the year. Employment income is deemed to be received on the *earliest* of:

(a) the date that the income is actually received by the employee

(b) the date that the employee becomes entitled to receive the income

and, for a company director only:

(c) the date that the income is credited to the director in the company's records

(d) the end of a period of account, if the amount of the director's income for that period is determined before it ends

(e) the date that the amount of the director's income for a period of account is determined, if this falls after the end of that period.

EXAMPLE 1

Barry (who is not a director) receives an annual salary of £45,000. His bonus for the year to 31 March 2012 was £7,350, received in May 2012. His bonus for the year to 31 March 2013 was £7,900, received in May 2013. Compute his employment income for 2012-13.

Solution

Employment income for 2012-13 is £52,350 (£45,000 + £7,350). The bonus received in May 2012 is taxed in 2012-13, even though it was earned before the year began.

Employment income

The term "employment income" includes practically anything that could conceivably be received by an employee in respect of an employment (e.g. wages, salaries, bonuses, commissions, fees, expense allowances, payments on the termination of employment, pensions arising from an employment and benefits in kind). Also, certain social security benefits† are taxed in the same way as employment income, including:

(a) the state retirement pension

(b) the job seeker's allowance

(c) statutory sick pay, maternity pay and paternity pay.

Note that it is not necessary for the employee to receive the income directly from the employer. So long as the income in question is received as a result of employment it is taxable as employment income, no matter who has paid it. For example, a waiter's tips are taxable, even though these are paid by customers rather than by the employer.

†*A special tax treatment now applies to child benefit (see later in this chapter).*

Non-taxable employment income

Certain forms of employment income are exempt from income tax. The main items of exempt income are as follows:

(a) luncheon vouchers of up to 15p per day (*abolished as from 6 April 2013*)

(b) free or subsidised meals in a staff canteen, if available to all employees

(c) a party or similar function paid for by the employer, so long as the function is open to staff generally and the cost does not exceed £150 per head, but note that:

  (i) if a function costs over £150 per head, the whole cost is taxable

  (ii) if there is more than one function during the year and their total cost exceeds £150 per head, functions totalling £150 per head or less are exempt from tax but any other functions are taxed in full

(d) the provision of a parking space at or near the employee's place of work

(e) the provision of a taxi home for an employee who is occasionally required to work later than usual and until at least 9pm (but no more than 60 journeys per year)

(f) the payment by an employer of the costs of an employee's journey home if the employee travels to work in a shared car (in accordance with a regular car-sharing arrangement) and is prevented from travelling home in the shared car because of unforeseen and exceptional circumstances

(g) "green commuting" benefits paid for by the employer and used by employees for travel between home and work, including the provision of:

  - bicycles and cycling safety equipment loaned to employees
  - meals provided on "cycle to work" days (*abolished as from 6 April 2013*)
  - works buses with a seating capacity for nine or more passengers
  - subsidies to public bus services

(h) contributions by an employer towards the additional household costs incurred by an employee who works at home (supporting evidence of these costs being required only if the contributions exceed £4 per week)

(i) approved mileage allowances (see below)

(j) the payment of an employee's personal incidental expenses (e.g. the cost of telephone calls home) when the employee is away from home overnight on business, of up to £5 per night for stays within the UK or up to £10 per night for stays outside the UK

(k) reasonable removal expenses (up to £8,000) paid by an employer when an employee first takes up an employment or transfers to a new location within the organisation

(l) reasonable gifts made by employer to employee in a personal capacity rather than as remuneration for services rendered (e.g. a wedding present)

(m) non-cash long-service awards, so long as the award is in respect of at least 20 years of service, does not cost the employer more than £50 per year of service and no such award has been made to the employee in the previous ten years

(n) non-cash gifts received by virtue of the employment from someone other than the employer, so long as the value of the gifts from any one source amounts to no more than £250 in the tax year and the gifts are not made in recognition of the performance of particular services in the course of the employment

(o) awards of up to £5,000 made under a staff suggestion scheme

(p) the cost of work-related training courses for an employee and payments of up to £15,480 per academic year to an employee who is attending a full-time course at a recognised educational establishment

(q) the provision of one mobile telephone (or smartphone) for an employee's use

(r) the provision of job-related living accommodation (see Chapter 8)

(s) the provision of workplace childcare, sports or recreation facilities

(t) up to £55 per week of childcare if the employer contracts directly with an approved childminder or provides childcare vouchers (reduced to only £28 per week for higher-rate taxpayers and £22 per week for additional-rate taxpayers who joined employer-supported childcare schemes on or after 6 April 2011)

(u) the provision of a low-interest or interest-free loan to an employee if the loan is of a type that qualifies for tax relief (see Chapter 4)

(v) the provision of eye tests and spectacles for VDU use and the provision of one health screening and one medical check-up per year

(w) the provision of pensions information and advice, if available to all employees and costing less than £150 per employee per year

(x) the private use of equipment or facilities provided to disabled employees to enable them to carry out the duties of their employment.

Approved mileage allowances

Employees who use their own vehicles on business may receive mileage allowances from their employers. These allowances are tax-free so long as they do not exceed the HMRC approved mileage allowance payment (AMAP) which is calculated by reference to a table of approved mileage rates. For 2012-13, these rates are:

	first 10,000 miles in the tax year	*each mile over 10,000 miles in the tax year*
Motor cars and vans	45p per mile	25p per mile
Motor cycles	24p per mile	24p per mile
Bicycles	20p per mile	20p per mile

If the mileage allowances paid to an employee exceed the amount calculated using these rates, then the excess is taxable. On the other hand, if the mileage allowances paid to an employee are less than the amount calculated using these rates, the deficit is an allowable expense. Tax relief cannot be claimed for any costs above the AMAP rate.

Employers may also pay employees up to 5p per mile tax-free for each passenger carried on a business trip. However, employees cannot claim tax relief if the employer pays less than this (or pays nothing at all).

EXAMPLE 2

Julie uses her own car when travelling on her employer's business. In 2012-13 she drives 12,000 business miles. Explain the taxation implications if her employer pays her:

(a) 47p per mile (b) 37p per mile (c) None.

Solution

(a) Having driven 12,000 business miles during the year, Julie may receive a tax-free mileage allowance of up to £5,000 (10,000 @ 45p + 2,000 @ 25p). She actually receives £5,640 (12,000 @ 47p) so her taxable mileage allowance is £640.

(b) If the mileage allowance is 37p per mile, Julie receives £4,440 from her employer. Therefore she has incurred an allowable expense of £560 (£5,000 – £4,440) which may be set against her income from employment.

(c) If Julie receives nothing, she has an allowable expense of £5,000.

Allowable expenses

If an employee incurs expenses by virtue of his or her employment, then one of two situations may arise:

(a) The employer does not reimburse the employee. In this case, the expenses (if they are allowable) will be deducted from the employee's income for tax purposes.

(b) The employer reimburses the employee. In this case, the amount reimbursed by the employer will be treated as part of the employee's income for tax purposes and the expenses, if allowable, will be deducted from that income.

However, reimbursed expenses may be ignored if HMRC grants a dispensation to this effect (a "notice of nil liability"). A dispensation is an agreement between HMRC and an employer which allows the employer to reimburse allowable expenses at an agreed rate without having to report the expenses to HMRC.

Expenses incurred by an employee are allowable for tax purposes only if they fall into one of the following categories:

(a) contributions to an occupational pension scheme, if deducted from the employee's pay by the employer (see Chapter 14)

(b) subscriptions to relevant professional bodies

(c) donations made under a payroll giving scheme (see later in this chapter)

(d) travel and subsistence expenses necessarily incurred in the performance of the duties of the employment (see below)
(e) other expenses incurred wholly, exclusively and necessarily in the performance of the duties of the employment.

The "wholly, exclusively and necessarily" rule is applied very stringently. In particular, the "necessarily" part of the rule means that an expense will not be allowed unless it can be shown that the duties of the employment concerned could not be performed (by anyone) if the expense were not incurred.

Travel between home and work

As stated above, travel and subsistence expenses are allowable for tax purposes only if they are necessarily incurred in the performance of the duties of the employment. This means that the cost of travel between home and work is normally disallowed on the grounds that the duties of the employment do not begin until the employee arrives at work. However, the following costs of travel between home and work are allowable:

(a) travel and subsistence costs incurred by a "site-based" employee (i.e. an employee who has no normal place of work) when travelling between home and the site
(b) travel and subsistence costs incurred by an employee who has a normal place of work, when undertaking business journeys which start from home
(c) travel and subsistence costs incurred by an employee who is seconded to a temporary place of work, so long as it is expected that he or she will return to the normal place of work within 24 months.

EXAMPLE 3

In which of the following cases will the expenses described be allowable against the employee's income for tax purposes?

(a) A bank manager voluntarily pays an annual subscription to a London club. He uses the club only for the purpose of meeting the bank's clients.

(b) A workman is required to provide his own tools and protective clothing.

(c) A clerk pays to attend a college course in the evenings, so as to gain qualifications and improve her career prospects.

(d) The finance director of a company pays an annual subscription to the Institute of Chartered Accountants.

(e) A college lecturer teaches at the main college building and then drives to one of the college's annexes to take his next class. He pays his own travel costs.

(f) A barrister living and practising in London is appointed Recorder of Portsmouth. He pays his own train fares between London and Portsmouth.

Solution

(a) The bank manager uses the club wholly and exclusively for business purposes, but it is not necessary for him to be a member of the club in order to perform his duties. Therefore the cost of the subscription will be disallowed. The facts of this case are similar to those of *Brown* v *Bullock* (1961).

(b) The cost of necessary tools and protective clothing will be allowed. In some cases, HM Revenue and Customs has agreed flat-rate tax allowances with the relevant trade union for such expenses as tools, protective clothing, uniforms and laundry costs.

(c) Whilst attending college, the clerk is not performing the duties of her employment. Therefore the cost of the college course will be disallowed. The facts of this case are similar to those of *Blackwell* v *Mills* (1945).

(d) Relevant professional subscriptions of this nature are specifically allowed by statute. Therefore the cost of the subscription will be allowed.

(e) Travel between the two buildings will be allowed, since the travel is necessary and is incurred in the performance of the duties of the employment.

(f) The duties of the employment are carried out entirely in Portsmouth. Whilst travelling from London, the barrister is not performing those duties so the expense will be disallowed. The facts of this case are similar to those of *Ricketts* v *Colquhoun* (1935).

Entertaining expenses

In general, entertaining expenses are not allowable against employment income and an employee who is obliged to defray such expenses personally cannot claim a deduction for them. However, if an employer either:

(a) reimburses an employee for entertaining expenses incurred, or

(b) pays the employee a specific entertaining allowance

then the entertaining expenses incurred by the employee may be set against the sums received from the employer. This rule is subject to the overriding rule that the entertaining expenses must be incurred wholly, exclusively and necessarily in the performance of the duties of the employment.

Payroll giving scheme

Employees whose employers operate an approved "payroll giving scheme" may make charitable donations by requesting that the donations should be deducted from their gross earnings. Income tax is then payable on the earnings which remain *after* the donations have been deducted, thus providing tax relief. The employer passes the donations on to an approved charity.

Payments made on termination of employment

Payments received by an employee on the termination of employment fall into three distinct categories:

(a) **Fully exempt**. The following types of termination payment are fully exempt from income tax:

  (i) payments made on the death of the employee

  (ii) payments made to the employee because of injury or disability

  (iii) lump sum payments under registered pension schemes.

  (iv) statutory redundancy pay.

(b) **Fully taxable**. If an employee receives a termination payment which does not fall into any of the categories listed above and which is made by way of reward for the employee's services, then the payment is fully taxable in the year in which it is received. This applies if the employee was contractually entitled to the payment or if there was a reasonable expectation that the payment would be made.

(c) **Partially exempt**. Payments of up to £30,000 made at the employer's discretion to compensate an employee for loss of employment ("ex gratia" payments) are exempt from income tax. Any excess over £30,000 is taxable in the year in which it is received. If the employee also receives statutory redundancy pay, the £30,000 exemption is reduced by the amount of SRP received.

The taxable part of a partially exempt termination payment is treated as the top slice of income, ranking above both savings income and dividends. This provision ensures that savings income and dividends are not moved out of the basic rate band and taxed at the higher rate (or additional rate) or at the dividend upper rate (or dividend additional rate) as a consequence of the taxpayer receiving a partially exempt termination payment.

EXAMPLE 4

Henrietta is made redundant in March 2013. She receives statutory redundancy pay of £2,500 and an ex gratia payment of £40,000 from her employer as compensation for loss of office. Her only other income in 2012-13 consists of her salary of £37,270 and UK dividends of £4,500. Calculate her tax payable for 2012-13, assuming that she claims only the basic personal allowance.

Solution

	Total	Non-savings	Dividends	Compensation
	£	£	£	£
Salary	37,270	37,270		
UK dividends £4,500 + £500	5,000		5,000	
Compensation £40,000 – £27,500	12,500			12,500
Total income	54,770	37,270	5,000	12,500
Less: Personal allowance	8,105	8,105		
Taxable income	46,665	29,165	5,000	12,500

Non-savings income and dividend income fall entirely into the basic rate band, leaving £205 of this band for the compensation. The remainder of the compensation is taxed at the higher rate.

Income tax due

Basic rate band	: Non-savings	29,165	@ 20%	5,833.00
	: Dividends	5,000	@ 10%	500.00
	: Compensation	205	@ 20%	41.00
Higher rate	: Compensation	12,295	@ 40%	4,918.00
		46,665		
Tax borne				11,292.00
Less: Tax credits on dividends				500.00
Tax payable				10,792.00

Notes:

(i) If the compensation payment had not been treated as the top slice of income, all of the dividends would have been moved out of the basic rate band and would have been taxed at the dividend upper rate of 32.5%. However, an extra £5,000 of the compensation would have been taxed at the basic rate of 20%. The "top-slicing" rule has saved tax of (£5,000 x (32.5% – 10%)) – (£5,000 x (40% – 20%)) = £125.00.

(ii) Any tax paid by means of the PAYE system would also be deducted.

High income child benefit charge

Child benefit is a social security benefit which is not generally taxable. However, as from 2012-13, a taxpayer who has adjusted net income (see Chapter 3) in excess of £50,000 per annum and receives child benefit (or whose partner receives child benefit) may be subject to the "high income child benefit charge". This income tax charge is equal to 1% of the child benefit award for each £100 of income between £50,000 and £60,000. The charge on taxpayers with income of more than £60,000 is 100% of the child benefit award.

This charge applies only to taxpayers whose income exceeds £50,000 for the tax year. If both of the partners to a domestic partnership have income exceeding £50,000, the charge applies only to the partner with the higher income.

The PAYE system

Under the Pay As You Earn (PAYE) system, employers are required to deduct income tax and National Insurance contributions from their employees when paying them their wages and salaries. The amounts deducted from employees, together with the secondary National Insurance contributions payable by the employer (see Chapter 16) must be paid to HMRC within 14 days of the end of the tax month in which the employees are paid (or 17 days if payment to HMRC is made electronically). A tax month runs from the 6th of one month to the 5th of the next month. Therefore employers generally make a payment to HMRC on or before the 19th (or 22nd) of each month. However, employers whose payments to HMRC do not exceed an average of £1,500 per month are allowed to make quarterly payments.

The PAYE system applies to all payments which are assessable as employment income, including wages, salaries, bonuses, commissions etc. The system also covers:

(a) payments taking the form of assets which are readily convertible into cash, such as shares, gold bars, coffee beans or other similar commodities, but excluding "own company" shares which are provided by the employer under an approved share scheme (see later in this chapter)

(b) vouchers exchangeable either for cash or for readily convertible assets

(c) remuneration schemes involving trade debts, whereby employers assign trade debts to employees, who then receive cash when the debts are settled.

Benefits in kind (see Chapter 8) are usually brought within the scope of PAYE by making an adjustment to the employee's tax code (see below).

Tax codes

The PAYE system is based upon the concept of "tax codes". It is HMRC's responsibility to issue a tax code for each employee for each tax year, representing the amount which the employee may earn in that year before becoming liable to income tax. The tax code takes into account a number of factors which may affect an employee's income tax liability, including the following:

(a) the personal allowances to which the employee is entitled

(b) the employee's tax reliefs (e.g. payments deductible from total income)

(c) the employee's allowable expenses

(d) adjustments made in order to collect tax on benefits in kind

(e) adjustments for tax overpaid or underpaid in previous years.

The tax code allocated to an employee is equal to one-tenth of the aggregate of the above items, rounded down to a whole number.

EXAMPLE 5

Henry is single and claims only the basic personal allowance. He makes a deductible payment of £100 per annum and pays an allowable subscription of £80 per annum. He has taxable benefits in kind amounting to £500 in 2012-13. Determine his tax code for 2012-13, assuming that his income for the year is not expected to exceed £100,000.

Solution

By virtue of his personal allowance, deductible payment and allowable expenses, Henry is entitled to earn £8,285 (£8,105 + £100 + £80) in the year before paying tax. But some of this will be set against his benefits in kind of £500, leaving only £7,785 to set against his salary. So Henry's tax code for the year would be 778 (i.e. one-tenth of £7,785, rounded down to a whole number).

The same result would be obtained if the aggregate figure (£7,785) were anywhere in the range £7,780 to £7,789, so tax codes are not precise. But dividing the aggregate figure by ten results in only one-tenth as many different tax codes as would be obtained otherwise and cuts down the size of the tax tables used by employers (see below).

Tax code suffixes

A tax code may also have a suffix comprising a letter of the alphabet. The most common suffix is L which stands for "low" and indicates that the employee is entitled to the basic personal allowance (currently £8,105). So Henry's full tax code in the above example would actually be 778L. Other suffixes include:

P - the employee is entitled to the personal allowance for those aged 65-74

Y - the employee is entitled to the personal allowance for those aged 75 or older.

Code BR instructs the employer to deduct basic rate tax from all payments made to the employee. Code NT instructs the employer not to deduct tax from the employee at all. Codes prefixed with the letter K are negative codes, used mainly for employees whose taxable benefits in kind exceed their allowances. Tax on the excess benefits is collected by increasing the amount of tax charged on the employee's wage or salary.

The purpose of tax code suffixes is to facilitate the recoding exercise which is needed whenever personal allowances are increased. When this happens, HMRC may instruct employers to increase all L codes by the amount required to reflect the increase in the basic personal allowance, to increase all P codes by the amount required to reflect the increase in the aged 65-74 personal allowance, and so forth. This avoids the need to recode every employee in the country individually.

Operation of the PAYE system

Employers who operate manual payroll systems are issued with sets of tax tables which enable them to calculate the amount of income tax that should be deducted from an employee in a given week or month. The main tables used are:

Table A — This table (also known as the Pay Adjustment Table) contains pages for each week or month of the year and shows, for each tax code, the amount of tax-free pay to which the employee is entitled for the year to date. In effect, the table spreads an employee's allowances evenly over the year, giving 1/12th of the allowances per month or 1/52th of the allowances per week.

Table B — This table (also known as the Taxable Pay Table) is used to look up an employee's income tax liability for the year to date, after the entitlement to tax-free pay has been taken into account.

In outline, the procedure followed for each employee in each week or month is:

(a) The employee's tax code is looked up in Table A, which shows the amount of tax-free pay to which the employee is entitled for the year to date.

(b) This is then subtracted from the employee's gross pay for the year to date giving the employee's taxable pay for the year to date.

(c) The employee's taxable pay for the year to date is then looked up in Table B, which shows the tax due for the year to date. Further tables are used if the employee is a higher rate taxpayer.

(d) Finally, the tax paid to date by the employee in previous weeks or months is subtracted from the tax due for the year to date, giving the employee's income tax liability for the current week or month.

The entire system is cumulative and requires employers to keep track of each of their employees' gross pay and income tax paid to date (i.e. since the beginning of the tax year on 6 April). Employers are provided with deductions working sheets (form P11) which facilitate the accumulation of the necessary "to date" figures.

In a computer-based payroll system, the tax tables become computer files and the weekly or monthly procedure is carried out by computer software. However, the operation of the PAYE system does not change in principle when a manual payroll system is replaced by a computer-based system.

PAYE forms

P2 — A notice of coding, sent by HMRC to both the employer and the employee.

P9D — An end-of-year return showing the benefits in kind and expenses of a lower-paid employee (see Chapter 8). Forms P9D must be submitted to HMRC by 6 July following the end of the tax year to which they relate and the employees concerned must be provided with copies by the same date.

P11 — Deductions working sheet (see above).

P11D	An end-of-year return showing the benefits in kind and expenses of a director or an employee earning at least £8,500. Forms P11D must be submitted to HMRC by 6 July following the end of the tax year and the employees concerned must be provided with copies by the same date.
P14	An end-of-year return showing an individual employee's gross pay, tax paid and National Insurance paid for the year. Sent to HMRC by the employer.
P35	An end-of-year return listing all employees in the tax year and showing each employee's gross pay, tax paid and National Insurance paid for the year. Sent to HMRC by the employer. The form P35, together with forms P14, must be submitted to HMRC by 19 May following the end of the tax year.
P45	A four-part form used when an employee leaves an employment, showing the employee's tax code, gross pay to date and tax paid to date. Part 1 of the form is sent to HMRC and the other three parts are given to the leaving employee. The employee gives parts 2 and 3 to his or her new employer who retains part 2 and sends part 3 to HMRC. The employee retains part 4.
P46	A form providing details of a new employee who does not have a P45 from a previous employment. Sent to HMRC by the employer.
P60	Certificate of gross pay and tax deducted, given to employees by employers at the end of the tax year. Forms P60 must be provided to employees by 31 May following the end of the tax year.

Notes:

(a) Online filing of "in-year" forms (P45s and P46s) and the end-of-year "annual return" (P14s and P35) is now mandatory for virtually all employers. Most of the other PAYE forms which must be submitted by employers to HMRC may also be filed online, including the end-of-year P9Ds and P11Ds.

(b) Employers are allowed to provide P60s to their employees by electronic means, as long as the employees concerned are able to access their P60s easily and securely.

(c) Employers with 250 or more employees are required to make their PAYE payments to HMRC by electronic means.

Real Time Information

The PAYE Real Time Information (RTI) system will be introduced by HMRC during tax year 2013-14. This system will require employers to send data about employees' pay and deductions (tax and NICs) to HMRC at the time that the employees are paid. Online data transmission will be mandatory. The RTI system will remove the need for an end-of-year P35 and an individual P14 for each employee. Furthermore, information about starters and leavers will also be transmitted as part of the normal RTI process, so that there will be no need for employers to submit P45s and P46s to HMRC.

Construction industry scheme

The construction industry scheme (CIS) may apply when a contractor makes payments to a subcontractor under a contract relating to construction operations. Subcontractors who rank as employees are dealt with via the PAYE system in the usual way, but it has proved necessary to introduce a special scheme in relation to subcontractors who do not rank as employees, so as to counter tax evasion. The main features of the CIS are as follows:

(a) Subcontractors are required to register as such with HMRC. They may apply to be paid gross by the contractors for whom they work or they may register to be paid under deduction of tax. To qualify for gross payment, a subcontractor must be running a business which:

  (i) is run in the UK and has a bank account (the "business test")
  (ii) has a construction turnover of at least £30,000 p.a. (the "turnover test")
  (iii) has complied with all of its tax obligations (the "compliance test").

(b) Subcontractors must give contractors their name, unique taxpayer reference and National Insurance number when they enter into a contract. The contractor then contacts HMRC to check on the subcontractor's status. This process is known as "verification".

(c) If the subcontractor is registered with HMRC, the contractor will be told either to pay the subcontractor gross or to apply the standard rate of deduction (20%). However, any payment which represents a reimbursement of the cost of materials supplied by the subcontractor is excluded from the amount which is subject to deduction of tax.

(d) If the subcontractor is not registered with HMRC, the contractor will be told to apply a higher rate of deduction (30%) when making payments to that subcontractor.

(e) Within 14 days of the end of each tax month, contractors must provide a statement to each subcontractor from whom a tax deduction has been made, showing details of the payments made and the amounts deducted.

(f) Also within 14 days of the end of each tax month, contractors must send a return to HMRC showing all of the payments made to subcontractors during the month, whether paid gross or under deduction of tax. Returns can be made on paper or electronically. Nil returns are required.

(g) All deductions made from subcontractors during a tax month must be paid over to HMRC within 14 days of the end of the tax month. Three further days are allowed if payment is made electronically.

Employee incentive schemes

An employee incentive scheme provides financial incentives for employees to improve their work performance. The main types of scheme which currently have income tax implications are:

(a) share incentive plans (SIPs)

(b) approved share option schemes

(c) enterprise management incentives (EMIs).

A brief description of each of these types of scheme is given below.

Share incentive plans

Share incentive plans (SIPs) offer employees a tax-efficient way of acquiring shares in the companies for which they work. SIPs were originally known as all-employee share ownership plans (AESOPs). The main features of these plans are as follows:

(a) Companies which set up a SIP may offer their employees:

  (i) *free shares* in the company worth up to £3,000 per annum per employee

  (ii) the opportunity to use salary of up to £1,500 per annum to buy *partnership shares* in the company (without having to pay either income tax or NICs on the salary used for this purpose)

  (iii) up to two free *matching shares* for each partnership share bought by an employee.

  This means that (each year) an employee who pays income tax at the basic rate could acquire up to £7,500 worth of shares at a cost of £1,200 (80% × £1,500). The cost would be reduced to £900 (60% × £1,500) for an employee paying tax at the higher rate and only £750 (50% × £1,500) for an employee paying tax at the additional rate. There would also be a saving in National Insurance contributions (see Chapter 16).

(b) The company may offer free shares only, partnership shares only, free shares and partnership shares only, partnership shares and matching shares only, or all three of these types of shares.

(c) Subject to certain conditions, the plan may link the provision of free shares to the achievement of employee performance targets.

(d) In general, all employees must be eligible to participate in the plan. However, the plan may specify that employees do not become eligible until they have been employed by the company (or employed by the group, in the case of a group of companies) for a qualifying period of not more than 18 months.

(e) Employees who hold over 25% of the company's ordinary shares (a "material interest") are not eligible to participate in the plan.

(f) The plan may allow (or compel) dividends of up to £1,500 per annum arising on an employee's shares to be reinvested tax-free in further *dividend shares*.

(g) All of an employee's shares leave the plan when he or she ceases to be employed by the company (or group). The plan rules may specify that employees who leave within three years should forfeit their free and matching shares. Additionally, employees may take some or all of their shares out of the plan as follows:

Free/matching shares	:	at any time after the end of the holding period specified by the plan, which must be between three and five years
Partnership shares	:	at any time (though any related matching shares may be forfeited if this occurs within three years)
Dividend shares	:	at any time after three years.

(h) If free, matching or partnership shares leave the plan within three years, a charge to income tax and NICs arises based on the market value of the shares when leaving the plan. If the shares leave the plan after three years but in less than five years, this charge is based upon the *lower* of the market value of the shares when originally awarded and the market value of the shares when leaving the plan.

(i) If dividend shares leave the plan within three years, a tax charge arises on a *notional dividend* equal to the cash dividend which was used to acquire the shares.

(j) No tax charge arises if shares of any type leave the plan after five years (or earlier if this is caused by the employee's death or by injury, disability or redundancy).

(k) Employees who keep their shares in the plan until they sell them incur no liability to capital gains tax. Employees who take their shares out of the plan and sell them later pay CGT on any increase in value since the shares were taken out.

Approved share option schemes

In general, a charge to income tax (and NICs) may arise if an employee who works for a company is granted an option to buy shares in that company. The charge arises when the option is exercised and is based upon the market value of the shares obtained, less the amount paid for the shares and less the amount (if any) which was paid to acquire the option. However, this charge can be avoided if the option falls within an approved share option scheme. Approved schemes are of two main types:

(a) **Savings-related share option schemes**. Under a savings-related scheme, employees are granted an option to buy shares and then save through a tax-free savings scheme in order to raise funds to exercise the option. The amount saved must be no more than £250 a month and the savings contract may last for three or five years. The scheme must be open to all employees who have worked for the company for a specified qualifying period (which cannot exceed five years). The price at which employees are given the option to buy shares must be at least 80% of the shares' market value at the time that the option is granted.

(b) **Company share option plans**. These schemes are less restrictive than savings-related schemes. The company can select the employees to whom it would like to offer share options and can set these employees performance targets which must be achieved before the options will be made available. The price at which an option may be exercised must not be manifestly less than the market value of the shares at the time that the option is granted and options must normally be exercised no earlier than three years and no later than 10 years after they are granted. However, options may be exercised within three years of being granted if an employee's participation in the scheme ends through injury, disability, redundancy or retirement. There is an upper limit of £30,000 on the value of the shares (at the time of the grant) for which an employee may hold options at any one time.

If a share option is granted under an approved scheme of either type and all necessary conditions are satisfied, then no income tax or NICs are payable on either the grant of the option or the exercise of the option. For capital gains tax purposes (see Chapter 18) the allowable cost of shares acquired under an approved share option scheme is the price actually paid for the shares by the employee.

Enterprise management incentives

Enterprise management incentives (EMIs) offer trading companies that have a permanent establishment in the UK the chance to reward selected employees with tax-free share options. In order to be eligible, a company must have fewer than 250 employees and gross assets not exceeding £30 million. The main features of the EMIs scheme are:

(a) The scheme allows a qualifying company to grant share options to any employee who works at least 25 hours per week for the company, or (if less) for at least 75% of his or her working time. The company may select the employees to whom it wishes to grant options and may award different amounts to different employees.

(b) Employees who own more than 30% of the company's ordinary share capital are excluded from the scheme.

(c) If the company so wishes, options may be granted to acquire shares at less than their market value at the time of grant or even at nil cost.

(d) No charge to income tax (or NICs) arises when an option is granted under the scheme. When the option is exercised, no charge arises if the shares are acquired at not less than their market value at the time of grant. Otherwise, a tax charge arises based on the *lower* of:

   (i) the excess of the market value of the shares at the time that the option was granted over the amount (if any) paid to acquire them

   (ii) the excess of the market value of the shares at the time that the option is exercised over the amount (if any) paid to acquire them.

(e) There is an upper limit of £250,000 (*£120,000 prior to 16 June 2012*) on the value of the shares (at the time of grant) for which an employee may hold unexercised options that have been granted under the scheme. At any time, the total value of the shares for which options have been granted cannot exceed £3 million.

(f) The sale of shares which were acquired under the scheme is a chargeable disposal for capital gains tax purposes. The Government's intention (also subject to EU approval) is that gains arising on or after 6 April 2012 from the exercise of EMIs options should be eligible for entrepreneurs' relief (see Chapter 22).

Summary

- Criteria have been established which may be used to distinguish employment from self-employment.
- The basis of assessment for employment income is the income actually received in the tax year.
- Income tax is payable on practically all of the income received in respect of an employment, including benefits in kind. Certain social security benefits are also taxed as if they were employment income. However, some minor items of employment income are exempt from income tax.
- In general, an employee's expenses are allowed only if they are incurred wholly, exclusively and necessarily in the performance of the duties of the employment.
- Any amount to which an employee is contractually entitled on the termination of employment is fully taxable. Certain termination payments (e.g. on death or injury) are fully exempt. Ex gratia termination payments are partially exempt.
- The PAYE system is used to deduct both income tax and NICs from employees' wages and salaries.
- The construction industry scheme (CIS) may apply when payments are made by a contractor to a sub-contractor in connection with a construction contract.
- Certain employee incentive schemes offer tax advantages. Share incentive plans provide employees with a tax-efficient means of acquiring shares in the companies for which they work. Share options may be granted tax-efficiently to employees by means of approved share option schemes and enterprise management incentives.

Exercises

7.1 List the criteria which might be used to distinguish employment from self-employment.

7.2 Malcolm's gross annual salary is £57,500. He also receives an annual bonus based on his employer's profits for the calendar year. His bonus for the year to 31 December 2011 was £8,350 (which he received on 9 April 2012). His bonus for the year to 31 December 2012 was £9,570 (which he received on 18 April 2013). Malcolm is not a company director. Calculate his employment income for 2012-13.

7.3 Which of the following forms of income from employment would be exempt from income tax in 2012-13?

(a) Luncheon vouchers of £2 per working day.

(b) Free meals in the company canteen.

(c) Removal expenses of £4,500.

(d) A cheque for £1,000 given to an employee on reaching 25 years of service with his employer.

(e) A canteen of cutlery given to an employee on his marriage.

(f) A mileage allowance of 35p per mile given to an employee who drives her own motor car for 2,500 business miles per year.

7.4 Which of the following expenses incurred by an employee would be deductible when computing employment income for tax purposes?

(a) Travel costs between work and home.

(b) Travel costs between employment sites.

(c) Subscriptions to professional bodies.

(d) The cost of protective clothing.

(e) The cost of a suit to wear at the office.

(f) Entertaining expenses.

***7.5** On 21 March 2013, Penny is made redundant by her employer. She receives statutory redundancy pay of £4,750 and an ex gratia payment of £32,000 from her employer as compensation for loss of employment. Her only other income in tax year 2012-13 is her salary (between 6 April 2012 and 21 March 2013) of £39,105 and net building society interest of £800.

Calculate the income tax payable by Penny for 2012-13 (before deducting tax paid under the PAYE system).

Chapter 8

Income from employment (2)

Introduction

As explained in Chapter 7, the term "employment income" includes any benefits in kind which an employee might receive. Benefits in kind consist of income received in the form of goods or services (rather than money) and include items such as living accommodation, company cars and interest-free loans. The purpose of this chapter is to explain how an employee's benefits in kind are calculated for tax purposes.

Benefits in kind

For the purpose of assessing benefits in kind, employees are divided into two classes. These are "P11D employees" and "lower-paid employees".

(a) P11D employees comprise those employees who earn at least £8,500 per annum and most company directors. The only exceptions are full-time working directors who earn less than £8,500 p.a. and control no more than 5% of their company's ordinary share capital. Employers must submit a form P11D to HM Revenue and Customs for each such employee for each tax year, listing the employee's benefits in kind and any reimbursed expenses (unless covered by a dispensation).

(b) All other employees are non-P11D employees or "lower-paid employees".

As a general rule, lower-paid employees are taxed only on benefits that are convertible into money, and then only on the amount of money that the employee could obtain in this way. In other words, lower-paid employees are taxed on the *second-hand value* of their benefits in kind. P11D employees are generally taxed on the *cost to the employer* of providing the benefits, whether or not these benefits are convertible into money.

When comparing an employee's earnings with the watershed figure of £8,500, it is necessary to take into account all earnings, including benefits in kind *valued as if the employee were a P11D employee*. No expenses may be deducted from earnings when making this comparison, apart from contributions to an occupational pension scheme or to a payroll giving scheme. If an employee works for more than one employer and the employers are connected in some way, earnings from the connected employers must be aggregated when deciding the employee's classification for benefits purposes.

EXAMPLE 1

Classify each of the following employees for benefits purposes:

(a) Joan works part-time and has a salary of £7,300 p.a. She also receives benefits which cost her employer £900 but which have a second-hand value of £500.

(b) Kate works part-time and has a salary of £8,320 p.a. She receives benefits which cost her employer £600 with a second-hand value of £300. Her allowable expenses are £535, including contributions of £416 to an occupational pension scheme.

(c) Lawrence is a company director. He has 10% of the company's share capital, works one day per week on company business and receives an annual director's fee of £8,000. Benefits cost his company £250 with a second-hand value of £150.

Solution

(a) Joan's salary, plus the cost of her benefits, total £8,200. This is less than £8,500 and therefore she is a lower-paid employee. She will be taxed on her salary and on the second-hand value of her benefits, a total of £7,800.

(b) Kate's salary, plus the cost of her benefits, total £8,920. Her pension contributions of £416 reduce this total to £8,504 but this is not less than £8,500 so she is a P11D employee. She will be taxed on her salary, plus the full cost of her benefits, less her allowable expenses i.e. £8,385 (£8,320 + £600 – £535).

(c) Lawrence is a P11D employee by virtue of being a company director who does not work full-time and who owns more than 5% of his company's share capital. He will be taxed on his fees, plus the full cost of his benefits i.e. £8,250.

Benefits assessable on all employees

The tax treatment of an employee's benefits in kind usually depends upon the employee's classification, as explained above. But certain benefits are assessable in the same way on all employees, regardless of classification. The two main benefits concerned are:

(a) vouchers which may be exchanged for goods or services
(b) living accommodation.

Vouchers for goods or services

All employees are taxed on the cost to their employer of providing vouchers which may be exchanged for goods or services, but no liability arises if a voucher is used to provide a benefit that would otherwise be exempt from tax. Note that:

(a) Entertainment and hospitality vouchers provided by a person other than the employer or someone connected with the employer are exempt from income tax unless provided as a reward for specific services rendered by the employee.

(b) The provision of a cash voucher results in a taxable benefit equal to the amount of cash into which the voucher can be converted.

Living accommodation

All employees are taxed in the same way on the value of any living accommodation provided for them by their employer. The rules are as follows:

(a) In the case of accommodation which is owned by the employer, the employee is taxed on the "annual value" of the accommodation. In practice, this is taken to be the accommodation's rateable value, which was used in the calculation of domestic rates before these were abolished. The rateable value of properties constructed since the abolition of domestic rates has to be estimated.

(b) In the case of accommodation rented by the employer, the employee is taxed on the greater of the rent paid by the employer and the accommodation's annual value.

In either case, the taxable benefit in kind is reduced by any contribution made by the employee. Accommodation costing the employer more than £75,000 is regarded as "expensive" and gives rise to an increase in the taxable benefit. This increase is calculated by applying an appropriate percentage to the amount by which the cost of the accommodation exceeds £75,000. Note the following points:

(a) The "appropriate percentage" used for this purpose is the same as the official rate of interest used in beneficial loan calculations (see later in this chapter) as that rate stood at the beginning of the tax year.

(b) The cost of providing accommodation is equal to the purchase price of the property concerned, plus the cost of any improvements made to the property before the start of the tax year, less any capital contribution made by the employee.

(c) If the property concerned was acquired by the employer more than six years before it was made available to the employee, then the purchase price of the property may be replaced for tax purposes by its market value on the date that it was first occupied by the employee.

EXAMPLE 2

As from 1 January 2012, an employee is provided by his employer with the use of a house which has an annual value of £5,300. The following information is relevant:

(a) The employer bought the house in 2009 at a cost of £170,000 and spent £35,000 on improvements in 2011. A further £10,000 was spent on improvements in July 2012.

(b) The employee pays £3,000 per annum to his employer in relation to this benefit.

Calculate the taxable benefit in 2012-13, assuming that the official rate of interest on 6 April 2012 was 4% per annum.

Solution

	£
Annual value	5,300
Add: 4% x (£170,000 + £35,000 – £75,000)	5,200
	10,500
Less: Employee contribution	3,000
Taxable benefit	7,500

Job-related accommodation

If accommodation provided by an employer for an employee is "job-related", then no taxable benefit arises. Accommodation is job-related if:

(a) it is necessary for the employee to reside in the accommodation for the proper performance of his or her duties (e.g. a caretaker who is required to live in a caretaker's flat on an employer's premises)

(b) the accommodation is provided for the better performance of the employee's duties and it is customary for such accommodation to be provided (e.g. a clergyman who lives in a vicarage provided by an employer)

(c) there is a special threat to the employee's security and the accommodation is provided as part of security arrangements.

Special rules for P11D employees

Certain benefits are assessed on P11D employees according to special rules. The main benefits for which special rules exist are:

(a) assets loaned to the employee for private use

(b) ancillary services connected with living accommodation

(c) cars provided for private use

(d) fuel provided for private use

(e) vans provided for private use

(f) beneficial loans.

Lower-paid employees would be taxed on these benefits only if they were capable of being converted into cash in some way, and then only on the amount of cash obtainable.

Assets loaned to the employee for private use

If an employer lends an asset to a P11D employee for his or her private use, the employee is taxed annually on 20% of the market value of the asset on the date of the loan. If the asset is subsequently sold or given to the employee, he or she is additionally taxed on the *greater* of:

(a) the market value of the asset when sold or given to the employee, less any amount paid for the asset by the employee, and

(b) the market value of the asset when first loaned to the employee, less the amounts already assessed to tax during the period of the loan, less any amount paid for the asset by the employee.

The loan of a bicycle and cycling safety equipment is exempt from tax if used wholly or mainly for travel between home and work.

EXAMPLE 3

On 6 April 2010, an employer purchases a music system for £800 and immediately lends the system to a P11D employee for his private use. The system remains in the employee's possession until 6 October 2012 when the employee buys it from his employer for £100, its market value on that day being £240. Calculate the taxable benefit in kind for tax years 2010-11 to 2012-13 inclusive.

Solution

			£
2010-11	20% of £800		160
2011-12	20% of £800		160
2012-13	20% of £800 x 6/12	80	
	plus, the greater of:		
	(i) £240 – £100 = £140		
	(ii) £800 – £160 – £160 – £80 – £100 = £300	300	380
Total benefit assessed to tax over period of the loan			700

Ancillary services connected with living accommodation

A P11D employee who is provided with living accommodation is taxed not only on the accommodation itself but also on the cost to the employer of providing any "ancillary services" in connection with that accommodation. Ancillary services include such items as heating and lighting, repairs and maintenance and cleaning. The provision of furniture for the employee's use is also included under the heading of ancillary services and is taxed as a loaned asset (see above). Note that:

(a) The taxable benefit in relation to ancillary services is reduced by any contribution made by the employee towards the cost of those services.

(b) If the accommodation is job-related, the taxable benefit with regard to ancillary services cannot exceed 10% of the employee's net earnings for the year, less any contribution made by the employee. Net earnings are defined for this purpose as total earnings for the year (apart from the ancillary services) less allowable expenses.

EXAMPLE 4

In 2012-13, an employer provides living accommodation for a P11D employee and also provides the following services in connection with this accommodation:

	£
Cleaning	1,040
Heating and lighting	850
Repairs and maintenance	1,235
Loan of furniture, cost to the employer	12,000

The employee contributes £100 per month towards the cost of these services. Compute the taxable benefit, given that the employee has net earnings for the year (excluding the ancillary services) of £42,500.

Solution

If the accommodation is not job-related, the taxable benefit is £4,325 (£1,040 + £850 + £1,235 + 20% of £12,000, less £1,200). If the accommodation is job-related, the taxable benefit is limited to 10% of £42,500, less £1,200 = £3,050.

Cars provided for private use

A P11D employee is taxed on the provision of a motor car unless the car is totally unavailable for the employee's private use. The taxable benefit is based upon the list price of the car when new (even if the employer bought the car for less than list price or bought it second-hand) and is adjusted according to the car's level of carbon dioxide emissions. The main features of the method of computation are as follows:

(a) The price of the car for the purpose of calculating the benefit in kind is the sum of:

   (i) the list price of the car when new, including standard accessories

   (ii) the cost of all optional accessories (other than mobile telephones) fitted to the car before it is made available to the employee

   (iii) the cost of any optional accessories (other than mobile telephones) costing £100 or more and fitted to the car after it is made available to the employee.

   Accessories which are designed for use only by a disabled person are ignored when calculating the price of the car. This exemption extends to any accessories required because of the employee's disability (e.g. power steering) and is not limited just to accessories designed for use solely by the disabled. A similar exemption applies to security enhancements (e.g. armour plating) for employees who can demonstrate that their employment creates a threat to their personal security.

(b) The taxable benefit is based upon the price of the car, less any capital contribution (up to a maximum of £5,000) made by the employee towards the car's cost.

(c) If the car is a "classic car", defined as a car which:

   (i) is over 15 years old at the end of the tax year, and

   (ii) has a market value at the end of the year exceeding £15,000 and exceeding the price calculated at (a) above

   then the car's market value at the end of the year is substituted for the car's price when calculating the taxable benefit.

(d) The taxable benefit for a tax year is calculated by applying a percentage to the figure calculated at (b) above. The applicable percentage depends upon the car's level of carbon dioxide emissions (rounded down to the nearest 5g/km if over 100g/km). For petrol-driven cars in 2012-13 this percentage is computed as follows:

Carbon dioxide emissions	*Applicable percentage*
Not exceeding 75g/km	5%
76g/km to 99g/km	10%
100g/km	11%
each additional 5g/km	1% increase

The percentage is increased by a further 3% for diesel-driven cars, but the maximum applicable percentage is 35% in all cases.

The applicable percentage for zero-emission cars (e.g. electric cars) is 0% up to and including tax year 2014-15.

(e) *In 2013-14*, the upper limit of the 10% band will decrease to 94g/km. Emissions of 95g/km or more will be rounded down to the nearest 5g/km. The percentage for cars with emissions of 95g/km will be 11% and this will then increase by 1% for each additional 5g/km up to a maximum of 35%.

In 2014-15, the applicable percentage for all cars with emissions exceeding 75g/km will increase by one percentage point (subject to a maximum of 35%).

(f) If a disabled employee is obliged by his or her disability to drive a car with automatic transmission, the taxable benefit is based upon the price (if lower) and emission rating (if lower) of the equivalent car with manual transmission.

(g) If a car is made available to the employee for only part of the year, the benefit in that year is reduced proportionately, depending upon the number of days for which the car is made available. This also applies if the car is unusable for a continuous period of at least 30 days in the year.

(h) Finally, the taxable benefit is reduced by any contribution which the employee pays to the employer for private use of the car.

EXAMPLE 5

(a) Throughout the whole of tax year 2012-13, Lucy (a P11D employee) is provided by her employer with a car with a list price of £12,400. She contributed £1,000 towards the car's cost and she pays £300 per annum to her employer for private use of the car. Calculate the taxable benefit arising in 2012-13 if the car is petrol-driven and has an emission rating of:

(i) 48g/km (ii) 77g/km (iii) 163g/km (iv) 232g/km.

Re-calculate the taxable benefit in each case if the car is diesel-driven.

(b) During 2012-13, Luke (a P11D employee) is provided by his employer with the use of a petrol-driven car first registered in 2009 with a list price at that time of £20,000. His employer bought the car for £15,700 in 2011. The car's emission rating is 166g/km. Calculate the taxable benefit in 2012-13 if:

(i) the car is available to Luke throughout the entire year
(ii) the car is made available to Luke only from 6 November 2012.

Solution

(a) Lucy's capital contribution reduces the price of the car to £11,400 and her annual contribution of £300 reduces the benefit accordingly. If the car is petrol-driven, the taxable benefit in each case is computed as follows:

(i) 5% x £11,400 = £570, less £300 = £270.
(ii) 10% x £11,400 = £1,140, less £300 = £840.
(Note that 77g/km is not rounded down to 75g/km)
(iii) 11% + 12% = 23% x £11,400 = £2,622, less £300 = £2,322.
(iv) 35% x £11,400 = £3,990, less £300 = £3,690.

If the car is diesel-driven, the applicable percentage is increased by a further 3% (but cannot exceed 35%). The revised taxable benefit in each case is:

(i) 5% + 3% = 8% x £11,400 = £912, less £300 = £612.
(ii) 10% + 3% = 13% x £11,400 = £1,482, less £300 = £1,182.
(iii) 11% + 12% + 3% = 26% x £11,400 = £2,964, less £300 = £2,664.
(iv) 35% x £11,400 = £3,990, less £300 = £3,690.

(b) The fact that Luke's employer bought the car for £15,700 is irrelevant. The benefit is based on the list price of the car and the applicable percentage is 24% (11% + 13%).

(i) 24% x £20,000 = £4,800.
(ii) 24% x £20,000 = £4,800 x 5/12 = £2,000.

Pool cars

The above provisions do not apply to "pool cars". A pool car is one which satisfies all of the following criteria:

(a) it is available for use by more than one employee and is not ordinarily used by one employee exclusively.

(b) it is not normally kept at an employee's residence overnight.

(c) any private use by an employee is merely incidental to its use for business purposes.

If all these criteria are satisfied, no taxable benefit will arise.

Fuel provided for private use

The taxable benefit described above covers the cost of providing the car itself, together with the costs of road fund licence, insurance and maintenance. But a separate taxable benefit arises if the employer also provides the employee with fuel for private motoring. Fuel benefit for a tax year is calculated by applying the same percentage as was used in the calculation of the car benefit to a fixed amount set by the Government for that tax year. *For 2012-13 this amount is £20,200*. The charge is reduced proportionately if the car is not made available to the employee for the whole of the tax year and is normally reduced if the employee receives fuel for private use for only part of the year. However, a full year's tax charge arises if fuel for private use ceases to be provided at some point during the tax year but is then provided again later in that same year.

It is important to appreciate that the taxable fuel benefit is *not* reduced by any partial contribution which the employee makes towards the cost of private fuel. There is no taxable benefit if the employee pays the full cost of all private fuel. Otherwise, the benefit is calculated as above, ignoring any partial contribution towards fuel costs.

EXAMPLE 6

Miranda (a P11D employee) was supplied throughout 2012-13 with a petrol-engined company car for both business and private use. The car had an emission rating of 184g/km and her employer paid all running costs. The cost of the fuel supplied for private motoring was £1,795. Calculate her taxable fuel benefit in 2012-13 if:

(a) she contributed nothing towards private fuel

(b) she reimbursed her employer for the cost of all private fuel

(c) she reimbursed her employer £1,750 towards the cost of the private fuel.

Solution

(a) 11% + 16% = 27% x £20,200 = £5,454.

(b) £nil, since the employer pays for no private fuel at all.

(c) Miranda's contribution is less than 100% and so the taxable benefit is £5,454.

Vans provided for private use

No taxable benefit arises if a motor van is made available to an employee mainly for business use and the employee is not allowed to use the van for private journeys other than ordinary commuting between home and work. But if a motor van is made available with no restrictions as to private use, the employee is normally liable to income tax on a taxable benefit (for 2012-13) of £3,000. Note that:

(a) The taxable benefit is reduced proportionately if the van is made available to the employee for only part of the tax year and is also reduced by any amount which the employee pays to the employer for private use of the van.

(b) A further taxable benefit arises if the employer provides fuel for private use, with no reduction for any partial contribution made by the employee towards the cost of such fuel. The amount of this taxable benefit for 2012-13 is £550.

(c) No taxable benefit arises in relation to a heavy goods vehicle (a van weighing more than 3,500kg) unless the vehicle is used wholly or mainly for private purposes.

The taxable benefit arising in the case of an electric van is reduced to £nil for tax years 2010-11 to 2014-15 inclusive.

Beneficial loans

A beneficial loan is one that is granted by an employer to an employee (or to a relative of the employee) either interest-free or at a low rate of interest. A loan is deemed to be made at a low rate of interest if the rate charged is less than the "official rate". P11D employees are taxed on the difference between the interest actually payable to the employer and the interest that would have been payable at the official rate. Note that:

(a) Loans made in the ordinary course of the employer's money-lending business and made on the same terms and conditions as loans made to the general public are ignored when calculating the benefit arising in connection with low-interest loans.

(b) Loans which qualify for tax relief (see Chapter 4) are also ignored.

(c) A loan made to a relative of an employee is ignored if it can be shown that the employee derives no personal benefit from the loan.

(d) No taxable benefit arises if the total amount outstanding on all beneficial loans made to an employee, apart from those covered by (a), (b) and (c) above, does not exceed £5,000 at any time during the tax year.

If a loan (beneficial or otherwise) made to a P11D employee is wholly or partly written off by the employer, the amount written off is assessed on the employee in the tax year in which the write-off takes place. However, no taxable benefit arises if the loan is written off on the death of the employee.

In fact, any amount which is written off a loan is generally classed as earnings (even in the case of lower-paid employees) and is therefore taxable, so long as the writing-off of the loan can only be ascribed to the fact that the borrower is an employee.

EXAMPLE 7

Adam (a P11D employee) has the following four loans from his employer:

(a) A £36,000 loan at 2.25% p.a. interest to enable Adam to buy his own home.
(b) An interest-free season ticket loan of £2,000.
(c) A £2,400 personal loan at 3.25% p.a. interest.
(d) A £6,000 loan to buy equipment for use in his employment.

The full amount of each loan was outstanding at 6 April 2012 and no repayments were made during 2012-13. Calculate Adam's taxable benefit in 2012-13 (assuming an official rate of interest of 4% per annum).

Solution

The £6,000 loan is a qualifying loan and is ignored. The remaining loans total more than £5,000 and so give rise to taxable benefits. The amount assessed to tax is:

	£
£36,000 x (4% – 2.25%)	630
£2,000 x 4%	80
£2,400 x (4% – 3.25%)	18
	728

Beneficial loans which vary during the year

In the above example, it was assumed that the amount of the loans did not vary during the tax year. However, if the amount of a beneficial loan does vary during the year, the taxable benefit can be calculated in one of two ways:

(a) **Normal method**. The amount of the loan at the start of the tax year (or when the loan began, if later) and at the end of the tax year (or when the loan ended, if earlier) are averaged and multiplied by the average official rate for the year. If the loan began or ended during the year, the result of this calculation is multiplied by the number of months for which the loan was outstanding in the year and divided by 12.

Interest actually paid by the employee (if any) is then subtracted, giving the taxable benefit.

(b) **Alternative method**. Interest at the official rate is calculated precisely on the day-to-day outstanding balance. Any interest paid by the employee is then subtracted, giving the taxable benefit.

The first method is usually quicker and easier and is generally used. However, either the employee concerned or HM Revenue and Customs may insist that the alternative method should be used. The employee will presumably do so if this results in a lower taxable benefit and HMRC may do so if it appears that the normal method is being deliberately exploited for tax avoidance purposes.

Summary

- The way in which an employee's benefits in kind are taxed depends upon whether or not the employee is a P11D employee, although some benefits in kind are taxable in the same way for all employees. A P11D employee is basically a company director or an employee earning at least £8,500 per annum.
- The taxable benefit arising in relation to living accommodation is generally based on the annual value of the property concerned. The benefit increases if the property cost more than £75,000. No taxable benefit arises if the accommodation is job-related.
- There are special rules for calculating the taxable amount of certain benefits if provided to P11D employees. These rules cover loaned assets, ancillary services connected with living accommodation, cars, fuel, vans and beneficial loans.
- An asset loaned to a P11D employee gives rise to an annual taxable benefit equal to 20% of the value of the asset on the date of the loan. A further benefit may arise if the asset is subsequently sold or given to the employee.
- P11D employees are taxed on ancillary services provided in connection with living accommodation. The tax charge is capped if the accommodation is job-related.
- The amount of the taxable benefit arising in relation to a motor car provided to a P11D employee for private use depends primarily on the car's list price and its carbon dioxide emissions. A further benefit will arise if the employee is also provided with fuel for private motoring.
- If a P11D employee is provided with a beneficial loan, the employee is generally taxed on the difference between the loan interest actually payable (if any) and the interest that would have been payable at the official rate.

Exercises

8.1 Kim is a part-time employee earning a salary of £7,000 per annum, out of which she pays 5% to her employer's occupational pension scheme. She has allowable expenses of £1,000 (all of which are reimbursed by her employer) and is provided with a company car on which the taxable benefit if she were a P11D employee would be £1,800. Is she a P11D employee or a lower-paid employee?

8.2 Throughout 2012-13, Niall (a P11D employee) is provided by his employer with a diesel-engined motor car which had a list price of £24,200 when new and has an emission rating of 187g/km. Niall's employer pays all of the car's running expenses including fuel for private use. Compute the taxable benefit in 2012-13.

8.3 Stephen is a P11D employee. On 1 June 2012, he was provided by his employer with an interest-free loan of £20,000. He repaid £5,000 of this loan on 1 January 2013 and then repaid £3,000 on 1 March 2013. Compute the taxable benefit in 2012-13 using:

(a) the normal method

(b) the alternative method.

Assume that the official rate of interest is 4% per annum. Perform all calculations to the nearest month and to the nearest pound.

***8.4** Emma is the sales director of a company. She earns an annual salary of £70,000 together with a bonus (received in September each year) based on the company's profits for the accounting year ending on the previous 30 June. She also receives a general expenses allowance of £8,000 per annum, which she uses for business travel and entertaining. The company provides her with a new BMW motor car every two years and pays all running costs. She has an interest-free loan from the company of £20,000 and the company pays her annual subscription to a private medical insurance scheme, costing £300. Explain the taxation implications of each of the elements of Emma's remuneration package.

***8.5** Jim is the managing director of a company and earns a basic salary in 2012-13 of £180,000. He receives benefits from the company during the year as follows:

(a) He is provided with the use of a company house which has an annual value of £9,750 and which cost his employer £250,000. Jim makes no contribution towards the cost of the house or towards its running costs which cost the company £2,300 in 2012-13. The company has also furnished the house at a cost of £8,500. Jim's occupation of the house is not job-related.

(b) He is provided with a petrol-engined company car which had a list price when new of £45,000 and which has an emission rating of 173g/km. The company pays all running costs.

(c) He is provided with a company loan of £50,000 on which he is charged interest at 1.25% per annum.

Calculate Jim's taxable benefits in 2012-13 (assuming an official rate of interest of 4% per annum).

Chapter 9

Income from self-employment: Computation of income

Introduction

This is the first of five chapters which deal with income from self-employment. The profits of a self-employed person are charged to income tax by the Income Tax (Trading and Other Income) Act 2005 and the main purpose of this chapter is to show how those profits are calculated for tax purposes. Subsequent chapters deal with related topics such as tax relief for capital expenditure, the tax consequences of making a loss and the taxation of partnerships.

A self-employed person may be conducting a trade or may be exercising a profession or vocation. However, the profits of trades, professions and vocations are all taxed in accordance with the same set of rules. Therefore, in this chapter and in subsequent chapters, references to "trades" and "trading" should be assumed to include professions and vocations. Similarly, the terms "trader" and "sole trader" will be used to refer to any self-employed person, regardless of whether that person is actually conducting a trade or is in fact exercising a profession or vocation.

The badges of trade

ITTOIA 2005 states that the trading profits of a person who is resident in the UK are chargeable to income tax wherever the trade is carried on. The trading profits of a non-UK resident are chargeable to income tax only if the trade is carried on wholly or partly in the UK (see Chapter 32). When deciding whether or not a person is trading it is necessary to make two important distinctions:

(a) the distinction between employment and self-employment (see Chapter 7)

(b) for a taxpayer who sells goods or other assets, the distinction between trading activities (which give rise to trading profits) and non-trading activities (which will usually fall within the scope of capital gains tax).

Section 989 of the Income Tax Act 2007 states that a "trade" includes "*any venture in the nature of trade*". This circular definition is of little real help and therefore it has been left largely to the courts to decide whether or not a given activity constitutes trading.

The main criteria which have arisen from case law decisions and which may be used to distinguish between trading and non-trading activities are known as the "badges of trade". They are as follows:

(a) **Subject matter of the transaction**

If a taxpayer sells assets of a type which might normally be acquired for personal enjoyment or held as a source of income, this may suggest that any profit arising on their sale should be treated as a capital gain rather than a trading profit.

But if the assets concerned do not provide personal enjoyment and do not yield income, it would seem that the only way in which they could be turned to advantage is by selling them. In these circumstances, any profit arising on their sale might be treated as a trading profit. In *Martin* v *Lowry* (1926), the taxpayer bought and sold a huge quantity of war surplus linen. In *Rutledge* v *CIR* (1929), the taxpayer bought and sold one million toilet rolls. In both of these cases, it was held that the subject matter of the transaction was such that the activity must be construed as trading.

(b) **Length of the period of ownership**

Trading stocks are normally retained for only a short period before being sold, whereas assets acquired for personal use or as a source of income are generally retained for longer. Therefore, if assets are bought and sold within a short space of time it is more likely that any profit made will be treated as a trading profit.

(c) **Frequency of transactions**

The more often that a taxpayer repeats a certain type of transaction, the more likely it is that the activity will be construed as trading. In *Pickford* v *Quirke* (1927), the taxpayer bought a cotton mill and sold off its assets at a profit. This was the fourth time that the taxpayer had carried out this particular type of transaction and therefore he was held to be trading.

(d) **Supplementary work**

A taxpayer who buys an asset, performs work on the asset so as to make it more saleable and then sells the asset is more likely to be regarded as trading than someone who simply buys and sells an asset without performing any supplementary work. In *Cape Brandy Syndicate* v *CIR* (1921), a group of individuals bought a large quantity of brandy which they first blended and then sold. They were held to be trading.

(e) **Reason for the sale**

The circumstances which have prompted the sale of an asset might be taken into account when deciding whether trading has occurred. A sale necessitated by a sudden urgent need for cash is less likely to be regarded as a trading activity than a sale made in the normal course of events.

(f) **Motive**

The presence of a profit motive in the mind of the taxpayer when acquiring an asset provides strong evidence of trading. In *Wisdom* v *Chamberlain* (1969), the taxpayer acquired silver bullion with the intention of selling it at a profit and eventually did so. He was held to be trading.

However, this test is not always conclusive. After all, many investments are bought at least partially with a view to their long-term sale at a profit and yet such profits are generally treated as capital gains. This point emphasises the need to consider the evidence provided by *all* of the badges of trade (not just one) when trying to decide whether or not trading has occurred.

Since trading requires the presence of a profit motive when the asset was acquired, the sale of an asset originally acquired by inheritance or by gift (or in any way otherwise than by purchase) is very unlikely to be construed as trading.

The calculation of trading profits

The computation of a self-employed person's trading profit begins with the net profit shown by that person's accounts. For tax purposes, trading profits must be calculated in accordance with generally accepted accounting practice, which means that income and expenditure must be measured on the accruals basis. Self-employed professionals were allowed at one time to calculate their profits for tax purposes on a cash basis† but this is no longer permissible, except for new barristers in their first seven years of practice.

It is usually necessary to make a number of adjustments to the net profit shown by the accounts in order to arrive at the trading profit for tax purposes These adjustments can be summarised as follows:

		£	£
Net profit shown by the accounts			xxx
Add:	Expenditure shown in the accounts but not deductible for tax purposes	xxx	
	Trading income not shown in the accounts	xxx	xxx
			xxx
Less:	Expenditure deductible for tax purposes but not shown in the accounts	xxx	
	Non-trading income shown in the accounts	xxx	xxx
Trading profit adjusted for tax purposes			xxx

Each of these adjustments is explained in this chapter.

† *The Government is currently consulting on the possibility of allowing small businesses to adopt the cash basis when calculating their profits for tax purposes. The introduction of simplified arrangements for certain expenses is also being considered.*

Deductibility of expenditure

In general, expenditure is deductible (allowable) when computing trading profits only if it is incurred *wholly and exclusively for the purposes of the trade*. This rule is not as restrictive as the "wholly, exclusively and necessarily" rule applied to the expenses of an employee (see Chapter 7) but it does have the following implications:

(a) Expenditure which has no connection with the trade is disallowed (the "remoteness test"). In *Strong & Co of Romsey Ltd* v *Woodifield* (1906), damages paid by a brewery to a hotel guest injured by a falling chimney were disallowed. These damages were incurred by the brewery in its capacity as a property owner, not in its capacity as a trader, and therefore failed the remoteness test.

(b) Expenditure which serves both a business purpose and a private purpose cannot be allowed in full (the "duality test"). If the expenditure can be apportioned with reasonable accuracy, then the private element is disallowed. However, in *Mallalieu* v *Drummond* (1983), the cost of black clothing worn in court by a lady barrister was wholly disallowed, since it was not possible to apportion the cost of the clothing between the part which satisfied professional standards of dress and the part which simply provided warmth and decency.

Even if expenditure passes both of these tests it may still be disallowed by statute.

Disallowed expenditure

Certain classes of expenditure are disallowed (either by statute or by case law) when computing trading profits. If any of these types of expenditure have been deducted in the accounts of a self-employed person, then the amount of the expenditure must be "added back" to the profit shown by the accounts in order to arrive at the trading profit for tax purposes. The main classes of disallowed expenditure are identified below.

Capital expenditure

Capital expenditure is specifically disallowed by ITTOIA 2005 but the Act does not provide a definition of the term "capital". Consequently, there is a great deal of case law on this subject, much of which is concerned with distinguishing between repairs (which are allowable) and improvements (disallowed as capital expenditure). In *Atherton* v *British Insulated & Helsby Cables Ltd* (1926), it was stated that capital expenditure is such that it brings an "enduring benefit" to the business, and this test is still widely used. The following capital-related expenses are also disallowed:

(a) legal or professional fees incurred in relation to an item of capital expenditure

(b) depreciation and amortisation charges, although capital allowances may be available instead (see Chapter 11)

(c) losses on the disposal of non-current assets.

Even repairs may be disallowed if they relate to a newly acquired asset and if the repairs are required in order to put the asset into usable condition. In *Law Shipping Co Ltd* v *CIR* (1923), the costs of putting a newly acquired ship into seaworthy condition were disallowed for this reason. However, repairs to a newly acquired asset which was usable before the repairs were carried out are generally allowed. In the case of *Odeon Associated Theatres Ltd* v *Jones* (1971), repairs to cinemas which had been bought in a state of disrepair (but were nonetheless usable) were allowed.

Appropriations of profit

Appropriations of profit made by the owner of a business (whether these are described as drawings, owner's salary or anything else) are disallowed. The owner's personal income tax payments and personal National Insurance contributions are also disallowed.

Provisions

Provisions are allowed so long as they are in respect of revenue expenditure and are made in accordance with generally accepted accounting practice. However, a provision will be disallowed if it cannot be estimated with sufficient accuracy.

Transfers to a general provision for doubtful debts (which is perhaps more correctly referred to as an "allowance" rather than a "provision") are usually disallowed when computing trading profits, since the amount involved is insufficiently accurate. The same is true of transfers to other general provisions. For example, a transfer to a general stock (or inventory) provision would usually be disallowed.

Entertainment and gifts

The cost of entertaining customers is disallowed. Staff entertaining costs are allowable but the employees concerned may incur an income tax liability if the amount involved is excessive (see Chapter 7). The cost of gifts is also disallowed, other than:

(a) gifts to employees, if made wholly and exclusively for trade purposes

(b) gifts to customers costing no more than £50 per customer per year, displaying a conspicuous advertisement for the business and not consisting of food, drink or tobacco

(c) gifts of trading stock (or inventory) or used plant and machinery to designated UK educational establishments, charities or community amateur sports clubs

(d) reasonably small gifts to local charities, if made wholly and exclusively for trade purposes (e.g. a charitable gift which attracts favourable publicity and enhances the firm's public image)

(e) contributions made to local enterprise agencies, training and enterprise councils and urban regeneration companies.

Charitable donations made within the Gift Aid scheme are given tax relief under the Gift Aid rules and are disallowed when computing trading profits (see Chapter 4).

Political donations

Political donations and subscriptions are usually not allowed. But political donations which result in a definite benefit to the trade may be allowed. In *Morgan* v *Tate & Lyle Ltd* (1954), the costs of a political campaign against nationalisation were allowed on the grounds that the campaign was waged for the survival of the trade.

Non-trade bad debts

Bad debts incurred in the course of trade are allowable. But loans written off are generally not allowable unless:

(a) the taxpayer is in the business of lending money and the loan concerned was made in the course of trade, or

(b) the loan was to an employee and was made by reason of the employment and for trade purposes; in this case, the amount of the written-off loan will usually be taxable on the employee as income from employment (see Chapter 8).

Transfers to a *specific* bad debts provision (or allowance) are allowable but transfers to a *general* provision are usually disallowed, as stated earlier. Bad debts recovered and reductions in a specific bad debts provision are both treated as trading income.

EXAMPLE

A sole trader's nominal ledger contains the following bad and doubtful debts account for the year ended 30 June:

	£	£		£	£
Trade debts written off		812	Allowances b/f at 1 July:		
Staff loan written off		50	General	432	
			Specific	312	744
Allowances c/f at 30 June:					
General	459		Trade debt recovered		42
Specific	288	747	Income statement		823
		1,609			1,609

The staff loan written off was not made for trade purposes. How much of the £823 charged to the income statement for the year should be added back when computing trading profits for tax purposes?

Solution

The figure of £823 charged to the income statement can be analysed as follows:

	£
Trade debts written off, less trade debts recovered (£812 – £42)	770
Staff loan written off	50
Increase in general allowance (£459 – £432)	27
Decrease in specific allowance (£312 – £288)	(24)
	823

The £50 staff loan written off and the £27 increase in the general allowance for doubtful debts are disallowed, so a total of £77 should be added back when calculating the trading profits for tax purposes.

Fines and penalties

Fines or penalties incurred because of infringements of the law are not regarded as trading expenses and are disallowed. An exception occurs if an employer pays parking fines incurred by employees whilst on their employer's business. Such payments are usually allowed when computing trading profits but may then be assessed on the employees as income from employment.

Criminal payments

A payment is disallowed if the making of the payment in itself constitutes a criminal offence (e.g. a bribe). Payments to blackmailers or extortionists are also disallowed.

Allowable expenditure

As explained earlier, expenditure is allowable when computing trading profits if it has been incurred wholly and exclusively for the purposes of the trade and is not specifically disallowed by statute. Apart from the disallowed items listed above, most of the expenditure shown in a typical income statement (or profit and loss account) will probably be allowable but the following points should be noted:

(a) **Interest**. Interest, including credit card and overdraft interest, is allowable if it is incurred for trade purposes. But interest paid on overdue tax is disallowed.

(b) **Legal and professional fees**. Legal and professional fees relating to capital expenditure are specifically disallowed (see above), but fees incurred for other trade purposes are normally allowable. For example, fees are allowed if incurred in connection with such matters as the collection of trade debts, the raising of loan finance, the renewal of a short lease (a lease of up to 50 years), a legal action for breach of contract or the preservation of trading rights.

Audit and accountancy fees incurred in relation to the preparation of accounts and the agreement of tax liabilities are normally allowed. Fees incurred in relation to a tax investigation by HMRC are incurred in the role of taxpayer rather than trader and are generally disallowed unless no profit adjustment arises from the investigation. The cost of tax appeals is disallowed, even if successful.

(c) **Short lease premiums**. A premium paid for the grant of a short lease of business premises (50 years or less) is discounted according to the length of the lease and is then allowed in equal annual instalments over the period of the lease (see Chapter 5). A reverse premium received by a tenant using premises for business purposes is taxable as trading income.

(d) **Damages**. Damages and compensation payments are allowed if incurred for the purposes of the trade.

(e) **Value added tax**. If a trader pays VAT in relation to an item of expenditure and is unable to reclaim that VAT (see Chapter 30), the amount of VAT suffered will be allowable so long as the item of expenditure is itself allowable.

(f) **Trade subscriptions**. Subscriptions payable to professional and trade associations are generally regarded as having been incurred for the purposes of the trade and are allowable. Political subscriptions are generally disallowed.

(g) **Employees' remuneration**. Remuneration paid to employees is allowable so long as it is genuinely expended for business purposes. In the case of *Copeman* v *Flood (William) & Sons Ltd* (1941), it was held that large salaries paid to family members could be allowed only to the extent that they were expended for trading purposes.

Remuneration which is not actually paid to employees within nine months of the end of the period of account in which it is accrued is disallowed in that period but allowed in the period of payment.

Employers' contributions to registered pension schemes (see Chapter 14) are allowed in the *period of account in which they are paid*.

Redundancy payments and compensation payments made for loss of employment are usually allowable, as are lump sum payments made to employees on retirement. On a cessation of trade, contractual redundancy payments, statutory redundancy payments and non-contractual redundancy payments of up to three times the statutory amount are all allowed.

The cost of educational courses provided for employees is allowable if incurred for trade purposes. The cost of retraining employees who are about to leave (or have recently left) is allowed subject to certain conditions. The cost of temporarily seconding an employee to a charity or educational establishment is allowable.

(h) **Staff defalcations**. Losses caused by the dishonesty of an employee are normally allowable. But, following the decision in *Curtis* v *J & G Oldfield Ltd* (1925), the defalcations of a person having control over the business (e.g. a business partner) are not allowed.

(i) **Travel expenses**. The cost of business travel is allowable but the cost of travelling between home and work is generally disallowed. In *Newsom* v *Robertson* (1952), the travelling expenses of a barrister between his home and his chambers were disallowed. But in *Horton* v *Young* (1971), the travelling expenses of a self-employed bricklayer between his home and the sites at which he worked was allowed, on the grounds that his business was conducted from his home.

Traders whose annual turnover does not exceed the VAT registration threshold (see Chapter 29) may use the approved employee mileage rates to calculate their expenses in relation to a motor vehicle (see Chapter 7). No other motor expenses or capital allowances may then be claimed in relation to the vehicle concerned.

(j) **Leased cars**. As from 6 April 2009, the amount of lease rental payments allowed in relation to a leased motor car is restricted if the car has an emission rating of more than 160g/km (*reduced to 130g/km as from 6 April 2013*). The restriction takes the form of a flat-rate disallowance of 15% of the lease rental payments. This restriction does not apply if a car is leased for no more than 45 days. Nor does it apply to cars acquired under hire purchase agreements (see Chapter 11).

Leases beginning before 6 April 2009

The above rules apply to cars leased on or after 6 April 2009 and replace a set of "old rules" which restricted relief on the cost of leasing "expensive" cars (cars with a retail price exceeding £12,000). Any lease which began before 6 April 2009 continues to be subject to the old rules until the end of the lease. These rules restrict the allowable amount of the cost of leasing an expensive car to:

$$\text{Lease rental payments} \times \frac{\pounds 12{,}000 + 1/2(\text{Retail price} - \pounds 12{,}000)}{\text{Retail price}}$$

For example, if lease rental payments of £3,600 are incurred in relation to the lease of a car with a retail price of £18,000 (and the lease began before 6 April 2009), the allowable expense is restricted to:

$$\pounds 3{,}600 \times \frac{\pounds 12{,}000 + 1/2(\pounds 18{,}000 - \pounds 12{,}000)}{\pounds 18{,}000} = \pounds 3{,}000.$$

This restriction does not apply to the lease of a low-emission car (currently defined as a car with an emission rating of 110g/km or less).

(k) **Patent royalties**. Patent royalties that are paid for trade purposes are allowable. The cost of registering a patent (or trademark) is also allowable.

(l) **Pre-trading expenditure**. Expenditure incurred during the seven years before starting to trade is treated as if incurred on the first day of trading and is allowable so long as the expenditure is of a type which would normally be allowable.

Trading income not shown in the accounts

The most common example of trading income being omitted from the accounts of a business occurs when the owner of the business appropriates trading stock (or inventory) for his or her personal use. This is referred to as "own consumption".

In this situation, generally accepted accounting practice (GAAP) suggests that the cost of the goods concerned, less any contribution made by the owner, should be credited to the income statement. But ITTOIA 2005 requires that own consumption of trading stock is accounted for at *market value*. This means that the profit of the business for tax purposes should be increased by the *selling price* of the goods, less any contribution made by the owner. For this purpose, "trading stock" consists of goods that are sold in the ordinary course of trade (including partially manufactured stock), but does not include:

- materials used in the manufacture, preparation or construction of trading stock
- services performed in the ordinary course of trade.

These items continue to be accounted for at cost price rather than selling price.

The above rule in ITTOIA 2005 puts onto a statutory basis the view that was originally expressed in the famous case of *Sharkey* v *Wernher* (1955). In this case, horses were transferred from a farm to the owner's private stables and it was held that the profits of the farm should be increased, for tax purposes, by the full market value of those horses.

Non-trading income shown in the accounts

Any non-trading income which is shown in the accounts of a business must be deducted when computing trading profits. The main categories of non-trading income which might be found in the accounts of a business are:

(a) income which is taxed under another heading (e.g. interest, property income)

(b) profits made on the disposal of non-current assets; these are normally depreciation adjustments but a genuine gain may be chargeable to capital gains tax

(c) decreases in general provisions or allowances.

Expenditure not shown in the accounts

The most common example of allowable expenditure not being shown in the accounts of a business is the trader's claim (if any) to capital allowances. The types of expenditure which attract capital allowances and the way in which capital allowances are calculated are considered in Chapter 11.

Another instance of allowable expenditure not shown in the accounts is a premium paid for the grant of a short lease. As explained earlier, part of such a premium is deductible from trading income in equal annual instalments over the lease period. If the premium is being amortised in the accounts, the amortisation charges are added back and the allowable amount of the premium (see Chapter 5) is deducted instead.

Post-cessation receipts

Post-cessation receipts are sums received after a person permanently ceases trading and which arise from the carrying on of the trade prior to cessation. Such receipts fall within the scope of ITTOIA 2005 and are treated as trading income.

Deductions are allowed for any expenses incurred which would have been deductible in calculating the profits of the trade if it had not ceased.

Summary

- A set of criteria known as the "badges of trade" may be used to distinguish between trading activities and non-trading activities.
- The net profit shown in the accounts of a self-employed person has to be adjusted in order to arrive at the trading profit for tax purposes.
- Expenditure is deductible when computing trading profits only if it is wholly and exclusively incurred for the purposes of the trade. Expenditure which is not so incurred is disallowed. Certain categories of expenditure are disallowed by statute.
- The amount of any disallowed expenditure which is shown in the accounts of a self-employed person must be added back to the profit shown by those accounts when computing the trading profit for tax purposes.
- If the owner of a business takes trading stock for personal use, the full market value of that stock (less any amount paid by the owner) must be added to the net profit shown by the accounts when computing the trading profit.
- Non-trading income included in the accounts of a business must be deducted from the net profit shown by those accounts when computing the trading profit.
- Any allowable expenditure not shown in the accounts (e.g. the deductible part of a premium paid for the grant of a short lease) must be deducted from the net profit shown by the accounts when computing the trading profit.
- Post-cessation receipts are treated as trading profits for tax purposes.

Exercises

9.1 List the six badges of trade.

9.2 State the general rule which governs whether or not expenditure is deductible when computing trading profits.

9.3 Which of the following items of expenditure would be allowed when computing trading profits?

(a) the salary paid to a sole trader's wife
(b) a Gift Aid donation
(c) a new lathe bought by an engineering business
(d) diaries costing £3 each given to customers
(e) the cost of the annual staff outing to Blackpool
(f) the black suit worn at work by a self-employed undertaker
(g) the legal costs of acquiring new freehold premises
(h) a subscription to the local chamber of commerce
(i) cases of wine costing £49.99 each given to customers at Christmas
(j) the legal costs of suing a trade debtor for non-payment.

9.4 Julian, a self-employed shopkeeper, takes goods costing £30 from his trading stock for his own personal use. If he had sold the stock to a customer he would have charged £45. When computing his trading profit, what adjustment would need to be made to the net profit shown by his accounts if:

(a) he pays nothing for the goods?
(b) he puts £30 of his own money into the till so as to pay for the goods?
(c) he puts £45 of his own money into the till?

9.5 (a) A motor car with a retail price of £21,000 is leased for four years at a cost of £280 per month. The car is used only for trade purposes and has an emission rating of 182g/km. How much of the monthly charge should be disallowed when calculating trading profits if:

(i) the lease began on 1 January 2012?
(ii) the lease began on 1 January 2009?

(b) A sole trader is granted a 15-year lease on premises which he uses for business purposes. He pays a premium of £15,000 and writes off £1,000 per year in his business accounts. How much of the £1,000 should be disallowed each year when calculating trading profits?

9.6 Linda's income statement (or profit and loss account) for the year ended 31 March 2013 is as follows:

	£	£
Sales		82,500
Less: Cost of sales		37,200
Gross profit		45,300
Add: Rents receivable	1,200	
Bank interest receivable	80	
Profit on sale of non-current asset	310	1,590
		46,890
Less: Wages and salaries	22,620	
Business rates and insurance	1,750	
Heating and lighting	2,170	
Repairs and renewals	4,280	
Telephone	880	
Motor expenses	3,250	
Sundry expenses	1,650	
Bad and doubtful debts	640	
Credit card interest	120	
Loss on sale of non-current asset	70	
Depreciation	2,500	39,930
Net profit for the year		6,960

Notes:

(a) Linda draws a salary of £200 per week from the business. This is included in the wages and salaries figure.

(b) Repairs and renewals are as follows:

	£
Decoration of business premises	400
Installation of new improved heating system	3,800
Minor repair	80
	4,280

(c) It has been agreed with HMRC that one-quarter of telephone costs and one-fifth of motor expenses relate to private use.

(d) Sundry expenses include business entertaining of £520.

(e) Trade debts written off in the year amount to £440 and £200 has been set aside as a general allowance (or provision) for bad and doubtful debts.

Compute Linda's trading profit (before deduction of capital allowances) for the year ended 31 March 2013.

***9.7** A sole trader's bad and doubtful debts account for the year ended 31 March 2013 is as follows:

	£	£		£	£
Trade debts written off		638	Allowances b/f		
Allowances c/f			General	200	
General	150		Specific	231	431
Specific	317	467			
			Staff loan recovered		500
			Income statement		174
		1,105			1,105

The staff loan recovered was not allowable as a trade expense when it was originally written off. How much of the £174 charged to the income statement for the year should be added back when calculating trading profit?

***9.8** Imran owns a business which operates from rented premises. He has a 10-year lease on the premises and paid a premium of £7,000 in order to obtain the lease. His income statement (or profit and loss account) for the year to 31 December 2012 is as follows:

	£	£
Gross profit for the year		52,618
Add: Interest receivable	212	
Surplus on sale of office equipment	300	512
		53,130
Less: Wages (see Note 1)	19,280	
Rent, rates and insurance (see Note 2)	6,915	
Electricity	4,328	
Telephone (see Note 3)	1,650	
Repairs (see Note 4)	2,286	
Printing and advertising	1,250	
Motor expenses (see Note 5)	5,712	
Legal and professional expenses (see Note 6)	3,000	
Sundry expenses (see Note 7)	4,777	
Bad and doubtful debts (see Note 8)	860	
Bank charges and interest	2,765	
Lease premium amortisation	700	
Depreciation	8,749	62,272
Net profit/(loss) for the year		(9,142)

Notes:

1. Wages include £5,800 for Imran's wife (who works part-time for the business) and £1,000 for his son (a student who does not work for the business at all). Also included is Imran's personal income tax of £3,384 and personal National Insurance contributions of £136.

2. Insurance includes Imran's private medical insurance premium of £409.

3. It has been agreed that one-sixth of telephone costs relate to private use.

4. Repairs include £750 for the cost of essential repairs to a newly-acquired second-hand forklift truck which could not be used until the repairs had been carried out.

5. Motor expenses are as follows:

	£
Vehicle servicing and repairs	1,165
Fuel and oil	2,815
Loss on disposal of motor vehicle	422
Road fund licences and insurance	610
Fine for speeding by Imran	700
	5,712

It has been agreed that one-tenth of motor expenses relate to private use.

6. Legal and professional expenses consist of:

	£
Fees relating to renewal of lease	500
Debt collection	1,500
Accountancy fees	1,000
	3,000

7. Sundry expenses are:

	£
Business entertaining	3,320
Staff Christmas dinner	312
Subscription to trade association	350
Donation to political party	200
Miscellaneous small items (all allowable)	595
	4,777

8. Trade debts of £500 were written off during the year. The general allowance for doubtful debts was reduced by £100 and the specific allowance for doubtful debts was increased by £460.

9. During the year, Imran appropriated trading stock costing £220 from the business for personal use, paying £220 of his own money into the business bank account. His gross profit percentage on turnover is 20%.

Compute Imran's trading profit (before deduction of capital allowances) for the year to 31 December 2012.

Chapter 10

Income from self-employment: Basis periods

Introduction

Income tax is charged for tax years (or "years of assessment") which run from 6 April to the following 5 April. It would therefore be convenient if all self-employed people were required to choose 5 April as their annual accounting date, so that the trading income for each tax year could easily be identified. However, self-employed people are free to choose any accounting date they wish and so it is necessary to devise some means of establishing a link between the periods of account for which trading profits are calculated and the tax years in which those profits are charged to tax.

The Income Tax (Trading and Other Income) Act 2005 states that "*the profits of a tax year are the profits of the basis period for the tax year*". The main purpose of this chapter is to explain the rules which are used to determine the basis period for a tax year.

The current year basis

The main principle of the self-employed basis period rules is that the basis period for a tax year is "*the period of 12 months ending with the accounting date in that tax year*". This is known as the "current year basis" (CYB). On this basis, the profits that are taxed in a tax year are normally the profits of the accounting year which ends in the tax year.

However, special rules apply when a business starts trading, ceases trading or changes its accounting date (see below).

EXAMPLE 1

(a) A trader prepares accounts to 31 December each year. Identify the basis period for tax year 2012-13.

(b) A trader prepares accounts to 30 September each year. For which tax year will the accounting year to 30 September 2013 be the basis period?

Assume in both cases that the special rules which are used on commencement, cessation or change of accounting date do not apply in any of the years concerned.

Solution

(a) The accounting year which ends during tax year 2012-13 is the year to 31 December 2012. Therefore this is the basis period for 2012-13. In other words, the profits of the year to 31 December 2012 are charged to income tax in tax year 2012-13.

(b) The accounting year to 30 September 2013 ends during tax year 2013-14 and is therefore the basis period for 2013-14. In other words, the profits of the year to 30 September 2013 are charged to income tax in tax year 2013-14.

Commencement of trade

Special rules are used to determine basis periods for the first two tax years when a new business starts trading. The first tax year in which trading profits are taxed is the tax year in which trade commences. When this tax year has been identified, basis periods for the opening tax years are determined in accordance with the following rules:

Tax year			*Basis period*
1			Date of commencement to the following 5 April (the "actual basis")
2	*either*	(a)	12 months to the accounting date in the second tax year (if possible)
	or	(b)	The first 12 months of trading (if the accounting date in the second tax year is less than 12 months after commencement)
	or	(c)	The actual tax year from 6 April to 5 April (if there is no accounting date in the second tax year)
3 etc.			Current year basis.

Note the following points:

(a) The basis period for the first tax year will often be less than 12 months long but the basis period for the second tax year will always be 12 months long.

(b) Basis periods for the opening tax years may overlap to some extent and therefore some of the profits made in the early years of trading may be the subject of more than one tax assessment (see below).

(c) If necessary, the trading profits for early periods of account are apportioned on a time basis in order to compute the amount of profit arising in each basis period.

(d) ITTOIA 2005 states that apportionments should be made by reference to the number of *days* in the period concerned, but adds that any other reasonable method of apportionment will be accepted so long as it is applied consistently. In practice, such calculations are usually made to the nearest month and this is the approach adopted in this book.

EXAMPLE 2

(a) Vera commences trading on 1 January 2011, preparing accounts annually to 31 December. Identify the basis periods for the first four tax years.

(b) Wilbur commences trading on 1 October 2011. He chooses 30 June as his annual accounting date and prepares his first accounts for the nine months to 30 June 2012. Identify the basis periods for the first four tax years.

(c) Yasmin commences trading on 1 February 2011 and chooses 30 April as her annual accounting date. She prepares her first accounts for the 15 months to 30 April 2012. Identify the basis periods for the first four tax years.

Solution

(a)	2010-11	Actual	1 January 2011 to 5 April 2011
	2011-12	12 months to a/c date in year 2	year to 31 December 2011
	2012-13	CYB	year to 31 December 2012
	2013-14	CYB	year to 31 December 2013
(b)	2011-12	Actual	1 October 2011 to 5 April 2012
	2012-13	First 12 months	1 October 2011 to 30 September 2012
	2013-14	CYB	year to 30 June 2013
	2014-15	CYB	year to 30 June 2014
(c)	2010-11	Actual	1 February 2011 to 5 April 2011
	2011-12	Actual	6 April 2011 to 5 April 2012
	2012-13	CYB	1 May 2011 to 30 April 2012
	2013-14	CYB	year to 30 April 2013

Notes:

(i) In each case, the basis period for the third tax year is the 12 months to the accounting date which occurs during that tax year. For Vera and Wilbur, this accounting date marks the end of a 12-month period of account and so the basis period for the third tax year coincides with that period of account.

(ii) For Yasmin, the accounting date which occurs during the third tax year marks the end of a 15-month period of account and so the basis period for the third tax year does not coincide with a period of account.

Overlap profits

If a business chooses 5 April as its annual accounting date, the basis periods used in the opening tax years will not overlap at all. Otherwise, opening basis periods will overlap and some profits will form the basis of more than one tax assessment. Such profits are known as "overlap profits".

ITTOIA 2005 states that accounts prepared to 31 March or to the 1st, 2nd, 3rd or 4th of April will usually be treated as if they were prepared to 5 April, so as to avoid very short overlap periods and very small amounts of overlap profits.

EXAMPLE 3

Albert begins trading on 1 May 2011 and has the following results:

	Adjusted trading profit
	£
15 months to 31 July 2012	16,800
year to 31 July 2013	21,600

Compute Albert's trading income for each of the first three tax years and also calculate the amount of any overlap profits.

Solution

Albert's first period of account is 15 months long and his first basis period comprises the 11 months from 1 May 2011 to 5 April 2012. Trading income for the first three tax years is as follows:

Year	*Basis*	*Basis period*	*Workings*	*Trading income*
				£
2011-12	Actual	1/5/11 to 5/4/12	£16,800 x 11/15	12,320
2012-13	12 months to a/c date in year 2	1/8/11 to 31/7/12	£16,800 x 12/15	13,440
2013-14	CYB	y/e 31/7/13		21,600

The overlap period consists of the eight months from 1 August 2011 to 5 April 2012, which are common to the basis periods for 2011-12 and 2012-13. Overlap profits are therefore £8,960 (£16,800 x 8/15).

Overlap relief

In general, overlap profits which arise in the opening years of a business are relieved by deduction from the trading profits that are charged to tax in the final tax year when trade ceases. Note the following points regarding "overlap relief":

(a) Overlap relief ensures that, over the entire lifetime of a business, the total of the trading profits which are charged to tax is equal to the total of the adjusted trading profits for each period of account.

(b) Overlap profits are not index-linked. Therefore the real value of overlap relief is eroded by inflation, especially in the case of businesses which trade for many years.

(c) If overlap profits exceed the trading profits which are charged to tax in the final tax year, the resulting loss is eligible for tax relief (see Chapter 12).

However, if a business changes its accounting date at some point during its lifetime, it is possible that some of the overlap profits arising in the opening years may be relieved by deduction from the trading profits that are taxed in the year of the change. It is also possible that further overlap profits might arise on a change of accounting date (see later in this chapter).

Cessation of trade

A cessation of trade occurs when the owner of a business retires or sells the business or dies. The final tax year in which trading profits are taxed is the tax year in which the cessation occurs. The basis period for this final tax year is determined as follows:

(a) If a business commences trading and ceases trading in the same tax year, the basis period for that year consists of the entire lifespan of the business.

(b) If a business ceases trading in its second tax year, the basis period for that year runs from 6 April at the start of the year up to the date of cessation. This rule overrides the usual commencement rules for the second tax year.

(c) Otherwise, the basis period for the final tax year runs from the end of the basis period for the previous tax year up to the date of the cessation. This basis period may be less than, equal to or more than 12 months in length.

If the final set of accounts prepared for a business covers a period which is of more than 12 months, it is possible that no accounting date at all falls into the penultimate tax year (the last year but one). This makes it impossible to apply the usual current year basis in that year. In these circumstances, the basis period for the penultimate tax year is the 12 months up to the normal accounting date falling in that year.

It is important to appreciate that income tax is charged on the owner of a business and not on the business itself. Therefore a change in the ownership of a business is treated for tax purposes as a cessation of one business followed by the commencement of another.

EXAMPLE 4

Carmen starts trading on 1 July 2011 and chooses 30 June as her annual accounting date. Identify the basis periods for her last two tax years if she ceases trading as follows:

	Date of cessation	*Final set of accounts*
(a)	31 March 2012	9 months to 31 March 2012
(b)	30 June 2012	year to 30 June 2012
(c)	30 June 2016	year to 30 June 2016
(d)	31 May 2016	11 months to 31 May 2016
(e)	30 April 2016	22 months to 30 April 2016

Solution

(a) Trade both commences and ceases in 2011-12. The basis period for this single tax year is the entire lifespan of the business i.e. 1 July 2011 to 31 March 2012.

(b) The cessation occurs in the second tax year. Basis periods are:

2011-12	Actual	1 July 2011 to 5 April 2012
2012-13	6 April to date of cessation	6 April 2012 to 30 June 2012

(c)	2015-16	CYB	y/e 30 June 2015
	2016-17	End of previous basis period up to date of cessation	y/e 30 June 2016
(d)	2015-16	CYB	y/e 30 June 2015
	2016-17	End of previous basis period up to date of cessation	1 July 2015 to 31 May 2016
(e)	2015-16	12 months to normal a/c date	1 July 2014 to 30 June 2015
	2016-17	End of previous basis period up to date of cessation	1 July 2015 to 30 April 2016

EXAMPLE 5

Damien starts trading on 1 July 2007 and chooses 31 December as his annual accounting date. He ceases trading on 30 September 2012 and has the following results:

	Adjusted trading profit
	£
6 months to 31 December 2007	8,400
year to 31 December 2008	9,200
year to 31 December 2009	10,500
year to 31 December 2010	7,500
year to 31 December 2011	6,400
9 months to 30 September 2012	5,800

Compute Damien's trading income for each tax year and show that the total of this income is equal to the total of the adjusted trading profits listed above.

Solution

Year	*Basis period*	*Workings*	*Trading income*
			£
2007-08	1/7/07 to 5/4/08	£8,400 + 3/12 x £9,200	10,700
2008-09	y/e 31/12/08		9,200
2009-10	y/e 31/12/09		10,500
2010-11	y/e 31/12/10		7,500
2011-12	y/e 31/12/11		6,400
2012-13	1/1/12 to 30/9/12	£5,800 – overlap relief £2,300	3,500
			47,800

The overlap period is from 1 January 2008 to 5 April 2008 (3 months) and the overlap profits are £2,300 (£9,200 x 3/12). The total of the trading income which is charged to tax is £47,800, the same as the total of the adjusted trading profits.

Change of accounting date

If a business changes its annual accounting date from one date (the "old date") to another date (the "new date"), special rules are used to determine the basis period for the year of change. The year of change is defined as the first tax year in which accounts are *not* made up to the old date or *are* made up to the new date (or both). There will be a change of basis period for a year of change so long as the following conditions are satisfied:

(a) The first set of accounts made up to the new date does not cover a period of more than 18 months.

(b) Notice of the change of accounting date is given to HMRC in a tax return which is not filed late.

(c) Either:
   (i) None of the previous five tax years has been a year of change resulting in a change of basis period, or
   (ii) HMRC is satisfied that the change of accounting date has been made for genuine commercial reasons and not for tax avoidance purposes.

If all of these conditions are satisfied, the basis period for the year of change is determined as follows:

(a) The "relevant period" is identified as the period beginning immediately after the end of the basis period for the previous tax year and ending with the new date in the year of change.

(b) If the length of the relevant period is less than 12 months, the basis period for the year of change is the 12 months to the new date in the year of change.

(c) If the length of the relevant period is not less than 12 months, the basis period for the year of change is the relevant period itself.

(d) In consequence, the basis period for a year of change will always be of at least 12 months' duration.

If all of the required conditions are *not* satisfied, the basis period for the year of change is the 12 months to the old date in that year. However, the following tax year is then regarded as a year of change (the taxpayer being treated as though this were the first year in which the new date had been used) and a change of basis period will occur in that year if all of the conditions are satisfied in relation to that year. A change of accounting date can be carried forward indefinitely in this way until such time as the necessary conditions for a change of basis period are satisfied.

If a taxpayer regularly prepares accounts to a particular *day* in the year (e.g. the last Saturday in June) rather than a particular *date*, the fact that the accounting date will change slightly in each year does not trigger the change of accounting date rules.

EXAMPLE 6

(a) Gary began trading many years ago, preparing accounts to 30 September each year. He decided to change his accounting date to 30 June and the first accounts made up to the new date were for the period from 1 October 2011 to 30 June 2012. The conditions necessary for a change of basis period were all satisfied. Identify the basis periods for years 2010-11 to 2013-14 inclusive.

(b) Audrey began trading on 1 January 2009, preparing accounts to 31 December each year. She decided to change her accounting date to 31 March and the first accounts made up to the new date were for the period from 1 January 2011 to 31 March 2012. The conditions necessary for a change of basis period were all satisfied. Identify the basis periods for years 2008-09 to 2013-14 inclusive.

(c) Grant began trading many years ago, preparing accounts to 30 June each year. He decided to change his accounting date to 31 December and the first accounts made up to the new date were for the period from 1 July 2012 to 31 December 2012. The conditions necessary for a change of basis period were all satisfied. Identify the basis periods for years 2011-12 to 2014-15 inclusive.

(d) Clare began trading on 1 March 2008, preparing accounts to 31 January each year. Her first accounts were for the period to 31 January 2009. She decided to change her accounting date to 30 April and the first accounts made up to the new date were for the period from 1 February 2011 to 30 April 2012. The conditions necessary for a change of basis period were all satisfied. Identify the basis periods for years 2007-08 to 2013-14 inclusive.

Solution

(a) The year of change is 2012-13 (the first year in which the old date was not used and the new date was used). The basis period for 2011-12 ended on 30 September 2011, so the relevant period is from 1 October 2011 to 30 June 2012. This is less than 12 months long so the basis period for 2012-13 is the 12 months to 30 June 2012. Basis periods for 2010-11 to 2013-14 are:

2010-11	year to 30 September 2010
2011-12	year to 30 September 2011
2012-13	year to 30 June 2012
2013-14	year to 30 June 2013

Note that there is an overlap between the basis periods for 2011-12 and 2012-13. The treatment of overlap profits on a change of accounting date is explained below.

(b) The year of change is 2011-12 (the first year in which the old date was not used and the new date was used). The basis period for 2010-11 ended on 31 December 2010, so the relevant period is from 1 January 2011 to 31 March 2012. This is not less than 12 months in length so the basis period for 2011-12 is the same as the relevant period. Basis periods for 2008-09 to 2013-14 are:

2008-09	1 January 2009 to 5 April 2009
2009-10	year to 31 December 2009
2010-11	year to 31 December 2010
2011-12	1 January 2011 to 31 March 2012
2012-13	year to 31 March 2013
2013-14	year to 31 March 2014

(c) The year of change is 2012-13 (the first year in which the new date was used). The basis period for 2011-12 ended on 30 June 2011, so the relevant period is from 1 July 2011 to 31 December 2012. This is not less than 12 months in length so the basis period for 2012-13 is the same as the relevant period. Basis periods are:

2011-12	year to 30 June 2011
2012-13	1 July 2011 to 31 December 2012
2013-14	year to 31 December 2013
2014-15	year to 31 December 2014

(d) The year of change is 2011-12 (the first year in which the old date was not used). The basis period for 2010-11 ended on 31 January 2011, so the relevant period is from 1 February 2011 to 30 April 2011. This is less than 12 months long so the basis period for 2011-12 is the 12 months to 30 April 2011, even though this accounting date was not used in 2011-12. Basis periods for 2007-08 to 2013-14 are:

2007-08	1 March 2008 to 5 April 2008
2008-09	1 March 2008 to 28 February 2009
2009-10	year to 31 January 2010
2010-11	year to 31 January 2011
2011-12	year to 30 April 2011
2012-13	year to 30 April 2012
2013-14	year to 30 April 2013

There is an overlap between the basis periods for 2010-11 and 2011-12 (as well as the usual overlaps arising on the commencement of trade).

Overlap profits on a change of accounting date

If a change of accounting date results in profits being taxed more than once, these overlap profits are added to any earlier overlap profits which arose in the opening years or on a previous change of accounting date. The total overlap profits are then carried forward for relief on cessation or on a subsequent change of accounting date.

On the other hand, if the basis period for a year of change exceeds 12 months, a part of the overlap profits brought forward from previous years may be relieved in the year of change. The amount to be relieved is calculated according to the following formula:

$$\text{Amount relieved} = A \times \frac{B - C}{D}$$

where: A = Total overlap profits brought forward and not yet relieved
B = Length of the relevant period
C = 12 (or 365 if daily apportionments are being used)
D = Total length of the overlap period(s) to which the total overlap profits brought forward relate.

EXAMPLE 7

(a) Byron began trading on 1 November 2008, preparing accounts to 31 October each year. He decided to change his accounting date to 31 August and the first accounts made up to the new date were for the period from 1 November 2010 to 31 August 2011. The conditions necessary for a change of basis period were all satisfied. The adjusted trading profits for Byron's first five periods of account were as follows:

	£
Year to 31 October 2009	12,000
Year to 31 October 2010	18,000
Period to 31 August 2011	16,000
Year to 31 August 2012	21,000
Year to 31 August 2013	24,000

Compute Byron's trading income for years 2008-09 to 2013-14.

(b) Michelle began trading on 1 January 2009, preparing accounts to 31 December each year. She decided to change her accounting date to 28/29 February and the first accounts made up to the new date were for the period from 1 January 2012 to 28 February 2013. The conditions necessary for a change of basis period were all satisfied. The adjusted trading profits for Michelle's first five periods of account were:

	£
Year to 31 December 2009	4,560
Year to 31 December 2010	5,250
Year to 31 December 2011	11,680
Period to 28 February 2013	14,390
Year to 28 February 2014	16,270

Compute Michelle's trading income for years 2008-09 to 2013-14.

Solution

(a) The year of change is 2011-12 (the first year in which the old date was not used and the new date was used). The basis period for 2010-11 ended on 31 October 2010, so the relevant period is from 1 November 2010 to 31 August 2011. This is less than 12 months in length so the basis period for 2011-12 is the 12 months to 31 August 2011. Trading income for 2008-09 to 2013-14 is:

Year	*Basis period*	*Workings*	*Trading income* £
2008-09	1/11/08 to 5/4/09	£12,000 x 5/12	5,000
2009-10	y/e 31/10/09		12,000
2010-11	y/e 31/10/10		18,000
2011-12	y/e 31/8/11	(£18,000 x 2/12) + £16,000	19,000
2012-13	y/e 31/8/12		21,000
2013-14	y/e 31/8/13		24,000

There are overlap profits of £5,000 (5 months) on the commencement of trade and a further £3,000 (2 months) on the change of accounting date. Total overlap profits carried forward are £8,000 (7 months).

(b) The year of change is 2012-13 (the first year in which the old date was not used and the new date was used). The basis period for 2011-12 ended on 31 December 2011, so the relevant period is from 1 January 2012 to 28 February 2013. This is not less than 12 months in length so the basis period for 2012-13 is the relevant period itself. Trading income for 2008-09 to 2013-14 is:

Year	*Basis period*	*Workings*	*Trading income* £
2008-09	1/1/09 to 5/4/09	£4,560 x 3/12	1,140
2009-10	y/e 31/12/09		4,560
2010-11	y/e 31/12/10		5,250
2011-12	y/e 31/12/11		11,680
2012-13	1/1/12 to 28/2/13	£14,390 – overlap relief £760	13,630
2013-14	y/e 28/2/14		16,270

There are overlap profits of £1,140 (3 months) on the commencement of trade. The relevant period is 14 months long, which exceeds 12 months by 2 months. Overlap relief in the year of change is calculated as £1,140 x 2/3 = £760. Overlap profits carried forward are £380 (1 month).

Transitional overlap relief

The basis period rules now in use were introduced by Finance Act 1994. Businesses which existed before 6 April 1994 used to be assessed on the *preceding year basis*, which meant that the basis period for a tax year was the accounting year ending in the *previous* tax year. The switch to the current year basis for these businesses occurred as from 1997-98.

One aspect of this transition which will remain relevant for many years is that these older businesses (which cannot claim overlap relief in the normal way) are eligible for *transitional overlap relief* on a change of accounting date or on the cessation of trade. An explanation of transitional overlap relief is provided on the website which accompanies this book. The website address is www.pearsoned.co.uk/melville.

Averaging of trading profits for farmers, market gardeners and creative artists

Certain trades, professions and vocations are more likely than others to experience profits which fluctuate considerably from one period of account to the next, giving rise to corresponding fluctuations in the trading income which is charged to tax. In particular, this problem may affect:

(a) farmers and market gardeners (who are at the mercy of the weather)
(b) creative artists.

The income tax system allows farmers, market gardeners and creative artists to smooth out fluctuating profits by making a claim for *averaging*. Trading income for two consecutive tax years may be averaged if the difference between the two income figures is at least 30% of the higher figure. The effect of an averaging claim is to replace the normal trading income for each of these two tax years by the average of the two figures. Note the following points in relation to the averaging process:

(a) If a loss has been incurred in either of the two years which are involved in a claim for averaging, this loss counts as zero in the averaging calculations. The loss is then eligible for tax relief (see Chapter 12).
(b) An averaging claim may not be made for the tax year in which trade commences or for the tax year in which trade ceases.
(c) If an averaging claim has been made for two tax years, the revised trading income for the second year may subsequently be used in another averaging claim. For example, if a claim has already been made for 2010-11 and 2011-12, then another claim may be made for 2011-12 and 2012-13. Overlapping claims of this nature must be made in chronological order.
(d) An averaging claim must be made by the first anniversary of the 31 January which follows the end of the second tax year to which the claim relates. For example, an averaging claim which relates to 2011-12 and 2012-13 must be made by 31 January 2015.

EXAMPLE 8

The recent adjusted trading profits of a self-employed farmer who began trading many years ago are as follows:

	£
year to 30 November 2011	54,200
year to 30 November 2012	18,640

He has no other income. May an averaging claim be made and would the farmer benefit from such a claim?

Solution

The tax years in question are 2011-12 and 2012-13. The difference between the trading income of the two years is £35,560, which exceeds 30% of £54,200 so an averaging claim may be made. If such a claim is made, trading income for both 2011-12 and 2012-13 is revised to £36,420 (the average of £54,200 and £18,640). The farmer benefits from this claim in the following ways:

(a) the likelihood of paying 40% tax for 2011-12 is removed, so reducing the total tax liability for the two years, and

(b) the farmer's cash flow situation is improved, since the 2011-12 tax liability is reduced and the 2012-13 tax liability is increased.

EXAMPLE 9

A market gardener who began trading many years ago has the following recent results:

	Adjusted trading profit/(loss)
	£
year to 31 December 2008	21,500
year to 31 December 2009	14,200
year to 31 December 2010	(5,400)
year to 31 December 2011	6,900
year to 31 December 2012	10,800

Compute the trading income for 2008-09 to 2012-13 inclusive, assuming that all possible averaging claims are made.

Solution

2008-09 and 2009-10

	£
Original trading income for 2008-09 (y/e 31/12/08)	21,500
Original trading income for 2009-10 (y/e 31/12/09)	14,200
Difference (more than 30% of £21,500)	7,300

Averaging gives revised trading income of £17,850 in 2008-09 and 2009-10.

2009-10 and 2010-11

	£
Revised trading income for 2009-10	17,850
Original trading income for 2010-11 (y/e 31/12/10)	0
Difference (more than 30% of £17,850)	17,850

Averaging gives revised trading income of £8,925 in 2009-10 and 2010-11.

2010-11 and 2011-12

	£
Revised trading income for 2010-11	8,925
Original trading income for 2011-12 (y/e 31/12/11)	6,900
Difference (less than 30% of £8,925)	2,025

No averaging is possible so trading income is unaltered.

2011-12 and 2012-13

	£
Original trading income for 2011-12 (y/e 31/12/11)	6,900
Original trading income for 2012-13 (y/e 31/12/12)	10,800
Difference (more than 30% of £10,800)	3,900

Averaging gives revised trading income of £8,850 in 2011-12 and 2012-13. Therefore the final trading income for all years concerned is as follows:

	£	
2008-09	17,850	
2009-10	8,925	
2010-11	8,925	
2011-12	8,850	
2012-13	8,850	(which may perhaps be averaged with 2013-14).

Marginal relief

As explained above, an averaging claim usually cannot be made if the difference between the trading income figures for the two tax years concerned is less than 30% of the higher figure. However, if the difference is at least 25% of the higher figure, a form of averaging known as "marginal relief" may be claimed. The effect of marginal relief is to reduce the higher income figure (H) and increase the lower income figure (L) by an amount given by the following formula:

$$3 \times (H - L) - 0.75 \times H$$

If the difference between H and L is exactly 30% of H, this formula has the same effect as an ordinary averaging claim. If the difference between H and L is exactly 25% of H, this formula has no effect at all.

EXAMPLE 10

A farmer's trading income for 2011-12 is £12,000. What averaging claims (if any) can he make if his 2012-13 trading income is:

(a) £7,600? (b) £8,600? (c) £9,600?

Solution

(a) The difference between the two income figures is £4,400, which is more than 30% of £12,000 so a normal averaging claim can be made, revising both of the income figures to £9,800 (the average of £12,000 and £7,600).

(b) The difference between the two income figures is £3,400, which is between 25% and 30% of £12,000 so marginal relief may be claimed. The adjustment to each figure is:

3 x (£12,000 – £8,600) – 0.75 x £12,000 = £1,200.

The income for 2011-12 is reduced by £1,200 to £10,800. The income for 2012-13 is increased by £1,200 to £9,800.

(c) The difference between the two income figures is £2,400, which is less than 25% of £12,000 so no averaging is possible at all.

Summary

- Trading profits are charged to income tax on the current year basis. This means that the basis period for a tax year is normally the accounting year which ends in that tax year. However, special basis period rules apply in the opening and closing tax years of a business and on a change of accounting date.
- The first tax year in which trading profits are taxed is the tax year in which trade commences. The basis period for the first tax year runs from the date of commencement to the following 5th April.
- If there is an accounting date in the second tax year and this date is at least 12 months after commencement, the basis period for the second tax year is the 12 months to that accounting date. But if this accounting date is not at least 12 months after commencement, the basis period for the second tax year is the first 12 months of trading.
- If there is no accounting date in the second tax year, the basis period for that tax year is the actual tax year from 6th April to the following 5 April.
- Overlap profits arising in the opening years of a new business are relieved either on the cessation of trade or on a change of accounting date. However, further overlap profits may arise on a change of accounting date
- The final tax year in which trading profits are taxed is the tax year in which trade ceases. In general, the basis period for the final tax year runs from the end of the basis period for the previous tax year up to the date of the cessation.
- Special rules are used in order to determine the basis period for the tax year in which a business changes its accounting date.
- Subject to certain conditions, farmers and market gardeners and creative artists may claim that the trading income of two consecutive tax years should be averaged.

Exercises

10.1 Under the *current year basis*, for which tax years would the following accounting years form the basis period?

(a) year to 31 October 2012
(b) year to 31 March 2013
(c) year to 30 April 2014
(d) year to 5 April 2014

10.2 Frank began trading on 1 July 2010. Identify the basis periods for his first four tax years if he:

(a) chooses 30 June as his annual accounting date and prepares his first accounts for the year to 30 June 2011
(b) chooses 30 April as his annual accounting date and prepares his first accounts for the 22 months to 30 April 2012
(c) chooses 30 April as his annual accounting date and prepares his first accounts for the 10 months to 30 April 2011.

Also identify any overlap periods which arise in each case.

10.3 Greta commences trading on 1 January 2011 and chooses 30 June as her annual accounting date. Her first accounts are made up for the 18 months to 30 June 2012 and show an adjusted trading profit of £27,300. Compute Greta's trading income for the first three tax years and calculate the amount of any overlap profits.

10.4 Hitesh has been trading for many years, preparing accounts to 31 January each year. His last full year of trading is the year to 31 January 2012. Identify the basis periods for the last three tax years in each of the following cases:

	Date of cessation	*Final set of accounts*
(a)	31 May 2012	4 months to 31 May 2012
(b)	31 March 2013	14 months to 31 March 2013
(c)	30 April 2013	15 months to 30 April 2013

10.5 Phillip starts trading on 1 June 2008 and ceases trading on 31 July 2013. He has adjusted trading profits as follows

	£
1 June 2008 to 30 September 2009	28,800
year to 30 September 2010	19,900
year to 30 September 2011	14,300
year to 30 September 2012	13,800
1 October 2012 to 31 July 2013	11,100

Compute Phillip's trading income for all tax years.

***10.6** Ivy begins trading as a market gardener on 1 January 2010, making up annual accounts to 31 December. Her adjusted trading profits in the opening years are as follows:

	£
year to 31 December 2010	21,600
year to 31 December 2011	15,030
year to 31 December 2012	13,710

(a) Compute Ivy's trading income for the first four tax years, assuming that no averaging claims are made.

(b) Compute Ivy's revised trading income for the first four tax years, assuming that all possible averaging claims are made.

***10.7** Ken starts trading on 1 October 2007 and chooses 30 April as his accounting date. He ceases trading on 31 January 2013 and has adjusted trading profits as follows:

	£
7 months to 30 April 2008	3,500
year to 30 April 2009	18,480
year to 30 April 2010	17,700
year to 30 April 2011	27,900
year to 30 April 2012	28,200
9 months to 31 January 2013	17,300

Compute Ken's trading income for all tax years.

***10.8** Belinda began trading on 1 March 2008 and chose 31 December as her accounting date. Her first accounts were for the period to 31 December 2008. She eventually decided to change her accounting date to 31 May and the first accounts made up to the new date were for the 17 months to 31 May 2012. The conditions necessary for a change of basis period were all satisfied. The adjusted trading profits for her first five periods of account were as follows:

	Adjusted trading profit
	£
1 March 2008 to 31 December 2008	43,700
year to 31 December 2009	52,590
year to 31 December 2010	54,300
1 January 2011 to 31 May 2012	71,060
year to 31 May 2013	68,200

Compute Belinda's trading income for 2007-08 to 2013-14 inclusive, showing the amounts of any overlap profits or overlap relief.

***10.9** Roger began trading on 1 January 2006, preparing accounts to 30 April each year. His first accounts were for the 16 months to 30 April 2007. In 2009 he decided to change his accounting date to 30 June. The first accounts made up to the new date were for the 14 months to 30 June 2009 and the conditions necessary for a change of basis period were all satisfied. Roger ceased trading on 31 May 2012. His adjusted trading profits were as follows:

	Adjusted trading profit
	£
1 January 2006 to 30 April 2007	33,920
year to 30 April 2008	29,700
1 May 2008 to 30 June 2009	33,300
year to 30 June 2010	41,600
year to 30 June 2011	37,900
1 July 2011 to 31 May 2012	23,500

Compute Roger's trading income for all tax years.

Chapter 11

Income from self-employment: Capital allowances

Introduction

Capital expenditure is generally not deductible when computing trading income but certain types of capital expenditure attract tax relief in the form of standardised depreciation allowances known as *capital allowances*. The purpose of this chapter is to define the categories of capital expenditure which are eligible for capital allowances and to explain how capital allowances are calculated for each of these categories.

Eligible expenditure

In order to be eligible for capital allowances, capital expenditure must usually fall into one of the following categories:

(a) plant and machinery
(b) industrial buildings and agricultural buildings (*abolished from 6 April 2011*)
(c) patent rights
(d) know-how
(e) research and development.

This chapter is primarily concerned with plant and machinery, which is the most important category. However, the other categories are considered briefly at the end of the chapter.

Chargeable periods

Capital allowances are calculated in respect of *chargeable periods*. For income tax purposes, each period of account generally ranks as a chargeable period and so there is usually one capital allowances computation per period of account. Note that:

(a) The capital allowances for a period of account are treated as a trading expense and are deducted when computing the adjusted trading profit for that period. The basis period rules are applied to the trading profit *after* deduction of capital allowances.

(b) A period of account lasting for more than 18 months is subdivided into one or more 12-month chargeable periods with (possibly) a short chargeable period at the end. Capital allowances are calculated separately for each of these chargeable periods and then aggregated to give the capital allowances due for the whole period of account.

(c) The chargeable periods of *companies*, which pay corporation tax rather than income tax, are determined according to a different set of rules (see Chapter 23).

EXAMPLE 1

Lee begins trading on 1 January 2012 preparing accounts to 31 December each year. His adjusted trading profit for the year to 31 December 2012 (before capital allowances) is £21,000 and capital allowances of £1,200 are claimed for that year. Compute his trading income for 2011-12 and 2012-13.

Solution

The adjusted trading profit for the year to 31 December 2012 (after deduction of capital allowances) is £19,800. Therefore trading income for the first two tax years is as follows:

Year	*Basis*	*Basis period*	*Workings*	*Trading income*
				£
2011-12	Actual	1/1/12 to 5/4/12	£19,800 x 3/12	4,950
2012-13	12 months to a/c date in year 2	y/e 31/12/12		19,800

Plant and machinery

Capital Allowances Act 2001 (the main statute concerned with capital allowances) does not provide a definition of the term "plant and machinery". Therefore it has been left mainly to case law to decide whether or not any given item should qualify as plant and machinery and so attract capital allowances. In *Yarmouth* v *France* (1887) it was stated that plant and machinery includes:

> "whatever apparatus is used by a businessman for carrying on his business, not his stock in trade which he buys or makes for sale, but all goods and chattels, fixed or moveable, live or dead, which he keeps for permanent employment in his business".

It is fairly clear that machinery of all types, motor vehicles and items such as office furniture and equipment all qualify as plant and machinery but difficulties arise in connection with expenditure on buildings and fixtures to buildings. Much case law has been concerned with the distinction between:

(a) assets which perform an *active function* in the carrying on of the business (i.e. the apparatus *with which* the business is carried on), and

(b) assets which perform a *passive function* in the carrying on of the business (i.e. the setting *in which* the business is carried on).

Assets in the first of these categories qualify as plant and machinery whilst assets in the second category do not, but the distinction between the categories can be a very fine one. Some of the more important case law decisions are as follows:

Held to be plant and machinery:

(a) a dry dock built for the repair and the maintenance of ships, in *CIR* v *Barclay Curle & Co Ltd* (1969)

(b) a swimming and paddling pool, in *Cooke* v *Beach Station Caravans Ltd* (1974)

(c) a concrete grain silo, in *Schofield* v *R & H Hall Ltd* (1975)

(d) decorative display screens placed in the window of a building society's offices and incorporating the name of the building society, in *Leeds Permanent Building Society* v *Proctor* (1982)

(e) moveable office partitions, in *Jarrold* v *John Good & Sons Ltd* (1962)

(f) display lighting in a store window, in *Cole Brothers Ltd* v *Phillips* (1982)

(g) light fittings, plaques and pictures on the walls of an hotel, in *IRC* v *Scottish and Newcastle Breweries Ltd* (1982)

(h) storage platforms built in a warehouse, in *Hunt* v *Henry Quick Ltd* (1992)

(i) a barrister's law books, in *Munby* v *Furlong* (1977).

Held *not* to be plant and machinery:

(a) prefabricated school buildings, in *St John's School* v *Ward* (1974)

(b) a moored ship used as a restaurant, in *Benson* v *The Yard Arm Club Ltd* (1979)

(c) a petrol station forecourt canopy, in *Dixon* v *Fitch's Garage Ltd* (1975)

(d) a football stand, in *Brown* v *Burnley Football and Athletic Co Ltd* (1980)

(e) a false ceiling built to hide electrical conduits, in *Hampton* v *Fortes Autogrill Ltd* (1979)

(f) a false ceiling, mezzanine floors, staircases, decorative floor and wall tiles all used to create ambience in a restaurant, in *Wimpey International Ltd* v *Warland* (1988).

In an attempt to clarify the distinction between buildings and plant, Capital Allowances Act 2001 provides a detailed list of types of expenditure on buildings or structures which are statutorily excluded from qualifying as plant. The Act also provides a detailed list of types of expenditure on buildings or structures which are not statutorily excluded from qualifying as plant and may therefore qualify if permitted by case law.

Expenditure statutorily deemed to be plant and machinery

By statute, expenditure of the following types always qualifies as plant and machinery:

(a) expenditure on the thermal insulation of a building
(b) expenditure incurred so as to comply with safety regulations at sports grounds
(c) expenditure on assets necessary to safeguard personal security
(d) expenditure on computer software
(e) expenditure on building alterations, incidental to installation of plant and machinery.

However, plant and machinery capital allowances on safety expenditure at sports grounds are to be abolished as from 6 April 2013.

Capital allowances on plant and machinery

With some exceptions (see later), capital allowances are not calculated individually for each item of plant and machinery acquired by a business. Instead, expenditure on plant and machinery is pooled together and capital allowances are calculated with reference to the value of the pool. In fact, there are two pools to consider. These are:

(a) **Main pool**. This is the pool to which most general plant and machinery is allocated (e.g. factory machines, office equipment etc.). Motor vans, motor cycles and lorries are also allocated to this pool. The situation with regard to motor cars is as follows:

 (i) In general, cars with emissions not exceeding 160g/km (*reduced to 130g/km as from 6 April 2013*) are allocated to the main pool. Cars with higher emissions are allocated to the special rate pool (see below).

 (ii) However, "low emission" cars (currently defined as those with emissions not exceeding 110g/km) are eligible for a 100% first year allowance and do not join any pool (see later in this chapter).

 A special treatment is accorded to cars acquired before 6 April 2009 and costing more than £12,000 (see later in this chapter).

(b) **Special rate pool**. This is a pool of assets arising from any or all of the following:

 (i) the acquisition of motor cars with emissions exceeding 160g/km

 (ii) the acquisition or replacement of certain "integral features" of a building; these are listed in CAA 2001 as electrical systems, water systems, heating and cooling systems, lifts, escalators/moving walkways and external solar shading

 (iii) expenditure on the thermal insulation of a building

 (iv) expenditure on assets with a working life of 25 years or more ("long-life" assets) but only if the business spends more than £100,000 a year on such assets.

The rate of capital allowances to which a business is entitled in relation to an item of plant and machinery depends upon the pool to which the item is allocated, as explained below.

Writing down allowance (WDA)

In general, a business may claim a *writing down allowance* for each of its pools of plant and machinery in each chargeable period. The procedure for computing the amount of the writing down allowance for each pool is as follows:

(a) The written down value (WDV) of the pool at the end of the previous chargeable period is brought forward.

(b) The cost of any plant and machinery which has been acquired during the chargeable period but which is not the subject of a claim for either first year allowance or annual investment allowance (see below) is added to the pool. Items of plant and machinery owned by the trader personally and then brought into the business at a later date are treated as if purchased at their market value on that date.

Plant and machinery acquired by hire purchase is treated as if bought for its cash price. A similar treatment applies to assets acquired under "long funding leases". In broad terms, these are finance leases with a term of more than five years.

(c) If any pool items have been disposed of during the chargeable period a disposal value is subtracted from the pool, equal to:

(i) sale proceeds, if the asset is sold in the open market

(ii) market value on the date of disposal, if the asset is given away or sold for less than market value (unless the new owner will be claiming capital allowances, in which case the sale proceeds are used)

(iii) scrap value or compensation received, if the asset is scrapped or destroyed.

But if the disposal value exceeds the original cost of the item, only the original cost is subtracted from the pool. The profit on the disposal may give rise to a capital gains tax liability (see Chapter 19).

(d) The available writing down allowance (WDA) is then calculated as a percentage of the pool balance. As from 6 April 2012, the applicable percentages are as follows:

Main pool	18% per annum
Special rate pool	8% per annum

Note that WDA is calculated at a percentage rate *per annum*. This refers to the length of the chargeable period for which capital allowances are being claimed and WDA is scaled up or down accordingly if the length of this period is not 12 months.

(e) The WDA claimed for the chargeable period is subtracted from the pool, leaving a WDV which is carried forward to the next period. This WDV will then attract WDAs in future chargeable periods (even if all the plant and machinery has now been sold).

It is not mandatory to claim the maximum WDA available for a chargeable period and a trader with low profits (or a loss) may wish to claim less than the maximum, usually to avoid wasting personal allowances. The effect of such a claim is to increase the WDVs carried forward, thus increasing the allowances available in future chargeable periods.

EXAMPLE 2

Joanne started a business on 6 April 2012, preparing annual accounts to 5 April. During the years to 5 April 2013 and 2014 she bought and sold plant and machinery as follows:

		£
8 April 2012	Bought motor car (emissions 160g/km)	8,600
27 October 2012	Bought motor car (emissions 150g/km)	10,400
31 July 2013	Sold motor car bought in April 2012	6,400
31 July 2013	Bought motor car (emissions 175g/km)	14,200

Prepare her capital allowances computation for the years to 5 April 2013 and 2014.

Solution

	Main pool	*Special rate pool*	*Allowances*
	£	£	£
y/e 5/4/13			
Additions (£8,600 + £10,400)	19,000		
WDA @ 18%	3,420		3,420
WDV c/f	15,580		
Total allowances			3,420
y/e 5/4/14			
WDV b/f	15,580		
Additions		14,200	
Disposals	(6,400)		
	9,180		
WDA @ 18%	1,652		1,652
WDA @ 8%		1,136	1,136
WDV c/f	7,528	13,064	
Total allowances			2,788

Notes:

(i) The motor cars bought for £8,600 and £10,400 enter the main pool because they both have emissions not exceeding 160g/km.

(ii) The motor car bought for £14,200 enters the special rate pool because its emissions exceed 160g/km.

Changes in the rates of WDA

Prior to 6 April 2012, the annual rates of WDA were 20% in the main pool and 10% in the special rate pool. Because of this, WDA for a chargeable period which spans 6 April 2012 has to be calculated at a "hybrid" rate. Hybrid rates of WDA are derived as follows:

$$\text{Main pool hybrid rate} = (20\% \times \frac{B}{CP}) + (18\% \times \frac{A}{CP})$$

$$\text{Special rate pool hybrid rate} = (10\% \times \frac{B}{CP}) + (8\% \times \frac{A}{CP})$$

where: B is the number of days in the chargeable period *before* 6 April 2012

A is the number of days in the chargeable period on or *after* 6 April 2012

CP is the number of days in the chargeable period.

Strictly speaking, hybrid rates of WDA should be calculated on a daily basis, as indicated by the above formulas. However, for the sake of simplicity, calculations in this book are made to the nearest month.

EXAMPLE 3

A trader prepares accounts to 31 December each year. Calculate the hybrid rates of WDA available for the year to 31 December 2012 in:

(a) the main pool (b) the special rate pool

Solution

(a) The hybrid rate in the main pool is (20% x 3/12) + (18% x 9/12) = 18.5%.
(b) The hybrid rate in the special rate pool is (10% x 3/12) + (8% x 9/12) = 8.5%.

EXAMPLE 4

A trader prepares accounts for the nine month period from 1 February 2012 to 31 October 2012. Calculate the hybrid rates of WDA available for this period in:

(a) the main pool (b) the special rate pool

Solution

(a) The hybrid rate in the main pool is (20% x 2/9) + (18% x 7/9) = 18.44%.
(b) The hybrid rate in the special rate pool is (10% x 2/9) + (8% x 7/9) = 8.44%.

Small pools of plant and machinery

If the balance in the main pool or in the special rate pool before calculating writing down allowance is £1,000 or less, the business concerned may claim a WDA of any amount up to the amount of that balance. This rule means that it is not necessary for businesses to carry forward very small pool balances for many years, claiming ever diminishing WDAs in each chargeable period.

Businesses with a balance of £1,000 or less in the main pool or special rate pool can claim a WDA of less than the full balance if they so wish.

EXAMPLE 5

Patrick prepares accounts to 31 August each year. The written down value of his main pool of plant and machinery after deducting capital allowances for the year to 31 August 2011 was £1,900. There was no special rate pool.

No plant and machinery was acquired during the year to 31 August 2012 but an item of plant that had been acquired for £3,000 in 2008 was sold in May 2012 for £1,250.

Required:

Prepare a capital allowances computation for the year to 31 August 2012, assuming that maximum allowances are claimed.

Solution

	Main pool	*Allowances*
	£	£
y/e 31/8/12		
WDV b/f	1,900	
Disposals	(1,250)	
	650	
WDA	650	650
WDV c/f	0	
Total allowances		650

Notes:

(i) The rate of WDA in the main pool for the year to 31 August 2012 would normally be (20% × 7/12) + (18% × 5/12) = 19.17%. So WDA would be normally be equal to 19.17% × £650 = £125.

(ii) However, since the WDV of the pool before calculating WDA is less than £1,000, a WDA of £650 may be claimed.

Annual investment allowance (AIA)

Expenditure on plant and machinery (other than motor cars) of up to a specified maximum amount each year qualifies for a 100% annual investment allowance (AIA). *As from 6 April 2012*, the AIA maximum amount is £25,000 per annum. This simplifies the capital allowances computations of smaller businesses whose annual expenditure on general plant and machinery does not exceed £25,000. The main features of the AIA are as follows:

(a) An AIA of 100% may be claimed in relation to qualifying expenditure that does not exceed the AIA maximum for the chargeable period.

(b) Expenditure on which the AIA is claimed does not enter any pool. If the qualifying expenditure for a chargeable period exceeds the AIA maximum, the excess enters the appropriate pool and is eligible for WDAs in the usual way.

(c) A business may allocate the AIA between items of expenditure in any way that it chooses. For example, if £20,000 is spent on main pool items and £10,000 on special rate pool items in a period in which the AIA maximum is £25,000, £10,000 of the AIA might be allocated to the special rate pool and the remaining £15,000 to the main pool. This would maximise allowances for the period, since the main pool attracts WDA at 18% whilst the special rate pool attracts WDA at only 8%.

    A business which spends no more than £25,000 a year on special rate items might use this approach to avoid having a special rate pool at all. But a special rate pool is unavoidable if the business acquires cars with emissions exceeding 160g/km, since cars are not eligible for AIA.

(d) The AIA maximum amount (£25,000 per annum from 6 April 2012) is increased or reduced proportionately for chargeable periods of more or less than 12 months.

(e) A business is not required to claim the full AIA to which it is entitled. Any qualifying expenditure which is not the subject of a claim for AIA enters the appropriate pool and is eligible for WDAs.

(f) If a person controls more than one business, these businesses are entitled to only one AIA between them if they are "related ". Businesses are related if they are conducted from shared premises or if their activities are within the same EU classification.

Change to the AIA maximum amount

Prior to 6 April 2012, the AIA maximum was £100,000 p.a. If a chargeable period spans 6 April 2012, the AIA maximum for the period is calculated proportionately.

For instance, if capital allowances are being calculated for the year to 30 June 2012, the maximum AIA which can be claimed is £81,250 (9/12 × £100,000 + 3/12 × £25,000). But the amount of expenditure which is eligible for AIA in the part of the period which falls after 5 April 2012 cannot exceed £25,000, scaled down according to the length of that part of the period (i.e. 3/12 × £25,000 = £6,250 in this case).

EXAMPLE 6

A trader prepares accounts to 31 October each year. Expenditure on general plant and machinery (excluding cars) in the year to 31 October 2012 is £52,500.

(a) Calculate the maximum AIA available for the year to 31 October 2012.

(b) Calculate the AIA that may be claimed for the year if:

  (i) the entire £52,500 is spent before 6 April 2012
  (ii) the entire £52,500 is spent on or after 6 April 2012
  (iii) £20,000 of the £52,500 is spent on or after 6 April 2012.

Solution

(a) Maximum AIA is £56,250 (5/12 × £100,000 + 7/12 × £25,000).

(b) (i) £52,500
  (ii) £14,583 (7/12 x £25,000)
  (iii) £47,083 (£32,500 + 7/12 x £25,000).

First year allowance (FYA)

A first year allowance of 100% is available in relation to certain classes of expenditure on plant and machinery. The main first year allowances are as follows:

(a) Expenditure on a motor car with emissions not exceeding 110g/km is eligible for a 100% FYA as long as the expenditure is incurred on or before 31 March 2013.

(b) Expenditure on a motor car with emissions not exceeding 95g/km will be eligible for a 100% FYA as long as the expenditure is incurred between 1 April 2013 and 31 March 2015.

(c) Expenditure on plant and machinery for use in the refuelling of vehicles with natural gas, biogas or hydrogen fuel is eligible for a 100% FYA as long as the expenditure is incurred on or before 31 March 2013 (*to be extended to 31 March 2015*).

(d) Expenditure incurred on certain classes of energy-saving and water-efficient plant and machinery qualifies for a 100% FYA.

A 100% FYA is also available in relation to expenditure on new (not second-hand) zero-emission goods vehicles acquired between 6 April 2010 and 5 April 2015 inclusive.

EXAMPLE 7

(a) Sharon started a business on 6 July 2011. She chose 5 April as her accounting date and her first accounts covered the period from 6 July 2011 to 5 April 2012. During this period she bought plant and machinery as follows:

		£
6 July 2011	Bought plant	6,000
19 August 2011	Bought motor car (emissions 142g/km)	8,400
17 March 2012	Bought plant	13,000

She claims maximum capital allowances in all chargeable periods. Prepare a capital allowances computation for the nine months to 5 April 2012.

(b) Sharon's purchases and sales of plant and machinery during the year to 5 April 2013 are as follows:

		£
8 April 2012	Bought plant	5,990
30 June 2012	Sold plant (original cost £3,500 on 6/7/11)	2,640

Prepare a capital allowances computation for the year to 5 April 2013.

Solution

(a)

		Main pool	*Allowances*
		£	£
6/7/11 - 5/4/12			
Additions not eligible for AIA		8,400	
WDA @ 20% x 9/12		1,260	1,260
		7,140	
Additions qualifying for AIA	19,000		
AIA @ 100%	19,000	-	19,000
WDV c/f		7,140	
Total allowances			20,260

Notes:

(i) The motor car is allocated to the main pool since it has emissions not exceeding 160g/km. Cars are not eligible for AIA.

(ii) Prior to 6 April 2012, the rate of WDA in the main pool was 20% per annum. WDA is scaled down by 9/12 for a nine-month period.

(iii) Prior to 6 April 2012, the AIA maximum was £100,000 per annum. Therefore the maximum AIA for this period is £75,000 (9/12 x £100,000). Sharon's AIA of £19,000 is well within this maximum.

(iv) Total capital allowances for the period are £20,260.

(b)

		Main pool	Allowances
		£	£
y/e 5/4/13			
WDV b/f		7,140	
Disposals		(2,640)	
		4,500	
WDA @ 18%		810	810
		3,690	
Additions eligible for AIA	5,990		
AIA @ 100%	5,990	-	5,990
WDV c/f		3,690	
Total allowances			6,800

Notes:

(i) The rate of WDA in the main pool as from 6 April 2012 is 18% per annum.

(ii) The maximum AIA for this 12-month period is £25,000. Sharon's AIA of £5,990 is well within this maximum.

(iii) Total capital allowances for the year are £6,800.

EXAMPLE 8

Ian prepares accounts to 31 December each year. The written down value of his main pool of plant and machinery after deducting capital allowances for the year to 31 December 2011 was £116,250. There was no special rate pool on that date. Purchases and sales of plant and machinery for the year to 31 December 2012 were as follows:

		£
3 January 2012	Bought electrical system	25,800
17 March 2012	Bought plant	60,700
5 May 2012	Bought car (emissions 105g/km)	12,700
25 August 2012	Sold plant bought for £1,000 in 2011	1,100
31 October 2012	Bought car (emissions 163g/km)	14,000

The electrical system bought in January 2012 qualifies as an "integral feature" of a building for capital allowances purposes.

Required:

Prepare a capital allowances computation for the year to 31 December 2012, assuming that maximum allowances are claimed. Perform all calculations to the nearest month.

Solution

		Main pool	*Special rate pool*	*Allowances*
		£	£	£
y/e 31/12/12				
WDV b/f		116,250		
Additions not eligible for AIA		42,750	14,000	
Disposal		(1,000)		
		158,000		
WDA @ 18.5%		29,230		29,230
WDA @ 8.5%			1,190	1,190
		128,770	12,810	
Additions eligible for AIA	43,750			
AIA @ 100%	43,750	-		43,750
Additions eligible for 100% FYA	12,700			
FYA @ 100%	12,700	-		12,700
WDV c/f		128,770	12,810	
Total allowances				86,870

Notes:

(i) Maximum AIA for the year is £43,750 (3/12 x £100,000 + 9/12 x £25,000). This could be allocated in any way between the expenditure of £25,800 on an electrical system in January and the expenditure of £60,700 on general plant in March.

(ii) Capital allowances for the year are maximised if the AIA is allocated first to the expenditure of £25,800, since this expenditure would otherwise enter the special rate pool and be eligible for WDA at a lower rate than in the main pool.

(iii) Setting the AIA first against the expenditure of £25,800 leaves £17,950 to set against the expenditure of £60,700. The balance of £42,750 is not eligible for AIA and therefore enters the main pool.

(iv) The disposal value of the plant sold in August 2012 is restricted to original cost.

(v) The hybrid rate in the main pool is (20% x 3/12) + (18% x 9/12) = 18.5%. The hybrid rate in the special rate pool is (10% x 3/12) + (8% x 9/12) = 8.5%.

(vi) The car bought in May 2012 has emissions not exceeding 110g/km and is therefore eligible for a 100% FYA.

(vii) The car bought in October 2012 has emissions exceeding 160g/km and is allocated to the special rate pool.

Balancing allowances and charges

If the disposal value of the plant and machinery disposed of during a chargeable period exceeds the balance of expenditure in the relevant pool before disposals are deducted, this indicates that the capital allowances given to date exceed the depreciation which has actually occurred. In these circumstances, the written down value of the pool is set to zero and a *balancing charge* is made, equal to the amount of the excess. A balancing charge is a negative capital allowance which is *added* to trading profits for tax purposes.

Balancing adjustments are also required when a business ceases trading (see later in this chapter) or when a non-pooled asset is disposed of. Non-pooled assets are assets which are treated individually for capital allowances purposes (see below). When a non-pooled asset is disposed of, a balancing adjustment is required so as to ensure that the total capital allowances granted in respect of the asset are exactly equal to its depreciation. If the asset's disposal value exceeds its WDV brought forward, a *balancing charge* is made, equal to the excess. If the asset's WDV brought forward exceeds disposal value, a *balancing allowance* is given, equal to the excess.

Non-pooled assets

Certain items of plant and machinery are not brought into the main pool or the special rate pool. Instead, these items are treated individually for capital allowances purposes, each item having its own "single asset pool". The items in question are:

(a) assets with some private use

(b) expensive motor cars acquired before 6 April 2009

(c) short-life assets.

The treatment of each of these items is explained below.

Assets with some private use

Any asset which is partly used for private purposes by the owner of a business is dealt with in a single asset pool. Capital allowances in relation to such an asset are calculated in the usual way and are deducted in full when calculating the WDV of the asset, but only the business proportion of these allowances may then be claimed. Note that:

(a) A balancing allowance or charge will arise on the disposal of an asset which is held in a single asset pool. The taxpayer may claim only the business proportion of any balancing allowance which arises in these circumstances and is taxed on only the business proportion of any balancing charge.

(b) Capital allowances are available in full on assets used for private purposes by an *employee* of the business, but the employee may then be assessed to income tax on a benefit in kind (see Chapter 8).

EXAMPLE 9

Allan prepares accounts to 5 April each year. His acquisitions and disposals of plant and machinery in the years to 5 April 2012 and 2013 include the following:

		£
8 April 2011	Bought Audi motor car (emissions 154g/km)	17,500
12 May 2011	Bought computer system	2,500
27 March 2013	Sold Audi motor car	14,600
27 March 2013	Bought BMW motor car (emissions 181g/km)	24,000

Private use of both cars is agreed to be 30%. There is 25% private use of the computer system. Compute the capital allowances available in relation to each of these items for the years to 5 April 2012 and 2013, assuming that Allan's entitlement to AIA in both years is fully used against other assets.

Solution

	Audi (30% p.u.)	*Computer (25% p.u.)*	*BMW (30% p.u.)*		*Allces*
	£	£	£		£
y/e 5/4/12					
Additions	17,500	2,500			
WDA @ 20%	3,500			x 70%	2,450
WDA @ 20%		500		x 75%	375
WDV c/f	14,000	2,000			
Total allowances					2,825
y/e 5/4/13					
Addition			24,000		
Disposal	(14,600)				
Balancing charge	(600)			x 70%	(420)
WDA @ 18%		360		x 75%	270
WDA @ 8%			1,920	x 70%	1,344
WDV c/f		1,640	22,080		
Total allowances					1,194

Notes:

(i) The Audi motor car has emissions which do not exceed 160g/km, so WDAs on this car for the year to 5 April 2012 are calculated at 20% per annum.

(ii) The BMW motor car has emissions which exceed 160g/km, so WDAs on this car for the year to 5 April 2013 are calculated at 8% per annum.

Expensive motor cars acquired before 6 April 2009

Motor cars (other than low emission cars) acquired before 6 April 2009 and costing more than £12,000 are dealt with on an individual basis. WDA is calculated at the same rate as in the main pool, subject to a maximum of £3,000 per car per annum.

Any unrelieved expenditure remaining in relation to an expensive car will be transferred to the main pool at the beginning of the first chargeable period starting on or after 6 April 2014. But this transfer will not occur if there is any private use of the car.

EXAMPLE 10

Bianca prepares accounts to 31 December each year. On 21 January 2009 she bought a motor car (not eligible for the 100% FYA) costing £19,750. Private use is 40%. Compute the capital allowances available on this car for the first four chargeable periods.

Solution

			Allces
	£		£
y/e 31/12/09			
Addition	19,750		
WDA (£19,750 @ 20% = £3,950, restricted to £3,000)	3,000	x 60%	1,800
WDV c/f	16,750		
y/e 31/12/10			
WDA (£16,750 @ 20% = £3,350, restricted to £3,000)	3,000	x 60%	1,800
WDV c/f	13,750		
y/e 31/12/11			
WDA @ 20% (no restriction necessary)	2,750	x 60%	1,650
WDV c/f	11,000		
y/e 31/12/12			
WDA @ 18.5% [(20% x 3/12) + (18% x 9/12)]	2,035	x 60%	1,221
WDV c/f	8,965		

Short-life assets

A trader may elect that an asset (other than a car) which would normally join the main pool should instead be treated as a "short-life asset". If this de-pooling" election is made, the asset is treated on an individual basis, and then:

(a) if the asset is not disposed of within eight years of the end of the period in which it is acquired, it is transferred to the main pool at its written down value at the end of those eight years and the short-life election will have had no effect

(b) if the asset is disposed of within the eight-year period, a balancing allowance will be given (or a balancing charge will be made).

Making a short-life election in relation to an asset which is likely to be sold for less than its WDV within eight years will generate a balancing allowance on disposal, so ensuring that capital allowances are given as quickly as possible. There is (of course) no point in making such an election if a 100% AIA is available in relation to the asset. Note that:

(a) A short-life election relating to expenditure incurred during a chargeable period must be made by 31 January in the second tax year following the tax year in which the chargeable period ends.

(b) One effect of a short-life election is that the asset concerned is kept out of the main pool. This increases the likelihood that disposals from that pool will have a disposal value which exceeds the pool balance, so triggering a balancing charge (see earlier in this chapter). This factor should be borne in mind when making a short-life election.

EXAMPLE 11

Anita starts trading on 6 April 2012, preparing accounts to 5 April each year. On 6 April 2012 she buys general plant costing £30,000 and a machine costing £40,000. She sells the machine on 31 March 2015 for £10,000. Compute capital allowances for the first three chargeable periods if:

(a) she does not make any short-life elections
(b) she makes a short-life election with regard to the machine (assuming that her AIA for the year to 5 April 2013 is set against the £30,000 expenditure on general plant).

Solution

(a)

		Main pool £	*Allowances* £
y/e 5/4/13			
Additions not eligible for AIA		45,000	
WDA @ 18%		8,100	8,100
		36,900	
Additions eligible for AIA	25,000		
AIA @ 100%	25,000	-	25,000
WDV c/f		36,900	
Total allowances			33,100
y/e 5/4/14			
WDV b/f		36,900	
WDA @ 18%		6,642	6,642
WDV c/f		30,258	

	Main pool	Allowances
	£	£
y/e 5/4/15		
WDV b/f	30,258	
Disposal	(10,000)	
	20,258	
WDA @ 18%	3,646	3,646
WDV c/f	16,612	

(b)

		Main pool	SL asset	Allowances
		£	£	£
y/e 5/4/13				
Additions not eligible for AIA		5,000	40,000	
WDA @ 18%		900	7,200	8,100
		4,100		
Additions eligible for AIA	25,000			
AIA @ 100%	25,000	-		25,000
WDV c/f		4,100	32,800	
Total allowances				33,100
y/e 5/4/14				
WDV b/f		4,100	32,800	
WDA @ 18%		738	5,904	6,642
WDV c/f		3,362	26,896	
y/e 5/4/15				
WDV c/f		3,362	26,896	
Disposal			(10,000)	
Balancing allowance			16,896	16,896
WDA @ 18%		605		605
WDV c/f		2,757		
Total allowances				17,501

Notes:

(i) Total allowances for the years to 5 April 2013 (£33,100) and 5 April 2014 (£6,642) are unaffected by the short-life election. But total allowances for the year to 5 April 2015 are increased by £13,855 (£17,501 – £3,646) if the short-life election is made.

(ii) If the short-life election is made, WDVs carried forward reduce by £13,855 (£16,612 – £2,757). This reduces future capital allowances.

Allowances on cessation of trade

When a business ceases trading and all of the plant and machinery is disposed of, capital allowances for the final chargeable period are computed as follows:

(a) Any items acquired in the final period are added into the relevant pool.

(b) No WDA, AIA or FYA is given in the final chargeable period.

(c) The disposal value of each pool (including single asset pools) is subtracted from the balance of unrelieved expenditure, giving rise to balancing allowances or balancing charges. Assets taken over personally by the trader are treated as if sold for their market value on the date they are taken over.

The balancing adjustments normally made on a cessation of trade can be avoided if the business is taken over by a connected person (e.g. the trader's spouse, civil partner or other relative) so long as an election to this effect is made by both parties. In this case, the final chargeable period is treated in exactly the same way as any other chargeable period and the assets are then transferred to the new owner at their WDVs.

EXAMPLE 12

Jake has been trading for many years, preparing accounts to 30 September each year. The written down value of his plant and machinery at 30 September 2011 was:

	£
Main pool	11,350
Motor car (20% private use by Jake)	13,200

Jake bought plant costing £1,150 in October 2011. This was his only transaction in plant and machinery until 30 June 2012, when he ceased trading and closed down his business. On that date, all of the items in his main pool were sold for a total of £12,850 (all items were sold for less than cost) and his car was sold for £12,000. Prepare Jake's capital allowances computation for the 9 months to 30 June 2012.

Solution

	Main pool	*Motor car (20% private)*	*Allowances*
	£	£	£
1/10/11 - 30/6/12			
WDV b/f	11,350	13,200	
Additions	1,150		
	12,500		
Disposals	(12,850)	(12,000)	
Balancing allowance/(charge)	(350)	1,200 x 80% = 960	610

Industrial buildings and agricultural buildings

Capital allowances referred to as *industrial buildings allowances* (IBAs) and *agricultural buildings allowances* (ABAs) have been available for many years in relation to expenditure on industrial buildings and agricultural buildings. However, these allowances have now been phased out and do not apply to chargeable periods beginning on or after 6 April 2011. If a chargeable period begins before 6 April 2011 and ends after that date, IBAs and ABAs are available only for the part of the period that falls before 6 April 2011.

A summary of the main features of IBAs and ABAs, together with a number of worked examples, may be found on the website which accompanies this textbook. The website address is www.pearsoned.co.uk/melville.

Miscellaneous capital allowances

Capital allowances are available in relation to some miscellaneous categories of capital expenditure. These include expenditure on:

(a) patent rights

(b) know-how

(c) research and development.

Furthermore, capital allowances may also be available in relation to expenditure on the renovation of business premises. Each of these matters is considered briefly below.

Patent rights

The treatment of purchased patent rights acquired for trade purposes is as follows:

(a) Patent rights are pooled together. The patent rights pool is adjusted in each chargeable period for acquisitions and disposals and then WDA is calculated at 25% per annum on the reducing balance.

(b) WDA is proportionately increased or decreased if the chargeable period is of more or less than 12 months.

(c) As with plant and machinery, disposal value is restricted to original cost.

(d) If the disposal value of a patent exceeds the balance of unrelieved expenditure in the pool, a balancing charge is made and the pool value is set to zero.

(e) On cessation of trade, there will be a balancing allowance if the patents are sold for less than the balance of unrelieved expenditure in the pool. There will be a balancing charge if the patents are sold for more than the balance of unrelieved expenditure.

Know-how

"Know-how" is defined as industrial information and techniques of use in either:

(a) manufacturing or the processing of goods or materials

(b) the working of mineral deposits

(c) agricultural, fishing or forestry operations.

All expenditure on know-how is pooled and capital allowances are calculated in much the same way as for patent rights. However, if know-how is sold for more than original cost, the disposal value used in the capital allowances computation is the *full sale proceeds*. Depending upon the balance of unrelieved expenditure in the pool prior to the disposal, this will either create a balancing charge or restrict the value of subsequent WDAs. In either case, the profit made on the disposal is (in effect) treated as trading income.

Research and development

Capital expenditure on research and development related to the claimant's trade attracts a first year allowance of 100%. Any proceeds subsequently received on the disposal of a research and development asset are treated as a trading receipt.

Business premises renovation allowance

A 100% allowance known as the Business Premises Renovation Allowance (BPRA) is available for capital expenditure on the renovation of certain business premises. In order to qualify for BPRA, the premises must be located in a disadvantaged area and must have been vacant for at least a year.

BPRA was originally available in relation to qualifying expenditure incurred on or after 11 April 2007 and the scheme was expected to last for five years. However, the BPRA scheme has now been extended for a further five years until 5 April 2017.

Summary

- Capital allowances are granted for chargeable periods. For income tax purposes, each period of account usually ranks as a chargeable period, but periods of account lasting more than 18 months are divided into two or more chargeable periods.
- In order to qualify as plant and machinery, an asset must perform an active function in the trade, not merely provide the setting in which the trade is carried on. There is extensive case law in relation to this distinction.
- With some exceptions, expenditure on plant and machinery is pooled together for capital allowances purposes. Most general plant and machinery is allocated to the main pool but certain items are allocated to the special rate pool.
- Motor cars with emissions in excess of 160g/km (*130g/km from 6 April 2013*) are allocated to the special rate pool. Cars with lower emissions are generally allocated to the main pool but cars with emissions not exceeding 110g/km (*95g/km from 1 April 2013*) attract a 100% FYA.
- Writing down allowances (WDAs) on plant and machinery are calculated at 18% per annum in the main pool and 8% per annum in the special rate pool. Prior to 6 April 2012, these rates were 20% and 10% respectively. WDA is scaled up or down if the chargeable period is not 12 months long.
- WDA for chargeable periods which span 6 April 2012 is calculated at hybrid rates.
- The first £25,000 per annum of expenditure on plant and machinery (other than cars) is eligible for a 100% annual investment allowance (AIA). Prior to 6 April 2012, the AIA maximum was £100,000 per annum. If a chargeable period spans 6 April 2012, the maximum AIA for that period is calculated proportionately.
- An asset which is used only partly for business purposes is dealt with in a single asset pool. Capital allowances are calculated in the usual way and are deducted in full when calculating the WDV of the asset, but only the business proportion of these allowances may be claimed.
- Cars acquired before 6 April 2009 and costing more than £12,000 are allocated to single asset pools. WDA in relation to such a car is restricted to £3,000 per annum.
- Short-life assets are allocated to single asset pools. A balancing allowance or charge will arise if a short-life asset is disposed of within eight years of the end of the period in which it was acquired.
- Balancing allowances and balancing charges will arise on a cessation of trade unless the business is taken over by a connected person.
- Capital allowances are also available in relation to patent rights, know-how, research and development expenditure and certain business premises renovations.

Exercises

It should be assumed in all of these exercises that maximum capital allowances are claimed.

11.1 Maurice prepares accounts to 5 April each year. The written down value of his main pool at 5 April 2012 was £10,300. There was no special rate pool. His purchases and sales of plant and machinery during the year to 5 April 2013 were as follows:

		£
7 April 2012	Bought plant	600
11 April 2012	Sold machinery (original cost £4,000 in 2011)	4,200
11 July 2012	Bought motor car (emissions 144g/km)	8,000
1 November 2012	Bought machinery	400
12 January 2013	Sold equipment (original cost £7,000 in 2009)	3,000

Compute the capital allowances which may be claimed for the year to 5 April 2013, assuming no private use of any of the assets.

11.2 Laura started a business on 1 October 2011. Her adjusted trading profit for the year to 30 September 2012 (before deduction of capital allowances) was £127,300. Her purchases of plant and machinery during the year were as follows:

		£
1 October 2011	Bought machinery	55,400
1 October 2011	Bought motor car (emissions 178g/km)	15,000
12 March 2012	Bought machinery	26,500
30 June 2012	Bought machinery	1,600

Compute her trading income for the first two tax years, assuming 40% private use of the car by Laura. Also compute the amount of any overlap profits.

11.3 Norma has prepared a set of accounts for the nine-month period to 31 March 2013. The written down value of her plant and machinery at 30 June 2012 was as follows:

	£
Main pool	178,400
Toyota motor car (50% private use by Norma)	18,200

Her purchases and her sales of plant and machinery during the period to 31 March 2013 were as follows:

		£
17 July 2012	Bought plant	64,450
1 August 2012	Sold Toyota motor car	15,000
1 August 2012	Bought Saab motor car (emissions 150g/km)	29,600
4 September 2012	Bought motor van	14,500
12 January 2013	Bought Ford motor car (emissions 105g/km)	11,600
3 February 2013	Bought Peugeot motor car (emissions 166g/km)	15,400
1 March 2013	Sold plant (original cost £10,000)	1,600

There was 50% private use (by Norma) of the Toyota and Saab motor cars. There was no private use of any of the other items. Prepare a capital allowances computation for the period to 31 March 2013.

***11.4** Talat prepares accounts to 30 September each year. The written down value of his plant and machinery after deducting capital allowances for the year to 30 September 2011 was as follows:

	£
Main pool	113,210
Special rate pool	9,900
VW motor car (30% private use by Talat)	14,500

He had the following transactions during the year to 30 September 2012:

		£
1 January 2012	Sold plant (original cost £4,200 in 2007)	1,310
23 February 2012	Bought air conditioning system	19,600
12 March 2012	Bought plant	56,300
5 July 2012	Sold main pool car (original cost £7,500 in 2009)	3,000
5 July 2012	Bought car (emissions 161g/km)	8,200
18 August 2012	Sold plant (original cost £1,000 in September 2011)	1,150
6 September 2012	Sold VW motor car	17,200
6 September 2012	Bought BMW motor car (emissions 154g/km)	32,000

The air conditioning system bought in February 2012 qualifies as an "integral feature" for capital allowances purposes. Private use by Talat of the VW and BMW motor cars has been agreed with HMRC to be 30%.

There were no capital transactions between 1 October 2012 and 31 March 2013, when Talat ceased trading and closed down his business. On 31 March 2013, the plant and machinery was disposed of as follows:

(i) All of the plant and machinery other than motor cars was sold for £107,000. This consisted of £95,000 for main pool items and £12,000 for special rate items.

(ii) Talat took over the BMW car. Its market value on 31 March 2013 was £29,000.

(iii) The only other car remaining was the one acquired in July 2012 and Talat gave this to his brother, who will be using it for private purposes. The market value of the car on 31 March 2013 was £6,300.

Prepare the capital allowances computations for the year to 30 September 2012 and for the period from 1 October 2012 to 31 March 2013.

***11.5** A trader prepares accounts to 31 January each year. For the year to 31 January 2013:

(a) Calculate the rates of WDA available in the main pool and the special rate pool.

(b) Calculate the maximum AIA which may be claimed and the amount of this which may be claimed in relation to expenditure incurred on or after 6 April 2012.

***11.6** Raymond started trading on 6 August 2011 and chose 5 April as his accounting date. His first accounts were for the period from 6 August 2011 to 5 April 2012. Purchases and sales of plant and machinery during the first two accounting periods were as follows:

		£
6 August 2011	Bought machinery	55,000
9 August 2011	Bought motor van (emissions 212g/km)	16,200
12 October 2011	Bought motor car (emissions 173g/km)	18,600
18 January 2012	Bought office equipment	4,800
4 April 2012	Bought motor car (emissions 142g/km)	9,200
12 May 2012	Sold car bought in April 2012	9,600
12 May 2012	Bought motor car (emissions 160g/km)	10,500
25 November 2012	Sold machinery (cost £11,500 in August 2011)	8,300
3 February 2013	Bought machinery	30,000

There was 25% private use (by Raymond) of the motor car purchased in October 2011 but there was no private use of any of the other assets.

Required:

Prepare a capital allowances computation for the period to 5 April 2012 and for the year to 5 April 2013.

Chapter 12

Income from self-employment: Trading losses

Introduction

If the computation of a self-employed person's adjusted trading profit for a period of account produces a negative result, then a trading loss has been incurred. This has two main consequences:

(a) the person's trading income for the relevant tax year is set to £nil

(b) tax relief may be claimed in respect of the loss.

Several forms of tax relief are available and each involves offsetting the trading loss against other income or gains of the person concerned, so reducing the amount of tax payable on that other income or on those gains. The purpose of this chapter is to explain the main features of each form of loss relief.

Relief for trading losses

The rules which grant tax relief in relation to trading losses are located in the Income Tax Act 2007. This Act provides the following main reliefs:

(a) **Carry-forward trade loss relief**. A trading loss may be carried forward to the future and set against future profits of the same trade. This is the relief which takes effect if no other tax relief is claimed in relation to a trading loss.

(b) **Trade loss relief against total income**. A trading loss may be set against the trader's total income for a period of up to two years.

(c) **Early trade losses relief**. This is a special tax relief which concerns trading losses incurred in the early years of trading.

(d) **Terminal trade loss relief**. This is a special tax relief which concerns trading losses incurred in the final year of trading.

Each of these forms of loss relief is described below.

Carry-forward trade loss relief

Unless a trader claims any other form of loss relief in relation to a trading loss, the loss is automatically carried forward and relieved against future trading profits. It is important to note the following points:

(a) Carry-forward relief is given against future *trading profits* only, not against any other form of income.

(b) Furthermore, relief is given only against future trading profits arising from *the same trade* as that in which the loss was incurred. So if a trader ceases one trade and commences another, the losses of the old trade cannot be carried forward and relieved against the future profits of the new trade. Similarly, if a trader carries on two trades simultaneously, a loss incurred in one of the trades cannot be carried forward and relieved against the future profits of the other trade.

(c) Relief must be given against the *first available* trading profits arising in the future. The maximum possible relief must be taken in each year until the loss is fully relieved, even if this leaves insufficient income to absorb personal allowances.

(d) Strictly speaking, relief is given by deduction from the trader's total income when computing his or her net income (see Chapter 2). But the amount of relief given in any tax year cannot exceed the trading profits for that year.

EXAMPLE 1

Carla incurred a trading loss of £42,000 in the year to 30 June 2010. Her trading profits for the following three years (adjusted for tax purposes) are as follows:

	£
year to 30 June 2011	15,000
year to 30 June 2012	26,000
year to 30 June 2013	60,000

Carla's only other income consists of interest (gross) of £500 per annum. Assuming that the trading loss is carried forward, calculate her net income (i.e. total income less reliefs) for tax years 2010-11 to 2013-14 inclusive.

Solution

	2010-11	*2011-12*	*2012-13*	*2013-14*
	£	£	£	£
Trading income	nil	15,000	26,000	60,000
Interest received	500	500	500	500
Total income	500	15,000	26,500	60,500
Less: Trading losses b/f	-	15,000	26,000	1,000
Net income	500	500	500	59,500

Notes:

(a) Carla's trading income for 2010-11 is £nil since there is a loss in the basis period for that year.

(b) The trading loss carried forward is relieved against future trading profits (not against the interest received) and maximum relief must be given in each year. This results in a waste of personal allowances in 2011-12 and 2012-13. Carla would probably prefer to carry forward the loss in its entirety to 2013-14, where it could be put to good use and save tax at the higher rate, but this is not permissible.

Capital allowances

As explained in Chapter 11, any capital allowances claimed for a period of account are treated as a trading expense of that period. Therefore capital allowances are included automatically in the calculation of a trading loss.

It is important to remember that it is not mandatory to claim the maximum capital allowances available for a chargeable period. If a trading loss has been incurred it may be advisable to claim less than the maximum capital allowances (or even none at all) so as to avoid wasting personal allowances when the trading loss is relieved. Disclaimed capital allowances are not lost permanently, since higher WDVs are carried forward than would otherwise have been the case and this results in higher capital allowances in future years.

EXAMPLE 2

Colin's adjusted trading profits/(losses) for the years to 31 August 2011 and 2012 are:

	Before capital allowances	*Capital allowances available*	*After capital allowances*
	£	£	£
year to 31 August 2011	(9,300)	2,100	(11,400)
year to 31 August 2012	17,300	5,700	11,600

He has no other income. If the trading loss is carried forward for relief against future profits of the same trade, should Colin claim maximum capital allowances in these two years?

Solution

If Colin claims maximum capital allowances in both years, relief in 2012-13 for trading losses brought forward will be £11,400. This will almost entirely absorb the trading profit of £11,600 assessed in that year, leaving only £200 against which to set the personal allowance, most of which will therefore be wasted.

It would be better to claim no capital allowances at all for the two years. The trading loss brought forward from 2011-12 would then be £9,300 and this would be relieved against the trading profit of £17,300 in 2012-13, leaving income of £8,000 against which to set Colin's personal allowance. There would be minimal waste of personal allowances and the capital allowances available to Colin in future years would be increased.

Trade loss relief against total income

As illustrated earlier, carrying trading losses forward for relief against future profits of the same trade does not always provide the most satisfactory form of loss relief. Problems associated with carry-forward relief include:

(a) Loss relief is delayed until sufficient profits arise from the same trade in future years (if, indeed, they ever do).

(b) The trader has no control over the amount of relief given in each year and therefore personal allowances may be wasted.

(c) If tax rates are falling, relief may be given at a lower rate than the rates which were in force when the loss was incurred.

An alternative form of loss relief which overcomes some of these problems is "trade loss relief against total income". This tax relief allows trading losses to be set against the trader's total income for a period of up to two years. It is important to note that:

(a) The trader is under no obligation to make a claim to set trading losses against total income. If no such claim is made, trading losses are automatically carried forward for relief against future trading profits.

(b) Any unrelieved losses remaining after a claim has been made to set trading losses against total income are automatically carried forward.

(c) Trading losses may be set against the trader's total income only if the business is being carried on "on a commercial basis" and "with a view to the realisation of profits". Furthermore, trading losses may not be set against total income if they arise in consequence of tax avoidance arrangements.

(d) In the case of *farmers and market gardeners*, a loss is usually not eligible for relief against total income if losses (calculated without regard to capital allowances) have also been incurred in each of the previous five tax years.

(e) If a claim is made to set trading losses against total income, relief is given by deducting the amount of the claim from the trader's total income when calculating his or her net income (see Chapter 2). Relief is given against non-savings income, savings income and dividends in the way which results in the lowest tax liability.

(f) ITA 2007 uses the term "sideways relief" to refer to the relief of trading losses against total income. This term is also used in connection with early trade losses relief (see later in this chapter).

Note that there are restrictions on the amount of sideways relief which may be claimed by a "non-active" trader (see later in this chapter).

Relieving a trading loss against total income

ITA 2007 states that relief against total income is available if a person who carries on a trade makes a trading loss "in the tax year". In most cases, the amount of the trading loss in a tax year is defined as the amount of the loss which was incurred in the basis period for that year. However, in order to prevent double counting, a trading loss incurred in an overlap period is treated as a loss of the earlier tax year only.

A trading loss incurred in a tax year may be set against the total income of:

either (i) the tax year in which the loss is incurred
or (ii) the previous tax year
or (iii) both of these years (if the loss is large enough for this).

A claim to set a trading loss against total income must be made by 31 January in the second tax year following the year in which the loss was made. For example, a claim in relation to a loss incurred in 2012-13 must be made by 31 January 2015. Note that:

(a) The trader can decide whether to make a claim for one of the available years, for both of these years, or for neither year. But partial claims are not allowed. A claim to set a trading loss against total income must be for as much of the loss as can be relieved, even if this leaves insufficient income to absorb personal allowances.

However, if a claim is made for both years, the trader can decide whether to claim maximum relief in the year of the loss (relieving the remainder of the loss in the previous year) or vice versa.

(b) A trading loss may be set against the total income of the previous tax year whether or not the loss-making trade was being carried on in that year.

(c) If a trader claims that two trading losses should be set against the total income of the same tax year (one claim for a loss incurred in that tax year and another claim for a loss incurred in the following tax year) then the claim in respect of the current year's trading loss takes priority.

EXAMPLE 3

Ashok has been trading for many years, preparing annual accounts to 31 July. Recent trading profits/(losses), adjusted for tax purposes, are as follows:

	£
year to 31 July 2010	32,400
year to 31 July 2011	10,450
year to 31 July 2012	(9,500)

He has investment income amounting to £6,500 (gross) per annum and claims only the basic personal allowance. Identify the claims which he could make in relation to the trading loss incurred in the year to 31 July 2012. Which of these loss relief claims (if any) might be recommended?

Solution

Ashok's trading income is:

Year	*Basis period*	*Trading income*
		£
2010-11	y/e 31/7/10	32,400
2011-12	y/e 31/7/11	10,450
2012-13	y/e 31/7/12	nil

He could make a claim to relieve the trading loss of £9,500 against his total income for 2012-13 only, 2011-12 only, both of these years, or neither year:

(a) A claim for 2012-13 only would relieve £6,500 of the loss against his other income, leaving no tax liability for the year and losses of £3,000 to carry forward against future trading profits. This would be a waste, since the other income of £6,500 would in any case have been covered by the personal allowance.

(b) A claim for 2011-12 only would relieve the entire loss against that year's total income of £16,950 (£10,450 + £6,500), leaving income of £7,450 (£16,950 – £9,500) against which to set the personal allowance. There would be some very minor wastage of the personal allowance but the tax liability for 2011-12 would become zero. This seems to be a fairly efficient way of relieving the loss.

(c) A claim for both years is pointless, since:

   (i) a claim giving relief in 2011-12 first would leave no losses to relieve in 2012-13

   (ii) a claim giving relief in 2012-13 first results in a waste of personal allowances in that year (see above).

(d) A claim for neither year would result in the entire loss being carried forward. This would mean that loss relief would be delayed until such time as sufficient profits of the same trade arose in future years.

On balance, a claim to set the trading loss against total income of 2011-12 might be recommended. This claim combines early relief of the loss with a very small wastage of personal allowances. The claim would have to be made by 31 January 2015.

However, this claim would relieve the loss at only 20%. If the first available future profits from the same trade are expected to be very high, it might be better to carry the loss forward and possibly obtain relief at a higher rate.

Relieving trading losses against capital gains

If a claim is made to set a trading loss against the total income of a tax year (or if no such claim is made because total income for that year is zero) the trader concerned may claim that any unrelieved part of the loss should be set against his or her capital gains. Such a claim must be made by 31 January in the second tax year following the tax year in which the trading loss was incurred. This relief is considered further in Chapter 17.

Early trade losses relief

Losses incurred in the early years of trading may (just like other trading losses) be carried forward against future trading profits or set against the trader's total income. But, in addition to these forms of tax relief, ITA 2007 allows trading losses incurred in *any of the first four tax years* to be set against the trader's total income of the three previous tax years. This is another form of "sideways relief" (see above). Note that:

(a) If this relief is claimed in relation to a trading loss, the loss is relieved against the trader's total income of the previous three tax years, *beginning with the earliest year*. For example, an early years trading loss incurred in 2012-13 could be set against the trader's total income of 2009-10, 2010-11 and 2011-12, in that order.

(b) A claim for early trade losses relief applies to *all* of the three years prior to the loss-making year. The trader cannot specify the years in which relief is to be given or the amount of relief to be given in each year. The maximum possible relief is given in each year and this may result in a waste of personal allowances.

(c) Relief is given by deducting the amount of the trading loss from total income when calculating the trader's net income (see Chapter 2). Relief is given against non-savings income, savings income and dividends in the way which results in the lowest tax liability.

(d) A loss incurred in an overlap period is treated as *a loss of the earlier tax year only*. This rule ensures that a loss is relieved only once.

(e) Early trade losses relief is not available in relation to a trading loss unless the trade is commercial. This means that the trade is carried on "on a commercial basis" and "in such a way that profits could reasonably be expected to be made in the basis period or within a reasonable time afterwards".

Early trade losses relief cannot be claimed in relation to trading losses which arise in consequence of tax avoidance arrangements.

(f) A claim for early trade losses relief must be made by 31 January in the second tax year following the loss-making tax year. The claim *cannot* be extended so as to set any unrelieved trading losses against capital gains.

As mentioned above, there is a restriction on the amount of sideways relief which may be claimed by a "non-active" trader (see later in this chapter).

EXAMPLE 4

Carl begins trading on 1 July 2011 and chooses 30 June as his accounting date. His tax-adjusted trading profits/(losses) for the first two accounting years are as follows:

	£
year to 30 June 2012	(43,200)
year to 30 June 2013	(12,400)

Now that he is self-employed, Carl has no other income. Prior to becoming self-employed his only income was from employment, as follows:

	£
2008-09	23,900
2009-10	18,760
2010-11	18,920
2011-12 (to 30 June 2011)	7,180

Assuming that Carl makes all possible early trade losses claims, calculate his net income (i.e. total income less reliefs) for years 2008-09 to 2011-12 inclusive.

Solution

The losses which are eligible for early trade losses relief are:

Year	*Basis period*	*Workings*	*Trading loss* £	*Early trade losses claim*
2011-12	1/7/11 to 5/4/12	£(43,200) x 9/12	(32,400)	08-09 *to* 10-11
2012-13	y/e 30/6/12	£(43,200) – overlap £(32,400)	(10,800)	09-10 *to* 11-12
2013-14	y/e 30/6/13		(12,400)	10-11 *to* 12-13

Trading income for 2011-12 through to 2013-14 is of course £nil. If all possible early trade loss claims are made, net income for years 2008-09 to 2011-12 is:

	2008-09 £	*2009-10* £	*2010-11* £	*2011-12* £
Employment income	23,900	18,760	18,920	7,180
Trading income	-	-	-	0
Total income	23,900	18,760	18,920	7,180
Less: Early trade losses:				
2011-12 loss	(23,900)	(8,500)		
2012-13 loss		(10,260)	(540)	
2013-14 loss			(12,400)	
Net income	-	-	5,980	7,180

Non-active traders

As mentioned earlier, there is a restriction on the amount of sideways relief which may be claimed by a "non-active trader". A non-active trader is a person who carries on a trade but who is not personally engaged in the activities of that trade for at least 10 hours per week. The restriction is that the total amount of the sideways relief given to a non-active trader in a tax year cannot exceed £25,000. This limit applies to the *total* amount of the following reliefs in any one tax year:

(a) trade loss relief against total income

(b) early trade losses relief

(c) relief for trade losses against capital gains.

However, this restriction does not affect the giving of sideways relief against profits of the same trade. So if (for example) a trade loss is carried back and set against total income of the previous year, the £25,000 limit does not apply to the amount of the loss (if any) which is set against profits of the same trade made in that previous year.

Terminal trade loss relief

In normal circumstances, a trader who incurs a trading loss may choose between carrying the loss forward against future profits of the same trade or relieving the loss against total income. But if a trading loss is incurred in the final year of trading, the first of these alternatives is not available since there can be no future profits against which to set the trading loss. In order to remedy this situation, ITA 2007 provides a tax relief known as "terminal trade loss relief" which permits a trading loss incurred in the last 12 months of trading to be set against the trading profits (if any) of the tax year in which the cessation occurs and the previous three tax years.

Calculating the terminal loss

The "terminal loss" eligible for terminal trade loss relief is the trading loss incurred in the final 12 months of trading, excluding any part of that loss which has already been relieved in other ways (i.e. by deduction from total income). The terminal loss is calculated by adding together the following components:

(a) the actual trading loss incurred from 6 April to the date of the cessation

(b) the actual trading loss incurred from a date 12 months before the date of the cessation to the following 5 April

(c) any available overlap relief (see Chapter 10).

If either (a) or (b) is a profit, this counts as a zero in the calculation of the terminal loss.

EXAMPLE 5

Andrea ceases trading on 31 October 2012. Her adjusted trading profits/(losses) for the closing periods of account are as follows:

	£
year to 31 December 2010	6,600
year to 31 December 2011	2,400
10 months to 31 October 2012	(22,500)

Overlap profits of £3,200 arose when Andrea began trading. Calculate the amount of the loss which is eligible for terminal trade loss relief, assuming that no claims are made to set trading losses against total income.

Solution

		£
Trading loss 6/4/12 to 31/10/12	£(22,500) x 7/10	(15,750)
Trading loss 1/11/11 to 5/4/12	£2,400 x 2/12 + £(22,500) x 3/10	(6,350)
Overlap relief		(3,200)
Terminal loss		(25,300)

Relieving the terminal loss

As stated above, the terminal loss may be relieved against the trading profits of the year of cessation and the three tax years preceding the year of cessation. Note that:

(a) Relief is given in later years first. For example, a terminal loss arising as a consequence of a business ceasing to trade during 2012-13 would be set against the trading profits of 2012-13, 2011-12, 2010-11 and 2009-10, in that order.

(b) The maximum possible relief must be given in each tax year even if this results in a wastage of personal allowances.

(c) Strictly speaking, relief is given by deduction from the trader's total income when computing his or her net income (see Chapter 2). But the amount of relief given in any tax year cannot exceed the trading profits for that year.

EXAMPLE 6

Brendan ceases trading on 30 September 2012. His recent trading profits/(losses) are:

	£
year to 31 January 2010	24,700
year to 31 January 2011	12,500
year to 31 January 2012	2,100
8 months to 30 September 2012	(21,840)

He has no other income. Overlap profits of £4,700 arose when Brendan began trading and no claims are made to set Brendan's trading loss against his total income. Calculate the amount of the terminal loss and show how this may be relieved.

Solution

The calculation of the terminal loss is as follows:

		£
Trading loss 6/4/12 to 30/9/12	£(21,840) x 6/8	(16,380)
Trading loss 1/10/11 to 5/4/12	£2,100 x 4/12 + £(21,840) x 2/8	(4,760)
Overlap relief		(4,700)
Terminal loss		(25,840)

The terminal loss may be relieved as follows:

	2009-10	*2010-11*	*2011-12*	*2012-13*
	£	£	£	£
Trading income	24,700	12,500	2,100	nil
Less: Terminal trade loss relief:				
(i) in 2011-12			(2,100)	
(ii) in 2010-11		(12,500)		
(iii) in 2009-10	(11,240)			
Net income	13,460	-	-	-

Post-cessation trade relief

As a general rule, post-cessation expenses which were not provided for in the final accounts of a business are relieved against any post-cessation receipts (which are taxed as trading income). If post-cessation receipts are insufficient to absorb all post-cessation expenses, the excess expenses are normally unrelieved.

However, certain categories of unrelieved post-cessation expenses may be set against the taxpayer's total income for the tax year in which the expenses are incurred. The main categories of post-cessation expenses which may be relieved in this way are:

(a) the costs of remedying defective work done whilst the business was operating, together with associated legal costs and insurance premiums

(b) bad debts which were not provided for in the accounts of the business, together with associated debt collection costs.

If the taxpayer's total income for a tax year is insufficient to absorb all of the post-cessation expenses eligible for relief in that year, the excess expenses may be set against the taxpayer's capital gains for the year.

Expenses incurred more than seven years after cessation are not eligible for post-cessation trade relief.

Transfer of a business to a company

If the owner of a business transfers that business to a limited company, there is a change in the legal ownership of the business and the vendor is deemed to have ceased trading. In consequence, any trading losses sustained by the vendor before the date of the transfer cannot be carried forward and set against the company's trading profits.

Relief for such losses might be obtained by deduction from the taxpayer's total income for the year of the loss and/or the previous year. Terminal loss relief might be available if the losses were incurred in the final 12 months of trading. But a further tax relief is offered by ITA 2007, which provides that:

(a) if a business is transferred to a limited company wholly or mainly in exchange for shares in that company, and

(b) the vendor of the business continues to hold those shares, and

(c) the company continues to carry on the transferred business

then the vendor may set unrelieved trading losses against the first available income that he or she receives from the company.

Losses on shares in unlisted trading companies

A person who subscribes for newly-issued shares in certain unlisted trading companies and then incurs a capital loss on the disposal of those shares may claim that this capital loss should be set against his or her total income as if it were a trading loss.

Tax relief under this provision is generally available only if the trading company concerned is of a type which would qualify for the purposes of the Enterprise Investment Scheme (see Chapter 6).

Summary

- A trading loss may be carried forward and relieved against future profits of the same trade. This will happen if no other form of tax relief is claimed in relation to the loss.
- A trading loss may be relieved against the trader's total income for a specified two-year period.
- Any trading loss which remains unrelieved after a claim has been made to set that loss against the trader's total income for a tax year may be set against any capital gains for that year.
- A trading loss incurred in any of the first four tax years may be set against the trader's total income of the three previous tax years.

- A trading loss incurred during the final 12 months of trading may be set against the trading profits of the tax year in which trade ceases and the previous three tax years.
- If a business is transferred to a company, the unrelieved trading losses of the vendor may (subject to certain conditions) be set against the first available income which the vendor receives from the company.
- Capital losses incurred on the disposal of shares in certain unlisted trading companies may (subject to certain conditions) be treated as trading losses.

Exercises

12.1 Sally, who has been trading for many years, incurs an adjusted trading loss of £40,000 in the year to 31 December 2012.

(a) What is her trading income for 2012-13?

(b) If she makes no claim in relation to her trading loss, how will it be relieved?

(c) How will the loss be relieved if she does make a claim?

12.2 Jane is self-employed. Her recent adjusted trading profits/(losses) are:

	£
year to 31 May 2009	(18,860)
year to 31 May 2010	4,710
year to 31 May 2011	6,210
year to 31 May 2012	14,810

Jane has other income of £6,000 per annum. Assuming that the trading loss is carried forward and set against future trading profits, calculate her net income (i.e. total income less reliefs) for tax years 2009-10 through to 2012-13.

12.3 Marcus begins trading on 1 January 2011 and has the following results:

	Adjusted trading profits/(losses) before capital allowances	*Capital allowances claimed*
	£	£
year to 31 December 2011	14,720	4,460
year to 31 December 2012	(7,480)	2,320

He has no other income.

(a) Compute his trading income (before loss relief) for 2010-11 to 2012-13.

(b) Identify the claims that could be made in relation to the trading loss, assuming that early trade losses relief is <u>not</u> claimed. Which (if any) of these claims should be recommended?

12.4 Nathan begins trading on 1 October 2010, making up accounts to 31 December each year. His first two sets of accounts show the following adjusted trading losses:

	£
15 months to 31 December 2011	(26,850)
year to 31 December 2012	(25,660)

He has had no other income since becoming self-employed but his income before he started trading was as follows:

	£
2007-08	15,100
2008-09	15,250
2009-10	16,400
2010-11 (to 30 September 2010)	8,450

Assuming that all possible early trade losses relief claims are made, calculate Nathan's net income (i.e. total income less reliefs) for years 2007-08 to 2010-11.

***12.5** Olive ceases trading on 31 May 2013. Her recent adjusted trading profits/(losses) are:

	£
year to 30 June 2009	37,450
year to 30 June 2010	39,190
year to 30 June 2011	16,120
year to 30 June 2012	(6,840)
11 months to 31 May 2013	(36,300)

Overlap relief of £7,140 is available. Calculate the terminal loss and show how this would be relieved, assuming that Olive has investment income of £20,000 per annum and that no claims are made to set trading losses against total income.

***12.6** Craig began trading on 1 August 2010 and has the following results:

	Adjusted trading profits/(losses) before capital allowances	*Capital allowances claimed*
	£	£
year to 31 July 2011	5,460	1,140
year to 31 July 2012	(27,400)	1,920

Before commencing to trade, Craig had only investment income. He sold all of his investments in October 2011 (realising a large capital gain) so as to raise extra working capital for his own business. His income from investments in recent years has been:

	£
2008-09	4,150
2009-10	4,940
2010-11	3,190
2011-12 (to October 2011)	2,510

(a) Compute Craig's trading income for 2010-11 to 2012-13.

(b) Explain the trading loss reliefs available to Craig. Which would you recommend?

Chapter 13

Income from self-employment: Partnerships

Introduction

The purpose of this chapter is to explain the taxation treatment of individuals who are members of a partnership. Most of the information given in the previous four chapters with regard to the computation of trading profit, basis periods, capital allowances and trading loss reliefs is applicable to partners as well as to sole traders. The main new problem which arises when dealing with partnerships is the problem of calculating each partner's share of the partnership profit or loss for taxation purposes and much of this chapter is devoted to that problem.

Note that a Limited Liability Partnership (LLP) which is regulated by the Limited Liability Partnership Act 2000 and which carries on a trade or profession is generally dealt with for tax purposes as a partnership rather than as a company.

Principles of partnership taxation

Under the partnership tax rules, a partnership is not regarded as a separate entity for taxation purposes and the partnership itself is not charged to tax. Instead, the profits of the partnership are allocated between the partners and then each partner is taxed as an individual. In detail, the procedure for each tax year is as follows:

(a) The partnership submits a tax return to HMRC. This return provides information on the profit or loss for the period of account ending in the tax year and gives details of the profit-sharing agreement in force during that period. The return is also used to:

  (i) claim capital allowances for the period of account, both on partnership assets and on individual partners' assets

  (ii) claim relief for any business expenses incurred by partners personally.

(b) The adjusted trading profit or loss of the partnership is calculated in the usual manner. Any drawings or other appropriations of profit made by the partners are disallowed. Capital allowances on partnership assets are treated as a trading expense.

(c) The adjusted trading profit or loss is then allocated between the partners according to the profit-sharing agreement in force during the period of account. If the agreement changes during the period of account, it is necessary to time-apportion the profit or loss, applying the old agreement to the pre-change profit or loss and the new agreement to the post-change profit or loss.

(d) Any capital allowances claimed on an individual partner's assets and any expenses incurred personally by a partner are deducted from the relevant partner's share of the adjusted trading profit or added to that partner's share of the adjusted trading loss.

(e) Partners are then assessed to tax individually, as if each partner's share of the partnership's trading profit or loss had arisen from a trade carried on by that partner alone. In effect, each partner is treated as a sole trader who:

    (i) begins trading when joining the partnership
    (ii) has the same periods of account as the partnership (except that a partner who joins or leaves the partnership part-way through a period of account will have an individual period of account which begins or ends part-way through a partnership period of account)
    (iii) ceases trading when leaving the partnership.

(f) Each partner is solely responsible for the tax due on his or her share of the partnership profit. Partners must include their share of the partnership profit or loss in their own tax returns and in their self-assessment calculations.

EXAMPLE 1

Tom, Dick and Harry begin trading as a partnership on 1 January 2011, sharing profits in the ratio 3:2:1. With effect from 1 January 2012, they agree that Harry should receive a salary of £20,000 per annum, that partners should be entitled to 4% per annum interest on capital and that remaining profits should be shared in the ratio 5:3:2. The adjusted trading profits of the partnership are:

	£
y/e 31 December 2011	90,000
y/e 31 December 2012	110,000

Fixed capitals are Tom £50,000, Dick £60,000, Harry £80,000. Compute each partner's trading income for 2010-11, 2011-12 and 2012-13.

Solution

The allocation of trading profit for each period of account is:

	Tom	*Dick*	*Harry*	*Total*
	£	£	£	£
y/e 31/12/11				
Profit (shared 3:2:1)	45,000	30,000	15,000	90,000
y/e 31/12/12				
Salary	-	-	20,000	20,000
Interest on capital	2,000	2,400	3,200	7,600
Remainder of profit (shared 5:3:2)	41,200	24,720	16,480	82,400
	43,200	27,120	39,680	110,000

Each partner is treated as a sole trader, commencing trade on 1 January 2011, making up accounts to 31 December and with trading profits for the first two accounting years as shown above. The trading income of each partner is:

Tom

Year	*Basis period*	*Workings*	*Trading income*
			£
2010-11	1/1/11 to 5/4/11	£45,000 x 3/12	11,250
2011-12	y/e 31/12/11		45,000
2012-13	y/e 31/12/12		43,200

Dick

Year	*Basis period*	*Workings*	*Trading income*
			£
2010-11	1/1/11 to 5/4/11	£30,000 x 3/12	7,500
2011-12	y/e 31/12/11		30,000
2012-13	y/e 31/12/12		27,120

Harry

Year	*Basis period*	*Workings*	*Trading income*
			£
2010-11	1/1/11 to 5/4/11	£15,000 x 3/12	3,750
2011-12	y/e 31/12/11		15,000
2011-13	y/e 31/12/12		39,680

Note:

In each case, the overlap period is from 1 January 2011 to 5 April 2011. Overlap profits are Tom £11,250, Dick £7,500 and Harry £3,750. These overlap profits will be relieved when the relevant partner leaves the partnership (or on a change of accounting date).

Notional profits and losses

Occasionally, the effect of taking into account partners' salaries and/or interest on capital is to allocate a trading loss to an individual partner, even though the partnership as a whole has made a trading profit. In these circumstances, that partner's share of the trading profit is set to £nil and then his or her "notional loss" is allocated between the remaining partners in proportion to their original profit allocations.

A similar procedure is followed if a partner is allocated a "notional profit" in a year in which the partnership as a whole has sustained a trading loss.

EXAMPLE 2

(a) Lock, Stock and Barrel are in partnership, making up accounts to 30 June each year. Their profit-sharing agreement specifies that Lock and Barrel should receive annual salaries of £20,000 and £24,000 respectively and that remaining profits or losses should be divided equally. The partnership has an adjusted trading profit of £26,000 in the year to 30 June 2012. Show how this will be allocated between the partners.

(b) Rod, Pole and Perch are in partnership, also making up accounts to 30 June each year. Their profit-sharing agreement specifies that Perch should receive an annual salary of £25,000 and that remaining profits or losses should be shared in the ratio 3:2:1. The partnership has an adjusted trading loss of £5,000 in the year to 30 June 2012. Show how this will be allocated between the partners.

Solution

(a)

	Lock	*Stock*	*Barrel*	*Total*
	£	£	£	£
Salaries	20,000	-	24,000	44,000
Remainder (£26,000 – £44,000)	(6,000)	(6,000)	(6,000)	(18,000)
	14,000	(6,000)	18,000	26,000
Stock's notional loss divided in the ratio 14,000:18,000	(2,625)	6,000	(3,375)	-
Allocation of trading profit	11,375	-	14,625	26,000

(b)

	Rod	*Pole*	*Perch*	*Total*
	£	£	£	£
Salaries	-	-	25,000	25,000
Remainder (£5,000 + £25,000)	(15,000)	(10,000)	(5,000)	(30,000)
	(15,000)	(10,000)	20,000	(5,000)
Perch's notional profit divided 15,000:10,000	12,000	8,000	(20,000)	-
Allocation of trading loss	(3,000)	(2,000)	-	(5,000)

Change in partnership composition

A change in partnership composition occurs if a new partner joins a partnership (or joins a sole trader to form a partnership) or if an existing partner dies or leaves the partnership. A change in composition has no tax effect on those persons who:

(a) were carrying on the trade beforehand (either alone or in partnership), and
(b) continue to carry on the trade after the change (either alone or in partnership).

Such persons are taxed on the current year basis as if the change had not taken place. But new partners have commenced trading and are subject to the commencement rules, whilst leaving partners have ceased trading and are subject to the cessation rules.

EXAMPLE 3

Red and White begin trading as a partnership on 1 October 2009, sharing profits equally. On 1 January 2011, they agree to admit Blue as a partner and to share profits in the ratio 3:2:1. The adjusted trading profits of the partnership are:

	£
y/e 30 September 2010	105,000
y/e 30 September 2011	120,000
y/e 30 September 2012	135,000

Compute each partner's trading income for the years 2009-10 through to 2012-13.

Solution

The allocation of trading profit for each period of account is:

	Red	*White*	*Blue*	*Total*
	£	£	£	£
y/e 30/9/10 (shared equally)	52,500	52,500	-	105,000
y/e 30/9/11				
1/10/10 - 31/12/10				
£120,000 x 3/12 (shared equally)	15,000	15,000	-	30,000
1/1/11 - 30/9/11				
£120,000 x 9/12 (shared 3:2:1)	45,000	30,000	15,000	90,000
	60,000	45,000	15,000	120,000
y/e 30/9/12 (shared 3:2:1)	67,500	45,000	22,500	135,000

For tax purposes, each partner is now treated as a sole trader and is assessed on his or her share of the partnership trading profit. The position of each partner is as follows:

(a) Red began trading on 1 October 2009, preparing accounts to 30 September. Each period of account is of 12 months' duration. Profits are £52,500 for the year to 30 September 2010, £60,000 for the year to 30 September 2011 and £67,500 for the year to 30 September 2012.

(b) White began trading on 1 October 2009, preparing accounts to 30 September. Each period of account is of 12 months' duration. Profits are £52,500 for the year to 30 September 2010, £45,000 for the year to 30 September 2011 and £45,000 for the year to 30 September 2012.

(c) Blue began trading on 1 January 2011, preparing accounts to 30 September. The first accounts cover the nine-month period from 1 January 2011 to 30 September 2011 with profits of £15,000. Profits are £22,500 for the year to 30 September 2012.

Each partner's trading income is as follows:

Red

Year	*Basis period*	*Workings*	*Trading income*
			£
2009-10	1/10/09 to 5/4/10	£52,500 x 6/12	26,250
2010-11	y/e 30/9/10		52,500
2011-12	y/e 30/9/11		60,000
2012-13	y/e 30/9/12		67,500

White

Year	*Basis period*	*Workings*	*Trading income*
			£
2009-10	1/10/09 to 5/4/10	£52,500 x 6/12	26,250
2010-11	y/e 30/9/10		52,500
2011-12	y/e 30/9/11		45,000
2012-13	y/e 30/9/12		45,000

Blue

Year	*Basis period*	*Workings*	*Trading income*
			£
2010-11	1/1/11 to 5/4/11	£15,000 x 3/9	5,000
2011-12	1/1/11 to 31/12/11	£15,000 + 3/12 x £22,500	20,625
2012-13	y/e 30/9/12		22,500

Note:

In the case of Red and White, the overlap period is from 1 October 2009 to 5 April 2010 and each partner has overlap profits of £26,250. In the case of Blue, there is an overlap period from 1 January 2011 to 5 April 2011 and another overlap period from 1 October 2011 to 31 December 2011. Overlap profits are £5,000 + (£22,500 x 3/12) = £10,625.

Non-trading income

A partnership which has trading income may also have non-trading income. For partnership tax purposes, non-trading income falls into two categories:

(a) **Taxed income**

For this purpose, "taxed income" is defined as income from which tax has been deducted at source (e.g. most interest) and dividends which have an attached tax credit. The amount of any taxed income arising in a period of account is divided between the partners in profit-sharing ratio and then each partner's share is apportioned between tax years and assessed to tax on the actual basis.

It is acceptable to allocate taxed income between tax years on the receipts basis if this would be more appropriate than time-apportionment.

(b) **Untaxed income**

For this purpose, "untaxed income" is defined as non-trading income which is not taxed income (e.g. income from property or interest received gross). The amount of any untaxed income arising in a period of account is allocated between the partners in profit-sharing ratio and is then assessed to tax using *the same basis periods as those used for the trading income*. The basis periods that would normally be applied if the income were received by an individual rather than a partnership are totally ignored. If this treatment results in non-trading income being taxed twice when a partner starts trading, overlap relief is available.

If a partnership does not carry on a trade or profession, the treatment described at (a) above applies to *all* of the partnership's non-trading income.

EXAMPLE 4

Hook, Line and Sinker begin trading as a partnership on 1 July 2010, sharing profits equally. The chosen accounting date is 30 June and the first accounts are made up for the year to 30 June 2011. In addition to its trading income, the partnership has non-trading income as follows:

	y/e 30/6/11	*y/e 30/6/12*
	£	£
Income from property	7,500	9,000
Net bank interest	2,400	3,600

(a) Compute each partner's income from property for tax years 2010-11, 2011-12 and 2012-13.

(b) Compute the gross amount of bank interest on which each partner is taxed in tax years 2010-11 and 2011-12.

Solution

(a) Each partner is allocated property income of £2,500 in the year to 30 June 2011 and £3,000 in the year to 30 June 2012. Property income per partner for each tax year is as follows:

Year	*Basis period*	*Workings*	*Property income* £
2010-11	1/7/10 to 5/4/11	£2,500 x 9/12	1,875
2011-12	y/e 30/6/11		2,500
2012-13	y/e 30/6/12		3,000

Each partner is entitled to overlap relief of £1,875.

(b) Each partner is allocated net bank interest of £800 in the year to 30 June 2011 and £1,200 in the year to 30 June 2012. When grossed-up at 100/80, these figures become £1,000 and £1,500 respectively. Therefore the gross amount of bank interest on which each partner is taxed (assuming time-apportionment between the tax years) is as follows:

Year	*Workings*	*Savings income* £
2010-11	£1,000 x 9/12	750
2011-12	(£1,000 x 3/12) + (£1,500 x 9/12)	1,375

The remaining 3/12ths of the bank interest received during the year to 30 June 2012 will be taxed in 2012-13, along with the first 9/12ths of any bank interest received in the year to 30 June 2013.

Trading losses

As explained above, a trading loss is allocated between the partners in the same way as a trading profit. In general, each partner is then entitled to precisely the same loss reliefs as a sole trader (see Chapter 12) with regard to his or her share of the loss.

EXAMPLE 5

Game, Set and Match begin trading in partnership on 1 August 2010, preparing accounts to 31 January each year and sharing profits equally. With effect from 1 March 2011, they agree to share profits in the ratio 1:2:2. The adjusted trading profits/(losses) of the partnership are as follows:

	£
period to 31 January 2011	43,050
y/e 31 January 2012	21,600
y/e 31 January 2013	(7,420)

Compute each partner's trading income for tax years 2010-11, 2011-12 and 2012-13 and explain how the trading loss incurred in the year to 31 January 2013 will be treated.

Solution

The allocation of trading profit or loss for each period of account is:

	Game	*Set*	*Match*	*Total*
	£	£	£	£
period to 31/1/11 (shared equally)	14,350	14,350	14,350	43,050
y/e 31/1/12				
1/2/11 - 28/2/11				
£21,600 x 1/12 (shared equally)	600	600	600	1,800
1/3/11 - 31/1/12				
£21,600 x 11/12 (shared 1:2:2)	3,960	7,920	7,920	19,800
	4,560	8,520	8,520	21,600
y/e 31/1/13 (shared 1:2:2)	(1,484)	(2,968)	(2,968)	(7,420)

Each partner's trading income is as follows:

Game

Year	*Basis period*	*Workings*	*Trading income*
			£
2010-11	1/8/10 to 5/4/11	£14,350 + 2/12 x £4,560	15,110
2011-12	y/e 31/1/12		4,560
2012-13	y/e 31/1/13		nil

Set

Year	*Basis period*	*Workings*	*Trading income*
			£
2010-11	1/8/10 to 5/4/11	£14,350 + 2/12 x £8,520	15,770
2011-12	y/e 31/1/12		8,520
2012-13	y/e 31/1/13		nil

Match

Year	*Basis period*	*Workings*	*Trading income*
			£
2010-11	1/8/10 to 5/4/11	£14,350 + 2/12 x £8,520	15,770
2011-12	y/e 31/1/12		8,520
2012-13	y/e 31/1/13		nil

Notes:

(i) The basis period for 2010-11 for each partner includes two months out of the year to 31 January 2012. The profit for these two months is calculated by taking 2/12ths of the partner's profit for that year. In the case of Game (for example) it would be wrong to take £600 + (1/11 x £3,960) as the profit of the period from 1/2/11 to 5/4/11.

(ii) Each partner has overlap profits, calculated in the usual way.

(iii) Each partner may choose individually how to relieve his or her share of the trading loss incurred in the basis period for 2012-13. Possibilities include carrying the loss forward against future trading profits, loss relief against total income or an early trade losses claim.

Treatment of certain interest as a loss

As explained in Chapter 4, certain types of loan interest are deductible from a partner's total income when computing his or her net income. The eligible loans are:

(a) a loan to purchase plant or machinery for use in the business of a partnership

(b) a loan to purchase an interest in a partnership.

If a partner's total income is insufficient to deduct such loan interest in full, the excess interest may be treated as a trading loss for the purposes of carry-forward trade loss relief and terminal trade loss relief (see Chapter 12).

Restrictions on trade loss relief for certain partners

Income Tax Act 2007 contains anti-avoidance rules which restrict the amount of tax relief that may be given for trading losses incurred by partners. These rules restrict the amount of sideways relief and capital gains relief that may be claimed by partners. As explained in Chapter 12, the term "sideways relief" refers to the relief of trade losses against total income, including early trade losses relief. The main restrictions are as follows:

(a) A limited partner or a member of an LLP is denied sideways relief or capital gains relief for a trading loss incurred in a tax year to the extent that the loss exceeds the partner's "contribution to the firm" as measured at the end of the basis period for that year. For this purpose, a partner's "contribution" is broadly equal to the amount of capital which the partner has contributed to the partnership, plus any share of profits that have not been withdrawn.

(b) Similarly, a "non-active" partner (one who is not personally engaged in the activities of the trade for at least ten hours per week) is denied sideways relief or capital gains relief for a trading loss incurred in an "early tax year", to the extent that it exceeds his or her contribution to the firm. For this purpose, an early tax year is defined as the tax year in which the partner began trading or one of the next three tax years.

(c) Furthermore, the total amount of sideways relief and capital gains relief given in relation to trading losses incurred by a limited partner or non-active partner is capped at £25,000 per tax year.

(d) Finally, trading losses incurred by any partner may not be set against total income or capital gains if the losses arise in consequence of tax avoidance arrangements.

Note that the restrictions on sideways relief do *not* restrict the extent to which a trading loss may be relieved against the partner's profits from the loss-making trade. For example, if a trading loss is relieved against total income of the previous tax year, there is no restriction on the amount of the loss which may be set against the partner's trading profit from the partnership in that year. The aim of the anti-avoidance rules is to restrict the extent to which losses may be relieved against other forms of income.

Summary

- Under the partnership tax rules, each partner is taxed individually on his or her share of the partnership profit and each partner is solely responsible for his or her own tax liability.
- The adjusted trading profit of a partnership is allocated between the partners in accordance with the profit-sharing agreement for the period of account in which the profit arises. Notional profits and losses allocated to a partner are redistributed among the remaining partners.
- In effect, each partner is treated as a sole trader who begins trading when joining the partnership, has the same accounting dates as the partnership and ceases trading when leaving the partnership.
- The tax treatment of the non-trading income of a partnership depends upon whether the income ranks as taxed income or untaxed income and whether or not the partnership also has trading income.
- The trading losses of a partnership are allocated between the partners in the same way as trading profits. Each partner may then choose individually how to relieve his or her share of the loss.

Exercises

13.1 Nickleby, Copperfield and Drood have traded as equal partners for many years, making up accounts to 31 December each year. As from 1 April 2012 they agree to share profits in the ratio 1:2:2. The adjusted trading profit for the year to 31 December 2012 is £183,000. Show how this profit is allocated between the partners.

13.2 Pickwick, Snodgrass and Tupman are in partnership, making up accounts to 31 March annually. Each partner receives 6% interest on fixed capital. Pickwick and Tupman are entitled to annual salaries of £40,000 and £30,000 respectively. Remaining profits or losses are divided equally. Fixed capitals are Pickwick £60,000, Snodgrass £100,000 and Tupman £50,000. The adjusted trading profit for the year to 31 March 2013 is £62,500. Show how this profit is allocated between the partners.

13.3 Dodson and Fogg began trading in equal partnership on 1 July 2009. On 1 July 2010, they admitted Jackson as a partner and agreed to share profits in the ratio 5:4:1. The adjusted trading profits of the partnership are:

	£
year to 30 June 2010	68,000
year to 30 June 2011	88,000
year to 30 June 2012	116,000

Compute each partner's trading income for 2009-10 through to 2012-13.

13.4 Wardle, Jingle and Trotter began trading on 1 October 2010, preparing accounts to 30 September each year and sharing profits in the ratio 7:2:1. Results for the first two years of trading are as follows:

	y/e 30/9/11	*y/e 30/9/12*
	£	£
Trading profit	117,460	136,540
Interest received gross	2,000	2,200
Interest received net (net amount received)	992	1,088

(a) Compute each partner's trading income for 2010-11, 2011-12 and 2012-13.

(b) Compute each partner's interest received gross for 2010-11, 2011-12 and 2012-13.

(c) Compute the gross amount of taxed interest on which each partner is charged to tax in 2011-12.

***13.5** Cluppins and Raddle form a partnership on 1 November 2008, preparing accounts to 31 May each year. Bardell is admitted as a partner on 1 January 2010. Cluppins leaves the partnership on 28 February 2011 and Winkle is admitted as a partner on 1 March 2011.

Profits and losses are shared as follows:

Cluppins and Raddle	1:2
Cluppins, Raddle and Bardell	7:8:5
Raddle, Bardell and Winkle	4:3:1

Adjusted trading profits are:

	£
1 November 2008 to 31 May 2009	60,000
year to 31 May 2010	120,000
year to 31 May 2011	30,000
year to 31 May 2012	80,000

Calculate each partner's trading income for 2008-09 through to 2012-13, identifying any overlap periods and profits.

Chapter 14

Pension contributions

Introduction

The most tax-efficient way of providing for a pension is to make contributions into a registered pension scheme. This might be an occupational pension scheme sponsored by an employer, a public service pension scheme established by the Government or a personal pension scheme taken out with a bank or insurance company. The main purpose of this chapter is to explain the tax reliefs which are available in relation to contributions made into registered pension schemes.

Registered pension schemes

The tax regime which now applies to pension schemes has been in effect since 6 April 2006 and was established by Finance Act 2004. This Act defines a pension scheme as "*a scheme ... to provide benefits to or in respect of persons -*

(a) on retirement,

(b) on death,

(c) on having reached a particular age,

(d) on the onset of serious ill-health or incapacity, or

(e) in similar circumstances."

A pension scheme may be either a "defined benefits" scheme or a "money purchase" scheme. In a defined benefits scheme, the benefits payable to a member are calculated by reference to earnings or length of service or some other such factor. An example of a defined benefits scheme is an occupational pension scheme in which an employee's pension rights are based upon his or her final salary. In a money purchase scheme, the benefits payable to a member are calculated by reference to the size of the pension fund built up during the member's working life.

Registration

A pension scheme which is registered with HMRC is known as a "registered pension scheme" and qualifies for various tax reliefs and exemptions. An application to register a pension scheme may be made if the scheme satisfies certain conditions and is either:

(a) an occupational pension scheme, or

(b) a public service pension scheme, or

(c) a pension scheme established by an insurance company, bank or similar institution.

An occupational pension scheme is one established by an employer or employers so as to provide benefits to employees. A public service pension scheme is (broadly) one established by the Government. The tax advantages of registration include:

(a) The scheme's investment income is exempt from income tax. Any capital gains made on the disposal of scheme investments are exempt from capital gains tax.

(b) Contributions made by scheme members attract tax relief (see below).

(c) Contributions made by employers attract tax relief (see below).

(d) Although pensions are chargeable to income tax, lump sums paid to scheme members by registered pension schemes are generally exempt from income tax, subject to the operation of the "lifetime allowance" (see below).

Except on ill-health grounds, a registered pension scheme must not allow members to take any pension benefits until they reach normal minimum pension age. This rose from 50 to 55 as from 6 April 2010. However, there is no requirement that members should actually retire before benefits are taken. Therefore, a member of an occupational pension scheme could draw a pension from his or her employer's scheme whilst continuing to work for that employer. Pension benefits must normally begin by the age of 75.

Unregistered pension schemes

A registered pension scheme must comply with many regulations with regard to its investments, the payments it makes to its members and a number of other matters. A pension scheme which does not wish to register is under no compulsion to do so and therefore these regulations can be avoided. However, unregistered schemes do not qualify for any of the tax reliefs and exemptions enjoyed by registered schemes.

National Employment Savings Trust (NEST)

The National Employment Savings Trust (NEST) is a state-sponsored pension scheme which is intended to act as a default scheme for those employees whose employers do not offer an occupational scheme. For taxation purposes, NEST is treated as an occupational pension scheme and can therefore register with HMRC.

Tax relief for contributions by scheme members

An individual may belong to as many pension schemes as he or she wishes and may make unlimited pension contributions. However, there are limits on the amount of contributions which can attract tax relief.

To be eligible for tax relief, an individual's contributions must be "relievable pension contributions" made into a registered pension scheme and the individual must be a "relevant UK individual" who is an "active member" of that scheme. Note that:

(a) Relievable pension contributions are contributions paid by the scheme member or by a third party on his or her behalf, excluding contributions made after the age of 75 and excluding employer contributions.

(b) An individual is a relevant UK individual for a tax year if *at least one* of a number of conditions is satisfied. The main conditions are that:

  (i) the individual has UK earnings that are chargeable to income tax for the year (i.e. income from employment or self-employment)

  (ii) the individual is resident in the UK at some time during the year.

  Income derived from the commercial letting of furnished holiday accommodation ranks as self-employment income for this purpose (see Chapter 5).

(c) An active member of a registered pension scheme is an individual who is accruing benefits under that scheme.

Tax relief can be claimed for a contribution only in the tax year in which payment is made. There are no provisions for carrying contributions back to previous tax years or forward to subsequent tax years.

Limit on tax relief

The maximum amount of pension contributions on which an individual can claim tax relief in any tax year is the *greater* of:

(a) 100% of the amount of the individual's UK earnings for the year that are chargeable to income tax

(b) the "basic amount", which is currently set at £3,600 (gross).

If an individual's earnings for a tax year are less than the basic amount, tax relief on the amount of any contributions beyond the level of earnings and up to the basic amount is available only if these contributions are made to a pension scheme which operates tax relief at source (see below).

EXAMPLE 1

Gordon is self-employed and a member of a registered pension scheme. His trading income for tax year 2011-12 is £31,600 but this falls to only £2,500 in 2012-13.

(a) How much may Gordon contribute to his pension scheme in each year ?

(b) How much of these contributions would attract tax relief?

Solution

(a) Gordon may make unlimited contributions to his pension scheme in both years.

(b) He may claim tax relief on contributions of up to £31,600 in 2011-12 and £3,600 in 2012-13 (assuming that the pension scheme operates tax relief at source).

Refund of excess contributions

If an individual makes pension contributions in a tax year which exceed the maximum amount on which tax relief can be claimed, then the excess contributions may be refunded (if the individual so wishes). Such a refund of pension contributions is known as a "refund of excess contributions lump sum".

A refund of excess contributions lump sum is not subject to income tax. This reflects the fact that the contributions which are being refunded by the pension scheme did not attract tax relief in the first place.

Methods of giving tax relief

There are three methods by means of which tax relief is given on member's pension contributions. The method adopted in any particular case will depend upon the type of pension scheme concerned and cannot be chosen by the member. The three methods of giving tax relief are as follows:

(a) **Relief at source**. If relief at source applies, the member's pension contributions are paid net of basic rate tax (20%) and the pension scheme administrator recovers the tax deducted at source from HMRC. Also, the member's basic rate limit and higher rate limit are both increased by the gross amount of the contributions, so ensuring that relief at the higher rate or additional rate is automatically given to higher rate and additional rate taxpayers. This is similar to the way in which higher and additional rate relief is given on Gift Aid donations (see Chapter 4). Another similarity with Gift Aid donations is that the member's "adjusted net income" (see Chapter 3) is reduced by the gross amount of the contributions.

If a scheme member makes pension contributions in excess of the maximum amount on which tax relief can be claimed (see above) and relief at source applies, the excess net contributions are treated as if they were actually gross contributions on which no tax relief is available.

(b) **Net pay arrangements**. The net pay arrangement applies if an employer deducts an employee's contributions to an occupational pension scheme from the employee's pay before operating the PAYE system. This automatically gives tax relief at the employee's marginal rate of income tax.

(c) **Relief on making a claim**. If it is not possible to use relief at source or the net pay arrangement, tax relief on a member's pension contributions is given by deducting those contributions from total income when computing the member's income tax liability for the year. This might apply (for example) in the case of contributions to a retirement annuity contract. Retirement annuity contracts were at one time an important means of providing for a pension but it has not been possible to take out a new retirement annuity contract since 30 June 1988. However, contributions may still be made in relation to contracts which were in existence at that date and retirement annuity contracts which have now become registered pension schemes are not obliged to operate relief at source.

EXAMPLE 2

(a) Wesley has no income for tax purposes in 2012-13. He belongs to a registered pension scheme which operates relief at source and he makes pension contributions during 2012-13 which are all eligible for tax relief. Compute the maximum amount of his net contributions in the year.

(b) Alana is self-employed. She has trading income of £62,000 in 2012-13 and no other income. She belongs to a registered pension scheme which operates relief at source and she makes contributions of £500 per month (gross) to this scheme in 2012-13. Explain how tax relief will be given in relation to these contributions.

(c) Bruce is self-employed and a member of a registered pension scheme to which he pays net contributions of £320 per month. His trading income for 2012-13 is £2,750 and he has no other earnings. Explain the tax treatment of his pension contributions for the year.

(d) Charlotte is employed at an annual salary of £24,000. She pays 7% of her salary each month into her employer's occupational pension scheme (which is a registered scheme). Explain how tax relief will be given in relation to her pension contributions.

Solution

(a) Gross contributions of up to £3,600 are eligible for tax relief in the year. Deducting basic rate (20%) tax relief at source gives maximum net contributions in the year of £2,880. Wesley is entitled to basic rate tax relief on these contributions even though he is a non-taxpayer.

(b) Alana pays net contributions of £400 per month (80% of £500). Her basic rate band will be extended by £6,000 (12 x £500) so she will pay higher rate tax on the excess of her taxable income over £40,370 (£34,370 + £6,000).

(c) Bruce is entitled to tax relief in 2012-13 on contributions of up to £3,600 (the greater of £2,750 and £3,600). Maximum net contributions are £2,880 (80% of £3,600). He has made payments totalling £3,840 (12 x £320) so excess contributions are £960. He will be treated as though he had made gross contributions of £4,560 (£3,600 + £960) with basic rate tax of £720 (20% of £3,600) deducted at source. This gives net contributions of £3,840. His pension scheme will recover £720 from HMRC.

(d) Charlotte earns £2,000 per month and makes monthly pension contributions of £140 (7% of £2,000). Her employer will deduct these contributions from her salary before operating the PAYE system, so she will pay income tax on only £1,860 per month.

Tax relief for contributions by employers

In general, contributions made by an employer into a registered pension scheme are deductible when computing the employer's trading profit for tax purposes. This is subject to the overriding condition that the contributions must be made wholly and exclusively for trade purposes. Note the following points:

(a) The amount of contributions which may be deducted when computing the trading profit for a period of account is usually the amount of the contributions *actually paid* by the employer in that period. However, "spreading" provisions may apply to especially large contributions (see below).

(b) There is no upper limit on the amount of contributions which may be deducted when computing an employer's trading profits. This is in contrast to the situation with regard to an individual's own contributions, which are subject to a limit on the amount which may attract tax relief in each tax year (see above).

(c) Contributions made by an employer in respect of an employee are disregarded when computing the *employee's* income for tax purposes.

Spreading of relief

If there is an unusually large increase in an employer's pension contributions between one period of account and the next, tax relief on excess contributions may be spread over a number of periods. Assuming that the current period and the previous period are of equal length, the required procedure is as follows:

(a) The contributions made by the employer in the current period are compared with those for the previous period. Certain contributions made in the current period are disregarded when making this comparison (e.g. contributions paid into the scheme so as to fund cost-of-living increases in current pensions).

(b) If the amount of contributions in the current period is more than 210% of the amount for the previous period, then there is an excess and this may need to be spread.

(c) The amount of the excess is calculated as the contributions made in the current period less 110% of the contributions made in the previous period. Spreading does not apply if this amount is less than £500,000. Otherwise, tax relief on the excess contributions is spread as follows:

Amount of the excess	*Tax relief spread equally over*
£500,000 to £999,999	current period and next period
£1,000,000 to £1,999,999	current period and next two periods
£2,000,000 or more	current period and next three periods

A further adjustment is required if the current period and previous period are of unequal length. Spreading does not apply if the employer made no contributions at all in the previous period (e.g. if a new scheme has been established in the current period).

EXAMPLE 3

During the year to 31 May 2012, an employer made contributions of £400,000 into a registered pension scheme. Explain how tax relief will be given on the contributions made during the year to 31 May 2013 if the amount of these contributions is:

(a) £800,000 (b) £920,000 (c) £1,000,000 (d) £2,640,000

Solution

(a) The current year contributions are 200% of those for the previous year. This does not exceed 210% so spreading does not apply. Tax relief on contributions of £800,000 will be given in the year to 31 May 2013.

(b) Current year contributions are 230% of those for the previous year but the excess of current year contributions over 110% of previous year contributions is only £480,000. This is less than £500,000 so spreading does not apply. Tax relief on contributions of £920,000 will be given in the year to 31 May 2013.

(c) Current year contributions are 250% of those for the previous year. The excess of current year contributions over 110% of previous year contributions is £560,000. This is between £500,000 and £999,999 so the excess must be spread equally over the current period and the next period.

Tax relief on contributions of £720,000 (£440,000 + £280,000) will be given in the year to 31 May 2013 and tax relief on the remaining £280,000 of contributions will be given in the year to 31 May 2014.

(d) Current year contributions are 660% of those for the previous year. The excess of current year contributions over 110% of previous year contributions is £2,200,000. This exceeds £2,000,000 so the excess must be spread equally over the current period and the next three periods.

Tax relief on contributions of £990,000 (£440,000 + £550,000) will be given in the year to 31 May 2013. Relief on contributions of £550,000 will be given in each of the three years to 31 May 2014, 2015 and 2016.

Annual allowance charge

If an individual is a member of one or more registered pension schemes, an income tax charge (the "annual allowance charge") arises if the "total pension input amount" for that individual in a tax year exceeds the annual allowance for the year. The annual allowance for tax year 2012-13 is £50,000. The annual allowance was also £50,000 in 2011-12, but was substantially higher in previous years.

If an individual's total pension input amount for a tax year exceeds the annual allowance for the year, the excess is charged to income tax at marginal rate (i.e. as if the amount of the excess were an additional slice of income on top of the individual's income from all other sources). This tax charge falls upon the individual concerned.

Pension input amount

An individual's total pension input amount for a tax year is found by calculating the pension input amount for each registered pension scheme to which the individual belongs and then aggregating these figures. The method of calculating pension input amount in relation to a pension scheme depends upon whether the scheme in question is a money purchase scheme or a defined benefits scheme. The rules are as follows:

(a) **Money purchase schemes**. Pension input amount for an individual for a tax year in relation to a money purchase scheme is equal to the total relievable contributions made by or in respect of that individual during the "pension input period" which ends during the tax year, together with any employer contributions.

(b) **Defined benefits schemes**. Pension input amount for an individual for a tax year in relation to a defined benefits scheme is equal to the increase in the value of the individual's pension rights under the scheme during the pension input period which ends during the tax year. For this purpose, the value of an individual's pension rights on a specified date is equal to:

   (i) the amount of any lump sum which would be payable to the individual if he or she became entitled to payment of it on that date, plus

   (ii) 16 times the amount of the annual pension which would be payable to the individual if he or she became entitled to payment of it on that date.

   Before calculating the increase in value of an individual's pension rights under a defined benefits scheme, the value of those rights at the start of the pension input period are adjusted for inflation. This adjustment reflects the annual increase in the Consumer Prices Index up to the September prior to the start of the tax year for which the calculation is being done.

There is no pension input amount for a tax year in respect of a pension scheme if the individual becomes entitled before the end of that year to all of the benefits which may be provided under the scheme. Nor is there any pension input amount for a tax year if the individual dies before the tax year ends.

Pension input periods

In general, the first pension input period for an individual in relation to a pension scheme begins on the date that the individual joins the scheme and ends on the first anniversary of that date. However, this period could end earlier (e.g. on the date up to which the pension scheme draws up its accounts) if this is thought to be more convenient. Each subsequent period then lasts for a year, except that the final period ends when the individual has become entitled to all of the benefits which may be provided under the scheme.

Carry forward of unused annual allowance

If an individual's pension input amount for a tax year is less than the annual allowance for that year, the individual has "unused annual allowance". As from tax year 2011-12, the available annual allowance for the current tax year is automatically increased by any unused annual allowance brought forward from the previous three years, so making it less likely that an annual allowance charge will apply. Note the following points:

(a) The individual must have been a member of a registered pension scheme during a tax year in order to carry forward unused annual allowance from that year.

(b) The current tax year's annual allowance must be set first against the total pension input amount for that year. Unused annual allowance from the three previous tax years may then be taken into account, beginning with the earliest of those years. For instance, an individual whose pension input amount for tax year 2012-13 exceeds the £50,000 annual allowance for that year may use unused annual allowance brought forward from 2009-10, 2010-11 and 2011-12, in that order.

(c) When determining whether or not there is any unused annual allowance in the three previous tax years, the annual allowance for each of those years is deemed to have been only £50,000, even though the actual annual allowance in some of those years may in fact have been considerably higher.

(d) The calculation of the amount of unused annual allowance from the previous three tax years that may be carried forward to the current year takes into account the fact that any unused annual allowance in those years may have been "used up" in any intervening tax year in which pension input amount has exceeded £50,000.

EXAMPLE 4

Calculate the annual allowance available in 2015-16 to an individual whose total pension input amounts for the three previous tax years are as follows:

2012-13 £35,000 2013-14 £72,000 2014-15 £41,000

Assume that the annual allowance is normally £50,000 in all tax years and that there is no unused annual allowance to bring forward from previous years.

Solution

Unused annual allowance is £15,000 in 2012-13 and £9,000 in 2014-15. But the pension input amount for 2013-14 exceeds the annual allowance by £22,000 and this uses up the £15,000 brought forward from the previous year. Therefore the available annual allowance for 2015-16 is £59,000 (current year £50,000 plus £9,000 brought forward from 2014-15).

EXAMPLE 5

Diane is a member of three registered pension schemes. Her pension input amounts for the two most recent pension input periods for each of these schemes are as follows:

Scheme A:
£92,000 (year to 30 June 2012) £95,000 (year to 30 June 2013)
Scheme B:
£71,000 (year to 5 April 2012) £86,000 (year to 5 April 2013)
Scheme C:
£98,000 (year to 30 April 2012) £65,000 (year to 30 April 2013)

Compute the annual allowance charge payable by Diane for tax year 2012-13, assuming that there is no unused annual allowance brought forward from the previous three years and that Diane's marginal rate of income tax for 2012-13 is 50%.

Solution

The pension input periods which are relevant when computing total pension input amount for 2012-13 are those which end during 2012-13. Total pension input amount is therefore £276,000 (£92,000 + £86,000 + £98,000). This exceeds the 2012-13 annual allowance of £50,000 by £226,000, so the annual allowance charge is £226,000 @ 50% = £113,000.

EXAMPLE 6

Compute the annual allowance charge payable by each of the following employees for tax year 2012-13, assuming in each case that the employee belongs to only one registered pension scheme and that there is no unused annual allowance brought forward. Assume that the Consumer Prices Index (CPI) rose by 3% in the year to September 2011.

(a) Jill belongs to a money purchase scheme. Her relievable contributions for the pension input period ending during 2012-13 are £40,000. Her employer's contributions on her behalf for the period are £70,000. Jill's marginal rate of tax for 2012-13 is 50%.

(b) Eric's scheme is a defined benefit scheme. When he retires he will receive an annual pension equal to 1/80th of his final salary for each year of pensionable service. He will also receive a lump sum equal to 3/80ths of final salary for each year of pensionable service. At the start of the pension input period ending during tax year 2012-13, Eric had completed 22 years of pensionable service and his salary was £72,000 per annum. His salary had risen to £76,000 by the end of the period. His marginal rate of tax for 2012-13 is 40%.

Solution

(a) Total pension input amount for the year is £110,000 and this exceeds the 2012-13 annual allowance by £60,000. Therefore the annual allowance charge payable by Jill for the year is £30,000 (£60,000 × 50%).

(b) If Eric became entitled to payment of his pension and lump sum at the start of the period, he would receive an annual pension of £19,800 (£72,000 x 22/80) and a lump sum of £59,400 (£72,000 x 66/80). The value of his pension rights at the start of the period is therefore £376,200 (£59,400 + (16 x £19,800)). Increasing this figure by 3% to reflect the change in CPI gives £387,486.

If Eric became entitled to payment of his pension and lump sum at the end of the period, he would receive an annual pension of £21,850 (£76,000 x 23/80) and a lump sum of £65,550 (£76,000 x 69/80). The value of his pension rights at the end of the period is therefore £415,150 (£65,550 + (16 x £21,850)).

Total pension input amount for the year is £27,664 (£415,150 – £387,486). This is less than the annual allowance of £50,000 for 2012-13 and therefore there is no annual allowance charge.

Lifetime allowance charge

There is no limit to the total level of benefits which an individual can receive from registered pension schemes during his or her lifetime. However, a charge to income tax known as the "lifetime allowance charge" will arise if total benefits exceed the lifetime allowance. Whenever pension benefits "crystallise" (e.g. when an individual starts taking a scheme pension) the value of the crystallised benefits is compared with the proportion of the lifetime allowance which remains unused. Any excess is chargeable to income tax. The lifetime allowance figures for tax years 2006-07 to 2012-13 are as follows:

2006-07	£1,500,000
2007-08	£1,600,000
2008-09	£1,650,000
2009-10	£1,750,000
2010-11	£1,800,000
2011-12	£1,800,000
2012-13	£1,500,000

Any excess of crystallised benefits over the available lifetime allowance is taxed at 55% if taken as a lump sum and at 25% otherwise. This tax charge falls jointly upon the individual and the scheme administrator. In practice, the tax will usually be paid by the scheme administrator and then deducted from the benefits paid to the individual.

Operation of the lifetime allowance

Whenever a "benefit crystallisation event" occurs, it is necessary to compare the value of the benefits that have crystallised with the proportion of the individual's lifetime allowance which remains unused after any previous such events. The main examples of a benefit crystallisation event are the payment of a lump sum and the commencement of a pension. Note the following points:

(a) The value of a lump sum is the amount paid to the scheme member. The value of a pension is generally equal to 20 times the amount of the pension which will be paid to the member during the first twelve months.

(b) On the first occasion that a benefit crystallisation event occurs, the value of the benefits that have crystallised is compared with the lifetime allowance as it stands on the date of the event. On a subsequent event, the value of the crystallised benefits is compared with the *proportion* of the lifetime allowance (if any) that remains after previous events. However, this proportion is applied to the lifetime allowance as it stands on the date of the subsequent event.

(c) If an individual becomes entitled to a scheme pension and a pension commencement lump sum from the same scheme on the same date, the payment of the lump sum is considered to be the earlier of the two events. This minimises the lifetime allowance charge, since the lifetime allowance is made available first to the lump sum (which would otherwise be taxed at 55%) rather than the pension.

EXAMPLE 7

Sharon is a member of two registered pension schemes. She receives no benefits from either of these schemes until 19 March 2008, when she takes a lump sum of £960,000 from one of her schemes. On 5 January 2013 she takes a lump sum of £710,000 from her other scheme. Calculate the lifetime allowance charge arising from these two events.

Solution

On 19 March 2008, the crystallised benefits absorb 60% of the lifetime allowance (which is £1,600,000 for events occurring during 2007-08). There is no lifetime allowance charge and 40% of the lifetime allowance remains unused.

On 5 January 2013, the crystallised benefits of £710,000 are compared with 40% of £1,500,000 (the lifetime allowance for events occurring during 2012-13). Crystallised benefits exceed the available allowance of £600,000 by £110,000. Therefore there is a lifetime allowance charge of £60,500 (55% of £110,000).

The lifetime allowance has now been fully used, so the full value of any further pension benefits will be subject to the lifetime allowance charge.

EXAMPLE 8

Stuart is a member of a registered pension scheme. He took no benefits from this or any other scheme until February 2013, when he received a lump sum of £320,000 and began to receive a pension of £65,000 per annum. Calculate the lifetime allowance charge arising from these events.

Solution

The value of the pension is £1,300,000 (20 x £65,000) so the total value of the benefits received is £1,620,000. This exceeds the lifetime allowance for 2012-13 by £120,000 and so there will be a lifetime allowance charge.

The lump sum is deemed to be the earlier of the two benefit crystallisation events, so it is the pension which has caused the lifetime allowance to be exceeded. Hence the excess is taxed at 25% and the lifetime allowance charge is £30,000 (25% of £120,000).

Summary

- In a defined benefits pension scheme, the benefits payable to members are usually based on final salary and length of service. In a money purchase scheme, the benefits payable to members are based upon the size of the pension fund built up during a member's working life.
- Registered pension schemes enjoy certain tax advantages when compared with unregistered schemes. A registered scheme's investment income is exempt from income tax. Any capital gains made on the disposal of scheme investments are exempt from capital gains tax. Tax relief is available in relation to contributions made by members and employers. Tax-free lump sums may be paid to members.
- Normal minimum pension age rose from 50 to 55 on 6 April 2010. Pension benefits from registered pension schemes must normally begin by the age of 75.
- The maximum amount of pension contributions on which an individual can claim tax relief in any tax year is equal to the greater of the individual's earnings for that year and £3,600. If earnings are less than £3,600, tax relief will be given on contributions beyond the level of earnings only if the pension scheme operates tax relief at source.
- Basic rate relief on an individual's pension contributions may be given by deduction at source. Relief at the higher rate and additional rate is then given by increasing the basic rate limit and higher rate limit by the gross amount of the contributions.
- Alternatively, tax relief may be given by deducting an employee's contributions from his or her gross pay before operating the PAYE system. Exceptionally, relief may be given by deduction from the individual's total income.

- In general, an employer's pension contributions are deducted when computing the employer's trading profit for the period of account in which the contributions are paid. However, tax relief on contributions which are unusually large may be spread over two or more periods.
- A tax liability will arise if an individual's total pension inputs for a tax year exceed the annual allowance. The excess is charged to income tax at marginal rate and this tax charge falls upon the individual concerned.
- A tax liability may arise when a benefit crystallisation event occurs. The most common examples of such an event are the payment of a lump sum to a member or the commencement of a pension. The value of the crystallised benefits is compared with the unused proportion of the lifetime allowance and any excess is charged to income tax. The tax charge is at either 55% or 25% (depending on whether the benefits are taken as a lump sum or a pension) and falls jointly upon the scheme administrator and the member concerned.

Exercises

14.1 State the maximum contribution to registered pension schemes on which an individual could obtain tax relief in 2012-13 if the individual's earnings for the year were:

(a) £120,000 (b) £1,200.

14.2 Freda is a member of a registered pension scheme which operates tax relief at source. She has income from self-employment of £60,000 in 2012-13 and makes pension contributions of £1,000 (gross) per month. Explain how tax relief will be given in relation to her pension contributions.

14.3 An employer's contributions into a registered pension scheme during the year to 30 June 2012 are £600,000. Explain how tax relief will be given on the contributions of £1,860,000 which the employer makes during the year to 30 June 2013.

14.4 Damon is a member of a defined benefit registered pension scheme. On retirement, he will receive an annual pension equal to 1/60th of final salary for each year of pensionable service. He will also receive a lump sum equal to 3/80ths of final salary for each year of pensionable service.

At the start of the pension input period ending during tax year 2012-13, Damon's annual salary was £360,000 and he had accumulated 20 years of pensionable service. By the end of this period his salary had risen to £450,000.

Damon's marginal rate of income tax for 2012-13 is 50% and he has no unused annual allowance brought forward from previous years. Calculate the annual allowance charge payable for 2012-13. (Ignore inflation).

14.5 Karen belongs to a number of registered pension schemes. Until tax year 2008-09 she had received no benefits from any of these schemes but in October 2008 she took a lump sum of £412,500 from one of her schemes. She received no further benefits until July 2012 when she took a lump sum of £1,188,000 from another of her schemes.

(a) Calculate the amount of any lifetime allowance charges arising in relation to either of Karen's lump sums.

(b) How would the situation change if the lump sum of £1,188,000 had been received in October 2008 and the lump sum of £412,500 had been received in July 2012?

***14.6** Edna's total pension input amounts for tax years 2012-13 to 2015-16 are as follows:

2012-13	£33,000
2013-14	£44,000
2014-15	£52,000
2015-16	£55,000

She has no unused annual allowance to bring forward from previous years. Calculate the annual allowance charge for 2015-16 and the amount of any unused annual allowance carried forward to 2016-17, assuming that the annual allowance is normally £50,000 in all years and that Edna's marginal rate of income tax in 2015-16 is 40%.

***14.7** Irma is self-employed. She was born in 1954. Her trading income for 2012-13 was £26,720 and during the year she made net contributions to a registered pension scheme of £6,000. Her only other income in 2012-13 comprised net bank interest of £27,208.

(a) Calculate Irma's income tax liability for 2012-13.

(b) Re-calculate Irma's income tax liability for 2012-13, now assuming that she was born in 1944.

Chapter 15

Payment of income tax, interest and penalties

Introduction

Interest is charged on income tax which is paid late. Conversely, interest may be added to repayments of income tax. The main purpose of this chapter is to identify the dates on which income tax is payable and to explain how the interest due on underpaid or overpaid tax is calculated. This chapter also considers financial penalties to which a taxpayer may become liable as a consequence of non-compliance with tax law.

Payment of income tax

Under the Self Assessment system (see Chapter 1) income tax which is not deducted at source is payable as follows:

(a) The taxpayer's income tax liability for the tax year in relation to all sources of income is aggregated. This tax liability is increased by the amount of any Class 4 National Insurance contributions (NICs) which are due for the year (see Chapter 16).

(b) Payments on account of the total liability (POAs) are due on 31 January in the tax year and on the following 31 July. For example, the POAs for 2012-13 are due on 31 January 2013 and 31 July 2013. Each POA is equal to 50% of the taxpayer's liability to income tax and Class 4 NICs for the *previous* tax year, less any tax which was paid by deduction at source. For this purpose, the term "deduction at source" includes tax paid via the PAYE system and any tax satisfied by the set-off of tax credits, as well as tax deducted at source from interest etc. Note that:

   (i) POAs are not required if the taxpayer's total liability to income tax and Class 4 NICs for the preceding year (less tax deducted at source) was under £1,000.

   (ii) POAs are also not required if more than 80% of the taxpayer's liability for the previous year was satisfied by deduction of tax at source.

   (iii) A taxpayer who believes that his or her liability for the current year will be less than in the previous year may claim to make reduced POAs. There are penalties for making such a claim fraudulently or negligently (see below).

(c) A balancing payment (or repayment) is normally due on 31 January following the end of the tax year. For example, the 2012-13 balancing payment is due on 31 January 2014. But note that:

(i) If a return notice is issued late (i.e. after 31 October following the end of the tax year to which it relates) and this has not been caused by the taxpayer's failure to notify his or her chargeability to tax, the balancing payment is due three months after the date of the notice.

(ii) If a self-assessment is amended by the taxpayer or by HMRC (or if a discovery assessment is raised) any additional amount payable is due 30 days after the date of its notification to the taxpayer or on 31 January following the end of the tax year, whichever is the later. However, this rule does *not* defer the date from which interest accrues on the additional tax.

The amount of the balancing payment is equal to the income tax and Class 4 NICs liability for the year, less any tax deducted at source and less the POAs. Any capital gains tax due for the year (see Chapter 17) is added to this payment.

(d) Taxpayers with employment income may request that an underpayment of income tax and/or capital gains tax of less than £3,000 should be collected via the PAYE system. Any amount paid in this way is treated as if paid on the first day of the tax year in which the tax is collected. For instance, an underpayment of tax which is collected via PAYE during tax year 2013-14 is treated as if paid on 6 April 2013.

Interest is charged if any payment is made after the due date. Late payment penalties (see below) may also be imposed. Taxpayers receive regular statements from HMRC showing the amounts due, the amounts paid to date and the amounts of any interest and penalties.

EXAMPLE 1

Warren's liability to income tax and Class 4 NICs for 2012-13 is £19,300, of which £16,100 has been paid by deduction at source. State the dates on which Warren should pay his outstanding liability for 2012-13 and compute the amount payable on each date if:

(a) his liability for 2011-12 was £17,200, of which £14,500 was deducted at source

(b) his liability for 2011-12 was £3,400, of which £2,500 was deducted at source.

Solution

(a) 84.3% of the liability for 2011-12 was deducted at source. This is over 80% and therefore no POAs are required for 2012-13. The remaining liability of £3,200 for 2012-13 (£19,300 – £16,100) is due for payment on 31 January 2014.

(b) 73.5% of the liability for 2011-12 was deducted at source. This is not over 80% but the remainder of the liability was only £900, which is under £1,000. Therefore no POAs are required for 2012-13. The remaining liability of £3,200 for 2012-13 is due for payment on 31 January 2014.

EXAMPLE 2

Barbara's liability to income tax and Class 4 NICs for 2012-13 is £34,000, of which £5,000 has been paid by deduction at source. Her liability for 2011-12 was £26,000, of which £4,000 was deducted at source. State the dates on which Barbara is required to pay her 2012-13 liability and compute the amount payable on each date.

Solution

Barbara paid 15.4% of her 2011-12 liability by deduction at source. This is not over 80% and the remainder of the liability (£22,000) was not less than £1,000. Therefore POAs are required for 2012-13. The required payments are as follows

(i) 31 January 2013, POA £11,000 (50% of (£26,000 – £4,000))

(ii) 31 July 2013, POA £11,000

(iii) 31 January 2014, balancing payment £7,000 (£34,000 – £5,000 – POAs £22,000).

Managed payment plans

Finance Act 2009 legislated for "managed payment plans" (MPPs) which would allow taxpayers to spread their tax payments over a period straddling the normal due dates. Under an MPP, a taxpayer would arrange with HMRC to make a tax payment by instalments which would be equally balanced on either side of the normal due date. If all of these instalments were paid on the agreed dates, the taxpayer would be treated as having paid the tax on the normal due date, so that no interest or late payment penalty would arise.

MPPs were expected to begin in 2011, once the necessary changes had been made to HMRC's computer and accounting systems, but implementation has now been deferred.

Late payment penalties

In addition to the interest that is charged on tax paid late (see below), a taxpayer who does not pay tax on time may also be liable to a late payment penalty. Broadly, the late payment penalty system imposes a penalty equal to 5% of any tax not paid within 30 days of the due date, with two further 5% penalties for tax remaining unpaid six months and 12 months after the due date. The detailed rules are as follows:

(a) If all or part of a balancing payment remains unpaid more than 30 days after the due date, a penalty is charged equal to 5% of the amount unpaid.

(b) Similarly, if a self-assessment is amended (or a discovery assessment is raised) and any of the additional amount which becomes payable remains unpaid more than 30 days after the due date, a penalty is charged equal to 5% of the amount unpaid.

(c) The "penalty date" is the date which falls 31 days after the due date of payment.

(d) If any tax under (a) and (b) above is not paid within the five-month period beginning on the penalty date, there is another penalty equal to 5% of the amount still unpaid.

(e) Finally, if any tax due under (a) and (b) above is not paid within the eleven-month period beginning on the penalty date, there is a further 5% penalty.

(f) If a taxpayer is liable to a late payment penalty, HMRC must issue the taxpayer with a penalty notice. Late payment penalties are due for payment within the 30-day period beginning with the day on which the penalty notice is served.

Note that the late payment penalty system does *not* apply to POAs.

EXAMPLE 3

Barbara (see Example 2 above) makes the following payments for 2012-13:

	£
31 January 2013	11,000
8 September 2013	11,000
17 February 2014	4,000
12 August 2014	2,000
3 February 2015	1,000

Compute the late payment penalties (if any) which Barbara would incur and state the dates by which these penalties should be paid.

Solution

- The first POA is paid in full and on time.
- The second POA is also paid in full but is paid late. However, late payment penalties do not apply to late POAs so there is no penalty.
- The penalty date for the balancing payment is 3 March 2014.
- £3,000 of the balancing payment is not paid before the penalty date. Therefore there is a late payment penalty of £150 (5% of £3,000).
- The five-month period beginning with the penalty date starts on 3 March 2014 and ends on 2 August 2014. £3,000 of the balancing payment is still unpaid at the end of this period and so there is another late payment penalty of £150 (5% of £3,000).
- The eleven-month period beginning with the penalty date starts on 3 March 2014 and ends on 2 February 2015. £1,000 of the balancing payment remains unpaid at the end of this period and so there is a late payment penalty of £50 (5% of £1,000).

Assuming that penalty notices are issued on 3 March 2014, 3 August 2014 and 3 February 2015 respectively, the first £150 penalty is payable on or before 1 April 2014, the second £150 penalty is payable on or before 1 September 2014 and the £50 penalty is payable on or before 4 March 2015.

Interest on income tax

Under the Self Assessment system, interest is charged on all late payments of tax and Class 4 NICs. Interest is also charged if a penalty is paid late. However, interest may be paid to the taxpayer when repayments are made of overpaid tax and Class 4 NICs.

Interest on overdue income tax

Interest charged on overdue income tax (and Class 4 NICs) is calculated as follows:

(a) In the case of late POAs and balancing payments, interest runs from the due date of payment up to the date on which the tax is actually paid.

(b) In the case of discovery assessments and amendments to self-assessments, interest runs from the date on which the balancing payment is due for the year to which the assessment relates (normally the 31 January which follows the end of that year) even though the tax itself might not be due for payment until a later date.

(c) Interest on a penalty runs from the due date of payment for that penalty (generally 30 days from its imposition).

(d) In practice, if a taxpayer submits a paper tax return by 31 October without calculating his or her tax liability (see Chapter 1) and HMRC does not notify the taxpayer of the amount due until after 31 December, interest on this tax starts to run 30 days after the date on which the taxpayer is notified.

(e) Interest is calculated on a daily basis at the official Bank of England rate plus 2.5% (currently 0.5% + 2.5% = 3% per annum). Apparently it is HMRC practice to use a denominator of 366 in such calculations, whether or not a leap year is involved.

EXAMPLE 4

Barbara (see Examples 2 and 3 above) pays all of her late payment penalties on 4 March 2015. Calculate the total interest payable by Barbara in relation to her income tax and Class 4 NICs for 2012-13, assuming an interest rate of 3% throughout.

Solution

(i) Interest on the second POA (39 days late) is £35.16 (£11,000 x 3% x 39/366).

(ii) The first £4,000 of the balancing payment is paid 17 days late. The next £2,000 is paid 193 days late and the final £1,000 is paid 368 days late. Interest is £67.38 ((£4,000 x 3% x 17/366) + (£2,000 x 3% x 193/366) + (£1,000 x 3% x 368/366)).

(iii) Interest on the first penalty (paid 337 days late) is £4.14 (£150 x 3% x 337/366).

(iv) Interest on the second penalty (paid 184 days late) is £2.26 (£150 x 3% x 184/366).

Total interest due is £108.94 (£35.16 + £67.38 + £4.14 + £2.26).

Interest on overpaid income tax

Repayments of overpaid income tax and Class 4 NICs attract interest. This is calculated on a daily basis at the *greater* of 0.5% per annum and the official Bank of England rate. Such interest is referred to as *repayment supplement* and is itself exempt from income tax.

Interest on overpaid income tax and Class 4 NICs runs from the "relevant date" to the date on which repayment is made to the taxpayer. The relevant date is:

(a) as regards POAs and any other payments of income tax and Class 4 NICs (other than tax deducted at source), the date of payment

(b) as regards income tax deducted at source (including PAYE), 31 January following the tax year for which the tax is deducted.

Repayments of income tax and Class 4 NICs for a year are attributed first to the balancing payment made for that year, secondly in two equal parts to the POAs for that year and finally to tax deducted at source for the year. Note that:

(a) If a repayment is triggered by a claim to carry back a loss or a payment from a later year to an earlier year (e.g. if a trading loss is carried back or if a Gift Aid donation is carried back) interest on this repayment runs from the 31 January following the later year, *not* the earlier year.

(b) Penalties repaid to a taxpayer also attract interest, running from the date of payment to the date of repayment.

(c) Apparently it is HMRC practice to use a denominator of 365 when computing interest on a repayment, whether or not a leap year is involved.

(d) Repayment supplement is not paid in relation to tax that has been deliberately overpaid by the taxpayer. This rule prevents taxpayers from using HMRC as a source of tax-free interest.

Penalties

A taxpayer who fails to comply with statutory requirements may become liable to a number of financial penalties, the most important of which are listed below. Some of these penalties are fixed in amount but HMRC often has the power to "mitigate" (i.e. reduce) the amount charged if it sees fit to do so. Whether or not a penalty is mitigated will usually depend mainly upon the seriousness of the taxpayer's offence and the degree to which the taxpayer has co-operated with HMRC. The main penalties are as follows:

(a) **Failure to notify chargeability to tax**. An individual must notify HMRC if he or she is liable to income tax for a tax year, even if a notice requiring a return has not been issued for that year (see Chapter 1). Notification must be made within six months of the end of the tax year concerned.

The penalty regime which applies to a "failure to notify" is not confined to income tax but covers a range of taxes, including capital gains tax, corporation tax and VAT. Under this regime, the penalty for a failure to notify liability to income tax for a tax year is expressed as a percentage of the tax which remains unpaid on 31 January following the end of that year. But no penalty is charged if the taxpayer has a reasonable excuse for the failure. The applicable percentage is determined as follows:

(i) For a "deliberate and concealed" failure to notify, where the failure is deliberate and the taxpayer has attempted to conceal it, the percentage is 100%.

(ii) For a failure which is "deliberate but not concealed" the percentage is 70%.

(iii) Otherwise, the percentage is 30%.

These penalties may be reduced if the taxpayer discloses the failure. There are greater reductions if the disclosure is "unprompted" than if it is "prompted". A disclosure is unprompted if it is made at a time when the taxpayer has no reason to believe that the irregularity has been discovered or is about to be discovered by HMRC.

(b) **Late submission of a tax return**. As from 6 April 2011, a new penalty regime takes effect in relation to the late submission of a self assessment tax return. This regime will eventually apply across a range of taxes. The late filing penalties are as follows:

(i) A £100 penalty is charged as soon as a tax return is late (by a single day). This applies whether or not the tax liability for the year has been paid and even if the taxpayer has no liability for that year or is owed a tax repayment for the year.

(ii) If a return is more than 3 months late, HMRC may charge a penalty of £10 per day whilst the return remains outstanding (up to a maximum of £900).

(iii) If a return is more than 6 months late, another penalty arises equal to the greater of £300 and 5% of the tax liability for the year.

(iv) If a tax return is more than 12 months late, a further penalty arises, again equal to the greater of £300 and 5% of the tax liability for the year. But if the taxpayer has deliberately withheld information from HMRC, the percentage used in the penalty calculation becomes 70% (not 5%). This rises to 100% if the withholding of information is deliberate and concealed. These higher penalties may be reduced if the taxpayer discloses the information which has been withheld.

The tax-geared penalties (i.e. penalties which are calculated as a percentage of the tax liability) have to be estimated by HMRC in the first instance. These penalties are then re-assessed when the taxpayer files the late return.

Note that none of the penalties listed above will be charged if the taxpayer has a reasonable excuse for failing to submit a return on time (e.g. serious illness).

(c) **Submission of an incorrect tax return**. A single penalty regime applies in relation to the submission of incorrect returns (and certain other documents) for the purposes of income tax and many other taxes. This common regime applies if an incorrect return or other document leads to an understatement of the amount of tax due and the inaccuracy was either careless or deliberate. No penalty is charged if the taxpayer has taken reasonable care. The regime also applies if an assessment issued by HMRC understates the amount of tax due and the taxpayer fails to take reasonable steps to notify HMRC of this fact within 30 days. The amount of any penalty under the regime is expressed as a percentage of the potential lost revenue and is determined as follows:

(i) For a "deliberate and concealed" inaccuracy, the percentage is 100%.

(ii) If an inaccuracy is "deliberate but not concealed" the percentage is 70%.

(iii) Otherwise, the percentage is 30%. The percentage is also 30% in cases where the taxpayer has failed to notify HMRC of an under-assessment.

As with the "failure to notify chargeability" penalties (see above) these penalties may be reduced if the taxpayer discloses the infringement and there are greater reductions if the disclosure is unprompted than if it is prompted.

(d) **Fraud or negligence when claiming reduced POAs**. A taxpayer who makes a claim for reduced POAs and does so fraudulently or negligently may be subject to a maximum penalty equal to the difference between the POAs actually made and the POAs that should have been made.

(e) **Failure to keep required records**. A taxpayer who fails to maintain or retain adequate records in support of the year's tax return may be subject to a penalty of up to £3,000.

In every case, the penalty described above is charged *in addition* both to the tax itself and to any late payment penalties or interest charged in relation to that tax.

Summary

- Under the Self Assessment system, income tax not collected at source or via the PAYE system is usually payable by means of two payments on account, followed by a balancing payment.
- Late payment penalties may be levied if a balancing payment is paid late and interest is payable on any tax paid late. Interest usually runs from the due date of payment up to the actual date of payment.
- Repayments of overpaid tax also attract interest, usually running from the date on which the tax was paid up to the date of repayment.
- Financial penalties may be imposed for various breaches of the tax law.

Exercises

15.1 For each of the following taxpayers, state the dates on which the 2012-13 income tax is due to be paid and calculate the amount payable on each date. (Ignore Class 4 NICs).

(a) Guy's 2011-12 income tax liability was £1,600, of which £1,150 was paid via the PAYE system and £50 was deducted at source from investment income. His income tax liability for 2012-13 is £1,750, of which £1,250 is paid via PAYE and £60 is deducted at source.

(b) Marie's 2011-12 income tax liability was £6,730, of which £4,370 was paid via PAYE and £20 was deducted at source. Her 2012-13 liability is £6,580, of which £4,810 is paid via PAYE and £35 is deducted at source.

(c) Majid's 2011-12 income tax liability was £14,850, of which £11,990 was paid via PAYE and £110 was deducted at source. His 2012-13 liability is £16,110, of which £12,370 is paid via PAYE and £140 is deducted at source.

15.2 Dorothy's income tax and Class 4 NICs liability for 2011-12 was £30,000, of which £6,000 was deducted at source. Her liability for 2012-13 is £35,000, of which £7,000 is deducted at source. She made a first POA in respect of 2012-13 on 27 February 2013 and a second POA on 12 September 2013. She also made a balancing payment for the year on 21 February 2014. All of her payments were for the correct amount.

(a) Calculate the amount of any late payment penalties payable by Dorothy in relation to 2012-13.

(b) Assuming an interest rate of 3% per annum, calculate the amount of any interest payable by Dorothy in relation to 2012-13.

15.3 Jabran did not receive a notice to file a tax return for 2011-12 but he was aware that he had income which had not been assessed to tax. He notified HMRC of this fact on 2 October 2012 and a return was issued to him on 15 November 2012. He completed the return and sent it back with the necessary payment on 7 April 2013.

Explain the penalties and interest which Jabran might be required to pay.

***15.4** Frances paid income tax and Class 4 NICs of £43,000 in 2011-12, of which £19,000 was deducted at source. Her total liability for 2012-13 is £63,000, of which £21,000 is deducted at source. Her payments for 2012-13 are as follows:

	£
15 February 2013	12,000
14 September 2013	12,000
3 February 2014	14,000
15 December 2014	4,000

Calculate the late payment penalties and interest payable for the year, assuming that any penalties are paid on 15 December 2014 and that interest is charged at 3% per annum.

Chapter 16

National Insurance contributions

Introduction

National Insurance contributions (NICs) are payable by employees, by employers and by those who are self-employed. Contributions are collected by the National Insurance Contributions Office (NICO) of HMRC and paid into a National Insurance Fund. This fund, supplemented if necessary by a grant from the Treasury, is then used to provide contributory social security benefits such as the state retirement pension.

The purpose of this chapter is to explain the circumstances in which NICs are payable and the way in which NICs are calculated.

Class 1 National Insurance contributions

Class 1 NICs are payable in relation to employees aged 16 or over. The employees themselves pay *primary* Class 1 NICs whilst employers pay *secondary* Class 1 NICs on their employees' behalf. Employees who continue to work after reaching state pension age pay no further primary contributions but employers must still pay secondary contributions in relation to such employees.

The amount of Class 1 NICs payable in relation to an employee depends upon the employee's earnings. For National Insurance purposes, an employee's earnings consist of his or her gross pay *before* deducting pension contributions, donations made under the terms of a payroll giving scheme or any other expenses borne by the employee. An employee's earnings for this purpose do *not* include:

(a) tips received directly from customers

(b) mileage allowances received from the employer if these are calculated at a rate which does not exceed the AMAP rate for the first 10,000 miles, regardless of the number of miles actually driven by the employee (see Chapter 7); but any excess forms part of the employee's earnings chargeable to Class 1 NICs

(c) pensions and redundancy pay

(d) employer contributions to a registered pension scheme

(e) business expenses paid for or reimbursed by the employer, including reasonable travel and subsistence expenses

(f) certain items which are paid for or provided by the employer, to the extent that these items are exempt from income tax; including relocation expenses, personal incidental expenses, workplace car parking, suggestion scheme awards, works buses, the loan of bicycles, employer-supported childcare etc. (see Chapter 7).

Benefits in kind which are not convertible into cash are generally not subject to Class 1 NICs. However, the *employer* may incur a liability to Class 1A NICs in relation to such benefits (see below). If an employee's remuneration is paid in the form of non-cash assets such as gold bars, coffee beans, fine wines or assigned trade debts, a liability to Class 1 NICs will arise if the assets are readily convertible into cash. Payments made in shares are generally liable to Class 1 NICs, unless they are "own company" shares provided under an approved share scheme or share option scheme (see Chapter 7).

Contribution periods

The main principles of the Class 1 National Insurance system are as follows:

(a) Primary and secondary Class 1 NICs are calculated according to the amount of an employee's earnings in a "contribution period". For those paid weekly or monthly, each week or month usually constitutes a contribution period. However, special rules apply to company directors (see later in this chapter).

(b) The liability to Class 1 NICs in a given contribution period is governed solely by the employee's earnings in that period and is totally unaffected by earnings in other periods. This is in contrast to the income tax PAYE system (see Chapter 7) which accumulates earnings over the year and calculates a tax liability each week or month based on the employee's total earnings for the tax year to date.

(c) If an employee has two or more employments in a contribution period, each of these employments is considered separately for the purpose of calculating the liability to Class 1 NICs. Earnings from two or more employments are aggregated only if the employments are with the same employer or associated employers.

(d) The percentage rate at which Class 1 NICs are calculated depends upon whether or not the employee is "contracted out" of the State Second Pension (S2P), which was formerly known as the State Earnings Related Pension Scheme (SERPS). Employees who are contracted out of S2P pay lower Class 1 NICs but are not entitled to receive the State Second Pension when they retire.

    In general, employees will be contracted out because they are members of their employer's contracted-out salary-related (COSR) occupational pension scheme. As from 6 April 2012, it is no longer possible for an employee to contract out of S2P on the basis of membership of a money-purchase pension scheme such as a defined contribution occupational pension scheme or a personal pension.

Primary Class 1 NICs

The primary Class 1 NICs payable by an employee for a contribution period falling during 2012-13 are calculated as follows:

(a) The employee's earnings in the period are compared with the *primary threshold*. The primary threshold for 2012-13 is £146 per week or £634 per month. No primary Class 1 NICs are payable for a contribution period if the employee's earnings in the period do not exceed this threshold.

(b) If earnings in the contribution period exceed the primary threshold, primary Class 1 NICs are generally payable at 12% on earnings between the primary threshold and the upper earnings limit (UEL). The UEL for 2012-13 is £817 per week or £3,540 per month. Any earnings beyond the UEL attract primary Class 1 NICs at 2%.

(c) However, if the employee is contracted out, the rate of primary Class 1 NICs payable on earnings between the primary threshold and the upper accruals point (UAP) is reduced to 10.6%. The UAP for 2012-13 is £770 per week or £3,337 per month.

(d) These rules may be summarised as follows:

	Not contracted out	*Contracted out*
Weekly-paid:		
On the first £146	0%	0%
On the next £624 (up to £770)	12%	10.6%
On the next £47 (up to £817)	12%	12%
On remaining earnings above £817	2%	2%
Monthly-paid:		
On the first £634	0%	0%
On the next £2,703 (up to £3,337)	12%	10.6%
On the next £203 (up to £3,540)	12%	12%
On remaining earnings above £3,540	2%	2%

It is worth noting that the UEL is aligned with the point at which higher rate income tax becomes payable. This occurs when a taxpayer's total income exceeds the sum of the personal allowance and the basic rate band. For 2012-13, this means that the UEL for the year is £42,475 (£8,105 + £34,370). Thus the UEL for a week is £817 (£42,475 ÷ 52) and the UEL for a month is £3,540 (£42,475 ÷ 12).

EXAMPLE 1

(a) Compute the primary Class 1 NICs payable by the following weekly-paid employees for the week ending 17 August 2012:

(i) Employee A has earnings in the week of £500 and is not contracted out.

(ii) Employee B has earnings in the week of £800 and is not contracted out.

(iii) Employee C has earnings in the week of £1,000 and is contracted out.

(b) Compute the primary Class 1 NICs payable by the following monthly-paid employees for the month of August 2012:
   (i) Employee D has earnings in the month of £2,500 and is contracted out.
   (ii) Employee E has earnings in the month of £3,500 and is contracted out.
   (iii) Employee F has earnings in the month of £4,500 and is not contracted out.

Solution

(a) (i) 12% x (£500 – £146) = £42.48
   (ii) 12% x (£800 – £146) = £78.48
   (iii) 10.6% x (£770 – £146) + 12% x (£817 – £770) + 2% x (£1,000 – £817) = £75.44

(b) (i) 10.6% x (£2,500 – £634) = £197.80
   (ii) 10.6% x (£3,337 – £634) + 12% x (£3,500 – £3,337) = £306.08
   (iii) 12% x (£3,540 – £634) + 2% x (£4,500 – £3,540) = £367.92

Secondary Class 1 NICs

The secondary Class 1 NICs payable by an employer in relation to an employee for a contribution period falling during 2012-13 are calculated as follows:

(a) The employee's earnings in the contribution period are compared with the *secondary threshold*. The secondary threshold for 2012-13 is £144 per week or £624 per month. No secondary contributions are payable if earnings in a contribution period do not exceed this threshold.

(b) If earnings in the period exceed the secondary threshold, secondary Class 1 NICs are generally payable at 13.8% on earnings above the threshold.

(c) However, if the employee is contracted out, the secondary Class 1 NICs payable on earnings between the secondary threshold and the UAP are calculated at 10.4%.

(d) These rules may be summarised as follows:

	Not contracted out	*Contracted out*
Weekly-paid:		
On the first £144	0%	0%
On the next £626 (up to £770)	13.8%	10.4%
On remaining earnings above £770	13.8%	13.8%
Monthly-paid:		
On the first £624	0%	0%
On the next £2,713 (up to £3,337)	13.8%	10.4%
On remaining earnings above £3,337	13.8%	13.8%

Secondary NICs holiday for new businesses

For a three-year period starting in September 2010, new businesses in certain regions of the UK are eligible for an NICs "holiday". Qualifying employers are not required to pay the first £5,000 of secondary NICs that would normally be payable in the first 12 months of employment for each of the first 10 employees hired in the first year of business.

EXAMPLE 2

Compute the secondary Class 1 NICs payable in relation to each employee in Example 1.

Solution

(a) (i) 13.8% x (£500 – £144) = £49.13

(ii) 13.8% x (£800 – £144) = £90.53

(iii) 10.4% x (£770 – £144) + 13.8% x (£1,000 – £770) = £96.84

(b) (i) 10.4% x (£2,500 – £624) = £195.10

(ii) 10.4% x (£3,337 – £624) + 13.8% x (£3,500 – £3,337) = £304.65

(iii) 13.8% x (£4,500 – £624) = £534.89

Directors' Class 1 NICs

The fact that NICs are calculated for each contribution period separately means that employees with identical annual earnings may pay very different amounts of primary contributions in the tax year, depending upon the distribution of their earnings over that year. Consider the following (rather extreme) example:

EXAMPLE 3

During 2012-13, an employee (not contracted out) earns a total of £48,000, paid at the rate of £4,000 each month.

(a) Calculate the total primary Class 1 NICs payable for the year.

(b) What would the total primary contributions be for the year if the employee received £48,000 in one month and nothing in the remaining 11 months?

Solution

(a) Primary contributions each month are equal to 12% x (£3,540 – £634) + 2% x (£4,000 – £3,540) = £357.92. This gives a total of £4,295.04 for the year.

(b) Primary contributions for the month in which the employee was paid £48,000 would be equal to 12% x (£3,540 – £634) + 2% x (£48,000 – £3,540) = £1,237.92.

Therefore the employee would save £3,057.12 in primary contributions (£4,295.04 – £1,237.92) if the entire year's salary were received in a single month.

Employees are not normally able to arrange for all of their year's earnings to be paid in one contribution period so as to avoid primary Class 1 NICs. However, company directors may well have sufficient influence to make such an arrangement. To counter this, the Class 1 contributions of company directors are calculated on an *annual* basis, regardless of the distribution of their earnings over the tax year. In effect, the entire year becomes a single contribution period. For 2012-13, the Class 1 NICs of a company director are payable according to the following rules:

(a) The primary threshold, upper accruals point (UAP) and upper earnings limit (UEL) for the year are £7,605, £40,040 and £42,475 respectively.

(b) The total primary contributions payable for the year by a director with earnings which exceed £7,605 are calculated as follows:

	Not contracted out	*Contracted out*
Annual earnings:		
On the first £7,605	0%	0%
On the next £32,435 (up to £40,040)	12%	10.6%
On the next £2,435 (up to £42,475)	12%	12%
On remaining earnings above £42,475	2%	2%

(c) The secondary threshold for the year is £7,488. The total secondary contributions payable for the year in relation to a director with earnings which exceed £7,488 are calculated as follows:

	Not contracted out	*Contracted out*
Annual earnings:		
On the first £7,488	0%	0%
On the next £32,552 (up to £40,040)	13.8%	10.4%
On remaining earnings above £40,040	13.8%	13.8%

EXAMPLE 4

Rework the previous example, given that the employee in question is a company director.

Solution

Regardless of the distribution of the director's earnings over the tax year, primary contributions would be equal to 12% x (£42,475 – £7,605) + 2% x (£48,000 – £42,475) = £4,294.90.

Class 1A National Insurance contributions

Benefits in kind which are not convertible into cash are generally exempt from Class 1 NICs. However, these benefits give rise to a Class 1A contribution instead, *payable only by the employer* (not by the employee). For 2012-13, this contribution is calculated as 13.8% of the amount of the benefit in kind which is assessed on the employee for income tax purposes (see Chapter 8).

EXAMPLE 5

In 2012-13, George (a P11D employee) is provided with a petrol-engined motor car by his employer who pays for all fuel and other running costs. The car had a list price when new of £21,700 and has an emission rating of 173g/km. George's employer also pays his private medical insurance premium of £600 per annum.

Calculate the Class 1A contribution payable by George's employer for the year.

Solution

The employee benefits assessed on George for income tax purposes are:

	£
Car (11% + 14% = 25% x £21,700)	5,425
Fuel (25% x £20,200)	5,050
Medical insurance premium	600
	11,075

Therefore the Class 1A contribution payable by George's employer is 13.8% x £11,075 = £1,528.35.

Class 1B National Insurance contributions

From time to time, an employer may enter into a PAYE Settlement Agreement (PSA) with HM Revenue and Customs. The effect of such an agreement is that the employer pays the income tax liability of employees in relation to minor or irregular benefits in kind. In these circumstances, the employer is liable to make a Class 1B National Insurance contribution calculated (in 2012-13) as 13.8% of the sum of the benefits in kind and the associated tax which is payable under the terms of the PSA.

Class 2 National Insurance contributions

Class 2 NICs are payable by self-employed people who are over 16 and under pensionable age. The contributions are payable at a flat rate (for 2012-13) of £2.65 per week. A person whose earnings from self-employment in a tax year are less than the "small earnings exception" (£5,595 for 2012-13) is not required to pay Class 2 NICs for that year but may do so voluntarily so as to maintain a full contributions record. Note that:

(a) For the purposes of Class 2 NICs, a self-employed person's earnings in a tax year are equal to the net profit, *before* adjustment for tax purposes, shown by that person's accounts for the year. The required figure is the actual net profit from 6 April to the following 5 April. Unless accounts are drawn up to 5 April, it will be necessary to apportion the net profits shown in two years' accounts to obtain this figure.

(b) If a self-employed person has two or more businesses, the profits of all of them are aggregated and a Class 2 NICs liability arises unless the aggregate profits are less than the small earnings exception.

EXAMPLE 6

(a) Alison is self-employed. Her accounts for the year to 5 April 2013 show a net profit of £5,500. Is she liable to pay Class 2 NICs for 2012-13?

(b) Amanda is also self-employed. Her accounts for the year to 31 December 2012 show a net profit of £5,400 and her accounts for the year to 31 December 2013 show a net profit of £6,480. Is she liable to pay Class 2 NICs for 2012-13?

Solution

(a) Alison's accounts (which coincide with tax year 2012-13) show a net profit which is less than the small earnings exception. Therefore she is not required to pay Class 2 NICs for 2012-13.

(b) Amanda's accounts do not coincide with the tax year so some apportionment is necessary. Her actual net profit in 2012-13 is £5,670 (£5,400 x 9/12 + £6,480 x 3/12). This is not less than the small earnings exception so she is required to pay Class 2 NICs for 2012-13.

Class 3 National Insurance contributions

Any individual (employed or self-employed) whose earnings are too low in a contribution period to require a National Insurance contribution may make a voluntary Class 3 contribution so as to maintain a full contributions record. For 2012-13, the amount of the Class 3 contribution is £13.25 per week.

Class 4 National Insurance contributions

In addition to the flat rate Class 2 liability described above, self-employed people who are over 16 and under pensionable age may also be liable to pay earnings-related Class 4 contributions. A self-employed person's Class 4 liability for a given tax year is based on the amount of trading income which is charged to income tax for that year. The Class 4 NICs are collected along with the income tax liability (see Chapter 15). Note that:

(a) The Class 4 liability is based on the person's trading income for the tax year *after* adjusting for capital allowances and trading losses but *before* deducting any pension contributions that are deducted from total income (see Chapter 14).

Trading losses which are set against the non-trading income of a tax year for tax purposes (see Chapter 12) are set instead against the first available trading income of that year or subsequent years for Class 4 purposes.

(b) If a self-employed person has more than one business, the earnings from all businesses for the year are aggregated.

(c) There is no liability to Class 4 NICs if trading income does not exceed the *lower profits limit* (£7,605 for 2012-13).

(d) If trading income exceeds the lower profits limit, Class 4 NICs are payable at 9% on profits between the lower profits limit and the upper profits limit. The upper profits limit for 2012-13 is £42,475. Any profits beyond the upper profits limit are charged to Class 4 NICs at 2%.

EXAMPLE 7

Calculate the Class 4 NICs payable for 2012-13 in each of the following cases:

(a) Shawn has trading income for 2012-13 of £14,880.

(b) Catherine has trading income for 2012-13 of £50,000.

(c) Paul has trading income for 2012-13 of £7,500.

Solution

(a) 9% x (£14,880 – £7,605) = £654.75.

(b) 9% x (£42,475 – £7,605) + 2% x (£50,000 – £42,475) = £3,288.80.

(c) Paul's profits are less than the lower profits limit so Class 4 NICs for the year are nil.

Annual maximum contributions

An individual who has more than one employment will normally be required to make Class 1 contributions in respect of each employment. Similarly, an individual who is both employed and self-employed will normally be required to make Class 1 contributions in respect of the employment and Class 2 and Class 4 contributions in respect of the self-employment. In these circumstances the total NICs payable could become onerous, but relief is available in the form of limits on the amount of NICs payable by any one person in any one year. In practice, the calculation of these limits can be very complex but a simplified outline of the rules is as follows:

(a) **Maximum Class 1 and 2 contributions**. In any one tax year, the total of the Class 1 contributions payable by an individual *at the main rate* (currently 12%) plus any Class 2 contributions is limited to the amount of the Class 1 contributions which would be payable by a weekly-paid employee who had 53 weeks of earnings equal to the UEL. For 2012-13, this gives a maximum contribution of £4,267.56 (53 × 12% × (£817 – £146)). A refund is made if this limit is exceeded, but the refund calculation takes into account the fact that earnings above the primary threshold which do not attract 12% contributions should attract 2% contributions instead.

(b) **Maximum Class 1, 2 and 4 contributions**. A refund of *Class 4 contributions only* is made if the total main rate (12%) Class 1 contributions, Class 2 contributions and main rate (9%) Class 4 contributions paid by an individual in any one tax year exceed the amount obtained by adding 53 Class 2 contributions to the maximum main rate Class 4 contribution for the year. For 2012-13 this limit is equal to £3,278.75 (53 @ £2.65 + 9% × (£42,475 – £7,605)). The refund calculation takes into account the fact that profits above the lower profits limit which do not attract Class 4 contributions at 9% should attract Class 4 contributions at 2% instead.

If an employee is contracted out, Class 1 contributions paid in the year are recalculated at the not-contracted-out rate before comparison is made with the above limits.

EXAMPLE 8

(a) Sabrina has two employments throughout 2012-13. Calculate the refund of NICs due for the year if she is not contracted out and her regular monthly earnings from the two employments are as follows:

(i) £850 and £1,250 (ii) £2,000 and £3,000 (iii) £4,000 and £4,500.

(b) Stephanie is employed at a monthly salary of £3,700. She is not contracted out. She also has a small business and pays 53 weekly Class 2 NICs in 2012-13. She pays no Class 4 NICs. Calculate the refund of NICs due for the year.

(c) Stewart is self-employed and pays 53 weekly Class 2 NICs in 2012-13. His trading income for 2012-13 is £35,230. He also receives directors' fees of £14,060 in the year. He is not contracted out. Calculate the refund of NICs due for the year.

Solution

(a) Sabrina will have paid *main rate* Class 1 NICs as follows:

	(i)	(ii)	(iii)
	£	£	£
First employment:			
12 x 12% x (£850 – £634)	311.04		
12 x 12% x (£2,000 – £634)		1,967.04	
12 x 12% x (£3,540 – £634)			4,184.64
Second employment:			
12 x 12% x (£1,250 – £634)	887.04		
12 x 12% x (£3,000 – £634)		3,407.04	
12 x 12% x (£3,540 – £634)			4,184.64
	1,198.08	5,374.08	8,369.28

In case (i), total contributions do not exceed the maximum, so no refund is due.

In case (ii), contributions exceed the maximum by £1,106.52 (£5,374.08 – £4,267.56) so Sabrina is entitled to a refund. However, the earnings which have given rise to the excess contributions are still subject to 2% contributions, so the refund is reduced by two-twelfths to £922.10.

In case (iii), Sabrina's contributions exceed the maximum by £4,101.72 (£8,369.28 – £4,267.56) so she is entitled to a refund of 10/12 x £4,101.72 = £3,418.10.

(b) Stephanie will have paid *main rate* Class 1 NICs and Class 2 NICs as follows:

	£
Class 1 (12 x 12% x (£3,540 – £634))	4,184.64
Class 2 (53 @ £2.65)	140.45
	4,325.09

This exceeds the maximum by £57.53 (£4,325.09 – £4,267.56). The refund can be made entirely out of Class 2 contributions so there will be no need to collect further 2% contributions on refunded main rate Class 1 contributions. The refund is £57.53.

(c) Stewart will have paid NICs as follows:

	£
Class 1 (12% x (£14,060 – £7,605))	774.60
Class 2 (53 @ £2.65)	140.45
Class 4 (9% x (£35,230 – £7,605))	2,486.25
	3,401.30

The total main rate Class 1 and Class 2 contributions are well within the maximum of £4,267.56. But the total of the main rate Class 1 contributions, Class 2 contributions and main rate Class 4 contributions exceeds the maximum of £3,278.75 by £122.55. Therefore Stewart is entitled to a refund of Class 4 contributions. However, the profits which have given rise to the excess contributions are still subject to 2% contributions, so the refund is reduced by two-ninths to £95.32.

Summary

- Primary Class 1 NICs are payable by employees. Secondary Class 1 NICs are payable by their employers. Both primary and secondary contributions are reduced if the employee is contracted out.
- Class 1 NICs are calculated with respect to earnings in a contribution period and each contribution period is considered independently.
- In 2012-13, primary Class 1 NICs are generally payable at 12% on earnings between the primary threshold and the upper earnings limit. But earnings between the primary threshold and the upper accruals point are charged at 10.6% (rather than 12%) if the employee is contracted out. Earnings that lie beyond the upper earnings limit attract primary Class 1 NICs at 2%.
- In 2012-13, secondary Class 1 NICs are generally payable at 13.8% on earnings that lie beyond the secondary threshold. But earnings between the secondary threshold and the upper accruals point are charged at 10.4% (rather than 13.8%) if the employee is contracted out.
- The Class 1 NICs of company directors are assessed on an annual basis and are unaffected by the distribution of the director's earnings over the year.
- Class 1A NICs are payable by employers in relation to benefits in kind which are not convertible into cash. Class 1B NICs are payable by employers in relation to PAYE Settlement Agreements.
- Class 2 NICs are payable at a flat rate by self-employed people whose profits exceed the small earnings exception.
- Class 4 NICs are paid by self-employed people and are earnings-related. In 2012-13, Class 4 NICs are payable at 9% on profits between the lower and upper profit limits and at 2% on profits beyond the upper limit.
- Class 3 NICs are paid voluntarily in order to maintain a full contributions record.
- There are annual maximum limits on the amount of NICs payable by an individual.

Exercises

16.1 Compute the primary and secondary Class 1 NICs payable in relation to the following employees (none of whom are contracted out):

(a) A earns £160 for the week ending 22 June 2012.

(b) B earns £780 for the week ending 22 June 2012.

(c) C earns £930 for the week ending 22 June 2012.

(d) D earns £550 for the month of September 2012.

(e) E earns £3,300 for the month of September 2012.

(f) F earns £6,000 for the month of September 2012.

16.2 Rework your answer to Exercise 15.1, assuming now that each of the employees is a member of a COSR occupational pension scheme.

16.3 Mark is self-employed and makes up his accounts annually to 30 November. His accounts for the year ended 30 November 2012 show a net profit of £7,270 and his accounts for the year ended 30 November 2013 show a net profit of £3,490. His 2012-13 trading income is £8,900. Calculate the NICs payable by Mark for 2012-13.

***16.4** Brenda is a company director and earns a regular monthly salary of £6,000. In December 2012 she received a £20,000 bonus. She is provided with a diesel-engined company car which has an emission rating of 218g/km and which had a list price when new of £26,000. The company pays all the running costs of the car, including fuel. Her BUPA subscription of £750 per year is paid by the company.

Calculate the NICs payable in respect of Brenda for 2012-13. She is a member of a COSR occupational pension scheme.

***16.5** Leonard is employed and receives a salary of £3,398 per month. He is not contracted out. He also has a small business and pays 53 weekly Class 2 NICs for 2012-13. His trading income for 2012-13 is £10,500. Calculate the refund of NICs due to Leonard for the year.

Review questions (Set A)

A1 Tom Tulliver has been appointed as sales director of Pembridge plc, a company in the building industry. In addition to a basic salary of £85,000, he has been offered a comprehensive benefits package. The proposed deal is:

(i) The company will provide him with a new car which, together with accessories, will cost £19,500. The car has an emission rating of 220g/km. Petrol for private use will be provided but Mr Tulliver must make a contribution of £1,000 per year towards its cost.

(ii) An interest-free loan of £5,250 will be made to him on appointment and need only be repaid on his leaving the company. The loan will be used to purchase various household items.

(iii) He has a choice of meals in the company canteen, which is open to all staff free of charge, or luncheon vouchers worth £5 per day, an amount equivalent to the normal cost of the meals. He has decided to accept the luncheon vouchers. The normal working year is 200 working days.

(iv) His son, aged three, is presently attending a nursery (which does not have approved childminder status) at a cost of £3,405 per year. Pembridge plc has offered to give his son a free place in their own nursery but Mr Tulliver would like to continue the existing arrangement and for Pembridge to pay the fees to the existing nursery.

Mr Tulliver's wife earns £15,000 per annum. She contributes 6% of her salary to her employer's occupational pension scheme (which operates the net pay arrangement).

Both Mr and Mrs Tulliver have building society accounts which will yield net interest of £6,400 and £2,712 respectively in 2012-13. Mr Tulliver receives UK preference dividends of £4,680 annually.

Mr Tulliver's appointment will begin on 1 April 2012 and he wishes to examine his and his wife's tax position before the start of fiscal year 2012-13.

Required:

(a) Advise Mr Tulliver on the taxation implications of his employment package.

(b) Advise him of any changes you consider that he should make to maximise the tax efficiency of the proposed package.

(c) Using your answer in (a) as to the amount of Mr Tulliver's income, advise him of the likely income tax borne by him and his wife for 2012-13 and, again, suggest how the tax position might be improved. (*Note*: Assume that the official rate of interest is 4%). *(Amended from AAT)*

A2 Jeremy, who has been married for many years, is 77 years old and receives a retirement pension of £20,260 per annum. He also receives dividend income of £6,750 per annum. In 2005 he purchased a life annuity from which a monthly income of £325 (gross) is paid. The capital element of each payment was agreed with HM Revenue and Customs at £300. Income tax is being deducted from the income element.

Jeremy owns a furnished cottage which he rents to holidaymakers. In tax year 2012-13 it was let for 20 weeks at a weekly rental of £300.

The following expenditure was incurred:

	£
Insurance (see note)	400
Water rates	500
Council tax	1,000

Note: An insurance premium of £400 for calendar year 2013 was paid on 1 January 2013. The insurance paid on 1 January 2012 was £360.

You are required:

To calculate the income tax payable by Jeremy for the year 2012-13, assuming that no elections have been made with respect to the married couple's allowance. *(ACCA)*

A3 Ae and Bee commenced in partnership on 1 July 2010 preparing accounts to 30 June. Cae joined as a partner on 1 July 2012. Profits have always been shared equally. The partnership's trading profits since the commencement of trading have been as follows:

	£
Year ended 30 June 2011	54,000
Year ended 30 June 2012	66,000
Year ended 30 June 2013	87,000

Dee commenced in self-employment on 6 April 2009. She initially prepared accounts to 5 April, but changed her accounting date to 31 July by preparing accounts for the four-month period to 31 July 2011. Dee's trading profits since she commenced trading have been as follows:

	£
Year ended 5 April 2010	35,160
Year ended 5 April 2011	32,880
Four months to 31 July 2011	16,240
Year ended 31 July 2012	54,120

Required:

(a) Calculate the trading income assessments of Ae, Bee and Cae for each of the tax years 2010-11, 2011-12 and 2012-13.

(b) Calculate the amount of trading profits that will have been assessed on Dee for each of the tax years 2010-11, 2011-12 and 2012-13.

(c) State the amount of Dee's unrelieved overlap profits as at 5 April 2013. *(ACCA)*

A4 In May 2012 Bernard, a self-employed plumber, and his son Gerald, a self-employed electrician, purchased 1,000 empty barrels from a Scottish whisky distillery. The barrels were over 100 years old and of no further use to the distillery. Bernard and Gerald sawed the barrels into halves and sold them to several local garden centres for use as ornamental flower tubs. Bernard and Gerald paid £10 per barrel to the distillery and sold a half-barrel for £8. Three-quarters of the barrels were sold by Bernard and Gerald in the summer of 2012 and the remainder in the summer of 2013.

You are required:

To prepare a list of points for consideration prior to writing a report to Bernard and Gerald on the liability to income tax on the profit generated by the venture. *(ACCA)*

A5 In each of the following situations, show the tax position assuming that the maximum potential reliefs are claimed as soon as possible. Then advise your client of any alternatives that might be available.

(i) Mr de Praet began trading on 1 January 2007, preparing accounts to 31 December annually. Recent results are:

	£	
Year to 31 December 2011	20,000	Profit
Year to 31 December 2012	(40,000)	Loss

He receives rents of £10,000 annually. It is estimated that the trading profits for the year to 31 December 2013 are likely to be £75,000.

(ii) Henry Percy started a business on 1 July 2006 and makes up accounts to 30 June annually. His adjusted trading results (before capital allowances) for the last two years have been:

	£	
Year to 30 June 2011	18,000	Profit
Year to 30 June 2012	(9,000)	Loss

Up to 31 December 2011 he always hired his plant and machinery but on 1 January 2012 he purchased a new machine for £7,360. He has no income other than his business profits. *(Amended from AAT)*

***A6** Roseanne starts business on 1 July 2012 and prepares accounts for the 16 months to 31 October 2013. The adjusted trading profit for this period is £26,720. Her only other income consists of interest received of £2,400 (net) per annum. In April 2013 she receives a notice to submit a tax return for 2012-13 but does not submit this return until 15 March 2014. The return is submitted electronically. Also on 15 March 2014, she pays all of the income tax and Class 4 NICs which fall due for payment on 31 January 2014.

Required:

(a) Calculate Roseanne's liability to income tax and Class 4 NICs for tax year 2012-13 and state the amount (or amounts) that fall due on 31 January 2014.

(b) Calculate any possible interest and penalties payable by Roseanne (assuming an interest rate of 3%).

***A7** Stephen is a UK resident taxpayer with two different sources of income. He works part-time as an IT consultant for a small number of clients, on a project management basis. A separate contract is drawn up for each project, specifying the deadline, expected output and the fee to be paid. Stephen uses his own laptop when necessary, and works from home most of the time.

Stephen also works two days a week (Thursdays and Fridays) for a nearby NHS Trust hospital where his wife (see below) works. He is given an office at the hospital, where he is required to be present between 8am and 6pm to work with the in-house IT team. In addition, the Trust provides 10 fully-paid days off in the year, and allows Stephen to invoice the Trust for the day even when he is sick.

Stephen's wife, Susan, is a pharmacist working in an NHS Trust hospital. Susan was born in 1969 and joined the company on 6 July 2012. Her gross pay for 2012-13 was £55,600 and income tax of £16,950 was deducted via PAYE.

Susan is provided with a company car for both business and private motoring. Details of the cars provided during 2012-13 were as follows:

	Make	**List price**	**Emissions**	**Fuel**
		£	g/km	
6 July 2012 to 5 October 2012	Ford	13,700	131	Petrol
6 October 2012 to 5 April 2013	BMW	30,910	146	Petrol

The company paid for all of the running costs of both these cars but Susan contributed £150 per month for private use of the BMW car. She also reimbursed her employer for all of the private fuel used by the Ford motor car (but not the BMW motor car).

On 6 August 2012, the company lent Susan £27,000 at an interest rate of 2% per annum. Susan repaid £18,000 of the loan on 6 March 2013.

Susan is provided with a mobile telephone and is allowed to use this telephone for both business and private calls. The company did not have to pay for the telephone itself but paid call charges of £391 during the year (of which £128 related to private calls).

Susan's other income for 2012-13 consisted of gross pay from her previous employer of £14,210 (PAYE £1,650), net dividends of £2,070 and ISA interest of £240.

Required:

(a) Discuss and apply the criteria which may be used to determine whether Stephen should be regarded as employed or self-employed.

(b) Prepare an income tax computation for Susan for tax year 2012-13. If any of her income is not taxable, explain why this is the case. (Assume that the official rate of interest is 4%).

(c) Calculate both Employers' and Employees' National Insurance Contributions (NICs) payable in relation to Susan for 2012-13. You should assume that Susan is not contracted out of the State Second Pension. *(CIPFA)*

***A8** Claud Chapperon is a self-employed wholesale clothing distributor who began trading on 1 July 2005. His summarised accounts for the year to 30 June 2012 are shown below (figures in brackets refer to notes).

	£	£
Sales (1)		400,000
Opening inventory (2)	40,000	
Purchases	224,000	
	264,000	
Closing inventory (2)	32,000	232,000
Gross profit		168,000
Wages and national insurance (3)	55,200	
Rent and rates	29,100	
Repairs and renewals (4)	3,490	
Miscellaneous expenses (5)	665	
Taxation (Claud's own income tax)	14,949	
Bad debts (6)	820	
Legal expenses (7)	1,060	
Depreciation	850	
Lease rental on Claud's car (8)	8,400	
Loss on sale of office furniture	60	
Gift Aid donations (9)	200	
Transport costs	3,861	
Interest (10)	990	
Running expenses of Claud's car (11)	2,000	
Premium on lease (12)	6,000	
Lighting and heating	1,250	
Sundry expenses (all allowable)	710	
Relocation expenditure (13)	2,395	132,000
Net profit		36,000

Notes:

1. Sales include £500 reimbursed by Claud's family for clothing taken from stock. The reimbursement represented cost price.

2. The basis of both the opening and closing inventory valuations was "lower of cost or market value" less a general reserve of 50%.

3. Included in wages are Claud's drawings of £100 per week, his NICs of £132 for the year and his wife's wages and NICs totalling £14,750. His wife works full-time in the business as a secretary.

4. The charge for repairs and renewals includes £3,100 for fitting protective covers over the factory windows and doors to prevent burglary.

5. Miscellaneous expenses comprise:

	£
Theft of money by employee	65
Political donation to Green Party	100
Gifts of 100 "Chapperon" calendars	500
	665

6. Bad debts comprise:

	£
Trade debt written off	720
Loan to former employee written off (not made for trade purposes)	250
Reduction in general allowance	(150)
	820

7. Legal expenses comprise:

	£
Defending action re alleged faulty goods	330
Costs re lease of new larger premises	250
Unsuccessful appeal against previous year's income tax assessment	200
Defending Claud in connection with speeding offence	190
Debt collection	90
	1,060

8. Claud's leased car had a retail price of £20,000 and was leased from 1 July 2011 to 30 June 2012. The car has emissions of 179g/km.

9. Gift Aid donations consist of £120 paid to the local children's hospital and £80 paid to Oxfam. Both payments were made on 30 April 2012.

10. Interest is as follows:

	£
Bank overdraft interest (business account)	1,020
Interest on overdue tax	130
Interest credited on NSB investment a/c (see note 14)	(160)
	990

11. HM Revenue and Customs has agreed that one-third of Claud's mileage is private. Included in the charge for motor running expenses is £65 for a speeding fine incurred by Claud whilst delivering goods to a customer.

12. The premium was for a lease of six years. The lease began on 1 July 2011.

13. The relocation expenditure was incurred in transferring the business to new and larger premises.

14. Interest recently credited to the NSB investment account is as follows:

	£
31 December 2011	160
31 December 2012	70

The following information is also provided:

(i) Capital allowances for the year to 30 June 2012 are £480.

(ii) Claud was born in 1956. He made net contributions of £11,800 to a registered pension scheme during 2012-13. His wife was also born in 1956.

You are required:

(a) To prepare a profit adjustment statement in respect of the period of account to 30 June 2012, showing the trading income for 2012-13.

(b) To calculate the Class 4 NICs payable by Claud for 2012-13.

(c) To prepare an estimate of Claud's income tax borne for 2012-13. *(ACCA)*

***A9** Iris starts business on 6 July 2012, preparing accounts to 5 April. Her adjusted trading loss for the nine months to 5 April 2013 is £15,000. However, she expects a trading profit of approximately £45,000 in the year to 5 April 2014.

Before starting her own business, Iris was in employment. Her recent employment income has been as follows

2008-09	£37,190
2009-10	£19,530
2010-11	£25,650
2011-12	£32,700
2012-13 (up to 5 July 2012)	£20,130

She has no other income in any year between 2008-09 and 2013-14 inclusive.

Required:

(a) Assuming for the sake of simplicity that tax rates, bands and allowances for all years are the same as those for 2012-13, calculate the effective percentage rate of tax relief that Iris would obtain if she claimed each of the following reliefs in relation to her trading loss:

- relief against total income for the year of the loss, or
- relief against total income for the previous year, or
- early trade losses relief, or
- carry-forward relief.

(b) Advise Iris as to the best course of action in relation to her loss.

***A10** Joseph Kent started business on 1 October 2010 as a joiner making conservatories. His tax-adjusted profits (before deduction of capital allowances) were as follows:

	£
Period to 31 December 2011	37,000
Year ended 31 December 2012	24,000
Year ended 31 December 2013	42,000

Capital additions and disposals were as follows:

		£
Additions		
1 October 2010	Plant and machinery	3,500
1 October 2010	Car (emissions 137g/km)	15,000
1 May 2011	Trailer	2,500
1 December 2012	Car (emissions 184g/km)	13,000
1 December 2013	Plant and machinery	2,400
Disposals		
1 December 2012	Car acquired 1/10/10	10,800
1 January 2013	Plant and machinery (at less than cost)	2,000

Private use of both cars has been agreed with HM Revenue and Customs at 20%. No claim is made to treat any of the assets as short-life assets.

Joseph's wife Sephora is a solicitor employed by a practising firm at a salary of £44,495 per annum. The following additional information is provided for 2012-13:

(i) A new petrol-engined car was provided for Sephora's use in August 2011. The list price at that time was £25,000. Of this amount, £4,000 was contributed by Sephora so that a better car could be provided. She was required to pay £25 per month towards the private use of the car but not towards the private fuel, all of which was provided by her employers. The car's emission rating is 172g/km.

(ii) Sephora has received a loan of £90,000 on the matrimonial home from her employers on which she pays interest at 1% per annum.

(iii) Sephora made a qualifying donation to the Oxfam charity on 1 July 2012 of £400 under the Gift Aid scheme.

(iv) Both Joseph and Sephora are under 65 years old.

You are required:

(a) To calculate Joseph's trading income for 2010-11 to 2013-14 inclusive.

(b) To calculate Sephora's income tax liability for 2012-13 (assuming an official rate of interest of 4% per annum). *(ACCA)*

Part 2

CAPITAL GAINS TAX

Chapter 17

Introduction to capital gains tax

Introduction

The next six chapters of this book are concerned with capital gains tax (CGT), which was introduced in 1965 with the aim of taxing any gains arising on the disposal of capital assets. Capital gains tax has undergone many changes since its inception and the changes that were made between 1965 and 1992 were consolidated into the Taxation of Chargeable Gains Act 1992. This Act has since been amended by subsequent Finance Acts.

Chargeable persons

A CGT liability may arise when a "chargeable person" makes a "chargeable disposal" of a "chargeable asset". The main categories of chargeable person are as follows:

(a) individuals who are resident or ordinarily resident in the UK

(b) business partners, who are each responsible for their share of the CGT due on the capital gains of a partnership

(c) the trustees of a trust or settlement

(d) the personal representatives of a deceased person.

Husbands and wives are assessed independently for CGT purposes, as are same-sex civil partners. The following are *not* chargeable persons for CGT purposes:

(a) companies and other corporate bodies, which pay corporation tax on their capital gains (not CGT) and therefore cannot incur a CGT liability

(b) registered charities and friendly societies, community amateur sports clubs, local authorities and local authority associations, registered pension schemes, unit trusts, investment trusts and approved scientific research associations, all of which are generally exempt from CGT (subject to certain restrictions).

Chargeable assets

All assets are regarded as chargeable assets except for those which are specifically exempted from CGT. The main exemptions are as follows:

(a) a taxpayer's principal private residence (see Chapter 21)

(b) motor cars, including vintage and veteran cars (but not personalised car registration plates); vehicles which are not covered by this exemption, such as vans, lorries and motor cycles, will generally fall within the scope of (d) below.

(c) items of tangible, movable property (referred to as "chattels") which are disposed of for £6,000 or less (see Chapter 19)

(d) chattels with a predictable useful life of 50 years or less ("wasting chattels") unless used in business and eligible for capital allowances (see Chapter 19)

(e) gilt-edged securities and qualifying corporate bonds (see Chapter 20)

(f) National Savings Certificates and Premium Bonds

(g) foreign currency (if acquired for private use)

(h) winnings from pools, lotteries, betting etc.

(i) decorations for valour (unless acquired by purchase)

(j) damages or compensation received for personal or professional injury and compensation received for mis-sold personal pension schemes

(k) life assurance policies (unless purchased from a third party)

(l) shares in a Venture Capital Trust (see Chapter 6)

(m) investments held in either an Individual Savings Account (ISA) or a Child Trust Fund (see Chapter 6).

It is important to realise that neither a chargeable gain nor an allowable loss can arise on the disposal of an asset that is not a chargeable asset. This means that any gains made on the disposal of such assets are not taxable but it also means that any losses which arise will not attract tax relief.

Chargeable disposals

The main and most obvious instance of a chargeable disposal occurs when a chargeable asset is sold. However, the sale of an asset in the course of trade (i.e. the sale of trading stock or inventory) does *not* constitute a chargeable disposal since any gain arising on such a sale is taxed as a trading profit (see Chapter 9).

Before CGT was introduced in 1965 there was a great incentive for taxpayers to show that the gain arising on the sale of an asset was a capital gain (not taxable) rather than a trading profit (taxable). This incentive diminished with the introduction of CGT. But it is still important to distinguish between capital gains and trading profits since the rules of computation for capital gains and trading profits are different, as are the rates of CGT and income tax (see later in this chapter).

As well as the sale of a chargeable asset, the following are also chargeable disposals:

(a) the sale of *part* of a chargeable asset

(b) the gift of all or part of a chargeable asset

(c) the loss or destruction of a chargeable asset

(d) the receipt of a capital sum derived from a chargeable asset (e.g. compensation received from an insurance company if an asset is damaged).

With regard to gifts, it is important to realise that CGT is basically a tax on the increase in value of an asset whilst owned by the taxpayer. This increase in value is chargeable to tax even if the taxpayer gives the asset away and receives nothing in return.

In general, the date on which a chargeable disposal is deemed to occur is the date on which ownership of the asset changes hands, regardless of the date on which any payment is made.

Non-chargeable disposals

The following types of disposal are *not* chargeable disposals and therefore any gains or losses arising on such disposals are exempt from CGT:

(a) gifts to charities and certain other bodies (e.g. art galleries and museums) and gifts of pre-eminent property to the nation (see Chapter 4)

(b) disposals caused by the death of the taxpayer.

Disposals between a husband and wife who live together at any time during the tax year in which the disposal occurs *are* chargeable disposals. However, such disposals are deemed to occur at a disposal value such that neither a chargeable gain nor an allowable loss arises on the disposal (see Chapter 18). This rule also applies to same-sex civil partners who have entered into a legally-recognised civil partnership.

A similar treatment may be accorded to gifts of national heritage property, subject to certain undertakings being received (e.g. with regard to reasonable public access).

Basis of assessment

A person's CGT liability for a tax year is based upon the chargeable disposals made by that person during the tax year. For example, the 2012-13 CGT assessment is based upon chargeable disposals made between 6 April 2012 and 5 April 2013 inclusive. No liability to CGT arises until an asset is disposed of, so the mere fact that an asset has appreciated in value will not of itself trigger a CGT assessment. The amount of the CGT assessment for a tax year is calculated as follows:

(a) The chargeable gain or allowable loss arising on each disposal made during the tax year is calculated separately (the method of calculation is described in great detail in subsequent chapters of this book).

(b) If total gains exceed total losses, the losses are subtracted from the gains to give the taxpayer's "net gains" for the year. If total losses exceed total gains, the gains are subtracted from the losses to give the "net losses" for the year.

(c) If there are net gains for the year, these are reduced first by any unrelieved losses brought forward from previous tax years or by any losses carried back on the death of the taxpayer (see later in this chapter).

(d) Net gains are then further reduced by the amount of the "annual exemption" for the year. The annual exemption for 2012-13 is £10,600. The amount of any net gains remaining after deduction of the annual exemption is the CGT assessment for the year. If net gains are too low to allow the whole of the annual exemption to be deducted, the CGT assessment for the year is £nil and the balance of the annual exemption is lost.

(e) If there are net losses for the year, the CGT assessment for that year is £nil and the whole of the annual exemption is lost. The net losses may then be carried forward for relief in future years, as described later in this chapter.

Husbands, wives and civil partners are each entitled to the full annual exemption. This exemption is also available to the trustees of a trust or settlement established for a mentally disabled person or for certain other infirm or disabled persons. For trustees of other settlements the annual exemption is lower (£5,300 for 2012-13). The personal representatives of a deceased person are entitled to the full annual exemption for the year of death and for the following two years.

EXAMPLE 1

Four taxpayers each make three chargeable disposals during 2012-13. Compute their CGT assessments for the year (assuming that there are no unrelieved losses brought forward or carried back) if these disposals give rise to the following gains and losses:

(a) Taxpayer A has gains of £2,900, £4,000 and £5,950.

(b) Taxpayer B has gains of £5,500, £6,340 and a loss of £350.

(c) Taxpayer C has gains of £950, £8,830 and a loss of £2,050.

(d) Taxpayer D has a gain of £8,950 and losses of £9,500 and £800.

Solution

(a) Total gains are £12,850 and there are no losses. Net gains are £12,850. Subtracting the annual exemption of £10,600 gives a CGT assessment for the year of £2,250.

(b) Total gains are £11,840. Total losses are £350 so net gains are £11,490. Subtracting the annual exemption of £10,600 gives a CGT assessment for the year of £890.

(c) Total gains are £9,780 and total losses are £2,050. Net gains are £7,730. This is less than the annual exemption of £10,600, so the CGT assessment for the year is £nil. The unused part of the annual exemption (£2,870) is lost.

(d) Total gains are £8,950 and total losses are £10,300. Net losses are £1,350. The CGT assessment for the year is £nil and the whole of the annual exemption is lost.

Rates of CGT

For tax year 2012-13, there are two main rates of CGT. These are the *standard rate* of 18% and the *higher rate* of 28%. However, a special rate of 10% applies to capital gains which qualify for "entrepreneurs' relief". In general terms, gains qualify for entrepreneurs' relief (ER) if they arise on the disposal of a business (see Chapter 22).

These rates of tax are applied to the gains which remain (if any) after capital losses and the annual exemption have been deducted. For individuals, the process is as follows:

(a) Gains which qualify for ER are taxed at 10%.

(b) If any of the individual's income is charged to income tax at the higher rate (40%) or dividend upper rate (32.5%), gains which do not qualify for ER are taxed at 28%.

(c) If none of the individual's income is taxed at the higher rate or at the dividend upper rate, the unused part of the basic rate band is first absorbed by any gains which qualify for ER (and which are taxed at 10%). Gains which do not qualify for ER are then taxed at 18% to the extent that they do not exceed any remaining part of the individual's basic rate band and at 28% otherwise.

The basic rate limit for 2012-13 is usually £34,370 (see Chapter 2) but this may be increased for Gift Aid donations (Chapter 4) or pension contributions (Chapter 14).

(d) Capital losses and the annual exemption may be deducted from capital gains in such a way that the CGT liability is minimised.

The rate of CGT applicable to trustees and personal representatives is 10% for gains which qualify for ER and 28% for all other gains.

EXAMPLE 2

Calculate the amount of CGT payable for 2012-13 by the following individuals. In each case, "taxable income" comprises the individual's total income, less reliefs which may be deducted from total income and less the personal allowance (see Chapter 2).

	Name	*Taxable income (£)*	*ER Gains (£)*	*Non-ER Gains (£)*	*Allowable losses(£)*
(a)	A	71,000	nil	11,800	nil
(b)	B	71,000	11,800	nil	nil
(c)	C	47,500	32,800	15,000	nil
(d)	D	52,700	27,600	4,200	1,000
(e)	E	29,300	nil	11,000	nil
(f)	F	32,570	nil	19,900	700
(g)	G	31,700	nil	22,300	12,900
(h)	H	24,270	£8,800	29,500	2,200

Assume that there are no unrelieved losses brought forward (or carried back on the death of the taxpayer) and no Gift Aid donations or pension contributions.

Solution

(a) Taxable income exceeds the basic rate limit, so gains which do not qualify for ER are taxed at 28%. CGT payable is (£11,800 – £10,600) x 28% = £336.

(b) Taxable income is not relevant since gains which qualify for ER are always taxed at 10%. CGT payable is (£11,800 – £10,600) x 10% = £120.

(c) The CGT liability is minimised if the annual exemption is set against the gains which do not qualify for ER, since these are taxed at a higher rate than gains which do qualify for ER. Taxable income exceeds the basic rate limit, so CGT payable is (£32,800 x 10%) + ((£15,000 – £10,600) x 28%) = £4,512.

(d) To minimise the CGT liability, the allowable losses of £1,000 are set against the gains of £4,200 which do not qualify for ER. Similarly, the annual exemption is set first against these gains. The remaining £7,400 of the exemption must then be set against the gains which qualify for ER. CGT payable is (£27,600 – £7,400) x 10% = £2,020.

(e) After deducting the annual exemption, the CGT assessment is £400 and this consists entirely of gains which do not qualify for ER. The unused part of the basic rate band is £5,070 (£34,370 – £29,300). This exceeds the CGT assessment of £400 so CGT payable is (£400 x 18%) = £72.

(f) The CGT assessment is £8,600 (£19,900 – £700 – £10,600) and this consists of gains which do not qualify for ER. The unused part of the basic rate band is £1,800 (£34,370 – £32,570). So CGT payable is (£1,800 x 18%) + (£6,800 x 28%) = £2,228.

(g) Net gains are £9,400 (£22,300 – £12,900). This is less than the annual exemption of £10,600 so the CGT assessment is £nil. £1,200 of the annual exemption is lost.

(h) The unused part of the basic rate band is £10,100 (£34,370 – £24,270). Gains which qualify for ER absorb £8,800 of this, leaving £1,300 available for the gains which do not qualify for ER. After deducting allowable losses and the annual exemption, these are £16,700 (£29,500 – £2,200 – £10,600), of which £1,300 is taxed at 18%. CGT payable is (£8,800 x 10%) + (£1,300 x 18%) + (£15,400 x 28%) = £5,426.

Relief for capital losses

If a taxpayer has net losses for a year, the CGT assessment for that year is £nil and the annual exemption is lost. The amount of the net losses may then be carried forward without time limit and set against the net gains of future years.

Losses carried forward must be offset against the first available net gains, but are offset only to the extent that those net gains exceed the annual exemption for the year in which they arise, so preventing the annual exemption from being wasted. Any losses remaining unrelieved are carried forward again to subsequent years. This method of preserving the annual exemption applies *only* to losses brought forward from a previous year. It is *not* possible to preserve the annual exemption by restricting the set-off of current year losses.

Since married couples and same-sex civil partners are taxed independently, the losses of one spouse (or partner) cannot be offset against the gains of the other spouse (or partner).

EXAMPLE 3

Four taxpayers each have £3,000 of capital losses brought forward. Calculate their CGT assessments for 2012-13 if their total gains and losses for the year are as follows:

(a) Taxpayer A has gains of £8,000 and losses of £1,300.

(b) Taxpayer B has gains of £10,800 and losses of £200.

(c) Taxpayer C has gains of £12,800 and losses of £500.

(d) Taxpayer D has gains of £16,700 and losses of £1,200.

Solution

(a) Net gains for the year are £6,700. This is less than the annual exemption of £10,600 so the CGT assessment for the year is £nil and the balance of the annual exemption is lost. There is no scope for relieving losses brought forward, so the entire £3,000 is carried forward to 2013-14.

(b) Net gains for the year are £10,600. This is exactly equal to the annual exemption so the CGT assessment for the year is £nil. There is no scope for relieving losses brought forward, so the entire £3,000 is carried forward to 2013-14.

(c) Net gains for the year are £12,300. This exceeds the annual exemption by £1,700 so £1,700 of the losses brought forward are relieved in 2012-13, giving a CGT assessment for the year of £nil. The remaining £1,300 of the losses are unrelieved and are therefore carried forward to 2013-14.

(d) Net gains for the year are £15,500. This exceeds the annual exemption by £4,900 so the entire £3,000 of losses brought forward are relieved in 2012-13, giving a CGT assessment for the year of £1,900. There are no unrelieved losses to carry forward.

Anti-avoidance rules relating to capital losses

TCGA 1992 contains the following anti-avoidance rules designed to prevent taxpayers from taking unfair advantage of the reliefs available in relation to capital losses:

(a) Capital losses incurred on a disposal to a connected person can be offset only against gains made on disposals to the *same person*, in the same or subsequent tax years. A taxpayer is deemed to be connected with a number of persons for CGT purposes, mainly relatives and business associates (see Chapter 18).

(b) A capital loss is not an allowable loss if it arises as a result of arrangements made by the taxpayer and a main purpose of those arrangements is to gain a tax advantage by creating an artificial capital loss.

Losses in the year of death

As stated earlier, disposals caused by the death of a taxpayer are exempt from CGT, although such disposals may give rise to an inheritance tax liability. But disposals made in the year of death (i.e. from 6 April up to the date of death) are *not* exempt from CGT and are taxed in the usual way, with a full annual exemption given for the year.

If a taxpayer suffers net losses in the year of death, such losses cannot (for obvious reasons) be carried forward. However, net losses incurred in the year of death may instead be carried back and set off against the net gains of the previous three years (most recent years first). As is the case with losses carried forward, losses carried back are set against a year's net gains only to the extent that those net gains exceed the annual exemption for the year in which they arise.

EXAMPLE 4

Sarah dies on 16 December 2012, having made net capital losses of £7,300 between 6 April 2012 and the date of her death. Her net gains in the previous three years (and the annual exemption for each of those years) were as follows:

	Net gains	*Annual exemption*
	£	£
2009-10	11,250	10,100
2010-11	2,800	10,100
2011-12	14,950	10,600

Calculate her CGT assessments for 2009-10 to 2012-13 inclusive.

Solution

Since losses in the year of death are carried back to the most recent year first, it is easier to begin with the year of death and then work backwards.

(a) In 2012-13, Sarah has net losses. Her CGT assessment for the year is therefore £nil and the annual exemption (available in full) is lost. The net losses of £7,300 may be carried back to 2011-12, 2010-11 and 2009-10, in that order.

(b) In 2011-12, Sarah's net gains of £14,950 exceed the annual exemption by £4,350 so £4,350 of the losses carried back are relieved in 2011-12, giving a CGT assessment for the year of £nil. The remaining £2,950 of the losses are carried back to 2010-11.

(c) In 2010-11, Sarah's net gains of £2,800 are less than the annual exemption of £10,100. Therefore the CGT assessment for the year is £nil and the balance of the annual exemption is lost. There is no scope for relieving losses carried back, so the £2,950 is now carried back to 2009-10.

(d) In 2009-10, Sarah's net gains of £11,250 exceed the annual exemption by £1,150 so £1,150 of the losses carried back are relieved in 2009-10, giving a CGT assessment for the year of £nil. The remaining £1,800 of the losses incurred in the year of death cannot be carried back any further and therefore cannot be relieved in any way.

Assuming that CGT assessments have already been made for 2009-10 and 2011-12, it will be necessary to revise these assessments to take into account the relief for losses carried back and to refund any CGT already paid for those years.

Relief for trading losses

If a taxpayer has claimed that a trading loss should be set against his or her total income for a tax year (or if no such claim can be made because total income for that year is zero) the taxpayer may further claim that any unrelieved part of the trading loss should be set against the capital gains of that year (see Chapter 12). If such a claim is made, the amount of the claim must be for the *lower* of the following two amounts:

(a) the amount of the unrelieved trading loss which is available for relief

(b) the "maximum amount", which is the amount of the CGT assessment, *disregarding the annual exemption*, that would have been raised for the year if the claim had not been made.

It is important to realise that the "maximum amount" is calculated as if the annual exemption simply did not exist. Not only is the annual exemption itself ignored in this calculation but so is the fact that capital losses brought forward might be restricted so as to preserve the exemption.

A trading loss which is set against capital gains is treated as a capital loss incurred in the year of the claim and is therefore relieved *before* giving relief for capital losses brought forward.

EXAMPLE 5

(a) Richard has net gains for 2012-13 of £16,800 and capital losses brought forward of £3,300. Calculate his CGT assessment for 2012-13.

(b) Richard has unrelieved trading losses (eligible for relief against his capital gains in 2012-13) of £27,500. Re-calculate his CGT assessment for 2012-13 if he claims that these losses should (as far as possible) be set against his capital gains.

(c) Now calculate the CGT assessment for 2012-13 if Richard's capital losses brought forward are £9,300 instead of £3,300.

Solution

(a) Without a trading losses claim for 2012-13, the CGT assessment for the year will be:

	£
Net gains	16,800
Less: Capital losses b/f	3,300
	13,500
Less: Annual exemption	10,600
CGT assessment	2,900

There will be no unrelieved capital losses to carry forward.

(b) A trading losses claim would have to be for the lower of:

(i) the unrelieved trading loss (£27,500)

(ii) the CGT assessment (disregarding the annual exemption) that would be raised if a trading losses claim were not made (£13,500).

Therefore the claim would be £13,500. This would be relieved in priority to capital losses brought forward. The CGT assessment would be:

	£
Net gains	16,800
Less: Trading losses	13,500
	3,300
Less: Annual exemption (restricted)	3,300
CGT assessment	nil

The remainder of the annual exemption (£7,300) would be lost. There would be no scope for relieving any of the capital losses brought forward, so the entire £3,300 would be carried forward to 2013-14. This claim would seem to be wasteful, since trading losses of £13,500 are sacrificed in order to reduce the CGT assessment by £2,900 and preserve capital losses of £3,300 (a total of £6,200).

(c) Without a trading losses claim, the CGT assessment would be calculated as follows:

	£
Net gains	16,800
Less: Capital losses b/f (restricted)	6,200
	10,600
Less: Annual exemption	10,600
CGT assessment	nil

There would be unrelieved capital losses of £3,100 carried forward. The maximum amount of a trading loss claim is £7,500 (£16,800 – £9,300) so the claim would have to be for £7,500 and the CGT assessment would be:

	£
Net gains	16,800
Less: Trading losses	7,500
	9,300
Less: Annual exemption (restricted)	9,300
CGT assessment	nil

The remainder of the annual exemption (£1,300) would be lost and the capital losses of £9,300 would be carried forward to 2013-14 in their entirety. The effect of the claim would be to preserve capital losses of £6,200 at the expense of sacrificing trading losses of £7,500. This might be worthwhile if Richard believes that he will have more chance of relieving capital losses than trading losses in future years.

Administration of CGT

The tax administration system which was described in Chapter 1 applies to CGT as well as to income tax. Note that:

(a) Taxpayers are normally not required to fill in the capital gains tax pages of their tax returns if both of the following conditions are satisfied:

   (i) total disposal proceeds for the year do not exceed four times the amount of the annual exemption (£42,400 for 2012-13)

   (ii) total chargeable gains for the year do not exceed the amount of the annual exemption (£10,600 for 2012-13).

   For this purpose, the term "total chargeable gains" means the total chargeable gains for the year *before* deduction of either current year losses or losses brought forward from previous years.

(b) Acquisitions of chargeable assets do not need to be entered on the tax return.

(c) A capital loss is not an allowable loss unless its amount is quantified and notified to HMRC. If the taxpayer receives a tax return for the year in which a loss is incurred, then notification must be made in that return. Otherwise, notification may be made in a later year's tax return or by sending a separate notice to HMRC. Capital losses are not allowed unless they are notified to HMRC within four years of the end of the tax year concerned.

Payment of CGT

CGT is normally payable on 31 January following the end of the tax year to which the tax relates. For instance, the date on which the 2012-13 CGT liability is normally payable is 31 January 2014. An important difference between the payment of CGT and the payment of income tax is that payments on account of the CGT liability are *not* required.

If the proceeds of a disposal are received by the taxpayer in instalments over a period of more than 18 months, the taxpayer may make a claim for the CGT due in relation to the disposal to be payable over the period of the instalments or over an eight-year period, whichever is the shorter.

Interest and penalties

The regime of interest and penalties which was described in Chapter 15 applies to both CGT and income tax.

Summary

- A liability to CGT may arise when a chargeable person makes a chargeable disposal of a chargeable asset. Individuals resident or ordinarily resident in the UK are chargeable persons. Companies are not chargeable persons.
- All assets are chargeable assets unless specifically exempted.
- A chargeable disposal occurs when all or part of a chargeable asset is sold (other than in the course of trade) or is given away, lost or destroyed.
- An individual's CGT liability for a tax year is based upon the chargeable disposals made by that individual during the year. For 2012-13, the first £10,600 of net gains are exempt from CGT.
- CGT for 2012-13 is generally payable at the standard rate of 18% or the higher rate of 28%. But gains which qualify for entrepreneurs' relief are taxed at only 10%.
- Net capital losses may be carried forward and set against the net gains of subsequent years. Net losses incurred in the year of death of a taxpayer may be carried back for up to three years.
- In certain circumstances, trading losses may be set against capital gains.
- CGT is normally payable on 31 January following the end of the tax year.

Exercises

17.1 Which of the following disposals might give rise to a CGT liability?

(a) the sale of freehold property by a UK company

(b) the gift of shares from husband to wife (assuming that the couple live together)

(c) the gift of an oil painting to a charity

(d) the sale of an oil painting by a charity

(e) the sale of an oil painting by an art dealer

(f) the sale of freehold property by a partnership.

17.2 Which of the following are chargeable assets for CGT purposes?

(a) shares in British Telecom plc

(b) gilt-edged securities

(c) an antique table worth £20,000

(d) an antique chair worth £5,000

(e) a taxpayer's home

(f) a vintage Bentley.

17.3 A taxpayer has capital losses of £2,500 in tax year 2012-13. There are no unrelieved losses brought forward from previous years. Compute the taxpayer's CGT assessment for 2012-13 if capital gains for the year are as follows:

either (a) £nil

or (b) £1,500

or (c) £8,250

or (d) £14,550.

17.4 In 2012-13, a taxpayer has capital gains of £262,600 and allowable losses of £12,300. He has no unrelieved capital losses brought forward from previous years. His taxable income for 2012-13 (after deduction of the personal allowance) is £27,270 and he has made no Gift Aid donations or pension contributions. Calculate his CGT liability for the year, assuming that the gains of £262,600 comprise:

(a) a single gain of £262,600 which does not qualify for entrepreneurs' relief (ER)

(b) a single gain of £262,600 which qualifies for ER

(c) a gain of £205,700 which qualifies for ER and a gain of £56,900 which does not qualify for ER.

17.5 A taxpayer has capital losses brought forward from previous years amounting to £4,800. Compute the CGT assessment for 2012-13 if total gains and losses for the year are as follows:

either (a) gains £9,700, losses £1,000

or (b) gains £11,500, losses £300

or (c) gains £16,600, losses £nil.

17.6 John dies on 3 March 2013. Between 6 April 2012 and 3 March 2013, he has capital gains of £1,200 and capital losses of £15,400. His net gains in recent tax years (and the annual exemption for each year) have been as follows:

	Net gains	*Annual exemption*
	£	£
2008-09	52,700	9,600
2009-10	16,600	10,100
2010-11	12,900	10,100
2011-12	3,150	10,600

Explain how (and to what extent) John's net losses in 2012-13 will be relieved.

17.7 On what date is CGT for 2012-13 normally due for payment?

***17.8** Rosemary's capital gains and losses in recent years (and the annual exemption for each year) have been as follows:

	Gains	*Losses*	*Annual exemption*
	£	£	£
2009-10	6,500	12,700	10,100
2010-11	9,500	2,350	10,100
2011-12	13,400	nil	10,600
2012-13	19,700	7,500	10,600

There were no unrelieved losses to bring forward from 2008-09 or earlier. Compute her CGT assessments for tax years 2009-10 to 2012-13 inclusive.

***17.9** Ahmed makes three disposals in 2012-13 (A, B and C). The gains on disposals A and B are £120,000 and £10,000 respectively. The allowable loss on disposal C is £24,400. He also has capital losses brought forward of £5,000.

Ahmed's taxable income for 2012-13 (after deduction of the personal allowance) is £19,370. He makes Gift Aid donations of £8,000 during the year. Compute the CGT payable for the year assuming that:

(a) Gain A qualifies for entrepreneurs' relief (ER) but Gain B does not qualify.

(b) Gain B qualifies for ER but Gain A does not qualify.

(c) Both gains qualify for ER.

(d) Neither gain qualifies for ER.

***17.10** Melissa is a sole trader. Her capital gains and capital losses for 2012-13 are £25,900 and £1,000 respectively. She also has capital losses brought forward from 2011-12 of £13,200 and unrelieved trading losses of £18,500 which are eligible for relief against capital gains in 2012-13.

Show Melissa's CGT assessment for 2012-13, assuming that:

(a) a claim to relieve trading losses against capital gains is not made

(b) a claim to relieve trading losses against capital gains is made.

Chapter 18

Computation of gains and losses

Introduction

The computation of the gain arising on the disposal of a chargeable asset is basically a matter of subtracting the acquisition cost of the asset from its disposal value. However, it may be necessary to adjust the gain to take account of a number of other costs incurred by the taxpayer and the calculation becomes more complex if only part of the asset has been disposed of. Also, a different method of computation applies if the asset was acquired on or before 31 March 1982.

The purpose of this chapter is to explain the basic method of computation and to show how this method is modified for disposals of older assets.

Layout of a CGT computation

The computation of the chargeable gain or allowable loss arising on a chargeable disposal occurring during tax year 2012-13 is laid out as follows:

	£	£
Disposal value		xxx
Less: Incidental costs of disposal		xxx
		xxx
Less: *Allowable expenditure*:		
Acquisition cost of asset	xxx	
Incidental costs of acquisition	xxx	
Enhancement expenditure	xxx	
Cost of defending the owner's title to the asset	xxx	
Valuation fees	xxx	xxx
Chargeable gain or allowable loss		xxx

Each of the terms used in this layout is explained below.

Disposal value

If a disposal consists of the sale of an asset, disposal value is generally taken to be the proceeds of the sale. But if a sale does not constitute a bargain made at arm's length, the sale proceeds are ignored and disposal value is taken to be the market value of the asset on the date of the sale. This rule applies particularly to transactions between "connected persons". For CGT purposes, a taxpayer is connected to his or her:

(a) spouse (husband or wife)

(b) relatives (brothers, sisters, ancestors, direct descendants) and their spouses

(c) spouse's relatives and their spouses

(d) business partners and their spouses and relatives.

All references to "spouse" in the above list should be taken to include same-sex civil partners who have entered into a legally-recognised civil partnership.

Market value is also used as disposal value if a disposal takes the form of a gift. But disposals between spouses or civil partners who live together are deemed to occur at a disposal value such that neither a gain nor a loss arises (see Chapter 17). This rule takes precedence over the usual rules concerning sales to connected persons and gifts.

In general, the market value of an asset is the amount which the asset would fetch if sold on the open market. Shares and securities which are listed on a recognised stock exchange ("listed" or "quoted" shares or securities) are valued for CGT purposes in the same way as they are valued for inheritance tax purposes (see Chapter 31).

The incidental costs of disposal which may be deducted when calculating a gain or loss include legal fees, estate agents' and auctioneers' fees, advertising costs etc.

Allowable expenditure

The following expenditure may be set against disposal value when calculating the gain or loss arising on a disposal:

(a) the acquisition cost of the asset (or its market value on the date of acquisition if it was acquired by gift or otherwise than by way of a bargain made at arm's length)

(b) incidental costs of acquisition (e.g. legal fees)

(c) "enhancement expenditure", which is expenditure on making improvements to the asset, so long as that expenditure is still reflected in the state of the asset at the time of disposal (but the costs of mere repairs and maintenance are disallowed)

(d) costs incurred in defending the owner's title to the asset (generally legal costs)

(e) valuation fees necessarily incurred for CGT purposes.

If an asset is acquired as the result of a disposal between spouses or civil partners who live together, the deemed acquisition cost for the spouse or partner receiving the asset is equal to the deemed disposal value for the spouse or partner who makes the disposal (see above).

EXAMPLE 1

(a) A chargeable asset was bought in June 2009 for £41,200 and sold in August 2012 for £73,350. Compute the chargeable gain.

(b) A chargeable asset was bought for £15,000 in August 2004. Legal costs of £500 were incurred when the asset was acquired. The owner of the asset incurred enhancement expenditure of £2,000 in May 2005 and £3,000 in June 2010. The asset was sold in July 2012 for £28,000. Legal costs of £700 were incurred on the sale. Compute the chargeable gain.

(c) A taxpayer bought a chargeable asset for £40,000 in February 2006. The asset was sold for £30,000 in October 2012. Compute the chargeable gain or allowable loss if:

(i) the asset was sold in an arm's length transaction

(ii) the asset was sold to the taxpayer's brother and had a market value of £45,000 on the date of the sale

(iii) the asset was sold to the taxpayer's wife and had a market value of £45,000 on the date of the sale.

Solution

(a)

	£
Sale proceeds	73,350
Less: Acquisition cost	41,200
Chargeable gain	32,150

(b)

	£	£
Sale proceeds		28,000
Less: Incidental costs of disposal		700
		27,300
Less: Acquisition cost	15,000	
Incidental costs of acquisition	500	
Enhancement expenditure (£2,000 + £3,000)	5,000	20,500
Chargeable gain		6,800

(c)

	(i)	(ii)	(iii)
	£	£	£
Disposal value	30,000	45,000	40,000
Less: Acquisition cost	40,000	40,000	40,000
Chargeable gain/(allowable loss)	(10,000)	5,000	-

In case (iii), disposal value is set to £40,000 so as to ensure that neither a gain nor a loss occurs on this disposal to the taxpayer's spouse.

Part disposals

If only *part* of a chargeable asset is disposed of, only part of its cost can be allowed when computing the gain or loss. The allowable part cost is the full cost of the asset multiplied by the following fraction:

$$\frac{A}{A+B}$$

where: A is the value of the part disposed of (i.e. the disposal value), and

B is the value of the part remaining in the taxpayer's ownership.

This part disposal fraction applies not only to the acquisition cost of the asset but also to any other items of allowable expenditure which relate to the whole asset. But any item of expenditure which relates only to the part of the asset which has been disposed of should be allowed in full.

EXAMPLE 2

Peter buys a chargeable asset for £26,000 in May 2003. He sells a one-quarter interest in the asset for £12,000 in August 2012, incurring incidental costs of disposal of £500. The value of the other three-quarters interest in the asset in August 2012 is £40,000. Calculate the chargeable gain.

Solution

	£
Sale proceeds	12,000
Less: Incidental costs of disposal	500
	11,500
Less: Part cost: $\frac{£12,000}{£12,000 + £40,000} \times £26,000$	6,000
Chargeable gain	5,500

Notes:

(i) The fact that Peter has sold a one-quarter interest in the asset is irrelevant. What is relevant is that he has sold £12,000 worth out of an asset currently worth £52,000, as indicated by the part disposal fraction.

(ii) If Peter disposes of the remaining three-quarters of the asset at some future time, the remaining £20,000 of the cost (£26,000 – £6,000) will then be allowable.

(iii) The incidental costs of disposal are allowed in full since these relate solely to the part of the asset which has been disposed of.

Small part disposals of land

An exception to the usual part disposal rules occurs when a taxpayer makes a small part disposal of land. A part disposal of land is "small" if the land is freehold, or held on a lease with more than 50 years left to run, and the following conditions are met:

(a) If the disposal is caused by a compulsory purchase order, the disposal proceeds must not exceed 5% of the value of the whole piece of land. However, it is the practice of HM Revenue and Customs to treat disposal proceeds of £3,000 or less as small for this purpose, regardless of whether or not the 5% test is satisfied.

(b) If the disposal is not caused by a compulsory purchase order, the disposal proceeds must not exceed 20% of the value of the whole piece of land and the total proceeds of all disposals of land in the year of assessment (excluding small disposals caused by compulsory purchases) must not exceed £20,000.

A taxpayer who makes a small part disposal of land which satisfies these conditions may claim that the disposal should not be treated as a chargeable disposal but that the proceeds of the disposal should instead be subtracted from the acquisition cost of the land. This claim has the following consequences:

(a) No gain or loss arises on the small part disposal.

(b) Since the acquisition cost of the land is reduced, the gain arising on a subsequent disposal of the remainder of the land is automatically increased.

In effect, the gain arising on the small part disposal is deferred until the remainder of the land is disposed of. Fairly obviously, the taxpayer should not make such a claim if the gain arising on the small part disposal would be covered by the annual exemption for the year.

Note that these rules apply only to small part disposals of *land*, whereas the more general part disposal rules explained earlier in this chapter apply to all types of chargeable asset.

EXAMPLE 3

In July 2003, Malcolm bought a piece of land for £40,000. In June 2008 he sold part of the land for £11,000. This disposal was not caused by a compulsory purchase and was his only disposal of land in 2008-09. The value of the remainder of the land in June 2008 was £50,000. Malcolm had substantial capital gains in 2008-09, sufficient to absorb his annual exemption for the year, and therefore decided to make a small part disposal claim.

Calculate the chargeable gain arising in January 2013 when Malcolm sells the remainder of the land for £60,000.

Solution

The small part disposal claim in 2008-09 was valid since the total value of the land immediately prior to the disposal was £61,000 and the disposal raised £11,000 which is less than 20% of £61,000. Furthermore, the proceeds of all land disposals in the year did not exceed £20,000.

No gain or loss arises on the June 2008 disposal but the sale proceeds of £11,000 are subtracted from the acquisition cost of the land. The gain on the January 2013 disposal is therefore as follows:

	£
Sale proceeds	60,000
Less: Reduced acquisition cost (£40,000 – £11,000)	29,000
Chargeable gain	31,000

Assets with negligible value

If the value of a chargeable asset has become negligible, the owner of the asset may make a "negligible value" claim. If this claim is accepted, the asset is treated as if it had been disposed of at its current, negligible value (giving rise to an allowable loss) and then immediately re-acquired at that value.

EXAMPLE 4

In September 2007, Gloria acquired 1,000 ordinary shares in a listed company for £7,000. Trading in the shares was suspended in December 2012 and Gloria claimed that the shares then had a negligible value of only 10p per share. This claim was accepted by HMRC. Compute the allowable loss.

Solution

	£
Deemed disposal value (1,000 x 10p)	100
Less: Cost	7,000
Allowable loss	(6,900)

If Gloria succeeds in selling the shares at some time in the future, their deemed acquisition cost for CGT purposes will be £100.

Assets held on 31 March 1982

CGT was originally introduced in 1965 and applied to disposals made on or after 6 April 1965, which was the "base date" for CGT. Gains which accrued before 6 April 1965 were not taxable. Therefore, if an asset was acquired before 6 April 1965 and disposed of after that date, only the part of the gain accruing after 6 April 1965 was taxable.

However, the CGT base date has since been changed to 31 March 1982. Therefore, if an asset which was held on 31 March 1982 is now disposed of, only the part of the gain accruing since 31 March 1982 is taxable. The calculation of the taxable part of the gain is achieved by means of a technique known as "rebasing" whereby the market value of the asset at 31 March 1982 is substituted for its acquisition cost in the CGT calculation.

Rebasing

Finance Act 2008 simplified the rebasing rules which apply to the disposal of assets held on 31 March 1982. The CGT treatment of such disposals is now as follows:

(a) The gain or loss arising on the disposal of an asset held on 31 March 1982 is calculated by comparing the asset's disposal value with its market value at 31 March 1982. Any enhancement expenditure incurred after 31 March 1982 is taken into account in the usual way when computing the gain or loss.

(b) The original acquisition cost of the asset is no longer relevant for CGT purposes and is entirely ignored. In fact, all costs incurred on or before 31 March 1982 (including any enhancement expenditure incurred up to that date) are ignored and are replaced in the CGT computation by the asset's market value at 31 March 1982.

(c) In effect, the owner of the asset is treated as if he or she had bought it on 31 March 1982 for its market value on that date.

Finance Act 2008 introduced a number of CGT reforms, including simplification of the rebasing rules. However, none of these reforms apply to companies. The rules which apply when a company makes a disposal of an asset held on 31 March 1982 are explained later in this book (see Chapter 24).

EXAMPLE 5

Alan bought a chargeable asset for £22,000 in April 1980. The asset was sold for £29,500 in January 2013. Compute the chargeable gain arising on this disposal if the asset's market value on 31 March 1982 was:

(a) £24,200 (b) £21,500 (c) £32,000

Solution

(a) The original cost of this asset is irrelevant and the gain or loss is calculated by means of rebasing. The chargeable gain is £5,300 (£29,500 – £24,200). Rebasing has worked in Alan's favour, since he is being taxed on only £5,300 out of a total gain of £7,500 during his period of ownership of the asset.

(b) The chargeable gain is £8,000 (£29,500 – £21,500). This time, rebasing has not worked in Alan's favour, since he is being taxed on £8,000 even though his total gain since 1980 is only £7,500. However, rebasing is mandatory and there is nothing that can be done about this.

(c) There is an allowable loss of £2,500 (£29,500 – £32,000). Rebasing has benefited Alan, since he has enjoyed a total gain of £7,500 during his period of ownership of the asset but is now being granted an allowable loss of £2,500.

Part disposals of assets held on 31 March 1982

When a part disposal is made of an asset which was held on 31 March 1982, the part disposal fraction which would normally be applied to the cost of the asset when computing the chargeable gain arising on the disposal (see earlier in this chapter) is applied instead to the asset's market value at 31 March 1982.

The gain or loss arising on such a part disposal is calculated by comparing disposal value with the appropriate part of the asset's market value at 31 March 1982. If there has been enhancement expenditure since 31 March 1982, the appropriate part of that expenditure is also taken into account when computing the gain or loss.

EXAMPLE 6

Hilary bought a chargeable asset in November 1978 for £3,000. The asset had a market value on 31 March 1982 of £5,000. She sold part of the asset for £8,000 in November 2012, at which time the remainder of the asset was valued at £12,000. Compute the chargeable gain arising on this disposal.

Solution

	£
Sale proceeds	8,000
Less: Part market value at 31 March 1982:	
$\frac{£8,000}{£8,000 + £12,000} \times £5,000$	2,000
Chargeable gain	6,000

Summary

- The disposal value of an asset is normally equal to sale proceeds, but if an asset is given away or is sold other than by way of a bargain at arm's length, the disposal value is normally deemed to be the market value of the asset on the date of disposal.
- Allowable costs include an asset's acquisition cost, incidental costs, enhancement expenditure, costs of defending the owner's title and valuation fees.
- On a part disposal, the allowable part cost is calculated by multiplying the full cost by the part disposal fraction. Special rules apply to small part disposals of land.
- A taxpayer may claim that an asset has negligible value, so triggering a disposal which gives rise to an allowable loss.
- Rebasing applies on the disposal of an asset which was held at 31 March 1982. The gain or loss on disposal is calculated by comparing disposal value with the market value of the asset at 31 March 1982.
- Finance Act 2008 made a number of reforms to the capital gains tax system. These include a simplification of the rebasing rules. None of these reforms apply to disposals made by companies.
- The gain or loss arising on the part disposal of an asset held on 31 March 1982 is calculated by comparing disposal value with the appropriate part of the asset's market value at 31 March 1982.

Exercises

18.1 Carol purchased a holiday flat in December 2003 for £100,000. She spent £5,000 on installing central heating in February 2004 and a further £750 on repainting the interior of the flat in March 2004. The flat was never Carol's main residence.

She sold the flat at auction in February 2013 for £172,000, paying a 5% fee to the auctioneer. Legal costs were £400 in December 2003 and £500 in February 2013. Compute Carol's chargeable gain on the disposal of the flat.

18.2 David was given a chargeable asset in November 2005 at which time the asset had a market value of £7,500. He sold the asset in January 2013. Compute the chargeable gain or the allowable loss if his sale proceeds were:

(a) £14,950

(b) £6,350

(c) £25,780.

18.3 Edwina bought a chargeable asset in August 2003 for £240,000, paying acquisition costs of £12,000. In June 2009 she sold a one-quarter interest in the asset for £100,000, incurring disposal costs of £5,000. The remaining three-quarters interest in the asset was valued at £500,000 in June 2009.

(a) Compute the chargeable gain arising in June 2009.

(b) Also compute the chargeable gain arising in January 2013, when Edwina sold her remaining three-quarters interest in the asset for £520,000.

18.4 Francis acquired an oil painting for £12,500 in March 1979. He sold the painting for £37,500 in March 2013. Compute the chargeable gain or allowable loss arising on this disposal if the painting's market value on 31 March 1982 was:

(a) £10,000 (b) £15,000 (c) £50,000.

18.5 In June 2004, Gillian was given shares with a market value at that time of £6,000. In November 2011 she made a successful claim to the effect that these shares now had a negligible value of only £80.

(a) Compute the allowable loss.

(b) Compute the chargeable gain arising in March 2013, when Gillian sold the shares for £120.

***18.6** Jon bought a chargeable asset for £23,000 in May 1979. He incurred enhancement expenditure of £10,000 in June 1981 and a further £14,000 in July 1996. The asset was valued at £58,500 on 31 March 1982 and was sold for £185,000 in February 2013.

(a) Compute the chargeable gain.

(b) Now re-compute the gain, assuming that the person who bought the asset from Jon in February 2013 was his wife (who lives with him).

***18.7** Karen bought a house in 1985 for £42,000. In November 1986 she spent £18,000 on dividing the house into two self-contained flats. In September 2010 she sold one of the flats for £95,000, at which time the other flat was valued at £105,000. In January 2013 she sold the second flat for £110,000. Karen never lived in either of the flats.

Compute the chargeable gains arising on Karen's two disposals.

Chapter 19

Chattels and wasting assets

Introduction

A "chattel" is an item of tangible, movable property. A "wasting asset" is an asset with a predictable useful life not exceeding 50 years. If an asset is both a chattel and a wasting asset (e.g. a TV set) it is referred to as a "wasting chattel". Special capital gains tax rules apply to disposals of chattels, wasting assets and wasting chattels. The purpose of this chapter is to explain these rules.

The chattels exemption

The disposal of a chattel for £6,000 or less is exempt from capital gains tax. This rule removes from charge a great many trivial disposals and ensures that CGT is levied only if the disposal is material. The following points relate to the chattels exemption:

(a) This exemption applies only to chattels, not to assets in general.

(b) The exemption means that gains arising on the disposal of a chattel for £6,000 or less are not chargeable to CGT. It also means that losses arising on such disposals are not generally allowable. However, special rules apply to chattels acquired for more than £6,000 and disposed of for £6,000 or less (see later in this chapter).

(c) The £6,000 figure relates to the *gross* disposal proceeds. These are the proceeds before deducting incidental costs of disposal.

(d) If the gross disposal proceeds of a chattel exceed £6,000, the chargeable gain cannot exceed five-thirds of the amount by which the disposal proceeds exceed £6,000. This "marginal relief" ensures that taxpayers who dispose of chattels for slightly more than £6,000 are not unduly penalised by the tax system.

EXAMPLE 1

In 2012-13, a taxpayer makes a number of disposals, as listed below. Which of these disposals would be exempt from CGT?

(a) An antique table sold for £5,000.

(b) A watercolour painting sold at auction. The auctioneer deducted his 10% commission from the selling price and sent the taxpayer a cheque for the remaining £5,670.

(c) A holding of shares sold for £4,500.

Solution

(a) The antique table is a chattel disposed of for £6,000 or less. Therefore the disposal is exempt from CGT.

(b) A watercolour painting is a chattel. The gross disposal proceeds must have been £6,300, since £6,300 less 10% = £5,670. The chattels exemption will not apply but the chargeable gain cannot exceed five-thirds of £300 (i.e. £500).

(c) A shareholding is not a chattel. Therefore the £6,000 exemption does not apply and the disposal will be chargeable to CGT.

EXAMPLE 2

In December 2012, Michael sells a piece of antique furniture for £6,360, paying incidental disposal costs of £320. He had acquired the furniture in January 2005 as a gift from his mother. Compute Michael's chargeable gain if the market value of the furniture in January 2005 was:

(a) £5,500 (b) £4,900

Solution

	(a)	(b)	
	£	£	
Sale proceeds	6,360	6,360	
Less: Incidental costs of disposal	320	320	
	6,040	6,040	
Less: Deemed acquisition cost	5,500	4,900	
Chargeable gain	540	1,140	(restricted to £600)

Notes:

(a) The maximum gain is £360 x 5/3 = £600. The gain of £540 in case (a) is less than £600, so the chargeable gain is £540.

(b) In case (b), £1,140 exceeds £600, so the gain is restricted to £600.

Chattels disposed of at a loss

If a chattel is disposed of at a loss, there are two possibilities. Either:

(a) the disposal proceeds exceed £6,000, in which case the allowable loss is calculated in the usual way, or

(b) the disposal proceeds are £6,000 or less, in which case the chattels exemption applies and it appears that no allowable loss could arise.

However, if a chattel is acquired for more than £6,000 and then disposed of for less than £6,000, the chattels exemption is overruled and an allowable loss is available. But the amount of this loss is restricted to the amount that would arise if the disposal proceeds were exactly £6,000.

EXAMPLE 3

In March 2013, Naomi sells an oil painting which she had acquired many years previously for £10,000. Compute the allowable loss if she sells the painting for:

(a) £7,200 (b) £5,700

Solution

(a) Naomi has disposed of a chattel for more than £6,000, so the disposal is not exempt from capital gains tax. The allowable loss is calculated in the usual way as £10,000 – £7,200 = £2,800.

(b) Naomi has disposed of a chattel for less than £6,000 and normally this disposal would be exempt from capital gains tax. However, since the asset was acquired for more than £6,000, a loss is allowed. This is calculated by substituting £6,000 for the disposal proceeds. The allowable loss is £10,000 – £6,000 = £4,000.

Part disposals of chattels

A part disposal of a chattel may be made in one of two ways. Either:

(a) a part interest in a chattel may be disposed of, or

(b) for chattels forming a set, one or more of the items in the set may be disposed of.

Each of these forms of part disposal is considered below.

Disposal of a part interest in a chattel

If a disposal is made of a part interest in a chattel, this part disposal will be exempt from capital gains tax only if the value of the *whole* chattel immediately prior to the part disposal is £6,000 or less.

If the value of the whole chattel exceeds £6,000 the disposal is not exempt from CGT and the usual part disposal calculation is performed. However, the chargeable gain on the part disposal is limited to five-thirds of the amount by which the value of the whole chattel exceeds £6,000, multiplied by the usual part disposal fraction.

EXAMPLE 4

In October 2006 Jackie bought a statuette for £3,500. In October 2012 she sells a one-third interest in the statuette for £2,000. Compute the chargeable gain if the value of the remaining two-thirds interest in October 2012 is:

(a) £4,000 (b) £5,000.

Solution

(a) The value of the whole chattel on the date of the part disposal is £6,000. Since this value does not exceed £6,000 the part disposal is exempt from CGT.

(b) The value of the whole chattel on the date of the part disposal is £7,000. Since this value exceeds £6,000 the part disposal is not exempt from CGT. The computation of the chargeable gain is as follows:

	£	
Sale proceeds	2,000	
Less: Part cost: $\frac{£2,000}{£2,000 + £5,000} \times £3,500$	1,000	
Chargeable gain	1,000	(restricted to £476)

The part disposal fraction cancels down to 2/7ths, so the gain is restricted to (£7,000 – £6,000) x 5/3 x 2/7 = £476.

Disposal of part of a set

If a taxpayer acquires a set of chattels (e.g. a set of dining chairs) and then disposes of them individually, each disposal is regarded as a part disposal and will in general be chargeable to CGT only if the disposal proceeds of an individual item exceed £6,000.

However, a taxpayer who wished to dispose of a set of chattels with a total value exceeding £6,000 could use this rule to avoid capital gains tax by disposing of the items one by one (with each disposal raising less than £6,000). In order to prevent such tax avoidance, a series of disposals of chattels which form part of a set *to the same person or to persons connected with each other or acting together* are treated as a single transaction for capital gains tax purposes. If the individual disposals occur in different tax years, any gain which results from this treatment is apportioned between tax years in proportion to the sale proceeds of each disposal.

EXAMPLE 5

Andrew acquired a set of six dining chairs in January 2006 for £1,300. In June 2012 he sold three of the chairs to a friend for £3,500 (the other three chairs also being valued at £3,500 at that time). In August 2012 he sold the remaining chairs to the friend's brother for £3,700. Compute the chargeable gain arising on these disposals.

Solution

If it were not for the rule introduced above, neither of these disposals would be chargeable to CGT since neither of them raises more than £6,000. However, the two disposals are made to connected persons and are therefore to be regarded as a single transaction for CGT purposes. The total disposal proceeds are £7,200 (£3,500 + £3,700). This exceeds £6,000 so the disposals are chargeable. The computation is as follows:

	£	
Sale proceeds	7,200	
Less: Cost	1,300	
Chargeable gain	5,900	(restricted to £2,000)

The maximum gain is (£7,200 – £6,000) x 5/3 = £2,000. £5,900 is greater than this, so the chargeable gain is restricted to £2,000.

Wasting chattels

Chattels which have a predictable useful life not exceeding 50 years in length are referred to as "wasting chattels" and are generally exempt from CGT. Therefore the disposal of a wasting chattel will usually give rise to neither a chargeable gain nor an allowable loss.

An exception to this rule occurs in the case of movable plant and machinery used in business and eligible for capital allowances. Plant and machinery is always regarded as having a predictable useful life not exceeding 50 years and therefore movable plant and machinery is a wasting chattel. Unless disposal proceeds are £6,000 or less (in which case the general chattels exemption applies) disposals of movable plant and machinery used in business and eligible for capital allowances are *not* exempt from CGT. One of two situations may arise on such a disposal:

(a) Disposal proceeds may be less than original cost. In this (the most likely) case, the allowable loss is reduced by the total capital allowances which have been available on the asset. This will reduce the loss to zero.

(b) Disposal proceeds may be greater than original cost. In this case, the total of the available capital allowances on the asset is zero and therefore capital allowances have no effect on the computation, which will proceed in the usual way.

In fact, these rules (other than the £6,000 exemption) also apply to fixed plant and machinery used in business and eligible for capital allowances.

It is worth noting that certain collectors' items such as antique clocks and watches and vintage motor cycles are regarded as plant and machinery. Consequently, these items are treated as wasting chattels, even though their useful lives may in fact considerably exceed 50 years. By virtue of this treatment, such items are exempt from CGT unless used in business and eligible for capital allowances.

EXAMPLE 6

An item of movable plant and machinery is bought in February 2010 for £8,000 and used solely for trade purposes. Capital allowances are available in relation to this item. Compute the chargeable gain arising if the item is sold in July 2012 and the sale proceeds are:

(a) £4,500 (b) £6,500 (c) £8,500 (d) £10,500.

Solution

In case (a), sale proceeds do not exceed £6,000 so the disposal is exempt from CGT. In cases (b), (c) and (d), the sale proceeds exceed £6,000 so there is no exemption. The computations are as follows:

	(b)	(c)	(d)
	£	£	£
Sale proceeds	6,500	8,500	10,500
Less: Acquisition cost	8,000	8,000	8,000
	(1,500)	500	2,500
Less: Available capital allowances	1,500	0	0
Chargeable gain/(allowable loss)	(nil)	500	2,500

Notes:

(i) In case (c), the maximum gain is £4,167 (£2,500 x 5/3). £500 is less than this, so the chargeable gain is £500.

(ii) In case (d), the maximum gain is £7,500 (£4,500 x 5/3). £2,500 is less than this, so the chargeable gain is £2,500.

Wasting assets

A wasting asset which is not a chattel is *not* exempt from CGT. Typical examples of such wasting assets include:

(a) intangible assets such as copyrights, patents and options with lives not exceeding 50 years in length

(b) short leases

(c) fixed plant and machinery (but see earlier in this chapter for the CGT treatment if plant and machinery is used in business and is eligible for capital allowances).

In general, the original cost of a wasting asset is deemed to waste away on a straight line basis over the asset's predictable life. The computation of the gain or loss arising on the disposal of such an asset is achieved by comparing the disposal value with the unexpired portion of the asset's cost at the time of disposal. However, special rules apply to the disposal of a lease (see later in this chapter).

EXAMPLE 7

In January 2003, Fiona acquired a 25-year copyright at a cost of £30,000. In January 2013 she sold the copyright for £35,500. Compute the chargeable gain.

Solution

When the copyright was bought it had a 25-year life. When it was sold there were 15 years remaining. Therefore the computation is as follows:

	£
Sale proceeds	35,500
Less: Unexpired portion of cost	
$\frac{15}{25}$ x £30,000	18,000
Chargeable gain	17,500

EXAMPLE 8

On 31 March 1978, Philip acquired a 45-year copyright at a cost of £75,000. The copyright was valued at £82,000 on 31 March 1982. On 31 March 2013, Philip sold the copyright for £47,000. Compute the chargeable gain.

Solution

Rebasing applies since the copyright was acquired before 31 March 1982. The copyright is treated as if it had been bought for £82,000 on 31 March 1982 (with 41 years of its life remaining). The original cost of £75,000 is ignored.

When the copyright was sold there were 10 years of its life remaining. Therefore the CGT computation is as follows:

	£
Sale proceeds	47,000
Less: Unexpired portion of market value at 31 March 1982:	
$\frac{10}{41}$ x £82,000	20,000
Chargeable gain	27,000

Leases

For capital gains tax purposes, leases are classified into long leases (those of more than 50 years) and short leases (those of 50 years or less). A chargeable disposal may occur in connection with a lease in any of the following ways:

(a) A taxpayer who has a long lease on a property assigns that lease to someone else.

(b) A taxpayer who has a short lease on a property assigns that lease to someone else.

(c) A taxpayer who owns the freehold of a property (or has a long head-lease) grants a long lease (or long sub-lease) to someone else, the property eventually reverting to the taxpayer concerned.

(d) A taxpayer who owns the freehold of a property (or has a long head-lease) grants a short lease (or short sub-lease) to someone else, the property eventually reverting to the taxpayer concerned.

(e) A taxpayer who has a short head-lease on a property grants a shorter sub-lease to someone else, the property eventually reverting to the taxpayer concerned.

Each of these cases is considered below. If a property is (or has been) the taxpayer's main residence, the gain arising on the disposal of a lease on the property may be subject to the principal private residence exemption described in Chapter 21.

Assignment of a long lease

The assignment of a long lease is treated as a disposal of the whole asset and therefore causes no CGT difficulties at all. The computation proceeds in precisely the same way as the computation on the disposal of any other whole asset.

EXAMPLE 9

In June 2007, Jim acquired a 99-year lease on a flat for £170,000. In January 2013, he assigned the lease to a third party for £192,000. The flat was never Jim's residence. Compute the chargeable gain.

Solution

The chargeable gain is simply £22,000 (£192,000 – £170,000). If the flat had been Jim's main residence for all or part of the period of ownership, the gain may have been reduced or eliminated by the principal private residence exemption.

Assignment of a short lease

A short lease is, by definition, a wasting asset. Therefore the computation of the gain arising on the disposal of a short lease should be achieved by comparing disposal proceeds with the unexpired portion of the lease's cost at the time of disposal.

However, unlike other wasting assets, the cost of a short lease is not deemed to waste away on a straight line basis. Instead, the cost of a short lease is deemed to waste away according to a table of percentages which is given in Schedule 8 of TCGA 1992 and is reproduced at the end of this chapter. The effect of this table is to write off the cost of a short lease slowly in the early years and more quickly in the closing years. The proportion of the cost of a short lease which is allowed in the CGT computation on its disposal is:

$$\frac{\text{\% relating to number of years lease has left to run on disposal}}{\text{\% relating to original length of lease}}$$

If the lease was originally a long lease but the taxpayer has owned it for some years so that the lease now being assigned is a short lease, the denominator in the above fraction is taken as 100%, corresponding to "50 or more" in the Schedule 8 table.

Schedule 8 gives percentages for whole numbers of years only. If the duration of a lease is not a whole number of years, then the appropriate percentage is calculated from the table on a pro rata basis.

EXAMPLE 10

Jean acquired a 30-year lease on a property in July 2002 for £132,000. In July 2012 she assigned the lease to a third party for £145,000. The property was never Jean's residence. Compute the chargeable gain.

Solution

When the lease was acquired it had a 30-year life (Sch 8 percentage 87.330%). When it was assigned there were 20 years remaining (Sch 8 percentage 72.770%). Therefore the computation is as follows:

	£
Sale proceeds	145,000
Less: Unexpired portion of cost	
$\frac{72.770}{87.330} \times £132,000$	109,992
Chargeable gain	35,008

EXAMPLE 11

A taxpayer assigns a lease of duration 12 years and 5 months. Calculate the appropriate percentage for use in the CGT computation on the disposal.

Solution

The percentage for 12 years is 53.191%. The percentage for 13 years is 56.167%. The difference between these percentages is 2.976%. Therefore the appropriate percentage for a lease of duration 12 years and 5 months is 53.191 + (2.976 x 5/12) = 54.431%.

EXAMPLE 12

Joan acquired a 40-year lease on a property on 31 May 1981 for £38,000. The market value of the lease on 31 March 1982 was £35,000. On 30 November 2012 she assigned the lease to a third party for £65,000. The property was never Joan's residence. Compute the chargeable gain.

Solution

Rebasing applies since the lease was acquired before 31 March 1982. On 31 March 1982 there were 39 years and 2 months of the lease term remaining (Sch 8 percentage 94.842 + 0.615 x 2/12 = 94.945%). When the lease was assigned there were only 8 years and 6 months remaining (Sch 8 percentage = 39.399 + (3.755 x 6/12) = 41.276%). Therefore the computation is as follows:

	£
Sale proceeds	65,000
Less: Unexpired portion of market value at 31 March 1982	
$\frac{41.276}{94.945}$ x £35,000	15,216
Chargeable gain	49,784

Note:

The original cost of £38,000 is ignored since rebasing applies.

Grant of a long lease

The grant of a long lease (or long sub-lease) out of a freehold (or a long head-lease) is treated as a part disposal for CGT purposes and the normal part disposal rules apply. The value of the part disposed of is usually equal to the proceeds of the disposal. The value of the part remaining takes into account both:

(a) the right of the taxpayer making the disposal to receive rents from the tenant, and

(b) the taxpayer's "reversionary interest", which is the right to take back the property when the lease (or sub-lease) finishes.

Grant of a short lease

The grant of a short lease (or short sub-lease) out of a freehold (or a long head-lease) is also treated as a part disposal for CGT purposes and therefore the part disposal rules apply again. However, part of the premium received on the grant of a short lease is assessable to income tax as property income (see Chapter 5) and therefore, in order to avoid double taxation, the disposal proceeds in the part-disposal computation are reduced by the amount of the premium which is assessable as property income.

EXAMPLE 13

Jeffrey acquired a freehold property in October 2004 for £234,000. In July 2012 he granted Jill a lease on the property for £160,000. The market value of the freehold after the lease had been granted was £200,000. The property was never Jeffrey's residence. Compute the chargeable gain, given that the lease granted to Jill was of duration:

(a) 99 years (b) 40 years.

Solution

(a) This is a part disposal with A = £160,000 and B = £200,000. The computation is as follows:

	£
Sale proceeds	160,000
<u>Less</u>: Part cost:	
$\frac{£160{,}000}{£160{,}000 + £200{,}000} \times £234{,}000$	104,000
Chargeable gain	56,000

(b) This is also a part disposal but £35,200 (£160,000 – (2% x £160,000 x 39)) of the disposal proceeds will be assessable as property income and this must be taken into account in the CGT computation. The computation is as follows:

		£
Sale proceeds (£160,000 – £35,200)		124,800
Less: Part cost:		
$\frac{£124,800}{£160,000 + £200,000} \times £234,000$		81,120
Chargeable gain		43,680

Note that the numerator of the part disposal fraction is taken as the disposal proceeds *after* deducting the property income assessment, whilst the denominator takes into account the disposal proceeds *before* deducting the property income assessment.

Grant of a short sub-lease out of a short head-lease

In essence, the grant of a short sub-lease out of a short head-lease is treated in a similar fashion to the assignment of a short lease, as discussed earlier in this chapter. As before, the TCGA 1992 Schedule 8 table of percentages is called into use to determine the part cost that should be deducted in the capital gains tax computation. But since the property will be returning to the original tenant when the sub-lease finishes, the proportion of the cost of the short head-lease which is allowed in the CGT computation on the granting of the sub-lease is equal to:

$$\frac{P1 - P2}{P3}$$

where:

P1 = % relating to the number of years left of the short head-lease when the sub-lease begins

P2 = % relating to the number of years left of the short head-lease when the sub-lease ends

P3 = % relating to original length of the short head-lease.

Since part of the premium received by the taxpayer on the grant of a short sub-lease will be assessable to income tax as property income, the capital gain arising is reduced by the amount of the property income assessment. However, this reduction cannot be used to convert a gain into a loss or to increase a loss.

EXAMPLE 14

Joanna acquired a 15-year lease on a property in September 2006 for £45,000. In September 2012 she granted a 4-year sub-lease to a third party for £20,000. The property was never Joanna's residence. Compute the chargeable gain.

Solution

The computation of the chargeable gain is as follows:

	£
Sale proceeds	20,000
Less: Proportion of cost	
$\frac{43.154 - 26.722}{61.617} \times £45{,}000$	12,001
	7,999
Less: Property income assessment (£10,160)	7,999
Chargeable gain	nil

Notes:

(i) P1 = 43.154 (9 years), P2 = 26.722 (5 years) and P3 = 61.617 (15 years)

(ii) The property income assessment (see Chapter 5) is:

	£
Premium received	20,000
Less: £20,000 x (4 – 1) x 2%	1,200
	18,800
Less: Relief for premium paid:	
$\frac{4}{15} \times (£45{,}000 - (£45{,}000 \times (15 - 1) \times 2\%))$	8,640
	10,160

(iii) The relief given for the property income assessment is restricted to £7,999 so as not to turn a gain into a loss.

Summary

- A chattel is an item of tangible, movable property. A wasting asset is an asset with a predictable useful life of 50 years or less. A wasting asset that is also a chattel is a wasting chattel.
- Chattels disposed of for £6,000 or less are exempt from CGT.
- If a chattel is disposed of for more than £6,000, the chargeable gain cannot exceed five-thirds of the amount by which disposal proceeds exceed £6,000.
- The allowable loss on chattels acquired for more than £6,000 and disposed of for less than £6,000 is restricted by substituting £6,000 for the disposal proceeds.
- Disposals of a part interest in a chattel are exempt from CGT if the value of the whole chattel is £6,000 or less.
- A series of disposals of chattels forming a set will be treated as a single transaction for CGT purposes if the disposals are to connected persons.
- Wasting chattels are exempt from CGT apart from movable plant and machinery used in business on which capital allowances are available.
- Wasting assets are not exempt from CGT. In general, the original cost of a wasting asset is written off over its predictable life using the straight line method. However, special rules apply to leases.
- An assignment of a long lease is regarded as the disposal of a whole asset.
- An assignment of a short lease is a disposal of a wasting asset. The original cost of a short lease is written off over its predictable life, using a table of percentages contained in Schedule 8, TCGA 1992.
- The grant of a long lease is treated as a part disposal.
- The grant of a short lease (or sub-lease) out of a freehold (or long head-lease) is treated as a part disposal. The part of the premium received which is taxable as property income is deducted from disposal proceeds in the CGT computation.
- The grant of a short sub-lease out of a short head-lease is a part disposal of a wasting asset. The Schedule 8 table is used to determine the allowable cost used in the CGT computation. The part of the premium received which is taxable as property income is deducted from the gain arising but cannot be used to convert a gain into a loss or to increase a loss.

Short lease amortisation table

(Schedule 8 of TCGA 1992)

Years	*Percentage*	*Years*	*Percentage*	*Years*	*Percentage*
50 or more	100	33	90.280	16	64.116
49	99.657	32	89.354	15	61.617
48	99.289	31	88.371	14	58.971
47	98.902	30	87.330	13	56.167
46	98.490	29	86.226	12	53.191
45	98.059	28	85.053	11	50.038
44	97.595	27	83.816	10	46.695
43	97.107	26	82.496	9	43.154
42	96.593	25	81.100	8	39.399
41	96.041	24	79.622	7	35.414
40	95.457	23	78.055	6	31.195
39	94.842	22	76.399	5	26.722
38	94.189	21	74.635	4	21.983
37	93.497	20	72.770	3	16.959
36	92.761	19	70.791	2	11.629
35	91.981	18	68.697	1	5.983
34	91.156	17	66.470	0	0

Exercises

19.1 Classify each of the following assets as either chattels, wasting assets or wasting chattels:

(a) A domestic washing machine.

(b) A gold ring.

(c) A personal computer.

(d) A 20-year lease on a building.

(e) A suit of clothes.

(f) An antique vase.

19.2 In October 2012 Keith sells an antique cabinet for £7,200. He incurs incidental costs of disposal amounting to £200. The cabinet cost Keith £2,300 in July 2004. Compute the chargeable gain.

19.3 In September 2012 Kevin sells a drawing for £2,000. He bought the drawing in February 2006 for £50,000 when it was thought (incorrectly) to be by a famous artist. Compute the allowable loss.

19.4 In January 2013 Karl sells a one-quarter interest in a painting for £25,000. The remaining three-quarters interest is valued at £85,000. The painting had cost Karl £38,500 in January 2004. Compute the chargeable gain.

19.5 In January 2010 Katrina buys an item of movable plant and machinery for use in her business. The plant costs her £50,000 and capital allowances are claimed. Compute the chargeable gain arising in March 2013 when she sells the plant, assuming that sale proceeds are:

(a) £65,000

(b) £35,000.

19.6 In June 2010 Katie acquired a 5-year option to buy a piece of land. The option cost her £10,000. In June 2012 she sold the option for £8,000. Compute the chargeable gain.

19.7 Katherine acquired a 40-year lease on a property on 31 August 1994 for £75,000. On 31 August 2012 she assigned the lease to a third party for £97,500. The property was never Katherine's residence. Compute the chargeable gain.

***19.8** In March 2005, Sean acquired a pair of matching antique silver candlesticks at a cost of £4,000. In August 2012 he sold one of the candlesticks to James for £6,750. At that time the other candlestick was valued at £5,750. In September 2012 he sold the other candlestick to Julia for £5,800. Calculate the chargeable gain arising on these two disposals if:

(a) James and Julia are unconnected.

(b) James and Julia are a married couple.

***19.9** On 31 March 1980, Estelle acquired a patent with a 42-year life at a cost of £21,000. The patent was valued at £22,000 on 31 March 1982 and Estelle sold the patent on 31 March 2013 for £13,000. Compute the chargeable gain.

***19.10** In May 2004, Edward paid £350,000 to buy a 20-year lease on a flat. In November 2012 he granted a 5-year sub-lease on the flat to a third party for £150,000. The flat was never Edward's principal private residence. Compute the chargeable gain.

Chapter 20

Shares and securities

Introduction

A disposal of shares or securities causes no CGT problems unless a taxpayer disposes of part of a shareholding which was built up over a period of time in a number of separate acquisitions. If this happens, it is impossible to identify the shares that have been disposed of, because shares of the same class in the same company are "fungible assets" (i.e. assets that cannot be individually distinguished). But the calculation of the gain or loss arising on the disposal cannot proceed until the cost of the shares has been established. Therefore TCGA 1992 specifies a set of *share identification* or *share matching* rules which are used to match disposals against acquisitions in these circumstances. The main purpose of this chapter is to explain these rules and to show how they are applied when calculating the gain or loss arising on a disposal of shares.

This chapter also explains the CGT rules relating to bonus issues, rights issues and capital distributions and outlines the CGT treatment of the share disposals which occur when one company is taken over by another company.

The share matching rules

For CGT purposes, disposals of shares or securities are matched against acquisitions of *the same class of shares in the same company* in the following order:

(a) First, against any acquisitions made on the same day as the day of the disposal.

(b) Next, against any acquisitions made during the following 30 days, matching with shares acquired earlier rather than later within that 30-day period. This rule is intended to counter the practice known as "bed and breakfasting", whereby shares are sold and then almost immediately re-acquired so as to trigger gains or losses for tax avoidance purposes.

(c) Finally, against shares forming the "Section 104 holding". This consists of a pool of all the shares of that class in that company that were acquired before the date of the disposal and which have not been matched against previous disposals.

It is important to note that the share matching rules which apply when a *company* makes a disposal of shares are different from those which apply for CGT purposes. The rules which have effect for corporation tax purposes are explained in Chapter 24.

EXAMPLE 1

Paul made the following acquisitions and disposals of ordinary shares in Crim plc:

Date		*Number of shares*
5 June 2009	acquisition	3,000
17 May 2010	acquisition	500
17 May 2010	disposal	800
9 June 2010	acquisition	200
13 March 2012	disposal	2,000
28 March 2012	acquisition	1,750
17 July 2013	disposal	1,000

No further shares were acquired during 2013. Against which acquisitions will each of the above disposals be matched?

Solution

(a) The 800 shares which were disposed of on 17 May 2010 are matched as follows:

- (i) first, against the 500 shares acquired on the same day
- (ii) next, against the 200 shares acquired in the next 30 days (on 9 June 2010)
- (iii) finally, against 100 of the shares that form the s104 holding; these are the 3,000 shares acquired on 5 June 2009 and there are 2,900 shares left in this holding after the 17 May 2010 disposal has been matched.

(b) The 2,000 shares disposed of on 13 March 2012 are matched as follows:

- (i) first, against the 1,750 shares acquired in the next 30 days (on 28 March 2012)
- (ii) finally, against 250 of the 2,900 shares that remain in the s104 holding (so there are 2,650 shares left in this holding after the 13 March 2012 disposal has been matched).

(c) The 1,000 shares disposed of on 17 July 2013 cannot be matched against shares acquired on the same day or during the following 30 days. Therefore these shares must be matched against 1,000 of the 2,650 shares that remain in the s104 holding.

The situation after these three disposals have been matched is that Paul is left with 1,650 shares in his s104 holding of ordinary shares in Crim plc.

The Section 104 holding

A taxpayer's "Section 104 holding" of shares of a certain class in a certain company is a pool containing any shares that were acquired before the date of the current disposal but which have not been matched against previous disposals. The name of this pool is derived from Section 104 of TCGA 1992, which provides the legal basis for its existence.

If it were not for the provisions of Section 104, it would be necessary to maintain detailed records of the date and cost of each individual share acquisition. However, the pooling arrangement provided by Section 104 eliminates the need to keep such detailed records. Instead, all that is required is a record of:

(a) the total number of shares in the s104 holding, and
(b) the total allowable expenditure in relation to those shares.

The allowable expenditure is normally equal to the cost (or CGT acquisition value) of the shares concerned. But if any of the shares in the s104 holding were acquired before 31 March 1982, their cost is replaced by their market value at that date. This is because rebasing applies to the disposal of assets held on 31 March 1982 and the cost of such assets is not relevant for CGT purposes.

Note that share acquisitions which are matched against same-day disposals or against disposals occurring within the previous 30 days (by virtue of the first two matching rules explained above) do not enter the s104 holding.

EXAMPLE 2

Pauline makes the following purchases of preference shares in Viole plc:

Date	*Number of shares*	*Cost* £
23 June 1980	1,000	1,000
14 May 1995	2,000	5,800
8 July 2012	3,000	8,700

The shares had a market value of £2 per share on 31 March 1982. There were no disposals on or before 8 July 2012. Show Pauline's s104 holding of preference shares in Viole plc at 8 July 2012.

Solution

	Number of shares	*Allowable expenditure* £
Acquired 23 June 1980	1,000	2,000
Acquired 14 May 1995	2,000	5,800
Acquired 8 July 2012	3,000	8,700
s104 holding c/f at 8 July 2012	6,000	16,500

Notes:

(i) The shares acquired before 31 March 1982 have been added into the s104 holding at their 31 March 1982 market value.

(ii) The three acquisitions forming the s104 holding have been combined into a single pool of 6,000 shares with total allowable expenditure of £16,500. It is now necessary to carry forward only these two "bottom line" figures, rather than the details of each individual acquisition.

(iii) On average, the allowable expenditure per share is £2.75 (£16,500 ÷ 6,000). When there is a disposal from the pool, this is the expenditure that will be allowed for each share that is disposed of (see below).

Disposals from the s104 holding

When there is a disposal of shares from the s104 holding, the number of shares that have been disposed of is deducted from the number of shares in the pool. It is then necessary to deduct a proportion of the allowable expenditure in the pool.

Strictly speaking, this proportion should be calculated using the part disposal fraction (see Chapter 18) which takes into account the value of the shares disposed of and the value of the remaining shares. In most cases, however, the value per share of the shares disposed of will be the same as the value per share of the shares that remain, so that the proportion of the allowable expenditure which should be deducted from the pool can be based upon the *number* of shares disposed of.

The gain or loss arising on a disposal from the s104 holding is calculated simply as the difference between the disposal value of those shares and the amount which has been subtracted from the allowable expenditure in the pool as a consequence of the disposal.

EXAMPLE 3

Paula makes the following acquisitions of ordinary shares in Idigo plc:

Date	*Number of shares*	*Cost*
		£
1 July 2006	5,000	6,300
2 August 2007	2,000	2,500
3 February 2010	1,200	2,300
4 January 2013	1,800	3,400

She sells 500 shares on 28 March 2013. No shares are acquired within the next 30 days.

(a) Show the s104 holding on 28 March 2013, just prior to and just after the disposal on that date.

(b) Compute the chargeable gain or allowable loss on the disposal if sale proceeds are:

(i) £1,300 (ii) £1,000 (iii) £700

Solution

(a) The s104 holding is as follows:

	Number of shares	*Allowable expenditure* £
Acquired 1 July 2006	5,000	6,300
Acquired 2 August 2007	2,000	2,500
Acquired 3 February 2010	1,200	2,300
Acquired 4 January 2013	1,800	3,400
	10,000	14,500
Sold 28 March 2013 (500/10,000ths)	(500)	(725)
s104 holding c/f	9,500	13,775

Notes:

1. The disposal in March 2013 must have come from the s104 holding since it cannot be matched against shares acquired on the same day or within the next 30 days.
2. The disposal is 500 shares out of a pool of 10,000 shares. Therefore 500 shares are deducted from the pool, along with 500/10,000ths of the allowable expenditure.
3. On average, the allowable expenditure in the pool is £1.45 per share and so the allowable expenditure deducted on the disposal (£725) is equal to 500 shares at £1.45 per share.

(b)

	(i) £	(ii) £	(iii) £
Sale proceeds	1,300	1,000	700
Less: Allowable expenditure	725	725	725
Chargeable gain/(allowable loss)	575	275	(25)

Bonus issues

A bonus issue occurs when a company issues free extra shares to its shareholders. The number of bonus shares received by a shareholder is generally in proportion to his or her existing shareholding. For instance, a "1 for 5" bonus issue would give each shareholder one free extra share for every five shares previously held.

For CGT purposes, a bonus issue is treated as a reorganisation of share capital, rather than as an issue of new shares. Accordingly, when a taxpayer receives bonus shares, the required CGT treatment is to uplift the number of shares in each of the taxpayer's previous acquisitions so as to reflect the bonus issue. Since all of these previous acquisitions are held together in the s104 holding, the desired effect can be achieved by simply adding the bonus shares into the "number of shares" column of the s104 holding. The allowable expenditure associated with this holding is not affected, since bonus shares are issued free of charge.

EXAMPLE 4

Sherjeel made the following acquisitions of ordinary shares in Trangle plc:

Date	*Number of shares*	*Cost*
		£
27 September 1981	1,200	2,400
28 July 1999	800	2,800
3 February 2004	500	2,000
5 July 2008	300	1,500

The market value of the company's shares on 31 March 1982 was £3 per share. On 1 September 2011, the company made a 1 for 10 bonus issue. Calculate the chargeable gain arising on 1 March 2013 when Sherjeel sold 1,400 shares for £6 each, assuming that he made no further acquisitions within the next 30 days.

Solution

The disposal cannot be matched against acquisitions on the same day or within the next 30 days, so it must come from the s104 holding. The s104 holding is as follows:

	Number of shares	*Allowable expenditure*
		£
Acquired 27 September 1981	1,200	3,600
Acquired 28 July 1999	800	2,800
Acquired 3 February 2004	500	2,000
Acquired 5 July 2008	300	1,500
s104 holding c/f	2,800	9,900

	Number of shares	*Allowable expenditure* £
s104 holding b/f	2,800	9,900
Bonus issue 1 September 2011	280	-
	3,080	9,900
Sold 1 March 2013 (1,400/3,080ths)	(1,400)	(4,500)
s104 holding c/f at 1 March 2013	1,680	5,400

The disposal proceeds are £8,400 (1,400 x £6). Therefore the chargeable gain is £3,900 (£8,400 – £4,500).

Notes:

(i) The shares acquired before 31 March 1982 are incorporated into the s104 holding at their market value at that date (£3 per share) and not at their cost.

(ii) The 280 bonus shares increase the number of shares in the s104 holding but do not increase the allowable expenditure in that holding.

Rights issues

A rights issue occurs when a company offers its shareholders the right to buy extra shares. Rights issues are similar to bonus issues in that the number of shares offered to each shareholder is generally in proportion to his or her existing shareholding. But rights shares are not issued free of charge. Shareholders who are offered rights shares may either:

(a) ignore the rights issue (in which case there is no CGT impact)

(b) sell their "rights" (see later in this chapter)

(c) buy the shares which they are offered.

For CGT purposes, a rights issue is treated in a very similar way to a bonus issue. If a taxpayer buys rights shares, the number of shares in each of the taxpayer's previous acquisitions is uplifted to reflect the rights issue. But since rights shares are not free, it is also necessary to increase the allowable expenditure for each of these acquisitions. This is achieved by adding the number of rights shares acquired into the s104 holding and increasing the allowable expenditure of this holding by the acquisition cost of these rights shares.

EXAMPLE 5

Tina made the following acquisitions of ordinary shares in Hombus plc:

Date	*Number of shares*	*Cost*
		£
15 August 1980	500	1,000
23 January 2000	700	2,800

The market value of the company's shares on 31 March 1982 was £2.50 per share. On 1 June 2011, the company made a 1 for 20 rights issue at £8 per share and Tina decided to buy the shares to which she was entitled. Calculate the chargeable gain arising on 12 November 2012 when Tine sold 840 shares for £7 each, assuming that she made no further acquisitions within the next 30 days.

Solution

The disposal cannot be matched against acquisitions on the same day or within the next 30 days, so it must come from the s104 holding. The s104 holding is as follows:

	Number of shares	*Allowable expenditure*
		£
Acquired 15 August 1980	500	1,250
Acquired 23 January 2000	700	2,800
	1,200	4,050
Rights issue 1 June 2011	60	480
	1,260	4,530
Sold 12 November 2012 (840/1,260ths)	(840)	(3,020)
s104 holding c/f	420	1,510

The disposal proceeds are £5,880 (840 x £7). Therefore the chargeable gain is £2,860 (£5,880 – £3,020).

Notes:

(i) The shares acquired before 31 March 1982 are incorporated into the s104 holding at their market value at that date (£2.50 per share) and not at their cost.

(ii) The 60 rights shares increase the number of shares in the s104 holding and also increase the allowable expenditure in that holding.

Capital distributions

A capital distribution occurs when shareholders are repaid part of their share capital, usually when a company goes into liquidation. Unless the amount of the distribution is small (see later in this chapter) a capital distribution is regarded as a part disposal for CGT purposes.

EXAMPLE 6

In March 2007, Vincent bought 10,000 ordinary shares in Apezium plc for £44,000. In June 2012, the company went into liquidation and Vincent received a first distribution of £0.50 per share. The market value of an ordinary share in Apezium plc just after this distribution was £0.75. Compute the allowable loss arising in June 2012.

Solution

The value of the part disposed of is £5,000 (10,000 @ £0.50) and the value of the part remaining is £7,500 (10,000 @ £0.75). The part disposal fraction is 5,000/12,500 which is equivalent to 2/5ths. The s104 holding is as follows:

	Number of shares	*Allowable expenditure* £
Acquired March 2007	10,000	44,000
Distribution June 2012 (2/5ths)	-	(17,600)
s104 holding c/f	10,000	26,400

The computation of the allowable loss is as follows:

	£
Disposal proceeds	5,000
Less: Allowable expenditure	(17,600)
Allowable loss	(12,600)

Sale of rights nil paid

Another example of a capital distribution occurs when a company makes a rights issue and a shareholder decides not to buy the shares concerned but instead to sell his or her rights to someone else (a "sale of rights nil paid"). When shareholders sell their rights they are *not* selling shares. What they are selling is the right to buy shares, often at an attractive price. The proceeds of such a sale are treated as a capital distribution. If the amount of money involved is small (see below) the amount received will be treated as a small capital distribution.

Small capital distributions

If the amount of a capital distribution is small when compared with the value of the shares concerned, the distribution is not treated as a disposal. Instead, the proceeds of the distribution are subtracted from the allowable expenditure relating to those shares. The effect of this is that the gain which would have been chargeable on the distribution is deferred until a subsequent disposal takes place. This is very similar to the treatment of small part disposals of land (see Chapter 18). Note that:

(a) A capital distribution is generally regarded as small if it consists of no more than 5% of the value of the company's shares just before the distribution. It is also HMRC practice to regard an amount of £3,000 or less as small for this purpose, even if the 5% test is not satisfied.

(b) HMRC will usually allow a small capital distribution to be treated as a disposal if this is to the taxpayer's advantage (e.g. if any gain is covered by the annual exemption).

EXAMPLE 7

In April 2010, Vanessa bought 100 shares in Entagon plc at a cost of £5 per share. The company went into liquidation and Vanessa received a first distribution of 40p per share in July 2012. The shares had a market value of £9.75 immediately after the distribution.

(a) Show how the distribution will be dealt with for CGT purposes.

(b) Calculate the chargeable gain arising in March 2013, when Vanessa received a second and final distribution of £9.82 per share.

Solution

(a) The value of the shares immediately prior to the distribution must have been £10.15 (£9.75 + £0.40). 40p is approximately 3.9% of £10.15 so the distribution ranks as a small capital distribution. The £40 received by Vanessa may be deducted from the £500 that she paid for her shares. This reduces the allowable cost on a subsequent disposal to £460.

(b) Assuming that the small capital distribution is not treated as a disposal, the s104 holding is as follows:

	Number of shares	*Allowable expenditure* £
Acquired April 2010	100	500
Distribution July 2012	-	(40)
	100	460
Disposal March 2013	(100)	(460)
s104 holding c/f	nil	nil

The gain arising on the disposal is:

	£
Disposal proceeds (100 @ £9.82)	982
Less: Allowable expenditure	460
Chargeable gain	522

Takeovers

A takeover occurs when one company acquires the shares of another company. Shareholders of the "target" company exchange their shares in return for cash, or shares of the acquiring company, or a combination of both cash and shares. The CGT treatment of such disposals is as follows:

(a) If a takeover is entirely for cash, the shareholders of the target company have sold their shares and have made chargeable disposals. The fact that shares have been sold as a consequence of a takeover is irrelevant and the gain or loss is computed in the usual way.

(b) If a takeover is entirely for shares (a "paper for paper" takeover), no chargeable disposals have taken place. A shareholder's newly-acquired shares in the acquiring company replace the shares originally held in the target company and are deemed for all CGT purposes to have been acquired on the same date and at the same cost as the original holding.

(c) If a takeover is partly for cash and partly for shares, a part disposal has taken place and a part disposal calculation is usually required. The value of the part disposed of is the amount of cash received and the value of the part remaining is the value of the shares received. However, if the amount of cash received by a taxpayer is no more than 5% of the total consideration (or no more than £3,000) the cash received may be treated as a small capital distribution.

EXAMPLE 8

In August 2006, Winston bought 8,000 shares in Hexago plc at a cost of £3 per share. In October 2012 Zircle plc made a takeover bid for Hexago plc, offering the Hexago shareholders three Zircle shares plus £1 in cash for every two Hexago shares. The offer was accepted on 29 October 2012 when the market value of shares in Zircle plc was £5 per share. Compute Winston's chargeable gain.

Solution

Winston received 12,000 shares in Zircle plc, worth £60,000, plus £4,000 in cash, a total of £64,000. The amount received in cash is 6.25% of the total and exceeds £3,000, so this cannot be treated as a small capital distribution. The s104 holding is as follows:

	Number of shares	*Allowable expenditure*
		£
Acquired August 2006	8,000	24,000
Distribution October 2012 (6.25%)	-	(1,500)
s104 holding after distribution	8,000	22,500
s104 holding (Zircle plc) c/f	12,000	22,500

The gain arising on the disposal is:

	£
Disposal proceeds	4,000
Less: Allowable expenditure	1,500
Chargeable gain	2,500

EXAMPLE 9

In June 2009, Darren bought 1,000 ordinary shares in Cubu plc for £8,400. In November 2012, Phere plc made a takeover bid for Cubu plc, offering two ordinary shares and one preference share in Phere for each ordinary share in Cubu. This offer was accepted on 21 November 2012 when the market value of ordinary shares in Phere plc was £4 per share and the market value of preference shares in Phere plc was £2 per share.

Show how Darren's cost of £8,400 should be allocated between the shares which he received by virtue of the takeover.

Solution

Darren received 2,000 ordinary shares worth £8,000 and 1,000 preference shares worth £2,000, giving a total consideration of £10,000. Since 80% of this total took the form of ordinary shares in Phere plc, these ordinary shares are deemed to have cost him 80% of £8,400 = £6,720. Similarly, the preference shares in Phere plc are deemed to have cost him 20% of £8,400 = £1,680. All of these shares are treated as if acquired in June 2009.

Gilts and qualifying corporate bonds

Gilt-edged securities and "qualifying corporate bonds" are not chargeable assets for CGT purposes. Therefore neither a chargeable gain nor an allowable loss can arise on their disposal. Note that:

(a) Gilt-edged securities ("gilts") are UK government securities such as Treasury Stock, Exchequer Stock etc.

(b) Qualifying corporate bonds consist of company debentures and other fixed-interest securities which are expressed in sterling and comprise a normal commercial loan.

(c) Gains and losses arising on the disposal of gilt-edged securities or corporate bonds by a *company* are assessed under the loan relationships rules for corporation tax purposes (see Chapter 23).

Summary

- Special matching rules are used to match disposals of shares and securities against acquisitions. Disposals are matched first against shares acquired on the same day as the disposal, then against shares acquired in the next 30 days and then against shares comprising the s104 holding.
- The s104 holding is a pool of shares of the same class in the same company that were acquired before the date of the current disposal but have not been matched against previous disposals. It is necessary to keep a record of the total number of shares in this pool and their total allowable expenditure.
- The CGT effect of a bonus issue is to increase the number of shares in the s104 holding. Allowable expenditure is not affected. The CGT effect of a rights issue which is taken up by the shareholder is to increase both the number of shares and the allowable expenditure in the s104 holding.
- A sale of rights nil paid is treated as a capital distribution.
- A capital distribution is treated for CGT purposes as a part disposal unless it ranks as a small capital distribution, in which case the amount of the distribution is deducted from the acquisition cost of the shares concerned.
- If a takeover is entirely for cash, the shareholders of the target company have made chargeable disposals. If a takeover is entirely for shares, no chargeable disposals have taken place. If a takeover is partly for cash and partly for shares, a part disposal has occurred unless the amount of cash can be treated as a small capital distribution.
- Gilt-edged securities and qualifying corporate bonds are not chargeable assets for CGT purposes.

Exercises

20.1 A taxpayer makes the following acquisitions of preference shares in Muvex Ltd:

Date	*No of shares purchased*
10 August 2012	1,000
20 October 2012	200
1 December 2012	150

No further shares are acquired during 2012 or 2013. How will the following disposals be matched against these acquisitions?

(a) 250 shares sold on 20 October 2012

(b) 420 shares sold on 12 November 2012

(c) 300 shares sold on 1 April 2013.

20.2 Sandra acquired the following ordinary shares in Pinker plc:

Date	*No of shares*	*Cost*
		£
29 January 1982	1,000	3,000
13 August 1996	1,000	9,500
4 October 2008	2,000	22,500

The market value of the shares on 31 March 1982 was £4 per share. On 26 June 2012, Sandra sold 700 of her shares in Pinker plc. Assuming that she acquired no further shares in the company during 2012, calculate the chargeable gain or allowable loss if her sale proceeds in June 2012 were:

(a) £8,400

(b) £6,300

(c) £5,200.

20.3 Jeremy acquired the following ordinary shares in Scarle plc:

Date	*No of shares*	*Cost*
		£
19 September 2006	4,000	16,000
20 October 2008	2,000	12,000
21 November 2010	1,000	7,000
22 December 2012	3,000	24,000
13 January 2013	5,000	55,000

He made no further acquisitions during 2013. On 22 December 2012, he sold 10,000 shares in the company for £10 per share. Calculate the chargeable gain or allowable loss arising on this disposal.

20.4 William made the following acquisitions of preference shares in Ptagon plc:

Date	*No of shares*	*Cost*
		£
17 February 2004	600	900
13 November 2008	200	400
9 October 2012	100	300

In January 2013, the company made a 1 for 4 bonus issue. In February 2013, William sold 450 shares for £4 per share. Calculate the chargeable gain, assuming that he made no acquisitions in the following 30 days.

20.5 Yvonne made the following acquisitions of ordinary shares in Rangle plc:

Date	*No of shares*	*Cost*
		£
30 September 2002	2,000	1,200
1 December 2006	3,000	3,600

In January 2013, the company made a 1 for 5 rights issue at £1 per share and Yvonne decided to buy the shares which she was offered. In March 2013, she sold one-half of her shares in the company for £1.80 per share. Calculate the chargeable gain arising in March 2013, given that no further shares were acquired within the following 30 days.

20.6 (a) In November 2002, Yorick bought 6,000 ordinary shares in Togon plc for £30,000. In March 2013, the company went into liquidation and Yorick received a first distribution of £1 per share. The market value of an ordinary share in Togon plc just after this distribution was £2. Compute the allowable loss.

(b) In January 2006, Yolande bought 300 ordinary shares in Lippex plc at a cost of £1.20 per share. In May 2012, when shares in Lippex plc had a market value of £2 each, the company made a rights issue. Yolande sold her rights, realising £25. Compute the chargeable gain arising in November 2012 when Yolande sold all of her shares for £780, assuming that no further shares were acquired within the following 30 days.

20.7 In June 2012, Walter bought 10,000 shares in Ovod plc at a cost of £7 per share. In September 2012, Rundu plc made a takeover bid for Ovod plc, offering the Ovod shareholders eight Rundu shares plus £4 in cash for every five Ovod shares. The offer was accepted on 2 September 2012 when the market value of shares in Rundu plc was £4.50 per share. Compute Walter's chargeable gain.

***20.8** Suzanne acquired the following ordinary shares in Quamarine plc:

Date	*No of shares*	*Cost*
		£
2 October 1979	200	600
10 January 1981	150	500
5 December 2000	400	1,420
8 November 2007	250	1,160
24 July 2012	300	1,400
10 August 2012	400	2,500
20 August 2012	350	2,600
31 August 2012	500	2,400

She made no further acquisitions. The shares were valued at £3.20 each on 31 March 1982. On 24 July 2012, Suzanne sold 1,200 shares for £7 per share. Compute the chargeable gain or allowable loss arising on this disposal.

***20.9** Saeed made the following purchases of ordinary shares in Hybola plc:

Date	*No of shares*	*Cost*
		£
24 August 1975	800	800
25 November 1980	1,200	1,350
26 February 1996	1,600	2,400
11 October 2005	400	800

The company's shares had a market value of £1.20 each on 31 March 1982. In June 2011, the company made a 1 for 20 rights issue at £1.50 per share and Saeed took up the shares which he was offered.

Calculate the chargeable gain arising in November 2012, when Saeed sold 1,260 shares at £3 each. Assume that no further shares were acquired within the following 30 days.

***20.10** Susan made the following purchases of ordinary shares in Semicle plc:

Date	*No of shares*	*Cost*
		£
11 January 2005	1,500	4,800
20 January 2012	1,140	5,700

In January 2013, the company went into liquidation and Susan received a first distribution of £2 per share. The market value of an ordinary share in Semicle plc just after this distribution was £1. Compute the allowable loss arising in January 2013.

***20.11** Steven made the following purchases of ordinary shares in Vexcon plc:

Date	*No of shares*	*Cost*
		£
9 May 2005	2,000	8,000
28 November 2010	500	2,500

In February 2013, Evvan plc made a takeover bid for Vexcon plc, offering the Vexcon shareholders two Evvan shares plus £2 in cash for every Vexcon share. The offer was accepted on 21 February 2013 when the market value of shares in Evvan plc was £4 per share. Compute Steven's chargeable gain or allowable loss.

Chapter 21

Principal private residences

Introduction

This chapter examines the CGT consequences of the disposal of a taxpayer's principal private residence. Although a principal private residence is not a chargeable asset for CGT purposes, a CGT liability may arise when a property is disposed of which has been used as a residence for only part of the period of ownership or which has been used partly as a residence and partly for other purposes.

Principal private residence

A dwelling which is a taxpayer's only or main residence is known as that taxpayer's principal private residence (PPR). A taxpayer's PPR is not a chargeable asset for CGT purposes. Therefore any gain which arises on the disposal of a PPR is not chargeable to tax and any loss which arises is not allowable. For a property to be regarded as a PPR, the taxpayer must actually occupy the property as a residence. Mere ownership is not sufficient. Furthermore, the term "residence" implies a degree of permanency and it is unlikely that the PPR exemption will apply to a property which has been used only as temporary accommodation. In *Goodwin* v *Curtis* (1998) a property which had been occupied by the taxpayer for only 32 days did not qualify as a residence.

The large majority of taxpayers own (at most) a single property and reside in that property, so that it is obvious that the property is the taxpayer's PPR. However, the following points may be relevant in more complex cases:

(a) A taxpayer may have only one PPR at any given time.

(b) A taxpayer who owns and lives in two (or more) properties may make an election to determine which property is to be regarded as the PPR. Such an election must be made within two years of the date from which it is to take effect.

(c) A married couple who live together may have only one PPR between them. This rule also applies to same-sex civil partners who live together and who have entered into a legally-recognised civil partnership.

(d) The PPR exemption covers the residence itself together with grounds or gardens of up to half a hectare (5,000 square metres) in area. Larger areas may be included in the exemption if they are warranted by the size of the residence.

(e) The requirement that there must be actual residence in the property is relaxed if the taxpayer is required to live in job-related accommodation (see Chapter 8). In these circumstances, the PPR exemption is extended to any property which the taxpayer owns so long as he or she intends to occupy the property in the future.

Partial exemption

If a property has been occupied as a PPR for only a part of the period of ownership, only a part of the gain realised on disposal will be exempt from CGT. The exempt part of the gain is equal to:

$$\frac{\text{length of period of residence}}{\text{length of period of ownership}} \times \text{whole gain}$$

The lengths of the periods of residence and ownership are usually calculated to the nearest month. Note the following important points:

(a) If the property was acquired before 31 March 1982, the period of ownership prior to that date and any period of residence prior to that date are ignored. This is because the base date for CGT is now 31 March 1982 (see Chapter 18).

(b) If a property has been the taxpayer's PPR at some time, the last 36 months of ownership always count as a period of residence, whether or not the taxpayer was actually resident then (so helping taxpayers who move house and have difficulty in selling their previous residence). This rule applies even if the taxpayer claims another property to be his or her PPR during the 36 months.

EXAMPLE 1

Allan bought a house in January 1979 for £20,000. The market value of the house on 31 March 1982 was £29,000. Allan lived in the house until 1 May 2009 on which date he bought another house and made this his principal private residence. The house he had bought in January 1979 was sold on 31 January 2013 for £145,000. Compute the chargeable gain.

Solution

In examples of this type it is necessary first to calculate the gain arising (ignoring any PPR exemption) and then to consider the PPR exemption as a second stage. The house was acquired before 31 March 1982, so rebasing applies. The gain arising is as follows:

	£
Sale proceeds	145,000
Less: Market value at 31 March 1982	29,000
Chargeable gain (before PPR exemption)	116,000

After 31 March 1982, Allan owned the house for 30 years and 10 months (370 months). He was actually resident for 27 years and 1 month (325 months) and the last 36 months of ownership also count as a period of residence, making a total of 361 months during which the PPR exemption applies. The chargeable gain is therefore as follows:

	£
Total gain (as above)	116,000
Less: $\frac{361}{370}$ x £116,000	113,178
Chargeable gain	2,822

Deemed residence

The period of residence in a property is deemed to include certain periods when the taxpayer was not actually resident, so long as:

(a) there is a period of actual residence both at some time before the period of absence and at some time after the period of absence, and

(b) the taxpayer claims no other property to be a PPR during the period of absence.

These periods of "deemed residence" are as follows:

(a) any periods of absence during which the taxpayer is working abroad

(b) a total of up to four years of absence during which the taxpayer is working elsewhere in the UK

(c) a total of up to three years of absence for any reason.

The requirement that the taxpayer must reside in the property at some time after the period of absence is waived if the absence is work-related and the terms of the taxpayer's employment prevent him or her from returning to the residence.

EXAMPLE 2

On 1 June 1990, Alice bought a house in Derby for £35,000.

- She occupied the house as her PPR until 1 May 1992 when she left to work in Exeter, living in rented accommodation.
- She returned to the house in Derby on 1 November 1993 and stayed until 1 July 1996 when she left to take up a post in the USA, again living in rented accommodation.
- She returned to Derby on 1 February 1999 and stayed until 1 December 2008 when she bought a house in Nottingham and made this her principal private residence.
- On 1 February 2013 she sold the house in Derby for £154,000.

Compute the chargeable gain.

Solution

	£
Sale proceeds	154,000
Less: Acquisition cost	35,000
Chargeable gain (before PPR exemption)	119,000

Alice's period of ownership of the house in Derby (a total of 272 months) can be broken down into the following periods:

(i)	1 June 1990 to 30 April 1992	23 months	Actual residence
(ii)	1 May 1992 to 31 October 1993	18 months	Working in UK
(iii)	1 November 1993 to 30 June 1996	32 months	Actual residence
(iv)	1 July 1996 to 31 January 1999	31 months	Working abroad
(v)	1 February 1999 to 30 November 2008	118 months	Actual residence
(vi)	1 December 2008 to 31 January 2013	50 months	Living in new PPR

Periods (i), (iii) and (v) are exempt since Alice was actually resident in the property during those periods. Period (ii) is exempt since Alice was working elsewhere in the UK, the four-year time limit has not been exceeded and she was resident in the property both before and after the absence. Similarly, period (iv) is exempt. The last 36 months of ownership are always exempt, which leaves the first 14 months of period (vi) to consider. During these 14 months Alice was claiming another property to be her PPR, so the period cannot count as a period of deemed residence and the gain arising during these 14 months is chargeable. The remaining 258 months benefit from the PPR exemption. The chargeable gain is therefore as follows:

	£
Total gain (as above)	119,000
Less: $\frac{258}{272}$ x £119,000	112,875
Chargeable gain	6,125

Letting relief

An extension to the PPR exemption, known as "letting relief", applies if a PPR has been let to tenants as residential accommodation. There are two situations to consider:

(a) A property might have been used entirely as a residence for part of the period of ownership but let to tenants during periods of absence by the owner. A chargeable gain will arise if the periods of absence are not entirely covered by the exemptions described above, but letting relief will then be available in relation to this gain.

(b) Part of a property might have been used as a residence whilst the other part has been let. In this case, the PPR exemption will generally cover:

  (i) the gain arising on the whole property in the last 36 months of ownership, and

  (ii) the remainder of the gain, to the extent that this is attributable to the part of the property which was occupied by the owner.

  The balance of the gain will be chargeable to CGT, but letting relief may then be available. In general, letting relief will *not* be granted if the part that has been let forms a dwelling which is entirely separate from the accommodation which forms the owner's residence (e.g. a self-contained flat with its own access from the road). Relief *will* normally be granted if the let accommodation forms part of the owner's dwelling and the owner previously resided in the entire premises.

Letting relief is calculated as the *lowest* of:

(a) the gain which relates to the let part of the property or to the letting period

(b) the gain which is exempt because of the PPR exemptions

(c) £40,000.

EXAMPLE 3

In relation to the previous example in this chapter, assume now that Alice always let her Derby house when she was not resident there. Compute the chargeable gain.

Solution

The only chargeable period was a period of 14 months during which a gain of £6,125 arose and during which the property was let. Letting relief is available as the lowest of:

(a) The part of the gain which relates to the letting period (£6,125)

(b) The part of the gain which is exempt because of the PPR exemptions (£112,875)

(c) £40,000.

Therefore letting relief is £6,125 and the chargeable gain is reduced to £nil.

EXAMPLE 4

Alistair bought a house on 1 April 1992 for £125,000 and occupied the entire house until 1 May 1999 when he rented the top floor (comprising one-half of the house) to tenants. He retained the ground floor as his own residence. This arrangement continued until 1 October 2012 when he sold the house for £615,000. Compute the chargeable gain.

Solution

	£
Sale proceeds	615,000
Less: Original cost	125,000
Chargeable gain (before PPR exemption)	490,000

Alistair owned the house for a total of 20 years and 6 months (246 months). Exemption is available for the 85 months during which he occupied the whole property and for the last 36 months (a total of 121 months). He was resident in half of the property for the remaining 125 months, so 50% of the gain arising during these 125 months is also exempt. The other 50% is chargeable but letting relief is available. The chargeable gain is as follows:

	£	£
Total gain (as above)		490,000
Less: PPR exemption:		
£490,000 x 121/246	241,016	
£490,000 x 125/246 x 1/2	124,492	365,508
		124,492
Less: Letting relief, lowest of:		
(a) £124,492		
(b) £365,508		
(c) £40,000		40,000
Chargeable gain		84,492

Business use

If a property is used partly as a residence and partly for business purposes, the gain which is attributable to the part used for business purposes is chargeable to CGT. No reliefs are available in relation to this gain. The usual exemption for the last 36 months of ownership does not apply to the part of the property which has been used for business purposes.

The entitlement to full PPR exemption is not restricted if an individual sets aside a part of their residence for the use of an adult for whom they are caring under a local authority adult placement scheme, even though the income derived from this activity is generally treated as trading income.

EXAMPLE 5

Ava bought a house on 1 July 1992 for £32,000. She occupied the entire property as her PPR until 1 August 1999 when she began using one-quarter of the house for business purposes. This continued until 1 November 2012 when she sold the house for £177,000. Compute the chargeable gain.

Solution

	£
Sale proceeds	177,000
Less: Acquisition cost	32,000
Chargeable gain (before PPR exemption)	145,000

Ava owned the house for 20 years and 4 months (244 months). For the first 7 years and 1 month (85 months) she occupied the entire house as her PPR. For the remaining 159 months she occupied three-quarters of the house. The chargeable gain is as follows:

	£	£
Total gain (as above)		145,000
Less: PPR exemption:		
£145,000 x 85/244	50,512	
£145,000 x 159/244 x 3/4	70,866	121,378
Chargeable gain		23,622

Summary

- A taxpayer's principal private residence (PPR) is exempt from CGT.
- A taxpayer with two or more residences may elect which property is to be regarded as his or her PPR.
- A married couple who live together may have only one PPR between them. This rule also applies to civil partners who live together.
- If a property has been occupied as a PPR for only a part of the period of ownership, only a part of the gain realised on disposal will be exempt from CGT.
- The last 36 months of ownership of a PPR always count as a period of residence.
- Certain periods of absence are deemed to be periods of residence.
- Letting relief may be available if a residence has been let to tenants as residential accommodation.
- If a residence is used partly for business purposes, the gain relating to the part used for business purposes is chargeable to CGT.

Exercises

21.1 Mohammed owns two properties - a flat in Central London and a country cottage in Sussex. In general he lives in his London flat during the week and spends the weekends in his Sussex cottage. Which of his two properties will be regarded as his principal private residence?

21.2 Melanie bought a house in November 1979 for £18,000. The house had a market value of £21,000 on 31 March 1982 and was sold on 31 October 2012 for £163,000. Compute the chargeable gain arising in each of the following cases:

(a) Melanie occupied the house as her principal private residence throughout the period of ownership.

(b) Melanie occupied the house throughout her period of ownership with the exception of the period between 1 June 1989 and 31 May 1993 when she lived with a friend. During this time the house stood empty.

(c) As (b) except that the house was let as residential accommodation during Melanie's absence.

21.3 Rupert bought a house in Manchester on 1 November 1990 for £55,000. He occupied the house until 1 November 1994 when he left to work abroad for a year, moving back into the house on 1 November 1995. He stayed until 1 February 1998 when he left again, this time to work in Aberdeen, where he stayed until his return on 1 May 2002. This time he stayed for only a month, leaving on 1 June 2002 to go to live with a friend. He never returned to the house and it was sold on 1 March 2013 for £232,000. During his absences, Rupert always let his house and he claimed no other property to be his principal private residence. Compute the chargeable gain arising on the disposal.

21.4 Samantha bought a house for £37,500 on 1 August 1991 and occupied the house as her principal private residence. On 1 June 1993 she began to use one-fifth of the house for business purposes. Unfortunately her business eventually failed and on 1 June 2000 she ceased trading. From that date onwards she resided in the entire house until it was sold on 1 August 2012 for £155,000. Compute the chargeable gain.

***21.5** Terry bought a house for £65,000 on 1 June 1992 and occupied the house as his principal private residence. He lived in the house until 1 June 1997 when he went to stay with relatives in Australia, letting the house in his absence. He did not return until 1 June 2001, when he began using one-quarter of the house for business purposes and the other three-quarters as his residence. This arrangement continued until 1 June 2012 when he sold the house for £190,000. Compute the chargeable gain.

Chapter 22

CGT reliefs

Introduction

A taxpayer's capital gains tax liability may sometimes be reduced or deferred by taking advantage of various CGT reliefs. The main reliefs available are concerned with:

(a) damaged or destroyed assets
(b) replacement of business assets
(c) gift of business assets
(d) transfer of a business to a limited company
(e) disposal of a business ("entrepreneurs' relief")
(f) reinvestment into EIS shares
(g) loans to traders.

The purpose of this chapter is to explain, for each of these reliefs, the circumstances in which the relief is available and the way in which the amount of relief is calculated.

Damaged assets

If an asset has been damaged and insurance money or other compensation is received in consequence, the situation is usually treated as a part disposal. The value of the part disposed of (A) is the amount of money received and the value of the part remaining (B) is the value of the asset on the date that the money is received. Any money spent on restoration is treated as enhancement expenditure.

However, in certain circumstances, the taxpayer may elect that the situation should *not* be treated as a part disposal and that the amount of money received should instead be deducted from the allowable expenditure relating to the asset. This has the effect of increasing the gain arising on a subsequent disposal and is very similar to the CGT treatment of small capital distributions (see Chapter 20). The circumstances in which a part disposal may be avoided are as follows:

(a) All of the money received is applied to restoring the asset, or

(b) The asset is not a wasting asset and all the money received is applied to restoring the asset except for an amount which is small in comparison with the amount received and which is not reasonably required for restoration purposes, or

(c) The asset is not a wasting asset and the amount of money received is small in comparison with the value of the asset.

For this purpose, a sum is regarded as "small" if it does not exceed £3,000 or 5% of the amount with which it is being compared, whichever is the higher.

A part disposal calculation is unavoidable if only part of the money received is spent on restoring the asset and neither of the "small" tests is satisfied. However, the taxpayer may elect that the calculation should relate only to the amount which is received but not spent on restoration. If this election is made, the remainder of the money received is deducted from the allowable expenditure relating to the asset.

EXAMPLE 1

In July 2006, Laura bought an oil painting for £120,000. In October 2012, the painting was damaged by fire. In February 2013, Laura received compensation from her insurance company of £30,000. Compute the chargeable gain or allowable loss arising in each of the following circumstances:

(a) Laura spent none of the insurance money on restoration and the damaged painting was valued at £170,000 in February 2013.

(b) Laura spent £30,000 on restoring the painting in November 2012 and elected that the situation should not be treated as a part disposal.

(c) Laura spent £29,000 on restoring the painting in November 2012 and elected that the situation should not be treated as a part disposal.

(d) Laura spent £20,000 on restoring the painting in November 2012 and elected that the part disposal should relate only to the retained £10,000. The restored painting was valued at £200,000 in February 2013.

Solution

(a) This is a part disposal, with A = £30,000 and B = £170,000. The computation is:

	£
Disposal proceeds	30,000
<u>Less</u>: Part cost:	
$\frac{£30,000}{£30,000 + £170,000} \times £120,000$	18,000
Chargeable gain	12,000

The balance of allowable expenditure carried forward and used in the calculation of the gain arising on a subsequent disposal is £102,000 (£120,000 – £18,000).

(b) The entire amount received is spent on restoration so the election to avoid a part disposal is valid. The balance of allowable expenditure is:

	£
Incurred July 2006	120,000
Incurred November 2012	30,000
	150,000
Less: Received February 2013 (and not treated as a disposal)	30,000
	120,000

(c) The £1,000 retained is small in comparison with the amount received and therefore the election to avoid a part disposal is valid (so long as the £1,000 is not required for restoration purposes). The balance of allowable expenditure is:

	£
Incurred July 2006	120,000
Incurred November 2012	29,000
	149,000
Less: Received February 2013 (and not treated as a disposal)	30,000
	119,000

(d) The amount retained is not small in comparison with the amount received and so a part disposal is unavoidable. However, by virtue of Laura's election, this will relate only to the retained £10,000, not to the entire £30,000 received. The computation is:

	£	£
Disposal proceeds		10,000
Less: Part original expenditure:		
$\frac{£10,000}{£10,000 + £200,000} \times £120,000$	5,714	
Part restoration expenditure:		
$\frac{£10,000}{£10,000 + £200,000} \times £20,000$	952	6,666
Chargeable gain		3,334

The balance of allowable expenditure carried forward in this case is:

	£
Incurred July 2006 (£120,000 – £5,714)	114,286
Incurred November 2012 (£20,000 – £952)	19,048
	133,334
Less: Received February 2013 (and not treated as a disposal)	20,000
	113,334

Without the election, the chargeable gain would be £11,739 (£30,000 – 30/230ths of £140,000). The balance of expenditure would be £121,739 (200/230ths of £140,000).

Destroyed assets

The loss or destruction of an asset is a chargeable disposal and usually results in a CGT computation in which disposal value is equal to the amount of any insurance money or other compensation received. However, if *all* of the money received is spent (within 12 months) on the purchase of a replacement asset, the taxpayer may claim that the disposal of the original asset should give rise to neither a gain nor a loss. The cost of the replacement asset is then reduced by the gain which would have been chargeable on the disposal of the original asset if this claim had not been made.

If only *part* of the money received is spent on the purchase of a replacement asset, the taxpayer may claim that the chargeable gain on the disposal of the original asset should be restricted to the amount of money retained (so long as this is less than the gain). The cost of the replacement asset is then reduced by the balance of the gain that would have been chargeable if the claim had not been made.

EXAMPLE 2

Maurice bought an item of jewellery in November 2007 for £125,000. In 2012 the jewellery was stolen. As a result, Maurice's insurance company paid him £141,500 in May 2012. In June 2012 he spent £150,000 on the purchase of replacement jewellery and claimed that neither a gain nor a loss should arise on the disposal of the original jewellery.

(a) Compute the chargeable gain arising in March 2015 when the replacement jewellery is sold for £180,000.

(b) How would this computation differ if the jewellery bought in June 2012 had cost only £140,000 and Maurice had made an appropriate claim?

Solution

(a) Without a claim, the gain arising on the loss of the original jewellery would be £16,500 (£141,500 – £125,000). The entire proceeds were spent on a replacement asset within 12 months so Maurice is entitled to make the claim. This reduces the deemed acquisition cost of the new jewellery to £133,500 (£150,000 – £16,500). The gain arising on the subsequent sale of the new jewellery is as follows:

	£
Disposal proceeds	180,000
Less: Deemed acquisition cost	133,500
Chargeable gain	46,500

(b) £1,500 of the insurance money was retained and so £1,500 of the gain arising on the stolen jewellery is immediately chargeable. The remaining £15,000 of the gain may be deducted from the acquisition cost of the new jewellery, reducing this cost to £125,000 (£140,000 – £15,000). The chargeable gain arising on the March 2015 disposal becomes £55,000 (£180,000 – £125,000).

Replacement of business assets

Subject to certain conditions, a taxpayer may claim that the gain arising on the disposal of a business asset (the "old asset") may be "rolled-over" against the cost of acquiring a replacement business asset (the "new asset"). The main effects of a claim for roll-over relief are as follows:

(a) The disposal of the old asset is deemed to give rise to neither a gain nor a loss.

(b) The cost of the new asset is reduced by the gain which would have been chargeable on the disposal of the old asset if the claim for roll-over relief had not been made.

Full relief is available only if the disposal proceeds of the old asset are *wholly* applied in acquiring the new asset. If only *part* of the disposal proceeds are used to acquire the new asset, the effect of a claim for roll-over relief is that the chargeable gain on the disposal of the old asset is restricted to the amount of money retained (so long as this is less than the gain). The cost of the new asset is then reduced by the balance of the gain that would have been chargeable if the claim had not been made. The conditions which must be satisfied if a roll-over claim is to be accepted are:

(a) Both the old asset and the new asset must be drawn from the following list (though they need not both be the same type of asset):

   (i) land, buildings and fixed plant and machinery

   (ii) goodwill

   (iii) ships, aircraft, hovercraft, satellites, space stations and spacecraft

   (iv) milk, potato and fish quotas and certain EU agricultural quotas

   (v) Lloyd's syndicate rights.

(b) The old asset must have been used only for trade purposes throughout the period of ownership and the new asset must be taken into trading use immediately upon its acquisition. But where a taxpayer operates two or more trades, there is no requirement that the old and new asset should be used in the same trade.

(c) The new asset must be acquired during the period beginning one year before and ending three years after the date of disposal of the old asset.

(d) The taxpayer must claim the relief within four years of the end of the *later* of the tax year in which the old asset is disposed of and the tax year in which the new asset is acquired.

Note that a similar relief is available to companies (which pay corporation tax on their chargeable gains) when a business asset is disposed of and a replacement business asset is acquired. For companies, however, the list of assets which are eligible for this relief excludes goodwill and quotas. These assets fall instead within the scope of the corporation tax intangible assets regime (see Chapter 23).

EXAMPLE 3

In May 2005, Janine bought a building for £187,525 for use in her business. In July 2012 she sold the building for £260,000 and, in the same month, bought another building for use in her business. Assuming that Janine claims roll-over relief, calculate the chargeable gain arising on the July 2012 disposal if the replacement building has a cost of:

(a) £270,000 (b) £240,000 (c) £185,000.

Solution

The gain on the disposal of the original building is computed as follows:

	£
Sale proceeds	260,000
Less: Acquisition cost	187,525
Chargeable gain	72,475

(a) The entire sale proceeds have been spent on a replacement building. None of the gain is immediately chargeable and the entire gain is rolled-over against the cost of the new building, reducing its allowable cost to £197,525 (£270,000 – £72,475).

(b) £20,000 of the sale proceeds have been retained. Therefore £20,000 of the gain is immediately chargeable. The remaining £52,475 may be rolled-over against the cost of the new building, reducing its allowable cost to £187,525 (£240,000 – £52,475).

(c) £75,000 of the sale proceeds have been retained. This exceeds the amount of the gain. Therefore the whole gain is immediately chargeable and no part of the gain may be rolled-over. The allowable cost of the new building is the full £185,000.

Replacement with a depreciating asset

If the new asset is a "depreciating asset" (an asset with an expected life of 60 years or less at the time of acquisition) the gain arising on the disposal of the old asset cannot be rolled-over and is *not* deducted from the cost of the new asset. Instead, the gain is temporarily deferred or "held-over" until it crystallises (becomes chargeable) on the *earliest* of the following three dates:

(a) the date on which the new asset is disposed of

(b) the date on which the new asset ceases to be used for trade purposes

(c) the 10th anniversary of the acquisition of the new asset.

Clearly, a gain which is held-over in these circumstances will become chargeable no more than ten years after the date of acquisition of the depreciating asset. However, if a suitable non-depreciating asset is acquired at any time before the earliest of the above three dates, the held-over gain may be transferred to this new asset, so converting a temporarily held-over gain into a permanently rolled-over gain.

EXAMPLE 4

In June 2012, Ian sold a freehold building for £200,000, realising a chargeable gain of £25,000. The building had been acquired in May 2007 and used only for trade purposes. In July 2012, he acquired fixed plant and machinery costing £220,000 and elected that the gain on the building should be held-over against the plant and machinery. Explain the way in which the held-over gain would be treated if:

(a) Ian sells the plant and machinery in October 2016.

(b) Ian sells the plant and machinery in March 2024.

Solution

(a) The replacement asset is sold before the 10th anniversary of its acquisition and so the deferred gain becomes chargeable in 2016-17.

(b) The replacement asset is still in Ian's possession ten years after its acquisition, so the held-over gain of £25,000 crystallises in July 2022 and forms part of Ian's chargeable gains in 2022-23.

EXAMPLE 5

Imagine now that Ian (in the above example) buys another freehold building for business use in November 2015 and elects to transfer the held-over gain on the plant and machinery to the new freehold building. Explain the treatment of the held-over gain if the new building costs:

(a) £250,000 (b) £190,000.

Solution

(a) The entire proceeds of the sale of the original building have been invested in a new building so the whole held-over gain of £25,000 can be converted into a rolled-over gain, reducing the allowable cost of the new building to £225,000.

(b) £10,000 out of the sale proceeds of the original building have not been invested in the new building and therefore cannot be rolled-over against its cost. This £10,000 will continue to be held-over against the plant and machinery and will become chargeable no later than July 2022. However, the remaining £15,000 is converted into a rolled-over gain, reducing the allowable cost of the new building to £175,000.

Gift of business assets

The gift of an asset is a chargeable disposal and this is the case whether or not the asset is used in business. However, subject to certain conditions, a claim may be made for the gain arising on a gift of business assets to be held-over until the transferee disposes of the assets concerned. If such a claim is made, the transferor's gain on the disposal is reduced to zero and the transferee's deemed acquisition cost is reduced by the amount of the gain that would have been chargeable on the transferor if the claim had not been made. The conditions which must be satisfied are as follows:

(a) Both the transferor and the transferee must elect for the gain arising on the gift to be held-over. This election must be made within four years of the end of the tax year in which the gift is made.

(b) The gifted assets must consist of either:

   (i) assets used in a trade, profession or vocation carried on by the transferor or by the transferor's *personal company* (a company of which at least 5% of the voting rights are held by the transferor), or

   (ii) shares or securities of a trading company which is unlisted or which is the transferor's personal company (so long as the *transferee* is not a company).

If the gift is of shares, rather than of individual business assets, the gain arising on the disposal is apportioned between the amount which relates to chargeable business assets owned by the company on the date of the gift and the amount which relates to other chargeable assets (e.g. investments). Only the part of the gain relating to chargeable business assets is eligible for hold-over relief.

Sale for less than market value

Gift relief is also available if a business asset is sold for less than market value (typically to a connected person). But if the actual consideration received by the transferor exceeds the original cost of the asset (so that part of the gain has been realised) the amount of the gain which may be held-over is reduced by the excess of the actual consideration over the asset's cost.

EXAMPLE 6

In March 2013, Jonathan gives a business asset to his daughter. Jonathan acquired the asset for £25,000 in May 2008 and its market value on the date of the gift is £60,000. Both Jonathan and his daughter elect that the gain arising should be held-over.

(a) Compute the gain arising on the gift and the amount which may be held-over.

(b) How would the computation differ if Jonathan's daughter paid him £32,000 for the asset?

Solution

(a) The chargeable gain is £35,000 (£60,000 – £25,000). The whole of this gain may be held-over, reducing Jonathan's daughter's deemed acquisition cost to £25,000 (£60,000 – £35,000).

(b) The chargeable gain is still £35,000, since this is not a bargain made at arm's length and therefore disposal value is taken to be the market value of the asset on the date of disposal. However, £7,000 of the gain (£32,000 – £25,000) has been realised in cash, so the amount of the gain which may be held-over is reduced to £28,000. The remaining £7,000 of the gain is immediately chargeable. The daughter's deemed acquisition cost is £32,000 (£60,000 – £28,000).

EXAMPLE 7

In July 2003, Kathy paid £60,000 to acquire 90% of the ordinary shares of an unlisted trading company. In May 2010, she gave all of the shares to her son and both Kathy and her son elected that the gain arising on this gift should (as far as possible) be held-over. The net assets of the company on the date of the gift (at market value) were as follows:

	£
Goodwill	100,000
Freehold building (used only for business purposes)	150,000
Listed investments	50,000
Net current assets (none of which are chargeable)	40,000
Total net assets	340,000

(a) Compute the gain arising on the gift and the amount which may be held-over.

(b) Compute the gain arising in March 2013 when Kathy's son sells all the shares for £350,000.

Solution

(a) Presumably, the value of the shares on the date of the gift was 90% of £340,000 = £306,000. So the gain arising on the gift was £246,000 (£306,000 – £60,000).

The company's chargeable assets on the date of the gift were £300,000 of which £250,000 were chargeable business assets. So £246,000 x 250,000/300,000 = £205,000 of the gain was held-over whilst the remaining £41,000 was chargeable.

(b) The gain arising in March 2013 is as follows:

	£
Sale proceeds	350,000
Less: Deemed acquisition cost (£306,000 – £205,000)	101,000
Chargeable gain	249,000

Transfer of a business to a limited company

Subject to certain conditions, the gain arising on the transfer of a business to a limited company in return for shares in that company is held-over until the transferor disposes of the shares. If this relief applies, the gain arising on the disposal of the business is deducted from the deemed acquisition cost of the shares. The required conditions are:

(a) The business is transferred as a going concern.

(b) All of the assets of the business (other than cash) are transferred to the company.

(c) The consideration received by the transferor consists wholly or partly of shares in the company.

This relief (known as "incorporation relief") applies automatically, so there is no need for the transferor to make a claim. However, the transferor may elect that incorporation relief should *not* apply. One situation in which such an election might be made is when the gain concerned is covered by the transferor's annual exemption.

If incorporation relief applies and the consideration for a transfer consists only partly of shares, then only part of the chargeable gain is held-over. In these circumstances, the held-over gain is calculated as follows:

$$\frac{\text{value of the shares received}}{\text{total consideration received}} \times \text{whole gain}$$

EXAMPLE 8

In November 2012, Leroy transfers his business to a limited company in exchange for £50,000 in cash and shares which are valued at £600,000. The gain arising on the transfer is £260,000. Leroy does not elect to disapply incorporation relief. Calculate the amount of the gain which is immediately chargeable and the amount which is held-over.

Solution

The held-over gain is £260,000 x 600,000/650,000 = £240,000. The remaining £20,000 of the gain is immediately chargeable. The deemed acquisition cost of the shares is reduced to £360,000 (£600,000 – £240,000).

Entrepreneurs' relief

A relief known as "entrepreneurs' relief" (ER) may apply to gains of up to £10 million made by an individual on a "material disposal" of business assets. In order for this relief to be available, the individual must dispose of either:

(a) all or part of a business (including a share in a partnership) which the individual has owned throughout the period of one year ending on the date of the disposal, or

(b) assets used by a business at the time at which it ceases trading, as long as the business was owned by the individual (or by a partnership in which the individual was a member) throughout the year ending on the date of cessation and the assets are disposed of within three years of that date, or

(c) shares or securities in a trading company which, throughout the period of one year ending on the date of the disposal, has been the individual's personal company and of which the individual has been an officer or employee.

In case (a) above, it is important to realise that the disposal must be the disposal of either a whole business or a significant part of a business. Merely disposing of a business asset does not qualify for ER. The following points should also be noted:

(a) In the first two cases above, ER is available only in respect of disposals of "relevant business assets". These include goodwill but exclude assets held as investments.

(b) A business qualifies for ER purposes if it is a trade, profession or vocation conducted on a commercial basis with a view to the realisation of profits.

(c) A trading company is "*a company carrying on trading activities whose activities do not include to a substantial extent activities other than trading activities*". HMRC will generally accept that a company is a trading company if no more than 20% of its activities are non-trading activities.

(d) A company qualifies as the individual's personal company for this purpose if the individual holds at least 5% of the company's ordinary shares and has at least 5% of the company's voting rights.

Entrepreneurs' relief is given only if the individual makes a claim. Claims must be made by the first anniversary of the 31 January following the tax year in which the qualifying disposal is made. For example, if a disposal occurs during tax year 2012-13, an ER claim must be made by 31 January 2015.

Associated disposals

If an individual qualifies for ER on a disposal of shares or securities or on a disposal of a share in a partnership, relief may also be available in relation to "associated disposals". An associated disposal is the disposal of an asset which is owned by the individual but has been used in the business of the company or partnership concerned.

Entrepreneurs' relief rate (10%)

If an ER claim is made in respect of a qualifying disposal, any losses arising in relation to that disposal must first be deducted from the gains arising in relation to the disposal. The resulting amount is then treated as a chargeable gain. This gain is subject to CGT *at the rate of 10%* rather than at the standard rate (18%) or the higher rate (28%).

The calculation of a taxpayer's CGT liability for a tax year may involve both gains which qualify for ER and gains which do not qualify. The taxpayer may also have capital losses in the year arising from non-ER disposals or capital losses brought forward from previous years. In these circumstances (as explained in Chapter 17):

(a) Non-ER capital losses, capital losses brought forward and the annual exemption may be set against gains in such a way that the CGT liability is minimised. This result is achieved if losses and the annual exemption are set first against non-ER gains (which are taxable at 18% or 28%) and only then against gains which qualify for ER.

(b) The unused part of the taxpayer's basic rate band (if any) is reduced by the amount of ER gains arising in the year. Non-ER gains are then taxed at 18% to the extent that they do not exceed any remaining part of the basic rate band and at 28% otherwise.

The worked examples given in Chapter 17 illustrate these points.

The lifetime limit

Entrepreneurs' relief is subject to a "lifetime limit". A taxpayer may claim ER more than once but this limit restricts the total gains eligible for relief during the taxpayer's lifetime.

The relief was originally introduced on 6 April 2008 with a lifetime limit of £1 million. This limit was subsequently increased to £2 million as from 6 April 2010, to £5 million as from 23 June 2010 and to £10 million as from 6 April 2011.

If an individual makes qualifying gains in excess of the lifetime limit and that limit is subsequently increased, retrospective relief is not given for the excess of those gains over the previous limit. However, if the individual then has further qualifying gains at some time in the future, ER may be claimed in relation to gains of up to the amount by which the limit has increased.

EXAMPLE 9

Three taxpayers have each made ER claims prior to 6 April 2011, as follows:

(a) Gemma has made an ER claim in relation to a gain of £600,000 arising in June 2009.

(b) Robin has made an ER claim in relation to a gain of £2,300,000 arising in May 2010

(c) Joyce has made ER claims relating to a gain of £750,000 arising in October 2008 and a further gain of £6 million arising in September 2010.

Calculate the maximum ER relief to which each of these taxpayers is entitled in relation to any qualifying disposals which arise or after 6 April 2011.

Solution

(a) Gemma's claim in June 2009 did not exceed the lifetime limit (which was £1 million at that time) and so ER was available in relation to the whole of the gain. As from 6 April 2011, she has £9,400,000 of the lifetime limit remaining.

(b) Robin's qualifying gain in May 2010 exceeded the lifetime limit of £2 million, so ER would have been available in relation to only £2 million of that gain. Although the limit has since increased to £10 million, there is no possibility of retrospective relief in relation to the remaining £300,000 of the May 2010 gain. However, £8 million of the lifetime limit is available for any qualifying gains arising on or after 6 April 2011.

(c) Joyce's October 2008 claim was within the lifetime limit of £1 million and so ER was available for the whole of the gain. By September 2010, the lifetime limit had risen to £5 million, so ER was available in relation to £4,250,000 of the September 2010 gain. Although the limit has since increased to £10 million, there is no retrospective relief for the remaining £1,750,000 of this gain, but £5 million of the lifetime limit is available for qualifying gains arising on or after 6 April 2011.

EXAMPLE 10

Calculate the CGT payable in respect of the following disposals, assuming in each case that the annual exemption is fully utilised against other gains, that there are no allowable losses other than those stated and that taxable income for 2012-13 exceeds the basic rate limit. Also assume that ER is claimed wherever possible.

(a) Wendy (who has never claimed ER before) sells her business in January 2013 and realised a chargeable gain of £720,000. She has owned the business since 1986.

(b) Tom sells his trading business in March 2013. He realises a gain of £300,000 on the disposal of his business premises but incurs a loss of £120,000 on the disposal of his goodwill. He has owned the business for 15 years and has made no previous ER claims.

(c) In August 2012, Henry sells a property which he has been letting unfurnished to the same tenant since 2006. The gain on this disposal is £150,000.

(d) Since 1996, Brenda has been a director of a trading company and has owned 20% of its ordinary shares. She sells her shares in October 2012 and realises a gain of £12,500,000. During 2009-10 she had claimed ER in relation to a gain of £900,000 arising on the disposal of a business.

Solution

(a) £720,000 does not exceed £10 million, so the whole of the gain qualifies for ER. The gain is taxed at 10%, giving CGT payable of £72,000.

(b) The loss on the goodwill must be deducted from the gain on the premises before computing ER. Tom's net gains are £180,000. This figure is taxed at 10%, so CGT payable is £18,000.

(c) Henry's use of this property does not qualify as a trade and therefore ER is not available. ER would have been available if the letting of the property had qualified as the commercial letting of furnished holiday accommodation (see Chapter 5). CGT payable is £42,000 (£150,000 x 28%).

(d) The disposal in 2009-10 used up £900,000 of the lifetime limit, so £9,100,000 of the gain arising in October 2012 is taxed at 10% and the remainder is taxed at 28%. CGT payable is £1,862,000 (£9,100,000 x 10% + £3,400,000 x 28%).

Interaction of entrepreneur's relief with other reliefs

A disposal which is eligible for entrepreneurs' relief may also qualify for the relief relating to a gift of business assets. But if a gift relief claim is made, no chargeable gain arises at the time of the disposal. Therefore an ER claim is inappropriate and cannot be made successfully. Similar comments apply to a disposal to which incorporation relief applies and a disposal which is the subject of a claim for rollover relief.

In all of these cases, the fact that no chargeable gain arises at the time of the disposal means that the opportunity to benefit from ER in relation to that disposal is lost. Whether or not a subsequent disposal (e.g. a disposal of gifted assets by the transferee) will qualify for ER will depend upon the circumstances of that disposal and whether the necessary conditions are satisfied at that time for ER to be available.

Reinvestment into EIS shares

The gain arising on the disposal of *any* asset may be deferred if an amount of money equal to the gain is used to subscribe for shares which are eligible under the rules of the Enterprise Investment Scheme (see Chapter 6). Note the following points:

(a) The shares must be subscribed for during the period starting one year before and finishing three years after the disposal concerned.

(b) A gain may be deferred if an amount equal to that gain is invested in eligible shares. It is *not* necessary to invest the entire disposal proceeds.

(c) There is no requirement that income tax relief should be available in relation to the investment. It follows that the taxpayer does not have to be unconnected with the company concerned and that the amount of a deferred gain can exceed the maximum amount on which income tax relief is granted.

(d) A taxpayer claiming this relief may restrict the amount of relief claimed so as to avoid wasting the annual exemption.

(e) The deferred gain usually becomes chargeable on the disposal of the EIS shares, but further deferral is possible if further EIS shares are then subscribed for.

Note also that the gain arising on the disposal of any asset in 2012-13 is exempt from CGT if the amount of the gain is invested (also in 2012-13) through the SEIS (see Chapter 6).

Loans to traders

If a taxpayer lends money to a trader and then finds that all or part of the loan is irrecoverable, the loss incurred may be treated as a capital loss and set against the taxpayer's capital gains. This relief is subject to the following conditions:

(a) the trader who has borrowed the money must be resident in the UK

(b) the money must have been borrowed for trade purposes (but not for the trade of money-lending)

(c) the debt must be unsecured.

Subject to these conditions, the amount lost is treated as a capital loss of the year in which the taxpayer makes the claim for relief, though a claim may be backdated for up to two years if it can be shown that the debt was irrecoverable then. If relief is given and then all or part of the loan is recovered, the amount recovered is treated as a capital gain of the year in which recovery takes place.

Summary

- If the compensation received on the loss or destruction of an asset is spent on the purchase of a replacement, the taxpayer may claim that the disposal should give rise to neither a gain nor a loss. The gain which would have been chargeable is then subtracted from the cost of the replacement asset.
- The gain arising on the disposal of a business asset may be rolled-over against the cost of acquiring a replacement.
- If a business asset is replaced by a depreciating asset, the gain arising cannot be permanently rolled-over but may be temporarily held-over instead. This gain will become chargeable no later than 10 years after the replacement asset was acquired (unless the gain is transferred to a non-depreciating asset in the meantime).
- The gain arising on the gift of a business asset may be held-over until the transferee disposes of the asset.
- The gain arising on the transfer of a business to a limited company is held-over until the transferor disposes of the shares which were received in exchange for the assets of the business. The transferor may elect that this relief should not apply.
- Subject to certain conditions, entrepreneurs' relief is available in respect of gains of up to £10 million arising on the disposal of the whole or part of a business. Gains which qualify for entrepreneur's relief are taxed at only 10%.
- The gain arising on the disposal of any asset may be deferred if the amount of the gain is used to subscribe for shares eligible under the rules of the EIS.
- The gain arising on the disposal of any asset in 2012-13 is exempt from CGT if the amount of the gain is invested (also in 2012-13) through the seed EIS.

Exercises

22.1 In October 2003, Matthew bought a piece of rare porcelain for £10,000. The porcelain was damaged in early 2009 and in March of that year Matthew spent £3,850 on restoration work. In July 2009, Matthew's insurance company paid him £4,000 and Matthew successfully claimed that this should not be treated as a part disposal. He sold the porcelain in March 2013 for £23,500. Compute the chargeable gain.

22.2 In February 2005, Maria bought a diamond necklace for £13,500. In 2007 the necklace was stolen and, as a result, an insurance payment of £14,000 was received in February 2008. In the same month, Maria spent £14,750 on the purchase of a replacement necklace and claimed that the disposal of the original necklace should give rise to neither a gain nor a loss. Compute the chargeable gain arising in January 2013 when the replacement necklace was sold for £20,000.

22.3 In September 2004, Pamela bought a building for business use at a cost of £150,000. In September 2012 she sold the building for £261,400 and immediately bought another building, again for business use. Assuming that Pamela claims roll-over relief, calculate the chargeable gain arising in September 2012 if the cost of the new building is:

(a) £258,900
(b) £149,800
(c) £276,800.

22.4 In August 2012, Susannah (a sole trader) gave a business asset to her son. The asset had been bought by Susannah for £91,500 in July 2003 and enhanced in May 2004 at a cost of £34,500. The asset's market value in August 2012 was £215,000. Both Susannah and her son elected that the gain arising should be held-over.

Compute the amount of the held-over gain. Also explain how the situation would differ if Susannah's son had paid her £150,000 for the asset.

***22.5** In January 1981, Norman bought a freehold building for use in his business at a cost of £120,000. The building had a market value on 31 March 1982 of £125,000. In June 2009 he sold the building for £875,000 and in August 2009 he spent £720,000 on buying another building for use in his business. This building was sold in December 2012 for £730,000. Compute the gains arising on the disposal of each building (assuming that Norman claims roll-over relief).

***22.6** In May 2007, Ruth sold a freehold building which she had used exclusively for business purposes. The building was sold for £220,000, realising a chargeable gain of £42,500. In the following month, Ruth acquired fixed plant for £220,000 and elected to hold-over the gain on the freehold property against this plant and machinery. In August 2012, she acquired another freehold building for £205,000 and elected to transfer the held-over gain to this new building. Explain the treatment of the £42,500 gain.

***22.7** Calculate the CGT payable in relation to each of the following disposals, assuming in each case that the annual exemption is fully utilised against other gains, that there are no allowable losses and that ER is claimed wherever possible. The taxpayers concerned have made no previous ER claims.

(a) On 31 May 2012, Roger sold all of his shares in a trading company, realising a gain of £351,000. He has owned 25% of the company's ordinary share capital since March 2007 and has been a director of the company since June 2008.

(b) On 31 July 2012, Dennis sold his business (which he has owned since May 1986) and realised gains of £15,250,000.

(c) On 31 August 2012, Denise sold her interest in a trading partnership and realised a gain of £140,000. She had been a member of the partnership for five years. Also on 31 August 2012, she sold a building which was owned by her personally but had been used by the partnership for business purposes since 2009. She realised a gain of £31,000 in relation to this building.

***22.8** In 2005, Shaun bought 20% of the ordinary shares of an unlisted trading company. The shares cost £140,000. He owned the shares until January 2013 when he gave all the shares to a friend. On the date of the gift, the shares had a market value of £500,000 and the company's assets were valued as follows:

	£
Freehold land and buildings	1,700,000
Goodwill	500,000
Investments	100,000
Motor cars	40,000
Net current assets	160,000

Calculate the chargeable gain, assuming that both Shaun and his friend elect that the gain arising should (as far as possible) be held-over.

Review questions (Set B)

B1 In March 2013, Vasco sold at auction an antique dressing-table. He received £11,960 after auctioneer's commission of 8%. He had purchased the table in January 2003 for £1,000.

Columbus sold one of his factories on 30 April 2012 for £900,000. The factory had been purchased in September 2004 for £566,700. In March 2013, Columbus purchased another factory for £700,000 and claimed roll-over relief in relation to the gain arising on the factory sold in April 2012.

You are required to:

(i) Calculate Vasco's chargeable gain.

(ii) Calculate the chargeable gain arising on the disposal made by Columbus in April 2012. Also calculate the base cost of the factory acquired in March 2013.

(ACCA)

B2 Yvonne had the following transactions in the shares of Scotia plc:

			£
18 August 2000	Bought	3,000 shares	6,000
19 September 2007	Bought	2,000 shares	5,000
13 March 2013	Sold	5,000 shares	23,000
28 March 2013	Bought	1,000 shares	4,400

Sally's capital gains tax position in 2012-13 was as follows:

	£
Capital gains arising in the year	37,000
Capital losses arising in the year	6,000
Capital losses brought forward	12,000

You are required to:

(a) Calculate Yvonne's chargeable gain.

(b) Calculate Sally's CGT liability for 2012-13, assuming that her taxable income for the year (i.e. total income less reliefs and the personal allowance) was:

(i) £20,000
(ii) £30,000
(iii) £40,000.

Also assume that none of Sally's gains qualify for entrepreneurs' relief and that she made no Gift Aid donations or pension contributions during 2012-13.

(ACCA)

B3 In August 2012, Samuel sold 20,000 ordinary shares in WQZ Ltd for £8 each. He had bought shares in the company as follows:

12 August 2004	10,000	shares cost £12,500
8 October 2006	5,000	shares cost £8,200
21 February 2008	35,000	shares cost £86,300

WQZ Ltd is an unlisted trading company with an issued share capital consisting of 120,000 ordinary shares, all of which have equal voting rights.

Samuel has been a director of WQZ Ltd since 2006. He claims entrepreneurs' relief (ER) in relation to the share disposal in August 2012 and has never claimed ER before. He has no other disposals in 2012-13 and has no allowable losses brought forward

You are required to:

(i) Calculate the gain arising in August 2012.

(ii) Explain why this gain is eligible for entrepreneurs' relief.

(iii) Calculate Samuel's CGT liability for 2012-13 and state the due date of payment.

B4 Consider each of the following situations:

(a) Marlene has chargeable gains for the year 2012-13 of £12,000 and capital losses for the year 2012-13 of £8,000.

(b) Moira has chargeable gains for the year 2012-13 of £12,000 and capital losses brought forward of £8,000.

(c) Marina has chargeable gains for the year 2012-13 of £3,000 and capital losses brought forward of £8,000.

(d) Melissa has chargeable gains for the year 2012-13 of £12,000, capital losses for the year 2012-13 of £8,000 and capital losses brought forward of £4,000.

You are required to:

For each situation, calculate the capital gains assessable for 2012-13 and state the amount of any losses carried forward. *(ACCA)*

B5 In the year to 5 April 2013, Thomas More made the following disposals:

(i) A flat in a house that he had purchased on 1 December 2002 for £80,000. It had never been occupied as the main residence and had been consistently let during his period of ownership. The property had been converted into two flats in September 2003 at a cost of £32,000. The flat was sold for £142,000 on 1 December 2012 and out of this legal fees of £4,000 were paid. It was agreed that the value of the other flat was £130,000 in December 2012.

(ii) 20,000 shares in ICI plc which cost £111,800 in December 2003 and were sold for £150,000 in December 2012. (No shares were acquired within the next 30 days).

Required:

(a) Calculate the capital gains tax payable on the sale of the flat and the shares in ICI plc. There were no other chargeable disposals in the year and no capital losses brought forward from previous years. Assume that Mr More's taxable income for 2012-13 exceeds the basic rate limit.

(b) If you were told at the start of 2012-13 that Mr More intended making the above disposals and that his wife had capital losses of £30,000 brought forward (and that she did not intend to make any disposals in 2012-13) would there be any advice that you would consider giving to Thomas? *(Amended from AAT)*

***B6** Mrs Laura Stapleton, a widow, has decided to dispose of her residence and retire to Canada, where she will live with her son, Danny.

She acquired her house on 1 June 1993 and lived there until 31 March 1994 when she left the UK in order to stay with Danny and his wife in Canada. Liking it there, she extended her stay and on 1 November 1994 she took a job at a local hospital until 31 December 1995 when she returned to the UK and resumed residence in her property.

She remained living in her house until 31 December 2007, when she left it permanently in order to live in a rented flat. Contracts were exchanged for the sale of the house on 31 May 2012.

The house originally cost £50,000 and an extension was completed in December 1996 at a cost of £20,000. The agreed sale proceeds are £300,000 and the expenses of sale are £5,200. Throughout the periods of Mrs Stapleton's absence, the property was let at a market rent.

Required:

Calculate the chargeable gain arising on the disposal of Mrs Stapleton's residence.

(Amended from AAT)

***B7** You have been consulted by Mr Christopher Rodrigues on two matters relating to capital gains tax. Extracts from his letter to you are:

"On 31 January 2013, I sold my shares in Fledgeby plc, a listed company. I had acquired them as follows:

1 January 2003	1,000	shares cost £4,200
19 June 2004	700	shares cost £2,950
31 December 2010	1,200	shares cost £5,620
11 August 2012	400	shares cost £2,100

I also took up a 1 for 4 rights issue at £3.50 per share on 31 May 2011. The shares were all sold for £38,000 on 31 January 2013 and I do not intend to buy any shares in the company in the future.

Also on 31 January 2013, I sold for £200,000 a plot of land that I acquired in January 1980 for £10,000. A friend has told me that the gain might be either a capital gain or a trading gain but, as capital gains and trading gains are both taxed, it doesn't really matter which way it is dealt with."

Required:

(a) Calculate the chargeable gain arising on the sale of the shares in Fledgeby plc.

(b) Do you agree with the statement of the other taxation practitioner? Draft brief notes that will form the basis of the letter that you will write to Mr Rodrigues.

(Amended from AAT)

***B8** On 1 May 1998, Nigel acquired a 30-year lease for £20,000. He assigned the lease on 1 November 2012 for £75,000.

Kay purchased a plot of land in February 2004 for £20,000. She sold part of the land for £18,000 in March 2013 when the value of the remainder of the land was £60,000.

Shirley had the following dealings in the shares of Wingfield plc, a listed company:

			£
January 1981	Bought	4,000 shares	18,000
March 1994	1 for 4 rights issue	1,000 shares	7,000
November 1996	Bought	3,000 shares	24,000
January 2007	1 for 2 bonus issue	4,000 shares	-
March 2013	Sold	7,000 shares	56,000

The shares had a market value of £8 per share on 31 March 1982. No further shares were acquired during 2013.

You are required to:

(i) Calculate Nigel's chargeable gain.

(ii) Calculate Kay's chargeable gain.

(iii) Calculate Shirley's chargeable gain. (ACCA)

***B9** Gillian purchased 10,000 ordinary shares in Downtown plc in January 2007 for £20,000. In October 2012, Upmarket plc acquired the whole of the share capital of Downtown plc following a take-over bid. The terms of the take-over offer were:

One ordinary share in Upmarket plc, and

Two preference shares in Upmarket plc, and

£3 cash

for every five shares held in Downtown plc. The share prices of Upmarket plc immediately after the take-over were:

Ordinary shares £10 each, and

Preference shares £3 each.

You are required to:

Calculate Gillian's chargeable gain arising in 2012-13. *(ACCA)*

***B10** Joan has been a full-time director of Sunnybank Pursuits Ltd (a trading company) since 1993 and has owned 10% of the company's ordinary shares since 1995. She retired in February 2013 and gave all of her shares in the company to her daughter, Sylvia. The capital gain on the gift was £400,000 before deducting any reliefs. This was her only disposal in tax year 2012-13.

Joan does not claim entrepreneurs' relief in relation to this disposal but Joan and Sylvia have jointly elected that the capital gain arising on the disposal should be held-over.

The market values of the company's chargeable assets at the time that the shares were gifted were:

	£
Land and buildings	4,000,000
Plant and machinery	2,000,000
Goodwill	1,000,000
Listed shares	1,000,000

All items of plant and machinery cost more than £6,000 each and are valued at more than £6,000 each in February 2013.

You are required to:

(i) Calculate Joan's assessable capital gain in 2012-13.

(ii) Assuming that Joan is a higher-rate taxpayer in 2012-13, calculate the CGT that would have been payable in relation to this share disposal if there had been no hold-over claim but Joan had claimed entrepreneurs' relief instead. *(ACCA)*

Part 3

CORPORATION TAX

Chapter 23

Introduction to corporation tax

Introduction

The next six chapters of this textbook deal with corporation tax, which is the tax that companies pay on their profits. The purpose of this first chapter is to provide an introduction to the basic principles of corporation tax. Relevant legislation can now be found mainly in the Corporation Tax Act 2009, the Corporation Tax Act 2010 and the Taxation of Chargeable Gains Act 1992, as amended by subsequent Finance Acts.

Scope of corporation tax

UK resident companies are liable to corporation tax on their "chargeable profits", no matter where in the world those profits arise. Companies which are not UK resident but which trade in the UK through a permanent establishment are liable to corporation tax on the income and gains of that establishment (see Chapter 32). Note that:

(a) A company's chargeable profits include its income and its chargeable gains. The term "chargeable gains" is normally used in preference to "capital gains".

(b) The main source of income for most companies is likely to be trading income. But a company may also have other sources of income. These could include bank interest, loan interest, property income etc.

(c) In general terms, a company's income is computed in a broadly similar way to that of an individual. The main differences between the assessment of a company's income and an individual's income are explained later in this chapter. The way in which a company's chargeable gains are calculated is considered in Chapter 24.

For corporation tax purposes, the word "company" is taken to mean any corporate body or unincorporated association, excluding partnerships, local authorities and local authority associations. As well as limited companies, this definition includes clubs and societies, which are liable to corporation tax on their income from non-members.

Organisations that are generally exempt from corporation tax (subject to various conditions and limits) include registered charities, agricultural societies, scientific research associations, friendly societies, trade unions, registered pension schemes and community amateur sports clubs.

Accounting periods

Corporation tax is charged in respect of "accounting periods" and it is very important to distinguish between accounting periods and periods of account. An *accounting period* is a period for which corporation tax is charged. A *period of account* is a period for which a company prepares a set of accounts.

Although accounting periods and periods of account are often the same thing, this is not always the case. An accounting period *begins* when:

(a) the company comes within the charge to corporation tax, or

(b) when the previous accounting period ends, so long as the company remains within the charge to corporation tax.

An accounting period *ends* on the *earliest* occurrence of any of a number of events. The main events which cause the end of an accounting period are:

(a) the expiration of 12 months from the beginning of the accounting period

(b) the end of a period of account

(c) the company starting or ceasing to trade

(d) the company ceasing to be within the charge to corporation tax

(e) the company becoming, or ceasing to be, UK resident

(f) the company entering administration or ceasing to be in administration.

These rules have the following general consequences:

(a) The length of an accounting period can never exceed 12 months.

(b) If a set of accounts covers a period of 12 months or less, the period of account forms a single accounting period and a corporation tax assessment is raised for this period.

(c) If a set of accounts covers a period of more than 12 months, the period covered by the accounts is broken down into two or more accounting periods, each giving rise to a separate corporation tax assessment. The first accounting period consists of the first 12 months of the period of account. The second accounting period consists of the next 12 months and so forth. If the period covered by the accounts is not an exact multiple of 12 months, the final accounting period will be of less than 12 months' duration.

EXAMPLE 1

Identify the accounting periods which relate to the following periods of account:

(a) A company prepares accounts for the year to 31 December 2012.

(b) A company prepares accounts for the six months to 31 October 2012.

(c) A company prepares accounts for the sixteen months to 31 December 2012.

(d) A company prepares accounts for the thirty months to 31 March 2013.

Solution

(a) The year to 31 December 2012 is an accounting period in its own right.

(b) The six months to 31 October 2012 is an accounting period in its own right.

(c) The sixteen months to 31 December 2012 is divided into two accounting periods - the 12 months to 31 August 2012 and the four months to 31 December 2012.

(d) The thirty months to 31 March 2013 is divided into three accounting periods. These are the 12 months to 30 September 2011, the 12 months to 30 September 2012 and the six months to 31 March 2013.

Chargeable profits

The main elements which are taken into account when computing a company's chargeable profits for an accounting period may be summarised as follows:

	£	£
Trading income	xxx	
Less: Trading losses brought forward	xxx	xxx
Income from property		xxx
Income from non-trading loan relationships		xxx
Non-trading income from intangible fixed assets		xxx
Miscellaneous income		xxx
Chargeable gains	xxx	
Less: Allowable capital losses	xxx	xxx
		xxx
Less: Property business losses	xxx	
Deficits on non-trading loan relationships	xxx	
Trading losses relieved against total profits	xxx	
Relief for qualifying charitable donations	xxx	xxx
Profits chargeable to corporation tax (PCTCT)		xxx

Most of the elements listed above are explained in this chapter but chargeable gains are dealt with in Chapter 24 and losses/deficits are considered in Chapter 26. The corporation tax treatment of foreign income is covered in Chapter 32. Note that:

(a) A company cannot be an employee and so cannot have employment income.

(b) There is no corporation tax equivalent of the personal allowances which are available to individuals who pay income tax.

Trading income

A company's trading income for an accounting period consists of its trading profit for that period, as adjusted for tax purposes. The starting point for the calculation is the company's pre-tax profit for the relevant period of account. This figure is then adjusted by excluding non-trading income and adding back disallowed expenses. The adjusted trading profit of a period of account lasting for more than 12 months is apportioned between the accounting periods of which it is composed (see later in this chapter). Capital allowances claimed for each accounting period are then deducted.

This process is very similar to the equivalent process which applies to self-employed individuals (see Chapter 9). However, the following points should be noted:

(a) When calculating a company's trading income, there is no need to disallow the private proportion of expenses. This is because a company does not have a private existence. Any private use *by employees* is treated simply as a cost of employing staff (who may then be liable to income tax on a benefit in kind). A similar argument applies if a company pays an employee's travel costs between home and work or provides an employee with any other goods or services.

(b) For a company, appropriations of profit consist mainly of dividends payable to shareholders and transfers to reserves.

(c) A company's Gift Aid donations are disallowed when computing trading income but are then treated as qualifying charitable donations and are deducted when calculating chargeable profits (see later in this chapter).

(d) Legal and other fees payable by a company in connection with the raising of loan finance are dealt with under the loan relationships regime (see later in this chapter).

(e) Losses caused by the dishonesty of a director are disallowed.

(f) A special corporation tax regime applies to a company's income and expenditure in relation to intangible fixed assets (see below). Any patent royalties payable or receivable by the company are dealt with under this regime.

(g) A company may be entitled to a special tax relief in relation to its research and development expenditure (see below).

(h) Accounts drawn up in accordance with International Financial Reporting Standards (IFRS) are generally valid for corporation tax purposes.

Corporation tax assessments are raised for accounting periods (not tax years) and so there is no need for any basis period rules. The basis period rules which apply to individuals (see Chapter 10) are completely irrelevant to companies. In particular, there are no special rules on commencement or cessation of trade or on a change of accounting date.

Capital allowances

A company's capital allowances are computed in much the same way as those of a self-employed individual (see Chapter 11). The only significant distinctions are as follows:

(a) Each accounting period ranks as a chargeable period when computing capital allowances for a company and so there is one capital allowances computation per accounting period. Since an accounting period cannot exceed 12 months in length, there will never be any need to scale *up* writing down allowances, but these are scaled *down* for accounting periods of less than 12 months.

(b) For companies, the reduction in the maximum AIA from £100,000 to £25,000 took effect as from 1 April 2012. Similarly, the reductions in WDA from 20% to 18% and from 10% to 8% also took effect as from 1 April 2012.

(c) A company may claim only one AIA, regardless of the number of businesses which it carries on. Companies under common control may claim only one AIA between them if they are "related". Two companies are related for this purpose if they carry on businesses from the same premises or if more than 50% of each company's turnover is derived from activities within the same EU classification.

(d) Companies which invest in energy-saving or environmentally-beneficial plant and machinery that qualifies for a 100% FYA may be able to claim a *first-year tax credit* in relation to the expenditure, rather than using the FYA in the normal way. This tax credit takes the form of a cash payment from the Government and is generally equal to 19% of the relevant expenditure. However, the available first-year tax credits for a chargeable period are capped at the greater of:

    (i) the total of the company's PAYE and NICs liabilities for that period, and
    (ii) £250,000.

    First-year tax credits are intended primarily for companies which make a trading loss in the chargeable period concerned and so have no trading profits against which to offset their FYAs. First-year tax credit cannot be claimed in relation to a 100% FYA to the extent that it has been (or could have been) relieved by offset against the company's trading profit for the period. It is expected that the first-year tax credits scheme will come to an end on 31 March 2018.

(e) As from 1 April 2012, 100% FYAs are available to trading companies which invest in plant and machinery for use in designated assisted areas within Enterprise Zones. To qualify for this FYA, the expenditure must be incurred by 31 March 2017.

(f) When computing a company's plant and machinery capital allowances, there will be no need to make any private use restrictions. Any private use of assets by employees is treated as part of the cost of employing staff and capital allowances are available in full in relation to such assets (though the employees concerned may then be liable to income tax on a benefit in kind).

Research and development tax credits

Small or medium-sized companies which incur research and development expenditure may (subject to certain conditions) claim tax relief on 225% of the amount of that expenditure. The expenditure must *not* be capital expenditure and must be relevant to the company's trade. Qualifying expenditure includes items such as staffing costs, consumables, payments to subcontractors and expenditure on power, fuel and water.

For this purpose, the definition of a "small or medium-sized company" is given by EU recommendations. Companies generally qualify as small or medium-sized if they have less than 500 employees and have either a turnover not exceeding €100 million or total assets not exceeding €86 million. Note that:

(a) In general, tax relief is given by deducting 225% of the qualifying expenditure when computing the company's trading income. If the effect of this deduction is to create or increase a trading loss, the company may (if it so wishes) claim a payment from HMRC equal to 11% of the "surrenderable loss". This is the *lower* of:

    (i) the amount of the trading loss
    (ii) 225% of the qualifying research and development expenditure.

    If such a claim is made, the surrendered loss is then ineligible for the loss reliefs that are normally available in relation to a company's trading losses (see Chapter 26).

(b) Prior to 1 April 2012, the rate of research and development expenditure tax relief for small and medium-sized companies was 200%. The rate at which payable tax credits were calculated was 12.5%.

(c) There is a cap of €7,500,000 *per project* on the amount of expenditure in respect of which a company may claim research and development tax credits.

Similarly, large companies may (subject to conditions) deduct 130% of their qualifying research and development expenditure when computing trading income. However, large companies cannot claim a payable tax credit from HMRC. The €7,500,000 cap does not apply to large companies.

Forthcoming changes to R&D tax credits

The Government intends to revise the research and development tax credits scheme as from 1 April 2013. Details of the revised scheme are subject to consultation. Legislation will be introduced in Finance Bill 2013.

Intangible fixed assets

Since April 2002, a special corporation tax regime has applied to a company's income and expenditure in relation to intangible fixed assets (IFAs) such as patents, trademarks, copyrights and goodwill. In outline, the system is as follows:

(a) Companies may obtain tax relief for the cost of IFAs created or acquired on or after 1 April 2002. In most cases, the amount of relief is equal to the amortisation charged in the company's accounts. If an asset is not amortised in the accounts or is amortised over a very long period, the company may elect for the asset to be subject to a fixed rate tax allowance calculated at 4% p.a.

(b) Capital allowances are no longer available to companies in respect of patent rights or know-how acquired on or after 1 April 2002. Computer software falls within the IFAs regime unless the company elects for capital allowances to apply.

(c) A loss on the disposal of an IFA which was created or acquired on or after 1 April 2002 is eligible for tax relief. Similarly, a profit on the disposal of such an asset is taxable income. But if an IFA is disposed of for more than original cost and the disposal proceeds are re-invested in newly-acquired IFAs, the amount by which disposal proceeds exceed original cost may be rolled-over against the cost of the new assets. The company is then taxed as if:

(i) the disposal proceeds of the old asset, and
(ii) the acquisition cost of the new asset (or assets)

were both reduced by the excess of disposal proceeds over original cost.

(d) Royalties payable or receivable for the use of IFAs (e.g. patent royalties) are within the scope of the IFAs regime. The tax treatment of royalties follows their accounting treatment, so that accruals and prepayments are taken into account.

(e) If royalties are paid net of basic rate income tax (see Chapter 25) the company must account to HM Revenue and Customs for the amount of tax deducted. Similarly, a company can reclaim any income tax suffered on royalties received. In both cases, the company's corporation tax computation will take into account the *gross* amount of royalties accrued in the accounting period.

(f) If IFAs are held or used for trade purposes, the related income and expenditure is taken into account when computing trading income. If IFAs are held or used for non-trade purposes, the income and expenditure is aggregated to produce an overall non-trading gain or loss. A gain forms part of the company's chargeable profits. A loss may be relieved in a number of ways (see Chapter 26).

(g) Gains or losses on the disposal of IFAs acquired before 1 April 2002 continue to be dealt with as chargeable gains or allowable losses. However, chargeable gains roll-over relief (see Chapter 22) is no longer available in relation to the replacement of an IFA by a company. Under transitional rules, gains arising on the disposal of an "old" IFA are eligible for the rollover relief described above.

EXAMPLE 2

A company's income statement for the year to 31 December 2012 is as follows:

	£	£
Turnover		1,640,430
Cost of sales		827,390
Gross profit		813,040
Other income		24,000
		837,040
Less: Distribution costs	187,770	
Administrative expenses	341,920	529,690
Profit for the year (before tax)		307,350

Notes:

1. The other income of £24,000 consists of rents receivable.
2. Distribution costs are as follows:

	£
Depreciation of distribution vans	18,530
Loss on disposal of distribution van	990
General distribution costs (all allowable)	168,250
	187,770

3. Administrative expenses are as follows:

	£
Depreciation of office equipment	12,680
Profit on disposal of office equipment	(3,710)
Loss on disposal of investments	27,000
Trade debts written off	10,600
Increase in general allowance for doubtful debts	8,400
Customer entertaining	2,760
Staff entertaining	5,550
Gift Aid donations	10,000
Legal fees re acquisition of new freehold offices	4,500
Motor expenses (one-half private motoring by employees)	59,060
Patent royalties payable for trade purposes	20,000
Embezzlement by director	50,000
General administrative expenses (all allowable)	135,080
	341,920

Compute the company's trading income (before deduction of capital allowances) for the year to 31 December 2012.

Solution

		£	£
Profit per accounts			307,350
Less:	*Non-trading income*:		
	Income from property	24,000	
	Profit on disposal of office equipment	3,710	27,710
			279,640
Add:	*Disallowed expenses*:		
	Depreciation of distribution vans	18,530	
	Loss on disposal of distribution van	990	
	Depreciation of office equipment	12,680	
	Loss on disposal of investments	27,000	
	Increase in general allowance for doubtful debts	8,400	
	Customer entertaining	2,760	
	Gift Aid donations	10,000	
	Legal fees re acquisition of new offices	4,500	
	Embezzlement by director	50,000	134,860
Trading income (before capital allowances)			414,500

Notes:

(i) The Gift Aid donations are disallowed when computing trading income but are treated as qualifying charitable donations instead (see later in this chapter).

(ii) Motor expenses incurred in relation to private motoring by employees are allowable when computing trading income, so long as the employees work in the trade.

(iii) Patent royalties payable for trade purposes are allowable.

EXAMPLE 3

After deducting capital allowances for the year to 31 December 2011, the tax written down values of a company's plant and machinery were as follows:

	£	
General pool	112,500	
Special rate pool	14,700	(BMW car bought May 2010, 170g/km)

The company's next set of accounts covered the 15-month period to 31 March 2013. Plant and machinery bought and sold during this period were:

		£
18 March 2012	Bought plant	40,000
31 August 2012	Sold plant (cost £20,000 in 2008)	8,500
6 November 2012	Sold BMW motor car	11,300
6 November 2012	Bought Audi motor car (emissions 203g/km)	25,600
29 January 2013	Bought motor car (emissions 107 g/km)	7,100
12 March 2013	Bought plant	5,400
15 March 2013	Sold plant (cost £2,000 in November 2011)	2,200

Calculate the capital allowances available for the 15 months to 31 March 2013, assuming 20% private use of the BMW and Audi motor cars by a director of the company.

Solution

The 15-month period of account must be broken down into two accounting periods, which are the year to 31 December 2012 and the three months to 31 March 2013. Each of these accounting periods is a chargeable period for capital allowances purposes and so there are two capital allowances computations.

		Main pool	*Special rate pool*	*Allowances*
		£	£	£
y/e 31/12/12				
WDV b/f		112,500	14,700	
Acquisition (no AIA)			25,600	
			40,300	
Disposals		8,500	11,300	
		104,000	29,000	
WDA @ hybrid 18.5%		19,240		19,240
WDA @ hybrid 8.5%			2,465	2,465
		84,760		
Acquisition	40,000			
AIA @ 100%	40,000	0		40,000
WDV c/f		84,760	26,535	
Total allowances				61,705
1/1/13 - 31/3/13				
WDV b/f		84,760	26,535	
Disposal		2,000		
		82,760		
WDA @ 18% x 3/12		3,724		3,724
WDA @ 8% x 3/12			531	531
		79,036		
Acquisition	5,400			
AIA @ 100%	5,400	0		5,400
Acquisition	7,100			
FYA @ 100%	7,100	0		7,100
WDV c/f		79,036	26,004	
Total allowances				16,755

Notes:

(i) Capital allowances are not restricted for private use by an employee.

(ii) Maximum AIA for the year to 31/12/12 is £43,750 (3/12 x £100,000 + 9/12 x £25,000) and for the period to 31/3/13 is £6,250 (3/12 x £25,000).

Income from property

In general, a company's income from property (or "property business profit") is calculated in much the same way as an individual's income from property (see Chapter 5). But the following important distinctions should be noted:

(a) Interest payable on a loan taken out by a company for the purpose of buying or improving let property is dealt with under the loan relationships rules and is therefore disallowed when computing property income.

(b) The loss reliefs available to a company which suffers a loss in relation to a property business are different from those available to an individual (see Chapter 26).

(c) Rent-a-room relief does not apply to companies.

UK-REITs

Subject to a number of conditions, a listed UK company with property income comprising at least 75% of total profits and property business assets (plus cash) comprising at least 75% of total assets may apply to become a UK Real Estate Investment Trust (UK-REIT).

The qualifying property income of a UK-REIT is exempt from corporation tax. Capital gains made on the disposal of investment property are also exempt from corporation tax. Such companies must distribute at least 90% of their tax-exempt profits to their shareholders, deducting basic rate tax at source (see Chapter 2).

Income from non-trading loan relationships

Income from non-trading loan relationships consists mainly of bank interest, building society interest and any other interest receivable by a company. Such interest is assessed on the *accruals* basis. The loan relationships rules are explained in detail later in this chapter. Note that:

(a) Unlike individuals, companies receive all bank and building society interest gross.

(b) Interest received by a UK company from another UK company is received gross.

(c) If (rarely) a company receives any interest net of income tax, the company may reclaim the income tax deducted at source (see Chapter 25) and is then assessed on the gross amount of interest accrued in the accounting period.

Miscellaneous income

CTA 2009 lists a number of categories of miscellaneous income on which corporation tax is charged. Perhaps the most important of these is foreign dividends (i.e. dividends from non-UK companies). However, changes introduced by Finance Act 2009 mean that most foreign dividends are now exempt from corporation tax (see Chapter 32).

EXAMPLE 4

A company prepares accounts to 31 December each year and lets two properties to tenants. The following information relates to the year to 31 December 2012:

(a) Property A is owned by the company. The property was let from 1 January 2012 to 30 June 2012 at an annual rent of £9,600, payable monthly in advance. However, the rent due on 1 May and 1 June 2012 was not paid and the tenant then absconded. The company has now written off this rent as a bad debt.

Having advertised for a new tenant (cost £200), the company re-let the property from 1 September 2012 at an annual rent of £10,200, payable monthly in advance. The rent due on 1 December 2012 was not received until 3 January 2013.

Apart from advertising, the only other expenses incurred by the company in relation to Property A during the year to 31 December 2012 were:

	£
Minor repairs	230
Interest on loan to acquire the property	8,400

This property is let unfurnished.

(b) Property B is a leasehold property which was acquired by the company on 1 October 2012. The company paid a premium of £120,000 for the grant of a 25-year lease but is not required to pay rent. As from 1 October 2012, this property was let to a tenant at an annual rent of £12,000. The first year's rent was paid in advance and the tenant also paid a premium of £40,000 for the grant of a 10-year lease.

This property is let furnished and the wear and tear allowance is claimed. No other expenses were incurred in relation to this property during the year.

Calculate the company's property business profit for the year to 31 December 2012.

Solution

	£	£
Rent receivable:		
Property A £9,600 x 6/12 + £10,200 x 4/12		8,200
Property B £12,000 x 3/12		3,000
Premium received £40,000 – (£40,000 x 2% x (10 – 1))	32,800	
Premium paid 10/25ths x (£120,000 – (£120,000 x 2% x (25 – 1)))	24,960	7,840
		19,040
Less: Bad debt £9,600 x 2/12	1,600	
Advertising	200	
Repairs	230	
Wear and tear allowance 10% x £3,000	300	2,330
Property business profit		16,710

Note that the loan interest is not deductible when computing property income but will be dealt with under the loan relationships regime.

Franked investment income

Dividends received from other UK companies are paid out of profits which have already been subject to corporation tax. Therefore, to avoid double taxation, such dividends are not included in the chargeable profits of the receiving company. The term "franked investment income" (FII) is used to refer to the UK dividends received by a company, together with the attached one-ninth tax credits. For example, a company which receives a UK dividend of £9,000 has FII of £10,000 (£9,000 + tax credit £1,000). FII does *not* form part of a company's chargeable profits.

Most foreign dividends received by UK companies are now exempt from corporation tax (see Chapter 32) and are treated exactly as if they were dividends received from other UK companies. Accordingly, an exempt foreign dividend is deemed to have an attached one-ninth tax credit and the amount of the dividend (plus tax credit) is treated as FII.

Relief for qualifying charitable donations

Certain charitable donations and gifts are referred to as "qualifying charitable donations" and are deductible when computing a company's chargeable profits. Qualifying charitable donations are as follows:

(a) donations made by a company under the Gift Aid scheme (see Chapter 4)
(b) gifts of listed shares or securities to a charity
(c) gifts of land and buildings to a charity.

The Gift Aid donations that are deducted when computing a company's chargeable profits for an accounting period are the donations actually *paid* during that period. Accruals and prepayments are ignored. Similarly, the amount deducted in relation to gifts of assets is the market value of the assets given in the period. Gift Aid donations made by a company are paid gross, so these donations are not grossed-up.

Charitable donations incurred by a company for trade purposes (and not within the Gift Aid scheme) are deductible when computing the company's trading income.

Loan relationships

A company is a party to a "loan relationship" if it is a debtor or creditor with regard to any debt which is a loan under general law. The main classes of debt to which the term refers are bank and building society deposits, bank overdrafts, Government securities ("gilts" or "gilt-edged" securities), corporate bonds (e.g. debentures) and other corporate debt. The tax treatment of income and expenditure relating to a loan relationship depends upon whether the relationship has been entered into for trade purposes. The loan relationships rules may be summarised as follows:

(a) **Trading loan relationships**. If a company has entered into a loan relationship for trade purposes, then:

  (i) Any interest payable (and any other cost relating to the debt) is treated as a trading expense.

  (ii) Any interest receivable (and other income relating to the debt) is treated as trading income. This will usually apply only if the company's trade is that of lending money.

(b) **Non-trading loan relationships**. If a company has entered into one or more loan relationships for non-trading purposes, then all of the "debits" and "credits" (costs and income) relating to such relationships are aggregated. Then:

  (i) If total credits exceed total debits, the net credits form part of the company's chargeable profits and are charged to corporation tax.

  (ii) If total debits exceed total credits, the net debits may be relieved in a variety of ways (see Chapter 26).

  Interest payable on underpaid corporation tax is treated as a non-trading debit. Similarly, interest receivable on a repayment of overpaid corporation tax is treated as a non-trading credit (see Chapter 25).

It is important to appreciate that the above treatment of costs and income relating to loan relationships applies to all such costs and income, *whether of a revenue or capital nature*. This means that the profit (or loss) arising on a disposal of Government securities or corporate bonds by a company is taxable (or allowable) even though such assets would not be chargeable assets for CGT purposes if held by individuals.

Accounting for loan relationships

In most cases, the amount of income and expenditure brought into account for a loan relationship is calculated on the *accruals basis*. Any receipts or payments made net of income tax must be grossed-up. Income tax deducted at source from the income received in an accounting period (now rare) may be reclaimed from HMRC. Similarly, income tax deducted at source from the payments made in an accounting period must be accounted for to HMRC (see Chapter 25).

EXAMPLE 5

A manufacturing company has the following results for the year to 31 March 2013:

	£
Trading income	883,000
Income from property	14,200
Bank interest (gross amount received)	6,200
Interest on Government securities (gross amount received)	28,000
Dividends from UK companies	18,450
Chargeable gains	123,000
Gift Aid donation	24,000

The following information is also relevant:

(a) Bank interest of £2,100 was owing to the company at the end of the year. The corresponding amount at the start of the year was zero.

(b) The Government securities were acquired on 1 July 2012. Interest of £28,000 (gross) is payable to the company on 30 June and 31 December each year.

Compute the company's chargeable profits for the year to 31 March 2013.

Solution

	£
Trading income	883,000
Income from property	14,200
Income from non-trading loan relationships	50,300
Chargeable gains	123,000
	1,070,500
Less: Qualifying charitable donations	24,000
Chargeable profits	1,046,500

Notes:

(i) The bank interest is income from a non-trading loan relationship and is assessed on the accruals basis. The amount that is charged to corporation tax for the year is £8,300 (£6,200 received + £2,100 accrued).

(ii) The interest on Government securities is income from a non-trading loan relationship and is assessed on the accruals basis. The gross income accrued in the year of £42,000 (£28,000 + £14,000) forms part of the company's chargeable profits for corporation tax purposes.

(iii) The dividends received from UK companies (plus the attached tax credits) are franked investment income and do not form part of the company's chargeable profits for corporation tax purposes.

(iv) The Gift Aid donation of £24,000 is a qualifying charitable donation.

EXAMPLE 6

A company produces the following income statement for the year to 31 March 2013:

		£	£
Gross profit brought down from trading account			758,950
Add:	Rental income (Note 1)	5,000	
	Loan interest receivable (Note 2)	2,600	
	Dividends received (Note 3)	18,750	
	Bank interest receivable (Note 4)	4,789	
	Patent royalties receivable (Note 5)	6,500	
	Profit on sale of building (Note 6)	6,000	43,639
			802,589
Less:	Operating expenses (Note 7)		568,912
Net profit for the year			233,677

Notes:

1. The property was let on 1 January 2013 at a rent of £20,000 per annum, payable annually in advance. The figure shown in the income statement represents the rent for the period 1 January 2013 to 31 March 2013. No allowable expenditure has been incurred in relation to the let property.
2. Gross loan interest of £1,950 was received during the year and a further £650 was owing to the company at the end of the year. None was owed to the company at the start of the year. The income statement shows the total of £2,600.
3. Dividends of £18,750 were received from other UK companies during the year.
4. Bank interest received in the year was £4,684. Of this, £1,000 was owed to the company at the start of the year. A further £1,105 was owing to the company at the end of the year but was not received until April 2013.
5. Patent royalties of £6,000 (gross) were received in the year and a further £500 was owing to the company at the end of the year. None was owed to the company at the start of the year. The income statement shows the total of £6,500. The patents are held for trade purposes.
6. The chargeable gain on the sale of the building is £2,350.
7. Operating expenses include:

	£
Directors' fees	100,000
Debenture interest (gross amounts):	
Paid 1 January 2013	4,000
Accrued at 31 March 2013	2,000
Depreciation of tangible fixed assets	102,500
Customer entertaining expenses	2,400
Gift Aid donation paid in the year	750

All of the remaining operating expenses are allowable as trading expenses. The debentures were issued on 1 July 2012 for trade purposes. The company claims capital allowances for the year of £87,450.

Required:

(a) Compute the company's trading income for the year to 31 March 2013.

(b) Compute the company's chargeable profit for the year to 31 March 2013.

Solution

(a) The company's trading income is as follows:

		£	£
Net profit per accounts			233,677
Less:	*Non-trading income*:		
	Income from property	5,000	
	Loan interest receivable	2,600	
	Dividends received	18,750	
	Bank interest receivable	4,789	
	Profit on sale of building	6,000	37,139
			196,538
Add:	*Disallowed expenses*:		
	Depreciation	102,500	
	Customer entertaining	2,400	
	Gift Aid donation	750	105,650
			302,188
Less:	Capital allowances		87,450
Trading income			214,738

(b) The chargeable profits for the year are:

	£
Trading income	214,738
Income from property	5,000
Income from non-trading loan relationships	7,389
Chargeable gain	2,350
	229,477
Less: Qualifying charitable donations	750
Chargeable profits	228,727

Notes:

(i) The computation of the company's trading income is performed in the same way as that of an individual. The starting point is the net profit shown by the accounts. Non-trading income included in this net profit is subtracted and disallowed expenses are added back. The aim is to separate out the company's trading profit from the total net profit shown in the accounts. The debenture interest is an allowable expense since the debentures were issued for trade purposes. The patent royalties receivable are trading income since the patents are held for trade purposes.

It is extremely important to classify the company's profits correctly and to arrive at a separate figure for each category of profit (e.g. trading income, rents, interest, chargeable gains etc.). This analysis is necessary because different rules of assessment apply to each category of profit and is especially vital if the company has incurred any losses (see Chapter 26).

(ii) Property income is computed on the accruals basis.

(iii) The accrued loan interest forms part of the company's income from non-trading loans (assuming that the loan was not made for trade purposes). The remainder of this figure is bank interest, received gross and assessed on the accruals basis.

(iv) FII is not chargeable to corporation tax.

(v) The chargeable gain on the sale of the building is fully chargeable to corporation tax since the company is not entitled to the annual exemption (see Chapter 24).

(vi) The Gift Aid donation is a qualifying charitable donation.

Long periods of account

As stated above, a period of account exceeding 12 months must be divided into two or more accounting periods, each of which will give rise to a separate corporation tax assessment. A company's profit for a long period of account is allocated between accounting periods as follows:

(a) Adjusted trading profits (before deduction of capital allowances) are usually time-apportioned. Capital allowances are then computed separately for each accounting period.

(b) Property income is also usually time-apportioned.

(c) A net credit on non-trading loan relationships is allocated between accounting periods on the accruals basis.

(d) Chargeable gains are allocated to the accounting period in which the disposals occur.

(e) Qualifying charitable donations are allocated to the accounting period in which they are made.

(f) Franked investment income is allocated to the accounting period in which it is received. Although a company's FII does not form part of its chargeable profits, this allocation may be important when determining the rate of corporation tax which must be paid by the company (see Chapter 25).

In practice, the time-apportionment method which is normally used for trading profits and property income may be replaced by a more accurate method of allocation if one is available. For instance, if trading profits have been earned as a result of a small number of transactions and the profit arising on each transaction can be calculated individually, trading profits may be allocated between accounting periods according to the transactions occurring in each period.

EXAMPLE 7

A company makes up accounts for the 21 months to 30 September 2012. The company's results for this period of account are as follows (all figures are shown gross):

	£
Adjusted trading profits (before capital allowances)	630,000
Non-trade loan interest receivable:	
Received 31 October 2011	600
Received 30 April 2012	600
Accrued to 30 September 2012	500
Chargeable gains:	
Disposal on 25 May 2011	2,300
Disposal on 12 December 2011	700
Disposal on 15 February 2012	10,500
Gift Aid donations:	
Paid 31 December 2011	4,000
Accrued to 30 September 2012	3,000

The loan interest receivable relates to a £12,000 loan made on 1 May 2011 at 10%. The company makes a £4,000 Gift Aid donation on 31 December every year. Show how the period of account will be divided into accounting periods and compute the company's chargeable profits for each accounting period. (Ignore capital allowances).

Solution

There are two accounting periods - the year to 31 December 2011 and the nine months to 30 September 2012. The chargeable profits for each accounting period are as follows:

	12 mths to 31/12/11	*9 mths to 30/9/12*
	£	£
Trading income (12:9)	360,000	270,000
Income from non-trading loan relationship	800	900
Chargeable gains	3,000	10,500
	363,800	281,400
Less: Qualifying charitable donations	4,000	nil
Chargeable profits	359,800	281,400

Notes:

(i) The loan interest is allocated on the accruals basis. Interest on the loan accrues at £100 per month so the interest for the period from 1 May 2011 to 31 December 2011 (eight months) is £800 and the interest for the period from 1 January 2012 to 30 September 2012 (nine months) is £900.

(ii) The chargeable gains are allocated according to the date of disposal and the Gift Aid donations are allocated according to the date of payment. The donations accrued at 30 September 2012 are ignored for now but will be taken into account when computing the chargeable profits of the accounting period in which they are paid.

Summary

- Corporation tax is charged on the worldwide profits of UK resident companies. Non-UK resident companies which trade in the UK through a permanent establishment are charged to corporation tax on the profits of that establishment.
- Corporation tax is charged in respect of accounting periods. The length of an accounting period can never exceed 12 months. A period of account which is longer than this is divided into two or more accounting periods.
- A company's chargeable profits consist of its income and chargeable gains, less any qualifying charitable donations.
- A company's trading income is calculated in a similar way to the trading income of an individual. However, special corporation tax rules apply to research and development expenditure and to income and expenditure relating to intangible fixed assets.
- A company's property income is assessed in a similar way to the property income of an individual. However, interest payable on a loan for the purchase or improvement of property is dealt with under the loan relationships rules. The reliefs available to a company which incurs a loss in relation to a property business are different from those available to an individual.
- The qualifying property income of a UK-REIT is exempt from corporation tax. Capital gains made on the disposal of investment property are also exempt.
- A company's income and expenditure relating to loan relationships entered into for trade purposes is taken into account when computing the company's trading income. Net credits on non-trading loan relationships form part of chargeable profits.
- Dividends received from other UK companies (plus the attached tax credits) are referred to as franked investment income and are not part of the chargeable profits of the receiving company. Most foreign dividends are now also deemed to have an attached tax credit and are treated as franked investment income.
- A company's qualifying charitable donations consist mainly of Gift Aid donations. These are relieved on the payments basis.

Exercises

23.1 Identify the accounting periods relating to the following periods of account:

(a) year to 30 November 2012
(b) 1 October 2011 to 31 July 2012
(c) 1 January 2013 to 31 January 2013
(d) 33 months to 31 August 2012
(e) 1 April 2011 to 30 September 2012.

23.2 On 1 January 2013, a company receives gross debenture interest of £1,600 from another UK company and pays net debenture interest of £8,640 to individuals.

(a) Outline the corporation tax treatment of each of these items.

(b) Explain how each of these items would appear in the company's accounts.

23.3 During the year to 31 March 2013, a company which qualifies as medium-sized spends £180,000 on research and development. This is qualifying expenditure under the R&D tax credits scheme. Explain the corporation tax treatment of this expenditure.

23.4 A company's accounts for the 17 months to 30 June 2012 include:

	£
Trading income	425,000
Debenture interest (gross amounts):	
Received 31 October 2011	2,400
Received 30 April 2012	2,400
Accrued to 30 June 2012	800
Income from property (let since 2008)	9,010
Chargeable gains:	
Disposal on 31 January 2012	28,700
Disposal on 1 February 2012	49,760
Dividend received from UK company	10,000
Gift Aid donations:	
Paid 31 July 2011	6,000
Paid 31 January 2012	6,000

The debentures were acquired (not for trade purposes) on 1 May 2011. Interest is payable half-yearly on 30 April and 31 October. Show how the company's period of account will be divided into accounting periods and compute the chargeable profits for each accounting period. Ignore capital allowances.

23.5 A company has the following results for the year to 31 March 2013:

	£	£
Trading profits, after capital allowances		1,561,400
Bank deposit interest (account opened 1 April 2012):		
Received 30 June 2012		19,820
Received 31 December 2012		44,670
Accrued to 31 March 2013		23,980
Chargeable gain on sale of factory		531,000
Dividends received from UK companies		132,000
Deed of covenant payable annually to a charity:		
Paid 1 October 2012, for year to 30 September 2013	9,000	
Less: Prepayment	4,500	4,500

The charitable covenant began on 1 October 2012 and falls within the Gift Aid scheme. Compute the company's chargeable profits for the year.

***23.6** A company's income statement for the year to 31 March 2013 is as follows:

	£	£
Gross trading profit		373,870
Receivable from other UK companies:		
Dividends		4,000
Debenture interest (Note 1)		6,000
Bank interest receivable (Note 2)		12,600
Income from property (Note 3)		4,000
Profit on sale of investments (Note 4)		22,490
		422,960
Less:		
Distribution costs (all allowable)	97,500	
Administrative expenses (all allowable)	101,150	
Directors' fees	50,000	
Interest on bank overdraft	23,780	
Debenture interest payable (Notes 5, 8)	50,000	
Patent royalties payable (Notes 6, 8)	7,500	
Depreciation of tangible fixed assets	108,300	438,230
Net loss for the year		15,270

Notes:

1. The company acquired £240,000 of 10% debentures (for non-trade purposes) on 1 January 2013. Interest is receivable half-yearly on 30 June and 31 December. No interest was received during the year to 31 March 2013.
2. Bank interest receivable includes interest of £1,450 which had accrued at 31 March 2013 but which was not received until April 2013. There was no accrued interest at 31 March 2012.
3. The property was let on 1 December 2012 at a rent of £1,000 per month payable quarterly in advance on 1 December, 1 March, 1 June and 1 September. There were no allowable expenses in the year to 31 March 2013.
4. The agreed chargeable gain on the sale of the investments was £8,450.
5. £500,000 of 10% debentures were issued (for trade purposes) on 1 April 2012. The interest is payable (net of income tax) on 1 January each year.
6. As from 1 July 2012, the company is required to pay patent royalties of £10,000 per annum, deducting basic rate income tax at source. The net amount paid in the year to 31 March 2013 was £4,000. The royalties are payable for trade purposes.
7. Capital allowances of £32,700 are claimed for the year.
8. All figures given in the income statement are gross.

Compute the company's chargeable profits for the year.

Chapter 24

Corporate chargeable gains

Introduction

A company's chargeable profits for an accounting period include any chargeable gains which arise from disposals made during that period. The chargeable gains of a company are computed in a similar way to the capital gains of an individual, but there are some important differences between the rules which apply to companies and the rules which apply to individuals. The purpose of this chapter is to explain how the chargeable gains of a company are determined for corporation tax purposes. The relevant legislation is in the Taxation of Chargeable Gains Act 1992, as amended by subsequent Finance Acts.

Chargeable disposals and chargeable assets

A chargeable gain or allowable loss may arise if a company makes a chargeable disposal of a chargeable asset. A company's chargeable assets will usually consist of non-current assets (fixed assets) such as land and buildings, plant and machinery or investments, but certain assets are entirely exempt from the chargeable gains legislation. The main exemptions for a company are:

(a) motor cars

(b) items of tangible, movable property ("chattels") worth £6,000 or less

(c) chattels with a predictable useful life of up to 50 years ("wasting chattels") unless used in business and eligible for capital allowances

(d) gilt-edged securities and qualifying corporate bonds, which are dealt with by the loan relationships regime (see Chapter 23).

A chargeable disposal generally occurs when the whole or part of a chargeable asset is sold or given away. However, the gift of a chargeable asset to a charity is exempt.

Basis of assessment

The chargeable gains figure which is included in a company's chargeable profits for an accounting period is based upon the disposals made during that period. This figure is calculated as follows:

(a) The chargeable gain or allowable loss arising on each disposal is calculated.

(b) If total gains exceed total losses, the losses are subtracted from the gains to give net chargeable gains for the accounting period.

(c) If total losses exceed total gains, the chargeable gains figure for the accounting period is £nil. The net losses are then carried forward for relief in subsequent accounting periods (see Chapter 26).

Companies are *not* entitled to the annual exemption which is available to individuals who pay capital gains tax (CGT).

Computation of gains and losses

The chargeable gains and allowable losses of a company are computed in a similar way to those of an individual (see Chapters 18-22) but the following important distinctions should be noted:

(a) (i) The gain arising on the disposal of a chargeable asset by a company is reduced by "indexation allowance", which adjusts the gain to take account of inflation. Indexation allowance used to be available when calculating the capital gains of individuals for CGT purposes, but this is no longer the case.

(ii) Rebasing does not always apply when a company disposes of an asset acquired before 31 March 1982.

The way in which indexation allowance is calculated and the corporation tax treatment of assets acquired before 31 March 1982 are both explained below.

(b) The share matching rules that are used when a company makes a disposal of shares or securities are different from the equivalent rules that apply when such a disposal is made by an individual. The share matching rules which are used for corporation tax purposes are explained later in this chapter.

(c) The principal private residence exemption does not apply to companies.

(d) With the introduction of the intangible fixed assets regime (see Chapter 23), goodwill and quotas acquired by a company are removed from the list of assets which qualify for chargeable gains rollover relief.

(e) Gift relief, incorporation relief, entrepreneurs' relief and EIS deferral relief do not apply to companies.

Indexation allowance

Indexation allowance was introduced in 1982 with the intention of ensuring that capital gains caused by inflation should not be charged to tax.

Indexation allowance is calculated separately for each item of allowable expenditure shown in a computation. The indexation allowance available on an item of expenditure is equal to the amount of that expenditure multiplied by an *indexation factor*, which is computed according to the following formula and is rounded to three decimal places:

$$\frac{RD - RI}{RI}$$

where: RD is the Retail Prices Index (RPI) for the month of disposal, and
RI is the RPI for the month in which the expenditure was incurred.

A table of RPIs is given at the end of this chapter.

EXAMPLE 1

A company bought a chargeable asset (not a chattel) in June 2001 (RPI 174.4) for £1,200 and sold the asset in August 2012 (RPI 244.2) for £4,350. Compute the chargeable gain.

Solution

	£
Sale proceeds	4,350
Less: Acquisition cost	1,200
Unindexed gain	3,150
Less: Indexation allowance	
$\frac{244.2 - 174.4}{174.4}$ = 0.400 x £1,200	480
Chargeable gain	2,670

EXAMPLE 2

A company bought a chargeable asset in November 1999 for £15,000. Enhancement expenditure was £2,000 in January 2001 and £3,000 in June 2005. The asset was sold in February 2013 for £38,000. RPIs are as follows:

November 1999	166.7
January 2001	171.1
June 2005	192.2
February 2013	247.8

Compute the chargeable gain.

Solution

	£	£
Sale proceeds		38,000
Less: Acquisition cost	15,000	
Enhancement expenditure (£2,000 + £3,000)	5,000	20,000
Unindexed gain		18,000
Less: Indexation allowance:		
(i) on acquisition cost $\frac{247.8 - 166.7}{166.7} = 0.487 \times £15{,}000$	7,305	
(ii) on enhancement January 2001 $\frac{247.8 - 171.1}{171.1} = 0.448 \times £2{,}000$	896	
(iii) on enhancement June 2005 $\frac{247.8 - 192.2}{192.2} = 0.289 \times £3{,}000$	867	9,068
Chargeable gain		8,932

Restrictions on indexation allowance

Note the following points about the indexation allowance:

(a) If RPI goes *down* between the month in which expenditure is incurred and the month of disposal, the indexation allowance available in relation to that expenditure is nil.

(b) No indexation allowance is available in respect of the incidental costs of disposal, even if they were incurred prior to the month of disposal.

(c) Indexation allowance cannot be used to convert a gain into a loss. Therefore, if the available indexation allowance (calculated in the normal way) exceeds the unindexed gain, the indexation allowance is restricted so as to give neither a gain nor a loss.

(d) Indexation allowance cannot be used to increase an unindexed loss. If there is an unindexed loss on a disposal then the indexation allowance is nil.

EXAMPLE 3

A company acquired a chargeable asset for £5,000 in February 2003 (RPI 179.3). The asset was sold in January 2013 (RPI 247.2). The asset was not a chattel. Compute the chargeable gain or allowable loss if the sale proceeds were:

(a) £9,000 (b) £5,500 (c) £4,800

Solution

	(a)	(b)	(c)
	£	£	£
Sale proceeds	9,000	5,500	4,800
Less: Acquisition cost	5,000	5,000	5,000
Unindexed gain or loss	4,000	500	(200)
Less: Indexation allowance			
$\frac{247.2 - 179.3}{179.3}$ = 0.379 x £5,000 = £1,895	1,895	500	nil
Chargeable gain or allowable loss	2,105	nil	(200)

Notes:

(i) In case (a), the indexation allowance can be given in full.

(ii) In case (b), the full indexation allowance would convert an unindexed gain of £500 into a loss of £1,395. Indexation allowance is restricted to £500 to prevent this.

(iii) In case (c) there is an unindexed loss, so indexation allowance is restricted to £nil.

Assets held on 31 March 1982

If an asset is disposed of which was acquired before 31 March 1982, only the part of the gain accruing since 31 March 1982 is charged to tax (see Chapter 18). The taxable gain is usually calculated by means of the "rebasing" technique, whereby the market value of the asset at 31 March 1982 is substituted for its acquisition cost.

However, although rebasing now always applies for individuals, this is not the case for companies. Under corporation tax rules, rebasing does *not* apply if the rebasing calculation results in a greater gain than the calculation based on original cost.

EXAMPLE 4

A company acquired a chargeable asset for £2,000 in April 1980 and sold the asset for £22,500 in May 2012. Compute the unindexed gain arising on this disposal if the market value of the asset at 31 March 1982 was:

(a) £4,200 (b) £500

Solution

(a) The unindexed gain over the entire period of ownership, based on the original cost of the asset, is £20,500 (£22,500 – £2,000). But the rebasing calculation gives a gain of only £18,300 (£22,500 – £4,200). This is less than the gain based on original cost so rebasing applies and the unindexed gain is £18,300.

(b) The rebasing calculation gives an unindexed gain of £22,000 (£22,500 – £500). This is more than the gain based on original cost so rebasing does not apply and the unindexed gain is £20,500.

Indexation allowance for pre-31 March 1982 assets

The rules for calculating the indexation allowance available to a company on the disposal of an asset held on 31 March 1982 are as follows:

(a) Indexation allowance is based on the change in RPI between March 1982 and the month of disposal. No further indexation allowance is available to compensate for the effects of pre-March 1982 inflation. This is why the table of RPIs given at the end of this chapter begins with the RPI for March 1982.

(b) In *both* the rebasing calculation and the calculation based on original cost, indexation allowance is calculated with reference to the *greater* of original cost and market value at 31 March 1982 (i.e. the same indexation allowance is given in both calculations).

EXAMPLE 5

Calculate the chargeable gain arising on the disposal described in the above example. RPIs are 79.44 for March 1982 and 242.4 for May 2012.

Solution

(a)

	Original cost	Rebasing
	£	£
Sale proceeds	22,500	22,500
Less: Original cost	2,000	
Market value 31/3/82		4,200
Unindexed gain	20,500	18,300
Less: Indexation allowance		
$\frac{242.4 - 79.44}{79.44}$ = 2.051 x £4,200	8,614	8,614
Chargeable gain	11,886	9,686

The rebasing calculation gives the lower gain, so rebasing applies and the chargeable gain is £9,686.

(b)

	Original cost	Rebasing
	£	£
Sale proceeds	22,500	22,500
Less: Original cost	2,000	
Market value 31/3/82		500
Unindexed gain	20,500	22,000
Less: Indexation allowance		
$\frac{242.4 - 79.44}{79.44}$ = 2.051 x £2,000	4,102	4,102
Chargeable gain	16,398	17,898

The rebasing calculation gives the higher gain, so rebasing does not apply and the chargeable gain is £16,398.

Losses on disposal of pre-31 March 1982 assets

If the rebasing calculation gives a gain and the original cost calculation also gives a gain, the chargeable gain is the *smaller* of these two gains. Similarly, if the rebasing calculation gives a loss and the original cost calculation also gives a loss, the allowable loss is the *smaller* of these two losses. Finally, if one of the calculations gives a gain and the other calculation gives a loss (or if either calculation gives a nil result) the situation is "no gain, no loss". In these circumstances there is no chargeable gain and no allowable loss.

EXAMPLE 6

A company acquired a chargeable asset (not a chattel) in 1979. The asset was sold in December 2012 (RPI 246.6) for £2,800. Compute the chargeable gain or allowable loss if the original cost of the asset and its market value on 31 March 1982 (RPI 79.44) were:

(a) £3,500 and £4,000 (b) £750 and £850 (c) £10 and £1,050.

Solution

(a)

	Original cost	*Rebasing*
	£	£
Sale proceeds	2,800	2,800
Less: Original cost	3,500	
Market value 31/3/82		4,000
Allowable loss	(700)	(1,200)

The rebasing calculation gives the higher loss, so rebasing does not apply and the allowable loss is £700. Indexation allowance was £nil in both calculations, since indexation allowance cannot be used to increase an unindexed loss.

(b)

	Original cost	*Rebasing*
	£	£
Sale proceeds	2,800	2,800
Less: Original cost	750	
Market value 31/3/82		850
Unindexed gain	2,050	1,950
Less: Indexation allowance		
$\frac{246.6 - 79.44}{79.44}$ = 2.104 x £850	1,788	1,788
Chargeable gain	262	162

The rebasing calculation gives the lower gain. Therefore rebasing applies and the chargeable gain is £162.

(c)

	Original cost	Rebasing
	£	£
Sale proceeds	2,800	2,800
Less: Original cost	10	
Market value 31/3/82		1,050
Unindexed gain	2,790	1,750
Less: Indexation allowance		
$\frac{246.6-79.44}{79.44}$ = 2.104 x £1,050 = £2,209	2,209	1,750
Chargeable gain	581	nil

The rebasing calculation gives a nil result, whilst the calculation based on original cost gives a gain. Therefore the situation is "no gain, no loss". Indexation allowance was restricted to £1,750 in the rebasing calculation so as to avoid converting a gain into a loss.

The rebasing election

A company may make an *irrevocable* election to the effect that gains and losses arising on all future disposals of assets held on 31 March 1982 should be calculated by the rebasing method, with no reference whatsoever to the costs incurred before 31 March 1982.

If this election is made, costs incurred before 31 March 1982 are completely ignored for all purposes, including calculation of the indexation allowance. Therefore indexation allowance will always be based upon market value at 31 March 1982, even if this is lower than the costs incurred before 31 March 1982.

Assets acquired before 6 April 1965

When the tax on chargeable gains was introduced, special rules applied to the disposal of an asset acquired before 6 April 1965. These rules no longer apply to individuals and are now rarely used for companies, as it becomes increasingly uncommon for a disposal to involve an asset acquired before 6 April 1965. Also, from the perspective of disposals made in the 21st century, the disposal of an asset acquired before 6 April 1965 must also be the disposal of an asset held on 31 March 1982. Therefore rebasing is available in relation to such disposals and rebasing will generally give a lower gain than the gain calculated according to the special rules mentioned above. However, these rules are still used for companies if they give the lower gain.

A summary of the treatment of assets acquired before 6 April 1965, together with a number of worked examples, can be found on the website which accompanies this book. The website address is www.pearsoned.co.uk/melville.

Disposals of shares or securities

The share matching rules which apply on a disposal of shares or securities by an individual were explained in Chapter 20 of this book. The main principle is that shares of the same class in the same company are pooled into the "Section 104 holding" and that disposals are generally matched against shares taken from this holding. Special rules apply if shares are bought and sold on the same day or if shares are sold and re-acquired within 30 days.

However, the share matching rules which are used when a *company* makes a disposal of shares or securities are not the same as the rules for individuals. A disposal of shares or securities by a company is matched against acquisitions in the following order:

(a) first, against acquisitions made on the same day

(b) next, against acquisitions made in the previous nine days (on a FIFO basis)

(c) next, against shares taken from the Section 104 holding, which (for companies) is the pool of shares acquired on or after 1 April 1982

(d) next, against the "1982 holding", which is a pool of shares acquired between 6 April 1965 and 31 March 1982 inclusive

(e) finally, against shares acquired before 6 April 1965 (on a LIFO basis).

These rules have to be more complex than their CGT equivalents because companies are entitled to indexation allowance and because rebasing does not always apply when a company disposes of a pre-31 March 1982 asset.

The Section 104 holding

A company's s104 holding of shares of a certain class in a certain company consists of the pool of shares which were acquired on or after 1 April 1982. Share acquisitions which are matched against disposals made on the same day or during the following nine days do not join the s104 holding.

The distinguishing characteristic of shares acquired on or after 1 April 1982 is that the indexation factor used on their disposal will differ according to the date of acquisition. If it were not for Section 104, it would be necessary to keep detailed records of the date and cost of each share acquisition made on or after 1April 1982, so that indexation allowance could be calculated correctly on a disposal. However, the pooling system provided by Section 104 eliminates the need to keep these records. All that is required is a record of:

(a) the total number of shares in the pool

(b) their total cost

(c) their total *indexed cost*, which consists of total cost plus all indexation allowance due up to the date of the most recent "operative event". An operative event occurs whenever shares enter or leave the pool.

The indexed cost of the s104 holding is calculated as follows:

(a) The number of shares in the pool at 1 April 1985 (if any) is totalled and the cost of these shares is also totalled. The indexed cost of the pool at 1 April 1985 is calculated as total cost, plus an indexation allowance for each acquisition forming part of the pool, based on the change in RPI between the date of the acquisition and April 1985.

(b) On the occurrence of a subsequent operative event, the indexed cost of the pool is increased by reference to the change in RPI since the previous operative event (if any) or since April 1985 (if the previous event was before April 1985). TCGA 1992 does not require the indexation factor used in this calculation to be rounded to 3 decimal places. The pool is then adjusted as follows:

    (i) If the event is an acquisition, the number of shares acquired is added to the number of shares in the pool and their cost is added to the cost and to the indexed cost of the pool.

    (ii) If the event is a disposal, the number of shares disposed of is subtracted from the number of shares in the pool. It is then necessary to deduct a proportion of the cost and indexed cost of the pool. Strictly speaking, this proportion should be calculated using the part disposal fraction (see Chapter 18) which takes into account the value of the shares disposed of and the value of the shares remaining. In most cases, however, the value per share of the shares disposed of will be the same as the value per share of the shares remaining, so that the proportion to be deducted from the cost and indexed cost of the pool can be based upon the *number* of shares disposed of.

The unindexed gain (or loss) arising on a disposal from the pool is calculated as the difference between the disposal proceeds and the amount which has been subtracted from the cost of the pool as a consequence of the disposal. The indexation allowance due on the disposal is the difference between the amount subtracted from the cost of the pool and the amount subtracted from the indexed cost of the pool. As usual, indexation allowance cannot be used to create a loss or to increase a loss.

EXAMPLE 7

A company makes the following acquisitions of ordinary shares in Juuj plc:

Date	*No of shares*	*Cost* £	*RPI*
1 July 1983	5,000	6,300	85.30
2 August 1984	2,000	2,500	89.94
3 February 1997	1,200	2,300	155.0
4 June 2003	1,800	3,400	181.3

The company sells 500 shares on 8 July 2012 (RPI 243.6).

(a) Calculate the cost and indexed cost of the s104 holding on 8 July 2012, just prior to and just after the above disposal (RPI for April 1985 is 94.78).

(b) Compute the chargeable gain or allowable loss on the disposal if sale proceeds are:

(i) £1,800 (ii) £1,000 (iii) £700

Solution

(a) The cost and indexed cost of the s104 holding on 8 July 2012 are calculated as follows:

	No of shares	*Cost* £	*Indexed cost* £
Bought 1 July 1983	5,000	6,300	6,300
Bought 2 August 1984	2,000	2,500	2,500
<u>Add</u>: Indexation to April 1985			
(a) $\frac{94.78 - 85.30}{85.30} = 0.111$			
0.111 x £6,300			699
(b) $\frac{94.78 - 89.94}{89.94} = 0.054$			
0.054 x £2,500			135
s104 holding at 5 April 1985	7,000	8,800	9,634
<u>Add</u>: Indexation to February 1997			
$\frac{155.0 - 94.78}{94.78}$ x £9,634			6,121
			15,755
Bought 3 February 1997	1,200	2,300	2,300
s104 holding at 3 February 1997	8,200	11,100	18,055

	No of shares	Cost	Indexed cost
		£	£
s104 holding at 3 February 1997	8,200	11,100	18,055
Add: Indexation to June 2003			
$\frac{181.3-155.0}{155.0}$ x £18,055			3,064
			21,119
Bought 4 June 2003	1,800	3,400	3,400
s104 holding at 4 June 2003	10,000	14,500	24,519
Add: Indexation to July 2012			
$\frac{243.6-181.3}{181.3}$ x £24,519			8,425
			32,944
Sold 8 July 2012 (500/10,000ths)	(500)	(725)	(1,647)
s104 holding c/f at 8 July 2012	9,500	13,775	31,297

Notes:

1. The indexation allowance calculated on operative events occurring after 5 April 1985 has not been rounded off to 3 decimal places.
2. The disposal in July 2012 must have come from the s104 holding since it cannot be matched against shares acquired on the same day or in the previous nine days.
3. The disposal is 500 shares out of a holding of 10,000. Therefore 500/10,000ths or 1/20th of the pool has been sold and so 1/20th of the cost and indexed cost are subtracted from the pool.
4. The cost of the shares disposed of is £725. Since the equivalent indexed cost is £1,647, the indexation allowance due on the disposal is £922 (£1,647 - £725).

(b)

	(i)	(ii)	(iii)
	£	£	£
Sale proceeds	1,800	1,000	700
Less: Cost	725	725	725
Unindexed gain or loss	1,075	275	(25)
Less: Indexation allowance (£922)	922	275	nil
Chargeable gain/(allowable loss)	153	nil	(25)

The 1982 holding

For a company, the 1982 holding is a pool of shares acquired between 6 April 1965 and 31 March 1982 inclusive. All of the shares in this pool attract the same rate of indexation allowance, based on the change in RPI between March 1982 and the date of disposal. This means that the calculation of this pool's value is much simpler than the calculation of the value of the s104 holding. All that is needed is a record of:

(a) the number of shares in the pool

(b) the total cost of these shares

(c) their market value at 31 March 1982.

When a disposal occurs, the number of shares in the pool is reduced and proportionate amounts are deducted from the pool's cost and from its market value at 31 March 1982. The gain or loss arising on the disposal is then calculated in the usual way, as for any disposal of a pre-31 March 1982 asset.

EXAMPLE 8

A company made the following acquisitions of ordinary shares in Cudij plc:

Date	*No of shares*	*Cost*
		£
1 June 1970	1,000	3,000
30 October 1975	800	2,500
15 August 1981	900	3,100

The shares had a market value of £1.80 per share on 31 March 1982 (RPI 79.44). The company made no further acquisitions and sold 750 of the shares on 18 January 2013 (RPI 247.2) for £8,500. Compute the chargeable gain.

Solution

The sale of 750 shares on 18 January 2013 cannot be matched against any acquisitions made on the same day or during the previous nine days and there is no s104 holding. The next step is to match against the 1982 holding, as follows:

	No of shares	*Cost*	*MV 31/3/82*
		£	£
Acquired 1 June 1970	1,000	3,000	1,800
Acquired 30 October 1975	800	2,500	1,440
Acquired 15 August 1981	900	3,100	1,620
	2,700	8,600	4,860
Sold 18 January 2013 (750/2,700ths)	(750)	(2,389)	(1,350)
1982 holding c/f	1,950	6,211	3,510

The sold shares are deemed to have cost £2,389 and their market value at 31 March 1982 was £1,350. The calculation of the gain arising on the disposal is:

	Original cost	*Rebasing*
	£	£
Sale proceeds	8,500	8,500
Less: Original cost	2,389	
Market value 31/3/82		1,350
Unindexed gain	6,111	7,150
Less: Indexation allowance		
$\frac{247.2 - 79.44}{79.44}$ = 2.112 x £2,389	5,046	5,046
Chargeable gain	1,065	2,104

The rebasing calculation gives the higher gain, so rebasing does not apply and the chargeable gain is £1,065.

Bonus issues and rights issues

As explained in Chapter 20, bonus issues and rights issues are regarded as reorganisations of share capital and shares acquired as a consequence of such issues are not treated as acquisitions in the normal way. Instead, the required treatment of bonus shares and rights shares is to uplift the number of shares in each of the taxpayer's existing holdings. In the case of rights issues, it is also necessary to increase the cost of those holdings, since rights shares (unlike bonus shares) are not acquired free of charge.

This treatment applies to companies as well as to individuals, but one complication that may arise in the case of a company is that rights shares acquired after 31 March 1982 might join the 1982 holding. If this occurs, the cost of the rights shares is treated as enhancement expenditure and it is necessary (for indexation purposes) to keep a separate record of the cost and acquisition date of those rights shares. The required procedure is illustrated in the following example.

EXAMPLE 9

A company made the following acquisitions of ordinary shares in Rujan plc:

Date	*No of shares*	*Cost*	*RPI*
		£	
15 August 1980	500	1,000	
23 January 1997	600	2,500	154.4

The market value of the shares on 31 March 1982 (RPI 79.44) was £2.50 per share. In June 2004 (RPI 186.8), Rujan plc made a 1 for 20 rights issue at £8 per share and the company decided to buy the shares it was offered. Calculate the chargeable gain arising in November 2012 (RPI 246.0) when the company sold 840 shares for £10 each.

Solution

The s104 holding:

	No of shares	Cost	Indexed cost
		£	£
Bought 23 January 1997	600	2,500	2,500
Add: Indexation to June 2004 $\frac{186.8-154.4}{154.4}$ x £2,500			525
			3,025
Rights issue June 2004 (1 for 20)	30	240	240
	630	2,740	3,265
Add: Indexation to November 2012 $\frac{246.0-186.8}{186.8}$ x £3,265			1,035
			4,300
Sold November 2012	(630)	(2,740)	(4,300)
s104 holding c/f	nil	nil	nil

The gain arising on the disposal of the s104 holding is:

	£
Sale proceeds (630 @ £10)	6,300
Less: Cost	2,740
Unindexed gain	3,560
Less: Indexation allowance (£4,300 - £2,740)	1,560
Chargeable gain	2,000

The 1982 holding:

	No of shares	Cost (original)	Cost (rights)	MV 31/3/82
		£	£	£
Acquired 15 August 1980	500	1,000		1,250
Rights issue June 2004 (1 for 20)	25		200	
	525	1,000	200	1,250
Sold November 2012 (210/525ths)	(210)	(400)	(80)	(500)
1982 holding c/f	315	600	120	750

The gain arising on the disposal from the 1982 holding is calculated on the basis that the company has sold an asset with a cost of £400 and a market value at 31 March 1982 of £500. The calculation also takes into account enhancement expenditure of £80 incurred in June 2004. The calculation of the gain is as follows:

	Original cost	Rebasing
	£	£
Sale proceeds (210 @ £10)	2,100	2,100
Less: Cost up to 31 March 1982	(400)	
Market value 31/3/82		(500)
Cost June 2004	(80)	(80)
Unindexed gain	1,620	1,520
Less: Indexation allowance		
$\frac{246.0 - 79.44}{79.44} = 2.097 \times £500$	(1,049)	(1,049)
$\frac{246.0 - 186.8}{186.8} = 0.317 \times £80$	(25)	(25)
Chargeable gain	546	446

The rebasing calculation gives the lower gain, so rebasing applies and the gain is £446. The total gain on the entire disposal of 840 shares is therefore £2,446 (£2,000 + £446).

Shares acquired before 6 April 1965

Special rules apply if a company disposes of shares which were originally acquired before 6 April 1965. However, these rules are now falling into disuse as it becomes increasingly uncommon for a disposal to involve shares acquired before that date.

A summary of the treatment of shares acquired before 6 April 1965, together with a number of worked examples, can be found on the website which accompanies this book. The website address is www.pearsoned.co.uk/melville.

Disposal of a substantial shareholding

A gain arising on the disposal of all or part of a "substantial shareholding" by a trading company or a member of a trading group is exempt from corporation tax so long as certain conditions are satisfied. Similarly, any loss arising on such a disposal is not an allowable loss. The main conditions which must be satisfied are:

(a) The company making the disposal must have held a substantial shareholding in the investee company throughout a 12-month period beginning not more than two years before the disposal takes place.

(b) The investee company must be a trading company or the holding company of a trading group.

For this purpose, a company holds a substantial shareholding in another company if it holds at least 10% of that company's ordinary share capital and is entitled to at least 10% of that company's profits and assets.

Summary

- A company's chargeable assets usually consist of non-current assets such as land and buildings, plant and investments. Non-chargeable assets include motor cars, chattels worth up to £6,000, wasting chattels, gilts and qualifying corporate bonds.
- A chargeable disposal occurs when the whole or part of a chargeable asset is sold or given away (unless given to a charity).
- If allowable losses for an accounting period exceed chargeable gains, the net losses are carried forward and relieved against chargeable gains in subsequent periods.
- Companies may claim indexation allowance but indexation allowance cannot be used to create or increase an allowable loss.
- Rebasing does not always apply when a company disposes of an asset acquired before 31 March 1982. It is necessary to perform a calculation based on original cost as well as the rebasing calculation. The chargeable gain (allowable loss) is the lower of the two gains (losses) given by these calculations.
- When a company makes a disposal of shares or securities, the disposal is matched first against shares acquired on the same day, then against shares acquired in the previous nine days, then against the s104 holding and then against the 1982 holding.
- The s104 holding consists of a pool of shares acquired on or after 1 April 1982. It is necessary to keep a record of the number of shares in this pool, their total cost and their total indexed cost.
- The 1982 holding is a pool of shares acquired between 6 April 1965 and 31 March 1982 inclusive. It is necessary to keep a record of the number of shares in this pool, their total cost and their market value at 31 March 1982.
- A gain arising on the disposal of a substantial shareholding by a trading company is exempt from corporation tax, subject to certain conditions.

Retail Prices Index (RPI)

(*Source*: Office for National Statistics)

	Jan	Feb	Mar	Apr	May	Jun	Jul	Aug	Sep	Oct	Nov	Dec
1982			79.44	81.04	81.62	81.85	81.88	81.90	81.85	82.26	82.66	82.51
1983	82.61	82.97	83.12	84.28	84.64	84.84	85.30	85.68	86.06	86.36	86.67	86.89
1984	86.84	87.20	87.48	88.64	88.97	89.20	89.10	89.94	90.11	90.67	90.95	90.87
1985	91.20	91.94	92.80	94.78	95.21	95.41	95.23	95.49	95.44	95.59	95.92	96.05
1986	96.25	96.60	96.73	97.67	97.85	97.79	97.52	97.82	98.30	98.45	99.29	99.62
1987	100.0	100.4	100.6	101.8	101.9	101.9	101.8	102.1	102.4	102.9	103.4	103.3
1988	103.3	103.7	104.1	105.8	106.2	106.6	106.7	107.9	108.4	109.5	110.0	110.3
1989	111.0	111.8	112.3	114.3	115.0	115.4	115.5	115.8	116.6	117.5	118.5	118.8
1990	119.5	120.2	121.4	125.1	126.2	126.7	126.8	128.1	129.3	130.3	130.0	129.9
1991	130.2	130.9	131.4	133.1	133.5	134.1	133.8	134.1	134.6	135.1	135.6	135.7
1992	135.6	136.3	136.7	138.8	139.3	139.3	138.8	138.9	139.4	139.9	139.7	139.2
1993	137.9	138.8	139.3	140.6	141.1	141.0	140.7	141.3	141.9	141.8	141.6	141.9
1994	141.3	142.1	142.5	144.2	144.7	144.7	144.0	144.7	145.0	145.2	145.3	146.0
1995	146.0	146.9	147.5	149.0	149.6	149.8	149.1	149.9	150.6	149.8	149.8	150.7
1996	150.2	150.9	151.5	152.6	152.9	153.0	152.4	153.1	153.8	153.8	153.9	154.4
1997	154.4	155.0	155.4	156.3	156.9	157.5	157.5	158.5	159.3	159.5	159.6	160.0
1998	159.5	160.3	160.8	162.6	163.5	163.4	163.0	163.7	164.4	164.5	164.4	164.4
1999	163.4	163.7	164.1	165.2	165.6	165.6	165.1	165.5	166.2	166.5	166.7	167.3
2000	166.6	167.5	168.4	170.1	170.7	171.1	170.5	170.5	171.7	171.6	172.1	172.2
2001	171.1	172.0	172.2	173.1	174.2	174.4	173.3	174.0	174.6	174.3	173.6	173.4
2002	173.3	173.8	174.5	175.7	176.2	176.2	175.9	176.4	177.6	177.9	178.2	178.5
2003	178.4	179.3	179.9	181.2	181.5	181.3	181.3	181.6	182.5	182.6	182.7	183.5
2004	183.1	183.8	184.6	185.7	186.5	186.8	186.8	187.4	188.1	188.6	189.0	189.9
2005	188.9	189.6	190.5	191.6	192.0	192.2	192.2	192.6	193.1	193.3	193.6	194.1
2006	193.4	194.2	195.0	196.5	197.7	198.5	198.5	199.2	200.1	200.4	201.1	202.7
2007	201.6	203.1	204.4	205.4	206.2	207.3	206.1	207.3	208.0	208.9	209.7	210.9
2008	209.8	211.4	212.1	214.0	215.1	216.8	216.5	217.2	218.4	217.7	216.0	212.9
2009	210.1	211.4	211.3	211.5	212.8	213.4	213.4	214.4	215.3	216.0	216.6	218.0
2010	217.9	219.2	220.7	222.8	223.6	224.1	223.6	224.5	225.3	225.8	226.8	228.4
2011	229.0	231.3	232.5	234.4	235.2	235.2	234.7	236.1	237.9	238.0	238.5	239.4
2012	238.0	239.9	240.8	242.5	242.4	*243.0*	*243.6*	*244.2*	*244.8*	*245.4*	*246.0*	*246.6*
2013	*247.2*	*247.8*	*248.4*									

Note:
RPIs for June 2012 and later months have been estimated by the author.

Exercises

24.1 A company made the following disposals during the year to 31 March 2013:

(a) A factory building was sold for £650,000 on 13 June 2012 (RPI 243.0). This building had cost £300,000 in August 2000 (RPI 170.5) and was extended in July 2002 (RPI 175.9) at a cost of £50,000.

(b) An office building was sold for £1,000,000 on 15 August 2012 (RPI 244.2) and was immediately replaced by another office building costing £925,000. The building sold in August 2012 had cost £600,000 in February 2002 (RPI 173.8). Rollover relief was claimed on the disposal of this building.

(c) A computer system was given to a charity on 14 July 2012 (RPI 243.6). This computer system had cost £5,000 in September 2009 (RPI 215.3) and had a market value of £500 in July 2012. Capital allowances had been claimed in relation to the computer system.

(d) A motor car was sold for £80,000 on 12 May 2012 (RPI 242.4). The car had cost £100,000 in June 2010 (RPI 224.1). Capital allowances had been claimed.

(e) An item of movable plant and machinery was sold for £30,000 on 16 September 2012 (RPI 244.8). This item had cost £70,000 in January 2007 (RPI 201.6) and capital allowances had been claimed in relation to the item.

(f) 8,000 ordinary shares in Exxak plc were sold for £80,000 on 18 December 2012 (RPI 246.6). Shares in Exxak plc had been bought as follows:

Date	*No. of shares*	*Cost* £	*RPI*
22 November 2002	4,000	16,000	178.2
14 December 2006	6,000	30,000	202.7
12 December 2012	3,000	36,000	246.6

(g) Government securities were sold for £40,000 on 17 October 2012 (RPI 245.4). These securities had cost £45,000 in October 2009 (RPI 216.0).

Compute the chargeable gain or allowable loss arising on each of the above disposals and outline any other corporation tax consequences of each disposal. Also compute the net chargeable gains figure which should be included in the company's chargeable profits for the year to 31 March 2013.

24.2 PCC Ltd is a manufacturing company which prepares accounts to 31 December each year. The company made the following disposals of chargeable assets in the year to 31 December 2012:

(i) On 12 September 2012, 7,500 ordinary shares in Epsilon plc were sold for £8.50 each. PCC Ltd had bought ordinary shares in Epsilon plc as follows:

		£
14 January 1981	Bought 2,000 shares	4,000
27 June 1991	Bought 3,000 shares	15,000
10 March 2001	Bought 4,000 shares	28,000

The shares had a market value on 31 March 1982 of £2.50 per share.

(ii) On 9 October 2012, two watercolour paintings (which do not form a set) were sold at auction. In each case, the auctioneer charged a 10% commission. The paintings had been acquired for £2,000 each in September 2002 and had been hanging in the company's reception area ever since. The net sale proceeds of the paintings (after deducting commission) were £5,175 and £5,805 respectively.

(iii) On 1 June 2012, a short lease was assigned for £7,000. The lease was originally acquired as a 20-year lease on 1 January 1998 at a cost of £20,000.

(iv) On 25 November 2012, a freehold property was sold for £115,000. The building had been acquired in August 2004 for £50,000. In February 2012 the company bought fixed plant for £100,000.

PCC Ltd has not made (and does not intend to make) a "re-basing" election to the effect that assets acquired before 31 March 1982 should be treated as if acquired on 31 March 1982 at a cost equal to their market value on that date. However, the company does intend to make any other election which will reduce the amount of gains chargeable to corporation tax in the year to 31 December 2012.

On 1 January 2012, the company had capital losses brought forward of £6,646.

Required:

Compute the chargeable gain or allowable loss arising on each of the above disposals. Hence compute the net chargeable gains figure which should be charged to corporation tax for the year to 31 December 2012. Assume Retail Price Indices as follows:

March 1982	79.44	August 2004	187.4
June 1991	134.1	June 2012	243.0
January 1998	159.5	September 2012	244.8
March 2001	172.2	October 2012	245.4
September 2002	177.6	November 2012	246.0

Extracts from the short lease amortisation table given in Schedule 8 of the Taxation of Chargeable Gains Act 1992 are as follows:

5 years	26.722	6 years	31.195	20 years	72.770

(CIPFA)

***24.3** Timberlake Ltd prepares accounts to 31 March each year. The company made the following disposals of chargeable assets in the year to 31 March 2013:

(i) In February 2013, a rare Bentley motor car used by the company's Managing Director was sold for £55,000. This car had cost £30,000 in November 2003.

(ii) In October 2012, an office building was sold for £670,000. The building had been acquired in January 1978 for £100,000 and was extended in July 1980 at a cost of £10,000 and again in September 1988 at a cost of £40,000. The market value of the building on 31 March 1982 was £135,000.

(iii) In May 2012, a plot of land was sold for £120,000. This land had cost £42,000 in November 2003 and had been used for trade purposes.

In June 2004, the company had sold land for £50,000 and had made a claim for rollover relief in relation to this disposal. This land had cost £10,000 in October 1999 and had been used for trade purposes.

(iv) In August 2012, gilt-edged stocks bought for £100,000 in January 2008 were sold for £110,500.

(v) In May 2012, plant and machinery bought for £19,500 in May 2011 was sold for £22,500. In March 2013, plant and machinery bought for £16,000 in March 2009 was sold for £9,000. Capital allowances had been claimed in relation to both of these items.

(vi) In February 2013, the company sold 500 ordinary shares in Theta plc for £10 per share. Timberlake Ltd had bought ordinary shares in Theta plc as follows:

		£
June 2001	Bought 2,500 shares	12,500
January 2008	Bought 3,000 shares	18,000

Timberlake Ltd has elected that assets acquired before 31 March 1982 should be treated as if acquired on 31 March 1982 at a cost equal to their market value on that date. The company had capital losses brought forward of £156,200 on 1 April 2012.

Required:

(a) Compute the chargeable gain or allowable loss arising on each of the disposals made during the year to 31 March 2013. Assume Retail Price Indices as follows:

March 1982	79.44	March 2009	211.3
September 1988	108.4	May 2011	235.2
October 1999	166.5	May 2012	242.4
June 2001	174.4	August 2012	244.2
November 2003	182.7	October 2012	245.4
June 2004	186.8	February 2013	247.8
January 2008	209.8	March 2013	248.4

(b) Compute the chargeable gains figure which should be included in the company's chargeable profits for the year to 31 March 2013.

(CIPFA)

Chapter 25

Computation and payment of the corporation tax liability

Introduction

Having ascertained a company's chargeable profits for an accounting period (including any chargeable gains) the next step is to compute the corporation tax liability arising in that period. The purpose of this chapter is to describe the way in which the corporation tax liability is computed and to explain the system by means of which the tax is collected.

Corporation tax financial years

Corporation tax rates are set for each *financial year*. A corporation tax financial year (FY) runs from 1 April to 31 March inclusive and is identified by the calendar year in which it begins. For example:

- FY2011 began on 1 April 2011 and ended on 31 March 2012
- FY2012 began on 1 April 2012 and ends on 31 March 2013

The fiscal year which applies to individuals (from 6 April to the following 5 April) is not relevant when dealing with corporation tax matters. Note that:

(a) If a company has an accounting period which coincides with a financial year (i.e. the year to 31 March) or is entirely contained within a financial year, the appropriate rate of corporation tax for that financial year is applied to the company's chargeable profits for the accounting period, giving the corporation tax liability.

(b) If an accounting period straddles 31 March, the chargeable profits for the period are time-apportioned between the two financial years involved and then charged to tax at the rates applicable to each financial year. A simple time-apportionment is always made in these circumstances. This is different from the way in which the profits of a long period of account are allocated between accounting periods (see Chapter 23).

It may seem obvious that the apportionment referred to above will be required only if corporation tax rates have changed from one financial year to the next. In practice, however, the amount of tax payable for each financial year has to be calculated separately in order to ascertain the figures required for the company's tax return.

EXAMPLE 1

A company has chargeable profits of £5,000,000 for an accounting period. Explain how the corporation tax liability for this period will be calculated if:

(a) the accounting period is the 12 months to 31 March 2013

(b) the accounting period is the nine months to 31 January 2013

(c) the accounting period is the ten months to 31 October 2012.

Solution

(a) The 12 months to 31 March 2013 coincide with FY2012, so the chargeable profits of £5,000,000 will be taxed at the rates applicable to FY2012.

(b) The nine months to 31 January 2013 are entirely contained within FY2012, so the chargeable profits of £5,000,000 will be taxed at the rates applicable to FY2012.

(c) The ten months to 31 October 2012 are contained partly within FY2011 (3 months) and partly within FY2012 (7 months). The chargeable profits of £5,000,000 will be time-apportioned between FYs as follows:

FY2011	1 Jan 2012 to 31 March 2012	£5,000,000 x 3/10	= £1,500,000
FY2012	1 April 2012 to 31 Oct 2012	£5,000,000 x 7/10	= £3,500,000

The profits of £1,500,000 falling into FY2011 will be taxed at FY2011 rates whilst the profits of £3,500,000 falling into FY2012 will be taxed at FY2012 rates.

Rates of corporation tax

There are two rates of corporation tax. These are the *main rate* and the *small profits rate*. Corporation tax rates in recent years have been as follows:

	FY2012	*FY2011*	*FY2010*	*FY2009*
Main rate	24%	26%	28%	28%
Small profits rate	20%	20%	21%	21%

The rate of corporation tax which applies to a company for an accounting period depends upon the size of the "augmented profits" for that period, where augmented profits are equal to the sum of chargeable profits and franked investment income (FII). Even though FII is not itself charged to corporation tax, FII *is* included in augmented profits and can therefore affect the rate of tax which a company pays on its chargeable profits.

The process of calculating a company's corporation tax liability for an accounting period which coincides with a financial year (or falls wholly within one) is as follows:

(a) Chargeable profits (PCTCT) for the period are calculated.

(b) Augmented profits are calculated by adding on any FII for the period. As explained in Chapter 23, a company's FII usually consists of UK dividends received (together with the attached tax credits) but may also include tax-exempt foreign dividends.

(c) The small profits rate applies if augmented profits for the period are less than or equal to the *lower limit* (£300,000). The main rate applies if augmented profits are greater than or equal to the *upper limit* (£1,500,000). The lower and upper limits are reduced proportionately for periods of less than 12 months.

(d) If augmented profits lie between the lower and upper limits, the company is taxed at the main rate but the liability is then reduced by *marginal relief*. The marginal relief calculation is explained later in this chapter.

(e) The rate of tax as determined above is applied to the company's chargeable profits, *not* to its augmented profits. Note that the applicable rate of corporation tax is applied to the *whole* of the company's chargeable profits. This differs from the income tax system, in which each band of income is taxed at a different rate. Note also that the lower and upper limits have remained unchanged for many years.

If an accounting period straddles 31 March, chargeable profits and augmented profits are both time-apportioned between the two financial years involved and a separate computation is performed for each financial year. The results of these two computations are then aggregated to give the tax liability for the period.

Rates of corporation tax for FY2013 and FY2014

The main rate of corporation tax will fall to 23% in FY2013 and to 22% in FY2014. The small profits rate for these years has not yet been determined.

EXAMPLE 2

Identify the applicable rate(s) of corporation tax payable in the following circumstances:

(a) A01 Ltd has augmented profits of £9 million for the year to 31 March 2013
(b) A02 Ltd has augmented profits of £200,000 for the year to 31 March 2013
(c) A03 Ltd has augmented profits of £500,000 for the year to 31 March 2013
(d) A04 Ltd has augmented profits of £1 million for the six months to 30 November 2012
(e) A05 Ltd has augmented profits of £1.6 million for the year to 31 December 2012.

Solution

(a) The accounting period coincides with FY2012 so FY2012 rates apply. Augmented profits exceed the upper limit, so chargeable profits for the period are taxed at the main rate (24%).

(b) The accounting period coincides with FY2012 so FY2012 rates apply. Augmented profits do not exceed the lower limit, so chargeable profits for the period are taxed at the small profits rate (20%).

(c) The accounting period coincides with FY2012 so FY2012 rates apply. Augmented profits are between the lower limit and the upper limit, so chargeable profits for the period are taxed at the main rate (24%), less marginal relief.

(d) The accounting period is wholly contained within FY2012 so FY2012 rates apply. The lower and upper limits for a six-month period are £150,000 and £750,000. Augmented profits exceed £750,000, so chargeable profits are taxed at the main rate (24%).

(e) The first three months of the accounting period fall into FY2011. Augmented profits for these three months are £400,000. This exceeds the upper limit of £375,000 for a three-month period. So chargeable profits for these three months are taxed at the FY2011 main rate of 26%.

The last nine months of the accounting period fall into FY2012. Augmented profits for these nine months are £1.2 million. This exceeds the upper limit of £1,125,000 for a nine-month period. So chargeable profits for these nine months are taxed at the FY2012 main rate of 24%.

EXAMPLE 3

Four companies each prepare a set of accounts for the year to 31 March 2013. Calculate the corporation tax liability of each company, given that:

(a) A06 Ltd has chargeable profits of £2,000,000 and has received no UK dividends
(b) A07 Ltd has chargeable profits of £143,000 and UK dividends of £9,000
(c) A08 Ltd has chargeable profits of £282,500 and UK dividends of £1,125,000
(d) A09 Ltd has chargeable profits of £7,500 and UK dividends of £270.

None of the companies have received any tax-exempt foreign dividends during the year.

Solution

	(a)	(b)	(c)	(d)
	£	£	£	£
Chargeable profits	2,000,000	143,000	282,500	7,500
FII (UK dividends + tax credits)	0	10,000	1,250,000	300
Augmented profits	2,000,000	153,000	1,532,500	7,800
Applicable rate of corporation tax	24%	20%	24%	20%
Corporation tax liability:				
£2,000,000 @ 24%	£480,000			
£143,000 @ 20%		£28,600		
£282,500 @ 24%			£67,800	
£7,500 @ 20%				£1,500

Notes:

(i) Each company's accounting period coincides with FY2012. Therefore the limits and rates of tax used are those for FY2012.

(ii) All of the dividends have an attached tax credit of one-ninth (see Chapter 2).

(iii) In each case, the augmented profits figure is used to determine the applicable rate of tax but this rate is then applied to the chargeable profits.

EXAMPLE 4

A company has chargeable profits of £1,430,000 for the eleven months to 30 November 2012 and received a UK dividend of £99,000 on 30 June 2012. Calculate the corporation tax liability for this period.

Solution

FII is £110,000 (£99,000 + tax credit £11,000) so augmented profits are £1,540,000. The first three months of the accounting period fall into FY2011 and the remaining eight months fall into FY2012. Chargeable profits, augmented profits and the lower and upper limits for the two FYs are as follows:

	FY2011 (1/1/12 to 31/3/12)	*FY2012 (1/4/12 to 30/11/12)*
Chargeable profits	£1,430,000 x 3/11 = £390,000	£1,430,000 x 8/11 = £1,040,000
Augmented profits	£1,540,000 x 3/11 = £420,000	£1,540,000 x 8/11 = £1,120,000
Lower limit	£300,000 x 3/12 = £75,000	£300,000 x 8/12 = £200,000
Upper limit	£1,500,000 x 3/12 = £375,000	£1,500,000 x 8/12 = £1,000,000

Notes:

(i) The date on which the FII was received is irrelevant to the apportionment process.

(ii) Augmented profits are above the upper limit in both FYs.

(iii) The corporation tax liability is £390,000 @ 26% + £1,040,000 @ 24% = £351,000.

(iv) From the size of the company's augmented profits for the period, it was obvious that augmented profits would exceed the upper limit in both FYs. Realising this would have saved the effort of apportioning the lower and upper limits between the FYs.

Marginal relief

As explained above, the main rate of corporation tax applies to companies with augmented profits that exceed the lower limit (£300,000). However, the tax liability is reduced by *marginal relief* if augmented profits do not exceed the upper limit (£1,500,000). Marginal relief is calculated according to the following formula:

$$F \times (U - A) \times \frac{N}{A}$$

where: F = the marginal relief fraction
U = the upper limit (scaled down for a period of less than 12 months)
A = augmented profits
N = non-augmented profits (i.e. chargeable profits)

The marginal relief fraction for FY2012 is 1/100. This fraction was 3/200 for FY2011 and was 7/400 for FY2010 and FY2009.

EXAMPLE 5

(a) A company has chargeable profits of £500,000 for the year to 31 March 2013 and receives no UK dividends. Compute the corporation tax liability for the year.

(b) A company has chargeable profits of £975,000 for the year to 31 March 2013 and receives UK dividends of £45,000. Compute the corporation tax liability for the year.

(c) A company has chargeable profits of £240,000 and UK dividends of £9,000 for the eight months to 31 January 2013. Compute the corporation tax liability for the period.

(d) A company has chargeable profits of £480,000 and UK dividends of £108,000 for the year to 31 December 2012. Compute the corporation tax liability for the year.

Assume in all cases that there are no tax-exempt foreign dividends.

Solution

(a) The accounting period coincides with FY2012. Augmented profits of £500,000 lie between the lower and upper limits. Chargeable profits (also £500,000) are taxed at the main rate and marginal relief is available. The computation is as follows:

	£
Corporation tax on £500,000 @ 24%	120,000.00
Less: Marginal relief:	
$\frac{1}{100}$ x (£1,500,000 – £500,000) x $\frac{£500,000}{£500,000}$	10,000.00
Corporation tax liability	110,000.00

(b) The accounting period coincides with FY2012. FII is £50,000 (£45,000 + £5,000) so augmented profits are £1,025,000 (£975,000 + £50,000). These lie between the lower and upper limits. The computation is as follows:

	£
Corporation tax on £975,000 @ 24%	234,000.00
Less: Marginal relief:	
$\frac{1}{100}$ x (£1,500,000 – £1,025,000) x $\frac{£975,000}{£1,025,000}$	4,518.29
Corporation tax liability	229,481.71

(c) The accounting period falls wholly within FY2012. FII is £10,000 (£9,000 + £1,000) so augmented profits are £250,000 (£240,000 + £10,000). The lower and upper limits for eight months are £200,000 (8/12 x £300,000) and £1,000,000 (8/12 x £1,500,000). Augmented profits lie between these limits so the computation is as follows:

	£
Corporation tax on £240,000 @ 24%	57,600.00
Less: Marginal relief:	
$\frac{1}{100} \times (£1{,}000{,}000 - £250{,}000) \times \frac{£240{,}000}{£250{,}000}$	7,200.00
Corporation tax liability	50,400.00

(d) FII is £120,000 (£108,000 + £12,000) and so augmented profits are £600,000. Three months of the accounting period fall into FY2011 and nine months fall into FY2012.

(i) For the three months which fall into FY2011, chargeable profits are £120,000 and augmented profits are £150,000. The lower and upper limits are £75,000 (3/12 x £300,000) and £375,000 (3/12 x £1,500,000). Augmented profits lie between these limits so tax is due at 26% less marginal relief.

(ii) For the nine months which fall into FY2012, chargeable profits are £360,000 and augmented profits are £450,000. The lower and upper limits are £225,000 (9/12 x £300,000) and £1,125,000 (9/12 x £1,500,000). Augmented profits lie between these limits so tax is due at 24% less marginal relief.

The computation is as follows:

	£	£
FY2011		
Corporation tax on £120,000 @ 26%	31,200.00	
Less: Marginal relief:		
$\frac{3}{200} \times (£375{,}000 - £150{,}000) \times \frac{£120{,}000}{£150{,}000}$	2,700.00	28,500.00
FY2012		
Corporation tax on £360,000 @ 24%	86,400.00	
Less: Marginal relief:		
$\frac{1}{100} \times (£1{,}125{,}000 - £450{,}000) \times \frac{£360{,}000}{£450{,}000}$	5,400.00	81,000.00
Corporation tax liability		109,500.00

Marginal rate

If augmented profits in FY2012 lie between the lower and upper limits, every £1 by which chargeable profits increase/decrease will generally cause an increase/decrease of 25p in the corporation tax liability, as long as augmented profits remain between the two limits. For instance, if the company in part (a) of the above example had an extra £2 of chargeable profits, its tax liability would rise by £0.50 (the calculation is left to the reader). Therefore this company is subject to a *marginal rate* of 25%. This is higher than the main rate of 24%, though the marginal rate would be somewhat reduced if the company also had FII.

Marginal rates are particularly significant when a company is trying to determine the most tax-efficient way of relieving a loss (see Chapters 26 and 28).

Due date of payment

A company's corporation tax liability for an accounting period is generally payable by means of a single payment which is due nine months and one day after the end of the period. However, certain large companies are required to pay their corporation tax by instalments. Note that:

(a) Electronic payment of corporation tax is now compulsory.

(b) Managed payment plans (MPPs) are to be introduced which will allow companies to spread their corporation tax payments over a period straddling the normal due dates. However, the implementation date for MPPs has not yet been determined.

EXAMPLE 6

(a) A company's period of account is the year to 31 July 2012. When is the corporation tax liability for this period due for payment?

(b) A company's period of account is the 18 months to 31 December 2012. When is the corporation tax liability for this period due for payment?

Assume in both cases that the company is not required to pay by instalments.

Solution

(a) The year to 31 July 2012 is a single accounting period. Corporation tax for the period is payable on 1 May 2013.

(b) This period of account breaks down into two accounting periods. The corporation tax for the year to 30 June 2012 is due on 1 April 2013. The corporation tax for the six months to 31 December 2012 is due on 1 October 2013.

Payment by instalments

As mentioned above, large companies are generally required to pay their corporation tax by instalments. The main features of the instalments system are as follows:

(a) A "large company" for this purpose is defined as one which pays corporation tax at the main rate, without deduction of marginal relief. However, a large company is *not* required to pay tax by instalments for an accounting period if:

(i) it has chargeable profits of £10 million or less for the accounting period and was not a large company in the 12 months preceding that period, or

(ii) it has a tax liability of less than £10,000 for the period but pays tax at the main rate, either because it has substantial amounts of dividend income or because it has a number of associated companies (see Chapter 28).

(b) Instalment payments are based on the company's own estimate of its corporation tax liability for the accounting period. When the tax liability for the year is finalised, the company is charged interest on any underpaid instalments and is paid interest on any overpaid instalments.

(c) For a 12-month accounting period there are four equal instalments. The first instalment falls due six months and 14 days from the start of the accounting period. The remaining three instalments then fall due at quarterly intervals. For instance, if the accounting period is the year to 31 December 2012, instalments fall due on 14 July 2012, 14 October 2012, 14 January 2013 and 14 April 2013.

If an accounting period is of less than 12 months' duration, the final instalment is always due three months and 14 days after the end of the period. Earlier instalments are due on the usual quarterly dates but only to the extent that those dates fall before the date of the final instalment. For instance, if an accounting period consists of the eight months to 30 September 2012, corporation tax is due in three instalments on 14 August 2012, 14 November 2012 and 14 January 2013.

In order to calculate the amount of each instalment, it is first necessary to multiply the corporation tax liability by 3/n, where n is the number of months in the accounting period. Each instalment is then equal to this figure, except that the final instalment may be lower than this in order to bring the total of the instalments to the correct amount.

EXAMPLE 7

A large company has a corporation tax liability of £720,000 for an accounting period. State the dates on which instalments are payable and compute the amount of each instalment if the accounting period is:

(a) the year to 31 March 2013 (b) the five months to 31 May 2012.

Solution

(a) Instalments are due on 14 October 2012, 14 January 2013, 14 April 2013 and 14 July 2013. Each instalment is equal to £720,000 x 3/12 = £180,000.

(b) Instalments are due on 14 July 2012 and 14 September 2012. The first instalment is equal to £720,000 x 3/5 = £432,000. The second and final instalment is £288,000, bringing the total to £720,000.

Gifts of pre-eminent property to the nation

As from 1 April 2012, a company which makes a gift of "pre-eminent property" to the nation (e.g. a work of art) is entitled (subject to certain conditions) to a corporation tax reduction equal to 20% of the value of that property.

Accounting for income tax deducted at source

Certain payments made by companies are made net of basic rate income tax. These consist principally of patent royalties paid to individuals and loan interest paid to individuals. A company which makes such a payment must account to HMRC for the tax deducted at source. The gross amount of the payment then attracts tax relief under the appropriate heading in the company's corporation tax computation.

Similarly, a company may receive income net of basic rate income tax. This is now rare but one instance occurs when a company receives patent royalties from an individual. In such a case, the company reclaims the income tax suffered at source. The gross amount of the income is then charged to corporation tax.

Quarterly accounting system

Companies are required to make periodic (usually quarterly) returns to HMRC of income tax deducted from payments and income tax suffered on taxed income. Returns are made on form CT61(Z). Nil returns are not required. Since it is now uncommon for companies to receive any taxed income, most of these returns will show only income tax deducted from payments. If this is the case, the company concerned must account for this income tax to HMRC within 14 days of the end of the return period. However, the procedure is rather more complex if the company also has taxed income.

Full details of the quarterly accounting system, together with several worked examples, can be found on the website which accompanies this textbook. The website address is www.pearsoned.co.uk/melville.

Shadow ACT

Until 6 April 1999, companies were obliged to pay Advance Corporation Tax (ACT) when paying dividends. Subject to certain conditions, the ACT paid for an accounting period was then treated as an advance payment of the corporation tax liability for that period, so reducing the amount of tax payable on the normal due date. ACT was abolished with effect from 6 April 1999 but some aspects of the ACT system are still relevant in a small number of cases. The present situation with regard to ACT (the "shadow ACT" system) is explained on website www.pearsoned.co.uk/melville.

Self Assessment

The system of Self Assessment for companies is similar in many ways to the equivalent system that applies for individuals (see Chapter 1). The main features of Corporation Tax Self Assessment (CTSA) are as follows:

(a) On the issue of a notice by HM Revenue and Customs, a company must file a corporation tax return (form CT600) for the accounting period specified in the notice, with supporting accounts and computations. The return must normally be filed with HMRC by the *latest* of the following dates:

   (i) 12 months after the end of the accounting period specified in the notice

   (ii) 12 months after the end of the period of account in which the last day of the specified accounting period falls (but periods of account which last for more than 18 months are treated for this purpose as ending after 18 months)

   (iii) 3 months after issue of the notice.

   Most companies prepare their accounts to the same date each year and notices are usually issued within a few weeks of the end of each period of account, so that the required filing date is normally 12 months after the end of the period of account. There is nothing to prevent a company from submitting an early return. Online filing is now compulsory.

(b) The CT600 return includes a formal self-assessment of the company's tax liability for the accounting period covered by the return. Unlike individuals, a company is *not* able to ask HMRC to calculate the tax liability.

(c) A company which is chargeable to corporation tax for an accounting period but has not received a notice requiring submission of a return must notify HMRC of its chargeability to tax within 12 months of the end of the period.

(d) HMRC has the right to amend a company's return (so as to correct obvious errors or omissions or anything else that is believed to be incorrect) within nine months of the date on which the return is filed. Similarly, the company has the right to amend its return and self-assessment within 12 months of the required filing date for that return.

   A company which believes that it has made an overpayment of corporation tax may make a claim for recovery of this overpaid tax (whether or not the alleged over-payment was caused by an error in a tax return). Such a claim must be made within four years of the end of the accounting period to which it relates. Depending upon the circumstances of the case, HMRC may or may not accept the claim.

(e) If HMRC wishes to open an enquiry into a company's tax return which is filed on or before the required filing date, then the enquiry must usually begin within 12 months of the date on which the return is filed. This means that the "enquiry window" for returns which are submitted early will close correspondingly early.

However, if a company's tax return is filed late or if the company amends its tax return, the deadline for starting an enquiry is extended to the quarter date (31 January, 30 April, 31 July or 31 October) which follows the first anniversary of the date that the return is filed or the amendment is submitted.

(f) Unless HMRC opens an enquiry into a company's tax return, the tax liability for the accounting period may usually be regarded as finalised when the enquiry window has closed. However, HMRC may raise a later "discovery assessment" if it is discovered that insufficient tax has been assessed.

The time limit for making a discovery assessment is normally four years after the end of the accounting period concerned. This increases to six years if the loss of tax has been caused by negligence on the part of the company (or a related person) and 20 years in the case of dishonesty.

(g) If a company fails to file a return by the required date, HMRC may make a determination of the amount of tax due. A determination can be displaced only if the company delivers the required return.

(h) A company is required to keep and preserve adequate records to substantiate the information entered on its tax return. These records must be retained for at least six years after the end of the accounting period concerned.

(i) Corporation tax appeals are dealt with in much the same way as income tax appeals (see Chapter 1). The tax avoidance disclosure regime which applies to income tax also applies to corporation tax.

Interest on underpaid and overpaid corporation tax

Interest on underpaid corporation tax generally runs from the date on which the tax should have been paid until the date on which it is actually paid. Interest on overpaid corporation tax generally runs from the date on which the tax was paid or (if later) the date on which it was due to be paid, until the date of repayment. Interest on overpaid corporation tax is calculated at a lower rate than interest on underpaid tax. Note that:

(a) It is HMRC practice to use a denominator of 366 when calculating interest on underpaid tax and a denominator of 365 when calculating interest on overpaid tax, whether or not a leap year is involved.

(b) Interest receivable on a repayment of overpaid corporation tax is taxable as a credit arising from a non-trading loan relationship. Similarly, interest payable on underpaid corporation tax is deductible as a non-trading debit.

(c) The interest rate which applies to underpaid instalments is generally lower than the normal rate during the period from the due date of the first instalment to the date which falls nine months and one day after the end of the accounting period.

Similarly, the interest rate applicable to overpaid instalments is generally higher than the normal rate during this period.

(d) If a company makes instalment payments on the assumption that it is a large company and this assumption later proves to be false, interest on any repaid instalments runs from the date on which a truly large company would have paid those instalments or (if later) the actual date of payment.

EXAMPLE 8

(a) A company calculates its corporation tax liability for the year to 30 September 2012 as £250,000 and pays this amount on the due date. The correct liability for the year eventually turns out to be £274,000 and the company pays a further £24,000 on 17 October 2013. Calculate the amount of interest payable by the company (assuming an interest rate of 3% per annum).

(b) A company calculates its corporation tax liability for the year to 30 November 2012 as £390,000 and pays this amount on the due date. The correct liability for the year eventually turns out to be only £333,000. The necessary repayment is made on 18 February 2014. Calculate the amount of interest payable to the company (assuming an interest rate of 0.5% per annum).

Neither company is a large company for the purposes of payment by instalments.

Solution

(a) The due date is 1 July 2013 (9 months and 1 day after 30 September 2012). Most of the corporation tax was paid on this date but the final £24,000 was paid on 17 October 2013, 108 days late. The interest payable by the company is:

$$£24{,}000 \times 3\% \times \frac{108}{366} = £212.46$$

(b) The overpaid tax of £57,000 was paid on the due date of 1 September 2013 and repaid on 18 February 2014, 170 days later. Interest payable to the company is:

$$£57{,}000 \times 0.5\% \times \frac{170}{365} = £132.74$$

Penalties

The main penalties which may be imposed in relation to corporation tax are as follows:

(a) **Late submission of tax return**. Penalties are charged if a company does not file its corporation tax return by the required date. These penalties are currently as follows:

   (i) If the return is up to three months late, a fixed penalty is charged of £100. This is increased to £500 for a third consecutive late return.

   (ii) If the return is over three months late, a fixed penalty is charged of £200. This is increased to £1,000 for a third consecutive late return.

   (iii) In addition to the above penalties, a further tax-geared penalty is charged if the return is submitted more than six months late. The penalty is expressed as a percentage of the amount of tax unpaid at the end of the six months, as follows:

   - If the return is made between six and 12 months late, the penalty is 10% of the tax unpaid six months after the return was due.
   - If the return is made more than 12 months late, the penalty rises to 20% of the tax unpaid six months after the return was due.

   It is important to note that a new penalty regime is being introduced in relation to late returns and late payment of tax (see Chapter 15). This regime will apply to a number of taxes but the date of implementation for corporation tax is not yet clear.

(b) **Failure to notify**. A penalty may be charged if a company which has not filed a tax return (and has not been issued with a notice requiring such a return) fails to notify HMRC of its chargeability to tax within 12 months of the end of the accounting period concerned. The penalty for a "failure to notify" is expressed as a percentage of the amount of tax which remains unpaid 12 months after the end of the period.

   As is the case for income tax (see Chapter 15) the applicable percentage varies from 30% to 100%, depending upon whether the failure to notify has been deliberate and/or concealed. The amount of any penalty is reduced if the failure is voluntarily disclosed and no penalty is charged if there is "reasonable excuse" for the failure.

(c) **Inaccurate tax returns**. A penalty may be charged if an inaccuracy in a tax return or other document leads to an understatement of the amount of corporation tax payable and the inaccuracy is either careless or deliberate. This penalty regime also applies if HMRC issues an assessment which understates the amount of tax payable and the company fails to take reasonable steps to notify HMRC of this fact within 30 days.

   As is the case for income tax (see Chapter 15) the amount of any penalty depends upon the company's degree of culpability and generally varies between 30% and 100% of the additional tax which becomes payable as a result of correcting the inaccuracy or understatement.

(d) **Failure to keep records**. A company which fails to keep and preserve adequate records is liable to a penalty of up to £3,000 per accounting period.

EXAMPLE 9

A company prepares accounts to 31 July each year. It calculates its corporation tax liability for the year to 31 July 2011 at £180,000 and pays this sum on 1 May 2012. Despite being issued with a notice by HMRC in August 2011, the company fails to submit its return for the year to 31 July 2011 until 31 March 2013. The corporation tax liability for the year was finally assessed at £206,000. Calculate the penalties that would be charged.

Solution

The return was made eight months late and tax of £26,000 was still outstanding six months after the return was due. Assuming that the company is not a persistent offender, a fixed penalty of £200 would be charged, together with a tax-geared penalty of £2,600 (10% of £26,000). Interest would also be charged on the unpaid tax.

Summary

- A corporation tax financial year runs from 1 April to the following 31 March and is identified by the calendar year in which it begins.
- There are two rates of corporation tax. These are the main rate and the small profits rate. The rate which applies to a company for an accounting period depends upon the company's augmented profits for that period.
- Marginal relief eases the transition from the small profits rate of corporation tax to the main rate of corporation tax.
- A company with augmented profits which lie between the lower and upper limits for FY2012 is subject to a marginal tax rate of 25%.
- The due date of payment for corporation tax is normally nine months and one day after the end of the accounting period. Large companies are required to pay their tax by instalments. Interest is charged on underpaid tax and is paid on refunds of overpaid tax.
- The system of Self Assessment for companies is similar in many ways to Self Assessment for individuals. However, a company must compute its own corporation tax liability and cannot require HMRC to calculate the tax due.
- Companies are usually required to file a CT600 return within 12 months of the end of each period of account. Online filing is now compulsory. Late submission results in a penalty fine and there are penalties for various other infringements of the law relating to corporation tax.

Exercises

25.1 A company has chargeable profits of £3,000,000 for the year to 30 June 2012. Compute the corporation tax liability for the year.

25.2 Four companies each have an accounting year ending on 31 March 2013. Compute the corporation tax liability of each company, given the following information:

(a) Comp1 Ltd has chargeable profits of £267,000 and UK dividends of £18,450.

(b) Comp2 Ltd has chargeable profits of £1,450,000 and UK dividends of £49,500.

(c) Comp3 Ltd has chargeable profits of £10,000,000 and no UK dividends.

(d) Comp4 Ltd has chargeable profits of £1,000 and no UK dividends.

Assume in each case that no tax-exempt foreign dividends are received.

25.3 A company has chargeable profits of £536,000 for the year to 31 March 2013 and UK dividends received of £36,900. There are no tax-exempt foreign dividends. Compute the corporation tax liability for the year.

25.4 Compute the corporation tax liability of each of the following companies:

(a) CompU Ltd has chargeable profits of £875,983 and FII of £32,800 for the year to 28 February 2013.

(b) CompV Ltd has chargeable profits of £200,000 for the six months to 31 December 2012 and has no FII.

(c) CompW Ltd has chargeable profits of £428,000 for the year to 31 March 2013 and has no FII.

For CompW Ltd, recalculate the corporation tax liability if chargeable profits were lower by £100,000 and demonstrate that the company's marginal rate is 25%.

25.5 A company calculates its corporation tax liability for the year to 31 August 2011 as £120,000 and pays this amount on 1 June 2012. The company's CT600 return is submitted during August 2012 and the tax liability for the year is finalised at £124,650. The balance of £4,650 is paid on 3 October 2012. The company is not a large company for the purposes of payment by instalments. Calculate the interest payable, assuming an interest rate of 3% per annum.

***25.6** A company has the following results for the year to 31 March 2013:

	£
Adjusted trading profit, after deduction of capital allowances	360,282
Bank deposit interest (a/c opened 1 July 2012):	
Received 31 December 2012	9,957
Accrued to 31 March 2013	3,000
UK dividend received in January 2013	24,300
Chargeable gains	295,327
Gift Aid donations:	
Paid 30 November 2012	24,600
Accrued to 31 March 2013	8,200

Compute the company's corporation tax liability for the year.

***25.7** A company has the following results for the 14 months to 31 December 2012:

	£
Adjusted trading profit, before deduction of capital allowances	1,413,508
Capital allowances claimed:	
Year to 31 October 2012	222,650
2 months to 31 December 2012	37,210
Capital gains:	
Disposal 12 May 2012	16,575
Disposal 6 November 2012	21,692
Building society interest:	
Received 31 December 2011	3,500
Received 31 December 2012	4,300
UK dividend received on 25 September 2012	3,150

Accrued building society interest was £3,000 on 31 October 2011, £4,000 on 31 October 2012 and £nil on 31 December 2012.

Compute the company's total corporation tax liability for the 14-month period.

Chapter 26

Corporation tax losses

Introduction

The loss reliefs which are available to a company incurring a trading loss are similar to those available to individuals (see Chapter 12) and generally involve either carrying the loss forward against future trading profits or setting the loss against the company's total profits for a specified period.

The main purpose of this chapter is to describe these loss reliefs and to explain the factors which might influence a company when choosing between them. The tax treatment of a company's non-trading losses is also considered in this chapter.

Relief for trading losses

The rules which grant tax relief in relation to a company's trading losses are now located in the Corporation Tax Act 2010. The main reliefs provided by this Act are as follows:

(a) **Carry forward of trade loss relief**. A trading loss may be carried forward and set against future profits of the same trade. This is the relief which takes effect if no other tax relief is claimed in relation to a trading loss.

(b) **Trade loss relief against total profits**. If a claim is made to this effect, a trading loss may be set against the company's total profits of:

   (i) the accounting period in which the loss arises (the "loss-making period"), and
   (ii) if the claim so requires, the 12 months prior to the accounting period in which the loss arises.

   Furthermore, a trading loss which is incurred in the 12 months before the company ceases to carry on that trade (a "terminal loss") may be set against the company's total profits of the preceding three years.

Each of these forms of loss relief is described below.

Carry forward of trade loss relief

Unless a company claims any other form of loss relief in relation to a trading loss, the loss is carried forward and relieved against the company's future trading profits. It is important to note the following points:

(a) Carry forward relief is given only against future *trading* profits, not against any other form of profits.

(b) Furthermore, relief is given only against future trading profits arising from *the same trade* as that in which the loss was incurred. If a company ceases one trade and commences another, the losses of the old trade cannot be carried forward and relieved against the future profits of the new trade. Similarly, if a company carries on two trades simultaneously, a loss incurred in one of the trades cannot be carried forward and relieved against the future profits of the other trade.

(c) Relief must be given against the *first available* future trading profits.

(d) There are restrictions on the carry-forward of trading losses when there is a change in the ownership of a company (see later in this chapter).

EXAMPLE 1

In the year to 31 March 2011, a company incurred a trading loss of £140,000 which was carried forward. The company's results for the next two years were:

	y/e 31 March 2012	*y/e 31 March 2013*
	£	£
Trading profits	110,000	1,850,000
Bank interest receivable	50,000	60,000
Chargeable gains	125,000	572,000
Franked investment income	nil	nil

Compute the company's chargeable profits for the years to 31 March 2012 and 2013 and identify the tax rate(s) at which the trading loss is relieved. How would the situation differ if the company's trading profits for the year to 31 March 2013 were lower by £1 million?

Solution

	y/e 31 March 2012	*y/e 31 March 2013*
	£	£
Trading profits	110,000	1,850,000
Less: Trading losses b/f	110,000	30,000
Trading income	0	1,820,000
Income from non-trading loans	50,000	60,000
Chargeable gains	125,000	572,000
Chargeable profits	175,000	2,452,000

Notes:

(i) In the year to 31 March 2012, trading losses are relieved to the fullest possible extent against the trading profits of the year. Chargeable profits and augmented profits are reduced from £285,000 to £175,000, saving corporation tax at 20% (the small profits rate for FY2011).

(ii) The losses of £30,000 which remain unrelieved cannot be offset against the bank interest or the chargeable gains of the year to 31 March 2012 but must be carried forward and relieved against the trading profits of the following year.

(iii) In the year to 31 March 2013, trading losses of £30,000 reduce chargeable profits and augmented profits from £2,482,000 to £2,452,000. This saves tax at 24% (the main rate for FY2012).

(iv) The total tax saved is £29,200 (£110,000 x 20% + £30,000 x 24%). Expressed as a percentage of the loss of £140,000, this equates to an overall effective rate of tax relief of 20.86%. If the company could defer the whole £140,000 of loss relief until the year to 31 March 2013, the total tax saved would be £33,600 (£140,000 x 24%), but carry forward relief must be given against the first available future trading profits.

(v) If trading profits were £1 million lower in the year to 31 March 2013, augmented profits would be under £1,500,000 and the company would pay tax for that year at 24%, less marginal relief. The marginal rate would be 25% (see Chapter 25) and therefore £30,000 of the loss would be relieved at 25%.

Unrelieved qualifying charitable donations

As stated in Chapter 23, certain charitable donations and gifts made by a company rank as "qualifying charitable donations". These are:

(a) Gift Aid donations

(b) gifts of listed shares or securities to a charity

(c) gifts of land and buildings to a charity.

In general, qualifying charitable donations are deducted when computing a company's chargeable profits and so serve to reduce the company's corporation tax liability. But if a trading loss is incurred in a period in which charitable donations are made, the company's total income and gains for that period may be insufficient to cover its donations, in which case some or all of these donations will be unrelieved. A similar situation might arise if trading losses brought forward are set against the trading profits of the period.

In these circumstances, the tax saving that the unrelieved donations would normally have provided is permanently lost. Qualifying charitable donations are eligible for relief only in the accounting period in which they are made and cannot be carried forwards for relief in subsequent periods or backwards for relief in previous periods.

EXAMPLE 2

A company has the following results for the three years to 31 March 2013:

	y/e 31/3/2011	*y/e 31/3/2012*	*y/e 31/3/2013*
	£	£	£
Trading profits/(losses)	(78,900)	36,300	64,900
Bank interest receivable	21,500	-	-
Gift Aid donations	1,000	1,000	1,000

Assuming that the trading loss of £78,900 is to be carried forward for relief against future trading profits, calculate the company's chargeable profits for each of the three years.

Solution

	y/e 31/3/2011	*y/e 31/3/2012*	*y/e 31/3/2013*
	£	£	£
Trading profits	-	36,300	64,900
Less: Trading losses b/f	-	36,300	42,600
Trading income	-	0	22,300
Income from non-trading loans	21,500	-	-
	21,500	0	22,300
Less: Qualifying charitable donations	1,000	-	1,000
Chargeable profits	20,500	0	21,300
Trading losses c/f	78,900	42,600	-
Unrelieved charitable donations	-	1,000	-

Notes:

(i) In the year to 31 March 2011, the qualifying charitable donations of £1,000 are set against the bank interest. The £78,900 of trading losses are carried forward.

(ii) In the year to 31 March 2012, the trading income of £36,300 is used to relieve part of the trading losses brought forward, leaving £42,600 to carry forward. The qualifying charitable donations for the year are completely unrelieved.

(iii) In the year to 31 March 2013, trading losses brought forward are fully relieved. The remaining profits of £22,300 are then reduced by the qualifying charitable donations of £1,000, leaving chargeable profits of £21,300 for the year.

Trade loss relief against total profits

CTA 2010 allows a trading loss to be relieved against a company's total profits. This relief applies only if claimed and is available in two parts:

(a) A company may claim that a trading loss incurred during an accounting period should be relieved against the total profits of that accounting period (*before* deducting qualifying charitable donations).

(b) The company may then further claim that any part of the trading loss which remains unrelieved after a claim has been made under (a) above, should be relieved against the total profits of accounting periods falling wholly or partly within the 12 months prior to the loss-making period. Note the following points:

   (i) This relief is also given *before* deducting qualifying charitable donations.

   (ii) If more than one accounting period falls wholly or partly into the 12 months preceding a loss-making period, relief is given in later accounting periods in priority to earlier accounting periods.

   (iii) If an accounting period falls only partly into the 12 months preceding a loss-making period, the profits of that period are time-apportioned and relief is available against only the profits which fall into the specified 12 months.

Trade loss relief against total profits is voluntary. A company wishing to relieve a trading loss in this way must make an appropriate claim within two years of the end of the loss-making accounting period. A claim may be made under (a) above without a further claim under (b). But a claim under (b) cannot be made without a prior claim under (a).

A company may not specify how much of its trading loss should be relieved against total profits. The effect of a claim is to relieve trading losses to the fullest possible extent in each affected accounting period. Any part of the loss which remains unrelieved after relief has been given against total profits is carried forward for relief against future profits of the same trade. If relief against total profits is not claimed, the entire loss is carried forward.

EXAMPLE 3

A company has the following results for the year to 31 December 2012:

	£
Trading loss	(112,500)
Building society interest receivable	14,000
Chargeable gains	103,000
Gift Aid donations	28,700

Assuming that a claim is made for the trading loss to be relieved against total profits, compute the company's chargeable profits for the year.

Solution

	£
Trading income	-
Income from non-trading loans	14,000
Chargeable gains	103,000
	117,000
Less: Trade loss relief against total profits	112,500
	4,500
Less: Qualifying charitable donations	4,500
Chargeable profits	0

Note:

Only £4,500 of the Gift Aid donations can be relieved. The remaining £24,200 is lost.

EXAMPLE 4

A company has the following results for the three years to 31 October 2012:

	y/e 31/10/10	*y/e 31/10/11*	*y/e 31/10/12*
	£	£	£
Trading profits/(losses)	112,500	110,700	(136,500)
Income from property	3,300	8,400	8,800
Gift Aid donations	2,000	2,000	2,000

Assuming that all possible claims are made to relieve the trading loss against total profits, calculate the company's chargeable profits for each of the three years.

Solution

	y/e 31/10/10	*y/e 31/10/11*	*y/e 31/10/12*
	£	£	£
Trading income	112,500	110,700	-
Income from property	3,300	8,400	8,800
	115,800	119,100	8,800
Less: Relief against total profits (a)	-	-	8,800
	115,800	119,100	0
Less: Relief against total profits (b)	-	119,100	-
	115,800	0	0
Less: Qualifying charitable donations	2,000	-	-
Chargeable profits	113,800	0	0
Trading loss c/f	-	-	8,600
Unrelieved charitable donations	-	2,000	2,000

Notes:

(i) In the year to 31 October 2012, the claim for relief against total profits must be for the maximum possible amount of £8,800. This leaves nothing against which to relieve the Gift Aid donations and therefore they are lost.

(ii) The remaining £127,700 of the trading loss is eligible for relief against total profits of the year to 31 October 2011. The claim must be for the maximum possible amount of £119,100. This leaves nothing against which to relieve the donations, which are lost.

(iii) The trading loss may not be carried back any further. The computation for the year to 31 March 2010 is therefore completely unaffected by loss reliefs..

(iv) A total of £127,900 (£8,800 + £119,100) of the trading loss has been relieved against total profits. The remaining £8,600 is carried forward for relief against future profits of the same trade.

EXAMPLE 5

A company has the following results for the three accounting periods to 31 March 2013:

	y/e 30/6/11	*9 months to 31/3/12*	*y/e 31/3/13*
	£	£	£
Trading profits/(losses)	13,400	69,900	(122,800)
Chargeable gains	1,200	3,500	38,600

Assuming that all possible claims are made to relieve the trading loss against total profits, calculate the company's chargeable profits for each of the three accounting periods.

Solution

		y/e 30/6/11	*9 months to 31/3/12*	*y/e 31/3/13*
		£	£	£
Trading income		13,400	69,900	-
Chargeable gains		1,200	3,500	38,600
		14,600	73,400	38,600
Less: Relief against total profits (a)		-	-	38,600
		14,600	73,400	0
Less: Relief against total profits (b)	(1)		73,400	
	(2)	3,650		
Chargeable profits		10,950	0	0
Trading losses c/f		-	-	7,150

Notes:

(i) £38,600 of the trading losses incurred in the year to 31 March 2013 are relieved against total profits of that period. This leaves losses of £84,200 which are eligible for carry-back relief. The carry-back period is the previous 12 months.

(ii) The nine-month accounting period to 31 March 2012 is entirely contained within the specified 12 months and so losses of £73,400 are relieved against total profits of that period. Losses relieved so far are now £112,000, leaving £10,800 still to be relieved.

(iii) Only three months of the year to 30 June 2011 fall into the specified 12 months. The maximum relief available is £3,650 (£14,600 x 3/12). The remaining £7,150 of the trading loss is carried forward for relief against future profits of the same trade.

Further points relating to relief against total profits

(a) A trading loss may be relieved against the total profits of an accounting period only if the loss-making trade is (or was) being carried on in that period.

(b) If more than one loss is eligible for relief against the total profits of an accounting period, earlier losses are relieved before later losses.

(c) Trading losses incurred by a company in the 12 months before the loss-making trade ceases may be carried back and set against total profits of the preceding three years.

(d) Relief against total profits is available only if the loss-making trade is being carried on "on a commercial basis" with a view to profit.

(e) In the case of *farming companies*, a loss is usually not eligible for relief against total profits if losses have also been incurred for the previous five years.

(f) There are restrictions on the carry-back of trading losses when there is a change in the ownership of a company (see below).

Repayments of corporation tax

If a claim to set a trading loss against total profits results in a repayment of corporation tax for an earlier accounting period, this repayment will attract interest. The amount of interest is calculated in the usual way (see Chapter 25) unless the accounting period for which repayment is being made began more than 12 months before the loss-making accounting period. In these circumstances, the interest is calculated as if the repayment were a repayment of tax for the loss-making accounting period itself.

EXAMPLE 6

A company which began trading on 1 April 2010 has the following results for its first three accounting periods:

	y/e 31/3/2011	*6 months to 30/9/2011*	*y/e 30/9/2012*
	£	£	£
Trading profits	180,000	120,000	nil
Franked investment income	nil	nil	nil

A trading loss of £290,000 was incurred in the year to 30 September 2012 and all possible claims were made to set this loss against the company's total profits. All corporation tax was originally paid on the due date and the necessary repayment of corporation tax is made on 1 August 2013.

Calculate the amount of the repayment and the interest which will accompany this repayment, assuming an interest rate of 0.5% per annum.

Solution

The trading loss is relieved against the £120,000 profit of the six months to 30 September 2011 and then against the £90,000 profit of the six months to 31 March 2011. The loss of £80,000 which remains unrelieved will be carried forward. The claim for trading loss relief against total income will generate the following repayment:

		£
6 months to 30 September 2011	120,000 @ 20%	24,000
y/e 31 March 2011	90,000 @ 21%	18,900
Total repayment		42,900

Notes:

(i) The six months to 30 September 2011 did not begin more than 12 months before the loss-making period so interest on the £24,000 will run from 1 July 2012 (the due date of payment for the six months to 30 September 2011).

(ii) The year to 31 March 2011 began more than 12 months before the loss-making period so interest on the £18,900 will run from 1 July 2013 (the due date of payment for the loss-making period itself).

(iii) The repayment takes place on 1 August 2013. This is 396 days after 1 July 2012 and 31 days after 1 July 2013. Therefore the interest due is:

$$(£24,000 \times 0.5\% \times \frac{396}{365}) + (£18,900 \times 0.5\% \times \frac{31}{365}) = £138.22.$$

Anti-avoidance legislation

Specific anti-avoidance legislation exists to prevent the following manoeuvre, which would otherwise be very tax-efficient:

(a) Acquire a company with substantial amounts of unrelieved trading losses.

(b) Revive the loss-making trade.

(c) Set the company's pre-acquisition trading losses against its post-acquisition trading profits, so avoiding corporation tax.

The legislation referred to above provides that if there is a change in the ownership of a company and certain conditions are satisfied, trading losses arising before the change cannot be set against trading profits arising after the change. Nor can trading losses arising after the change be set against total profits arising before the change. The required conditions are that:

(a) a change in ownership has occurred at a time when the company's business has become negligible and then (at any time after the change) there has been a significant revival of the company's business, or

(b) a change in ownership and a major change in the nature or conduct of the company's business have both occurred within the same three-year period.

For this purpose, a change in ownership is deemed to occur if over half of the company's ordinary share capital is acquired either by one person or by a group of people, each acquiring at least a 5% shareholding.

Choice of loss relief

A company which incurs a trading loss must choose between carrying the loss forward against future trading profits or relieving the loss against the total profits of the current period and (possibly) the total profits of the previous 12 months. Some of the main criteria which will influence this choice are as follows:

(a) the likelihood and expected amount of future profits arising from the same trade as that in which the loss was incurred

(b) the company's cash flow situation (a cash shortage may dictate that loss relief should be obtained as soon as possible)

(c) the rates of corporation tax payable by the company in earlier accounting periods and the expected rates payable in future periods

(d) the possibility that loss relief may reduce the augmented profits of an accounting period to such an extent that the rate of tax payable for that period is changed

(e) the possibility that qualifying charitable donations may be unrelieved

(f) in general, the desire to maximise the tax saved as a result of loss relief claims.

Non-trading losses

A company may incur non-trading losses in a number of ways. The main classes of non-trading loss and the reliefs available for each are as follows:

(a) **Property business losses**. A loss incurred by a company on its property business is set against the company's total profits for the accounting period in which the loss occurs. To the extent that the loss cannot be relieved in this way, it is either:

   (i) carried forward and set against the company's total profits in succeeding accounting periods (as long as the property business is still being carried on in those accounting periods), or

   (ii) relieved by means of group relief (see Chapter 28).

   These reliefs are more generous than their income tax equivalents (see Chapter 5). Note that there are restrictions on the carry-forward of property losses when there is a change in the ownership of a company. These restrictions are similar to those relating to trading losses (see earlier in this chapter).

(b) **Net debits on non-trading loan relationships**. If a company incurs a deficit on its non-trading loan relationships (see Chapter 23), a claim may be made for the deficit to be relieved in any of the following ways:

   (i) by set-off against the company's total profits for the accounting period in which the deficit occurs (*after* deducting any trading losses brought forward but *before* deducting any trading losses relieved against total profits and *before* deducting qualifying charitable donations)

   (ii) by group relief (see Chapter 28)

   (iii) by set-off against the company's income from non-trading loan relationships in the previous 12 months.

   Part of the deficit may be relieved in one way and part in another, if the company so wishes. Claims must be made within two years of the end of the accounting period in which the deficit occurs. Any part of the deficit which is not subject to such a claim is carried forward automatically and set against non-trading profits of subsequent accounting periods.

(c) **Non-trading losses on intangible fixed assets**. A company which incurs a non-trading loss on intangible fixed assets in an accounting period (see Chapter 23) may claim that all or part of the loss should be set against the company's total profits for that period. Any part of the loss which is not subject to such a claim and which is not relieved by means of group relief (see Chapter 28) is carried forward and treated as non-trading expenditure of the next accounting period.

(d) **Capital losses**. A company's capital losses are treated in a similar way to those of an individual (see Chapter 17). Capital losses are relieved first against chargeable gains of the same accounting period and then against the chargeable gains of subsequent accounting periods. Since companies are not entitled to the annual exemption, there is no need to restrict capital losses brought forward so as to conserve the exemption. Capital losses cannot be relieved against any other form of income.

Summary

- A company's trading losses are carried forward and relieved against the first available profits of the same trade, unless the company makes a claim for trading loss relief against total profits.
- Qualifying charitable donations which cannot be relieved in the accounting period in which they are paid are lost and cannot be carried forwards or backwards for relief in subsequent or previous accounting periods.
- A company may claim that a trading loss should be relieved against the total profits of the loss-making accounting period.
- If a trading loss has been set against total profits of the loss-making period and part of the loss remains unrelieved, this part of the loss may be set against the total profits of the previous 12 months.
- If a claim to relieve a trading loss against total profits results in a repayment of corporation tax for an earlier accounting period, this repayment will attract interest.
- Loss reliefs are also available in relation to property business losses, net debits on non-trading loan relationships, non-trading losses on intangible fixed assets and capital losses.

Exercises

26.1 A company has the following results for the three years to 31 May 2012:

	y/e 31/5/10	*y/e 31/5/11*	*y/e 31/5/12*
	£	£	£
Trading profits/(losses)	(32,200)	23,800	40,300
Gift Aid donations	400	500	600

Assuming that the trading loss is to be carried forward for relief against future trading profits, calculate the company's chargeable profits for each of the three years, showing the amount of the losses carried forward at the end of each year.

26.2 A company has the following results for the year to 31 October 2012:

	£
Trading loss	(232,300)
Income from property	190,200
Chargeable gains	45,540
Gift Aid donations	24,000

Assuming that a claim is made to relieve the trading loss against total profits of the loss-making accounting period, calculate the chargeable profits for the year.

26.3 Which of the following statements is true?

(a) Capital losses may be carried forward and relieved against future trading profits.

(b) Trading losses may be carried forward for relief against future chargeable gains.

(c) Trading losses may be relieved against chargeable gains of the same period.

(d) Capital losses may be relieved against trading profits of the same period.

26.4 A company has the following results for its three most recent accounting periods:

	y/e 31/5/11	*eight months to 31/1/12*	*y/e 31/1/13*
	£	£	£
Trading profits/(losses)	59,700	73,600	(155,700)
Chargeable gains	8,400	-	48,700
Gift Aid donations	1,000	1,000	1,000

Assuming that all possible claims are made to relieve the trading loss against total profits, calculate the company's chargeable profits for each of the three periods.

26.5 In the year to 31 March 2013, a company has chargeable profits of £800,000. In the nine months to 31 December 2013, the company incurs a trading loss of £600,000 and has no other income or gains. There is no franked investment income in either period and there are no qualifying charitable donations.

(a) Explain the corporation tax effects of a claim to relieve the trading loss against total profits.

(b) Calculate the effective rate of tax relief obtained in relation to the trading loss if such a claim is made.

***26.6** A company has the following results for the four years to 31 March 2013:

	y/e 31/3/10	*y/e 31/3/11*	*y/e 31/3/12*	*y/e 31/3/13*
	£	£	£	£
Trading profits/(losses)	61,900	77,400	64,200	(172,500)
Chargeable gains/(capital losses)	(7,500)	4,300	2,700	5,700
Gift Aid donations	3,400	3,400	3,400	3,400

Calculate the total repayment of corporation tax (with interest) to which the company is entitled, assuming that:

(a) all possible claims are made to relieve the trading loss against total profits

(b) any repayment of corporation tax which is generated by these claims is made on 14 January 2014

(c) corporation tax for the three years to 31 March 2012 was all paid on the due dates

(d) the company has received no dividends in any of the four years

(e) the rate of interest paid on repayments of corporation tax is 0.5%.

Also explain how the situation would differ if the company had ceased trading on 31 March 2013 (computations are <u>not</u> required).

Chapter 27

Close companies and companies with investment business

Introduction

In general terms, a "close company" is one which is controlled by a small number of people and a "company with investment business" is one whose business consists wholly or partly of making investments. Special corporation tax rules apply to each of these types of company and the main purpose of this chapter is to explain the nature of these rules.

This chapter also considers the taxation consequences which should be borne in mind when deciding whether to trade as an unincorporated business or as a close company.

Close companies

The essence of a close company is that its affairs can be controlled and manipulated by a small group of people, possibly for tax-avoidance purposes. In fact, most companies in the UK are close companies. Certain anti-avoidance legislation exists in relation to close companies and the main points of this legislation are explained later in this chapter. The first step, however, is to provide a precise definition of the term "close company".

Definition of a close company

A close company is a UK resident company which satisfies certain conditions. The main instance of a close company is a company which is under the *control* of:

(a) five or fewer *participators*, or

(b) any number of participators who are also *directors* of the company.

The rights of a participator's *associates* are aggregated with that participator's own rights for the purpose of determining whether a company is a close company. Some important terms used in this definition are explained below.

Control

Persons are deemed to have "control" over a company if, taken together, they:

(a) own over 50% of the company's issued share capital, or

(b) have over 50% of the company's voting power, or

(c) would receive over 50% of the company's income, if it were all distributed, or

(d) would receive over 50% of the company's assets, if the company were wound up.

Participators

A "participator" is defined as someone who has a share or interest in the capital or income of the company. In many cases, a company's only participators are its shareholders, but other persons (e.g. option holders, loan creditors) might also rank as participators.

Directors

A "director", for this purpose, is any person:

(a) who occupies the position of director (whether called a director or not), or

(b) whose directions or instructions are normally obeyed by the directors, or

(c) who is a manager of the company and (possibly together with associates) controls at least 20% of the company's ordinary share capital.

Associates

The main "associates" of a participator are:

(a) the participator's business partners

(b) the participator's relatives

(c) the trustees of a settlement established by the participator or by his/her relatives.

For this purpose, a participator's relatives comprise his or her spouse (or civil partner), parents and remoter ancestors, children and remoter issue, brothers and sisters.

EXAMPLE 1

A company's issued share capital consists of 1,000 £1 ordinary shares, held as follows:

	No of shares		*No of shares*
David	200	Helen	50
Emma	50	Ian	30
Frederick	100	Jacqueline	40
George	50	Others (1 share each)	480

None of the shareholders are associated in any way and no shareholder is also a director.

(a) Is the company a close company?

(b) Would the company be a close company:

  (i) if David were Jacqueline's brother, or

  (ii) if Emma married Ian, or

  (iii) if David were Jacqueline's brother and Emma married Ian?

Solution

(a) The five largest shareholders own 45% of the share capital, so the company is not under the control of five or fewer participators. The company is also not under the control of its directors. Therefore the company is not a close company.

(b) (i) If David were Jacqueline's brother, her 4% holding would be aggregated with his and the five largest shareholders would control 49% (45% + 4%) of the share capital. The company would not be a close company.

  (ii) If Emma married Ian, his 3% would be aggregated with hers and the five largest shareholders would control 48% (45% + 3%) of the share capital. The company would still not be a close company.

  (iii) If David were Jacqueline's brother and Emma married Ian, the five largest shareholders would control 52% (45% + 4% + 3%) of the share capital. The company would then be a close company.

EXAMPLE 2

A company's issued share capital consists entirely of ordinary shares, held as follows:

	% holding	*Director*
Keith	7	Yes
Leonora	7	Yes
Martin	7	Yes
Norma	7	Yes
Oliver	7	Yes
Penny	16	No
Richard	4	No
Others (all non-directors owning under 1%)	45	
Total	100	

None of the shareholders are associated in any way.

(a) Is the company a close company?

(b) Would the company be a close company:

  (i) if Penny were a manager, or

  (ii) if Penny were Richard's daughter, or

  (iii) if Penny were both a manager and Richard's daughter?

Solution

(a) The five largest shareholders own 44% of the share capital, so the company is not under the control of five or fewer participators. The company is also not under the control of its directors, who own 35% of the share capital. Therefore the company is not a close company.

(b) (i) If Penny were a manager, she would not rank as a director since her shareholding is less than 20%. The situation would be unaltered and the company would not be a close company.

(ii) If Penny were Richard's daughter, then his 4% holding would be aggregated with hers and the five largest shareholders would control 48% (44% + 4%) of the share capital. The company would still not be a close company.

(iii) If Penny were both a manager and Richard's daughter, then her deemed 20% holding (16% + 4%) would make her a director. The six directors would control 55% of the share capital and the company would then be a close company.

Exceptions

Certain types of company are statutorily excepted from close company status, even if they are controlled by five or fewer participators or by the participator-directors. The main exception consists of listed companies with a substantial public interest. In order for this exception to apply, a company must satisfy all of the following conditions:

(a) The company's voting shares must have been both dealt in and listed on a recognised stock exchange within the 12 months prior to the date on which the company's status is being determined.

(b) The total voting power possessed by the *principal members* of the company must not exceed 85% of the total voting power.

(c) At least 35% of the company's voting power must be in the hands of the public.

For this purpose, a "principal member" is a shareholder who (possibly with associates) has more than 5% of the voting power of the company and is also one of the top five shareholders. If two or more shareholders, each holding more than 5%, tie for fifth place, there will be more than five principal members.

The "public" excludes the company's directors, their associates, pension schemes for the company's own employees and most principal members. But principal members which are non-close companies or pension schemes (apart from pension schemes for the company's own employees) *are* included within the definition of the public.

EXAMPLE 3

A company's issued share capital consists entirely of ordinary shares. These shares have been listed on a recognised stock exchange for many years and there have been frequent dealings in them within the last 12 months. The company's shares are owned as follows:

	% holding	*Director*
ABBQ Ltd (a non-close company)	13	-
DFFK Ltd (a close company)	7	-
Terry	8	Yes
Ursula	10	Yes
Vincent (a manager)	33	No
Wendy	4	No
Others (all non-directors owning under 1%)	25	
Total	100	

None of the shareholders are associated in any way. Is the company a close company?

Solution

At first sight, the company seems to be a close company. It is under the control of its directors (since Vincent ranks as a director) and it is also under the control of five or fewer participators. However, the company is listed on a recognised stock exchange and its shares have been dealt in within the past 12 months. Furthermore, its principal members (the top five shareholders, each owning more than 5% of the voting shares) hold only 71% of the company's voting power and the public (ABBQ Ltd, Wendy and the others) hold 42%. Therefore the company is excepted from being a close company.

Consequences of close company status

There are several tax consequences of close company status. These include:

(a) Benefits in kind provided by the company to its participators or their associates are generally treated as distributions.

(b) Loans made to participators or their associates are assessed to tax.

(c) The small profits rate of corporation tax is not available to a close company which is also a close investment-holding company (see later in this chapter).

Each of these consequences is explained below. Note also that special loan relationships rules apply if a close company enters into a loan relationship with one of its participators or with an associate of a participator.

Benefits in kind provided to participators

Benefits in kind provided by a close company to its participators (or their associates) are generally regarded as distributions. The taxation effects of this are as follows:

(a) The cost to the company of providing the benefit is disallowed when computing its corporation tax liability.

(b) The company is deemed to have made a distribution equal to the amount which would be assessed on a director or employee earning at least £8,500 per annum if the benefit had been received by such a employee (see Chapter 8).

(c) The person receiving the benefit is taxed as if he or she had received a dividend of the same amount as the deemed distribution.

A benefit in kind provided to a participator is *not* treated as a distribution if it is already assessable as employment income. This will be the case if the participator is a director of the company or an employee earning at least £8,500 per annum (see Chapter 8).

EXAMPLE 4

On 31 August 2012, a close company provides one of its part-time employees with a holiday costing £3,600. This is charged as an expense in the company's income statement for the year to 31 March 2013. The employee concerned earns a salary of £5,000 and is also one of the company's shareholders. Explain the tax treatment of this item.

Solution

The £3,600 is disallowed in the company's tax computation for the year to 31 March 2013. The company is deemed to have made a distribution of £3,600 and the recipient of the holiday is taxed as if he/she had received a dividend of £3,600 (tax credit £400).

Loans made to participators

If a close company makes a loan to a participator (or associate), the tax consequences are as follows:

(a) The company is required to pay an amount of tax which is calculated at 25% of the amount of the loan. This tax is payable nine months and one day after the end of the accounting period in which the loan is made. However, no tax is payable in relation to any part of a loan which is repaid to the company before the date on which the tax falls due.

(b) The tax paid when the loan was made is repaid to the company if the participator repays the loan or if the loan is written off. This tax repayment is made nine months and one day after the end of the accounting period in which the loan is repaid or written off.

(c) If a loan to a participator is wholly or partly written off, the amount written off is *not* treated as a debit arising under a loan relationship and therefore the company is denied tax relief in relation to this amount. Furthermore, the participator is deemed to have received income equal to the amount written off. This income is treated as if received net of income tax at the dividend ordinary rate (currently 10%).

The tax which is deemed to have been deducted at source from this income is not repayable to the participator, even if he or she is a non-taxpayer. However, further tax at the dividend upper (or additional) rate is payable on any part of the grossed-up income which, when added to the participator's other income, falls beyond the basic rate limit (or higher rate limit).

In the case of a participator who is also an employee, this tax charge takes priority over the usual rules which apply to employee loans written off (see Chapter 8).

(d) Certain loans are excluded from the treatment described above. These include loans made to a participator in the normal course of the company's business and loans not exceeding £15,000 made to a participator who is a full-time employee or director of the company, so long as that participator (with associates) has no more than a 5% interest in the company.

EXAMPLE 5

On 1 May 2011, a close company which prepares accounts to 31 March each year lends £30,000 to Ravi, who is one of its directors. No interest is charged on this loan. Ravi owns 25% of the company's ordinary share capital. Explain the tax treatment of this loan if:

(a) Ravi repays the loan in full on 15 February 2013

(b) Ravi repays £12,000 of the loan on 15 February 2013 and the remaining £18,000 is written off by the company on the same day.

Solution

Tax of £7,500 (25% of £30,000) is payable by the company on 1 January 2013. Since the loan is interest-free, it is treated as a beneficial loan and Ravi is subject to income tax on the related benefit in kind. As regards the eventual repayment or write-off of the loan:

(a) The tax of £7,500 is repaid to the company on 1 January 2014.

(b) The £7,500 is repaid on 1 January 2014 but the company cannot claim tax relief in relation to the £18,000 of the loan which has been written off.

Ravi is treated as if he had received income in 2012-13 of £20,000 (gross) with tax deducted at source of £2,000. This is taxed in the same way as dividend income and so might give rise to further income tax at 32.5% or 42.5% if Ravi's total income is sufficient for him to pay tax at the higher rate or the additional rate.

Close investment-holding companies

A close company is also a close investment-holding company (CIC) unless it exists wholly or mainly for one or more of a number of purposes defined by statute. The main purposes which except a company from CIC status are:

(a) the carrying on of a trade on a commercial basis, or

(b) the letting of property (other than to connected persons).

A close investment-holding company is subject to the usual close company rules described above, but is also subject to further provisions. The most important of these is that a CIC is not entitled to the small profits rate of corporation tax. Nor can it benefit from marginal relief. A CIC always pays corporation tax at the main rate, no matter how small its chargeable profits.

Companies with investment business

A "company with investment business" is defined by the Corporation Tax Act 2009 as "*a company whose business consists wholly or partly of making investments*". The investment income of such a company will normally consist of:

(a) income from property

(b) net credits on non-trading loan relationships

(c) chargeable gains.

The company may also receive franked investment income but of course this is not chargeable to corporation tax. The expenses incurred by a company in relation to its investment business fall into two categories:

(a) expenses which are directly related to one of the company's sources of income and which may be set against that income (e.g. property expenses offset against property income, debits on non-trading loan relationships set against credits)

(b) management expenses, which are not related to any particular source of income but which may be set against the company's total income.

Note that only genuine management expenses are allowed. For example, in *L G Berry Investments Ltd* v *Attwooll* (1964), excessive directors' remuneration included in management expenses was disallowed.

To the extent that management expenses cannot be relieved in the accounting period in which they are incurred they may be carried forward (without time limit) to future periods. There are restrictions on the carry-forward of management expenses when there is a change in the ownership of a company. These restrictions are similar to those relating to the carry-forward of trading losses (see Chapter 26).

Unincorporated business vs close company

An individual who starts trading is faced with a choice between two alternatives:

(a) To trade as an unincorporated business, either as a sole trader or in partnership with others. In this case the individual is self-employed and the business profits are assessed to income tax as trading income.

(b) To trade as a limited company (probably a close company) with the individual concerned being a director and/or shareholder of the company. In this case, the company's profits are assessed to corporation tax and the individual's earnings and dividends from the company are assessed to income tax.

The choice between these two alternatives will be determined partly (though not solely) by taxation considerations. A full analysis of these considerations is beyond the scope of this book but some of the main factors which should be taken into account when deciding whether to trade as an unincorporated business or as a company include:

(a) the rates of income tax and corporation tax
(b) the NI contributions which are payable by the self-employed and by employees and employers
(c) the tax effects of distributing profits to the owner of the business
(d) the tax reliefs available on pension contributions
(e) the dates on which tax and NI contributions are due for payment
(f) the tax reliefs available in relation to trading losses
(g) the taxation of chargeable gains
(h) the tax treatment of loans made to the owner of the business.

Each of these factors is discussed below.

Rates of tax

The entire profits of an unincorporated business are charged to income tax, whether or not the profits are drawn out of the business. Rates of tax in 2012-13 are 20%, 40% or 50%, depending upon the owner's taxable income. A marginal rate of 40% applies if the owner's taxable income exceeds £34,370 (a relatively small sum) and the 50% rate applies if the owner's taxable income exceeds £150,000.

By contrast, the profits of a company for FY2012 are charged to corporation tax at 20% or 24% with a marginal rate of 25% if augmented profits lie between the lower and upper limits. The 25% rate does not apply until profits reach £300,000. The 24% rate does not apply until profits reach £1,500,000. Furthermore, the owners of a company can determine the amount of profits to be paid out as directors' remuneration and can therefore control the extent to which profits are assessed to income tax rather than corporation tax.

Note, however, that retaining profits in a company so as to minimise the tax liability in the short term will increase the value of the company's shares. This will result in an increased capital gains tax (CGT) liability in the longer term when shareholders dispose of their shares, though the gains made on such disposals might be eligible for entrepreneurs' relief and/or other CGT reliefs.

National Insurance

In 2012-13, the self-employed pay flat-rate Class 2 NICs of £2.65 per week. Class 4 contributions are also payable, calculated as 9% of profits between £7,605 and £42,475 and 2% of profits beyond £42,475.

The total amount of the Class 1 NICs payable in respect of directors' remuneration can be much higher than this. A director who is not contracted out pays primary contributions at 12% on earnings between £7,605 and £42,475 and at 2% on any further earnings. In addition, the company pays 13.8% secondary contributions on all earnings in excess of £7,488. However, these secondary contributions are deductible when calculating the company's profits for corporation tax purposes.

Distribution of profits

The amount of income tax payable on the profits of an unincorporated business is entirely unaffected by the level of the owner's drawings. But the distribution of profits by a company (either as directors' remuneration or as dividends) has tax implications:

(a) The payment of directors' remuneration reduces the company's corporation tax liability at the expense of increasing the income tax liability of the directors concerned and creating a liability to both primary and secondary NICs.

(b) The payment of a dividend avoids the NI liability and a dividend has an attached tax credit. But dividends are an appropriation of profit and are not allowed in the company's corporation tax computation.

The decision as to whether to pay out a company's profits as directors' remuneration or dividends (or a mixture of both) is a complex one and should take into account the personal circumstances of the shareholders and directors as well as all of the factors listed above. A constraint which should be borne in mind is the need to pay sufficient directors' remuneration to comply with National Minimum Wage regulations.

EXAMPLE 6

A close company which prepares accounts to 31 March each year is owned and managed by a single shareholder/director who is paid a salary of £5,000 per month. In addition to this salary, the company's owner intends to withdraw £20,000 from the company on 31 March 2013. Two approaches are being considered:

(a) that the company should make an extra salary payment to the owner, such that the total of this payment and the related secondary NICs will equal £20,000

(b) that the company should pay a dividend to the owner, such that the total of this dividend and the company's extra corporation tax liability (when compared with the other approach) will equal £20,000.

Consider the tax-effectiveness of each of these two approaches. For the approach which involves the payment of a dividend, show separately the situation which will apply if the company's marginal rate of corporation tax for the year is 20%, 24% or 25%. Perform all calculations to the nearest £ and assume that the owner has no income apart from income derived from the company.

Solution

	Extra salary £	*Dividend (20%)* £	*Dividend (24%)* £	*Dividend (25%)* £
Payments made by company:				
Salary	17,575			
Secondary Class 1 NICs @ 13.8%	2,425			
Corporation tax on £20,000		4,000	4,800	5,000
Dividend		16,000	15,200	15,000
Total payments	20,000	20,000	20,000	20,000
Amount received by owner:				
Gross salary	17,575			
Dividend + tax credit (1/9th)		17,778	16,889	16,667
Primary Class 1 NICs @ 2%	(351)			
Income tax @ 40%	(7,030)			
Income tax @ 32.5%		(5,778)	(5,489)	(5,417)
Income remaining after tax	10,194	12,000	11,400	11,250

Notes:

(i) The owner's regular salary is sufficient to ensure that any further income is subject to primary Class 1 NICs at 2% and income tax at the higher rate or dividend upper rate.

(ii) The payment of a dividend to the owner seems to be more tax-effective than the payment of extra salary. However, this distinction becomes less marked as the company's marginal rate of corporation tax increases.

Pension contributions

In 2012-13, a self-employed individual may obtain tax relief on pension contributions of up to £3,600 or 100% of self-employment income (whichever is the greater). Similarly, a company director may obtain tax relief on pension contributions of up to £3,600 or 100% of director's remuneration (whichever is the greater) whilst the company itself may make unlimited pension contributions on the director's behalf and deduct these contributions when computing chargeable profits. However, this deduction is available only if the contributions are paid wholly and exclusively for trade purposes. If the contributions are made in respect of a controlling director, the "wholly and exclusively" test will not be satisfied unless the contributions are in line with those which would have been paid in respect of an ordinary employee in a similar situation.

Dividends do not rank as earnings and therefore dividends received are ignored when computing the maximum pension contributions on which an individual may obtain tax relief. Furthermore, a shareholder in a company is not (per se) an employee of that company. So a company cannot make employer's pension contributions in relation to one of its shareholders unless that shareholder is also a director or other employee.

Dates of payment of tax and NICs

A self-employed person must make payments on account of his or her liability to income tax and Class 4 NICs. These payments are due on 31 January in the tax year and on the following 31 July. The balance of the liability (if any) is payable on the following 31 January. Note that:

(a) Choosing an accounting date early in the tax year (e.g. 30 April) maximises the delay between earning profits and paying tax on them. For example, the tax on profits for the year to 30 April 2012 (basis period for 2012-13) is payable on 31 January 2013 and 31 July 2013 with a balancing payment on 31 January 2014.

(b) However, choosing an accounting date early in the tax year has the adverse effect of maximising the amount of overlap profits which are assessed twice on the commencement of trade.

(c) Class 2 NICs of £2.65 per week are payable throughout the tax year.

In general, close companies will pay their corporation tax nine months and one day after the end of the accounting period. Income tax and Class 1 NICs in relation to directors' remuneration must be accounted for via the PAYE system.

Relief for trading losses

For both individuals and companies, trading losses may be carried forward and set against future profits of the same trade. The main distinctions between trading loss reliefs for individuals and trading loss reliefs for companies are concerned with the opportunities to set such losses against total income:

(a) The trading losses of a self-employed individual may be set against that person's total income for the year of the loss, the previous year or both of these years.

In the case of a company, a claim to set trading losses against total profits of the previous 12 months cannot be made unless a claim has already been made to set trading losses against total profits of the current accounting period.

(b) Both for self-employed individuals and for companies, terminal losses incurred in the 12 months prior to a cessation of trade may be carried back for three years. For individuals, terminal losses may be relieved only against profits of the same trade (see Chapter 12). For companies, terminal losses are set against the company's total profits, not just profits of the same trade (see Chapter 26).

(c) In certain circumstances, the trading losses of an individual may be set against capital gains (see Chapter 12). A company receives a similar relief by virtue of the fact that a company's chargeable gains are automatically included in its total profits.

(d) Trading losses of an individual incurred in the opening years of a business may be relieved against total income of the previous three years. There is no equivalent relief for companies.

Note that a company's losses can be relieved only against the company's own income and gains, not against the income and gains of individual shareholders.

Chargeable gains

If an unincorporated business disposes of a chargeable asset, any gain that arises is assessed to capital gains tax on the owner of the business. The rate of tax for disposals occurring during tax year 2012-13 is 18% or 28%. The annual exemption is available.

The computational rules which apply when a company makes a chargeable disposal are somewhat different from those which apply for CGT. In particular, indexation allowance is available to companies but not to individuals. Gains arising in FY2012 are subject to corporation tax at either 20%, 24% or 25%. No annual exemption is available. Gains retained in the company increase the value of the company's shares, so resulting in an increased CGT liability when shareholders eventually dispose of their shares. In effect a chargeable gain may be taxed twice, first to corporation tax and then to CGT.

Close company loans to participators

As explained earlier in this chapter, close companies must pay tax when making loans to participators. A tax charge of this type can sometimes be triggered accidentally if a director who is also a shareholder overdraws his or her current account with the company. These provisions have no relevance to unincorporated businesses.

Incorporation

If the initial choice is to trade as an unincorporated business, the trader may still consider incorporation at some future time. Some of the main tax consequences of incorporation are as follows:

(a) The transfer of the assets of a business to a company might give rise to a CGT liability. However, subject to certain conditions, the gains arising may be held-over until the shares which were acquired in exchange for the business assets are disposed of (see Chapter 22).

(b) If the company is under the control of the person who was previously the owner of the unincorporated business, assets which are eligible for capital allowances can be transferred at their written down values for capital allowances purposes, so avoiding the need for balancing adjustments (see Chapter 11).

(c) The transfer of assets to the company will not be treated as a supply for VAT purposes so long as the business is transferred as a going concern and the company is a taxable person at the time of the transfer (see Chapter 29).

(d) If the proprietor of the unincorporated business has unrelieved trade losses, these cannot be carried forward and used by the company. However, subject to certain conditions, such unrelieved losses may be relieved against the proprietor's income from the company (see Chapter 12).

Summary

- A close company is one which is under the control of five or fewer participators or any number of participator-directors. The rights of the associates of a participator are aggregated with the participator's own rights when determining whether or not a company is a close company.
- Certain types of company (mainly listed companies with a substantial public interest) are excepted from close company status.
- Benefits in kind provided to the participators of a close company are treated as distributions. Loans to the participators are charged to tax.
- A close company is also a close investment-holding company unless it exists wholly or mainly for the purposes of trading or the letting of property. A close investment-holding company always pays corporation tax at the main rate.
- A company with investment business is a company whose business consists wholly or partly of making investments. Management expenses incurred by such companies are generally set against total income.

Exercises

27.1 Andrew Pearson is a shareholder of Andrew Pearson (Nottingham) Ltd. Which of the following (if any) are his associates for the purposes of deciding whether the company is a close company?

(a) his sister
(b) his brother-in-law
(c) his nephew
(d) his father
(e) his partner in a firm of solicitors.

27.2 A company's share capital consists of 5,000 ordinary shares, held as follows:

	Number of shares
Sejanus (a manager)	900
Claudius (a director)	400
Agrippa (a director)	300
Cleopatra (a director)	300
Tiberius (a director)	200
Gaius (a director)	200
Ptolemy	190
Livia (the grandmother of Claudius)	190
Apicata (the wife of Sejanus)	120
Others (all non-directors owning 10 shares or less)	2,200
Total	5,000

Is the company a close company?

27.3 On 31 October 2012, a close company which prepares accounts to 31 March each year provides one of its full-time working directors with:

(a) an interest-free loan of £12,000 (the company does not provide loans in the ordinary course of its business)

(b) a season ticket for the opera, costing the company £1,800.

Explain the tax treatment of these two items, assuming that the director in question owns 10% of the company's ordinary share capital.

***27.4** On 19 April 2011, a close company (which makes up accounts to 31 March annually) lends £100,000 to Siobhan, who is a director of the company and who owns 30% of its ordinary share capital. The company does not provide loans in the ordinary course of its business. Siobhan pays a commercial rate of interest on this loan until 1 October 2012, when she repays £55,000. She then continues to pay a commercial rate of interest on the remainder of the loan until it is written off by the company on 31 March 2013. Explain the tax implications of these transactions.

***27.5** A close company has the following results for the year to 31 March 2013:

	£
Income from letting property	89,000
Chargeable gains	600
Franked investment income	1,200

(a) Compute the corporation tax payable for the year.

(b) Would it make any difference if the property income were trading income instead?

(c) Would it make any difference if the property income were a net credit on non-trading loan relationships instead?

Chapter 28

Groups of companies and reconstructions

Introduction

For corporation tax purposes, groups of companies are divided into a number of categories and each category enjoys certain tax advantages. These advantages may include:

(a) the transfer of trading losses and certain other deficits between group members

(b) the transfer of chargeable assets from one group member to another in such a way that no chargeable gain arises on the transfer.

However, group companies also incur certain tax disadvantages, principally a reduction in the lower and upper limits which are used to determine the applicable rate of corporation tax. The main purpose of this chapter is to describe the categories of group which exist and the extent to which these advantages and disadvantages apply to each category.

The tax implications of company reconstructions are also considered very briefly at the end of this chapter.

Associated companies

For taxation purposes, two companies are associated if one of the companies is under the control of the other or if they are both under the control of a third party, which may be an individual, a partnership or a company. In this context, the word "control" means the same as it does with regard to close companies (see Chapter 27). Control over a company is deemed to accompany:

(a) ownership of over 50% of the company's issued share capital or voting power, or

(b) entitlement to over 50% of the company's income or assets.

The main consequence of two or more companies being associated is that the lower and upper limits (currently £300,000 and £1,500,000 respectively) are divided equally between the companies concerned. This is an anti-avoidance measure, designed to block the practice of breaking large companies into several smaller ones in order to take advantage of the small profits rate.

Counting associated companies

When determining the lower and upper limits which apply to a company for an accounting period, it is necessary to count the number of other companies with which the company was associated in that period. Note that:

(a) An associated company is counted even if it was associated with the taxpayer company for only part of the period. Furthermore, two or more associated companies are counted even if they were associated with the taxpayer company for different parts of the period but never simultaneously.

(b) Associated companies which are dormant are ignored.

(c) Associated companies are counted whether or not they are resident in the UK. For instance, if a UK company has nine overseas subsidiaries, the upper and lower limits will be divided between all ten of the companies concerned, even though the overseas subsidiaries are outside the charge to UK corporation tax.

(d) If a company controls a second company which in turn controls a third company, then (for this purpose) the first company also controls the third company, even though it may own (indirectly) less than 50% of the third company's shares.

(e) If an accounting period straddles 31 March and the lower and upper limits differ between the two financial years with which the period overlaps, the two parts of the accounting period which fall either side of 31 March are treated as two separate "notional accounting periods" for the purpose of counting associated companies. The number of associated companies in each notional period is then taken into account when calculating the tax liability for that notional period.

This rule is generally implemented by the Finance Act for the year in which the limits change. However, these limits have not changed since 1994.

EXAMPLE 1

Co01 Ltd owns 100% of the issued share capital of Co02 Ltd and 70% of the issued share capital of Co03 Ltd. Co03 Ltd owns 70% of the issued share capital of Co04 Ltd.

(a) Which companies are associated with Co01 Ltd?

(b) If Co02 Ltd acquired 60% of the issued share capital of an overseas company, would this overseas company also become an associated company of Co01 Ltd?

Solution

(a) Co01 clearly controls Co02 and Co03. Even though Co01 (indirectly) owns only 49% of the issued share capital of Co04 (70% x 70%), Co04 is controlled by Co03 which is controlled by Co01. So Co01 controls Co04. Therefore Co02 Ltd, Co03 Ltd and Co04 Ltd are all associated with Co01 Ltd.

(b) Co01 Ltd would control the overseas company and so this company would become one of its associated companies (despite not being a UK company).

EXAMPLE 2

Sub01 Ltd has chargeable profits of £120,000 for the six months to 30 September 2012 and no franked investment income.

Until 1 July 2012 the company had no associated companies but, on that date, its entire share capital was acquired by Hold01 Ltd. This company has five other wholly-owned subsidiaries, two of which are dormant. Compute the corporation tax liability of Sub01 Ltd for the six months to 30 September 2012.

Solution

Sub01 Ltd is deemed to have had four associated companies (Hold01 Ltd and its three active subsidiaries) throughout the entire accounting period. So the lower and upper limits are reduced to £60,000 and £300,000 respectively (one-fifth of their usual values). These are annual figures, which are multiplied by 6/12 for a six-month accounting period, giving £30,000 and £150,000. Augmented profits of £120,000 fall between these limits, so tax is payable at the main rate less marginal relief. The corporation tax computation is:

FY2012	£
£120,000 @ 24%	28,800.00
Less: Marginal relief:	
$\frac{1}{100}$ x (£150,000 – £120,000) x $\frac{£120,000}{£120,000}$	300.00
Corporation tax liability	28,500.00

Transfer pricing

For many years, the UK tax system has contained "transfer pricing" rules which prevent UK companies from gaining a tax advantage by carrying out transactions at artificial prices with connected companies overseas (see Chapter 32). The transfer pricing rules require companies to compute their profits for tax purposes as if such transactions had been carried out at "arm's length". This means that profits must be computed using the prices which would have applied between unconnected parties.

The original transfer pricing rules applied only to transactions with connected companies situated overseas, but these rules have now been extended to cover transactions between connected UK companies. Broadly, companies are connected for this purpose if one controls the other or they are under common control. The rules require an adjustment for tax purposes to the profits of the company which gains a potential tax advantage from the transactions and a corresponding adjustment to the profits of the other company.

Small and medium-sized companies are generally exempt from all of the transfer pricing legislation.

51% groups

Company B is said to be a 51% subsidiary of Company A if *all* of the following conditions are satisfied:

(a) Company A owns (directly or indirectly) over 50% of the ordinary share capital of Company B, and

(b) Company A is entitled to more than 50% of the profits available to the ordinary shareholders of Company B, and

(c) Company A would be entitled to more than 50% of the assets available to the ordinary shareholders of Company B if Company B were to be wound-up.

Two companies are members of a 51% group if one company is a 51% subsidiary of the other or they are both 51% subsidiaries of a third company.

By definition, members of a 51% group are also associated companies and so suffer from a reduction in the lower and upper limits, as described above. On the other hand, 51% groups used to enjoy certain tax advantages. Most of these advantages have now ceased to exist but there are still some tax provisions which relate specifically to 51% groups. These are as follows:

(a) Franked investment income received from a 51% subsidiary or fellow 51% subsidiary is disregarded when computing the augmented profits of the receiving company for the purpose of determining the applicable rate of corporation tax (see Chapter 25).

(b) If at least one of the companies in a 51% group is liable to pay corporation tax by instalments (see Chapter 25) one of the group members may be nominated to pay all of the corporation tax due from all of the group members. In these circumstances, instalments are based upon the estimated tax liability of the group as a whole. When the total liability of each group member is finally determined, the instalments already paid may be allocated between the group members in such a way as to minimise any interest payable on underpaid instalments.

75% groups

Company B is said to be a 75% subsidiary of Company A if *all* of the following conditions are satisfied:

(a) Company A owns (directly or indirectly) at least 75% of the ordinary share capital of Company B, and

(b) Company A is entitled to at least 75% of the profits available to the ordinary shareholders of Company B, and

(c) Company A would be entitled to at least 75% of the assets available to the ordinary shareholders of Company B if Company B were to be wound-up.

Two companies are members of a 75% group if one company is a 75% subsidiary of the other or they are both 75% subsidiaries of a third company.

The "UK related" members of a 75% group benefit from two main tax reliefs. These are the right to transfer certain losses and deficits between group members ("group relief") and the transfer of chargeable assets between group members in such a way that no chargeable gain arises on the transfer. These reliefs are described below.

A company is regarded as "UK related" if it is UK resident or if it carries on a trade in the UK through a permanent establishment.

EXAMPLE 3

PNT Ltd is the parent company of a small group. All companies in the group are UK resident and all of the issued shares of each company are ordinary shares. Shareholdings within the group are as follows:

(a) PNT Ltd owns 80% of Qsub Ltd, 100% of Rsub Ltd and 60% of Tsub Ltd.

(b) Qsub Ltd owns 90% of Vsub Ltd.

(c) Tsub Ltd owns 70% of Wsub Ltd.

Identify associated companies, 51% subsidiaries and 75% subsidiaries within this group structure.

Solution

PNT Ltd controls Qsub Ltd, Rsub Ltd and Tsub Ltd. Furthermore, Qsub Ltd controls Vsub Ltd and Tsub Ltd controls Wsub Ltd. So all six companies are associated.

PNT Ltd owns (indirectly) 72% of the ordinary share capital of Vsub Ltd (80% x 90%) and 42% of the ordinary share capital of Wsub Ltd (60% x 70%). Therefore:

(i) Qsub Ltd and Rsub Ltd are 75% subsidiaries (and 51% subsidiaries) of PNT Ltd.

(ii) Tsub Ltd and Vsub Ltd are 51% subsidiaries of PNT Ltd.

(iii) Vsub Ltd is a 75% subsidiary (and a 51% subsidiary) of Qsub Ltd.

(iv) Wsub Ltd is a 51% subsidiary of Tsub Ltd.

Group relief

Group relief consists of the surrender of trading losses and/or certain other items by one member of a 75% group (the "surrendering company") to another member of the same group (the "claimant company"). The main items which may be surrendered are:

(a) trading losses and deficits on non-trading loan relationships

(b) property business losses, non-trading losses on intangible fixed assets and qualifying charitable donations.

Capital losses cannot be surrendered under the group relief rules, but a capital loss can in effect be transferred from one group company to another by a different means (see later in this chapter). Note the following points with regard to group relief:

(a) The surrender may be in whole or in part as best meets the requirements of the surrendering company and the claimant company. Trading losses and deficits on non-trading loan relationships may be surrendered even if they could instead have been set against the profits of the accounting period in which they are incurred. The other items are available for surrender only to the extent that (in aggregate) they exceed the surrendering company's gross profits for the period in which they are incurred.

    For this purpose, a company's "gross profits" are its profits before deducting amounts which are eligible for group relief and before deducting losses or other amounts carried forward or back from any other period.

(b) A surrender may be made from subsidiary to parent, from parent to subsidiary or from subsidiary to fellow subsidiary.

(c) Only current-period losses (or other items) are eligible for group relief and these must be set against the claimant company's profits for an *overlapping* accounting period. If the accounting periods of the surrendering company and the claimant company do not correspond exactly, group relief is available only in respect of the period of overlap between the two periods. The losses of the surrendering company and the profits of the claimant company are time-apportioned so as to determine the amounts which fall into the overlap period. A similar time-apportionment is required when a company joins or leaves a group part-way through an accounting period.

(d) The amount of losses and other items surrendered to a claimant company cannot exceed that company's profits for the corresponding accounting period, *before* deduction of any reliefs derived from a subsequent period but *after* deduction of:

    - trading losses brought forward
    - current-period trading losses which are relieved (or which could have been relieved) against the total profits of the period
    - property business losses of the current period or previous periods
    - deficits on non-trading loan relationships which are set against profits of the current period or brought forward from previous periods

- non-trading losses on intangible fixed assets which are set against profits of the current period or brought forward from previous periods
- qualifying charitable donations for the period.

The reference to "reliefs derived from a subsequent accounting period" means that group relief is given before relief for trading losses carried back and before relief for deficits on non-trading loan relationships carried back.

(e) A group relief claim must be made within two years of the end of the claimant company's accounting period. Any amount paid to the surrendering company by the claimant company in return for the surrendered items is ignored for tax purposes so long as the payment does not exceed the amount of the surrendered items.

(f) There are restrictions on group relief if the surrendering company is UK related (with a permanent establishment in the UK) but is not UK resident. Restrictions also apply to the surrender of losses incurred by an overseas permanent establishment of a UK resident company (see Chapter 32).

(g) In certain circumstances, group relief may be claimed by UK parent companies in relation to losses incurred by their foreign subsidiaries (see Chapter 32).

EXAMPLE 4

Low1 Ltd is a wholly-owned subsidiary of High1 Ltd. Both companies are UK resident and prepare accounts to 31 March each year. Results for the year to 31 March 2013 are:

	High1 Ltd	*Low1 Ltd*
	£	£
Trading profit/(loss)	100,000	(180,000)
Chargeable gains	5,000	75,000
Gift Aid donations	12,000	-

Show how the trading loss sustained by Low1 Ltd may be relieved.

Solution

High1 Ltd has chargeable profits of £93,000 (£100,000 + £5,000 – £12,000). This sets a ceiling on the amount of group relief which may be claimed. The trading loss sustained by Low1 Ltd may be relieved in a number of ways. For example:

(a) The entire loss could be carried forward for relief against future trading profits.

(b) £75,000 of the loss could be relieved against the company's chargeable gains and the balance of £105,000 could then be carried forward. Alternatively, the remaining £105,000 of the loss could be relieved against the total profits of Low1 Ltd for the previous 12 months.

(c) Group relief of anything up to £93,000 could be claimed and the balance of the loss then dealt with as above.

EXAMPLE 5

Low2 Ltd prepares accounts to 31 March each year and is a 75% subsidiary of High2 Ltd which prepares accounts to 31 December. Both companies are UK resident. Recent results are as follows:

	High2 Ltd	*Low2 Ltd*
	£	£
Trading loss for year to 31 March 2012		(40,000)
Chargeable profits year to 31 December 2011	35,000	
Chargeable profits year to 31 December 2012	56,000	

Compute the amount of group relief that may be claimed.

Solution

The accounting periods of High2 Ltd and Low2 Ltd do not correspond, so it is necessary to time-apportion profits and losses, as follows:

	1/4/11 - 31/12/11 (9 months)	*1/1/12 - 31/3/12 (3 months)*
	£	£
(i) High2 Ltd profit	26,250	14,000
(ii) Low2 Ltd loss	(30,000)	(10,000)

The group relief available in each period is the lower of (i) and (ii). Therefore, High2 Ltd may claim that group relief of up to £26,250 should be set against its 2011 profits and that group relief of up to £10,000 should be set against its 2012 profits. The remaining £3,750 of the loss is not eligible for group relief.

Using group relief effectively

Group relief should be used to ensure that trading losses (and other eligible items) are relieved as tax-effectively as possible and that the group's overall tax liability is minimised. Points to bear in mind are:

(a) Losses should be surrendered first to claimant companies which pay corporation tax (in FY2012) at the marginal rate of 25%, then to companies paying tax at the main rate of 24% and finally to companies paying tax at the small profits rate of 20%.

(b) Claimant companies should consider claiming less than the full amount of capital allowances available for an accounting period, so maximising the profits available for group relief set-off.

(c) A company which has incurred a trading loss should use the loss itself in a claim against total profits if this would save more tax than surrendering the loss to another group company.

Transfer of chargeable assets within a group

If a chargeable asset is transferred from one member of a 75% group to another, the transfer is deemed to have occurred at a value giving rise to neither a gain nor a loss. When an asset which has been transferred between group members in this way is finally disposed of outside the group, the chargeable gain arising on the disposal is then (in effect) calculated with reference to the original cost of the asset to the group.

The definition of a 75% group for this purpose is less rigorous than the definition given above in relation to group relief. A *capital gains group* consists of a principal company plus its 75% subsidiaries (as previously defined) plus the subsidiaries' 75% subsidiaries and so forth, subject to the over-riding requirement that the principal company must have more than a 50% interest in each member of the group.

EXAMPLE 6

J100 Ltd owns 80% of the ordinary share capital of K101 Ltd, which owns 80% of the share capital of L102 Ltd, which owns 80% of the share capital of M103 Ltd, which owns 80% of the share capital of N104 Ltd. All of these companies are UK resident. Which of the companies belongs to a capital gains group with J100 Ltd as the principal company?

Solution

At first sight, all five companies seem to belong to the capital gains group which has J100 Ltd at its head. However, J100 Ltd must have more than a 50% interest in each member of the group. J100 Ltd's actual interests in each member are as follows:

K101 Ltd	80%
L102 Ltd	80% x 80% = 64%
M103 Ltd	80% x 80% x 80% = 51.2%
N104 Ltd	80% x 80% x 80% x 80% = 40.96%

Therefore, N104 Ltd is not a member of this capital gains group.

Roll-over relief for capital gains groups

For the purposes of roll-over relief on the replacement of a business asset (see Chapter 22) all of the companies in a capital gains group are treated as a single company. This means that a gain arising on the disposal of a business asset by one member of a group can be rolled-over against the cost of a qualifying business asset acquired by any other member of the same group.

It is important to note that the qualifying business asset against which a gain is rolled-over must be an asset which has been newly acquired *by the group as a whole*. It is not possible to roll-over a gain against an asset which has been acquired by one group member from another.

Degrouping charge

A chargeable gain or allowable loss may arise in connection with an intra-group transfer if a company has a chargeable asset transferred to it from another group member and then leaves the group within six years of the date of the transfer. The company leaving the group (the "transferee company") is deemed to have sold the asset on the date of the intra-group transfer for its market value on that date (triggering a gain or loss) and then to have immediately re-acquired the asset on the same date and for the same amount.

The tax treatment of such a "degrouping" gain or loss depends upon the circumstances which have caused the transferee company to leave the group, as follows:

(a) If the transferee company has left the group because of a disposal of shares made by another company in the group, then:

   (i) any degrouping gain is added to disposal proceeds when computing the gain or loss arising on that share disposal, and

   (ii) any degrouping loss is treated as allowable expenditure when computing the gain or loss arising on that share disposal.

   The event that most frequently causes a company to leave a group is the disposal by a parent company of its shares in a subsidiary. Such a disposal necessitates the above treatment of degrouping gains or losses, so that (in effect) any such gains or losses arising when the subsidiary leaves the group are passed on to the parent.

   However, it is important to note that the disposal by a parent company of shares in a subsidiary is likely to qualify as the disposal of a "substantial shareholding". Since gains arising on such disposals are exempt from tax (see Chapter 24), this means that any degrouping gains arising in these circumstances would also be exempt.

(b) If the transferee company has *not* left the group because of a disposal of shares by another company in the group, then any degrouping gain or loss is treated as if it had arisen in the accounting period in which the transferee company leaves the group and is usually taken into account when computing the transferee company's corporation tax liability for that period. However, as explained later in this chapter, any gain or loss (including a degrouping gain or loss) may be treated for tax purposes as if it had accrued instead to another company in the group.

   These provisions would apply if (for example) a subsidiary company left a group because it had made a share issue and, as a result of that issue, its parent company no longer owned at least 75% of the subsidiary's shares.

EXAMPLE 7

Sub01 Ltd and Sub02 Ltd belong to a capital gains group. In May 2009, Sub01 Ltd transferred a chargeable asset to Sub02 Ltd. This asset had originally cost £10,000 and its market value in May 2009 was £25,000. Indexation allowance of £1,350 would have been available in May 2009 If the asset had been sold outside the group. Sub02 Ltd (which prepares accounts to 31 December) left the group in March 2013.

(a) Calculate the degrouping gain arising on the departure of Sub02 Ltd.

(b) Explain the tax treatment of this gain.

Solution

(a) Sub02 Ltd is deemed to have sold the asset for £25,000 in May 2009 and then immediately to have re-acquired it for the same amount. The sale would have given rise to a chargeable gain of £13,650 (£25,000 – £10,000 – £1,350) so a degrouping gain of £13,650 arises when Sub02 Ltd leaves the group.

(b) The treatment of this gain depends upon the circumstances in which Sub02 Ltd has left the group. If this departure has been caused by a share disposal made by another member of the group (probably Sub02's parent), then £13,650 is added to disposal proceeds when calculating the gain or loss arising on that share disposal. Otherwise, the degrouping gain is treated as a chargeable gain of £13,650 accruing to Sub02 Ltd in the year to 31 December 2013.

Capital losses

Capital losses cannot be surrendered to another member of the group. This is in contrast to trading losses and certain other items which can be surrendered. At one time, the only way around this problem was to transfer assets between group members in such a way that chargeable gains and capital losses arose in the same company. Imagine that Company L and Company G were both members of a capital gains group, that Company L had capital losses and that Company G was about to dispose of an asset and realise a chargeable gain. Company L's capital losses could be set against this gain in the following way:

(a) Company G could transfer its asset to Company L (on a no gain/no loss basis).

(b) Company L could then dispose of the asset. The gain would be realised by Company L rather than Company G, so allowing Company L's losses to be set against it.

However a simpler procedure is now available. Two companies that are members of a 75% group may jointly elect that all or part of the gain (or loss) arising on a disposal by one of the companies should be treated as if it had been realised (or incurred) by the other company. This allows gains and losses to be brought together in the same company without having to actually transfer assets between group members. The election must be made within two years of the end of the accounting period in which the disposal occurs.

Pre-entry capital losses

A group which anticipates making disposals which will give rise to substantial chargeable gains might try to shelter those gains from tax by acquiring a "capital loss company". This is a company which has capital losses brought forward and/or assets which would realise capital losses on disposal. The intention of the acquisition would be to set these capital losses against the group's chargeable gains (by means of the procedure outlined above) and so reduce the group's overall corporation tax liability.

However, anti-avoidance legislation exists which prevents groups from gaining a tax advantage in this way. This legislation applies only if certain conditions are satisfied. The main conditions are as follows:

(a) There must be a change of ownership of the company concerned. This condition is satisfied if the company joins a group.

(b) The change of ownership must occur in connection with "arrangements", of which one of the main purposes is to secure a tax advantage.

If these conditions are satisfied, the anti-avoidance legislation applies and it is not possible to set the acquired capital losses against the group's chargeable gains.

Even if these conditions are *not* satisfied, there is in any case a restriction on the relief available in relation to a company's *pre-entry capital losses*. Pre-entry capital losses are defined as capital losses incurred by the company before joining a group. Such losses may be set only against gains arising on disposals of:

(a) assets which the company owned before it joined the group ("pre-entry assets"), or

(b) assets acquired by the company *from outside the group* since joining the group.

Consortia

A company is owned by a consortium and is known as a *consortium company* if at least 75% of its ordinary share capital is owned by other companies (which are known as *consortium members*) each of which:

(a) owns at least 5% but less than 75% of the consortium company's ordinary share capital, and

(b) is entitled to at least 5% of the profits available to the consortium company's ordinary shareholders, and

(c) would be entitled to at least 5% of the assets available to the consortium company's ordinary shareholders on a winding-up.

A 90% subsidiary of a consortium company is also a consortium company.

Group relief for a consortium

Group relief is available in either direction between a consortium member and a consortium company, so long as both companies are UK related and the consortium company is either a trading company or a company whose business consists wholly or mainly of holding shares in trading companies which are its 90% subsidiaries. Note the following points with regard to group relief for a consortium:

(a) The relief is restricted in proportion to the consortium member's shareholding in the consortium company. For instance, if ConsCom Ltd is a consortium company and ConsMem Ltd is a consortium member which owns p% of ConsCom Ltd, then:

  (i) If ConsMem Ltd is the claimant company, it may claim up to p% of ConsCom Ltd's losses.

  (ii) If ConsMem Ltd is the surrendering company, it may surrender to ConsCom Ltd losses of up to p% of ConsCom Ltd's profits.

(b) A group relief claim must be agreed by all the consortium members.

(c) The amount of a consortium company's trading loss which is available for group relief is the amount of that loss less any potential claim for relief against total profits of the loss-making period, whether or not such a claim is actually made.

EXAMPLE 8

The ordinary share capital of Wcom Ltd (which is a trading company) is owned 30% by Xmem Ltd, 25% by Ymem Ltd and 45% by Zmem Ltd. All companies are UK resident and prepare accounts to 31 March. Results for the year to 31 March 2013 are as follows:

	Wcom Ltd	*Xmem Ltd*	*Ymem Ltd*	*Zmem Ltd*
	£	£	£	£
Trading profit/(loss)	(62,000)	41,000	11,000	38,000
Chargeable gains	10,000	-	-	-

What are the maximum possible group relief claims which may be made?

Solution

Wcom Ltd could claim that £10,000 of its trading loss should be set against its total profits of the loss-making period. Therefore, whether or not such a claim is made, the amount of the loss which is available for group relief is £52,000 (£62,000 – £10,000). This amount is shared between the consortium members in proportion to their shares in the consortium company, as follows:

	Xmem Ltd	*Ymem Ltd*	*Zmem Ltd*
	£	£	£
Share of Wcom Ltd available loss	15,600	13,000	23,400
Chargeable profits	41,000	11,000	38,000
Maximum group relief claim	15,600	11,000	23,400

Company reconstructions

If a company transfers a trade to another company, this ranks as a cessation of that trade and unrelieved trading losses incurred before the date of the transfer cannot normally be carried forward and set against the subsequent profits of the transferred trade.

But if a trade is transferred between two companies (both within the charge to UK corporation tax in respect of that trade) and at least 75% of the trade is effectively owned by the same persons both:

(a) at some time within the year before the date of the transfer, and

(b) at some time within the two years after the date of the transfer

then any unrelieved trading losses of the transferor company may be carried forward and set against subsequent profits (from the same trade) of the transferee company. For instance, this "succession of trade" relief would be available if a company created a 75% subsidiary and then transferred a trade to that subsidiary. However, this relief does not extend to non-trading losses or capital losses, neither of which can be carried forward from the transferor company to the transferee company.

Subject to certain conditions, the following provisions also apply to such "company reconstructions":

(a) For capital allowances purposes, assets are transferred at their tax-written down values, with no balancing adjustments.

(b) Chargeable assets are transferred to the transferee company on a no-gain, no-loss basis, as long as the transferor company receives no consideration for the assets and the assets remain within the scope of UK corporation tax.

Summary

- Two companies are associated if one of the companies is under the control of the other, or if they are both under the control of a third party.
- The upper and lower limits which are used to determine the applicable rate of corporation tax are shared equally between associated companies.
- Transfer pricing rules apply to transactions carried out an artificial prices between group companies.
- Trading losses and certain other items may be surrendered between members of a 75% group. This is known as "group relief".
- Chargeable assets may be transferred between members of a capital gains group without giving rise to a chargeable gain.
- Subject to certain conditions, group relief is available between consortium members and consortium companies.
- If a trade is transferred between two companies, the unrelieved trading losses of the transferor company may (subject to certain conditions) be carried forward and set against the subsequent trading profits of the transferee company.

Exercises

28.1 Arm1 Ltd and Arm2 Ltd are both 100% subsidiaries of Headco Ltd, which has no other subsidiaries. They are all UK resident. How will the relationship of the three companies affect the way in which they are taxed?

28.2 Alphant Ltd is a subsidiary of Betant Ltd, which has two other subsidiaries (one of which is dormant). In the year to 31 March 2013, Alphant Ltd has the following results:

	£
Trading profits	220,000
Bank deposit interest	6,000
Income from property	4,000
UK dividend received from non-group company	27,000
Gift Aid donations	17,000

Compute the corporation tax liability for the year.

28.3 Basenote Ltd is a wholly-owned subsidiary of Apexine Ltd. Both companies are UK resident and prepare accounts to 31 March each year. The results for the year to 31 March 2013 are as follows:

	Apexine Ltd	*Basenote Ltd*
	£	£
Trading profit/(loss)	120,000	(90,000)
Trading losses brought forward	(42,000)	(19,000)
Income from property	7,000	3,000
Gift Aid donations	12,000	4,000

Calculate the maximum group relief that may be claimed for the year by Apexine Ltd.

28.4 Z11 Ltd owns 90% of the ordinary share capital of Z12 Ltd. Z12 Ltd owns 80% of the ordinary share capital of Z13 Ltd and 70% of the ordinary share capital of Z14 Ltd. All companies are UK resident. Which of these companies form a capital gains group with Z11 Ltd as its principal company?

28.5 The ordinary share capital of PPPX Ltd (which is a trading company) is owned 32% by CM01 Ltd, 35% by CM02 Ltd and 23% by CM03 Ltd. The remaining 10% is owned by various individuals, none of whom own more than 1%. All companies are UK resident and prepare accounts to 31 July. Results for the year to 31 July 2012 are as follows:

	PPPX Ltd	*CM01 Ltd*	*CM02 Ltd*	*CM03 Ltd*
	£	£	£	£
Trading profit/(loss)	(96,000)	41,000	38,000	11,000
Chargeable gains	-	15,000	-	-
Bank interest receivable	12,000	6,000	11,000	4,000
Gift Aid donations	-	(3,000)	(2,000)	(1,000)

Compute the maximum possible group relief claims.

***28.6** TTX1 Ltd has owned 90% of the ordinary share capital of BBX2 Ltd for many years. Both are UK resident. Recent results for the two companies are as follows:

	TTX1 Ltd	*TTX1 Ltd*	*BBX2 Ltd*
	y/e 31/3/2012	*y/e 31/3/2013*	*y/e 30/11/2012*
	£	£	£
Trading profit/(loss)	190,000	130,000	(174,000)
Chargeable gains	25,000	13,000	3,000
Gift Aid donations	5,000	5,000	-

No dividends have been paid or received by either company in any of these accounting periods and maximum group relief is claimed. Calculate the corporation tax which is payable by each company for each accounting period, making and stating any necessary assumptions.

Review questions (Set C)

C1 Tolbooth Ltd is a small manufacturing company. It commenced trading on 1 April 2011 and prepared its first set of accounts for the 18 month period to 30 September 2012. As the accounting technician responsible for preparing the tax computation, you have extracted the following information from the audit file:

		£
(i)	Trading profits (before capital allowances)	390,000
(ii)	Rental income:	
	£20,000 per year from property rented on 1 April 2011.	
	Rent received annually in advance on 1 April.	
(iii)	Bank deposit interest:	
	Received 30 June 2011	2,000
	Received 31 December 2011	2,000
	Accrued to 31 March 2012	1,000
	Received 30 June 2012	12,000
	Accrued to 30 September 2012	4,000
(iv)	Plant and machinery was purchased on 30 June 2011, costing	126,250
(v)	Gift Aid donations:	
	£5,000 every six months as from 31 December 2011	
	Paid 31 December 2011	5,000
	Accrued to 31 March 2012	2,500
	Paid 30 June 2012	5,000
	Accrued to 30 September 2012	2,500
(vi)	Chargeable gain on disposal 1 August 2012	6,500

Required:

(a) State how the first period of account to 30 September 2012 will be divided into accounting periods.

(b) Calculate the corporation tax liability for each accounting period.

(Amended from AAT)

C2 Quadrant Ltd has the following results for its three most recent accounting periods:

	y/e 30/6/11	*1/7/11 to 31/3/12*	*y/e 31/3/13*
	£	£	£
Trading profit/(loss)	2,050,000	260,000	(895,000)
Bank interest receivable	51,600	39,000	28,700
Chargeable gains/(losses)	32,000	(3,000)	47,000
Gift Aid donations	10,000	8,000	5,000

Notes:

1. There were no trading losses brought forward on 1 July 2010.
2. Capital losses brought forward on 1 July 2010 were £67,300.
3. No dividends were paid or received in any of the accounting periods.
4. Following a bad trading result for the year to 31 March 2013, the company expects to return to making a sizeable trading profit in future years.

Required:

(a) Compute the company's corporation tax liability for each of the three accounting periods, assuming that no claims are made in relation to the trading loss of £895,000.

(b) Compute the company's corporation tax liability for each of the three accounting periods, assuming that claims are made to relieve the £895,000 trading loss at the earliest possible opportunity. Also compute the amount of any trading losses carried forward.

(c) Calculate the amount of tax which would be saved in consequence of the claims referred to in (b) above.

(CIPFA)

C3 LimAA Ltd, LimBB Ltd and LimCC Ltd have the following results for the year to 31 March 2013:

	LimAA Ltd	***LimBB Ltd***	***LimCC Ltd***
	£	£	£
Trading profits	1,230,400	167,800	852,500
Bank interest receivable	16,300	-	15,000
Property income	-	5,000	-
Chargeable gains	46,400	13,600	37,300
Allowable capital losses	(2,900)	(77,400)	-
UK dividends received	216,000	1,800	90,000
Gift Aid donations paid	5,200	1,000	4,800

None of the companies has any associated companies.

Required:

Compute each company's corporation tax liability for the year.

C4 Unusual Urns Limited is a UK resident company. It has no associated companies. Recent results are as follows:

	Year to 30 September 2011	*6 months to 31 March 2012*
	£	£
Trading profit/(loss)	210,000	(150,000)
Gift Aid donations	1,500	750

The company's chargeable profits for the year to 31 March 2013 are expected to be approximately £700,000, derived mostly from trading income. The company receives no dividends.

You are required:

(a) to state the alternative methods by which the company can obtain relief for the loss of £150,000 sustained in the period to 31 March 2012, and

(b) to state, with your reasons, which of these alternatives you would choose so as to obtain the maximum tax advantage when claiming relief in respect of the £150,000 loss. You should also state the effect that your proposed treatment will have on the Gift Aid donations paid by the company. *(ACCA)*

C5 Antietam Ltd makes up accounts to 31 March annually. Results for the 12 months to 31 March 2013 are as follows:

	£
Trading profits (before capital allowances)	170,000
Capital allowances	32,000
Rental income	46,000
Chargeable gains	6,400

The company has capital losses brought forward from previous accounting periods of £1,400 and made a Gift Aid donation of £20,000 on 31 March 2013. It also received a dividend from ICI plc on 16 December 2012 of £14,400.

Required:

(a) Calculate the corporation tax liability of Antietam Ltd for the year to 31 March 2013.

(b) Recalculate the liability if you are told that the company has one subsidiary company. *(Amended from AAT)*

***C6** Undulating Uplands Ltd is a UK resident manufacturing company with no associated companies. It had always made up accounts to 30 November but decided to change the year end from November to February. The company's results for the period from 1 December 2011 to 28 February 2013 are as follows:

	Notes	£
Adjusted trading profit		750,000
Dividends received from UK companies	1	45,000
Bank interest received	2,5	13,500
Building society interest received	3,5	8,400
Gift Aid donations	4	16,000
Capital allowances on plant and machinery	8	65,000

The following additional information is available:

1. Dividends were received from UK companies as follows:

	£
30 December 2011	7,200
30 March 2012	10,800
30 September 2012	9,000
30 January 2013	18,000

2. Bank interest was credited by Natland Bank plc as follows:

	£
21 December 2011	4,900
20 June 2012	3,800
21 December 2012	4,800

   Accrued interest was £4,500 on 30 November 2011, £4,300 on 30 November 2012 and £4,000 on 28 February 2013.

3. Building society interest was credited by Northshires Building Society as follows:

	£
31 March 2012	4,000
30 September 2012	4,400

   The account was opened on 1 December 2011 and closed on 30 September 2012.

4. The Gift Aid donations were paid as follows:

	£
15 May 2012	8,000
15 November 2012	8,000

5. The amounts shown for bank and building society interest received are the actual amounts received.

6. The company had trading losses brought forward of £400,000 on 1 December 2011.

7. The company had capital losses brought forward of £15,000 on 1 December 2011.

8. The capital allowances figure of £65,000 comprised:

	£
12 months to 30 November 2012	39,000
3 months to 28 February 2013	26,000

9. In May 2012, the company bought a building for business use. This building cost £450,000. In January 2013, another building was sold for £350,000. This building had been bought in January 2007 for £150,000 and used exclusively for business purposes. An appropriate claim was made to minimise the chargeable gain arising on this disposal. (RPI was 201.6 in January 2007 and 247.2 in January 2013).

You are required:

To calculate the corporation tax liability for the period to 28 February 2013 and to state when this is payable (perform all calculations to the nearest month). *(ACCA)*

***C7** R Ltd is a small company engaged in the manufacture and distribution of plumbing equipment. Following a period of poor trading results, its annual chargeable profit in recent years has been approximately £180,000. Early in 2012 the directors estimated that the chargeable profit for the year to 31 March 2013 would be £220,000.

In March 2012, the directors were considering the possibility of R Ltd acquiring a controlling interest in two other small companies in the same trade - S Ltd and T Ltd. The chargeable profit of each of these companies for the year to 31 March 2013 was estimated at £20,000.

You are required:

To advise the directors of the differing aggregate corporation tax liabilities which will arise for the year to 31 March 2013 if:

(i) the above plan is adopted

(ii) R Ltd acquires the businesses of S Ltd and T Ltd - taking over their assets, trades and workforces, but not acquiring a shareholding. S Ltd and T Ltd would then be wound up. *(CIMA)*

***C8** On 1 August 2009 X Ltd granted a 20-year lease to Y Ltd on the following terms:

- An annual rental of £20,000 which is payable quarterly in advance on 1 August, 1 November, 1 February and 1 May each year.
- A premium of £80,000 payable by Y Ltd on 1 August 2009.

On 1 April 2012, Y Ltd intends sub-letting the premises to Z Ltd on the following terms:

- A term of five years, at the end of which Y Ltd will resume occupancy.
- An annual rental of £28,000, payable in advance each year on 1 April.
- A premium of £45,000 payable by Z Ltd on 1 April 2012.

You are required:

(a) To compute, for the year to 31 March 2010, the amount of property income assessed to corporation tax on X Ltd and the amount of the premium which Y Ltd may deduct in arriving at its trading profits chargeable to corporation tax. Assume that both companies make up accounts annually to 31 March.

(b) To compute the amount of property income assessed to corporation tax on Y Ltd for its year to 31 March 2013.

(c) To comment briefly on the chargeable gains implications of the above transactions.

(CIMA)

***C9** Mr B has been production manager in a large engineering firm for several years, earning approximately £50,000 p.a. He has recently decided to start up his own business and seeks your advice on all of the differences, from a taxation point of view, between trading as a sole trader or as a limited company. It is possible that his wife will become involved in the running of the business.

He has estimated that during the first year, while the business is developing, it is unlikely that any profit will result. Indeed, it is possible that a loss will arise. Thereafter he anticipates that profits will rise rapidly to approximately £70,000 p.a. His living expenses amount to about £20,000 per year and initially this will be provided from his savings.

You are required:

To prepare a list of headings which would be contained in a report designed to highlight these differences. Under each heading, you should give a brief description of the difference between trading as a sole trader or as a company. You are not required to write the complete report. *(CIMA)*

***C10** HD Ltd owns 80% of the ordinary share capital of SD Ltd. These shares were acquired during 1998. Both companies are UK resident for tax purposes and neither has any other associated companies. Their most recent results have been:

	HD Ltd	*SD Ltd*
	y/e 31/12/12	*9 months to 31/3/13*
	£	£
INCOME		
Trading profit	890,000	-
Trading loss	-	(102,000)
Bank interest	6,000	4,000
Property income	2,000	8,000
Chargeable gains	-	20,000
Capital losses brought forward	(15,000)	-
Dividend from SD Ltd	27,000	
Dividends from UK companies		32,000
PAYMENTS		
Gift Aid donations	4,000	5,000
DIVIDEND PAID	327,000	33,750

You are required:

(a) To compute the corporation tax payable by each company for the above accounting periods, assuming that maximum group relief is claimed by HD Ltd.

(b) To suggest a more tax-efficient way in which HD Ltd and SD Ltd might have dealt with the capital gains and losses shown above.

(CIMA)

Part 4

MISCELLANEOUS

Chapter 29

Value added tax (1)

Introduction

This is the first of two chapters concerned with value added tax (VAT). Value added tax is an indirect tax which was introduced in 1973 and which is charged on the supply of a wide variety of goods and services. Current legislation is to be found in the Value Added Tax Act 1994 (VATA 1994), as amended by subsequent Finance Acts.

VAT was administered by HM Customs and Excise until the Inland Revenue and HM Customs and Excise were merged in 2005. The tax is now administered by HM Revenue and Customs (HMRC).

The principle of VAT

The basic principle of VAT is that tax should be charged at each stage of the production and distribution process but that the total tax due should be borne by the final consumer of the product. This is achieved as follows:

(a) Traders who are registered for VAT (see below) are required to charge VAT on their sales and must account for this *output tax* to HMRC, but

(b) such traders are allowed to recover from HMRC the *input tax* which they pay to their own suppliers, so that

(c) in effect, registered traders suffer no VAT and the total VAT is borne by the consumer at the end of the distribution chain.

EXAMPLE 1

QuCo Ltd owns a quarry. It extracts stone from this quarry and sells the stone to SlabCo Ltd for £10,000 plus VAT. SlabCo Ltd converts all the stone into paving slabs and sells these slabs to GarCen Ltd for £18,000, plus VAT. GarCen Ltd owns and runs a garden centre, where the slabs are sold to the general public for a total of £32,000, plus VAT. Show how VAT is charged and collected at each stage of this process, assuming that VAT is to be calculated at 20% throughout.

Solution

	Cost price before VAT	*Input tax*	*Selling price before VAT*	*Output tax*	*Paid to HMRC*
	£	£	£	£	£
QuCo Ltd	-	-	10,000	2,000	2,000
SlabCo Ltd	10,000	2,000	18,000	3,600	1,600
GarCen Ltd	18,000	3,600	32,000	6,400	2,800
Total VAT charged					6,400

Note:

None of the three companies involved suffers any net VAT. In each case, the total of input tax paid to suppliers and the amount due to HMRC is precisely equal to the output tax received from customers. The final consumers, who are unable to reclaim the VAT which they pay, bear the total VAT of £6,400.

Taxable persons

Formally, UK VAT is chargeable when a *taxable supply* of goods or services is made in the UK by a *taxable person* in the course of business. The term "person" can refer to an individual, partnership or company, as well as to any other body which supplies goods or services in the course of business. There is no need for a profit motive to exist, just that goods or services are supplied for a consideration, so the term "person" can also refer to a charity, a club etc. A *taxable person* is a person making taxable supplies who is, or should be, registered for VAT. Persons must register if their turnover of taxable items exceeds a prescribed registration threshold and might register voluntarily even if turnover is below this threshold (see later in this chapter).

A taxable person should charge VAT to customers when making taxable supplies, must account for this output tax to HMRC and may reclaim the tax suffered on inputs. A person who is not a taxable person can neither charge VAT to customers nor reclaim input tax. The main national museums and art galleries are an exception to this general rule, in that they are allowed to reclaim input tax even though they provide free admission to the public and so do not operate a business.

Taxable supplies

A *taxable supply* is any supply of goods or services in the UK other than a supply which is specifically exempted from VAT. VAT is charged on a taxable supply at the standard rate of 20%, unless the supply attracts tax at the reduced rate (5%) or at the zero rate (0%).

The types of supply which are exempt from VAT and the types of supply which are taxable at the reduced rate or the zero rate are listed later in this chapter.

Supply of goods

A supply of goods is deemed to occur when the ownership of goods passes from one person to another. In general, a supply of goods will fall within the scope of VAT only if it is made for a consideration (i.e. in return for money or payment in kind) but the following are also deemed to be supplies of goods for VAT purposes:

(a) gifts of business assets on which input tax has been reclaimed, other than:
   (i) gifts made to any one person in any rolling 12-month period costing in total no more than £50
   (ii) gifts consisting of samples (where a "sample" is a specimen of a product which is intended to promote sales of that product)

(b) goods permanently taken out of a business for private use by the owner or an employee of the business, in respect of which input tax has been reclaimed.

The sale of goods on hire purchase terms is deemed to be a supply of goods but VAT is charged on the cash price of the goods, not the HP price.

Supply of services

Any supply which is made for a consideration but which is not a supply of goods is deemed to be a supply of services. However, a gift of services is not a taxable supply. The hiring of goods to a customer is a supply of services, not a supply of goods, since the ownership of the goods does not pass to the customer. A supply of services is also deemed to occur if the owner or an employee of a business:

(a) temporarily makes private use of goods owned by the business, in respect of which input tax has been reclaimed, or

(b) makes private use of services which have been supplied to the business, in respect of which input tax has been reclaimed.

However, the private use of a business motor car is generally not a taxable supply.

Self-supply

A "self-supply" occurs when a taxable person makes a supply to himself or herself. For example, a self-supply of a motor car occurs if a motor manufacturer produces a car and then uses it instead of supplying it to a customer. The Treasury is empowered to order that, for VAT purposes, self-supplied goods or services are regarded as both:

(a) a taxable supply made *by* the business, and

(b) a taxable supply made *to* the business.

The effect of such an order is that output tax must be accounted for in relation to the supply but that an equal amount of input tax is deemed to have been suffered. This input tax may then be irrecoverable in whole or part (see Chapter 30).

Exempt supplies

A supply of goods or services is an exempt supply if it falls within one of fifteen exemption groups. In summary, these exemption groups are as follows:

Group 1 The sale or lease of land and buildings, *other than*:

(i) the sale (or lease for more than 21 years) of new and certain second-hand buildings for residential or charitable use (zero-rated)

(ii) the sale of new or uncompleted commercial buildings or of land to be used for their construction (standard-rated)

(iii) the grant of gaming or fishing rights; the provision of hotel or holiday accommodation or seasonal caravan and camping pitches; the grant of timber rights; the provision of parking facilities or facilities for the storage or mooring of aircraft, ships etc; the grant of the right to occupy a box or a seat at a theatre, sports ground etc; the letting of sports facilities (all standard-rated)

(iv) any supply which would otherwise be exempt, but in respect of which an election has been made to waive exemption (the "option to tax")

Group 2 Insurance

Group 3 Public postal services provided by the Royal Mail

Group 4 Betting, gaming and lotteries

Group 5 Financial services (e.g. bank charges, stockbroking, underwriting)

Group 6 Education provided by schools, universities and further education colleges

Group 7 Health and welfare services

Group 8 Burial and cremation services

Group 9 Subscriptions to trade unions and professional bodies

Group 10 Sports competition entry fees paid to non-profit making bodies

Group 11 Disposals of works of art to approved bodies (e.g. the National Gallery)

Group 12 Certain fund-raising events organised by charities

Group 13 Cultural services

Group 14 Supplies of goods where input tax cannot be recovered

Group 15 Investment gold

The tax implications of a supply of goods or services being exempt are as follows:

(a) VAT cannot be charged on an exempt supply.

(b) A person who makes only exempt supplies cannot register for VAT, charges no output tax, is not a taxable person and cannot reclaim input tax.

(c) In effect, a person making only exempt supplies is in an identical position with regard to VAT as the final consumer at the end of a distribution chain.

Option to tax

The inability to reclaim input tax when making exempt supplies of land and buildings might lead the supplier to elect for the "option to tax" (see above). If such an election is made, the supplier charges output tax on the supply at the standard rate but may then reclaim input tax. The customer will of course have to pay VAT, but if the customer is also a taxable person then he or she will be able to reclaim the tax paid and therefore may not object to the arrangement.

The option to tax is not available in relation to certain supplies of land and buildings, including buildings intended for residential or charitable use. However, the option would be available in relation to (for example) the sale of a used commercial building.

Reduced rate supplies

A supply of goods or services is charged to VAT at the reduced rate of 5% if it falls within one of eleven reduced-rate groups. These groups are as follows:

Group 1	Fuel and power supplied for domestic or charity use
Group 2	Installation of energy-saving materials
Group 3	Grant-funded installation of heating or security equipment
Group 4	Women's sanitary products
Group 5	Children's car seats and car seat bases
Group 6	Certain residential conversions
Group 7	Certain residential renovations and alterations
Group 8	Contraceptive products (unless exempt from VAT)
Group 9	Certain welfare advice or information supplied by a state-regulated private welfare institution or by a charity (unless exempt from VAT)
Group 10	Installation of mobility aids for the elderly
Group 11	Smoking cessation products

Zero rate supplies

A supply of goods or services is charged to VAT at the zero rate (0%) if it falls within one of sixteen zero-rate groups. These groups are as follows:

Group 1	Food (other than luxury foods and food supplied in the course of catering)
Group 2	Water and sewerage services unless supplied for industrial use
Group 3	Books, newspapers and journals (but stationery is standard-rated)
Group 4	Talking books and wireless sets for the blind and handicapped

Group 5	The sale (or lease for more than 21 years) of new buildings for residential or charitable use and second-hand buildings converted for residential use
Group 6	The sale (or lease for more than 21 years) of protected buildings that have been substantially reconstructed for residential or charitable use
Group 7	Certain categories of international services
Group 8	Passenger transport (but transport in vehicles seating less than 10 people and certain types of pleasure transport are standard-rated)
Group 9	Certain caravans and houseboats
Group 10	Gold supplied by a central bank to another central bank or to a member of the London Gold Market
Group 11	Bank notes
Group 12	Drugs and medicines prescribed by a medical practitioner and certain aids for the handicapped
Group 13	Exports
Group 14	Sales in tax-free shops before 1 July 1999
Group 15	The sale *by* a charity of donated goods and certain supplies made *to* a charity
Group 16	Children's clothing and footwear and protective boots and helmets

The tax implications of a supply of goods or services being zero-rated are as follows:

(a) The supply is a taxable supply but the VAT due is calculated at 0%.

(b) A person who makes only zero-rated supplies is nonetheless making taxable supplies and must register as a taxable person if taxable turnover exceeds the prescribed threshold. Having registered (and this may be done voluntarily if taxable turnover is less than the threshold) the person will then be able to reclaim input tax.

The value of a supply

The *value* of a taxable supply is the amount on which the VAT charge is based and this is normally equal to the price (before VAT) charged for the supply. For example, if a standard-rated supply is made at a price of £1,000 plus VAT at 20%, the value of the supply is £1,000 and the consideration given for the supply is £1,200.

For standard-rated supplies, the VAT component of the consideration can be found by multiplying the consideration by the "VAT fraction". With a standard rate of 20%, this is 20/120 = 1/6th. Note that:

(a) If a supply consists of a gift of business assets, the value of the supply is deemed to be the price (excluding VAT) which the person receiving the gift would have to pay to purchase goods identical in every respect to the goods concerned. This rule also applies if assets are taken permanently out of a business for private use by the owner or an employee of the business.

(b) If the owner or an employee temporarily makes private use of business assets, the value of the resulting supply of services is generally based on the amount by which the assets have depreciated whilst being used for private purposes.

(c) If private use is made of services which have been supplied to the business, the value of the resulting supply of services is equal to an appropriate proportion of the value of the supply which was made to the business.

(d) If the consideration for a supply is paid in kind or if the supply is made to a connected person for less than market value, the value of the supply is taken to be the market value of the goods or services supplied.

EXAMPLE 2

(a) On 1 August 2012, a standard-rated supply is made with a value of £180. Calculate the VAT charged and the consideration for the supply.

(b) On 2 January 2013, a standard-rated supply is made for a consideration of £1,776. Calculate the VAT element and the value of the supply.

Solution

(a) The VAT charged is £36.00 (£180 x 20%) and the total consideration is £216.00.

(b) The VAT element is £296 (£1,776 x 1/6) and the value of the supply is £1,480.

Cash discounts

If a customer is offered a cash discount in return for prompt payment, the value of the supply is the price (before VAT) charged by the supplier, less the maximum cash discount which the customer might receive. This is the case whether or not the customer actually takes advantage of the discount.

Note that the VAT fraction cannot be used to calculate the VAT component of the consideration if a cash discount is offered but not taken.

EXAMPLE 3

A standard-rated supply is made at a price of £4,000, plus VAT. The customer is offered a 3% discount if payment is made within 30 days. Calculate the value of the supply and the VAT charged on the supply, assuming a standard rate of 20%.

Solution

The value of the supply is £3,880 (£4,000, less 3%) and the VAT charged is £776 (£3,880 x 20%). If the customer pays within 30 days, the consideration will be £4,656. If the customer pays after 30 days, the consideration will be £4,776 (£4,000 + £776).

Mixed supplies

A "mixed supply" occurs if a mixture of goods and/or services is invoiced together at a single inclusive price. If all of the items in the mixture are chargeable to VAT at the same rate, the value of the supply and the related output tax can be calculated in the usual way. Otherwise, it is necessary to apportion the price charged between the various elements of the mixture in order to calculate the output tax due.

There is no standard way of achieving this apportionment but the method used must be fair and justifiable.

EXAMPLE 4

A VAT-exclusive price of £320 is charged for a mixed supply of goods. The goods concerned consist of standard-rated goods which cost the supplier £141 (excluding VAT) and zero-rated goods which cost the supplier £19. Calculate the output tax due, assuming a standard rate of 20%.

Solution

From the information given, the only way of apportioning the price of the mixed supply into the standard-rated element and the zero-rated element is to split the price according to the cost of each element to the supplier. On this basis, the value of the supply represented by standard-rated goods is £320 x 141/160 = £282. VAT at 20% of this figure gives £56.40. Therefore the total price charged should be £376.40.

Composite supplies

A "composite supply" occurs if a mixture of goods and/or services is supplied together in such a way that it is not possible to split the supply into its component parts. In this case, the nature of the supply as a whole must be considered in order to determine the rate of tax due (if any). For example, in the case of *Mander Laundries Ltd* (1973) it was held that the services of a launderette consist of a single, standard-rated supply of services, not a mixed supply of water, heat, hire of washing machines etc.

Imports and exports

The VAT treatment of imports and exports depends upon whether the transactions involve goods or services and whether the transactions are between the UK and a country which is not a member of the European Union (EU) or between the UK and another EU member.

A brief summary of this complex area is given below.

Imports of goods to the UK from non-EU countries

VAT is charged on the import of goods from outside the EU at the same rate as if the goods had been supplied in the UK and must be paid by the person to whom the goods are supplied, whether or not that person is a taxable person. Note that:

(a) The VAT on imported goods is normally payable at the point of entry to the UK, but businesses which import goods may defer immediate payment and pay by direct debit once a month. HMRC will usually require a guarantee from an approved bank or insurance company before allowing an importer to defer payments in this way.

(b) For importers who are taxable persons, the VAT due on postal imports with a value not exceeding £2,000 may be deferred until the VAT return is submitted for the tax period which includes the date of importation.

(c) VAT suffered by taxable persons on imported goods may be treated as input tax.

(d) No VAT is charged on any consignment of goods (other than alcohol, tobacco and perfumes) which is imported from outside the EU and which has a value that does not exceed the "low value consignment relief" (LVCR) threshold of £15. As from 1 April 2012, LVCR does not apply to goods sent to the UK from the Channel Islands.

Exports of goods from the UK to non-EU countries

Exports of goods from the UK to non-EU countries are zero-rated.

Goods traded between EU countries

If a registered person in one EU country supplies goods to a registered person in another EU country and the customer's VAT registration number is obtained and shown on the sales invoice, then:

(a) The supply is zero-rated in the country of origin, so the supplier does not have to account for any output tax in relation to the supply.

(b) The customer must account for VAT on the "acquisition" (the term "import" is not used) at whatever rate is applicable to those goods in the destination country.

(c) The VAT suffered by the customer may then be treated as input tax.

If the customer's registration number is not known, or if the customer is not a registered person, the supplier will charge VAT at the rate applicable in the country of origin.

International services

International services are services which are supplied in the UK by an overseas supplier or supplied overseas by a UK supplier. The VAT treatment of international services depends upon the "place of supply" of those services. The general rules relating to the place of supply of international services are as follows:

(a) Business to business (B2B) supplies are taxed at the place where the *customer* is established. Furthermore, it is the responsibility of the customer (not the supplier) to account for any output tax relating to such supplies. This is known as the "reverse charge" procedure.

(b) Business to consumer (B2C) supplies are taxed at the place where the *supplier* is established. For this purpose, a "consumer" is either a person who receives a supply of services wholly for private purposes, or a charity, government department etc. that has no business activities.

The main effects of these rules are as follows:

(a) If a UK business supplies services to a business customer located in an EU member state (but outside the UK) the supply is subject to the VAT rules of that member state and is outside the scope of UK VAT. If the customer is located outside the EU, the supply is outside the scope of VAT altogether.

(b) If a UK business supplies services to a non-business customer located overseas, the supply is subject to the normal UK rules (as if the customer had been in the UK).

(c) If a UK business *receives* services from overseas, the UK business must operate the reverse charge procedure and account for output tax at the appropriate rate for the services concerned. The VAT suffered by taxable persons as a result of this procedure is then treated as input tax. Input tax is generally recoverable, but certain classes of input tax are irrecoverable (see Chapter 30).

Reverse charge procedure within the UK

A reverse charge procedure similar to the one described above in relation to international services applies to certain supplies made within the UK. This procedure applies when a supply of *mobile telephones or computer chips* with a total value of £5,000 or more (supplied together and on a single invoice) is made within the UK to a VAT-registered person. Under this procedure, it is the responsibility of the purchaser (not the seller) to account to HMRC for the output tax due on the supply. The VAT suffered by the purchaser as a result of the reverse charge procedure may then be treated as input tax.

The aim of this procedure is to deal with so-called "missing trader" fraud, whereby VAT is charged on a supply but the supplier fails to account for this tax to HMRC and then cannot be traced. This type of fraud is commonly associated with the supply of mobile telephones and computer chips. The reverse charge procedure also applies to the supply of emissions allowances (or "carbon credits").

Registration

The total value of the taxable supplies made by a person is known as that person's *taxable turnover*. A person whose taxable turnover in a 12-month period exceeds the registration threshold (£77,000 from 1 April 2012) must register with HMRC. Online registration is mandatory as from 31 October 2012. A person who registers is issued a VAT registration number which must then be quoted on that person's tax invoices (see next chapter).

A person who is liable to register but who fails to do so is still a taxable person and is personally responsible for the output tax due in relation to supplies made since the date on which registration should have occurred.

When deciding whether or not the registration threshold has been exceeded, it is necessary to aggregate the taxable turnover from all of a person's business activities. The registration relates to the person, *not* to an individual business. It is important to bear in mind the definition of the word "person" for VAT purposes (see above) and to aggregate taxable supplies only if they are made by the same person.

EXAMPLE 5

(a) Jim is a sole trader with a taxable turnover of £65,000 per annum. Is he required to register with HMRC?

(b) Pearl and Dean are in partnership, operating a business with a taxable turnover of £85,000 per annum. Is anyone required to register?

(c) Julia is a sole trader with a taxable turnover of £50,000 per annum. She is also in partnership with Julie, operating a business with a taxable turnover of £70,000 per annum and sharing profits equally. Is anyone required to register?

Solution

(a) No. Jim's taxable turnover does not exceed the registration threshold.

(b) Yes. The partnership of Pearl and Dean is one "person" for VAT purposes and has a taxable turnover exceeding the registration threshold. Therefore the partnership must register.

(c) No. Julia as a sole trader is one person, whilst the partnership of Julia and Julie is another, quite separate, "person". Neither of these persons has a taxable turnover exceeding the registration threshold so neither of them is required to register.

Business splitting

"Business splitting" or "disaggregation" occurs when a business with a taxable turnover exceeding the registration threshold is divided into two or more smaller businesses, each operated by a different person and each with a taxable turnover not exceeding the registration threshold, in the hope of avoiding registration.

If this type of manoeuvre were successful, supplies could be made to customers without charging VAT and the administrative costs associated with making VAT returns and maintaining VAT records (see next chapter) could be avoided. The only disadvantage would be that input tax could not be reclaimed but in the case of a business with mainly exempt or zero-rated inputs this disadvantage would be slight.

However, if a business has been split artificially, HMRC may direct that the persons conducting the split businesses should be treated as a single taxable person for VAT purposes. In fact, this direction may be made even if the split businesses have never been operated as a single unit, so long as HMRC is satisfied that only one business really exists.

When to register

A person is required to register for VAT if, at the end of any calendar month, the value of that person's taxable supplies for the year ended on the last day of the month exceeds the registration threshold (£77,000 as from 1 April 2012). If the person has been making taxable supplies for less than twelve months, registration is required if the value of taxable supplies made to date is greater than the registration threshold. HMRC must be notified within 30 days of the end of the relevant month. Registration will then usually take effect after the end of the month following the relevant month. However, registration is not required if HMRC is satisfied that the person's taxable turnover for the following twelve months will not exceed the deregistration threshold (£75,000 as from 1 April 2012).

Registration is also required if there are reasonable grounds for believing that taxable turnover during the next 30 days alone will exceed the registration threshold. In this case, HMRC must be notified by the end of the 30-day period and registration will take effect from the beginning of that period.

For the purpose of deciding whether the registration threshold has been or will be exceeded, supplies consisting of the capital assets of the business are excluded from taxable turnover. However, such supplies normally receive no special treatment, so that the sale of a non-current asset will be a taxable supply unless the asset falls into one of the exemption groups.

EXAMPLE 6

Kevin begins trading on 1 January 2011. Taxable turnover during the first two years of trading is as follows:

2011	£	*2012*	£
January	1,800	January	6,800
February	2,100	February	5,400
March	2,800	March	5,900
April	2,600	April	7,400
May	2,400	May	7,900
June	2,900	June	7,700
July	3,300	July	8,000
August	3,500	August	7,900
September	4,200	September	7,800
October	5,500	October	8,100
November	6,900	November	8,300
December	6,200	December	9,700

The turnover in January 2012 includes £2,000 relating to the sale of machinery previously used in the trade. The VAT registration threshold was £70,000 until 1 April 2011 and £73,000 until 1 April 2012. State the date on which Kevin must register for VAT.

Solution

At the end of each month, cumulative taxable turnover during the previous 12 months (or since the start of trade, if less) are as follows:

2011	£	*2012*	£
January	1,800	January	47,200
February	3,900	February	50,500
March	6,700	March	53,600
April	9,300	April	58,400
May	11,700	May	63,900
June	14,600	June	68,700
July	17,900	July	73,400
August	21,400	August	77,800
September	25,600	September	81,400
October	31,100	October	84,000
November	38,000	November	85,400
December	44,200	December	88,900

The cumulative figure at the end of January 2012 is turnover for the months of February 2011 to January 2012 inclusive, less the £2,000 relating to the sale of a capital asset.

The registration threshold is passed at the end of August 2012. Kevin must notify HMRC by 30 September 2012 and registration will probably take effect as from 1 October 2012.

Transfer of a business to an unregistered person

If a taxable person transfers a business as a going concern to a person who is not registered for VAT, supplies made by the business before the transfer date are deemed (for the purpose of deciding whether or not the transferee should register) to have been made by the transferee. So if the transferred business, together with any other business operated by the transferee, had a taxable turnover exceeding the registration threshold in the 12 months prior to the transfer, the transferee must register for VAT immediately.

Voluntary registration

A person making taxable supplies which do not exceed the registration threshold may nonetheless register for VAT voluntarily. This enables the person concerned to recover input tax but means that output tax must be charged when taxable supplies are made to customers. However, if the supplies are mainly zero-rated, or consist of standard-rate or reduced-rate supplies made wholly or mainly to customers who are themselves taxable persons, the fact that output tax must be charged will probably not deter customers.

Being registered for VAT will add to the administrative costs of running the business but this factor may be outweighed by the benefit of being able to recover input tax.

EXAMPLE 7

Lindsey is not registered for VAT. In the year to 31 March 2013, she has inputs costing £10,000 plus VAT at 20%. Her outputs total £35,000.

(a) How much profit does she make for the year?

(b) If she had registered for VAT voluntarily, how much profit would she have made?

(c) Does it matter whether the supplies that she makes are all:

- (i) zero-rated?
- (ii) standard-rated supplies made to VAT-registered businesses?
- (iii) standard-rated supplies made to the general public?

Solution

(a) Her profit is £23,000 (£35,000 – £12,000).

(b) If she had registered for VAT (and outputs had remained at £35,000) she would have been able to reclaim her input tax, giving a profit of £25,000 (£35,000 – £10,000).

(c) (i) If she makes only zero-rated supplies, voluntary registration has no effect on her selling prices and, therefore, no effect on her sales.

- (ii) If she makes only standard-rated supplies to VAT-registered businesses, her prices will increase by 20% but her customers will be able to reclaim the extra tax paid and so there should be no effect on her sales.
- (iii) If she makes only standard-rated supplies to the general public, increasing her prices may entail a loss of custom and she may prefer not to register.

Exemption from registration

HMRC may grant exemption from registration to a person making supplies which exceed the registration threshold, so long as these supplies are all zero-rated. An application for exemption might be made if the amount of input tax which could be reclaimed if the person were registered is small in comparison with the increased administrative costs associated with VAT registration.

Pre-registration input tax

VAT incurred before registration is not input tax. Nonetheless, it can be treated as input tax so long as certain conditions are satisfied. These conditions vary according to whether the VAT is incurred on a supply of goods or a supply of services:

(a) **Goods**. VAT suffered on a pre-registration supply of goods may be treated as input tax so long as the goods were supplied to the taxable person for business purposes within the four years prior to the date of registration and were not sold or consumed before that date.

(b) **Services**. VAT suffered on a pre-registration supply of services may be treated as input tax so long as the services were supplied to the taxable person for business purposes no more than six months before the date of registration.

Group registration

A group of associated companies (see Chapter 28) may apply for the group to be registered as a single taxable person, rather than each company in the group being registered individually. Group registration has the following consequences:

(a) The input tax suffered by the group as a whole is set against the output tax charged by the group as a whole.

(b) One of the group companies is nominated as the "representative member" and takes responsibility for submitting VAT returns and accounting for VAT on behalf of the entire group. However, any other company in the group can be held liable if the representative member fails to pay the VAT which is due.

(c) Supplies between group members are not regarded as taxable supplies and are ignored for VAT purposes.

Individual group companies may register separately and choose not to join the VAT group. This may improve the cash flow position of a company with mainly zero-rated supplies which makes monthly VAT returns (see next chapter). It is also possible for a group of associated companies to form two or more VAT groups, with some of the companies belonging to one VAT group and some belonging to another.

Group registration offers tax avoidance opportunities in certain cases and HMRC may remove a company from a VAT group if avoidance is suspected.

Deregistration

Deregistration may be either voluntary or compulsory:

(a) A registered person may deregister voluntarily if HMRC is satisfied that taxable turnover, excluding supplies of capital assets, will not exceed the deregistration threshold (£75,000 from 1 April 2012) in the next 12 months.

(b) Compulsory deregistration is triggered when a registered person entirely ceases to make taxable supplies. The person must notify HMRC within 30 days that this has occurred and deregistration will normally take effect as from the date on which taxable supplies ceased.

(c) Deregistration is also compulsory on a change of legal status (e.g. when a sole trader admits a partner or when the business of a partnership is taken over by a company).

On deregistration, the person concerned is deemed to make a supply of all the tangible assets of the business and output tax is charged accordingly. However, assets on which no input tax was reclaimed are excluded from this deemed supply and the output tax due is not collected if it does not exceed £1,000 in total. The deemed supply does *not* take place if the business is sold as a going concern to another taxable person.

Summary

- VAT is chargeable when a taxable person makes a taxable supply of either goods or services in the course of business.
- A taxable supply is any supply of goods or services other than an exempt supply and may be charged to value added tax at either the standard rate, the reduced rate or the zero rate.
- A taxable person is a person who makes taxable supplies and who is (or should be) registered for VAT. A taxable person may be an individual, a partnership, a company, a charity, a club or an association.
- A person making taxable supplies which exceed the registration threshold must register with HM Revenue and Customs. A person making taxable supplies which do not exceed the threshold may register voluntarily.
- A taxable person must account to HM Revenue and Customs for the output tax charged to customers but may recover the input tax charged by suppliers.
- A person making only exempt supplies cannot charge VAT to customers and is unable to recover input tax.

Exercises

29.1 Classify each of the following supplies as either taxable at the standard rate, taxable at the reduced rate, taxable at the zero rate or exempt:

(a) a theatre ticket
(b) a loaf of bread
(c) bank charges
(d) electricity supplied for business use
(e) a taxi ride
(f) a taxation textbook
(g) gas supplied for domestic use
(h) a subscription to a professional body
(i) an insurance premium
(j) a new commercial building
(k) a meal in a restaurant
(l) a train ticket
(m) exports to a non-EU country
(n) writing paper.

29.2 A standard-rated supply is made in May 2012 at a price of £340, plus VAT. Calculate the VAT chargeable and the consideration for the supply if:

(a) no discount is offered
(b) a 2% discount is offered for prompt payment and the customer takes advantage of this discount
(c) a 2% discount is offered for prompt payment but the customer decides not to take advantage of this discount.

29.3 In each of the following cases, is anyone required to register with HM Revenue and Customs? If so, who?

(a) Lorna is a sole trader, making taxable supplies of £85,000 per annum.
(b) Mike owns two distinct businesses. One has a taxable turnover of £40,000 per annum and the other has a taxable turnover of £50,000 per annum.
(c) Pat and Phil are in partnership. Their taxable turnover is £60,000 per annum. Phil also owns another business with a taxable turnover of £45,000 per annum.
(d) SmiCo Ltd has a taxable turnover of £250,000 per annum. The company's shares are owned entirely by John Smith and his wife.

29.4 Rosemary owns a business which has an annual turnover (excluding any VAT) of £80,000. Describe her VAT position if:

(a) she makes wholly exempt supplies
(b) she makes wholly standard-rated supplies
(c) she makes wholly zero-rated supplies.

29.5 Explain the VAT consequences of making a "self-supply".

***29.6** Answer the following questions:

(a) who should register for VAT?

(b) when should registration occur?

(c) what are the consequences of failing to register?

(d) when may a taxable person deregister?

(e) why might someone choose to register voluntarily?

***29.7** Sanjay began trading on 1 February 2012, selling standard-rated goods and services. He decided not to register for VAT voluntarily. His turnover (excluding VAT) for the first 16 months of trading was as follows:

2012	£	**2013**	£
February	2,550	January	8,080
March	3,660	February	7,920
April	3,880	March	6,780
May	4,240	April	5,100
June	4,860	May	4,890
July	5,290		
August	5,430		
September	6,320		
October	7,410		
November	8,050		
December	9,270		

In January 2013, he sold a machine (which had been used as a non-current asset) for £800. This is *not* included in the above turnover figures.

Sanjay is worried that his monthly turnover has started to fall and he is considering offering customer discounts in an attempt to reverse this trend.

Required:

(a) Explain the term "taxable person" for VAT purposes.

(b) State the circumstances in which VAT registration is compulsory and explain why some persons may choose to register voluntarily.

(c) State the date by which Sanjay would be required to register for VAT. Would registration be necessary if his monthly turnover for the remainder of 2013 seemed likely to continue on a downward trend?

(d) Explain the VAT consequences which would ensue if Sanjay began offering trade discounts or cash discounts to his customers.

(CIPFA)

Chapter 30

Value added tax (2)

Introduction

The previous chapter outlined the main principles of value added tax and explained the processes of registration and deregistration. This chapter is concerned with the procedures used to account for VAT to HMRC and the way in which the tax is administered. Other matters considered in this chapter include non-recoverable input tax, the VAT position of persons who make both taxable and exempt supplies and a number of schemes which exist in order to simplify the workings of the VAT system.

Accounting for VAT

At regular intervals (usually quarterly) registered persons must submit a VAT return to HMRC, showing input tax and output tax for the period covered by the return. Any excess of output tax over input tax is payable to HMRC. Any excess of input tax over output tax is repayable by HMRC. Note that:

(a) A VAT return must be submitted within one month of the end of the "tax period" to which it relates, together with any tax due. Online filing and electronic payment are mandatory for all businesses as from 1 April 2012.

(b) A registered person making supplies which are wholly or mainly zero-rated will be entitled to a VAT repayment in most tax periods. Such a person may opt to submit VAT returns monthly rather than quarterly, so speeding up tax repayments at the expense of making twelve returns per year rather than four.

Payments on account

A registered person who makes quarterly returns and whose annual VAT liability exceeds £2.3 million is obliged to make payments on account to HMRC. The first payment is due one month before the end of the quarter and a second payment is due at the end of the quarter. A balancing payment is made one month after the end of the quarter. All of these payments must be made electronically.

Each of the two payments on account is usually calculated as 1/24th of the total VAT liability for the previous year. However, the business may choose to pay its actual VAT liability for each month rather than the set POAs.

The tax point

The date on which a supply is deemed to occur is known as the "tax point" of that supply. The tax point of a supply determines:

(a) for outputs, the tax period in which the tax on that supply must be accounted for

(b) for inputs, the tax period in which the tax on that supply may be reclaimed

(c) the rate of VAT applicable to the supply (if VAT rates change).

For a supply of goods the "basic tax point" is the date on which the goods are removed or made available to the customer. For a supply of services the basic tax point is the date on which the services are performed. However, the actual tax point of a supply will differ from the basic tax point in the following circumstances:

(a) If the supplier issues a tax invoice or receives payment on a date which is earlier than the basic tax point, then the actual tax point is the date on which the invoice is issued or payment is received, whichever occurs first.

(b) Otherwise, if the supplier issues a tax invoice within 14 days after the basic tax point, then the invoice date becomes the actual tax point.

HMRC may extend the 14-day rule mentioned above if asked to do so by a registered person who is genuinely unable to issue invoices within 14 days of the basic tax point. This may occur if customer invoice prices cannot be determined until the business has received suppliers' invoices for materials etc.

Tax invoices

If a taxable person makes a taxable supply to another taxable person, a "tax invoice" must be issued. The main purpose of this invoice is to provide documentary evidence of the transaction, so allowing the person receiving the supply to reclaim the input tax related to that supply. The required contents of a valid tax invoice (which may be on paper or issued electronically) are:

(a) the invoice number, date and tax point

(b) the name, address and VAT registration number of the supplier

(c) the name and address of the customer

(d) for each invoice item, a description of the goods or services supplied

(e) for each description, the quantity of the goods or the extent of the services, the unit price, the amount payable (before VAT) and the rate of VAT applicable.

(f) the total amount due, before VAT

(g) the rate of any cash discount available

(h) the total amount of VAT chargeable.

The issue of a tax invoice is optional if a supply is made to a customer who is not a taxable person. Retailers are not required to issue a tax invoice unless asked for one by the customer and may then issue a less detailed tax invoice if the consideration for the supply does not exceed £250. A less detailed tax invoice need show only:

(a) the name, address and VAT registration number of the retailer

(b) the tax point

(c) a description of the goods or services supplied

(d) the total amount payable by the customer, including VAT

(e) for each rate of VAT chargeable, the gross amount payable (including VAT) and the rate of tax which is applicable.

Note that some minor changes will be made to the VAT invoicing rules as from 1 January 2013 so as to implement changes required by the EU Invoicing Directive.

Accounting records

Every taxable person must keep such records as are required by HMRC. The main records which must be kept are as follows:

(a) business and accounting records (including orders, delivery notes, business correspondence, purchases and sales books, cashbooks and other account books, till rolls, bank statements, paying-in slips and annual accounts)

(b) a VAT account

(c) a copy of each tax invoice issued

(d) all tax invoices received (although tax invoices are not required for payments of £25 or less relating to telephone calls, car park charges, toll charges or purchases made through coin-operated machines)

(e) documentation relating to imports and exports.

HMRC may also specify additional record-keeping requirements for all businesses of a particular description and (in cases where additional records might assist in identifying supplies on which VAT might otherwise go unpaid) for individual businesses.

All records must be retained for a period of six years or for such lesser period as HMRC may allow. HMRC is empowered to require a taxable person to provide their VAT records for inspection and is also empowered to inspect these records at the business premises.

Special schemes

The VAT system offers a number of special schemes which are intended to simplify the workings of the VAT system, especially for smaller businesses. The main schemes are as follows:

(a) the cash accounting scheme

(b) the annual accounting scheme

(c) the flat-rate scheme for small businesses

(d) the flat-rate scheme for farmers

(e) the margin scheme for second-hand goods.

Each of these schemes is explained below. There are also several special schemes for use only by retailers. The "retail schemes" are briefly considered later in this chapter.

Cash accounting scheme

A registered person whose taxable turnover is not expected to exceed £1,350,000 in the next 12 months may opt to join the cash accounting scheme. Those who join this scheme account for output tax in the tax period in which *payment is received* from the customer and reclaim input tax in the tax period in which *payment is made* to the supplier. The tax point is ignored when allocating inputs and outputs to tax periods.

Joining this scheme allows a registered person to delay the payment of output tax to HMRC until the tax has actually been received from customers, which is beneficial if customers are given extended credit. The scheme also provides automatic relief for bad debts. On the other hand, input tax cannot be reclaimed until the tax has actually been paid to suppliers. A person may not join the cash accounting scheme unless:

(a) the person's taxable turnover (excluding sales of capital items) is not expected to exceed £1,350,000 in the next 12 months

(b) the person's VAT returns are up to date

(c) all amounts due to be paid to HMRC have in fact been paid, or the person has come to an arrangement for such payments to be made

(d) within the previous 12 months, the person has not been convicted of a VAT offence or assessed to a penalty for VAT evasion involving dishonest conduct.

A person who belongs to the cash accounting scheme must withdraw from the scheme at the end of a tax period if taxable turnover for the 12 months to date has exceeded £1,600,000. HMRC will allow such a person to remain in the scheme only if it can be demonstrated that the high turnover is not expected to recur and that taxable turnover for the next 12 months is expected to be no more than £1,350,000.

The cash accounting scheme cannot be used for supplies of goods and services which are invoiced before the supply is made or for supplies where payment is not due for more than six months after the date of the invoice.

Annual accounting scheme

A person with a taxable turnover which is not expected to exceed £1,350,000 in the next 12 months may apply to join the annual accounting scheme and submit only one VAT return per year. The scheme operates as follows:

(a) During the year the person makes nine interim payments to HMRC, each equal to 10% of the VAT liability for the previous year. These payments must be made by direct debit or by other electronic means and begin in the fourth month of the year.

(b) Optionally, the person may choose to make three interim payments in months four, seven and ten rather than the nine payments referred to above. In this case, each payment is equal to 25% of the VAT liability for the previous year.

(c) If a person joins the annual accounting scheme when first registering for VAT (or less than 12 months after registration), the interim payments are based initially upon the person's expected VAT liability for the year.

(d) At the end of the year the annual return is submitted together with a final payment consisting of the balance of the VAT liability. The return and payment must be made within two months of the end of the year.

(e) A person who operates the annual accounting scheme must withdraw from the scheme if taxable turnover exceeds £1,600,000 for the previous year.

The advantages of the scheme include a reduction in the number of VAT returns each year (from four to one) and more predictable cash flows. There is also an extra month at the end of the year in which to complete the annual return and to pay any VAT which is due.

Flat-rate scheme for small businesses

An eligible business which is registered for VAT may opt to join the flat-rate scheme (FRS) for small businesses. This scheme enables a small business to calculate its VAT liability as a flat-rate percentage of total turnover and so avoids the need to keep detailed records of input tax and output tax. The FRS operates as follows:

(a) Output tax is charged to customers at the normal rate for the supply. Similarly, input tax is paid to suppliers at the normal rate. But the output tax charged to customers is not paid over to HMRC and (in general) input tax cannot be recovered.

(b) In each tax period, a flat-rate percentage is applied to the VAT-inclusive turnover for the period (including the value of any exempt supplies). The result of this calculation is the amount of VAT payable to HMRC for the period.

(c) The applicable flat-rate percentage depends upon the trade sector in which the business operates. With a standard rate of 20%, the flat-rate percentage currently ranges from 4% to 14.5%.

(d) Input tax on the purchase of capital assets costing at least £2,000 (including VAT) can be reclaimed in the usual way, in which case output tax must be accounted for in the usual way on the eventual disposal of the asset.

(e) The FRS can be used in conjunction with the annual accounting scheme. It *cannot* be used in conjunction with the cash accounting scheme or a retail scheme (see later in this chapter). However, the FRS offers an optional cash-based turnover method and an optional retailer's turnover method.

The FRS is available to businesses with a taxable turnover which is not expected to exceed £150,000 in the next 12 months. A business must leave the FRS if its VAT-inclusive income exceeds £230,000 during any 12-month period ending on an anniversary of the date that it joined the scheme.

Flat-rate scheme for farmers (Agricultural flat-rate scheme)

In general, a farmer making taxable supplies which exceed the registration threshold is liable to register for VAT in the normal way. Similarly, a farmer whose taxable supplies are below the threshold may register voluntarily. Since farmers make mainly zero-rated supplies, a farmer who is registered will usually receive regular repayments of input tax, at the expense of maintaining the necessary VAT records.

An alternative to registration is the flat-rate scheme for farmers. This scheme is available to farmers regardless of the size of their taxable turnover and is intended to reduce administrative costs. The scheme operates as follows:

(a) A farmer who joins the scheme does not register for VAT. This reduces administrative costs but deprives the farmer of the opportunity to reclaim input tax.

(b) In compensation, the farmer is allowed to add a flat-rate 4% to his or her selling prices and to retain this addition. The flat-rate addition may be charged only when selling designated goods or services to VAT-registered persons.

(c) From the point of view of a taxable person buying goods from a flat-rate farmer, the flat-rate addition is treated as input tax and may be reclaimed, subject to the usual rules and restrictions (see later in this chapter).

A farmer may not join this scheme if the total of the flat-rate additions which would be charged if the farmer were a member of the scheme exceeds the total amount of input tax which the farmer would otherwise be entitled to reclaim by £3,000 per annum or more.

Margin scheme for second-hand goods

In general, VAT is charged on the full value of goods sold, regardless of whether those goods are new or second-hand. However, subject to certain conditions, a taxable person selling second-hand goods may choose to sell them through the margin scheme and charge VAT only on his or her profit margin. The scheme operates as follows:

(a) Output tax is charged only on the seller's profit margin. This is the difference between the price at which the goods were obtained and their selling price. No output tax is charged to the customer unless the goods are sold at a profit.
(b) The seller's profit margin is deemed to be VAT-inclusive, so that the amount of tax due is calculated by multiplying this margin by the VAT fraction. Expenses incurred by the seller (e.g. the costs of restoration, repairs and spare parts) are ignored when establishing the amount of the profit margin.
(c) The buyer of the goods cannot reclaim the input tax suffered, even if he or she is a taxable person.

The main conditions which must be satisfied for the margin scheme to be used are that the goods concerned are second-hand and that they were acquired either on a supply on which no VAT was chargeable (e.g. from a member of the public) or from someone who also sold the goods under the margin scheme. The sales invoice must include an indication that the margin scheme has been applied.

EXAMPLE 1

An antiques dealer buys a table from a member of the public for £2,000. The dealer spends a further £750 on restoration work and then sells the table for £5,000. Compute the output tax which must be accounted for in relation to this sale, assuming that the table is sold through the margin scheme and that the sale occurs in December 2012.

Solution

The dealer's margin is £3,000, ignoring restoration costs. The output tax due is therefore £3,000 x 1/6 = £500.

Retail schemes

Retailers are those who supply goods and services directly to the public. A retailer's sales will often consist of a very large number of relatively small transactions and in these circumstances it would sometimes be difficult and expensive to keep detailed records of each transaction for VAT purposes. In response to this problem, retail schemes have been devised which enable retailers to calculate their output tax in a fairly straightforward way. The standard retail schemes are as follows:

(a) point of sale scheme
(b) apportionment scheme 1
(c) apportionment scheme 2
(d) direct calculation scheme 1
(e) direct calculation scheme 2.

Full information on the detailed workings of the standard schemes is given on the website which accompanies this book. The website address is www.pearsoned.co.uk/melville.

Retailers with an annual taxable turnover exceeding £130 million cannot use any of these standard schemes. If such retailers wish to use a retail scheme they must negotiate an individual "bespoke retail scheme" with HMRC.

It should be noted that the growing use of information technology by large retailers and by many small retailers means that it is now much easier to record individual sales than it was when VAT was introduced in 1973. This means that the original rationale for the retail schemes has been diminished over the years. Accordingly, retailers may not use any of these schemes unless permitted to do so. HMRC permission will be granted only if a retailer cannot reasonably be expected to account for VAT in the normal way, so that the use of a retail scheme is strictly necessary.

Bad debts

If a taxable person uses the cash accounting scheme, the output tax relating to a supply is not accounted for until the consideration for that supply has been received and so automatic relief is given for bad debts. But persons who do not use the cash accounting scheme might account for the output tax relating to a supply before the consideration for that supply is received and then find that a bad debt has occurred. In these circumstances, a claim may be made for a refund of the VAT lost, so long as:

(a) goods or services have been supplied for a consideration and the related output tax has been accounted for to HMRC

(b) the value of the supply was no more than its open market value

(c) the debt has been written off in the books of account

(d) at least six months have elapsed since both the date of the supply and the date that payment was due

(e) the claim for bad debt relief is made within four years and six months from the later of the date of the supply and the date that payment was due.

A business that recovers input tax relating to a supply, but does not pay the supplier within six months of the date of supply or the date that payment was due (if later) must repay the input tax to HMRC, whether or not the supplier makes a claim for bad debt relief.

As a further simplification, a business which was de minimis for the previous year may treat itself as provisionally de minimis for each VAT period in the current year and review its de minimis status only at the end of the current year. This simplification does not apply to businesses which expect to incur more than £1 million of input tax in the current year.

EXAMPLE 3

(a) During the quarter to 31 August 2012, Justin makes taxable supplies of £30,000 and exempt supplies of £20,000. Input tax incurred is £1,500. Does he pass either of the two simplified de minimis tests for the quarter?

(b) During the year to 31 March 2013, Margaret makes taxable supplies of £140,000 and exempt supplies of £60,000. Input tax incurred is £27,600, of which £22,800 is directly attributable to taxable supplies. Does she pass either of the two simplified de minimis tests for the year?

Solution

(a) Input tax averages £500 per month and exempt supplies are 40% of total supplies. Therefore Justin passes the first test and may provisionally reclaim all of his input tax for the quarter.

(b) Input tax averages £2,300 per month and so Margaret fails the first test. But total input tax less input tax directly attributable to taxable supplies averages only £400 per month and exempt supplies are 30% of total supplies. Therefore Margaret passes the second test and may reclaim all of her input tax for the year.

Administration of VAT

Overall responsibility for administration of the VAT system lies with the Commissioners for Revenue and Customs. VAT registration and the collection of VAT are dealt with by the VAT Central Unit. The main functions of this unit are:

(a) to maintain registration records

(b) to process VAT returns

(c) to collect the VAT due from registered persons and to make repayments of tax where necessary.

There is also a network of local offices throughout the UK which deal with local VAT administration matters. HMRC officials from these offices may visit the business premises of registered persons in their area to check the accuracy of VAT returns and to ensure that the VAT system is being operated correctly.

VAT assessments

VAT is largely a self-assessed tax and so it is not normally necessary to raise formal VAT assessments. But HMRC may issue such an assessment if a taxable person has failed to make a VAT return or has made a return which is incorrect or incomplete.

VAT assessments cannot usually be raised any later than four years after the end of the tax period to which they relate, but this time limit is extended to twenty years if the taxable person has behaved dishonestly or fraudulently. Any claim for a refund of overpaid VAT must also be made within four years in most cases.

Appeals

A person who disagrees with an "appealable" VAT decision made by HMRC may ask for the decision to be internally reviewed. The person concerned also has the right of appeal to a tribunal. Appeals are permitted in relation to most VAT matters, but certain matters cannot be the subject of an appeal.

The internal review process and the appeals system are very similar to their direct tax counterparts (see Chapter 1). In summary:

(a) A request that an appealable HMRC decision should be reviewed must normally be made in writing within 30 days of the date of the decision. A request may be accepted later than this if the person concerned has a reasonable excuse for failing to meet the 30-day time limit.

(b) An internal review is carried out by an HMRC officer who has not previously been involved with the decision in question. The review is normally completed within 45 days. The review officer then writes to the person concerned to inform him or her of the review's conclusions.

(c) If no internal review is requested, an appeal to a tribunal may be made within 30 days of the date of the original decision. Otherwise, an appeal to a tribunal may be made within 30 days of the date of the review conclusion letter.

(d) Most VAT appeals are dealt with by the Tax Chamber of the First-tier Tribunal. The Finance and Tax Chamber of the Upper Tribunal hears appeals against decisions made by the First-tier Tribunal.

(e) If either HMRC or the person concerned is dissatisfied with a decision made by the Upper Tribunal, a dispute on a point of law may be referred to the Court of Appeal.

Avoidance schemes

Businesses with a taxable turnover exceeding £600,000 are required to notify HMRC if they make use of certain designated VAT avoidance schemes which are listed on a statutory register. Similarly, businesses with a taxable turnover exceeding £10 million are required to notify HMRC if they make use of schemes which bear certain hallmarks of VAT avoidance.

Penalties, surcharges and interest

The main penalties which may be imposed in relation to VAT are as follows:

(a) **Criminal fraud**. A person who attempts to evade VAT in such a way that his or her conduct amounts to criminal fraud may, on a summary conviction obtained before a magistrate, be imprisoned for up to six months. The person may also be liable to pay a fine of up to £5,000 (the "statutory maximum") or three times the amount of tax evaded, whichever is the greater. If the conviction is on indictment, the person may be imprisoned for up to seven years and there is no limit to the size of any fine.

(b) **Failure to notify**. A taxable person who fails to notify HMRC of his or her liability to register, or makes late notification, is liable to a penalty. This penalty is assessed in accordance with a penalty regime which applies to any failure to notify HMRC of a taxable activity. This penalty regime is not confined to VAT but covers a range of direct and indirect taxes.

Under this regime, the penalty for a failure to notify liability to register is calculated as a percentage of the "potential lost revenue". This is the amount of VAT for which the taxable person is liable between the date on which registration should have taken place and the date on which registration actually takes place. The percentage varies between 30% and 100%, depending upon the degree of culpability of the person in question but may be reduced if the person voluntarily discloses the failure to notify. (See Chapter 15 for further details).

(c) **Incorrect VAT returns**. A taxable person who submits an incorrect VAT return is liable to pay a penalty. This penalty is assessed in accordance with a penalty regime which applies to the submission of incorrect tax returns generally and which covers a wide range of taxes. Under this regime, a penalty may be charged if an incorrect VAT return leads to an understatement of the amount of tax due and the inaccuracy was either careless or deliberate. A penalty may also be charged if a VAT assessment issued by HMRC understates the amount of tax due and the taxable person fails to take reasonable steps to inform HMRC of this fact within 30 days.

The amount of any penalty imposed depends upon the person's degree of culpability and will usually vary between 30% and 100% of the additional tax which is payable as a result of correcting the inaccuracy or the understatement. But these penalties are substantially reduced if the taxable person voluntarily discloses the inaccuracy or the failure to inform HMRC of an under-assessment.
(See Chapter 15 for further details).

(d) **Default surcharge**. A "default" occurs if a taxable person submits a late VAT return and/or makes a late payment of VAT. In these circumstances, HMRC will usually issue a surcharge liability notice specifying a surcharge period running for 12 months from the end of the tax period concerned. If a further default is made within this period, then:

- the surcharge period is extended to the first anniversary of the tax period to which the new default relates, and
- if the new default has resulted in any VAT not being paid on time, a default surcharge will be levied, calculated as the greater of £30 and a percentage of the tax paid late. The surcharge percentage is 2% for the first default within the surcharge period, 5% for the second default, 10% for the third default and 15% for the fourth and any subsequent default. However, surcharges are not imposed at the 2% or 5% rate for an amount of less than £400.

A surcharge period comes to an end only when no defaults have occurred for a continuous 12-month period. Automatic late payment penalties do not apply to businesses with a turnover not exceeding £150,000 per year. Such businesses are initially offered help and advice if they are late with their VAT payments.

It is important to note that a new penalty regime is being introduced in relation to late returns and late payment of tax (see Chapter 15). This penalty regime will apply to a range of taxes and is being phased in over a period of several years. The date of implementation for VAT has not yet been determined.

(e) **VAT wrongdoing**. A VAT "wrongdoing" penalty is charged if a person makes an unauthorised issue of a VAT invoice. This situation would arise if VAT invoices were issued by a person who is not registered for VAT.

The amount of the penalty varies from 30% to 100% of the amount shown as VAT on the unauthorised invoice, with substantial reductions if the person concerned voluntarily discloses the wrongdoing.

(f) **Breaches of regulations**. A taxable person who fails to comply with sundry VAT regulations will initially receive a written warning from HMRC. If non-compliance is continued, the person is liable on a first offence to a penalty of £5 per day until the breach is remedied. The penalty rises to £10 per day on a second offence within a period of two years and again to £15 per day on a third or subsequent offence. The maximum penalty which may be charged is equal to 100 times the daily rate and the minimum penalty is £50.

Certain penalties may be mitigated (i.e. reduced or not charged at all) if the taxable person has a reasonable excuse for his or her conduct. As noted above, some penalties may also be mitigated if the person concerned has voluntarily disclosed any non-compliance and has co-operated fully with HMRC.

Interest

"Default interest" is charged on VAT which has been assessed (see above) or which could have been assessed but for the fact that payment was made before an assessment was raised. Such interest runs from the date on which the tax should have been paid to the date of payment. Conversely, if a taxable person makes an overpayment of VAT and this has been caused by an HMRC error, the person is paid interest on the tax that is refunded.

When a taxable person discovers that an error on a previous VAT return has resulted in an underpayment of VAT, default interest is not charged if the error is corrected in a later return. This is permissible as long as the error does not exceed a "de minimis" limit. This limit is equal to the greater of £10,000 and 1% of taxable turnover for the return period, subject to a maximum of £50,000.

Repayment supplement

If a taxable person is entitled to a repayment of VAT for a tax period, this repayment is increased by a "repayment supplement" of 5% (or £50, if greater) so long as:

(a) the return for the relevant tax period is submitted on time, and

(b) the amount stated to be repayable in the return is either correct or does not exceed the correct figure by more than 5% or £250 (whichever is greater), and

(c) HMRC fails to issue written instructions for the repayment to be made within 30 days from the date on which the return was received.

Summary

- VAT is normally accounted for to HMRC on a quarterly basis, although a person who is entitled to a VAT repayment in most tax periods may submit monthly returns.
- The date on which a supply is deemed to occur is known as the "tax point".
- A tax invoice must normally be issued if a taxable person makes a taxable supply to another taxable person.
- There are several special schemes which simplify the workings of the VAT system. These include the cash accounting scheme, the annual accounting scheme, the flat-rate scheme for small businesses, the flat-rate scheme for farmers and the margin scheme. There are also several special schemes for retailers.
- The input tax suffered in relation to certain types of supply is not recoverable. Special rules apply to car fuel bought by a business and then used for private motoring.
- A person making a mixture of taxable supplies and exempt supplies is "partially exempt" and may reclaim only part of the input tax suffered.
- The VAT system is administered by HM Revenue and Customs. Penalties are imposed for non-compliance with VAT regulations.

Exercises

30.1 List the required contents of a valid VAT invoice.

30.2 Describe the main features of the VAT cash accounting scheme and the VAT annual accounting scheme.

30.3 The following information relates to the VAT return of Toucan Ltd for the three months to 30 November 2012. All figures are VAT-exclusive unless stated otherwise.

(i) Standard-rated supplies made to customers were £28,800. A cash discount of 2.5% was offered to customers who paid within 28 days and this discount was taken by customers who bought 50% of the supplies made during the quarter.

The figure of £28,800 includes a £1,600 sale made to a customer in September 2012. This customer went bankrupt in November 2012 and a bad debt of £1,600 was written off in the company's books on 30 November 2012.

On 15 November 2012, a customer was invoiced for £4,800 in relation to a sale of standard-rated goods. The customer paid for these goods on 4 December 2012 and the goods were made available to the customer on 10 December 2012. This sale is NOT included in the above figure of £28,800 and was NOT eligible for the 2.5% cash discount.

(ii) Standard-rated goods bought for resale or consumption cost £9,280. Standard-rated services cost £5,200.

(iii) On 1 September 2012, the company was charged VAT of £1,960 on the purchase of a motor car with emissions of 132g/km. Private use of this car by one of the company's employees accounts for 50% of its mileage. Maintenance charges in relation to the car were £280 for the quarter and fuel costs were £520. The company wishes to reclaim VAT on fuel as far as possible.

(iv) In October 2012, the company bought a new non-current asset for a VAT-inclusive price of £14,100.

The company is now considering an application to join the flat-rate scheme for small businesses. Standard-rated sales are expected to run at £11,500 per month from now on and purchases of standard-rated items (other than non-current assets) on which VAT may be reclaimed are expected to be £5,500 per month. The company also anticipates the acquisition of a single non-current asset at a cost of £5,000 during 2013. All of these figures exclude VAT. The flat-rate percentage applicable to Toucan Ltd is 9.5%.

Required:

(a) Compute the VAT payable to (or repayable by) HMRC for the three months to 30 November 2012 and state the date on which any amount payable would fall due.

(b) Explain the main features of the flat-rate scheme for small businesses. Would Toucan Ltd be eligible to join this scheme? If so, would it be beneficial for the company to join the scheme?

(CIPFA)

30.4 Sebastian is self-employed. He drives a car with an emission rating of 203 g/km and he charges the cost of all the petrol used to his business bank account. In the quarter to 31 July 2012 he drives 3,800 miles on business and 1,400 miles for private purposes. The VAT-inclusive cost of all the petrol bought in the quarter is £798. How should Sebastian deal with petrol in his VAT return for the quarter?

***30.5** During the quarter to 31 December 2012, a taxable person makes the following supplies:

	£
Standard-rated supplies (including VAT)	326,400
Zero-rated supplies	88,000
Exempt supplies	440,000

Input tax for the quarter is £118,000, attributed as follows:

	%
Attributed to taxable supplies	35
Attributed to exempt supplies	40
Unattributed	25

Compute the VAT provisionally payable to or reclaimable from HMRC for the quarter.

***30.6** Tracey is a sole trader. She has the following transactions during the quarter to 31 December 2012 (all amounts shown are VAT-exclusive):

	£
Sales to UK customers:	
Standard-rated	34,475
Zero-rated	12,600
Exports of goods:	
To non-EU members	8,600
To EU members (all customers are VAT registered)	17,300
Purchases:	
Standard-rated	25,800
Zero-rated	6,200
Expenses:	
Wages and salaries	22,450
Car repairs	120
Insurances	260
Entertaining UK customers	420
Other expenses (all standard-rated)	9,700
Capital transactions:	
Purchase of new plant and machinery	8,000
Purchase of motor van	12,000

Tracey drives a car with an emission rating of 174 g/km and charges the cost of all the petrol used by this car, whether for business or private motoring, to her business bank account. Calculate the amount of VAT due for the quarter.

Chapter 31

Inheritance tax

Introduction

This chapter provides a basic introduction to inheritance tax (IHT). An IHT liability can arise in a number of ways but the events which most commonly trigger such a liability are the transfer of assets on the death of their owner and the gift of assets during the lifetime of their owner.

IHT was introduced in 1986 to replace capital transfer tax. Current IHT legislation is to be found in the Inheritance Tax Act 1984 (originally the Capital Transfer Tax Act 1984) as amended by subsequent Finance Acts.

Chargeable transfers of value

The main situation in which a charge to IHT may arise is when a *transfer of value* of *chargeable property* is made by a *chargeable person*.

Transfers of value

A transfer of value occurs when a transferor makes a "disposition" such that his or her estate is lower in value than it was before the disposition occurred. The value of a transfer for IHT purposes is equal to the reduction in the value of the transferor's estate. If the transferor also pays the IHT in relation to the transfer, this further reduces the value of the estate, so that the total value of the transfer is then equal to the amount of the disposition plus the associated IHT.

A disposition is a disposal of property or an interest in property. This includes disposals made during the lifetime of the transferor ("lifetime transfers") as well as disposals caused by the death of the transferor. However, certain dispositions are not regarded as transfers of value for IHT purposes and so cannot give rise to an IHT liability. The most significant of these dispositions are:

(a) dispositions without gratuitous intent (i.e. genuine commercial transactions which give rise to a loss and so cause a reduction in the value of the transferor's estate)

(b) dispositions made during the transferor's lifetime which are allowable expenditure for income tax or corporation tax purposes or which consist of pension contributions made by an employer for the benefit of employees

(c) dispositions made during the transferor's lifetime for the maintenance of his or her family (including spouses, civil partners, children and dependent relatives)

(d) dispositions caused by the fact that the transferor has died whilst on active service.

Chargeable property

For IHT purposes, the word "property" encompasses all types of asset, including legally enforceable rights and interests of any description. All property is chargeable property unless specifically excluded from charge. The main exclusions are:

(a) property situated outside the UK and owned by a person who is domiciled outside the UK (i.e. a person whose permanent home is situated outside the UK)

(b) government securities issued on terms which grant tax exemption under certain conditions and held by a person who satisfies those conditions (e.g. government securities which give tax exemption to persons who are not ordinarily resident in the UK and held by someone who is not ordinarily resident)

(c) "heritage property" designated as such by the Treasury, so long as undertakings are given with regard to maintenance of the property and the provision of public access

(d) a reversionary interest in a trust or settlement, unless acquired by purchase (see later in this chapter for more information on trusts and types of trust).

Chargeable persons

An individual who is domiciled in the UK (i.e. whose permanent home is in the UK) is a chargeable person and is liable to IHT in relation to all of his or her chargeable property situated throughout the world An individual who is not domiciled in the UK is liable to IHT only in relation to property situated in the UK. Note that:

(a) Husbands and wives (and civil partners) are assessed to IHT independently.

(b) A partnership is not a chargeable person. Each partner is individually liable to IHT in relation to his or her share of the partnership assets.

(c) A company is not a chargeable person. But the participators of a close company (see Chapter 27) may incur IHT in relation to transfers made by that company.

(d) The life tenants of an interest in possession trust created before 22 March 2006 are regarded for IHT purposes as owning the assets of the trust, divided between them in proportion to their interests. The trust itself is not a chargeable person. However, most other trusts are chargeable to IHT (see later in this chapter).

Exempt transfers

Certain transfers are wholly exempt from IHT. In other cases, an exemption or relief may reduce the value of a transfer for IHT purposes. The main exemptions and reliefs are:

(a) business and agricultural property reliefs (see later in this chapter)

(b) exemptions for transfers made to certain transferees (see below)

(c) exemptions available to the transferor (see below).

These exemptions and reliefs are applied to a transfer in the order given above.

Exemptions for transfers made to certain transferees

The following transfers are wholly exempt from IHT whether made on death or during the lifetime of the transferor:

(a) transfers to the transferor's spouse (husband or wife) or same-sex civil partner (so long as a legally-recognised civil partnership has been established)

(b) gifts to charities, community amateur sports clubs or political parties

(c) gifts made for national purposes to designated bodies (e.g. museums) and gifts of pre-eminent property to the nation (see Chapter 4)

(d) subject to certain conditions, transfers made into a settlement established for the maintenance, repair or preservation of designated heritage property.

In the case of transfers between spouses, there is no requirement that the husband and wife should live together, only that the marriage should be valid under UK law. This exemption ceases when the marriage is dissolved by a decree absolute.

Exemptions available to the transferor

The following exemptions are available in relation to lifetime transfers only:

(a) **Normal expenditure out of income**. Transfers consisting of "normal expenditure out of income" (e.g. birthday and Christmas presents) are wholly exempt from IHT. In order for a transfer to benefit from this exemption, HM Revenue and Customs must believe that the transfer:

   (i) is part of the normal expenditure of the transferor, and

   (ii) is made out of income rather than capital, and

   (iii) leaves the transferor sufficient income to maintain his or her usual standard of living.

(b) **Small gifts**. Gifts to individuals with a value of up to £250 per transferee per tax year (from 6 April to 5 April) are wholly exempt from IHT. This exemption cannot be used to exempt part of a gift which has a value exceeding £250.

(c) **Gifts in consideration of marriage**. Gifts made to a bride or to a bridegroom in consideration of their marriage are exempt from IHT up to the following limits:

   (i) £5,000 if made by a parent of the bride or groom
   (ii) £2,500 if made by the grandparent or remoter ancestor of the bride or groom
   (iii) £2,500 if made by the bride to the groom or vice versa
   (iv) £1,000 in any other case.

   The above exemptions are per transferor per marriage and can be used to exempt part of the value of larger gifts. Similar rules now also apply to gifts made on the registration of a civil partnership.

(d) **Annual exemption**. The first £3,000 of lifetime transfers made in any tax year is exempt from IHT. Note that:

   (i) If the total of the lifetime transfers made in a tax year exceeds £3,000, the exemption is set against the year's transfers in chronological order.
   (ii) Any unused part of the annual exemption may be carried forward to the following tax year (but no further) and set against the excess of that year's lifetime transfers over that year's annual exemption.
   (iii) It is HM Revenue and Customs practice to set the annual exemption against potentially exempt transfers (see below) as well as chargeable lifetime transfers, even though potentially exempt transfers may never become chargeable to inheritance tax. There is some doubt as to whether this practice is statutorily correct but it has been followed in this book.

EXAMPLE 1

Tania makes no transfers during 2010-11. Her only transfers during 2011-12 and 2012-13 are as follows:

		£
2011-12		
June 2011	Gift to her son on his marriage	6,000
October 2011	Gift to her granddaughter	4,500
January 2012	Gift to Oxfam	10,000
March 2012	Gift to a friend	100
2012-13		
July 2012	Gift to her nephew	1,000
August 2012	Gift to her cousin	3,500

Calculate the value of each of the above transfers after deduction of all the relevant exemptions. None of the gifts are regarded as normal expenditure out of income.

Solution

(AE = Annual exemption)

	Value before AE	*AE for current year*	*AE for previous year*	*Value after AE*
	£	£	£	£
2011-12				
Gift to son on marriage (£6,000 – £5,000)	1,000	1,000	-	-
Gift to granddaughter	4,500	2,000	2,500	-
Gift to charity (exempt)	-	-	-	-
Gift to friend (exempt as a small gift)	-	-	-	-
	5,500	3,000	2,500	-
2012-13				
Gift to nephew	1,000	1,000		-
Gift to cousin	3,500	2,000		1,500
	4,500	3,000		1,500

Note:

£500 of the 2010-11 annual exemption remains unused but cannot be carried forward beyond 2011-12. The 2011-12 and 2012-13 annual exemptions are fully utilised.

Potentially exempt transfers (PETs)

If a lifetime transfer is not exempt from IHT as a result of the various exemptions listed above, the transfer will be either a "chargeable lifetime transfer" or a "potentially exempt transfer". Chargeable lifetime transfers are charged to IHT immediately. But potentially exempt transfers (PETs) are charged to IHT only if the transferor dies within seven years of the date of the transfer.

A potentially exempt transfer is a lifetime transfer made by an individual to any of the following:

(a) another individual

(b) a trust for the benefit of a disabled person

(c) a trust for the benefit of a bereaved minor (in certain cases).

Most lifetime transfers are in fact PETs. But lifetime transfers made to trusts other than those mentioned above are chargeable lifetime transfers.

Types of trust

The above definition of a PET makes reference to various types of trust. Trusts were introduced briefly in Chapter 6 but are explained again below:

(a) A trust (or settlement) is an arrangement whereby property is held by persons known as trustees for the benefit of other persons known as beneficiaries.

(b) If one or more persons are entitled to the lifetime use of the trust property or to the income generated by the trust property, those persons are "life tenants" and the trust is a trust with an "interest in possession" (IIP). A person whose interest in the trust property will not take effect until some future event occurs (e.g. the death of a life tenant) is said to have a "reversionary interest".

(c) A trust with no interest in possession is sometimes referred to as a "discretionary trust". The trustees of such a trust have the discretion to distribute as much or as little of the trust income to the beneficiaries as they see fit.

For IHT purposes, most trusts are classified as "relevant property trusts" and are subject to a special IHT regime. This involves a "periodic" tax charge on the trust property every ten years and an "exit" charge whenever property leaves the trust.

However, trusts for the disabled and trusts for bereaved minors are generally not relevant property trusts. Nor are IIP trusts set up before 22 March 2006 (until the life interest at that date comes to an end). In these cases, the trust is not liable to the periodic or exit charges.

EXAMPLE 2

Consider each of the following lifetime transfers and classify each one as either an exempt transfer, a PET or a chargeable lifetime transfer. Assume in each case that the transfer was made during 2012-13 and that the annual exemption for both the current year and the previous year have been set against earlier transfers.

(a) a gift of £10,000 made by a husband to his wife

(b) a gift of £20,000 made by a mother to her son on his marriage

(c) a gift of £50,000 made to a trust for the benefit of a disabled person

(d) a gift of £100,000 made to a relevant property trust.

Solution

(a) wholly exempt

(b) exempt £5,000; PET £15,000

(c) PET

(d) chargeable lifetime transfer.

IHT payable on chargeable lifetime transfers

The amount of IHT payable on a chargeable lifetime transfer depends upon:

(a) the value of the transfer (less any relevant exemptions), which must be grossed-up if the tax is paid by the transferor

(b) the rates of IHT in force on the date of the transfer

(c) the total (including the current transfer) of the gross chargeable lifetime transfers made during the seven years ending on the date of the current transfer.

Grossing-up

IHT is chargeable on the *gross* value of a transfer. This is the reduction in the value of the transferor's estate which the transfer has caused. If the transferee pays the tax due on a transfer, the gross value of the transfer is simply the amount received by the transferee (less any exemptions). However, if the tax due is paid by the transferor, the amount received by the transferee (less exemptions) is only the net value of the transfer and this must be grossed-up at the appropriate rates to find the gross value.

In general, any capital gains tax payable by the transferor in relation to the transfer is ignored when calculating the reduction in value of the transferor's estate.

Rates of IHT applicable to chargeable lifetime transfers

The rates of IHT applicable to chargeable lifetime transfers made on or after 6 April 2012 are as follows:

Gross chargeable lifetime transfers for the seven years to date	*Rate of tax*	*Grossing-up fraction*
first £325,000 ("nil-rate band")	0%	nil
remainder after the first £325,000	20%	100/80

The rates of tax have been 0% and 20% for many years but the threshold beyond which 20% tax is payable is normally increased in each tax year, so increasing the width of the nil-rate band. Recent values of the threshold have been:

Date of transfer	£
6 April 2005 to 5 April 2006	275,000
6 April 2006 to 5 April 2007	285,000
6 April 2007 to 5 April 2008	300,000
6 April 2008 to 5 April 2009	312,000
6 April 2009 to 5 April 2010	325,000
6 April 2010 to 5 April 2011	325,000
6 April 2011 to 5 April 2012	325,000

Note that the IHT threshold has not been increased since 2009-10. In fact, Finance Act 2010 fixed this threshold at £325,000 until the end of tax year 2014-15.

For each transfer, the calculation of the tax due involves the following steps:

(a) The total gross value of previous chargeable lifetime transfers made during the seven years to date is brought forward.

(b) If the total brought forward has utilised the whole of the nil-rate band, tax is due at 20% on the gross value of the current transfer.

(c) If the total brought forward has not utilised the whole of the nil-rate band, the balance of that band is set against the current transfer. If this does not absorb the whole of the transfer, tax is due at 20% on the gross value of the remainder.

EXAMPLE 3

On 1 July 2012, Violet makes a chargeable lifetime transfer (after deduction of relevant exemptions) of £48,000. Her only previous chargeable lifetime transfer was made in 2008 and had a gross value (after exemptions) of £283,000. Calculate the IHT due if:

(a) the transferee agrees to pay the tax due

(b) the tax due is paid by Violet.

Solution

The total of transfers brought forward is £283,000, leaving £42,000 of the nil-rate band to set against the current transfer.

(a) If the transferee pays the tax, the gross value of the transfer is £48,000 and the IHT due is £42,000 @ 0% + £6,000 @ 20% = £1,200. The total of gross transfers for the seven years to 1 July 2012 is now £331,000.

(b) If Violet pays the tax, the net value of the transfer is £48,000. The gross value and the tax due are calculated as follows:

	Net	*Gross*	*Tax*
	£	£	£
£42,000 grossed up @ 0%	42,000	42,000	0
£6,000 grossed up @ 20%	6,000	7,500	1,500
Totals	48,000	49,500	1,500

The gross value of the transfer is £49,500 and the tax due is £1,500. The total of gross transfers for the seven years to 1 July 2012 is now £332,500.

IHT payable on death

The IHT payable on death consists of:

(a) additional tax on any chargeable lifetime transfers made by the deceased person during the seven years ending on the date of death

(b) tax on any PETs made by the deceased person during those seven years

(c) tax on the estate of the deceased person as at the date of death, to the extent that the transfers made on death are not exempt from IHT.

Tax on chargeable lifetime transfers and PETs

The tax payable on death in respect of the chargeable lifetime transfers and PETs made in the seven years ending on the date of death is calculated as follows:

(a) The transfers are considered in chronological order with no distinction made between chargeable lifetime transfers and PETs.

(b) Tax is recalculated on the gross value of each transfer using the IHT bands and rates in force *on the date of death* and taking into account any other chargeable transfers made in the seven years ending on the date of the transfer. For deaths occurring on or after 6 April 2012 the applicable rates are as follows:

Gross chargeable transfers for the seven years to date	*Rate of tax*
first £325,000 ("nil-rate band")	0%
remainder after the first £325,000	40%

Note that the nil-rate band available on death in relation to a deceased person may be increased by a transfer of unused nil-rate band from a previously deceased spouse or civil partner (see later in this chapter).

(c) The tax calculated at (b) for each transfer may then be reduced by *taper relief*, depending upon the number of years which have elapsed between the date of the transfer and the date of death. Taper relief is given as follows:

Period between transfer and death	*Percentage tax reduction*
3 years or less	0%
Over 3 but not more than 4 years	20%
Over 4 but not more than 5 years	40%
Over 5 but not more than 6 years	60%
Over 6 but not more than 7 years	80%

(d) Finally, for each transfer, any tax paid during the lifetime of the transferor is subtracted, leaving a balance of tax due on that transfer. This tax liability is the responsibility of the transferee. No repayment is given if the lifetime tax paid in relation to a transfer exceeds the liability on death.

EXAMPLE 4

Wilson dies on 20 December 2012, having made only the following transfers during his lifetime:

		£
6 June 2002	Gift to daughter	50,000
4 May 2008	Gift to relevant property trust	503,400
11 June 2009	Gift to son on marriage	50,000

Calculate the IHT payable during Wilson's lifetime (if any) in relation to each of the above transfers, assuming that Wilson paid this tax himself. Also calculate any further IHT payable in relation to these transfers on Wilson's death.

Solution

The value of each gift after deduction of exemptions is as follows:

		Value before AE	*AE for current year*	*AE for previous year*	*Value after AE*
		£	£	£	£
2002-03	Daughter	50,000	3,000	3,000	44,000
2008-09	Relevant property trust	503,400	3,000	3,000	497,400
2009-10	Son (£50,000 – £5,000)	45,000	3,000	-	42,000

Lifetime tax liability

The gifts to Wilson's son and daughter were PETs and gave rise to no immediate tax liability but the gift to the trust was a chargeable lifetime transfer. There were no other such transfers during the seven years to date so the whole of the nil-rate band (£312,000 at that time) was set against the gift. The tax due was £46,350, calculated as follows:

	Net	*Gross*	*Tax*
	£	£	£
£312,000 grossed up @ 0%	312,000	312,000	0
£185,400 grossed up @ 20%	185,400	231,750	46,350
Totals	497,400	543,750	46,350

Tax liability on death

The June 2002 PET is more than seven years old at the time of Wilson's death. This PET is exempt from tax and can be completely ignored for IHT purposes. The tax due on the other two transfers is calculated as follows:

(i) *Transfer made on 4 May 2008*

The gross value of this transfer is £543,750 and there were no other chargeable transfers in the seven years to date (5 May 2001 to 4 May 2008). The tax due at the death rates applicable on 20 December 2012 is:

	£
£325,000 @ 0%	0
£218,750 @ 40%	87,500
	87,500
Less: Taper relief (4-5 years) @ 40%	35,000
	52,500
Less: Lifetime tax paid	46,350
IHT payable by transferee	6,150

The tax liability calculated on death (£52,500) exceeds the lifetime tax paid on the transfer (£46,350) by £6,150. This amount is payable by the transferee.

(ii) *Transfer made on 11 June 2009*

The gross value of this transfer is £42,000. Previous gross chargeable transfers in the seven years to date (12 June 2002 to 11 June 2009) were £543,750, completely absorbing the nil-rate band. Therefore the tax due at the death rates applicable on 20 December 2012 is:

	£
£42,000 @ 40%	16,800
Less: Taper relief (3-4 years) @ 20%	3,360
	13,440
Less: Lifetime tax paid	0
IHT payable by transferee	13,440

Tax on the deceased person's estate

IHT on the deceased person's estate (to the extent that the transfers made on death are not exempt from IHT) is calculated using the rates of tax applicable on death. The calculation proceeds as follows:

(a) First, the nil-rate band is reduced by the total of gross chargeable transfers (including any PETs) made in the seven years ending on the date of death. Note that a deceased person's nil-rate band may be higher than usual because of a transfer of unused nil-rate band from a previously deceased spouse or civil partner (see below).

(b) The remainder of the nil-rate band (if any) is then set against the value of the estate and tax at 40% is calculated on the balance.

(c) The tax due is divided by the value of the estate and the result (expressed as a percentage) is the "estate rate" i.e. the average rate of tax borne by the estate.

However, as from 6 April 2012, a lower rate of IHT applies to an estate if at least 10% of the net estate (after deducting IHT exemptions, reliefs and the nil-rate band) is left to charity. The rate of IHT which applies in these circumstances is 36%.

EXAMPLE 5

Toby dies on 2 March 2013, leaving an estate valued at £400,000. None of the transfers made on death are exempt from IHT. Calculate the IHT due on the estate if the total of the gross chargeable transfers made by Toby in the seven years up to his death was:

(a) Nil (b) £125,000 (c) £370,000.

Solution

(a) £325,000 @ 0% + £75,000 @ 40% = £30,000. (Estate rate 7.5%)

(b) £200,000 @ 0% + £200,000 @ 40% = £80,000. (Estate rate 20%)

(c) £400,000 @ 40% = £160,000. (Estate rate 40%).

EXAMPLE 6

Rose dies on 10 July 2012, leaving an estate valued at £525,000. None of the transfers made on death are exempt from IHT apart from a bequest to the RSPCA (a charity). Rose made no chargeable transfers in the seven years prior to her death. Calculate the IHT due on the estate if the amount of the bequest to the RSPCA was:

(a) £10,000 (b) £30,000.

Solution

(a) The gift to charity is an exempt transfer and the nil-rate band is available in full, so IHT is due on £190,000 (£525,000 – £10,000 – £325,000). The total of this amount and the gift to charity is £200,000 and the gift is only 5% of this total. Therefore the lower rate does not apply and IHT due is £76,000 (£190,000 @ 40%).

(b) IHT is due on £170,000 (£525,000 – £30,000 – £325,000). The total of this amount and the gift to charity is £200,000 and the gift is 15% of this total. This is not less than 10% so the lower rate applies and IHT due is £61,200 (£170,000 @ 36%).

Transfer of unused part of nil-rate band

A transferable nil-rate band arises when one party to a marriage or civil partnership dies and the amount that is chargeable to IHT on his or her death (including any transfers made in the previous seven years) does not use up all of the nil-rate band. In these circumstances, the unused part of the nil-rate band may be transferred to the surviving spouse or civil partner for use on his or her death. Note that:

(a) The transferred part of the nil-rate band may be used only when the surviving spouse or civil partner dies and cannot be used to reduce the lifetime tax payable on any chargeable lifetime transfers made by the survivor.

(b) The amount available for transfer is calculated by determining the proportion of the nil-rate band which was unused when the survivor's spouse or civil partner died. This proportion is then applied to the amount of the nil-rate band which is in force on the date of the survivor's death.

EXAMPLE 7

Harriet died on 21 October 2012. Her husband had died previously and his estate on death (including transfers made in the last seven years of his life) had absorbed £110,000 of the nil-rate band at that time. Calculate the nil-rate band which is available when calculating the IHT due on Harriet's death, assuming that her husband died in:

(a) May 2005 (b) July 2007.

Solution

(a) When Harriet's husband died, the nil-rate band was £275,000. His estate absorbed £110,000 of this, leaving £165,000 (i.e. 60% of the nil-rate band) unused. Therefore Harriet's nil-rate band on death is £325,000 + 60% of £325,000 = £520,000.

(b) When Harriet's husband died, the nil-rate band was £300,000. His estate absorbed £110,000 of this, leaving £190,000 (19/30ths of the nil-rate band) unused. Therefore Harriet's nil-rate band on death is £325,000 + 19/30ths of £325,000 = £530,833.

Quick succession relief

Quick succession relief (QSR) is available when property which is transferred on death was transferred to the deceased person within the previous five years and was charged to IHT at that time. The tax (if any) payable in relation to the transfer made on death is reduced by an amount which depends upon the value of the earlier transfer and the amount of IHT paid on that transfer. The relief is calculated as:

$$\frac{\text{net value of earlier transfer}}{\text{gross value of earlier transfer}} \times \text{IHT paid on earlier transfer} \times \text{QSR\%}$$

The QSR percentage depends upon the date of the earlier transfer, as follows:

Period between earlier transfer and death	*QSR percentage*
1 year or less	100%
Over 1 but not more than 2 years	80%
Over 2 but not more than 3 years	60%
Over 3 but not more than 4 years	40%
Over 4 but not more than 5 years	20%

Gifts with reservation

A "gift with reservation" is a gift of any property made in such a way that either:

(a) possession and enjoyment of the property is not bona fide assumed by the donee at or before the start of the "relevant period", or

(b) the property is not enjoyed to the entire exclusion of the donor throughout the whole of the relevant period.

For this purpose, the "relevant period" is the period which ends on the date of the donor's death and which begins seven years before that date or (if later) on the date of the gift.

If there were no special rules relating to gifts with reservation, taxpayers would be able to divest themselves of property (so reducing the IHT charge on death) whilst continuing to benefit from that property. This is prevented by legislation which ensures that:

(a) property which is subject to a reservation at the date of the donor's death is treated as part of the donor's estate, and

(b) if any property ceased to be subject to a reservation before the donor's death, the donor is treated as having made a PET on the date that the reservation ceased to exist.

These rules are supplemented by regulations which deal with the possibility of a double tax charge arising if the gift is also a chargeable transfer.

Valuation

As stated at the beginning of this chapter, the value of a transfer for IHT purposes is equal to the reduction in value of the transferor's estate as a result of that transfer. In general, this is equivalent to the open market value of the transferred assets on the date of the transfer but it should not be assumed that this will always be the case. For instance, if the transferor disposes of:

(a) a single item from a matching set of such items, or

(b) a small number of shares in a company, sufficient to convert a majority shareholding into a minority shareholding

it is likely that the true reduction in value of the transferor's estate (and therefore the value of the transfer for IHT purposes) will exceed the market value of the transferred assets. This caveat aside, determining the market value of the transferred assets may in itself cause difficulty and special valuation rules are sometimes required. The most important of these rules are described below.

Listed shares

Shares which are listed on a recognised stock exchange (referred to as "listed shares" or "quoted shares") are valued at the *lower* of:

(a) the lower of the two prices quoted for those shares on the day of the transfer, plus one-quarter of the difference between these two prices (the "quarter-up" rule)

(b) the average of the highest and lowest prices at which bargains have been recorded on that day (if any).

If listed shares are transferred on a non-working day (for which prices are unavailable) the shares are valued as if transferred on the last working day before the date of the transfer or the first working day after it, whichever gives the lower figure.

EXAMPLE 8

On 1 June 2012, Shirley gives 5,000 shares in a listed company to her daughter. Shares in the company are quoted at 189p - 197p on that date, with recorded bargains at 190p, 192p and 196p. Calculate the market value of the shares for IHT purposes.

Solution

The quarter-up rule gives 189p + 1/4 x (197p – 189p) = 191p. The average of the highest and lowest recorded bargains is 193p, so the shares are valued at 191p and the transfer has a market value of 5,000 x £1.91 = £9,550.

Related property

When calculating the value of a transfer for IHT purposes, the existence of any "related property" may be taken into account. Related property consists of property which:

(a) is owned by the transferor's spouse or civil partner, or

(b) is owned (or has been owned within the previous five years) by a charity, political party etc. as a result of an exempt transfer made either by the transferor or by his or her spouse or civil partner.

Under the related property rules, the property being transferred and the related property are valued together (as a whole) and then part of that value is apportioned to the property being transferred. These rules are intended to prevent taxpayers from avoiding IHT by fragmenting the ownership of an asset and will only be used if the valuation given by the related property rules is greater than the valuation that would be calculated normally.

EXAMPLE 9

Roy owns 3,500 ordinary shares in an unlisted company which has an issued share capital of 10,000 ordinary shares. Roy's wife owns a further 1,600 shares. Shareholdings in the company are valued as follows:

	£		£
500 shares	5,000	4,600 shares	64,400
3,000 shares	33,000	5,100 shares	96,900
3,500 shares	43,750		

Roy now transfers 500 of his shares to a relevant property trust. Calculate the value of this transfer for IHT purposes.

Solution

Ignoring related property, Roy's estate has reduced in value by £10,750 (£43,750 – £33,000) and this would normally be the value of the transfer. But taking related property into account, the value of the transfer is calculated as follows:

	£
Value of Roy's holding before the transfer (£96,900 x 3,500/5,100)	66,500
Value of Roy's holding after the transfer (£64,400 x 3,000/4,600)	42,000
Value of the transfer	24,500

Since £24,500 exceeds £10,750, the value of the transfer is £24,500.

Overseas property

Property situated outside the UK is valued in the appropriate foreign currency. This value is then converted into sterling, using the exchange rate for the day of the transfer which gives the lowest sterling value.

Business property relief

Business property relief of either 100% or 50% is available in relation to a transfer which meets *all* of the following conditions:

(a) the property transferred consists of "relevant business property"

(b) the business is a "qualifying business" (investment businesses do not qualify)

(c) the property has been owned by the transferor for at least two years, or has replaced other relevant business property, such that the combined period of ownership of both the original and replacement property is at least two years out of the five years preceding the date of the transfer.

The main categories of relevant business property, together with the applicable rates of relief, are as follows:

		Rate of relief
(a)	Property consisting of a business or an interest in a business	100%
(b)	Securities in an unlisted company which gave the transferor control of the company immediately before the transfer	100%
(c)	Shares in an unlisted company	100%
(d)	Shares transferred from a controlling holding in a listed company	50%
(e)	Land, buildings, plant and machinery which, immediately before the transfer, were used for business purposes by a partnership in which the transferor was a partner or by a company of which he/she had control	50%
(f)	Land, buildings, plant and machinery which, immediately before the transfer, were used in the transferor's business and owned by a trust of which the transferor was a life tenant.	50%

No relief is given in relation to "excepted assets". These are assets which have not been used for business purposes throughout the two years prior to the transfer and which are not required for the future use of the business.

Agricultural property relief

Agricultural property relief of either 100% or 50% is available in relation to a transfer of agricultural property so long as that property has been either:

(a) occupied by the transferor and used for agricultural purposes throughout the two years preceding the transfer, or

(b) owned by the transferor throughout the seven years preceding the transfer and occupied by the transferor or someone else for agricultural purposes throughout those seven years.

For this purpose, agricultural property consists mainly of agricultural land and pasture, woodlands and associated buildings. Land managed according to the terms of certain wildlife habitat schemes (together with associated buildings) is also eligible for agricultural property relief. The rates of relief are:

(a) 100% if, immediately before the transfer, the transferor enjoys vacant possession of the property or the right to obtain it within the following 12 months

(b) Otherwise, 100% if the property is let on a tenancy starting after 31 August 1995 and 50% if the property is let on a tenancy starting before 1 September 1995.

These rates apply only to the "agricultural value" of the property. This is the value that the property would have if it could only ever be used for agricultural purposes. If a property qualifies for both business property relief and agricultural property relief, agricultural property relief is given first.

Administration of IHT

Inheritance tax is administered by HMRC. For chargeable lifetime transfers and transfers caused by the death of the transferor, an "account" must be delivered to HMRC, giving details of the transfers made and their value. Details of this procedure are as follows:

(a) **Chargeable lifetime transfers**. The transferor must deliver an account to HMRC within 12 months of the end of the month in which the transfer occurred. There is no need to deliver an account if the transfer is exempt or potentially exempt, or if:

   (i) for chargeable lifetime transfers consisting wholly of cash or quoted stocks and securities, the total of all chargeable transfers made in the seven years to date does not exceed the IHT threshold

   (ii) for chargeable lifetime transfers not consisting wholly of cash or quoted stocks and securities, the total of all chargeable transfers made in the seven years to date does not exceed 80% of the IHT threshold.

(b) **Death**. The personal representatives of a deceased person must deliver an account to HMRC within 12 months of the end of the month in which the death occurred. But there is no need to deliver an account if the person was UK-domiciled and:

   (i) the gross value of the estate, plus transfers made during the seven years prior to death, does not exceed the IHT threshold (or double this threshold if 100% of the nil-rate band was transferred to the deceased person on the prior death of a spouse or civil partner), and

   (ii) no more than £100,000 of the estate is situated outside the UK, and

   (iii) any trust assets included in the estate of the deceased person are held in a single trust and do not exceed £150,000 in value, and

   (iv) there have been no chargeable lifetime transfers or PETs made within the seven years to date, other than transfers consisting of cash, listed securities or land and buildings (and contents) with a total gross value not exceeding £150,000.

   If the deceased person was not UK-domiciled (and never had been) an account is not required so long as the value of UK assets transferred on death does not exceed £150,000 and these assets consist solely of cash, listed shares or listed securities.

When a transfer gives rise to an IHT liability, the HMRC Capital Taxes Office issues a notice showing the value of the transfer for IHT purposes and the amount of tax payable. Appeals may be lodged within 30 days of the date of the notice.

Payment of IHT

The IHT relating to a transfer is usually payable six months after the end of the month in which the transfer (or the death) occurred. However, the tax on chargeable lifetime transfers made in roughly the first half of the tax year (6 April to 30 September) is not payable until 30 April in the following tax year.

It is notable that the tax on a transfer is usually due for payment before the end of the 12-month period within which an account of the transfer must be delivered to HMRC. Since interest is charged on tax paid late, there is an incentive to deliver the account (and pay the tax due) on or before the due date of payment.

Summary

- The main occasion on which IHT is charged is when a transfer of value of chargeable property is made by a chargeable person. A transfer may be a lifetime transfer or a transfer made on death.
- The value of a transfer is equal to the reduction in value of the transferor's estate as a result of the transfer. The value of a transfer for IHT purposes may be reduced by business property relief and/or agricultural property relief.
- Transfers made to certain transferees (e.g. spouses, civil partners, charities and political parties) are exempt from IHT.
- Lifetime transfers comprising small gifts, gifts made out of income and gifts made on marriage or civil partnership are wholly or partly exempt from IHT. The first £3,000 of lifetime transfers made in any tax year is exempt from IHT.
- A potentially exempt transfer (PET) is not chargeable to IHT unless the transferor dies within seven years. A chargeable lifetime transfer may be charged to IHT when the transfer is made (depending upon the total of the transfers made in the previous seven years) and may attract additional tax when the transferor dies.
- The amount of IHT charged on the estate of a deceased person depends upon the size of the estate and the total of any chargeable transfers made in the seven years before the person's death.
- The IHT on a transfer is normally payable six months after the end of the month in which the transfer takes place.

Exercises

31.1 Phoebe made the following transfers during 2012-13:

		£
12 April 2012	Gift to grandson	50
17 May 2012	Gift to her nephew on his marriage	3,000
3 August 2012	Gift to her husband	25,000
31 October 2012	Gift to a relevant property trust	10,000
1 January 2013	Gift to the Labour Party	5,000

None of the gifts are regarded as normal expenditure out of income. Phoebe made no transfers at all during 2011-12. Calculate the value of each of her 2012-13 transfers after deduction of all the available exemptions.

31.2 Classify each of the following lifetime transfers as either exempt, potentially exempt, or chargeable:

(a) a gift to the transferor's favourite charity

(b) a gift to a relevant property trust

(c) a gift to the transferor's grandfather.

31.3 On 5 December 2012, Nicholas makes a gift of £80,000 (after deduction of all relevant exemptions) to a relevant property trust. His only previous chargeable lifetime transfers were in June 2003 (gross chargeable value £200,000) and July 2007 (gross chargeable value £281,000). Calculate the lifetime IHT payable in relation to the £80,000 gift and state the due date of payment:

(a) if the trustees pay the tax (b) if Nicholas pays the tax.

31.4 On 31 August 2006, Martha gave £500,000 to her daughter as a wedding present. On 1 June 2008 she gave £500,000 to a relevant property trust. Martha died on 1 January 2013, having made only these two transfers during her life.

(a) Calculate any lifetime tax due on each of the above transfers and state the due date of payment, assuming that Martha paid this tax herself.

(b) Calculate any further tax due on Martha's death in relation to these transfers and state the due date of payment. (Assume that there is no unused nil-rate band to be transferred from a previously deceased spouse or civil partner).

31.5 On 29 September 2012, Hyacinth makes a transfer consisting of 1,000 shares in a listed company. The shares are quoted at 572p - 588p on that date, with recorded bargains at 572p, 577p and 578p. Calculate the market value of the transfer for IHT purposes.

***31.6** On 12 November 2002, Hazel made a gross chargeable transfer to a relevant property trust of £266,000 (after deduction of exemptions). On 1 April 2008 she gave £300,000 to her grandson. These were her only transfers. She died on 17 December 2012.

Calculate the tax payable by her grandson as a result of Hazel's death. (Assume that there is no unused nil-rate band to be transferred from a previously deceased spouse or civil partner).

***31.7** Tony died on 11 July 2012, leaving an estate valued at £500,000. None of the transfers made on his death were exempt from IHT. He had made the following transfers during his lifetime:

		£
3 May 2004	Gift to relevant property trust (tax paid by trustees)	100,000
1 July 2005	Gift to daughter	250,000
1 August 2005	Gift to son	250,000
10 June 2008	Gift to relevant property trust (tax paid by Tony)	450,000

Calculate the tax payable as a result of Tony's death. (Assume that there is no unused nil-rate band to be transferred from a previously deceased spouse or civil partner).

Chapter 32

Overseas aspects of taxation

Introduction

The main purpose of this final chapter is to consider the way in which the UK tax system deals with the overseas income and gains of UK resident individuals and companies. The treatment of non-resident individuals and companies with income or gains arising in the UK is also briefly considered.

The chapter begins by explaining the factors which affect an individual's UK tax status and then continues with a brief review of the overseas aspects of income tax, capital gains tax and inheritance tax. Overseas aspects of corporation tax are dealt with towards the end of the chapter.

Residence, ordinary residence and domicile

The extent to which an individual is chargeable to UK tax depends entirely upon that individual's *residence*, *ordinary residence* and *domicile*. These three key concepts are explained below. It should be noted that an individual's nationality is usually *not* an important factor when determining that individual's UK tax status.

Residence

The term "residence" is not clearly defined in statute law (though a statutory definition is expected to be introduced in April 2013) and so the meaning of the term for tax purposes has evolved mainly from case law. The circumstances in which an individual is normally deemed to be UK resident are as follows:

(a) An individual who is physically present in the UK for at least 183 days during a tax year is deemed to be resident in the UK for the whole of that tax year. Any day on which the individual is present in the UK at midnight generally counts as a day of presence. However, there is an exemption for passengers who are in transit between two places outside the UK but find themselves in the UK at midnight. Days spent in transit are not counted as days of presence unless the individual engages in activities on that day that are unrelated to his or her passage through the UK (e.g. attending a business meeting).

(b) An individual who is in the habit of making regular visits to the UK averaging at least 91 days per tax year (excluding days that are spent in the UK because of circumstances beyond the individual's control, such as illness) is usually regarded as UK resident. Two situations are possible:

   (i) An ex-resident who has now left the UK but who makes regular visits as described above is deemed to be UK resident for the whole of each tax year during which the visits continue.

   (ii) An individual who was not previously a UK resident but who begins making regular visits as described above is normally deemed to be UK resident with effect from the fifth year of the visits. However, if it is clear from the outset that the visits are going to be regular, the individual may be regarded as UK resident with effect from the first year of the visits.

It is important to appreciate that the concept of UK residence normally applies to *whole* tax years. An individual is deemed to be UK resident for the whole of a tax year or for none of it and it is not usually possible to apportion a tax year into periods of residence and non-residence. The significance of this will become clear when the tax implications of residence and non-residence are described (see below). However, such apportionment is permitted in the following cases:

(a) in the year of arrival, if an individual takes up permanent residence in the UK or comes to stay in the UK for at least two years

(b) in the year of departure, if an individual leaves the UK in order to take up permanent residence abroad or to live abroad for at least three years

(c) in the years of departure and return, if an individual leaves the UK in order to take up employment abroad under a contract of employment for at least a whole tax year; in this case the individual concerned is normally regarded as being non-resident throughout the period of the contract, so long as UK visits during that period do not exceed 183 days in any one tax year or 91 days per year on average.

If a tax year is apportioned into periods of residence and non-residence, any personal allowances to which the individual is entitled are available in full for that year.

Ordinary residence†

The term "ordinary residence" is also without a statutory definition. In general terms, an individual is ordinarily resident in the UK if he or she is habitually UK resident (i.e. resident year after year). In a given tax year, it is quite possible to be resident but not ordinarily resident, or vice versa.

An individual who is ordinarily resident in the UK but who is temporarily abroad during a particular tax year (i.e. not present for at least 183 days but not absent for the entire tax year either) is deemed to be resident in the UK for the whole of that tax year.

† *The Government has announced that it intends to abolish the concept of ordinary residence for tax purposes as from 6 April 2013.*

EXAMPLE 1

(a) Pierre, who has lived in France for the whole of his life, arrives in the UK on 1 May 2012 and remains in the UK until 31 March 2013, when he returns permanently to France. What is his UK residence status for 2012-13?

(b) Peter, who has lived in the UK for the whole of his life, leaves the UK on 1 May 2012 and returns permanently on 31 March 2013. What is his UK residence status for 2012-13?

(c) Petra, who has lived in the UK for the whole of her life, leaves the UK on 1 April 2012 and returns permanently on 30 April 2013. She makes no visits to the UK during her time abroad. What is her UK residence status for 2012-13?

Solution

(a) Pierre is *resident* in 2012-13 (spending at least 183 days in the UK during the year) but he is *not ordinarily resident.*

(b) Peter does not spend at least 183 days in the UK during 2012-13. However, he does spend at least some time in the UK during the year and he is *ordinarily resident.* Therefore he is also *resident* for the year.

(c) Petra is *ordinarily resident.* However, she is absent from the UK for the whole of 2012-13 and therefore she is *not resident* for that year.

Domicile

An individual's domicile is the country in which the individual has his or her permanent home. It is not possible to have more than one domicile at a time.

Individuals acquire a "domicile of origin" on birth. This is usually the domicile of the father or other person on whom the individual is dependent and is not necessarily the country of birth. Having reached the age of 16, an individual may then change domicile and acquire a "domicile of choice", but such a domicile can only be acquired by settling in the chosen country.

If an individual acquires a domicile of choice, that domicile is also acquired by anyone under the age of 16 who is dependent on that individual. A domicile acquired in this way is known as a "domicile of dependency".

Income tax - general rules

The general rules governing an individual's liability to UK income tax are as follows:

(a) Individuals who are *resident* in the UK for a tax year are liable to pay UK income tax on all of their income for that year, including any overseas income. Note that:

  (i) Overseas employment income is taxed in accordance with the rules of ITEPA 2003 (see later in this chapter). Overseas trading income, property income and investment income are taxed by ITTOIA 2005.

  (ii) ITTOIA 2005 provides that the "relevant foreign income" of a UK resident who is not domiciled in the UK may be taxed only to the extent that the income is remitted to the UK (the "remittance basis"). The term "relevant foreign income" covers most of the forms of overseas income to which ITTOIA 2005 applies.

  In general, an individual who wishes that the remittance basis should apply for a tax year must make a claim to that effect. However, the remittance basis is automatically assumed to apply to an individual whose unremitted income and gains are less than £2,000 in the year concerned (unless the individual notifies HMRC that he/she does not wish the remittance basis to apply).

  (iii) Individuals who claim the remittance basis and have been UK resident for more than seven of the past ten tax years are liable to an annual tax charge of £30,000. This charge increases to £50,000 for those who have been resident in the UK for at least 12 of the last 14 years. Since this rule applies only to those who *claim* the remittance basis, it does not apply to individuals whose unremitted income and gains are less than £2,000 for the tax year.

  (iv) Personal allowances are generally available to UK residents. But individuals who claim the remittance basis are not entitled to personal allowances. Again, this rule applies only to those who *claim* the remittance basis.

  (v) As from 6 April 2012, individuals who are taxed on the remittance basis may remit overseas income to the UK without incurring an income tax liability if this income is used to make a commercial investment in a qualifying business.

(b) Individuals who are *not resident* in the UK are liable to pay UK income tax on their UK income only. Note that:

  (i) The property income of non-residents is usually payable after deduction of basic rate income tax by the letting agent or tenant.

  (ii) Personal allowances may be claimed by certain non-residents, principally those who are citizens of the European Economic Area (see Chapter 3).

(c) If a tax year is apportioned into periods of residence and non-residence, the above rules apply to the two periods as if they were separate tax years.

These general rules are subject to a number of exceptions, depending upon the type of income involved (see below).

Unremittable income

A UK resident who would normally be liable to income tax on income arising from an overseas source may make a claim to the effect that the income is "unremittable". Such a claim may be made if the income cannot be remitted to the UK because of:

(a) the laws of the country in which the income arises, or

(b) the executive actions of the government of that country, or

(c) the impossibility of obtaining foreign currency in that country which could be transferred to the UK.

The effect of the claim is that the income is not taxed in the year in which it arises but is taxed instead in the year in which it ceases to be unremittable (if that occurs).

Double taxation relief (DTR)

The rules given above are likely to lead to a number of situations in which income is taxed twice. For example, the overseas income of a UK resident will be taxed in the UK and might also be taxed in the country in which the income arises, depending upon that country's tax laws. Similarly, the UK income of a non-resident will be taxed in the UK and might also be taxed overseas. In order to avoid this situation, the UK has made "double taxation treaties" with many overseas countries. Typically, such a treaty might provide that certain forms of income should be exempt from income tax in the country of origin (or charged at a reduced rate) if receivable by a non-resident.

Unilateral double tax relief

Unless double tax relief is available (or prohibited) under the terms of a double taxation treaty with the country concerned, the UK tax system provides "unilateral double tax relief" for foreign tax suffered by a UK resident who receives overseas income. Overseas income which is received net of foreign tax is grossed-up and charged to UK income tax in the usual way, but the taxpayer is then given tax relief equal to the *lower* of:

(a) the amount of foreign tax suffered (the "withholding tax") and

(b) the amount of UK tax due on the overseas income.

The amount of UK tax due on the overseas income is equal to the difference between the tax due on the taxpayer's total income (including overseas income) and the tax which would be due if the overseas income were ignored. If the foreign tax suffered exceeds the UK tax due, part of the foreign tax suffered will be unrelieved.

Unilateral relief is available only if the taxpayer has taken all reasonable steps to minimise the amount of the foreign tax liability.

EXAMPLE 2

Vicky's income for 2012-13 consists of her salary from UK employment of £43,360 and rents from overseas property (net of 30% withholding tax) of £3,500. Vicky is UK resident in 2012-13. Calculate her UK income tax liability for the year.

Solution

Property income is £5,000 (£3,500 x 100/70). Therefore total income is £48,360 (£43,360 + £5,000) and taxable income is £40,255 (£48,360 – £8,105). The income tax liability is:

		£
34,370	@ 20%	6,874.00
5,885	@ 40%	2,354.00
40,255		9,228.00
Less:	Double tax relief, lower of:	
	(a) foreign tax (£1,500)	1,500.00
	(b) UK tax on foreign income (40% x £5,000)	
UK tax liability		7,728.00

Income from employment

Income from employment is taxed according to detailed rules contained in the Income Tax (Earnings and Pensions) Act 2003. Broadly, the extent to which an individual's income from employment is taxable depends upon the individual's residence status and whether the duties of the employment are performed in the UK or overseas. The rules are briefly summarised as follows:

(a) **Employee resident in UK**. Unless the remittance basis applies to the individual concerned (see below) the entire employment income of an individual who is UK resident is taxable on the receipts basis, regardless of whether the duties of the employment are performed in the UK or overseas.

(b) **Employee resident in UK (remittance basis)**. As explained earlier in this chapter, the remittance basis may apply to a UK resident individual who is not domiciled in the UK. If the remittance basis applies, then the extent to which employment income is taxable depends upon whether the individual is ordinarily resident in the UK. The situation is as follows:

    (i) If the individual is ordinarily resident in the UK, any employment income that is classified as "chargeable overseas earnings" is taxed on the remittance basis. All other employment income is fully taxable (on the receipts basis). Chargeable overseas earnings are those which are derived from a foreign employer in respect of duties performed wholly outside the UK.

(ii) If the individual is *not* ordinarily resident in the UK, employment income that is classified as "foreign earnings" is taxed on the remittance basis. All other employment income is fully taxable (on the receipts basis). Foreign earnings are those which are in respect of duties performed wholly outside the UK.

(c) **Employee not resident in UK**. The employment income of an individual who is not resident in the UK is taxable (on the receipts basis) only to the extent that the income is in respect of duties performed in the UK.

Note that the income tax on *foreign pensions* received by a UK resident is calculated on only 90% of the amount arising unless the remittance basis applies, in which case the whole of the amount remitted to the UK is taxable.

Travelling and subsistence expenses

If the duties of an employment are performed abroad, the employee is both resident and ordinarily resident in the UK and the earnings from the employment are not classed as "chargeable overseas earnings" (see above), then the following expenses may be deducted from the employee's earnings for tax purposes:

(a) where duties are performed wholly abroad:

- (i) the costs of travelling abroad at the start of the employment and travelling back to the UK at the end of it
- (ii) the costs of overseas board and lodging provided or reimbursed by the employer to enable the employee to perform the duties of the overseas employment

(b) where duties are performed partly in the UK and partly abroad, travelling and subsistence expenses paid for or reimbursed by the employer (and assessable as earnings) relating to:

- (i) travel by the employee between the UK and the overseas place of work
- (ii) travel by the employee's spouse and minor children, if the employee is working abroad for a continuous period of 60 days or more, but limited to two return journeys per person per tax year.

Similar deductions to those described at (b) above are available to non-UK domiciled individuals who are working in the UK but these deductions are available for only five years, beginning with the date of arrival in the UK.

The 100% deduction for seafarers

If the duties of a *seafarer* who is resident and ordinarily resident in the UK are performed wholly or partly outside the UK throughout a continuous qualifying period of 365 days or more, a 100% deduction is given against all of the earnings for that period (including earnings relating to any work performed in the UK). In effect, the earnings attributable to such a qualifying period are exempt from UK income tax.

A qualifying period begins when an individual leaves the UK to work abroad as a seafarer and the period is treated as continuous even if the individual returns to the UK from time to time, so long as:

(a) no visit in the UK during the period lasts for more than 183 days, and

(b) on each day of return to the UK, the total number of days present in the UK since the period began is no more than one-half of the total length of the period so far.

As from 6 April 2011, the seafarers' earnings deduction (SED) is extended to seafarers who are not resident or ordinarily resident in the UK but who are resident in a state of the European Economic Area other than the UK. Such seafarers are liable to UK income tax on duties performed in the UK (e.g. in the UK's territorial waters) but are now able to claim SED in relation to their earnings during a qualifying period.

Trading income

The extent to which the profits of a trade, profession or vocation are charged to UK income tax depends upon whether or not the owner of the business is UK resident and whether the business is carried on in the UK or overseas. The rules are as follows:

(a) Trading profits arising to a UK resident are charged to income tax wherever in the world the trade is carried on. Therefore UK residents are taxed on the profits of businesses which are carried on wholly or partly overseas.

(b) If a business is carried on wholly overseas, then income arising from that business ranks as "relevant foreign income" (see above). Therefore a UK resident who is not domiciled in the UK may claim that the income concerned should be taxed on the remittance basis.

(c) Trading losses arising from a business carried on wholly overseas may be carried forward in the usual way (see Chapter 12). Such losses are also eligible for terminal loss relief if incurred in the final year of trading. But "sideways relief" against total income is available only against overseas income which is not charged on the remittance basis and which consists of:

    (i) trading profits arising from a business which is carried on wholly overseas

    (ii) employment income ranking as "chargeable overseas earnings" (see above)

    (iii) overseas pensions.

(d) Trading profits arising to a non-UK resident are charged to income tax only if the trade is carried on wholly or partly in the UK. In the case of a trade which is carried on only partly in the UK, the profits which are charged to income tax are the profits arising from the UK part of the trade.

Travelling and subsistence expenses

If a trade is carried on wholly overseas and the owner of the business is absent from the UK wholly and exclusively for business purposes, then the expenses listed below are allowable deductions when computing trading profits (so long as those profits are not taxed on the remittance basis):

(a) expenses incurred by the trader in travelling between the UK and the location of the overseas business

(b) overseas board and lodging expenses

(c) expenses relating to travel by the proprietor's spouse and minor children, if the proprietor is abroad for a continuous period of 60 days or more, but limited to two return journeys per person per tax year.

Income from property and investments

Income from property and income from savings and investments are charged to UK income tax according to the following rules:

(a) Income from property situated in the UK is taxable whether or not the person to whom the income arises is UK resident. Income from property situated overseas is taxable only if the person to whom the income arises is UK resident.

(b) Savings and investment income from a UK source is generally taxable whether or not the person to whom the income arises is UK resident. However, interest on UK Government securities is exempt from UK income tax if the recipient is *not ordinarily resident* in the UK. Savings and investment income from an overseas source is taxable only if the person to whom the income arises is UK resident.

(c) Overseas property income and overseas savings and investment income generally rank as "relevant foreign income" (see above). Therefore a UK resident who is not domiciled in the UK may claim that these forms of income should be taxed on the remittance basis. However, overseas savings and investment income which is taxed on the remittance basis is taxed as if it were non-savings income and so cannot benefit from the starting rate for savings (10%) or the dividend lower, upper and additional rates (10%, 32.5% and 42.5%).

(d) Dividends received from UK companies by UK resident individuals (and by certain non-residents, mainly EEA citizens) carry a one-ninth tax credit.

One-ninth tax credits are also available in relation to dividends received from a non-UK company, as long as the individual who receives the dividend owns less than 10% of the company's shares or the company is resident in a "qualifying territory" with which the UK has an appropriate double taxation treaty.

Capital gains tax - general rules

The general rules which govern an individual's liability to UK capital gains tax (CGT) are as follows:

(a) Individuals who are resident or ordinarily resident in the UK for a tax year are liable to CGT in relation to all disposals of chargeable assets which occur in that year, no matter where in the world the assets are situated. Double tax relief may be available.

(b) Individuals who are neither resident nor ordinarily resident in the UK are not liable to CGT at all, even in relation to disposals of assets situated in the UK.

There are three main exceptions to these general rules:

(a) A non-UK domiciled individual who is resident or ordinarily resident in the UK is fully liable to CGT on the disposal of assets situated in the UK. However, gains arising from disposals of assets situated overseas may (in certain circumstances) be taxable only on the remittance basis. No annual exemption is available for a tax year in which an individual claims that the remittance basis should apply.

    As from 6 April 2012, individuals who are taxed on the remittance basis may remit overseas gains to the UK without incurring a CGT liability if these gains are used to make a commercial investment in a qualifying business.

(b) An individual who is neither resident nor ordinarily resident in the UK but who carries on a business in the UK is chargeable to CGT in relation to disposals of business assets situated in the UK.

(c) Individuals who acquire assets before temporarily leaving the UK (for up to five tax years) and then dispose of those assets whilst abroad remain chargeable to CGT in relation to these disposals. Gains arising in the tax year of departure are taxed in that year. Later gains are taxed in the year in which residence resumes.

A claim may be made to defer a CGT assessment relating to a disposal of overseas assets if it can be shown that the gain in question cannot be remitted to the UK. The conditions which must be satisfied in order that such a claim should be successful are the same as the equivalent conditions for income tax (see above). The taxpayer must show that the gain cannot be remitted to the UK because of either:

(a) the laws of the country in which the gain arises, or

(b) the executive actions of the government of that country, or

(c) the impossibility of obtaining foreign currency in that country.

If the conditions preventing remittance of the gain to the UK subsequently cease to exist, the gain is chargeable in the year in which this occurs.

Inheritance tax - general rules

An individual who is domiciled in the UK is liable to inheritance tax (IHT) in relation to all of his or her chargeable property, wherever in the world that property is situated. An individual who is not domiciled in the UK is liable to IHT only in relation to property situated in the UK. The definition of "domicile" for IHT purposes is broader than the general definition given earlier in this chapter. An individual is treated as domiciled in the UK on the date of a transfer if that individual:

(a) was domiciled in the UK at any time within the previous three years, or

(b) was UK resident for at least seventeen of the twenty tax years ending with the year in which the transfer takes place.

In general, transfers between spouses or civil partners are exempt from IHT. But transfers made by a UK-domiciled spouse/partner to a spouse/partner who is not domiciled in the UK are exempt only up to a cumulative total of £55,000. The Government has announced that it intends to increase this figure in tax year 2013-14.

Corporation tax - general rules

A company's liability to UK corporation tax depends upon whether or not it is resident in the UK. A company is regarded as resident in the UK if it is incorporated in the UK or if its central management and control is situated in the UK. The general rules which govern a company's liability to UK corporation tax are as follows:

(a) A UK resident company is chargeable to UK corporation tax on all of its profits, no matter where in the world those profits are earned. Note the following points:

  (i) The profits of a trade conducted through a permanent establishment situated overseas (e.g. an overseas branch) are treated as trading income. Trading losses may be relieved as usual and group relief is generally available. But the losses of an overseas establishment may be surrendered only to the extent that those losses are not relievable in the overseas country.

  However, a company may now make an irrevocable election to the effect that the profits of *all* its overseas branches (including any chargeable gains) should be exempt from UK corporation tax. If this election is made, no relief will be available for foreign branch losses.

  (ii) Most foreign dividends received by UK companies are exempt from corporation tax (with certain exceptions) and are treated as if they were dividends received from other UK companies. An exempt foreign dividend is deemed to have an attached one-ninth tax credit and the dividend (plus tax credit) is treated as FII.

  (iii) Gains arising on the disposal of overseas assets are generally chargeable gains and form part of the company's chargeable profits.

(b) A non-UK resident company is chargeable to UK corporation tax only if it carries on a trade through a permanent establishment situated in the UK. If so, the company is taxed on:

   (i) the trading profits of the UK establishment
   (ii) income from property in the possession of the UK establishment
   (iii) gains arising from the disposal of assets used by the UK establishment.

   The trading losses of a UK permanent establishment of a non-UK resident company may generally be set against any other profits of the establishment or may be carried forward against the establishment's future trading profits. The establishment may also surrender its losses to UK resident companies in the same group, so long as those losses are not relievable in the overseas country. Similarly, the establishment may claim losses surrendered by other UK resident group companies. Also, assets transferred between such an establishment and a UK resident group company are transferred on a no-gain, no-loss basis, so long as the assets concerned remain within the charge to UK corporation tax.

   A non-UK resident company is not generally entitled to the small profits rate of corporation tax or to marginal relief. But this rule will not apply if it is over-ridden by a double taxation treaty between the UK and the country in which the non-UK company is resident.

Overseas subsidiaries

The profits of a non-UK resident subsidiary of a UK resident parent company may be subject to overseas tax but are not generally subject to UK tax unless the subsidiary is treated as a controlled foreign company (see later in this chapter). The UK resident parent company is of course liable to corporation tax on any non-exempt income received from the overseas subsidiary (e.g. interest) and the subsidiary will also count as an associated company, so causing a reduction in the upper and lower limits.

As explained in Chapter 28, groups of companies enjoy a number of corporation tax reliefs, including (subject to certain conditions):

(a) transfer of trading losses and certain other items between group members
(b) transfer of chargeable assets between group members on a no-gain, no-loss basis.

These reliefs are generally available only to "UK related" companies (see Chapter 28) and do not usually apply to an overseas subsidiary. However, the losses of a subsidiary which is resident in the European Economic Area (EEA) or carries on a trade in the EEA may be surrendered to a UK company, but only after all possibilities of relief in any other country have been exhausted. In order to obtain relief against UK profits, the losses of the EEA subsidiary must be re-computed under UK tax rules.

Company migration

A UK resident company may wish to "migrate" overseas in order to escape paying UK corporation tax on its worldwide profits. This is only possible for companies which are incorporated outside the UK and involves moving the central management and control of the company from the UK to an overseas location. A company wishing to take this step must:

(a) notify HMRC of its intentions, specifying the date on which it intends to become non-resident, and

(b) provide HMRC with a statement of all the tax payable up to that date, specifying the arrangements which will be made to ensure that this tax is paid.

On the date that a company becomes non-resident it is deemed to make a disposal of all its assets at their market value on that date. This deemed disposal is likely to result in a sizeable chargeable gain, which is sometimes referred to as the "exit charge". However, this charge is not made in full in the following circumstances:

(a) If the company retains a permanent establishment in the UK, the deemed disposal does not include assets which are situated in the UK and which are used for trade purposes by that establishment.

(b) If the company is a 75% subsidiary of a UK resident company (termed the "principal company") the gains arising in connection with the deemed disposal of the company's *foreign* assets may be postponed, so long as both companies make an election in writing to that effect. The postponed gains will crystallise if:

    (i) within the following six years, any of the foreign assets are disposed of, or

    (ii) at any time, the company which is migrating ceases to be a 75% subsidiary of the principal company, or

    (iii) at any time, the principal company ceases to be UK resident.

    Any gains which crystallise are chargeable on the principal company.

Transfer pricing

A UK resident company might try to reduce its corporation tax liability by transferring goods at an artificially low price to an overseas subsidiary. This would have the effect of lowering the UK company's profits (which are liable to UK tax) and increasing the subsidiary's profits (which are not liable to UK tax).

However, this tax avoidance manoeuvre is blocked by "transfer pricing" legislation which requires that a true market price should be substituted for the transfer price in these circumstances and that the UK company should make the necessary adjustment when completing its self-assessment tax return (see Chapter 28). Small and medium-sized companies are generally exempt from the transfer pricing legislation.

Controlled foreign companies (CFCs)

A UK resident company which wishes to operate overseas may choose to do so through a separate non-UK resident company which is under its control (an overseas subsidiary).

Since the profits of a non-UK company are generally not chargeable to UK corporation tax, this would seem to be beneficial (especially if the operation is carried on in a country with low tax rates). Furthermore, any dividends paid by the overseas subsidiary to its UK parent would usually be tax-exempt. However, some of these tax advantages are lost if the overseas subsidiary ranks as a *controlled foreign company* (CFC).

As an anti-avoidance measure, the profits of a CFC are apportioned between its shareholders for tax purposes and any CFC profits apportioned to a UK company are charged to corporation tax. This tax is calculated at the average rate payable by the UK company for the accounting period in which the CFC's accounting period ends. Double taxation relief is available. But no assessment is raised on a UK company to which less than 25% of a CFC's profits are apportioned. A CFC is a company which:

(a) is resident overseas but is under UK control, and

(b) is subject to a level of taxation in the country in which it is resident which is less than 75% of the corresponding UK tax, or

(c) is resident in one of a number of countries which (effectively) allow companies to choose their own "designer rate" of tax as a means of side-stepping the CFC rules.

However, the profits of a CFC for an accounting period are *not* apportioned between its shareholders if any of the following conditions are satisfied for that period:

(a) The accounting profits of the CFC do not exceed £200,000 per annum.

(b) The chargeable profits of the CFC do not exceed £50,000 per annum.

(c) The CFC is engaged in certain exempt activities.

(d) The CFC was not set up mainly to achieve a reduction in UK tax.

The CFC rules do not apply to profits which arise from "genuine economic activities" conducted from a business establishment located in the European Economic Area (EEA).

Reform of the CFC rules

Finance Act 2012 introduces a revised CFC tax regime which takes effect for accounting periods beginning on or after 1 January 2013. The new regime makes many detailed changes to the CFC rules but retains most of the basic principles to be found in the current regime. In particular, the definition of a CFC is broadly unchanged and the "25% rule" is retained. The changes are mainly concerned with the conditions (and thresholds) which are considered when determining whether or not a company is exempt from CFC status. The aim of these changes is to target only those situations in which profits have been artificially diverted away from the UK for tax reasons.

The new regime will also apply to exempt foreign branches of UK companies with profits taxed at a lower rate than in the UK.

Double taxation relief for companies

Unless double tax relief is available (or prohibited) under the terms of a double taxation treaty with the country concerned, the UK tax system provides unilateral double tax relief for foreign tax suffered by a UK company which receives income from overseas.

Unilateral relief takes the form of a tax credit equal to the *lower* of the amount of foreign tax suffered and the amount of UK corporation tax payable on the foreign income. Any excess foreign tax is unrelieved, but it may be possible to carry the excess back or forward to other accounting periods (see below).

EXAMPLE 3

In the year to 31 March 2013, a UK resident company had UK trading profits of £5,200,000 and overseas property income (net of 35% withholding tax) of £130,000. Compute the corporation tax liability for the year.

Solution

	UK	*Overseas*	*Total*
	£	£	£
Trading income	5,200,000		5,200,000
Property income £130,000 x 100/65		200,000	200,000
Chargeable profits	5,200,000	200,000	5,400,000
Corporation tax @ 24%	1,248,000	48,000	1,296,000
Less: Unilateral DTR		(48,000)	(48,000)
Corporation tax due	1,248,000	-	1,248,000

The unilateral relief given is restricted to the UK tax due on the overseas income. The remaining £22,000 (£70,000 – £48,000) of foreign tax paid is unrelieved.

Unrelieved foreign tax

Unrelieved foreign tax arising in connection with trading income derived from an overseas permanent establishment (i.e. an overseas branch) may be carried back for up to three years or may be carried forward without time limit. Note that:

(a) When unrelieved foreign tax is carried back or forward, it is treated as if it were foreign tax paid in respect of the trading income of the same overseas branch in the accounting period to which it is carried. But if the rate of foreign tax suffered on such income is consistently higher than the UK tax rate, it is unlikely that there will be any scope for relieving unrelieved foreign tax from other accounting periods.

(b) These provisions are not relevant to a company which has elected that the profits of all its overseas branches should be exempt from UK tax (see earlier in this chapter).

Underlying DTR

If a UK resident company owns at least 10% of the voting power of an overseas company from which it receives a non-exempt dividend, then an additional form of unilateral double taxation relief, known as "underlying relief", is available. The idea of underlying DTR is to give relief for the foreign tax suffered on the profits out of which the dividend has been paid. Underlying relief is calculated by the formula:

$$\frac{D}{P} \times T$$

where: D = the gross dividend received

P = the profit available for distribution as shown in the accounts for the period to which the dividend relates

T = the overseas tax actually paid on the profits of that period.

However, since most foreign dividends received by UK companies are now exempt from corporation tax, underlying double tax relief applies only in the minority of cases where a company receives a non-exempt foreign dividend.

EXAMPLE 4

On 1 November 2012, a UK company receives a non-exempt dividend from an overseas company (in which it has 15% voting power) of £10,500, net of 30% withholding tax. The income statement of the overseas company for the year to which the dividend relates is:

	£
Profit before tax	400,000
Less: Provision for taxation liability	150,000
Profits after tax	250,000
Dividends	100,000
Retained profits c/f	150,000

The actual tax liability of the overseas company is finally agreed at £160,000. Compute the maximum unilateral double tax relief available in respect of the £10,500 dividend.

Solution

(i) D = £10,500 x 100/70 = £15,000. P = £250,000. T = £160,000

(ii) Withholding tax = £4,500

(iii) Underlying tax = $\frac{D}{P} \times T = \frac{£15,000}{£250,000} \times £160,000 = £9,600$

(iv) Maximum unilateral DTR = £4,500 + £9,600 = £14,100. Therefore the gross dividend is £24,600 (net £10,500 + tax £14,100).

Unilateral expense relief

A company may waive the right to claim unilateral "credit relief" (where DTR takes the form of a tax credit) and opt for unilateral "expense relief" instead. A company which opts for expense relief is assessed on the *net* foreign income, so that the foreign tax is treated as if it were an expense. Unilateral expense relief may be attractive if a company makes a claim to set a trading loss against its total profits, so that it has no corporation tax liability on the foreign income and cannot obtain any credit relief.

EXAMPLE 5

A UK company has a trading loss of £50,000 for the year to 31 March 2013. During the year, the company receives overseas property income of £12,000, net of 40% withholding tax. Show the corporation tax computation for the year if:

(a) unilateral credit relief is claimed

(b) unilateral expense relief is claimed.

The company claims trading loss relief against total profits of the year to 31 March 2013.

Solution

	Credit relief	*Expense relief*
	£	£
Trading income	0	0
Property income (gross)	20,000	
Property income (net of foreign tax)		12,000
	20,000	12,000
Less: Trading loss	(20,000)	(12,000)
Chargeable profits	0	0
Corporation tax liability	0	0
Unrelieved trading losses	30,000	38,000
Unrelieved foreign tax	8,000	nil

Notes:

(i) No unilateral credit relief is available since the overseas income is absorbed by the trading loss, leaving a UK tax liability of £nil.

(ii) Credit relief gives £8,000 of unrelieved foreign tax.

(iii) Expense relief eliminates the unrelieved foreign tax. The trading losses available for carry-back against total profits of the previous 12 months or carry-forward against future trading profits are increased by £8,000.

Interaction of charitable donations, loss reliefs and DTR

A company's chargeable profits are reduced by the qualifying charitable donations made in the accounting period (see Chapter 23) and by the amount of any trading losses relieved against the total profits of the period (see Chapter 26). Normally, it is sufficient simply to subtract donations and trading losses from the company's total income (and gains) without allocating these deductions to any particular source of income. However, if unilateral double tax relief is claimed, such an allocation must be made so that the amount of UK tax payable on the foreign income can be calculated.

If any donations or trading losses are set against the foreign income, this will have the effect of reducing the UK tax due on that foreign income and so reducing the maximum unilateral DTR available. Therefore, donations and trading losses should be set first against UK income, then against foreign income. If a company has more than one source of foreign income, donations and trading losses should be set against foreign income which has suffered low rates of foreign tax in preference to foreign income which has suffered high rates of foreign tax.

EXAMPLE 6

In the year to 31 March 2013, a UK company has UK trading profits of £4,800,000 and overseas property income (net of 45% withholding tax) of £2,750,000. Gift Aid donations of £100,000 are made in the year. Compute the corporation tax liability for the year.

Solution

	UK	*Overseas*	*Total*
	£	£	£
Trading income	4,800,000		4,800,000
Income from property:			
£2,750,000 x 100/55		5,000,000	5,000,000
	4,800,000	5,000,000	9,800,000
Less: Donations	100,000	-	100,000
Chargeable profits	4,700,000	5,000,000	9,700,000
Corporation tax @ 24%	1,128,000	1,200,000	2,328,000
Less: Unilateral DTR		(1,200,000)	(1,200,000)
Corporation tax liability	1,128,000	-	1,128,000

Notes:

(i) The donations are set against the UK income so as to maximise double tax relief on the overseas income.

(ii) DTR is limited to the UK tax due on the overseas income. Foreign tax paid is £2,250,000, of which £1,050,000 is unrelieved.

Summary

- An individual's liability to UK tax depends upon that individual's residence, ordinary residence and domicile.
- Individuals who are resident in the UK for a tax year are liable to UK income tax on their worldwide income for that year. Non-residents are liable to tax on their UK income only.
- Double taxation relief may be available if income is subject to both UK tax and overseas tax.
- The extent to which an individual's income from employment is taxable depends upon the individual's residence status and whether the duties of the employment are performed in the UK or overseas.
- Trading profits arising to a UK resident are charged to income tax wherever in the world the trade is carried on. Trading profits arising to a non-resident are charged to income tax only if the trade is carried on wholly or partly in the UK.
- Income from UK property and investments is generally taxable whether or not the person to whom the income arises is UK resident. Income from overseas property and investments is taxable only if the person to whom the income arises is UK resident.
- Individuals who are resident or ordinarily resident in the UK for a tax year are liable to UK CGT on their disposals throughout the world in that year.
- Individuals who are domiciled in the UK are liable to UK IHT. The definition of "domicile" for IHT purposes is broader than the general definition.
- UK resident companies are liable to UK corporation tax on their worldwide profits. A non-UK resident company is liable to UK corporation tax only if it carries on a trade through a permanent establishment situated in the UK.
- Most foreign dividends received by UK companies are exempt from corporation tax.
- The profits of a controlled foreign company may be apportioned between the controlling UK companies and assessed to UK corporation tax.
- Double tax relief for companies may take the form of credit relief, underlying tax relief or expense relief.

Exercises

32.1 Jean-Paul is a Canadian citizen. He owns a house in Canada and regards Canada as his home but he lives in London for nearly all of tax year 2012-13. His income for the year is derived from the following sources:

(a) a part-time employment with a UK company (the duties of which are performed entirely in London)

(b) a second part-time employment with a Belgian company (the duties of which are performed entirely in Brussels, which he visits on one day each month)

(c) dividends from stocks and shares held in Canada

(d) interest on UK Government securities.

To what extent is any of his income chargeable to UK income tax?

32.2 Amy is domiciled in the UK and has lived in the UK all her life. On 1 January 2011 she leaves to work in Australia for three years. Explain her UK income tax status for tax years 2010-11 to 2013-14 inclusive.

32.3 Cara is a UK resident. She receives a pension of £10,000 per annum from the Italian company for whom she used to work when she lived in Italy. Explain how the UK income tax system will treat this pension if Cara is:

(a) domiciled in the UK

(b) domiciled in Italy.

32.4 How would a UK resident company proceed if it wished to "migrate" overseas? Why might this be a desirable step?

32.5 Explain the term "controlled foreign company" (CFC). In what circumstances are the profits of a CFC chargeable to UK corporation tax?

32.6 Brist Ltd is a UK resident company which prepares annual accounts to 31 March. In the year to 31 March 2013, the company had a UK trading profit of £2,120,000 and received overseas property income of £98,000 (this figure is net of 30% withholding tax).

(a) Compute the company's corporation tax liability for the year and explain the treatment of any unrelieved foreign tax.

(b) Would the situation be any different if the overseas property income was replaced by trading income from an overseas branch?

***32.7** Donald is domiciled, resident and ordinarily resident in the UK. He has the following income in 2012-13:

	£
UK trading profits	37,405
UK bank interest (net amount received)	1,600
Income from foreign property (net of 45% withholding tax)	2,200

Donald claims only the personal allowance. Compute the amount of income tax payable for 2012-13.

***32.8** A UK resident company has 19 subsidiaries, five of which are situated abroad. In the year to 31 March 2013, the company had the following results:

	£
UK trading profits	720,000
UK dividends received	40,000
UK chargeable gains	120,000
Overseas bank interest (net of 40% withholding tax)	10,800
Gift Aid donations paid	80,000

None of the dividends received were from any of the company's subsidiaries. Calculate the company's corporation tax liability for the year to 31 March 2013.

Review questions (Set D)

D1 You have received a letter from the managing director of Wakem & Co. Ltd, a company making wholly standard rated supplies. Extracts from the letter are as follows:

"During the course of the last quarter, sales have been very good. In particular, we sold £30,000 worth of goods to St. Oggs Inc, an American company, and we also sold £20,000 worth of goods to Rappit Ltd in Scotland. Mr Jakin, the managing director of Rappit Ltd, drove a hard bargain and to secure the order we had to allow a 5% discount for prompt settlement. As we closed down the box manufacturing line, we sold off the machinery and made a useful £15,000. The electrical equipment remaining has been hired to Mudport Ltd for £1,000 per month. One piece of bad news is that Garum Furs plc has gone into liquidation owing us £14,000, though there is a possibility of recovering part of that amount in the liquidation."

Required:

Explain the significance for VAT purposes of the events described in this letter.

(Amended from AAT)

D2 M Ltd, a UK resident trading company, owns 6% of the share capital of Z Inc and 8% of the share capital of X S.A. Neither of these companies is resident in the UK for tax purposes. In addition, M Ltd has a controlling interest in two UK resident companies - N Ltd and O Ltd. The following information relates to M Ltd's 12-month accounting period ended 31 March 2013:

	£
INCOME	
Trading income	500,000
Non-exempt dividend received from Z Inc (after 30% withholding tax)	35,000
Non-exempt dividend received from X S.A. (after 5% withholding tax)	38,000
PAYMENTS	
Gift Aid donations	10,000

You are required:

To compute the corporation tax liability of M Ltd for the above period, showing clearly the relief for double taxation. *(CIMA)*

D3 A Ltd is the holding company for a group of five companies. The relationships between the companies in the group are shown in the diagram below:

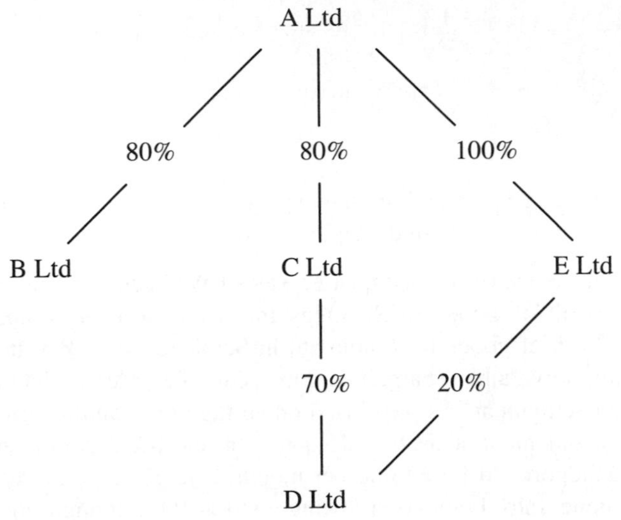

All of the companies are UK resident except for E Ltd which is resident in a non-EEA country where the rate of tax is 5%. E Ltd does not carry on a trade in the UK (or elsewhere in the EEA) and can be regarded as a Controlled Foreign Company. All of the companies have an accounting year ended 31 March 2013 and their incomes/(losses) for the year were as follows:

	Trading income	*Bank interest*
	£	£
A Ltd	90,000	-
B Ltd	100,000	15,000
C Ltd	(90,000)	12,000
D Ltd	(5,000)	-
E Ltd	15,000	-

You are required to:

(a) Identify the companies which are treated as associated companies.

(b) Identify the companies which form a group (or groups) for group relief purposes.

(c) Compute the corporation tax liability of each company, assuming that the most efficient use is made by the group of any trading losses. Assume also that none of the companies paid or received any dividends during the year. *(CIMA)*

D4 Your company has a number of branches and subsidiaries trading outside the UK. The board is about to offer contracts to employees working in UK locations which will allow them to transfer to foreign locations on a temporary basis, with all of their duties being performed outside the UK. There are two contracts being offered - one lasting nine months and one lasting eighteen months. The employees concerned are all currently resident, ordinarily resident and domiciled in the UK.

You are required:

To draft a report to the board on the taxation implications, for the employees, of each of the possible contracts. *(CIMA)*

***D5** David Deans started trading as a painter and decorator on 1 July 2012. He has notified you of his turnover each month which, up to November 2012, has been as follows:

	£
July 2012	6,500
August 2012	7,500
September 2012	8,500
October 2012	9,700
November 2012	13,000

In anticipation of a meeting with Mr Deans, you have received a letter from him, of which the following is an extract:

"In preparation for our meeting, I have some further information for you and some questions which I hope you will be able to answer for me. I anticipate that my turnover is likely to be £15,000 in December 2012 and £17,500 in January 2013. It must be reaching the time at which I need to be registered for VAT. Could you give me some idea of when this might be and whether I could delay it in order to improve my cash flow?

Since starting business I have purchased substantial quantities of stock. Will I be able to recover any of the VAT I have paid?

In June next year, I intend to buy a new van and a new car for the business. Their cost, including VAT, will be £14,000 and £8,000 respectively. I assume that I will be able to recover the VAT on both items. The van will be used wholly for business and the car for both business and private use. The firm will pay for all the petrol used by both vehicles.

As yet, I have not suffered any bad debts but as the business expands there is always the risk that they might arise. Are there any special VAT arrangements to deal with them?"

Required:

Draft notes in preparation for the meeting with Mr Deans, responding to the queries which he has raised. *(Amended from AAT)*

***D6** Mrs Lammle, who is registered for VAT, has traded as a manufacturer of standard-rated items since 1 June 1996. She has decided to retire on 31 May 2012, her 65th birthday, and you are asked to finalise her tax position up to that date. You are provided with the following information:

(i) Mrs Lammle has always prepared accounts to 31 May each year. Overlap profits of £37,500 arose on commencement.

(ii) The last accounts will be for the year to 31 May 2012. Interim accounts have been prepared to 29 February 2012, revealing the following:

	£
Sales	100,200
Cost of sales	24,700
Gross profit	75,500
Expenses	29,000
Net profit	46,500

All of the above figures are net of VAT and contain no disallowable items.

(iii) For the last three months to 31 May 2012 (which is also the last VAT quarter), you have extracted the following figures from the accounting records:

	£
Sales:	
To UK customers	30,654
To overseas customers	8,000
Materials purchased:	
Standard-rated	4,098
Zero-rated	2,000
Exempt	800
Expenses:	
General (all standard-rated)	6,120
Wages	7,000
Hire of machinery	612
Business bank charges	500
Entertaining UK clients	400

All of the above include VAT if appropriate. There was no stock at 1 March 2012 and there is no outstanding stock left at 31 May 2012. All of the general expenses are allowable for income tax purposes.

(iv) The tax written down value of the plant and machinery carried forward after capital allowances had been calculated for the year to 31 May 2011 was:

	£
Plant and machinery main pool	12,375
Special rate pool (car with no private use)	5,250

No plant and machinery was acquired during the year to 31 May 2012.

(v) The business was sold as a going concern on 31 May 2012. The items sold were:

	£
Freehold shop	200,000
Freehold workshop	130,000
Goodwill	180,000
Plant (no item worth more than £6,000)	25,000
Car	6,000

The shop and the workshop were acquired on 1 June 1996 for £30,000 and £21,000 respectively.

Required:

(a) Calculate the VAT due for the quarter to 31 May 2012.

(b) Calculate the final adjusted profit for the year to 31 May 2012, after deduction of capital allowances.

(c) Calculate Mrs Lammle's trading income for 2012-13.

(d) Calculate the capital gains tax due on the disposal of the business, assuming that entrepreneurs' relief is claimed. Mrs Lammle has made no previous claims for this relief, has no other disposals in 2012-13 and has no capital losses brought forward.

(Amended from AAT)

***D7** You are the chief accountant of Z Ltd, a UK resident company, whose activities to date have been confined wholly to the UK. The company is about to acquire three UK resident subsidiaries and the members of the newly-formed group will engage, for the first time, in import and export activities (all with non-EU countries).

You are required:

To draft a brief report to the board on the VAT implications of the above changes.

(CIMA)

***D8** The group structure below shows holdings in ordinary shares in other companies. All of the companies are UK resident except for O Inc which is resident in a non-EEA country.

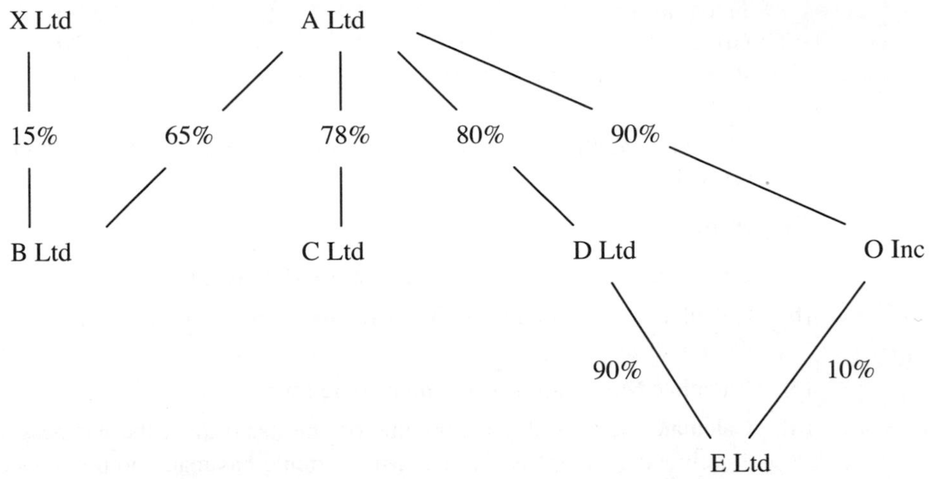

The results for each of the above companies for the accounting year ended 31 March 2013 are as follows (all profits and losses are trading profits and losses):

		£			£
X Ltd	Loss	(40,000)	D Ltd	Profit	35,000
B Ltd	Profit	60,000	O Inc	Loss	(30,000)
A Ltd	Profit	103,000	E Ltd	Loss	(2,000)
C Ltd	Loss	(70,000)			

O Inc does not trade in the UK or in any other EEA country.

You are required:

(a) To identify the associated companies and state the upper and lower limits for each of the companies shown.

(b) To identify any groups and consortia in the above structure qualifying for group relief.

(c) To compute the corporation tax liability of each company, assuming that loss relief has been claimed in the most efficient manner.

(d) To advise the directors of A Ltd on the weakness, from a tax point of view, of the existing structure. *(CIMA)*

Part 5

ANSWERS

Answers to exercises

Chapter 2

2.1

(a) £1,830 @ 20% = £366.00.

(b) £32,300 @ 20% = £6,460.00.

(c) £34,370 @ 20% + £34,333 @ 40% = £20,607.20.

(d) £34,370 @ 20% + £115,630 @ 40% + £170,000 @ 50% = £138,126.00.

2.2

(a)

	Total	Non-savings	Savings
	£	£	£
Business profits	23,710	23,710	
Bank interest £720 × 100/80	900		900
Total income	24,610	23,710	900
Less: Personal allowance	8,105	8,105	
Taxable income	16,505	15,605	900

Income tax due

Non-savings income	: Basic rate	15,605	@ 20%	3,121.00
Savings income	: Basic rate	900	@ 20%	180.00
		16,505		
Tax borne				3,301.00
Less: Tax deducted at source				180.00
Tax payable				3,121.00

(b)

	Total	Non-savings	Savings
	£	£	£
Business profits	30,840	30,840	
Building society interest £8,000 × 100/80	10,000		10,000
Bank interest £2,300 × 100/80	2,875		2,875
Total income	43,715	30,840	12,875
Less: Personal allowance	8,105	8,105	
Taxable income	35,610	22,735	12,875

Income tax due

Non-savings income	: Basic rate	22,735	@ 20%	4,547.00
Savings income	: Basic rate	11,635	@ 20%	2,327.00
	: Higher rate	1,240	@ 40%	496.00
		35,610		
Tax borne				7,370.00
Less: Tax deducted at source				2,575.00
Tax payable				4,795.00

(c)

	Total (all savings income)
	£
Bank interest £130,604 × 100/80	163,255
Total income	163,255
Less: Personal allowance	0
Taxable income	163,255

Income tax due

Savings income	: Starting rate	2,710	@ 10%	271.00
	: Basic rate	31,660	@ 20%	6,332.00
	: Higher rate	115,630	@ 40%	46,252.00
	: Additional rate	13,255	@ 50%	6,627.50
		163,255		
Tax borne				59,482.50
Less: Tax deducted at source				32,651.00
Tax payable				26,831.50

2.3

	Total	Non-savings	Savings	Dividends
	£	£	£	£
Employment income	28,755	28,755		
Income from property	13,330	13,330		
Bank interest £144 × 100/80	180		180	
NSB investment a/c interest	20		20	
UK dividends £225 + tax credit £25	250			250
Total income	42,535	42,085	200	250
Less: Personal allowance	8,105	8,105		
Taxable income	34,430	33,980	200	250

Note: NSB investment a/c interest is received gross and so does not need to be grossed-up.

Income tax due				
Non-savings income	: Basic rate	33,980	@ 20%	6,796.00
Savings income	: Basic rate	200	@ 20%	40.00
Dividend income	: Ordinary rate	190	@ 10%	19.00
	: Upper rate	60	@ 32.5%	19.50
		34,430		
Tax borne				6,874.50
Less: Tax credits on dividends				25.00
Tax payable				6,849.50
Less: Tax deducted at source				36.00
Tax payable				6,813.50

Note: Stephanie would also be given credit for any PAYE tax paid.

2.4

	Total	*Non-savings*	*Savings*
	£	£	£
Retirement pension	7,395	7,395	
Bank interest £416 × 100/80	520		520
Total income	7,915	7,395	520
Less: Personal allowance	7,915	7,395	520
Taxable income	0	0	0

£190 of the personal allowance (£8,105 – £7,915) is unused. Tax borne is £nil and Ernest is entitled to repayment of the £104.00 of tax deducted at source. If he received dividends of £468, dividend income of £520 (£468 + £52) would replace the bank interest but he would not be able to claim payment of the £52 tax credit.

Chapter 3

3.1

(a) £8,105

(b) £3,105 (£8,105 – 1/2 × £10,000)

(c) £8,105 – 1/2 × £20,000 gives a negative figure, so the personal allowance is £nil.

3.2

(a) This taxpayer is in the 65-74 age group and is entitled to a PA of £10,500 for the year.

(b) This taxpayer is over 75 and has an income which exceeds the limit by £1,000, giving a PA of £10,160 (£10,660 – 1/2 × £1,000).

(c) This taxpayer reaches the age of 65 during tax year 2012-13 and has an income which exceeds the limit by £8,600. This would give a PA of £6,200 (£10,500 – 1/2 × £8,600) but the allowance is not reduced to less than the PA for those under 65 so the taxpayer will claim £8,105.

3.3

(a) The husband is over 75 and therefore receives a PA of £10,660. His wife is over 65 but her income exceeds the limit by £300, giving her a PA of £10,350 (£10,500 – 1/2 × £300). MCA is £7,705 (which is not reduced, since the husband's income does not exceed the limit).

(b) The husband is over 75 but his income exceeds the limit by £700, giving him a PA of £10,310 (£10,660 – 1/2 × £700). His wife is over 75 and is entitled to a PA of £10,660 (of which £590 is unused). An MCA of £7,705 is also available. This is not reduced at all since the reduction required because of the husband's income has already been made in full against his PA.

(c) The husband is over 75 but his income exceeds the limit by £6,400. Therefore he must lose a total of £3,200 in allowances. His own PA is reduced from £10,660 to £8,105 (a reduction of £2,555). The remaining £645 is deducted from the MCA of £7,705 giving an MCA of £7,060. His wife is over 65 and is therefore entitled to a PA of £10,500.

3.4

	(a)	(b)	(c)
	£	£	£
HUSBAND			
Net income	17,300	9,500	10,995
Less: Personal allowance	10,660	9,500	10,660
Taxable income	6,640	0	335
Income tax			
£6,640 @ 20%	1,328.00		
£0 @ 20%		0.00	
£335 @ 20%			67.00
Less: MCA £7,705 @ 10%	770.50		
MCA £7,705 @ 10% = £770.50 (£703.50 transferred to wife)			67.00
Tax borne	557.50	0.00	0.00
WIFE			
Net income	18,600	14,535	18,465
Less: Personal allowance	10,660	10,660	10,660
Taxable income	7,940	3,875	7,805
Income tax			
£7,940 @ 20%	1,588.00		
£3,875 @ 20%		775.00	
£7,805 @ 20%			1,561.00
Less: MCA £7,705 × 8/12 @ 10% (higher-income partner)		513.67	
MCA transferred from husband			703.50
Tax borne	1,588.00	261.33	857.50

3.5

(a) No MCA is available if both taxpayers were born on or after 6 April 1935.

(b) The MCA is reduced to £7,705 × 2/12 = £1,284.

(c) The wife has the higher net income and this is £1,600 over the limit. She cannot claim age-related PA so the MCA of £7,705 is reduced by £800 (1/2 × £1,600), giving £6,905. This is further reduced to £6,905 × 4/12 = £2,302.

3.6

		Total	Non-savings	Savings
		£	£	£
Retirement pension		9,640	9,640	
Bank interest £912 × 100/80		1,140		1,140
Total income		10,780	9,640	1,140
Less: Personal allowance		10,660	9,640	1,020
Taxable income		120	0	120
Income tax due				
£120 @ 10%	12.00			
Less: Tax deducted at source	228.00			
Refund due	(216.00)			

3.7

	Richard	Patricia
	£	£
Business profits	31,760	
UK dividends £3,600 + £400		4,000
Less: Personal allowance	8,105	4,000
Taxable income	23,655	0
Income tax		
£23,655 @ 20%	4,731.00	
£0 @ 10%		0.00
Less: MCA £7,080 @ 10%	708.00	
Tax borne	4,023.00	0.00
Less: Tax credits on dividends		0.00
Tax payable	4,023.00	0.00

Notes:

(i) Richard's income exceeds the limit by £6,360 so he must lose £3,180 in allowances. His own PA is reduced from £10,660 to £8,105 (a reduction of £2,555) and the remaining £625 is subtracted from the MCA, giving an MCA of £7,080 (£7,705 – £625).

(ii) Patricia is entitled to a PA of £10,500 but can use only £4,000 of this. She cannot claim payment of the £400 tax credits on dividends.

Chapter 4

4.1

	£
Total income	22,810
Less: Payment £200 × 100/80	250
Net income	22,560
Less: Personal allowance	8,105
Taxable income	14,455
Income tax	
Tax borne @ 20%	2,891.00
Add: Tax deducted from payment	50.00
Tax liability	2,941.00

4.2

				(a)	(b)
				£	£
Total income				46,580	46,580
Less: Interest paid				1,600	
Net income				44,980	46,580
Less: Personal allowance				8,105	8,105
Taxable income				36,875	38,475
Income tax					
	(a)	(b)			
	34,370	34,370	@ 20%	6,874.00	6,874.00
	2,505	4,105	@ 40%	1,002.00	1,642.00
	36,875	38,475			
Tax liability				7,876.00	8,516.00

Paul's tax liability is reduced by £640 if he pays the interest. The cost of the interest to him is therefore only £960 (amount paid £1,600 less reduction in tax liability £640). In effect, the interest paid of £1,600 is reduced by tax relief at 40% (£640), leaving £960 as the cost to Paul.

4.3

Rose's net income for the year is £8,070 (£8,095 – £25). This is covered by her personal allowance of £8,105 (of which £35 is wasted) so taxable income is £nil and the tax liability is zero. In fact the tax liability would also have been zero if the £25 payment had not been made, since Rose's total income is less than her personal allowance. The payment has had no effect on her tax liability and so tax relief on the payment is zero.

4.4

(a) 23% (b) marginal rate (c) 10% (d) 30%

4.5

(a) The donation is deemed to be made net of 20% income tax. Charities are not liable to income tax so the charity concerned recovers a further £240 (£960 × 20/80) from HMRC, making the donation worth £1,200 in total.

(b) If the taxpayer does not pay income tax for 2012-13 of at least £240, the income tax liability for the year will be increased to exactly £240.

(c) The taxpayer's basic rate and higher rate limits for 2012-13 are both increased by £1,200. This results in a tax saving of up to £240 (20% × £1,200) for a higher rate taxpayer and up to £360 (30% × £1,200) for an additional rate taxpayer.

4.6

	£
Business profits	26,400
Less: Personal allowance	10,175
Taxable income	16,225
Income tax	
Tax liability @ 20%	3,245.00

Notes:

(i) The grossed-up donation is £350 (£280 × 100/80) and the tax deemed deducted is £70.

(ii) Adjusted net income is £26,050 (£26,400 – £350). This is £650 over the income limit, so the personal allowance is £10,175 (£10,500 – 1/2 × £650).

(iii) Raj pays income tax of more than £70 so there is nothing more to be done.

4.7

	Matthew £	*Widow* £
Non-savings income	26,510	17,900
Less: Gift of shares to charity		500
Net income	26,510	17,400
Less: Personal allowance	10,105	8,105
Taxable income	16,405	9,295

Matthew £	*Widow* £			
16,405	9,295	@ 20%	3,281.00	1,859.00
Less: MCA £7,705 @ 10%			770.50	
Tax liability			2,510.50	1,859.00

(See notes overleaf)

Notes:

(i) Matthew is over 75 years old. The personal allowance is available in full in the year of death. His income exceeds the limit by £1,110 (£26,510 – £25,400) so the personal allowance is (£10,660 – 1/2 × £1,110) = £10,105.

(ii) MCA is available since Matthew was born before 6 April 1935 and is given in full in the year of death. Although Matthew's income exceeds £25,400, the necessary reduction in allowances has already been made against his own PA, so the MCA is not reduced.

(iii) The Gift Aid donation is deemed to be paid net of £25.00 tax (£100 × 20/80). Matthew's widow pays more income tax than this so there is nothing more to be done.

Chapter 5

5.1

The property income assessable in 2012-13 (i.e. the income accrued for the year) is £8,200 (£8,000 × 9/12 + £8,800 × 3/12). The amount actually received is not relevant.

5.2

	£	£	£
Rents received £220 × 48			10,560
Less: Expenses allowed in full:			
Advertising		35	
Repairs to furniture		50	
Apportioned expenses:			
Council tax	1,400		
Gardener's wages	1,040		
Insurance	230		
	$\frac{48}{52}$ × 2,670	2,465	
Wear and tear (see below)		927	3,477
Property income			7,083

Note:
The wear and tear allowance is 10% of (£10,560 – (£1,400 × 48/52)) = £927.

5.3

(a) Premiums received in relation to the granting of long leases (i.e. leases of more than 50 years) are not assessable to income tax.

(b) £12,000 – (49 × 2% of £12,000) = £240.

(c) £12,000 – (19 × 2% of £12,000) = £7,440.

5.4

The income tax assessment on the landlord is £12,300 (£15,000 – (9 × 2% of £15,000)). Therefore Jasper will be allowed an annual deduction from his trading profits of £1,230 for each of the ten years of the lease.

5.5

All three flats pass the 210-day test. However, Flat 1 does not pass the 105-day test and so will not be regarded as a furnished holiday let unless it can be averaged with one or more of the other flats. Possible averaging claims are:

(a) Flat 1 with Flat 2. This is no use since the average number of days let is only 103.

(b) Flat 1 with Flat 3. This is no use since the average number of days let is only 104.

(c) Flat 1 with Flat 2 and Flat 3. This is beneficial since the average number of days let is 105.

Chapter 6

6.1

	Total	*Savings*	*Dividends*
	£	£	£
BSI £15,772 × 100/80	19,715	19,715	
UK dividends £36,468 + tax credit £4,052	40,520		40,520
Total income	60,235	19,715	40,520
Less: Personal allowance	8,105	8,105	
Taxable income	52,130	11,610	40,520

Income tax due				
Savings income	: Starting rate	2,710	@ 10%	271.00
	: Basic rate	8,900	@ 20%	1,780.00
Dividend income	: Ordinary rate	22,760	@ 10%	2,276.00
	: Upper rate	17,760	@ 32.5%	5,772.00
		52,130		
Tax borne				10,099.00
Less: Tax deducted at source and tax credits				7,995.00
Tax payable				2,104.00

6.2

	Total	Non-savings	Savings	Dividends
	£	£	£	£
Retirement pension	10,046	10,046		
Bank interest £384 × 100/80	480		480	
UK dividends £585 + tax credit £65	650			650
Total income	11,176	10,046	480	650
Less: Personal allowance	10,660	10,046	480	134
Taxable income	516	0	0	516

Income tax is due of £51.60 (£516 @ 10%), less tax credit on dividends of £51.60, leaving a tax liability of zero. Anne cannot claim payment of the remaining £13.40 of the tax credits but she is entitled to a refund of the £96 tax deducted at source from her bank interest.

Note: The ISA interest is exempt from tax.

6.3/6.4

See text.

6.5

	Total	Non-savings	Savings
	£	£	£
Retirement pension	20,970	20,970	
NSB interest	60		60
BSI £3,784 × 100/80	4,730		4,730
Total income	25,760	20,970	4,790
Less: Personal allowance	10,320	10,320	
Taxable income	15,440	10,650	4,790

Income tax due				£
Non-savings income	: Basic rate	10,650	@ 20%	2,130.00
Savings income	: Basic rate	4,790	@ 20%	958.00
		15,440		
Tax borne				3,088.00
Less: Tax deducted at source				946.00
Tax payable				2,142.00

Notes:

(a) Bernice reaches her 65th birthday during 2012-13 and is therefore entitled to the personal allowance of £10,500 for the year. However, her income exceeds the income limit by £360, so the allowance is reduced by £180 to £10,320.

(b) Any PAYE tax deducted from the pension will be subtracted when calculating tax payable.

Chapter 7

7.1

See text.

7.2

The basis of assessment for employment income is the receipts basis. The assessable income for 2012-13 is therefore £65,850 (£57,500 + £8,350).

7.3

(a) 15p per day would be exempt. The remaining £1.85 per day would be taxable.

(b) Free meals in the company canteen are exempt if available to all employees.

(c) Removal expenses of up to £8,000 are exempt if reasonable and incurred on first taking up an appointment or transferring to a new location.

(d) Long-service awards made in cash are taxable.

(e) A gift made in a personal capacity (rather than for services rendered) is exempt so long as it is reasonable in amount.

(f) The mileage allowance is exempt since it is less than the standard figure of 45p per mile for the first 10,000 miles. The employee has an allowable expense of £250 (2,500 @ 10p).

7.4

(a) Not generally allowable since not incurred in performing the duties of the employment. But see the chapter for exceptions to this rule in the case of site-based employees, employees undertaking business journeys from home and employees who are seconded to a temporary place of work.

(b) Allowable so long as necessarily incurred.

(c) Allowable if relevant to the employment.

(d) Allowable.

(e) Not allowable, even if worn only at the office. A suit provides warmth and decency and is therefore not purchased exclusively for the purposes of the employment.

(f) Not allowable unless reimbursed or paid out of a specific entertaining allowance. The expenses must also be wholly, exclusively and necessarily incurred.

Chapter 8

8.1

For the purpose of deciding Kim's classification it is necessary to take into account all of her earnings (valued as if she were a P11D employee) and to ignore expenses other than the pension contributions. This gives total earnings of £9,450 (95% of £7,000 + £1,000 + £1,800). This total exceeds £8,500, so Kim is a P11D employee.

8.2

The applicable percentage is 31% (11% + 17% + 3%) so the taxable car benefit is £7,502 (31% of £24,200). There is a further taxable fuel benefit of £6,262 (31% of £20,200).

8.3

(a) The amount outstanding at the end of the tax year is £12,000. Therefore the average amount of the loan between 1 June 2012 and 5 April 2013 is (£20,000 + £12,000)/2 = £16,000. The loan was in existence for 10 months of the year, so the taxable benefit is (£16,000 × 4% × 10/12) = £533.

(b) The taxable benefit is (£20,000 × 4% × 7/12) + (£15,000 × 4% × 2/12) + (£12,000 × 4% × 1/12) = £607.

Chapter 9

9.1

- subject matter
- length of ownership
- frequency of transactions
- supplementary work
- reason for sale
- motive

9.2

Expenditure must be incurred wholly and exclusively for the purposes of the trade.

9.3

(a) allowable so long as the salary is commensurate with the work done
(b) not allowable when computing trading profits, but relieved under the Gift Aid rules
(c) not allowable (capital expenditure)
(d) allowable so long as the diaries carry a prominent advertisement for the business
(e) allowable
(f) not allowable (fails the duality test)
(g) not allowable (related to capital expenditure)
(h) probably allowable as a trade subscription
(i) not allowable (food, drink or tobacco)
(j) allowable (relates directly to trading).

9.4

(a) add £45 (b) add £15 (c) no adjustment required.

9.5

(a) (i) Disallow 15% × £280 = £42.

(ii) The allowable amount is given by:

$$£280 \times \frac{£12{,}000 + 1/2(£21{,}000 - £12{,}000)}{£21{,}000} = £220 \text{ (so disallow £60).}$$

(b) The amount assessed on the landlord is (£15,000 – (14 × 2% of £15,000)) = £10,800. So the amount allowable in each year is £720 (1/15th of £10,800) and the amount to be disallowed each year is £280 (£1,000 – £720).

9.6

	£	£
Net profit for the year		6,960
<u>Add</u>: *Disallowed expenditure*:		
Proprietor's salary	10,400	
Cost of new heating system	3,800	
Telephone (1/4th of £880)	220	
Motor expenses (1/5th of £3,250)	650	
Entertaining	520	
General allowance for bad debts	200	
Loss on sale of non-current asset	70	
Depreciation	2,500	18,360
		25,320
<u>Less</u>: *Non-trading income*:		
Rents receivable	1,200	
Bank interest receivable	80	
Profit on sale of non-current asset	310	1,590
Trading profit (before capital allowances)		23,730

Chapter 10

10.1

(a) 2012-13 (b) 2012-13 (c) 2014-15 (d) 2013-14

10.2

(a)

2010-11	Actual	1/7/10 to 5/4/11
2011-12	12 months to a/c date in year 2	y/e 30/6/11
2012-13	CYB	y/e 30/6/12
2013-14	CYB	y/e 30/6/13

There is an overlap period between 1 July 2010 and 5 April 2011.

(b)

2010-11	Actual	1/7/10 to 5/4/11
2011-12	Actual	6/4/11 to 5/4/12
2012-13	CYB	1/5/11 to 30/4/12
2013-14	CYB	y/e 30/4/13

There is an overlap period between 1 May 2011 and 5 April 2012.

(c)

2010-11	Actual	1/7/10 to 5/4/11
2011-12	First 12 months	1/7/10 to 30/6/11
2012-13	CYB	y/e 30/4/12
2013-14	CYB	y/e 30/4/13

There is an overlap period between 1 July 2010 and 5 April 2011. There is another overlap period between 1 May 2011 and 30 June 2011.

10.3

				£
2010-11	Actual	1/1/11 to 5/4/11	£27,300 × 3/18	4,550
2011-12	Actual	6/4/11 to 5/4/12	£27,300 × 12/18	18,200
2012-13	CYB	1/7/11 to 30/6/12	£27,300 × 12/18	18,200

There is an overlap period between 1 July 2011 and 5 April 2012 (9 months). The overlap profits are 9/18 × £27,300 = £13,650.

10.4

(a)	2010-11	CYB	y/e 31/1/11
	2011-12	CYB	y/e 31/1/12
	2012-13	End of previous basis period to date of cessation	1/2/12 to 31/5/12
(b)	2010-11	CYB	y/e 31/1/11
	2011-12	CYB	y/e 31/1/12
	2012-13	End of previous basis period to date of cessation	1/2/12 to 31/3/13
(c)	2011-12	CYB	y/e 31/1/12
	2012-13	12 months to normal a/c date	1/2/12 to 31/1/13
	2013-14	End of previous basis period to date of cessation	1/2/13 to 30/4/13

10.5

Year	*Basis period*	*Workings*	*Trading income* £
2008-09	1/6/08 to 5/4/09	£28,800 × 10/16	18,000
2009-10	1/10/08 to 30/9/09	£28,800 × 12/16	21,600
2010-11	y/e 30/9/10		19,900
2011-12	y/e 30/9/11		14,300
2012-13	y/e 30/9/12		13,800
2013-14	1/10/12 to 31/7/13	£11,100 – £10,800	300
			87,900

Note:

There is an overlap period from 1 October 2008 to 5 April 2009 with profits of 6/16 × £28,800 = £10,800. Therefore overlap relief of £10,800 is given in the tax year in which trade ceases.

Chapter 11

11.1

		Main pool	Allowances
		£	£
y/e 5/4/13			
WDV b/f		10,300	
Additions (ineligible for AIA)		8,000	
		18,300	
Disposals (£3,000 + £4,000)		(7,000)	
		11,300	
WDA @ 18%		2,034	2,034
		9,266	
Additions qualifying for AIA (£600 + £400)	1,000		
AIA @ 100%	1,000	-	1,000
WDV c/f		9,266	
Total allowances			3,034

11.2

		Main pool	Motor car (40% p.u.)		Allowances
		£	£		£
y/e 30/9/12					
Additions (ineligible for AIA)		21,000	15,000		
WDA @ 19%		3,990			3,990
WDA @ 9%			1,350	× 60% =	810
		17,010	13,650		
Additions qualifying for AIA	62,500				
AIA @ 100%	62,500	-			62,500
WDV c/f		17,010	13,650		
Total allowances					67,300

Notes:

(i) Maximum AIA for this period is [(£100,000 × 6/12) + (£25,000 × 6/12)] = £62,500, of which no more than £12,500 can be claimed in relation to expenditure on or after 6 April 2012.

(ii) Total expenditure on plant and machinery (excluding cars) is £83,500 (£55,400 + £26,500 + £1,600). Therefore £21,000 of this total is ineligible for AIA.

(iii) WDA hybrid rate in the main pool is [(20% × 6/12) + (18% × 6/12)] = 19%. The hybrid rate in the special rate pool would be [(10% × 6/12) + (8% × 6/12)] = 9%.

(iv) WDA for the car is calculated at 9% because it has emissions in excess of 160g/km.

The adjusted trading profit is now £60,000 (£127,300 – £67,300). Trading income for the first two tax years is as follows:

Year	*Basis period*	*Workings*	*Trading income*
			£
2011-12	1/10/11 to 5/4/12	£60,000 × 6/12	30,000
2012-13	1/10/11 to 30/9/12		60,000

The overlap period is 1 October 2011 to 5 April 2012. Overlap profits are £30,000.

11.3

		Main pool	*Special rate pool*	*Allowances*
		£	£	£
9 months to 31/3/13				
WDV b/f		178,400		
Additions (ineligible for AIA)		60,200	15,400	
Disposals		(1,600)		
		237,000		
WDA @ 18% × 9/12		31,995		31,995
WDA @ 8% × 9/12			924	924
		205,005		
Additions eligible for AIA	18,750			
AIA @ 100%	18,750	-		18,750
Additions eligible for 100% FYA	11,600			
FYA @ 100%	11,600	-		11,600
WDV c/f		205,005	14,476	
Total allowances				63,269

Notes:

(i) The Peugeot motor car is allocated to the special rate pool because it has emissions in excess of 160g/km.

(ii) The motor van is allocated to the main pool. Total additions to the main pool are £78,950 (£64,450 + £14,500). Deducting the AIA of £18,750 (9/12 × £25,000) leaves expenditure of £60,200 which is not eligible for AIA.

(iii) The very low emission car attracts a 100% FYA.

(iv) WDAs are restricted because the chargeable period is only nine months long.

(v) Capital allowances on the two private use cars are £3,598 (see below).

(vi) Total capital allowances for the year are £66,867 (£63,269 + £3,598).

	Toyota (50% p.u.)		*Saab (50% p.u.)*		*Allowances*
	£		£		£
9 months to 31/3/13					
WDV b/f	18,200				
Additions (ineligible for AIA)			29,600		
Disposals	(15,000)				
Balancing allowance	3,200	× 50% =			1,600
WDA @ 18% × 9/12			3,996	× 50% =	1,998
WDV c/f			25,604		
Total allowances					3,598

Notes:

(i) The Saab motor car attracts WDA at 18% because its emissions do not exceed 160g/km.

(ii) WDA is restricted because the chargeable period is only nine months long.

(iii) The emission rating of the Toyota motor car is irrelevant (for this chargeable period) since it has been disposed of and so does not attract WDA in the period.

Chapter 12

12.1

(a) £nil.

(b) The loss will be carried forward and set against the first available profits of the same trade.

(c) The loss may be set against her total income of 2012-13 and/or 2011-12.

12.2

	2009-10	*2010-11*	*2011-12*	*2012-13*
	£	£	£	£
Trading income	-	4,710	6,210	14,810
Other income	6,000	6,000	6,000	6,000
Total income	6,000	10,710	12,210	20,810
Less: Trading losses b/f	-	(4,710)	(6,210)	(7,940)
Net income	6,000	6,000	6,000	12,870

12.3

(a)

Year	*Basis period*	*Workings*	*Trading income*
			£
2010-11	1/1/11 to 5/4/11	(£14,720 – £4,460) × 3/12	2,565
2011-12	y/e 31/12/11	£14,720 – £4,460	10,260
2012-13	y/e 31/12/12		nil

(b) The trading loss of 2012-13 is £9,800 (£7,480 + £2,320). A claim could be made to set this loss against total income in 2012-13 or 2011-12 or in both of these years:

(i) A claim for 2012-13 is pointless since there is no income in that year.

(ii) A claim for 2011-12 would reduce total income for that year to £460 (£10,260 – £9,800) and so eliminate the income tax liability for the year. The personal allowance would be largely wasted.

(iii) A claim for both years is pointless since a claim in 2012-13 is pointless.

The 2011-12 claim would be less wasteful if Marcus declined to claim any capital allowances in either of the first two years of trading. Trading income for 2011-12 would become £14,720 and the 2012-13 loss would become £7,480. Claiming relief against total income in 2011-12 would then leave income of £7,240 for the year, which would absorb most of the personal allowance.

12.4

The losses eligible for early trade losses relief are:

Year	*Basis period*	*Workings*	*Trading loss* £	*Early trade losses claim*
2010-11	1/10/10 to 5/4/11	£(26,850) × 6/15	(10,740)	07-08 *to* 09-10
2011-12	1/1/11 to 31/12/11	£(26,850) × 12/15 – overlap		
		£(26,850) × 3/15	(16,110)	08-09 *to* 10-11
2012-13	y/e 31/12/12		(25,660)	09-10 *to* 11-12

If all possible early trade losses relief claims are made, total income is:

		2007-08 £	*2008-09* £	*2009-10* £	*2010-11* £
Trading income		-	-	-	nil
Other income		15,100	15,250	16,400	8,450
Total income		15,100	15,250	16,400	8,450
Less: Early trade losses:	2010-11 loss	(10,740)			
	2011-12 loss		(15,250)	(860)	
	2012-13 loss			(15,540)	(8,450)
Net income		4,360	-	-	-

Notes:

(a) Personal allowances are totally wasted in 2008-09 to 2010-11.

(b) The loss incurred in 2012-13 has been only partly relieved. The remaining £1,670 of the loss (£25,660 – £15,540 – £8,450) is eligible for early trade losses relief in 2011-12 but there is no income in this year against which to set the loss. The loss will be carried forward and set against future trading profits.

Chapter 13

13.1

	Nickleby £	*Copperfield* £	*Drood* £	*Total* £
1/1/12 - 31/3/12				
(£183,000 × 3/12 = £45,750)	15,250	15,250	15,250	45,750
1/4/12 - 31/12/12				
(£183,000 × 9/12 = £137,250)	27,450	54,900	54,900	137,250
Allocation of profit for the year	42,700	70,150	70,150	183,000

13.2

	Pickwick £	*Snodgrass* £	*Tupman* £	*Total* £
Interest on capital	3,600	6,000	3,000	12,600
Salaries	40,000	-	30,000	70,000
Remainder (shared equally)	(6,700)	(6,700)	(6,700)	(20,100)
	36,900	(700)	26,300	62,500
Notional loss divided 36,900:26,300	(409)	700	(291)	-
Allocation of profit for the year	36,491	-	26,009	62,500

13.3

The allocation of profit for each period of account is:

	Dodson £	*Fogg* £	*Jackson* £	*Total* £
y/e 30/6/10 (shared equally)	34,000	34,000	-	68,000
y/e 30/6/11 (shared 5:4:1)	44,000	35,200	8,800	88,000
y/e 30/6/12 (shared 5:4:1)	58,000	46,400	11,600	116,000

Each partner's trading income is:

Dodson

Year	*Basis period*	*Workings*	*Trading income* £
2009-10	1/7/09 to 5/4/10	£34,000 × 9/12	25,500
2010-11	y/e 30/6/10		34,000
2011-12	y/e 30/6/11		44,000
2012-13	y/e 30/6/12		58,000

Fogg

Year	*Basis period*	*Workings*	*Trading income* £
2009-10	1/7/09 to 5/4/10	£34,000 × 9/12	25,500
2010-11	y/e 30/6/10		34,000
2011-12	y/e 30/6/11		35,200
2012-13	y/e 30/6/12		46,400

Jackson

Year	*Basis period*	*Workings*	*Trading income*
			£
2010-11	1/7/10 to 5/4/11	£8,800 × 9/12	6,600
2011-12	y/e 30/6/11		8,800
2012-13	y/e 30/6/12		11,600

Note:

Dodson and Fogg each have overlap profits of £25,500. Jackson has overlap profits of £6,600.

13.4

(a) Trading profit of £117,460 for the year to 30 September 2011 is allocated Wardle £82,222, Jingle £23,492, Trotter £11,746. Trading profit of £136,540 for the year to 30 September 2012 is allocated Wardle £95,578, Jingle £27,308 Trotter £13,654. The partners' trading income is:

	Wardle	*Jingle*	*Trotter*
	£	£	£
2010-11 (6/12 × y/e 30/9/11)	41,111	11,746	5,873
2011-12 (y/e 30/9/11)	82,222	23,492	11,746
2012-13 (y/e 30/9/12)	95,578	27,308	13,654

(b) The untaxed interest of £2,000 for the year to 30 September 2011 is allocated Wardle £1,400, Jingle £400, Trotter £200. The untaxed interest of £2,200 for the year to 30 September 2012 is allocated Wardle £1,540, Jingle £440, Trotter £220. Each partner's untaxed interest is:

	Wardle	*Jingle*	*Trotter*
	£	£	£
2010-11 (6/12 × y/e 30/9/11)	700	200	100
2011-12 (y/e 30/9/11)	1,400	400	200
2012-13 (y/e 30/9/12)	1,540	440	220

(c) The taxed interest of £1,240 (gross) for the year to 30 September 2011 is allocated Wardle £868, Jingle £248, Trotter £124. The taxed interest of £1,360 (gross) for the year to 30 September 2012 is allocated Wardle £952, Jingle £272, Trotter £136. The gross amount on which each partner is charged to tax in 2011-12 (assuming time-apportionment between tax years) is:

	£
Wardle (£868 × 6/12 + £952 × 6/12)	910
Jingle (£248 × 6/12 + £272 × 6/12)	260
Trotter (£124 × 6/12 + £136 × 6/12)	130

Chapter 14

14.1

(a) £120,000.

(b) £3,600 (so long as at least £2,400 is paid to a scheme which operates relief at source).

14.2

She will pay net contributions of £800 per month, so obtaining relief at the basic rate. Her basic rate limit and higher rate limit will both be increased by £12,000.

14.3

Current year contributions are 310% of those in the previous year. This exceeds 210% so spreading may be required. The excess of current year contributions over 110% of previous year contributions is £1,200,000, which is between £1,000,000 and £1,999,999. Therefore this excess must be spread over the current period and the next two periods. Tax relief on contributions of £1,060,000 (£660,000 + £400,000) will be given in the year to 30 June 2013. Relief on contributions of £400,000 will be given in each of the years to 30 June 2014 and 2015.

14.4

If Damon became entitled to payment of his pension and lump sum at the start of the pension input period, he would receive an annual pension of £120,000 (£360,000 × 20/60) and a lump sum of £270,000 (£360,000 × 60/80). The value of his pension rights at the start of the period is therefore £2,190,000 (£270,000 + (16 × £120,000)).

If he became entitled to payment of his pension and lump sum at the end of the period, he would receive an annual pension of £157,500 (£450,000 × 21/60) and a lump sum of £354,375 (£450,000 × 63/80). The value of his pension rights at the end of the period is therefore £2,874,375 (£354,375 + (16 × £157,500)).

Total pension input amount for 2012-13 is £684,375 (£2,874,375 – £2,190,000). This exceeds the annual allowance of £50,000 by £634,375. Therefore the annual allowance charge is £317,187.50 (50% of £634,375).

14.5

(a) The first lump sum absorbs 25% of the 2008-09 lifetime allowance of £1,650,000. There is no lifetime allowance charge and 75% of the lifetime allowance remains unused. The second lump sum of £1,188,000 exceeds 75% of the 2012-13 lifetime allowance of £1,500,000 by £63,000. There is a lifetime allowance charge of £34,650 (55% of £63,000).

(b) The first lump sum now absorbs 72% of the 2008-09 lifetime allowance. The second lump sum is less than 28% of the 2012-13 lifetime allowance and therefore there is no lifetime allowance charge on either lump sum.

Chapter 15

15.1

(a) No POAs are required because the 2011-12 liability (less tax deducted at source) was less than £1,000. A balancing payment of £440 (£1,750 – £1,250 – £60) is payable on 31 January 2014.

(b) The amount paid by deduction at source in 2011-12 (£4,390) was not more than 80% of the total liability for the year and the remainder (£2,340) was not less than £1,000. Therefore POAs are required for 2012-13. A first POA of £1,170 (one-half of £2,340) is due on 31 January 2013 and a second POA of £1,170 is due on 31 July 2013.

A balancing *repayment* of £605 (£6,580 – £4,810 – £35 – £2,340) will be due on 31 January 2014. Marie could have made a claim to pay reduced POAs for 2012-13 if she had known that the POAs based on her 2011-12 liability were likely to be excessive.

(c) No POAs are required because more than 80% of the 2011-12 tax liability was satisfied by deduction at source. A balancing payment of £3,600 (£16,110 – £12,370 – £140) is payable on 31 January 2014.

15.2

(a) The balancing payment was not more than 30 days late so there are no late payment penalties.

(b) The first POA of £12,000 was paid 27 days late, the second POA of £12,000 was paid 43 days late and the balancing payment of £4,000 was paid 21 days late. The interest payable is:

	£
£12,000 × 3% × 27/366	26.56
£12,000 × 3% × 43/366	42.30
£4,000 × 3% × 21/366	6.89
	75.75

15.3

(a) Jabran notified HMRC of his chargeability to tax within the permitted six months and so incurs no penalty in relation to this notification.

(b) His tax return was due to be submitted to HMRC within three months of the issue date. He filed the return late (but not more than three months late) and so incurs a penalty of £100.

(c) The balancing payment was due three months after the issue date of the tax return. His payment was more than 30 days late and therefore he incurs a 5% late payment penalty.

(d) Interest is payable on the tax paid late and interest is payable on the late payment penalty if it is not paid within 30 days of the date of its imposition.

Chapter 16

16.1

(a) Primary : 12% × (£160 – £146) = £1.68
Secondary : 13.8% × (£160 – £144) = £2.21

(b) Primary : 12% × (£780 – £146) = £76.08
Secondary : 13.8% × (£780 – £144) = £87.77

(c) Primary : 12% × (£817 – £146) + 2% × (£930 – £817) = £82.78
Secondary : 13.8% × (£930 – £144) = £108.47

(d) Primary : nil (earnings do not exceed the primary threshold)
Secondary : nil (earnings do not exceed the secondary threshold)

(e) Primary : 12% × (£3,300 – £634) = £319.92
Secondary : 13.8% × (£3,300 – £624) = £369.29

(f) Primary : 12% × (£3,540 – £634) + 2% × (£6,000 – £3,540) = £397.92
Secondary : 13.8% × (£6,000 – £624) = £741.89

16.2

(a) Primary : 10.6% × (£160 – £146) = £1.48
Secondary : 10.4% × (£160 – £144) = £1.66

(b) Primary : 10.6% × (£770 – £146) + 12% × (£780 – £770) = £67.34
Secondary : 10.4% × (£770 – £144) + 13.8% × (£780 – £770) = £66.48

(c) Primary : 10.6% × (£770 – £146) + 12% × (£817 – £770) + 2% × (£930 – £817) = £74.04
Secondary : 10.4% × (£770 – £144) + 13.8% × (£930 – £770) = £87.18

(d) Primary : nil (earnings do not exceed the primary threshold)
Secondary : nil (earnings do not exceed the secondary threshold)

(e) Primary : 10.6% × (£3,300 – £634) = £282.60
Secondary : 10.4% × (£3,300 – £624) = £278.30

(f) Primary : 10.6% × (£3,337 – £634) + 12% × (£3,540 – £3,337) + 2% × (£6,000 – £3,540) = £360.08
Secondary : 10.4% × (£3,337 – £624) + 13.8% × (£6,000 – £3,337) = £649.65

16.3

Mark's profit for Class 2 purposes in 2012-13 is £6,010 (£7,270 × 8/12 + £3,490 × 4/12). This exceeds the small earnings exception so Mark is liable to pay Class 2 contributions of £2.65 per week. His profit for Class 4 purposes in 2012-13 is £8,900 so Class 4 contributions are payable of £116.55 (9% × (£8,900 – £7,605)).

Chapter 17

17.1

(a) Companies are not chargeable persons, so the sale will not give rise to a CGT liability.

(b) Disposals between husband and wife who are living together are deemed to occur at a disposal value such that neither a gain nor a loss arises. So there will be no CGT liability on the gift.

(c) Gifts to charities are exempt from CGT.

(d) In general, charities are not chargeable persons and therefore disposals by charities do not give rise to a CGT liability (subject to certain restrictions).

(e) The sale is made in the course of trade. Therefore the profit arising will be a trading profit and not a capital gain.

(f) The partnership is not a chargeable person but the partners are. Any CGT liability arising on the disposal of the freehold property will be divided between them.

17.2

(a) Shares and securities are chargeable assets (apart from gilt-edged securities and certain corporate bonds).

(b) Gilt-edged securities are not chargeable assets.

(c) A table is a chattel. Chattels disposed of for more than £6,000 are chargeable assets.

(d) A chair is a chattel. Chattels disposed of for £6,000 or less are not chargeable assets.

(e) A taxpayer's principal private residence is not a chargeable asset.

(f) Motor cars are not chargeable assets.

17.3

(a) Net losses are £2,500. The annual exemption is lost and the CGT assessment is £nil.

(b) Net losses are £1,000. The annual exemption is lost and the CGT assessment is £nil.

(c) Net gains are £5,750. The unused part of the annual exemption (£4,850) is lost and the CGT assessment is £nil.

(d) Net gains are £12,050. The annual exemption of £10,600 is fully used. The CGT assessment is £1,450.

17.4

(a) The CGT assessment is £239,700 (£262,600 – £12,300 – £10,600) and the unused part of the basic rate band is £7,100 (£34,370 – £27,270). Therefore the CGT liability is (18% × £7,100) + (28% × £232,600) = £66,406.

(b) The CGT liability is (10% × £239,700) = £23,970.

(c) The losses and the annual exemption are set against the gain of £56,900, leaving £34,000. The gain which qualifies for ER absorbs the whole of the unused part of the basic rate band so the CGT liability is (10% × £205,700) + (28% × £34,000) = £30,090.

17.5

(a) Net gains are £8,700. £1,900 of the annual exemption is lost and the CGT assessment is £nil. The losses brought forward of £4,800 remain unrelieved and are carried forward to 2013-14.

(b) Net gains are £11,200. This exceeds the annual exemption by £600, so £600 of the losses brought forward are relieved and the CGT assessment is £nil. The remaining £4,200 of the losses brought forward are carried forward to 2013-14.

(c) Net gains are £16,600. This exceeds the annual exemption by £6,000, so all of the losses brought forward are relieved. The CGT assessment is £1,200 (£16,600 – £4,800 – £10,600). There are no unrelieved losses to carry forward.

17.6

Net losses in 2012-13 are £14,200. The annual exemption is lost and the CGT assessment for the year is £nil. The net losses may be offset against the net gains of 2011-12, 2010-11 and 2009-10, in that order, to the extent that those net gains exceed the annual exemption. Relief is £nil in 2011-12, £2,800 (£12,900 – £10,100) in 2010-11 and £6,500 (£16,600 – £10,100) in 2009-10. Total relief is £9,300. The remaining £4,900 of net losses in 2012-13 cannot be relieved at all.

17.7

31 January 2014.

Chapter 18

18.1

		£
Sale proceeds		172,000
Less: Incidental costs of disposal:		
Auctioneer's fee	8,600	
Legal fees	500	9,100
		162,900
Less: Acquisition cost	100,000	
Incidental costs of acquisition:		
Legal fees	400	
Enhancement expenditure	5,000	105,400
Chargeable gain		57,500

(The repainting costs do not rank as enhancement expenditure).

18.2

	(a)	(b)	(c)
	£	£	£
Sale proceeds	14,950	6,350	25,780
Less: Deemed acquisition cost	7,500	7,500	7,500
Chargeable gain/(allowable loss)	7,450	(1,150)	18,280

18.3

(a)

	£
Sale proceeds (June 2009)	100,000
Less: Incidental costs of disposal	5,000
	95,000
Less: Part cost: $\frac{£100{,}000}{£100{,}000 + £500{,}000} \times £240{,}000$	(40,000)
Part incidental costs of acquisition: $\frac{£100{,}000}{£100{,}000 + £500{,}000} \times £12{,}000$	(2,000)
Chargeable gain	53,000

(b)

	£
Sale proceeds (January 2013)	520,000
Less: Remainder of cost (£240,000 – £40,000)	(200,000)
Remainder of costs of acquisition (£12,000 – £2,000)	(10,000)
Chargeable gain	310,000

18.4

	(a)	(b)	(c)
	£	£	£
Sale proceeds	37,500	37,500	37,500
Less: Market value 31 March 1982	10,000	15,000	50,000
Chargeable gain/(allowable loss)	27,500	22,500	(12,500)

Notes:

(i) The asset's cost is ignored, since the gain or loss is computed by means of rebasing.

(ii) In case (a), Francis is taxed on a gain of £27,500 even though his total gain over the entire period of ownership of the asset is actually only £25,000 (£37,500 – £12,500).

(iii) In case (c), Francis is granted an allowable loss of £12,500 even though he has made a gain of £25,000 during his period of ownership of the asset.

18.5

(a)

	£
Deemed disposal proceeds	80
Less: Deemed acquisition cost	6,000
Allowable loss	(5,920)

(b)

	£
Disposal proceeds	120
Less: Deemed acquisition cost (November 2011)	80
Chargeable gain	40

Chapter 19

19.1

(a) Wasting chattel.
(b) Chattel.
(c) Wasting chattel.
(d) Wasting asset.
(e) Wasting chattel.
(f) Chattel.

19.2

	£	
Sale proceeds	7,200	
Less: Incidental disposal costs	200	
	7,000	
Less: Acquisition cost	2,300	
Chargeable gain	4,700	(restricted to £2,000)

The gain is restricted to (£7,200 – £6,000) × 5/3 = £2,000.

19.3

	£
Deemed sale proceeds	6,000
Less: Acquisition cost	50,000
Allowable loss	(44,000)

19.4

	£
Sale proceeds	25,000
Less: Part cost:	
$\frac{£25{,}000}{£25{,}000 + £85{,}000} \times 38{,}500$	8,750
Chargeable gain	16,250

The maximum gain is (£110,000 – £6,000) × 5/3 × 25/110 = £39,394. The actual gain is far less than this so the chargeable gain is £16,250.

19.5

	(a)	(b)
	£	£
Sale proceeds	65,000	35,000
Less: Acquisition cost	50,000	50,000
	15,000	(15,000)
Less: Available capital allowances	0	15,000
Chargeable gain or allowable loss	15,000	(0)

19.6

	£
Sale proceeds	8,000
Less: Unexpired portion of cost $\frac{3}{5} \times £10{,}000$	6,000
Chargeable gain	2,000

19.7

When the lease was acquired it had a 40-year life (Sch 8 percentage 95.457%). When the lease was assigned there were 22 years remaining (Sch 8 percentage 76.399%). Therefore the computation is as follows:

	£
Sale proceeds	97,500
Less: Unexpired portion of cost	
$\frac{76.399}{95.457} \times £75{,}000$	60,026
Chargeable gain	37,474

Chapter 20

20.1

(a)	20 October 2012	200	(bought on same day)
	10 August 2012	50	(s104 holding)
(b)	1 December 2012	150	(next 30 days)
	10 August 2012	270	(s104 holding)
(c)	10 August 2012	300	(s104 holding)

20.2

There were no acquisitions on the same day as the disposal or within the following 30 days, so the disposal must have come from the s104 holding. The s104 holding is as follows:

	Number of shares	*Allowable expenditure*
		£
Acquired 29 January 1982	1,000	4,000
Acquired 13 August 1996	1,000	9,500
Acquired 4 October 2008	2,000	22,500
	4,000	36,000
Sold 26 June 2012 (700/4,000ths)	(700)	(6,300)
s104 holding c/f	3,300	29,700

Notes:

(i) The shares acquired before 31 March 1982 are added into the s104 holding at their market value on that date.

(ii) On average, the allowable expenditure in the pool is £9 per share. The allowable expenditure deducted on the June 2012 disposal (£6,300) is equal to 700 shares at £9 per share.

The gain or loss arising on the disposal is as follows:

	(a)	(b)	(c)
	£	£	£
Sale proceeds	8,400	6,300	5,200
Less: Allowable expenditure	6,300	6,300	6,300
Chargeable gain/(allowable loss)	2,100	0	(1,100)

20.3

The 10,000 shares disposed of on 22 December 2012 are matched as follows:

(a) The first match is against the 3,000 shares acquired on the same day as the disposal. These 3,000 shares were acquired for £24,000 and sold for £30,000 (3,000 × £10), so the chargeable gain on these 3,000 shares is £6,000.

(b) The next match is against the 5,000 shares acquired within the next 30 days. These 5,000 shares were acquired for £55,000 and sold for £50,000 (5,000 × £10), so the allowable loss on these 5,000 shares is £5,000.

(c) The third and final match is against 2,000 of the shares in the s104 holding. The s104 holding is as follows:

	Number of shares	*Allowable expenditure*
		£
Acquired 19 September 2006	4,000	16,000
Acquired 20 October 2008	2,000	12,000
Acquired 21 November 2010	1,000	7,000
	7,000	35,000
Sold 22 December 2012 (2,000/7,000ths)	(2,000)	(10,000)
s104 holding c/f	5,000	25,000

These 2,000 shares were acquired for £10,000 (the allowable expenditure deducted from the s104 holding on their disposal) and sold for £20,000 (2,000 × £10). Therefore the chargeable gain is £10,000.

Overall, the chargeable gain on the 22 December 2012 disposal of 10,000 shares is £11,000 (£6,000 – £5,000 + £10,000).

20.4

There were no acquisitions on the same day as the disposal or within the following 30 days, so the disposal must have come from the s104 holding. The s104 holding is as follows:

	Number of shares	*Allowable expenditure* £
Acquired 17 February 2004	600	900
Acquired 13 November 2008	200	400
Acquired 9 October 2012	100	300
	900	1,600
Bonus issue January 2013	225	-
	1,125	1,600
Sold February 2013 (450/1,125ths)	(450)	(640)
s104 holding c/f	675	960

The 450 shares which were disposed of in February 2013 were acquired for £640 (the allowable expenditure deducted from the s104 holding) and were sold for £1,800 (450 × £4). Therefore the chargeable gain is £1,160.

20.5

There were no acquisitions on the same day as the disposal or within the following 30 days, so the disposal must have come from the s104 holding. The s104 holding is as follows:

	Number of shares	*Allowable expenditure* £
Acquired 30 September 2002	2,000	1,200
Acquired 1 December 2006	3,000	3,600
	5,000	4,800
Rights issue January 2013	1,000	1,000
	6,000	5,800
Sold March 2013 (3,000/6,000ths)	(3,000)	(2,900)
s104 holding c/f	3,000	2,900

The 3,000 shares which were disposed of in March 2013 were acquired for £2,900 (the allowable expenditure deducted from the s104 holding) and were sold for £5,400 (3,000 × £1.80). Therefore the chargeable gain is £2,500.

20.6

(a) The value of the part disposed of is £6,000 (6,000 × £1) and the value of the part remaining is £12,000 (6,000 × £2) so there has been a 6,000/18,000 (1/3rd) part disposal. One-third is more than 5% and the amount received is more than £3,000, so this cannot be treated as a small capital distribution. The s104 holding is as follows:

	Number of shares	*Allowable expenditure* £
Acquired November 2002	6,000	30,000
Distribution March 2013 (one-third)	-	(10,000)
s104 holding c/f	6,000	20,000

The allowable loss is £4,000 (£6,000 – £10,000).

(b) The value of Yolande's shares immediately prior to the sale of rights was £600. £25 is less than 5% of £600, so the sale of rights ranks as a small capital distribution. Assuming that this distribution is not treated as a disposal, the s104 holding is as follows:

	Number of shares	*Allowable expenditure* £
Acquired January 2006	300	360
Distribution May 2012	-	(25)
	300	335
Sold November 2012	(300)	(335)
s104 holding c/f	-	-

The chargeable gain is £445 (£780 – £335).

20.7

Walter received 16,000 shares worth £72,000, plus £8,000 in cash, a total of £80,000. The amount received in cash is 10% of the total. This exceeds 5% and the amount exceeds £3,000. Therefore this does not rank as a small capital distribution and the situation must be treated as a part disposal. The s104 holding is as follows:

	Number of shares	*Allowable expenditure* £
Acquired June 2012	10,000	70,000
Distribution September 2012 (10%)	-	(7,000)
s104 holding after distribution	10,000	63,000
s104 holding (Rundu plc) c/f	16,000	63,000

The chargeable gain is £1,000 (£8,000 – £7,000).

Chapter 21

21.1

So long as Mohammed actually resides in both properties he may choose which is to be regarded as his PPR. Whichever property he bought and lived in first was automatically regarded as his PPR. After he bought the second property (and began residing in it) he could, if he wished, elect that this property should become his PPR for CGT purposes. He would do this if he thought that the gain arising on the disposal of the second property would exceed the gain arising on the disposal of the first property. The election would have to be made within two years of the date from which it is to take effect.

21.2

	£
Sale proceeds	163,000
Less: Market value 31 March 1982	21,000
Chargeable gain (before PPR exemption)	142,000

The chargeable gain (before considering the PPR exemption) is £142,000. Considering each of the three cases individually:

(a) The house is not a chargeable asset and therefore the disposal is exempt from CGT. The gain is £nil.

(b) After 31 March 1982, Melanie owned the house for 30 years and 7 months (367 months) and was absent for 48 months. There is no indication that the absence was work-related and this absence exceeds the permissible maximum "absence for any reason" by 12 months. Therefore the PPR exemption is £142,000 × 355/367 = £137,357 and the chargeable gain is £142,000 × 12/367 = £4,643.

(c) Letting relief is available and is the lowest of £4,643, £137,357 and £40,000, which is £4,643. This reduces the chargeable gain to £nil.

21.3

	£
Sale proceeds	232,000
Less: Acquisition cost	55,000
Chargeable gain (before PPR exemption)	177,000

Rupert's period of ownership (a total of 268 months) is broken down as follows:

(i)	1 November 1990 to 31 October 1994	48 months	Actual residence
(ii)	1 November 1994 to 31 October 1995	12 months	Working abroad
(iii)	1 November 1995 to 31 January 1998	27 months	Actual residence
(iv)	1 February 1998 to 30 April 2002	51 months	Working in UK
(v)	1 May 2002 to 31 May 2002	1 month	Actual residence
(vi)	1 June 2002 to 1 March 2013	129 months	Living with friend

Periods (i), (iii) and (v) are exempt (actual residence) and period (ii) is exempt (working abroad). Period (iv) exceeds the four-year maximum allowable for working in the UK but the remaining three months of this period are exempt as part of the 36 months allowed for any reason. The last 36 months of ownership are exempt but the remaining 93 months of period (vi) cannot be exempt since they are not followed by a period of actual residence. The chargeable gain is:

	£
Total gain (as above)	177,000
Less: PPR exemption:	
£177,000 × 175/268	115,578
	61,422
Less: Letting relief (lowest of £61,422, £115,578 and £40,000)	40,000
Chargeable gain	21,422

21.4

	£
Sale proceeds	155,000
Less: Acquisition cost	37,500
Chargeable gain (before PPR exemption)	117,500

Samantha owned the house for a total of 21 years (252 months). For 7 years (84 months) the house was used partly for business purposes. The computation of the chargeable gain is as follows:

	£	£
Total gain (as above)		117,500
Less: PPR exemption:		
£117,500 × 168/252	78,333	
£117,500 × 84/252 × 4/5	31,333	109,666
Chargeable gain		7,834

Chapter 22

22.1

The allowable expenditure in relation to the porcelain is £9,850 (£10,000 in October 2003, plus £3,850 in March 2009, less £4,000 received July 2009). The computation of the gain arising in March 2013 is:

	£
Sale proceeds	23,500
Less: Allowable expenditure	9,850
Chargeable gain	13,650

22.2

The gain arising on the theft of the original necklace would have been:

	£
Disposal proceeds	14,000
Less: Acquisition cost	13,500
Chargeable gain	500

The allowable cost of the new necklace is reduced to £14,250 (£14,750 – £500). The gain arising on its disposal is as follows:

	£
Disposal proceeds	20,000
Less: Deemed acquisition cost	14,250
Chargeable gain	5,750

22.3

The gain on the disposal of the original building is computed as follows:

	£
Sale proceeds	261,400
Less: Acquisition cost	150,000
Chargeable gain	111,400

(a) £2,500 of the sale proceeds have been retained. Therefore £2,500 of the gain is immediately chargeable. The remaining £108,900 may be rolled-over against the cost of the new building, reducing its allowable cost to £150,000 (£258,900 – £108,900).

(b) £111,600 of the sale proceeds have been retained. This exceeds the gain. Therefore the whole gain is immediately chargeable and no part of the gain may be rolled-over. The allowable cost of the new building is the full £149,800.

(c) The entire sale proceeds have been spent on a replacement building. Therefore none of the gain is immediately chargeable and the entire gain may be rolled-over against the cost of the new building, reducing its allowable cost to £165,400 (£276,800 – £111,400).

22.4

The amount of the held-over gain is computed as follows:

		£
Disposal value		215,000
Less: Acquisition cost	91,500	
Enhancement expenditure	34,500	126,000
Held-over gain		89,000

The son's deemed acquisition cost is £126,000 (£215,000 – £89,000). If he had paid his mother £150,000 for the asset, the held-over gain would be reduced by £24,000 (£150,000 – £126,000) to £65,000 and his deemed acquisition cost would be £150,000 (£215,000 – £65,000).

Chapter 23

23.1

(a) The year to 30 November 2012 is an accounting period.

(b) The period from 1 October 2011 to 31 July 2012 does not exceed 12 months and is therefore an accounting period.

(c) The period from 1 January 2013 to 31 January 2013 does not exceed 12 months and is therefore an accounting period.

(d) The 33 months to 31 August 2012 is divided into three accounting periods. These are the 12 months to 30 November 2010, the 12 months to 30 November 2011 and the nine months to 31 August 2012.

(e) The 18 months to 30 September 2012 is divided into two accounting periods. These are the 12 months to 31 March 2012 and the six months to 30 September 2012.

23.2

(a) (i) Assuming that the debentures were acquired for non-trading purposes, the debenture interest receivable is a credit on a non-trading loan relationship. The gross amount of debenture interest accrued during the accounting period is aggregated with other debits and credits arising on non-trading loan relationships. Net credits are chargeable to corporation tax. Net debits are eligible for tax relief (see Chapter 26).

(ii) The income tax of £2,160 (£8,640 × 20/80) deducted at source from the debenture interest paid must be accounted for to HMRC, but the gross interest accrued during the accounting period is allowed either as an expense when computing the company's trading income or as a debit when computing the net credit or debit arising from non-trading loan relationships (depending on whether or not the loan is for trade purposes).

(b) Both items would normally be shown gross in the company's income statement.

23.3

The company may deduct £405,000 (£180,000 × 225%) in relation to this R&D expenditure when computing its trading income for the year to 31 March 2013. If the effect of this deduction is to create or increase a trading loss, the company may claim a payment from HMRC equal to the *lower* of 11% of the trading loss and 11% of £405,000 (i.e. £44,550).

23.4

The 17 months to 30 June 2012 will be divided into two accounting periods. These are the 12 months to 31 January 2012 and the five months to 30 June 2012. The chargeable profits for each accounting period are as follows:

	12 months to 31/1/12	*5 months to 30/6/12*
	£	£
Trading income (time apportioned)	300,000	125,000
Debenture interest receivable	3,600	2,000
Income from property (time apportioned)	6,360	2,650
Chargeable gains	28,700	49,760
	338,660	179,410
Less: Qualifying charitable donations	12,000	-
Chargeable profits	326,660	179,410

Notes:

(a) The debenture interest receivable is allocated on the accruals basis. Interest accrues at £400 per month. In the first accounting period, interest is due for the nine months from 1 May 2011 to 31 January 2012. In the second accounting period, interest is due for the five months from 1 February 2012 to 30 June 2012.

(b) The chargeable gains are allocated according to the dates of the disposals. Even though the two disposals are on consecutive days, they fall into different accounting periods.

(c) The Gift Aid donations are allocated according to the date of payment.

23.5

The chargeable profits for the year to 31 March 2013 are as follows:

	£
Trading income	1,561,400
Income from non-trading loan relationships (£19,820 + £44,670 + £23,980)	88,470
Chargeable gains	531,000
	2,180,870
Less: Qualifying charitable donations	9,000
Chargeable profits	2,171,870

Chapter 24

24.1

(a) *Disposal of factory building*

		£	£
Sale proceeds			650,000
Less:	Acquisition cost	300,000	
	Enhancement expenditure	50,000	350,000
Unindexed gain			300,000
Less:	Indexation allowance:		
	(i) on acquisition cost		
	$\frac{243.0 - 170.5}{170.5} = 0.425 \times £300{,}000$	127,500	
	(ii) on enhancement expenditure		
	$\frac{243.0 - 175.9}{175.9} = 0.381 \times £50{,}000$	19,050	146,550
Chargeable gain			153,450

(b) *Disposal of office building*

		£
Sale proceeds		1,000,000
Less:	Acquisition cost	600,000
Unindexed gain		400,000
Less:	Indexation allowance:	
	$\frac{244.2 - 173.8}{173.8} = 0.405 \times £600{,}000$	243,000
		157,000
Less:	Rolled-over gain (£157,000 – £75,000)	82,000
Chargeable gain		75,000

£75,000 of the sale proceeds have been retained and therefore £75,000 of the gain is immediately chargeable. The base cost of the replacement building is reduced to £843,000 (£925,000 – £82,000).

(c) *Disposal of computer system*

There is no chargeable gain or allowable loss in relation to this disposal, since gifts to charity are not chargeable disposals.

The company's plant and machinery capital allowances computation for the year to 31 March 2013 will show a disposal of £500 and this will generate a balancing adjustment if the computer is being treated as a short-life asset (see Chapter 11).

Gifts of used plant and machinery to a charity are allowable as trading expenses and so there will be a deduction of £500 from the company's trading profit (see Chapter 9).

(d) *Disposal of motor car*

There is no chargeable gain or allowable loss in relation to this disposal, since cars are not chargeable assets

When the car was acquired it entered either the main pool or the special rate pool, depending upon its emission rating. A disposal value of £80,000 is subtracted from the relevant pool in the year to 31 March 2013.

(e) *Disposal of plant and machinery*

This plant and machinery is a wasting chattel. Wasting chattels are normally exempt assets but this item has been used in business and capital allowances have been claimed, so the exemption does not apply. However, the loss of £40,000 is reduced to £nil by capital allowances of the same amount.

The company's plant and machinery capital allowances computation for the year to 31 March 2013 will show a disposal of £30,000.

(f) *Disposal of shares in Exxak plc*

The disposal is matched first against the 3,000 shares acquired within the previous nine days. These shares cost £36,000 and were sold for £30,000, so there is an allowable loss of £6,000.

The remaining 5,000 shares of the disposal are matched with shares taken from the s104 holding, as follows:

	No of shares	*Cost*	*Indexed cost*
		£	£
Bought 22 November 2002	4,000	16,000	16,000
Add: Indexation to December 2006			
$\frac{202.7 - 178.2}{178.2} \times £16,000$			2,200
			18,200
Bought 14 December 2006	6,000	30,000	30,000
s104 holding at 14 December 2006	10,000	46,000	48,200
Add: Indexation to December 2012			
$\frac{246.6 - 202.7}{202.7} \times £48,200$			10,439
			58,639
Sold 18 December 2012	(5,000)	(23,000)	(29,320)
s104 holding c/f at 18 December 2012	5,000	23,000	29,319

These 5,000 shares were sold for £50,000 so the chargeable gain arising on their disposal is £20,680 (£50,000 – £29,320).

(g) *Disposal of Government securities*

There is no chargeable gain or allowable loss in relation to this disposal, since disposals of Government securities (or "gilt-edged" securities) by a company are dealt with by means of the loan relationships regime.

Assuming that the securities were not held for trade purposes, there will be a debit on non-trading loan relationships of £5,000.

Total chargeable gains are £249,130 (£153,450 + £75,000 + £20,680) and allowable losses are £6,000. Therefore net chargeable gains for the year to 31 March 2013 are £243,130.

24.2

(i) *Disposal of shares in Epsilon plc*

The s104 holding is as follows:

	No of shares	*Cost*	*Indexed cost*
		£	£
Bought 27 June 1991	3,000	15,000	15,000
Add: Indexation to March 2001			
$\frac{172.2 - 134.1}{134.1} \times £15,000$			4,262
			19,262
Bought 10 March 2001	4,000	28,000	28,000
	7,000	43,000	47,262
Add: Indexation to September 2012			
$\frac{244.8 - 172.2}{172.2} \times £47,262$			19,926
			67,188
Sold 12 September 2012	(7,000)	(43,000)	(67,188)
s104 holding c/f	0	0	0

These 7,000 shares were sold for £59,500 (7,000 × £8.50) so the unindexed gain arising on the disposal is £16,500 (£59,500 – £43,000). The available indexation allowance is £24,188 but this is restricted to £16,500 and the chargeable gain is zero.

The 1982 holding is as follows:

	No of shares	*Cost*	*MV 31/3/82*
		£	£
Bought 14 January 1981	2,000	4,000	5,000
Sold 12 September 2012	(500)	(1,000)	(1,250)
1982 holding c/f	1,500	3,000	3,750

Indexation allowance on this disposal is (244.8 – 79.44)/79.44 = 2.082 × £1,250 = £2,603. Rebasing gives the lower gain. The shares were sold for £4,250 (500 × £8.50). The chargeable gain is £397 (£4,250 – £1,250 – £2,603).

(ii) *Disposal of watercolour paintings*

The gross disposal proceeds of the paintings are £5,750 (£5,175 × 100/90) and £6,450 (£5,805 × 100/90) respectively. The first painting is disposed of for less than £6,000 and is exempt. The gain arising on the disposal of the second painting is as follows:

		£
Sale proceeds		6,450
Less:	Incidental costs of disposal	645
		5,805
Less:	Acquisition cost	2,000
Unindexed gain		3,805
Less:	Indexation allowance:	
	$\frac{245.4-177.6}{177.6}$ = 0.382 × £2,000	764
Chargeable gain		3,041 (restricted to £450 × 5/3 = £750)

(iii) *Disposal of short lease*

When it was assigned, the lease had 5 years and 7 months left to run. The Sch. 8 percentage is 29.331 (26.722 + 7/12 × 4.473). The loss on the disposal is as follows:

		£
Sale proceeds		7,000
Less:	Cost (29.331/72.770 × £20,000)	8,061
Allowable loss		(1,061)

(iv) *Disposal of freehold property*

Assuming that the building and the plant are used for business purposes, all except £15,000 of the gain on the disposal of the building may be held over. The computation is as follows:

		£
Sale proceeds		115,000
Less:	Acquisition cost	50,000
Unindexed gain		65,000
Less:	Indexation allowance:	
	$\frac{246.0-187.4}{187.4}$ = 0.313 × £50,000	15,650
		49,350
Less:	Held-over gain	34,350
Chargeable gain		15,000

Total gains are £16,147 (£397 + £750 + £15,000). Allowable losses are £1,061 so net gains are £15,086. These are reduced by capital losses brought forward of £6,646 to £8,440.

Chapter 25

25.1

Chargeable profits for the year are apportioned between financial years as follows:

FY2011	1 July 2011 to 31 March 2012	£3,000,000 × 9/12 = £2,250,000
FY2012	1 April 2012 to 30 June 2012	£3,000,000 × 3/12 = £750,000

The company's augmented profits must exceed the upper limit, so corporation tax is due at the main rate. The liability is [(26% × £2,250,000) + (24% × £750,000)] = £765,000.

25.2

(a)

	£
Chargeable profits	267,000
FII (£18,450 + £2,050)	20,500
Augmented profits	287,500

Augmented profits do not exceed the lower limit of £300,000. Therefore the small profits rate for FY2012 applies and the corporation tax liability is £53,400 (20% × £267,000).

(b)

	£
Chargeable profits	1,450,000
FII (£49,500 + £5,500)	55,000
Augmented profits	1,505,000

Augmented profits exceed the upper limit of £1,500,000. Therefore the main rate for FY2012 applies and the corporation tax liability is £348,000 (24% × £1,450,000).

(c) Augmented profits and chargeable profits are both £10,000,000. Augmented profits exceed the upper limit of £1,500,000. Therefore the FY2012 main rate applies and the corporation tax liability is £2,400,000 (24% × £10,000,000).

(d) Augmented profits and chargeable profits are both £1,000. Augmented profits do not exceed the lower limit of £300,000. Therefore the small profits rate for FY2012 applies and the corporation tax liability is £200 (20% × £1,000).

25.3

Augmented profits are £577,000 (£536,000 + (£36,900 + £4,100)), a figure which lies between the lower and upper limits. Therefore the company's chargeable profits (£536,000) are taxed at the main rate and marginal relief is available. The computation is:

	£
Corporation tax on £536,000 @ 24%	128,640.00
Less: Marginal relief:	
$\frac{1}{100} \times (£1{,}500{,}000 - £577{,}000) \times \frac{£536{,}000}{£577{,}000}$	8,574.14
Corporation tax liability	120,065.86

25.4

(a) CompU Ltd has chargeable profits of £875,983 and augmented profits of £908,783 (£875,983 + £32,800) for this accounting period which falls partly into FY2011 and partly into FY2012. It is necessary to apportion between the two FYs. The computation is as follows:

	£	£
FY2011 (1 month)		
Corporation tax on £72,999 @ 26%	18,979.74	
Less: Marginal relief:		
$\frac{3}{200} \times (£125{,}000 - £75{,}732) \times \frac{£72{,}999}{£75{,}732}$	712.35	18,267.39
FY2012 (11 months)		
Corporation tax on £802,984 @ 24%	192,716.16	
Less: Marginal relief:		
$\frac{1}{100} \times (£1{,}375{,}000 - £833{,}051) \times \frac{£802{,}984}{£833{,}051}$	5,223.89	187,492.27
Corporation tax liability		205,759.66

Notes:

(i) The question gave a figure for FII, *not* a figure for UK dividends. By definition, FII includes the tax credits that are attached to dividends. Therefore there is no need to add tax credits a second time to the FII figure of £32,800.

(ii) The lower and upper limits for the part of the accounting period which falls into FY2011 (one month) are scaled down to 1/12th of their annual amounts. Similarly, the lower and upper limits for the part of the accounting period which falls into FY2012 (11 months) are scaled down to 11/12ths of their annual amounts. Hence the figures of £125,000 (1/12th of £1,500,000) and £1,375,000 (11/12ths of £1,500,000) used in the marginal relief calculations.

(b) CompV Ltd has chargeable profits and augmented profits of £200,000 for this six-month accounting period which falls wholly within FY2012. The lower and upper limits are scaled down to £150,000 and £750,000 respectively for a six-month period and the company's augmented profits lie between these scaled-down limits. Therefore corporation tax is due at 24% less marginal relief. The computation is as follows:

	£
Corporation tax on £200,000 @ 24%	48,000.00
Less: Marginal relief:	
$\frac{1}{100} \times (£750{,}000 - £200{,}000)$	5,500.00
Corporation tax liability	42,500.00

(c) CompW Ltd has chargeable profits and augmented profits of £428,000 for this accounting period which coincides with FY2012. Augmented profits lie between the lower and upper limits, so chargeable profits are taxed at the main rate and marginal relief is available. The computation is:

	£
Corporation tax on £428,000 @ 24%	102,720.00
Less: Marginal relief:	
$\frac{1}{100} \times (£1{,}500{,}000 - £428{,}000)$	10,720.00
Corporation tax liability	92,000.00

If chargeable profits and augmented profits were both £328,000, the computation would be:

	£
Corporation tax on £328,000 @ 24%	78,720.00
Less: Marginal relief:	
$\frac{1}{100} \times (£1{,}500{,}000 - £328{,}000)$	11,720.00
Corporation tax liability	67,000.00

The tax liability is reduced by £25,000, which is 25% of £100,000. Therefore the company is subject to a marginal corporation tax rate of 25%. This applies as long as augmented profits remain between the lower and upper limits.

25.5

The due date of payment is 1 June 2012 (nine months and one day after 31 August 2011). The final payment of £4,650 was made on 3 October 2012, i.e. 124 days late. The interest due is:

$$£4{,}650 \times 3\% \times \frac{124}{366} = £47.26.$$

Chapter 26

26.1

	y/e 31/5/10	*y/e 31/5/11*	*y/e 31/5/12*
	£	£	£
Trading profits	-	23,800	40,300
Less: Trading losses b/f	-	23,800	8,400
Trading income	-	0	31,900
Less: Qualifying charitable donations	-	-	600
Chargeable profits	0	0	31,300
Trading losses c/f	32,200	8,400	-
Unrelieved charitable donations	400	500	-

26.2

	£
Trading income	-
Income from property	190,200
Chargeable gains	45,540
	235,740
Less: Trade loss relief against total profits	232,300
	3,440
Less: Qualifying charitable donations	3,440
Chargeable profits	0
Unrelieved charitable donations	20,560

26.3

Statements (a), (b) and (d) are false. Statement (c) is true. The reasons for this are as follows:

(a) Capital losses which are carried forward may be relieved only against future chargeable gains, not against future trading profits.

(b) Trading losses which are carried forward may be relieved only against future trading profits of the same trade, not against future chargeable gains.

(c) Trading losses may be relieved against total profits (including chargeable gains) of the accounting period in which the loss is incurred.

(d) Capital losses are relieved against chargeable gains of the same accounting period but not against trading profits of that period.

Therefore the correct answer is (c).

26.4

	y/e 31/5/11	*eight months to 31/1/12*	*y/e 31/1/13*
	£	£	£
Trading income	59,700	73,600	-
Chargeable gains	8,400	-	48,700
	68,100	73,600	48,700
Less: Trade loss relief (a)	-	-	48,700
	68,100	73,600	0
Less: Trade loss relief (b)	22,700	73,600	-
	45,400	0	0
Less: Qualifying charitable donations	1,000	-	-
Chargeable profits	44,400	0	0
Trading losses c/f	-	-	10,700
Unrelieved charitable donations	-	1,000	1,000

Notes:

(i) The trading loss may be carried back for 12 months. The period to 31 January 2012 is wholly within these 12 months. But only four months out of the year to 31 May 2011 fall within the 12 months so maximum relief available in this year is £22,700 (£68,100 × 4/12).

(ii) Losses of £145,000 (£48,700 + £73,600 + £22,700) are relieved, leaving losses to carry forward of £10,700.

26.5

(a)/(b)

The main effects of a claim to relieve the trading loss against total profits are as follows:

(i) Augmented profits for the year to 31 March 2013 are reduced to £200,000 and the company pays corporation tax at the FY2012 small profits rate of 20%. Without the claim, the company would pay corporation tax at the main rate of 24%, less marginal relief.

(ii) The original tax liability for the year to 31 March 2013 would have been £185,000. This is £800,000 × 24%, less marginal relief of (1/100 × (£1,500,000 – £800,000)).

The revised liability is £40,000 (£200,000 × 20%). This is a tax saving of £145,000. The loss of £600,000 has been relieved at an effective rate of 24.17%.

Note that an alternative way of calculating the saving is to recognise that the first £500,000 of loss relief reduces profits from £800,000 to £300,000 (the lower limit) and so saves tax at the marginal rate of 25%. The remaining £100,000 of loss relief saves tax at 20%. So the total saving is £500,000 × 25% + £100,000 × 20% = £145,000.

(iii) The corporation tax refund due for the year to 31 March 2013 carries interest dating from 1 January 2014 (or the date on which the tax was originally paid, if later).

Chapter 27

27.1

(a), (d) and (e) are associates, (b) and (c) are not.

27.2

The top five shareholders are Sejanus (with Apicata) 1,020 shares, Claudius (with Livia) 590 shares, Agrippa 300 shares, Cleopatra 300 shares and Tiberius 200 shares, totalling 2,410 shares. So the company is not under the control of five or fewer shareholders.

Sejanus is ranked as a director (since he is a manager and, with his wife, owns 20.4% of the share capital). So the directors are Sejanus (with Apicata) 1,020 shares, Claudius (with Livia) 590 shares, Agrippa 300 shares, Cleopatra 300 shares, Tiberius 200 shares and Gaius 200 shares, totalling 2,610 shares. The company is under the control of its participator-directors and is therefore a close company.

27.3

(a) The director owns more than 5% of the company's share capital so the loan is taxable. The company must pay tax of £3,000 (25% of £12,000) by 1 January 2014 (unless the loan is repaid before then). Once paid, this tax is not refundable until nine months and one day after the end of the accounting period in which the loan is repaid or written off. The director will be subject to income tax on loan interest calculated at the official rate. If the loan is eventually written off (wholly or partly) the director will be taxed on the amount written off and the company will be denied any tax relief in relation to this amount.

(b) The director will be subject to income tax on a benefit in kind of £1,800. But if the ticket had been given to a shareholder who was not a director or other employee earning at least £8,500 per annum, it would have been treated as a distribution. The cost of the ticket would have been disallowed in the company's accounts and the shareholder would have been charged to income tax as if he or she had received a dividend of £1,800 (tax credit £200).

Chapter 28

28.1

(a) They are associated companies and so the upper and lower limits are shared equally between the three companies.

(b) The transfer pricing legislation applies to transactions carried out at artificial prices between group companies, though small and medium-sized companies are generally exempt from this legislation.

(c) The augmented profits of Headco Ltd are calculated without regard to dividends received from Arm1 Ltd and Arm2 Ltd.

(d) They also form a 75% group so trading losses and other items may be surrendered by a group member to any other group member.

(e) Chargeable assets are transferred between the three companies on a no-gain, no-loss basis.

28.2

	£	£
Trading profits	220,000	
Income from non-trading loan relationship	6,000	
Income from property	4,000	
Qualifying charitable donations	(17,000)	
Chargeable profits	213,000	
FII (£27,000 + £3,000)	30,000	
Augmented profits	243,000	
Lower limit (£300,000 × 1/3)	100,000	
Upper limit (£1,500,000 × 1/3)	500,000	
Corporation tax on £213,000 @ 24%		51,120.00
Less: Marginal relief: $\frac{1}{100} \times (£500,000 - £243,000) \times \frac{£213,000}{£243,000}$		2,252.72
Corporation tax due		48,867.28

Note:
Lower and upper limits are shared between Alphant Ltd, Betant Ltd and the other active subsidiary.

28.3

Basenote Ltd has current year trading losses of £90,000 and excess donations of £1,000, giving a total of £91,000. But Apexine Ltd has chargeable profits of only £73,000 (£120,000 – £42,000 + £7,000 – £12,000) so the maximum group relief that may be claimed is £73,000.

28.4

Z11 Ltd owns at least 75% of Z12 Ltd and Z12 Ltd owns at least 75% of Z13 Ltd, of which Z11 Ltd (indirectly) owns more than 50%. Therefore Z11 Ltd, Z12 Ltd and Z13 Ltd form a capital gains group. Z12 Ltd does not own at least 75% of Z14 Ltd, so Z14 Ltd is not a member of the group, even though Z11 Ltd does (indirectly) own more than 50% of its ordinary share capital.

28.5

The amount of the loss of PPPX Ltd which is available for group relief is £84,000 (£96,000 less a potential claim for relief against total profits of £12,000). This is shared between the consortium members as follows:

	CM01 Ltd	*CM02 Ltd*	*CM03 Ltd*
	£	£	£
Share of PPPX Ltd available loss	26,880	29,400	19,320
Chargeable profits	59,000	47,000	14,000
Maximum group relief claim	26,880	29,400	14,000

Chapter 29

29.1

(a) standard rate
(b) zero rate
(c) exempt
(d) standard rate
(e) standard rate
(f) zero rate
(g) reduced rate
(h) exempt
(i) exempt
(j) standard rate
(k) standard rate
(l) zero rate
(m) zero rate
(n) standard rate.

29.2

(a) The value of the supply is £340. VAT charged is 20% of £340 = £68 and the consideration for the supply is £408.

(b) The value of the supply is £333.20 (£340 less 2%). VAT charged is 20% of £333.20 = £66.64 and the consideration for the supply is £399.84.

(c) VAT chargeable remains at £66.64 but the consideration for the supply is £406.64.

29.3

(a) Lorna must register since her taxable turnover exceeds the registration threshold.

(b) Mike must register since his aggregate taxable turnover exceeds the registration threshold.

(c) No-one need register. The partnership of "Pat and Phil" is not the same person as "Phil" so the turnover of the two businesses is not aggregated.

(d) The taxable "person" in this case is the company (not the shareholders) and therefore the company must register.

29.4

(a) She is not a taxable person, may not register for VAT and cannot reclaim input tax.

(b) She is a taxable person and must register for VAT. She must account for output tax and may reclaim input tax.

(c) She is a taxable person and must register for VAT unless granted an exemption by HMRC. If she registers she may reclaim input tax. If she is granted exemption she will not be able to reclaim input tax but she will avoid the administrative burden associated with VAT registration.

29.5

See text.

Chapter 30

30.1

See text.

30.2

See text.

30.3

(a)

	£	£
Output tax:		
Standard-rated supplies (£28,800 × 97.5% × 20%)		5,616
Supply invoiced 15 November 2012 (£4,800 × 20%)		960
Fuel scale charge (1/6 × £266)		44
		6,620
Input tax:		
Standard-rated goods (£9,280 × 20%)	1,856	
Standard-rated services (£5,200 × 20%)	1,040	
Car maintenance (£280 × 20%)	56	
Car fuel (£520 × 20%)	104	
Non-current asset (1/6 × £14,100)	2,350	5,406
Payable to HMRC by 31 December 2012		1,214

Notes:

(i) Output tax is calculated on the price charged to customers less the maximum cash discount available, regardless of whether customers take advantage of this discount.

(ii) Output tax is payable in relation to the sale to the bankrupt customer. Bad debt relief cannot be claimed until at least 6 months have elapsed.

(iii) The tax point of the £4,800 supply is the invoice date (earlier than the date of payment or the date on which the goods were made available).

(iv) Input tax cannot be reclaimed in relation to a car not used wholly for business purposes.

(b) The flat-rate scheme for small businesses (FRS) is available to businesses with a taxable turnover which is not expected to exceed £150,000 in the next 12 months. Toucan Ltd seems likely to satisfy this requirement. Membership of the scheme would allow Toucan Ltd to calculate its VAT liability as a flat-rate percentage of its total turnover and so avoid the need to keep detailed records of input tax and output tax. The FRS operates as follows:

(i) Output tax is charged to customers at the normal rate for the supply. Similarly, input tax is paid to suppliers at the normal rate. However, the output tax charged to customers is not paid over to HMRC and (in general) input tax is not recoverable.

(ii) In each tax period, a flat-rate percentage is applied to the VAT-inclusive turnover for the period. The result of this calculation is the amount of VAT payable to HMRC.

(iii) Input tax on the purchase of non-current assets costing at least £2,000 (including VAT) can be reclaimed in the usual way.

If Toucan Ltd joined the FRS, its average monthly VAT liability would be £1,311 (£11,500 × 1.2 × 9.5%). If the company did not join the scheme, the average liability would be £1,200 ((£11,500 - £5,500) × 20%). In both cases, input tax could be reclaimed on the expected non-current asset purchase of £5,000. It would appear, therefore, that Toucan Ltd would not benefit from joining the FRS unless administrative savings exceeded £111 per month.

30.4

Input tax reclaimed is £798 × 1/6 = £133.00. The scale figure for this type of car for a 3-month period is £500, so output tax of £500 × 1/6 = £83.33 must be accounted for.

Chapter 31

31.1

	Value before AE	*AE for 2012-13*	*AE for 2011-12*	*Value after AE*
	£	£	£	£
Gift to grandson (exempt as a small gift)	-	-	-	-
Gift on marriage (£3,000 – £1,000)	2,000	2,000	-	-
Gift to husband (spouse exemption)	-	-	-	-
Gift to relevant property trust	10,000	1,000	3,000	6,000
Gift to Labour Party (exempt)	-	-	-	-
	12,000	3,000	3,000	6,000

31.2

(a) exempt (b) chargeable (c) PET.

31.3

The total of transfers brought forward in the seven years to date is £281,000, leaving £44,000 of the nil-rate band to set against the current transfer.

(a) If the trustees pay the tax, the gross value of the transfer is £80,000 and the IHT due is £44,000 @ 0% + £36,000 @ 20% = £7,200, payable on 30 June 2013.

(b) If Nicholas pays the tax, the net value of the transfer is £80,000. The gross value and the tax due are as follows:

	Net	*Gross*	*Tax*
	£	£	£
£44,000 grossed up @ 0%	44,000	44,000	0
£36,000 grossed up @ 20%	36,000	45,000	9,000
Totals	80,000	89,000	9,000

The tax due is £9,000, payable on 30 June 2013.

31.4

The value of each gift after deduction of exemptions is as follows:

		Value before AE	*AE for current year*	*AE for previous year*	*Value after AE*
		£	£	£	£
2006-07	Daughter (£500,000 – £5,000)	495,000	3,000	3,000	489,000
2008-09	Relevant property trust	500,000	3,000	3,000	494,000

Lifetime tax liability

The gift to Martha's daughter was a PET, so no lifetime tax was payable. The lifetime tax on the gift to the trust was £45,500, payable on 30 April 2009 and calculated as follows:

	Net	*Gross*	*Tax*
	£	£	£
£312,000 grossed up @ 0%	312,000	312,000	0
£182,000 grossed up @ 20%	182,000	227,500	45,500
Totals	494,000	539,500	45,500

Tax liability on death

(i) *Transfer made on 31 August 2006*

The gross value of this transfer is £489,000 and there were no other chargeable transfers in the seven years ending on the date of the transfer. Tax due at death rates applicable on 1 January 2013:

	£
£325,000 @ 0%	0
£164,000 @ 40%	65,600
	65,600
<u>Less</u>: Taper relief (6-7 years) @ 80%	52,480
	13,120
<u>Less</u>: Lifetime tax paid	0
IHT payable by daughter on 31 July 2013	13,120

(ii) *Transfer made on 1 June 2008*

The gross value of this transfer is £539,500 and previous gross chargeable transfers in the seven years ending on the date of the transfer (2 June 2001 to 1 June 2008) were £489,000, using the whole of the nil-rate band. Tax due at death rates applicable on 1 January 2013:

	£
£539,500 @ 40%	215,800
<u>Less</u>: Taper relief (4-5 years) @ 40%	86,320
	129,480
<u>Less</u>: Lifetime tax paid	45,500
IHT payable by trustees on 31 July 2013	83,980

31.5

The quarter-up rule gives 572p + 1/4 × (588p – 572p) = 576p. Average of the highest and lowest recorded bargains is 575p, so the shares are valued at 575p and the transfer has a market value of 1,000 × £5.75 = £5,750.

Chapter 32

32.1

Jean-Paul is a UK resident during 2012-13 but he is neither ordinarily resident nor domiciled in the UK. His UK income tax position is as follows:

(a) The earnings from his UK employment are fully taxable.

(b) If the remittance basis applies to him for 2012-13, the earnings from his Belgian employment are taxable on the remittance basis. Otherwise, these earnings are fully taxable.

(c) If the remittance basis applies to him for 2012-13, the dividends on the Canadian shares are taxable on the remittance basis. Otherwise, these dividends are fully taxable.

(d) The interest on UK Government securities is exempt from UK income tax since Jean-Paul is not ordinarily resident in the UK.

32.2

Normally, a person is regarded as being either resident for the whole of a tax year or non-resident for the whole of that year, but a person who leaves the UK to take up employment abroad for at least an entire tax year (as Amy has done) is regarded as resident for the part of the tax year before the date of departure and non-resident thereafter. Amy's situation is therefore as follows:

(a) In 2010-11 she is resident until 31 December 2010 and non-resident from 1 January 2011. She will receive full personal allowances for 2010-11 to set against her income for that year. Her income for UK tax purposes after 31 December 2010 will consist only of any income arising in the UK (e.g. rents from letting her house whilst away). Her Australian salary will not be subject to UK tax.

(b) In 2011-12 and 2012-13 she is non-resident. Her Australian salary will not be subject to UK tax and she will be taxed only on her UK income, if any. As a citizen of the European Economic Area, she is entitled to personal allowances.

(c) In 2013-14 she is resident from 1 January 2014. She will receive full personal allowances for 2013-14 to set against her income for the year. Her income for UK tax purposes before 1 January 2014 consists only of her UK income. Once again, her Australian salary will not be subject to UK tax.

However, if Amy visits the UK for 183 days or more in any one tax year she will be resident for that year and her worldwide income will be subject to UK income tax. Similarly, she may be regarded as resident if she visits the UK for 91 days or more per annum.

32.3

(a) 90% of the pension is subject to UK income tax.

(b) If the remittance basis applies to Cara for a tax year, only the amount of the pension remitted to the UK in that year is subject to UK income tax. Otherwise, 90% of the pension is taxable.

32.4

See text.

32.5

See text.

32.6

(a)

	UK	*Overseas*	*Total*
	£	£	£
Trading income	2,120,000		2,120,000
Property income			
(£98,000 × 100/70)		140,000	140,000
Chargeable profits	2,120,000	140,000	2,260,000
Corporation tax @ 24%	508,800	33,600	542,400
Less: Unilateral DTR		(33,600)	(33,600)
Corporation tax due	508,800	-	508,800

Unilateral double tax relief is restricted to the UK tax payable on the foreign income. The remaining £8,400 (£42,000 – £33,600) of foreign tax is unrelieved. This arises because the foreign tax rate exceeds the UK rate by 6% (6% × £140,000 = £8,400). The unrelieved foreign tax is lost.

(b)

If the overseas income consisted of trading income from an overseas branch, the unrelieved foreign tax of £8,400 could be carried back for up to three years or carried forward without time limit. The unrelieved tax would then be treated as foreign tax paid in respect of the overseas branch in the accounting period to which it was carried back or carried forward. If the UK rate of tax exceeded the foreign rate of tax in any such accounting period, this would offer an opportunity to relieve some or all of the unrelieved foreign tax.

However, the company may have made an irrevocable election to the effect that the profits of all of its overseas branches should be exempt from UK corporation tax. In this case, the overseas income would be totally ignored in the company's tax computation and there would be no relief for any foreign tax paid.

Answers to review questions

Set A

Question A1

(a)

	£
Car (35% of £19,500)	6,825
Fuel (35% of £20,200)	7,070
Loan (4% of £5,250)	210
LVs (200 @ £4.85)	970
Nursery fees	3,405
	18,480

(b) (i) Consider a car with a lower emission rating. The car on offer has an emission rating which gives the highest possible tax charge. Each 5g/km reduction would save income tax on £397 (1% × (£19,500 + £20,200)).

(ii) If the £1,000 contribution is made towards running costs of the car such as maintenance, insurance etc. (not towards private fuel) it will reduce the taxable car benefit.

(iii) Reduce the loan to £5,000, so that no taxable benefit arises.

(iv) Take the canteen meals instead of LVs. No taxable benefit will arise.

(v) Transfer the son to the in-house nursery. No taxable benefit will arise. Alternatively, up to £28 per week of childcare can be received tax-free (by a higher-rate taxpayer) if the employer contracts with an approved childminder or provides vouchers for paying an approved childminder.

(c)

	Mr Tulliver				*Mrs Tulliver*		
	Total	*Non-savings*	*Savings*	*Divs*	*Total*	*Non-savings*	*Savings*
	£	£	£	£	£	£	£
Salary	85,000	85,000			15,000	15,000	
Less: Pension cont.					900	900	
					14,100	14,100	
Benefit package	18,480	18,480					
BSI (× 100/80)	8,000		8,000		3,390		3,390
UK divs £4,680 + £520	5,200			5,200			
	116,680	103,480	8,000	5,200	17,490	14,100	3,390
Less: PA	0	0			8,105	8,105	
Taxable income	116,680	103,480	8,000	5,200	9,385	5,995	3,390

Income tax

Mr T	*Mrs T*			
34,370	9,385	@ 20%	6,874.00	1,877.00
77,110		@ 40%	30,844.00	
5,200		@ 32.5%	1,690.00	
116,680	9,385			
Tax borne			39,408.00	1,877.00

Tax could be saved by switching investments from Mr T to Mrs T, using the rest of her basic rate band, where savings income would be taxed at only 20% and dividends at only 10%. This would also reduce Mr T's income to the point where he would receive a personal allowance.

Question A2

	Total	*Non-savings*	*Savings*	*Dividends*
	£	£	£	£
Employment income	20,260	20,260		
Property income	3,680	3,680		
Annuity £25 × 12	300		300	
UK divs £6,750 + tax credit £750	7,500			7,500
Total income	31,740	23,940	300	7,500
Less: Personal allowance	8,105	8,105		
Taxable income	23,635	15,835	300	7,500

Income tax due

Non-savings income	: Basic rate	15,835	@ 20%	3,167.00
Savings income	: Basic rate	300	@ 20%	60.00
Dividend income	: Ordinary rate	7,500	@ 10%	750.00
		23,635		
				3,977.00
Less: MCA £7,090 @ 10%				709.00
Tax borne				3,268.00
Less: Tax credits (£750) and tax deducted at source (£60)				810.00
Tax payable				2,458.00

Notes:

1. Rents received are £6,000. Insurance is £370 (9/12 × £360 + 3/12 × £400). The wear and tear allowance is £450 (10% × (£6,000 – £500 – £1,000)) so total expenses are £2,320 (£370 + £500 + £1,000 + £450). Property income is £3,680 (£6,000 – £2,320).
2. Total income exceeds the limit for age-related allowances by £6,340 so allowances are reduced by £3,170 (£6,340 × 1/2). £2,555 is deducted from the personal allowance of £10,660, bringing it down to the lowest possible figure of £8,105. The remaining £615 is deducted from the MCA of £7,705, giving £7,090.

Question A3

(a)

		Ae	Bee	Cae
		£	£	£
2010–11	1 July 2010 to 5 April 2011			
	£54,000 × 9/12 × 1/2	20,250	20,250	
2011-12	year ended 30 June 2011			
	£54,000 × 1/2	27,000	27,000	
2012-13	year ended 30 June 2012			
	£66,000 × 1/2	33,000	33,000	
	1 July 2012 to 5 April 2013			
	£87,000 × 9/12 × 1/3			21,750

(b)/(c)

		Dee
		£
2010-11	year ended 5 April 2011	32,880
2011-12	1 August 2010 to 31 July 2011	
	(£32,880 × 8/12) + £16,240	38,160
2012-13	year ended 31 July 2012	54,120

Overlap profits of £21,920 arise in respect of the eight months from 1 August 2010 to 5 April 2011.

Question A4

If the transactions are of a trading nature, the profits made by the partnership of Bernard and Gerald will be charged to income tax as trading income. The "badges of trade" will be used to decide whether they are trading, as follows:

(a) *Subject matter*. It appears that the subject matter of the transaction is of a type normally associated with a trading venture, rather than of a type more normally associated with investments or personal consumption.

(b) *Frequency of transactions*. There was only one purchase but there were several sales. The fact that sales were made to a number of different garden centres gives the impression of trading.

(c) *Length of ownership*. This was a fairly short-term venture. Most of the barrels had been sold within a few months and this again gives the impression of trading.

(d) *Supplementary work*. The barrels were sawn in half and Bernard and Gerald canvassed garden centres in the hope of finding customers. These activities constitute supplementary work and support the view that they were trading.

(e) *Motive*. It seems clear that the barrels were bought with only one view in mind - resale at a profit. This is a clear indicator of trading.

(f) *Acquisition*. The barrels were not inherited or gifted. They were purchased by Bernard and Gerald. This supports the view that they were trading.

It seems clear that this was an adventure in the nature of trade. Bernard and Gerald will be charged to income tax on their trading profits in tax years 2012-13 and 2013-14.

Question A5

(i) *Mr de Praet*

	2011-12	*2012-13*
	£	£
Trading income	20,000	nil
Income from property	10,000	10,000
Total income	30,000	10,000
Less: Trading losses relieved against total income	30,000	10,000
Net income	nil	nil

The personal allowance is lost in both years. Tax savings are achieved at basic rate. If the loss had been carried forward, there would have been no loss of personal allowances and tax savings would have been achieved at higher rate (assuming that the estimate of future trading profits is accurate).

(ii) An AIA of £7,360 (100% × £7,360) is available in the year to 30 June 2012. This increases the loss to £16,360. A claim to set this loss against total income for 2011-12 will leave net income of £1,640 (£18,000 – £16,360), so wasting personal allowances.

It would be better to restrict the capital allowances claim to £1,525. This reduces the trading loss claim to £10,525, leaving net income of £7,475 which exactly absorbs the 2011-12 personal allowance. The unclaimed capital allowances increase the WDV carried forward and so result in higher capital allowances in future years.

Set B

Question B1

(i)

	£
Sale proceeds	13,000
Less: Auctioneer's commission (8%)	1,040
	11,960
Less: Acquisition cost	1,000
Chargeable gain	10,960

The maximum gain is 5/3 × £7,000 = £11,667, so the chargeable gain remains at £10,960.

(ii)

	£
Sale proceeds	900,000
Less: Acquisition cost	566,700
Chargeable gain	333,300

£200,000 of the sale proceeds were not reinvested in the new factory. Therefore £200,000 of the gain is immediately chargeable. The rolled-over gain is £133,300. The base cost of the new factory is £566,700 (£700,000 – £133,300).

Question B2

(a) The disposal is matched first with the 1,000 shares bought in the following 30 days. These shares were sold for £4,600 and bought for £4,400, giving a chargeable gain of £200.

The disposal is then matched with 4,000 of the shares in the Section 104 holding. This holding is as follows:

	Number of shares	*Allowable expenditure*
		£
Bought 18 August 2000	3,000	6,000
Bought 19 September 2007	2,000	5,000
	5,000	11,000
Sold 13 March 2013 (4/5ths)	(4,000)	(8,800)
s104 holding c/f	1,000	2,200

These 4,000 shares were sold for £18,400, so the chargeable gain on their disposal is £9,600 (£18,400 – £8,800). The total chargeable gain is £9,800 (£200 + £9,600).

(b) Sally's net gains for 2012-13 are £31,000. Deducting losses brought forward of £12,000 leaves £19,000. Deducting the annual exemption of £10,600 leaves £8,400. CGT is due as follows:

(i) 18% × £8,400 = £1,512

(ii) (18% × £4,370) + (28% × £4,030) = £1,915

(iii) 28% × £8,400 = £2,352.

Question B3

(i) The s104 holding consists of 50,000 shares at a total cost of £107,000. Therefore the gain on the August 2012 disposal is as follows:

	£
Sale proceeds	160,000
Less: Acquisition cost (2/5ths of £107,000)	42,800
Chargeable gain	117,200

(ii) The gain is eligible for entrepreneurs' relief because it arises on a disposal of shares in a trading company which (throughout the previous 12 months) has been Samuel's personal company and of which he has been an officer or employee. WQZ Ltd is his personal company because he owns at least 5% of its ordinary shares and has at least 5% of its voting rights.

(iii) Deducting the annual exemption of £10,600 leaves £106,600. The CGT liability is £10,660 (10% × £106,600). This is due for payment on 31 January 2014.

Question B4

(a) Marlene has net gains of £4,000. These are covered by £4,000 of the annual exemption, leaving a CGT assessment of £nil. The remaining £6,600 of the annual exemption is wasted. There are no losses carried forward.

(b) Moira has net gains of £12,000. Losses brought forward of £1,400 are subtracted from these gains, leaving £10,600. This is covered by the annual exemption, leaving a CGT assessment of £nil. Losses carried forward are £6,600 (£8,000 – £1,400).

(c) Marina has net gains of £3,000. These are covered by £3,000 of the annual exemption, leaving a CGT assessment of £nil. The remaining £7,600 of the annual exemption is wasted. The losses brought forward of £8,000 are carried forward to next year.

(d) Melissa has net gains of £4,000. These are covered by £4,000 of the annual exemption, leaving a CGT assessment of £nil. The remaining £6,600 of the annual exemption is wasted. The losses brought forward of £4,000 are carried forward to next year.

Question B5

(a) *Disposal of flat*

	£
Sale proceeds	142,000
Less: Incidental costs of disposal	4,000
	138,000
Less: Part cost: $\frac{£142,000}{£142,000 + £130,000} \times £80,000$	(41,765)
Part conversion costs: $\frac{£142,000}{£142,000 + £130,000} \times £32,000$	(16,706)
Chargeable gain	79,529

Disposal of ICI shares

The chargeable gain is £38,200 (£150,000 – £111,800).

Total gains are £117,729 (£79,529 + £38,200). After deducting the 2012-13 annual exemption of £10,600, the CGT assessment for the year is £107,129. CGT due at 28% is £29,996.12.

(b) Mr More might consider the transfer of assets to Mrs More (at no gain, no loss). She could then dispose of them and any gain arising would be taxed in her name. For example, he could transfer the shares in ICI plc to her. If she then disposed of them and realised the gain of £38,200, this would be entirely covered by her losses brought forward and her annual exemption, so saving a substantial amount of CGT.

Set C

Question C1

(a) The accounting periods are the year to 31 March 2012 and the six months to 30 September 2012.

(b)

	y/e 31/3/12	*6 months to 30/9/12*
	£	£
Trading profits (time apportioned)	260,000	130,000
Less: Capital allowances:		
£100,000 + 20% × £26,250	105,250	
18% × £21,000 × 6/12		1,890
Trading income	154,750	128,110
Income from property	20,000	10,000
Income from non-trading loan relationships:		
£2,000 + £2,000 + £1,000	5,000	
£12,000 – £1,000 + £4,000		15,000
Chargeable gains		6,500
	179,750	159,610
Less: Qualifying charitable donations	5,000	5,000
Chargeable profits	174,750	154,610
Corporation tax @ 20%	34,950.00	
Corporation tax @ 24%		37,106.40
Less: 1/100 × (£750,000 – £154,610)		5,953.90
Corporation tax liability	34,950.00	31,152.50

The lower and upper limits for the second accounting period are £150,000 (£300,000 × 6/12) and £750,000 (£1,500,000 × 6/12) respectively.

Question C2

(a)

	y/e 30/6/11	9 mths to 31/3/12	y/e 31/3/13
	£	£	£
Trading income	2,050,000	260,000	-
Income from non-trading loans	51,600	39,000	28,700
Chargeable gains	-	-	8,700
	2,101,600	299,000	37,400
Less: Gift Aid donations	10,000	8,000	5,000
Chargeable profits	2,091,600	291,000	32,400
Tax @ 28%	439,236		
Tax @ 26%/26%/20%	135,954	75,660	6,480
Less: 3/200 × (£1,125,000 – £291,000)		12,510	
Corporation tax liability	575,190	63,150	6,480

Notes:

(i) Capital losses carried forward at 30 June 2011 are £35,300 (£67,300 – £32,000). Therefore net chargeable gains for the year to 31 March 2013 are £8,700 (£47,000 – £35,300 – £3,000).

(ii) The first nine months of the year to 30 June 2011 falls into FY2010 (main rate 28%) and the last three months fall into FY2011 (main rate 26%).

(iii) For the nine months to 31 March 2012, the lower and upper small company rate limits are £225,000 (£300,000 × 9/12) and £1,125,000 (£1,500,000 × 9/12) respectively.

(b)

	y/e 30/6/11	9 mths to 31/3/12	y/e 31/3/13
	£	£	£
Trading income	2,050,000	260,000	-
Income from non-trading loans	51,600	39,000	28,700
Chargeable gains	-	-	8,700
	2,101,600	299,000	37,400
Less: Trading losses	525,400	299,000	37,400
	1,576,200	0	0
Less: Gift Aid donations	10,000	0	0
Chargeable profits	1,566,200	0	0
Corporation tax liability @ 28%/26%	430,705	0	0

Notes:

(i) Only three months of the year to 30 June 2011 fall into the 12 months prior to the loss-making period. Therefore loss relief in this year is restricted to £525,400 (£2,101,600 x 3/12).

(ii) Trading losses c/f are £33,200 (£895,000 – £37,400 – £299,000 – £525,400).

(c)

The reduction in the liability for the year to 30 June 2011 is £144,485 (£575,190 – £430,705) so the total tax saved as a result of the loss relief claims is £214,115 (£144,485 + £63,150 + £6,480).

Question C3

	LimAA Ltd	*LimBB Ltd*	*LimCC Ltd*
	£	£	£
Trading profits	1,230,400	167,800	852,500
Income from non-trading loans	16,300	-	15,000
Property income	-	5,000	-
Chargeable gains	43,500	-	37,300
	1,290,200	172,800	904,800
Less: Gift Aid donations	5,200	1,000	4,800
Chargeable profits	1,285,000	171,800	900,000
Franked investment income	240,000	2,000	100,000
Augmented profits	1,525,000	173,800	1,000,000
Tax @ 24%/20%/24%	308,400	34,360	216,000
Less: Marginal relief			4,500
Corporation tax liability	308,400	34,360	211,500

Notes:

(i) The tax rate of 24% or 20% is applied to chargeable profits, *not* to augmented profits.

(ii) Marginal relief is 1/100 × (£1,500,000 – £1,000,000) × £900,000/£1,000,000 = £4,500.

Question C4

(a) The company has two alternatives. One alternative is to carry the loss back and set it against the total profits (before donations) of the year to 30 September 2011. The other is to carry the loss forward and set it against the trading profits of the year to 31 March 2013.

(b) The main deciding factor is the company's marginal rate of corporation tax for the period in which loss relief is given. The company's marginal rate of tax for the year to 30 September 2011 is 20.5% [(21% × 6/12 + (20% × 6/12)]. The company's marginal rate of tax for the year to 31 March 2013 is 25%.

Therefore the better alternative is to carry the loss forward and save tax at 25%. The donations of £750 will be unrelieved whatever the company does.

Question C5

(a)

	£
Trading profits	170,000
Less: Capital allowances	32,000
Trading income	138,000
Income from property	46,000
Chargeable gains £6,400 – £1,400	5,000
	189,000
Less: Qualifying charitable donations	20,000
Chargeable profits	169,000
FII (£14,400 + £1,600)	16,000
Augmented profits	185,000
Corporation tax at 20% on £169,000, due 1 January 2014	33,800

(b) If the company has one subsidiary, the lower and upper limits are divided by two. The lower limit becomes £150,000 and the upper limit becomes £750,000. Corporation tax is due as follows:

	£
£169,000 @ 24%	40,560.00
Less: $\frac{1}{100} \times (£750{,}000 - £185{,}000) \times \frac{£169{,}000}{£185{,}000}$	5,161.35
Corporation tax due 1 January 2014	35,398.65

Set D

Question D1

(i) The sale to St Oggs Inc is an export to a non-EU country and is zero-rated, even though the goods in question are normally standard-rated. HMRC may require documentary evidence that the goods have actually been exported.

(ii) Scotland is not outside the UK so the sale to Rappit Ltd is not an export and the supply is standard-rated. The value of the supply is £19,000 (£20,000 less 5%) and the related output tax (with a standard rate of 20%) is £3,800 (20% of £19,000). This is the case whether or not Rappit Ltd takes advantage of the discount offered.

(iii) The sale of the machinery is a taxable supply of goods, even though the machinery was a fixed (non-current) asset rather than stock in trade.

(iv) The hire of electrical equipment is a taxable supply of services.

(v) Unless Wakem & Co. Ltd operates the cash accounting scheme, output tax relating to supplies of goods to Garum Furs plc will have been paid over to HMRC at the end of the tax periods in which the supplies took place. This VAT can be recovered from HMRC so long as at least six months have elapsed since the date of supply and Wakem & Co. Ltd has written off the debt in its books. If part-payment is eventually received from the liquidator, part of the recovered VAT will be repayable to HMRC.

Question D2

	UK income	*Income from Z Inc*	*Income from X S.A.*	*Total*
	£	£	£	£
Trading income	500,000	-	-	500,000
Dividend income	-	50,000	40,000	90,000
	500,000	50,000	40,000	590,000
Less: Donations	10,000	-	-	10,000
Chargeable profits	490,000	50,000	40,000	580,000

M Ltd, N Ltd and O Ltd are associated companies, so the upper and lower limits are divided equally between them. Each company has an upper limit of £500,000 and a lower limit of £100,000. The chargeable profits of M Ltd are £580,000, so tax is due at 24%.

	UK income	*Income from Z Inc*	*Income from X S.A.*	*Total*
	£	£	£	£
Corporation tax at 24%	117,600	12,000	9,600	139,200
Less: DTR	-	12,000	2,000	14,000
Corporation tax liability	117,600	0	7,600	125,200

Question D3

(a) A Ltd controls B Ltd, C Ltd, D Ltd and E Ltd, so all five companies are associated companies.

(b) A Ltd controls 75% or more of B Ltd, C Ltd and D Ltd so these four companies form a 75% group. E Ltd is not UK related and so cannot belong to the group for group relief purposes. It is also worth noting that E Ltd is not EEA resident (and does not carry on a trade in the EEA) and so it would not be able to surrender a trading loss to a UK company.

(c) The chargeable profits of E Ltd (a CFC) do not exceed £50,000, so there is no allocation of E Ltd's profits to A Ltd. The profits of £15,000 are not chargeable to UK corporation tax at all.

Both A Ltd and B Ltd will pay tax at the marginal rate of 25% unless their chargeable profits are reduced to the lower limit of £60,000 (£300,000 × 1/5). Therefore the first priority when dealing with the losses of C Ltd and D Ltd is to use them to reduce the profits of A Ltd and B Ltd to £60,000 each. This absorbs £85,000 of losses. The remaining losses of £10,000 could be set against the bank interest of C Ltd or surrendered to A Ltd or B Ltd, saving tax at 20% in each case. Assuming that a claim is made to set this £10,000 against the total profits of C Ltd, the corporation tax liability of each company is as follows:

	A Ltd	*B Ltd*	*C Ltd*	*D Ltd*
	£	£	£	£
Trading income	90,000	100,000	-	-
Bank interest	-	15,000	12,000	-
	90,000	115,000	12,000	-
Less: Group relief	30,000	55,000	-	-
Trading loss relief	-	-	10,000	-
Chargeable profits	60,000	60,000	2,000	-
Tax @ 20%	12,000	12,000	400	-

Question D4

(a) Employees on a nine-month contract will not be absent from the UK for a whole tax year and so, for tax purposes, these employees will be both resident and ordinarily resident in the UK throughout the nine months. Their earnings whilst working abroad will be fully assessable to UK income tax, but double tax relief will be available.

(b) Employees on an 18-month contract which includes an entire tax year will usually be treated as both non-resident and not ordinarily resident for the duration of the contract. Their earnings from duties performed overseas (and any other foreign income) will not be subject to UK income tax and they will not be liable to UK capital gains tax. They will, however, be liable to UK income tax on any income arising in the UK during their absence (e.g. rents from letting their homes whilst working abroad).

(c) Employees on an 18-month contract which does not include an entire tax year will be treated as resident in the UK throughout the 18 months. Their overseas earnings will therefore be assessed to UK income tax, but double tax relief will be available.

Employees who are treated as non-resident but who are citizens of the EEA will be able to claim personal allowances to set against their UK income.

Index